WORLD BUSINESS: GLOBALIZATION, ANALYSIS AND STRATEGY

First Edition

John S. Hill

University of Alabama

THOMSON

SOUTH-WESTERN

Australia · Canada · Mexico · Singapore · Spain · United Kingdom · United States

THOMSON

SOUTH-WESTERN

World Business: Globalization, Strategy, and Analysis

John S. Hill

VP/Editorial Director:
Jack W. Calhoun

VP/Editor-in-Chief:
Michael Roche

Senior Publisher:
Melissa S. Acuña

ExecutiveEditor:
John Szilagyi

Developmental Editor:
Emma F. Guttler

Marketing Manager:
Jacquelyn Carrillo

Production Editor:
Stephanie Blydenburgh

Manager of Technology:
Vicky True

Technology Project Editor:
Kristen Meere

Media Editor:
Karen Schaffer

Manufacturing Coordinator:
Rhonda Utley

Production House:
Shepherd, Inc.

Printer:
Edwards Brothers
Ann Arbor, MI

Design Project Manager:
Anne Marie Rekow

Internal Designer:
Anne Marie Rekow

Cover Designer:
Anne Marie Rekow

Cover Images:
Image 100

BRIEF CONTENTS

CONTENTS

᭤

To my family. My wife Linda and sons Christopher and Richard have been brilliant. Too often they have asked: "Where's Dad?" The response has always been the same: "He's at the office doing his book." This work is dedicated to them.

Preface

Jnternational business became a recognized academic discipline in the 1960s. From those times, textbooks followed a template that separated topics into environmental factors (economic, political, cultural, legal, financial); global factors (exchange rates, the international monetary system) and strategy (market entry methods, marketing, manufacturing, human resources, finance, accounting). This approach was academically convenient but left the integrating of the topics to instructors and students.

This text, *World Business: Globalization, Analysis and Strategy* is multidisciplinary. It integrates history, geography, political science, economics, anthropology and other social sciences into its explanations of how markets function and how managers can best make appropriate decisions in world markets.

Organization

World Business: Globalization, Analysis and Strategy starts with a three-chapter examination of the globalization process. This emphasis helps students understand the underlying forces at work in the world marketplace. Chapter One demonstrates that globalizing influences have been at work for hundreds of years, and how these influences have accelerated since 1980. Chapter Two explores globalizing influences in detail. In particular, it underscores the role of the United Nations in providing, through its specialized agencies, vital services to link world markets and facilitate commercial interactions. Chapter Three examines the consequences of globalization and its effects on country cultures and values.

Part Two focuses on world business analyses. In Chapters Four and Five, major emphases are placed on history and geography in explaining how regions and countries have developed, and what tools are useful in their analysis. These explanations go beyond detailing current conditions (the usual approach), and probe the origins of regional and national development. This helps students understand *why* regions and countries evolved the ways they did. Chapters Six and Seven look at how global industries and competitors are analyzed, and how individual companies review their global situations in the planning process.

Part Three deals with strategy. The logical jump-off point is corporate globalization. This is examined from both internal perspectives (Chapter Eight), and external viewpoints through Chapter Nine coverage of market entry strategies. The focus then shifts to global and multi-market strategies: how companies execute strategies across national markets and orchestrate their supply chains for maximum global effectiveness. No other international text has this contemporary approach. Finally, localization issues are examined in Chapters Twelve and Thirteen. The Chapter Twelve treatment of cultural differences includes extensive materials on religion—how Islam, Buddhism, Hinduism, Confucianism, and Taoism affect daily and business behaviors among the four billion non-Christians in world markets. This contrasts with current texts that give spartan coverage to this important topic. Chapter Thirteen addresses stakeholder and supply chain issues at the local level. Again, the integrative approach is used to give students comprehensive perspectives on localization strategies.

Throughout this text, efforts have been made to give equal treatment to all world regions and countries. The U.S. is undoubtedly a very important market in the global economy, but over-emphasis on the Americas should not come at the expense of other markets. The book's title, *World Business: Globalization, Analysis and Strategy,* reflects this orientation.

Differentiating Features

This book is significantly different from current international business texts across eight dimensions. These dimensions are as follows.

	Usual IB Approach	*World Business: Globalization, Analysis and Strategy* Approach
Text Organization	A series of loosely related topics	Chapter topics revolve around globalization, diffusion, and economic development themes, with linkages to environmental analyses and global/local strategies.
Globalization	Is usually defined with some discussion	Is explored historically and with respect to globalizing forces and effects
Change Orientation	Markets, environments, and strategies examined "as is." Little depth or explanatory power.	Change is the one constant of world markets, and is examined from institutional, individual, industry, and corporate perspectives.
Market Analyses	Examined from convenient academic perspectives: economic, political, cultural, legal forces as separate analyses	Evaluated as managers see them—from geographic perspectives: global, regional forces affecting national markets
Industries and Competitors	Rarely assessed from global perspectives	Analyzed as companies see them—from global, regional and national market perspectives
Strategy Implementation	Analyzed from functional perspectives: marketing, manufacturing, financial, etc.	Assessed according to strategic needs: global/multi-market and localization strategies
Topic Presentation Within Chapters	Not integrated	Chapter outlines and figures show topics and their interrelatedness
Relation to Broader Themes: the World at Large	Occasionally attempted	Quotations bring in outside commentaries to reinforce text principles and concepts

1. *Globalization as an underlying text theme:* Most texts in this field present a series of chapters on related topics without any unifying theme of how it all fits together. This book has an underlying rationale—a framework that links chapters in a logical and progressive manner. This is explained in Chapter One and reinforced throughout the text. This rationale is that globalization, technology transfers, and modernization take time to diffuse both across world markets and within individual countries. As firms transfer goods and services into similar (often developed) markets, the need for adaptations diminishes and standardized global strategies may be appropriate. But as companies move into developing countries, environmental differences become pronounced, particularly in heavily populated rural areas. These necessitate strategic changes as local needs must be accommodated. To varying degrees, all overseas business requires some adaptation as peoples from national cultures interact, and as firms combine corporate needs for scale economies with adaptive touches—global-local strategies.

2. *A comprehensive look at globalization:* Many political scientists, economists, politicians, businesspeople, and writers in the popular press have commented about globalization from their particular vantage points. This text examines this very important topic in-depth—its historical origins, what factors cause it, and its effects. Readers will start to understand some underlying controversies: why foreign franchises of U.S. companies have been attacked; why Islamic (and many other) nations are suspicious of westernization; and, perhaps most importantly, why the changes globalization promotes are disruptive to national cultures.

3. *Understanding and managing change:* The one constant in world markets is change, and change is what most executives must understand and manage if they are to be successful. Yet most texts are static—they simply describe the present. This text tackles change head-on. We explore the past through history, and students can see linkages to current situations. We examine economic and cultural change to see where nations have been, where they are, and where they would like to be. Similarly, we look at changes in corporate outlooks and market development as countries adapt (or not) to the challenge of globalization.

4. *Looking at markets the way that managers do, as geographic entities:* Executives analyze regions and countries holistically. They know that most nations have unique histories, and that those histories significantly affect their current situations and outlooks on life. Likewise, geography is also a major determinant of economic development. Most importantly, managers know that they must examine political, economic, cultural, and other factors together *as a group* to understand why regions and markets behave the ways they do.

5. *Looking at industries and competitors from a global perspective:* Managers know that to be effective across world markets, they must analyze industry behaviors and market rivals from a worldwide vantage point. No other perspective is valid. Similarly, executives know that global planning is a "must" as they allocate their limited resources in effective man-

ners. Unlike competing books, this text recognizes these most important of management tasks and provides guidelines to help students understand how international firms undertake this process.

6. *Implementing strategies in multidisciplinary ways:* This text responds to contemporary trends in business and replaces the old functional approaches of marketing, manufacturing, and HRM with integrated approaches to demand management and to supply chain organization, both at the global/multi-market and local levels. This represents a major shift in how international business should be taught and, as importantly, it is more in step with current management thinking and academic practices. From a practical perspective, follow-on international courses that use functional field breakouts will not seem as repetitive to both students and instructors.

7. *Integrated chapter outlines:* Topic integration facilitates learning as students see "how it all fits together." Not only does this text integrate world business topics around the globalization theme at the chapter level, it has frameworks to integrate the various themes within chapters.

8. *How world business topics relate to broader themes:* This is achieved through quotations from famous (and infamous) personalities from all walks of life. As importantly, they lighten the reading load and reinforce key principles and concepts throughout the text.

Distinguishing Pedagogical Features

Introductory Vignettes   The opening vignettes for each chapter define the chapter topics and set the stage for further chapter reading.

The Global Web   This resource provides users with the opportunity to engage in more in-depth research via the Internet.

In-text Quotations   Quotations from well-known politicians, economists, businesspeople, philosophers, poets, and writers give the reader perspectives from additional voices. Some of these quotations reinforce key text points; others provide an opposing viewpoint and some are humorous anecdotes.

Casettes   Small cases at the end of each chapter cover mainstream topics and can be focal points for class discussion or used in individual study.

Comprehensive Cases   These cases appear at the end of each Part to more thoroughly explore the Part concepts while utilizing real world companies.

Instructor Resources

Instructor's Manual with Test Bank (ISBN: 0-324-23651-4)   An in-depth Instructor's Manual with Test Bank, devised to provide major assistance to the professor, accompanies the text. The material in the manual includes a variety of features, including detailed case notes.

PowerPoint Lecture Presentation Software An asset to any instructor, the lectures provide outlines for every chapter, graphics of the illustrations from the text, and additional examples providing instructors with a number of learning opportunities for students. The PowerPoint Lecture Presentations are available on the IRCD in Microsoft 2000 format and as downloadable files on the text support site.

ExamView Available on the Instructor's Resource CD-ROM, ExamView contains all of the questions in the printed test bank. This program is an easy-to-use test creation software compatible with Microsoft Windows. Instructors can add or edit questions, instructions, and answers, and select questions (randomly or numerically) by previewing them on the screen. Instructors can also create and administer quizzes online, whether over the Internet, a local area network (LAN), or a wide area network (WAN).

Instructor's CD-ROM (ISBN: 0-324-23690-5) Key instructor ancillaries (instructor's manual, test bank, ExamView and PowerPoint slides) are provided on CD-ROM, giving instructors the ultimate tool for customizing lectures and presentations.

Videos (ISBN: 0-324-20354-3) Videos compiled specifically to accompany *World Business* utilize real-world companies to illustrate international business concepts as outlined in the text. Focusing on both small and large businesses, the video gives students an inside perspective on the situations and issues that global corporations face.

Website *World Business*'s Web site at *http://hill.swlearning.com/* provides a multitude of student resources. Additional supplementary materials are included on a password-protected site for instructors.

TextChoice: Management Exercises and Cases TextChoice is the home of Thomson Learning's online digital content. TextChoice provides the fastest, easiest way for you to create your own learning materials. South-Western's Management Exercises and Cases database includes a variety of experiential exercises, classroom activities, management in film exercises, and cases to enhance any management course. Choose as many exercises as you like and even add your own material to create a supplement tailored to your course. Contact your South-Western/Thomson Learning sales representative for more information.

ECoursepacks Create a tailor-fit, easy-to-use online companion for any course with eCoursepacks, from Thomson companies South-Western and Gale. eCoursepacks gives educators access to content from thousands of current popular, professional, and academic periodicals, as well as NACRA and Darden cases, and business and industry information from Gale. In addition, instructors can easily add their own material with the option of even collecting a royalty. Permissions for all eCoursepack content are already secured, saving instructors the time and worry with securing rights.

eCoursepacks online publishing tools also save time and energy by allowing instructors to quickly search the databases to make selections, organize all the content, and publish the final online product in a clean, uniform, and full-color format. eCoursepacks is the best way to provide current information quickly and inexpensively. To learn more, visit: *http://ecoursepacks.swlearning.com*.

InfoTrac College Edition Included with each new copy of the text is four months of free access to InfoTrac College Edition, an online library of more than 4,000 academic journals and periodicals. Through its easy to use search engine and other user-friendly features, InfoTrac College Edition puts cutting edge research and the latest headlines at students' fingertips.

ACKNOWLEDGMENTS

Winston Churchill noted, "Writing a book is an adventure. To begin with, it is a toy and an amusement. Then it becomes a mistress, then it becomes a master, then it becomes a tyrant." As this book moved through the various phases into the master and tyrant phases, many helped to bring it finally to fruition.

In the beginning, my thanks go to my extended family in Leicester, England. They kept the home fires burning as I moved to the U.S. and fulfilled many academic and professional objectives.

In the U.S., it was the late Richard R. Still at the University of Georgia who taught me to write in a coherent fashion, to think beyond the status quo, and how to write textbooks.

At the University of Alabama, many generations of students stimulated my thought processes and provided the enthusiasm that continues to inspire all of us in the teaching profession. My day-to-day professional colleagues have been wonderful and have helped create an atmosphere conducive to superior scholarly output. A special tribute also to Professor Art Thompson, a veteran text writer, whose encouragement was welcomed, and who has constantly demonstrated the dedication, thoroughness, and professionalism that must accompany textbook writing.

To the reviewers who provided their valuable feedback: Josiah Baker, University of Central Florida; Richard Baldwin, Cedarville University; Jonathan Brookfield, Texas A&M University; Peggy Chaudhry, Villanova University; Les Dlabay, Lake Forest College; Jonathan Doh, Villanova University; Robert Grosse, Thunderbird, The American Graduate School of International Management; Masaaki Kotabe, Temple University; Carol Lopilato, California State University–Dominguez Hills; Roderick Matthews, University of Wisconsin–Madison; Pallab Paul, University of Denver; and Hongxin Zhao, St. Louis University.

At Thomson Learning, it was Sales Representative Pamela Boyd's enthusiasm for this project that got the ball rolling. Kudos also to John Szilagyi who took this project on when others were skeptical. To Emma Guttler, my developmental editor, and Stephanie Blydenburgh and Mary Grivetti, the production editors, I extend my profound thanks. It goes without saying that they are better organizers of textbooks than I.

To the students who read this preface (and those who do not!), I salute you. World business is an adventure. Enjoy your studies. As you absorb the principles within this book cover, I hope your enthusiasm for global studies is enhanced, and that your interest in international activities and events continues throughout your lifetimes. Understanding the world about us has become an imperative for good citizenship in all nations. May your minds, extended through globalization, never go back to narrow-minded parochialism.

To the professors astute enough to adopt this text—thank you! It is a new approach to world business and one that I hope you will enjoy teaching from. No discipline can move forward without those willing to overthrow the ways of our academic forefathers. Let me have your comments and suggestions at *jhill@cba.ua.edu.* I cannot promise to implement all of them, but, like you, I constantly strive for excellence.

As always, there are thousands of facts that go into a textbook. I believe all of them to be correct, but the responsibility for errors is ultimately mine alone.

ABOUT THE AUTHOR

John S. Hill is Miller Professor of International Business at the University of Alabama in Tuscaloosa, Alabama. Born and bred in England, he completed his bachelor's and master's degrees at the Universities of Aston in Birmingham and the University of Lancaster before obtaining his doctorate at the University of Georgia in the U.S. in international business. Prior to coming to the U.S., he worked in the rubber and plastics industry, as a market researcher, and as a financial analyst in England.

Professor Hill has published in more than twenty-five journals, including the *Harvard Business Review,* the *Columbia Journal of World Business,* the *Journal of International Business Studies, Long Range Planning, European Journal of Marketing, International Marketing Review,* and the *Journal of International Marketing.*

PART ONE

The Globalization Process: Background, Causes, and Effects

❧

Globalization is the trend toward increasing interdependencies among world markets and the diffusion of new ideas, technologies, products, services, and lifestyles among world markets. The first three chapters of this text examine the globalization process.

Chapter 1 looks at the world business challenge, the diversity of international markets, and the change that occurs as a result of international business activities. First, we look at the evolution of world business from earliest times up to the present day and how technological developments allowed the systematic exploration of world markets. Then, examination is made of the diffusion of technologies and ideas among and within international markets and the reasons some nations have benefited and developed faster than others. Finally, the effects of globalization on company strategies are explored: when standardized approaches are appropriate and when localized strategies are optimal.

Chapter 2 looks at the development of linkages among nations—the building of a world infrastructure to facilitate international business dealings. The influence of public institutions such as the United Nations' agencies is examined—

the World Trade Organization, the International Monetary Fund, the World Bank, as well as the institutions that have encouraged specific aspects of world business, such as the International Telecommunications Union (telecommunications), the International Civil Aviation Authority, the International Maritime Organization (air and sea travel), and others. The private sector contribution is also evaluated: the roles of global retailers, transportation companies, and international media in facilitating transfers of products, services, and ideas among nations.

The effects of globalization—the cumulative impact of the transfers of new ideas, philosophies, technologies, products, and lifestyles—are assessed in Chapter 3. How technology transfers affect economic development and how, as countries develop, they move from traditional to modern political and economic institutions and behaviors. The development process also results in changes in industry, company, and consumer behaviors as market competition increases. Finally, because economic and cultural change is disruptive, resistance occurs. The causes and reasons for such resistance are examined.

Chapter One

The World Business Challenge

⚭

THE WORLD IN A NUTSHELL

If we could shrink the earth's population to a village of precisely 100 people, with existing human ratios remaining the same, there would be:

- *57 Asians, 21 Europeans, 8 Africans;*
- *14 from the Western Hemisphere (north and south);*
- *52 would be female, 48 male;*
- *70 would be non-white, 30 white;*
- *70 would be non-Christian;*
- *89 would be heterosexual, 11 homosexual;*
- *59% of the entire world's wealth would be held by 6 people—all 6 would be U.S. citizens;*
- *80 would live in substandard housing;*
- *30 would be unable to read;*
- *20 would suffer from malnutrition;*
- *1 would be near death, 1 would be near birth;*
- *1 would have a college education;*
- *1 would own a computer.*

> —*Donella L Meadows*
> *Dartmouth College*

The diversity of the world's population is stunningly apparent from these statistics. The task of world business courses is to enable students to appreciate global diversity and the extent of global change in the world marketplace, and to prepare them to manage successfully in it. Commerce and the exchange of ideas is the essence of world business, and global corporations are instruments of change and development.

Hence, in this chapter you will learn:

- What world business is and how it contributes to the well-being of countries, companies, and individuals.
- The world business challenge: political, economic, and cultural diversity and change in the international marketplace, and how executives respond to the challenge with knowledge and understanding derived from the business disciplines and from political science, anthropology, economic development, sociology, religion, geography, and history.

- Historic perspectives on world business: early efforts to harness technologies and take products into foreign markets; the impact of diffusion catalysts such as mega languages, writing, printing technologies, transportation innovations, broadcast, electronic media, and retailing institutions; the emergence of modern corporations.
- The globalization movement: how international trade, trade blocs, foreign direct investment, movements toward global capitalism, technology, and global media have contributed to the dissemination of products, services, ideas, and lifestyles in world markets; how the developing world lags economically; and how the global diffusion process contributes to explanations about developmental differences among and within international markets.
- How the diffusion process affects strategy formulation and implementation. Why firms pursue global and multi-market strategies in some markets and localize products, services, and supply chains in others; and why global-local strategies are often optimal.

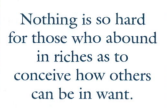

Nothing is so hard for those who abound in riches as to conceive how others can be in want.

—*Jonathan Swift, 17th–18th-century English satirist*

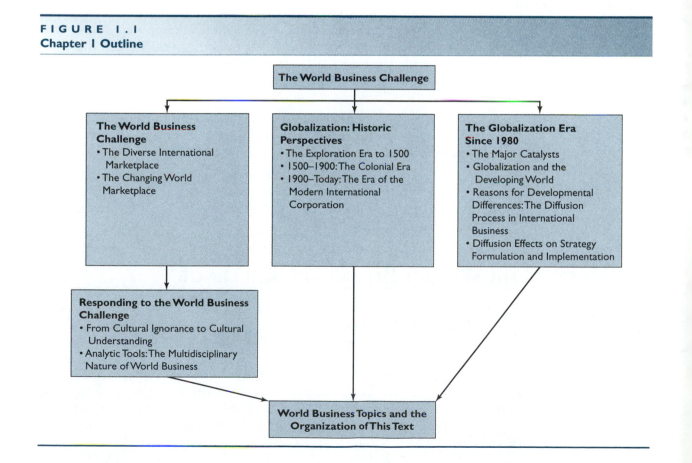

FIGURE 1.1
Chapter 1 Outline

INTRODUCTION

The term *world business* refers to commercial activities performed to promote the transfer of technologies, goods, services, and ideas across national boundaries. World business occurs under many different formats, from the movement of goods from one country to another (exporting and trade), to contractual agreements giving firms in foreign nations legal permissions to use products, services, and processes from other nations (franchising, licensing, subcontracting production), and finally to companies setting up sales, manufacturing, research and development, and distribution facilities in foreign markets. The study of world business helps students understand how and why technologies, goods, services, and ideas cross national borders, and what factors affect their acceptance (or rejection) in foreign markets.

> Commerce is the great civilizer. We exchange ideas when we exchange fabrics.
>
> —*Robert Ingersoll,*
> *19th-century U.S. lawyer*

The flows of goods, services, technologies, and ideas among markets have major effects on countries and their governments, companies, and individuals.

- At the nation-state level, participation in world business activities helps countries take advantage of national expertise in commerce to deliver goods and services into the international marketplace. It also increases the varieties of goods and services available in national markets and exposes consumers to new lifestyles and ideas. Over time, these exposures affect national cultures (political, economic institutions) and impact behaviors, attitudes, and lifestyles. Governments have major effects on international business activities in determining how open (or closed) national economies are to external influences such as trade and investment.

- For companies, world business increases competition in domestic markets and opens up new opportunities abroad. Global competition forces firms to be more innovative and efficient in their use of resources.

- For consumers, international business brings increased varieties of goods and services into the world marketplace and enhances living standards. As importantly, open borders mean increased exposures to new ideas, technologies, and ways of doing things.

THE WORLD BUSINESS CHALLENGE

As business people survey the world marketplace, they are both impressed and intimidated by the diversity and change they see in the 200+ national markets and their 6+ billion people. Yet this is the marketplace they must understand in order to build products and services for worldwide customers in the face of increasing international competition. Successful international corporations are those that recognize the diversity of the world marketplace and are able to cope with the uncertainties of doing business in continually changing market environments. Figure 1.2 summarizes the international business challenge.

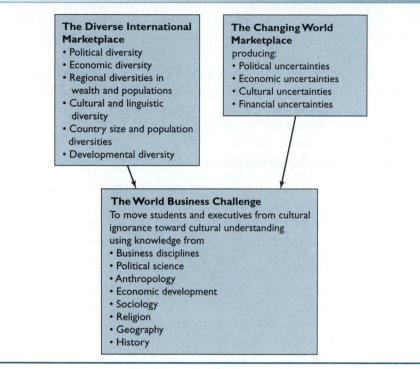

FIGURE 1.2
The World Business Challenge

FIGURE 1.2
The World Business Challenge

The Diverse International Marketplace
• Political diversity
• Economic diversity
• Regional diversities in wealth and populations
• Cultural and linguistic diversity
• Country size and population diversities
• Developmental diversity

The Changing World Marketplace
producing:
• Political uncertainties
• Economic uncertainties
• Cultural uncertainties
• Financial uncertainties

The World Business Challenge
To move students and executives from cultural ignorance toward cultural understanding using knowledge from
• Business disciplines
• Political science
• Anthropology
• Economic development
• Sociology
• Religion
• Geography
• History

The Diverse International Marketplace

The task of understanding the world marketplace is immense. International executives must cope with:

- *Political diversity* as world markets are governed by both autocracies (chiefs, kings, dictators, one-party-governments) and democracies

- *Economic diversity* as national wealth disparities vary from $100 per capita per year (Ethiopia) to almost $40,000 per capita (Switzerland)

- *Regional diversity* in distributions of wealth and population: North America has 5–6 percent of the world population but controls about one-third of world gross domestic product; Asia has almost 60 percent of the world population, but only about a quarter of world GDP (10 percent without Japan).

- *Cultural and linguistic diversity:* The world's 200 nations are divided into about 10,000 linguistic/cultural groups,[1] a crude average of some fifty languages or ethnic groups per country. The Sudan has 600 ethnic groups and 400 different languages spread across its 31 million population. India has Hindi and English as its major languages, but supports many hundreds of dialectic versions across its regions.

> Equality may perhaps be a right, but no power on earth can ever turn it into a fact.
>
> —*Honore de Balzac, 19th-century French novelist*

- *Diversities in country size and populations:* The number of countries in the world economy numbered about sixty at the start of the twentieth century. This rose to ninety-six by 1960 and to over 200 as the millennium drew to a close. These vary from Mainland China and India with 1.3 and 1 billion inhabitants respectively to forty-three nations with less than one million inhabitants.[2]

- *Developmental diversities* between industrialized nations (80 percent urban populations, 3 percent of GDP from agriculture) and industrializing nations, such as those in sub-Saharan Africa and parts of Asia that are 30 percent urbanized and obtain over 30 percent of their GDPs from agriculture.[3]

The Changing World Marketplace

The world marketplace is characterized by constant change, resulting in major political, economic, cultural, and financial uncertainties.

Political change occurs as nations seek to establish stability and order within their national borders. In democratic nations, there are uncertainties as voters decide what political directions their countries should take. On average, there are national elections somewhere in the world almost every week. Companies with major trade or investment commitments in those markets pay attention to national, regional, and local elections to determine how these elections will impact business—whether new governments are likely to support commercial developments and how they are likely to impact national demands for products and services. In some developing countries, especially where democracies are not established, there are uncertainties as rival ethnic, religious, or social groups compete for political recognition (for example, in Somalia, Sudan, Ethiopia). In democratic nations, account must be taken of splinter groups (e.g., environmental "greens" in Western Europe, fundamentalist Muslim groups in Iran, leftist guerillas in Colombia). Wherever there are major differences in political opinions, there is the potential for political unrest.

Economic change has become increasingly important with the growing interdependences among national economies. Economic downturns in North America or Western Europe reverberate throughout the world economy. Developing country problems (such as the U.N.–Iraq war in 1990–91 and the Asian financial crisis over 1997–99) caused downturns in worldwide economic activity. Executives must be able to analyze global and regional economic trends and appreciate their impacts on corporate activities. At the nation-state level, managers must recognize symptoms of governmental mismanagement of the economy: unbalanced budgets (insufficient income from taxes to support government spending), corruption (e.g., in government contracts and spending), unfair tax structures, balance of payments problems, etc. Two major economic problems are inflation (which causes erosions of savings, consumer purchasing power, and living standards) and high unemployment. Both can result in public discontent and political unrest.

Cultural change creates uncertainties through its effects on political and economic climates. Religious problems in particular have caused strife at national and international levels. Within nations, religious conflicts are highly disruptive

> Nothing endures but change.
>
> —*Heraclitus, 5th-century*
> B.C. *Greek philosopher*

> There is nothing wrong with change, if it is in the right direction.
>
> —*Winston Churchill, 20th-century British statesman*

(e.g., Protestants and Catholics in Northern Ireland, Hindus and Muslims in the Kashmir in India, Christians and Muslims in Nigeria and Indonesia, and fundamentalist and mainstream Muslim groups in Iran, Pakistan, Saudi Arabia, Egypt, Algeria, the Palestine). For many peoples of the world, religion is the most important part of their lives, more important than money and wealth, more important than country affiliations, more important than any other worldly issues. This causes problems as religion often supercedes national allegiances and makes religious conflicts among the most difficult to resolve.

Financial changes occur as international businesses conduct transactions in a world marketplace with over 180 currencies. When most international business transactions occur, exchange rates (the price of one currency in terms of another) are involved. Firms must monitor two types of financial change. First, the values of many currencies fluctuate with respect to each other, affecting pricing and asset valuations as goods and resources cross national borders. Second, country abilities to make payments to foreigners are variable. Only a minority of national currencies (the dollar, yen, euro, and a few others) are fully acceptable (convertible) in all world markets. Many developing country currencies for example, are unacceptable to nonresidents as means of payment (inconvertible). As increasing numbers of developing markets enter the international marketplace, a key issue is how they can pay for needed goods and services. Many (e.g., Argentina) have built up major debts as they have fallen behind in their ability to pay import bills. Others undergo significant economic turmoil as they strive to make their currencies acceptable (convertible) internationally. The 1997–99 Asian financial crisis occurred as key nations in that region realigned their national currencies in efforts to make them convertible.

Coping with political, economic, and cultural diversity and change is what international business is all about. The task of international managers to understand foreign markets and to craft strategies to satisfy customers and out-compete rivals in the world marketplace requires not only understanding the principles underlying sound business strategies, but also having in-depth knowledge of the world markets—their characteristics, behaviors, and trends.

RESPONDING TO THE WORLD BUSINESS CHALLENGE: HOW EXECUTIVES COPE WITH GLOBAL DIVERSITY AND CHANGE

From Cultural Ignorance to Cultural Understanding

Implementing strategies across world markets requires in-depth understandings of national cultures and international trends. Anyone can read the local or international press and find out what is going on in a particular country, and, while that knowledge is important, it is not sufficient for making important resource allocation or strategy decisions. International business managers must know not only *what* is

> We have just enough religion to make us hate, but not enough to make us love one another.
>
> —*Jonathan Swift, 17th–18th-century English satirist*

> Change, not habit, is what gets most of us down; habit is the stabilizer of human society, change accounts for all its progress.
>
> —*William Feather, U.S. author and publisher*

> The recipe for perpetual ignorance is: Be satisfied with your opinions and content with your knowledge.
>
> —*Elbert Hubbard, 19th-century U.S. writer*

going on but *why*. They must be able to interpret international events and assess their significance in wider national, regional, or worldwide contexts. It is impossible for managers to know everything about national cultures and international trends, but the relentless accumulation of worldwide market knowledge is the hallmark of all top international executives. They never stop learning. To be effective, however, managers must also have suitable frameworks to aid interpretations of market trends and events. The principal objective of world business courses is to provide these frameworks. The progression from cultural ignorance to understanding has four distinct stages:

> To know one's ignorance is the best part of knowledge.
>
> —*Lao-Tzu, 6th-century* B.C. *Chinese philosopher*

1. *Cultural ignorance* exists when individuals have no knowledge of cultural differences. Business people at this stage are liabilities to their companies and may do more harm than good on overseas assignments.

2. *Cultural awareness* takes place when people know there are cultural differences and are looking for them. Business people at this stage are less likely to commit social or cultural blunders.

> If you wish to please people, you must begin by understanding them.
>
> —*Charles Reade*

3. *Cultural knowledge* is an extension of cultural awareness. Business people know how to offer appropriate greetings (i.e., the bow of Japan) and what behaviors to expect in foreign markets. They observe, catalog, and analyze foreign behaviors and look for the reasons behind them.

4. *Cultural understanding* occurs when business people not only know what behaviors are appropriate but also understand why those behaviors are occurring. Individuals at this stage are often fluent in the local language and are aware of the behavioral and attitudinal subtleties of a culture.

Analytic Tools: The Multidisciplinary Nature of World Business

Understanding world markets requires knowledge from a broad range of social scientific disciplines. Business studies draws heavily from the social sciences of economics, sociology, and psychology in its examinations of corporate, social, and individual behaviors. When the study of business goes beyond national borders, the conceptual foundation of world business extends to include the following areas of study.

> Democracy substitutes election by the incompetent many for appointment by the corrupt few.
>
> —*George Bernard Shaw, 19th–20th-century British playwright*

Political science is the study of politicians, political institutions, and their effects on business and society. Democracies are present in many countries, but over 40 percent of nations are autarchies—hereditary monarchies, dictatorships, chiefs, shahs, and the like. In autarchies, the leader's word is law, and their control is often absolute. In democracies, politicians control national destinies, but they are accountable to voters. Therefore, international businesses must routinely monitor political changes via elections, wars, and coups d'etat. Politicians have major impacts on economic conditions—whether national markets grow or contract (major influences on corporate sales and profit levels), and governments control corporate access to national markets via trade and investment policies. As importantly, governments provide the legal frameworks that ultimately control business behaviors within their national borders.

Anthropology is the study of the evolution of mankind in its various environments. The evolution of human behaviors during economic development from traditional to modern societies entails major disruptions to political and economic institutions and to group and individual behaviors. One key to understanding world markets is appreciating how economic-development changes affect business operations in changing markets.

Economic development occurs as nations industrialize and grow economically. As they progress toward higher living standards, significant changes occur in national institutions and behaviors. These changes in political, economic and cultural institutions affect behaviors and values at all levels of society. Knowledge of these institutions and the development process helps business people understand changes in foreign markets and provides insights as to how a country's past affects its present and future prospects. Understanding the economic and cultural development process requires insights from the anthropological, sociological, and economic development fields to illustrate the multi-faceted nature of change as nation-states move from simple self-sufficient societies to complex nation-states producing varieties of goods and services. Exhibit 1-1 details a multi-country study of the major cultural changes occurring during the modernization process. Note the importance of industrialization and the enduring effects of religion on national values and behaviors.

Sociology is the study of group behaviors in society. In tradition-based societies, extended family units are common and familial obligations run deep in business behaviors, the awarding of contracts, and employment opportunities. Another group behavior—social class—determines societal hierarchies. In traditional societies, hereditary criteria (family pedigree) and seniority (equated with wisdom) are major sources of social status. But as countries urbanize, industrialize, and modernize, money and the accumulation of wealth become key indicators of social-class standing. Finally, as countries industrialize, gender roles change, and male-oriented (patriarchal) societies come under pressure as female contributions to societal well-being outside of the home are recognized.

Religion is a primary determinant of behaviors and attitudes in all countries. In North America and Western Europe, Christian religions (including Protestantism and Roman Catholicism) provide behavioral and ethical guidelines to followers, but their effects on daily lives are not as pronounced as in other parts of the world. In the developing world, religion tends to have profound effects on daily lives. It is difficult to understand the Middle East without significant knowledge of the Islamic (Muslim) faith. Similarly, attitudes and behaviors in India are best understood when placed in their Hindu context. Both Islamic and Hindu religions have followings of over one billion people. Some religions are non-theistic (that is, they do not recognize or worship one or more gods); instead, they are life-guiding philosophies that affect behaviors. Confucianism and Taoism have affected Chinese behaviors for centuries. Buddhism, another non-theistic religion, affects daily behaviors in many Asian nations (e.g., Korea, Thailand, Laos, Cambodia, China, Japan). Thus, understanding world markets requires in-depth appreciations of the world's major religions and their effects.

> Change is inevitable in a progressive country. Change is constant.
>
> —*Benjamin Disraeli, 19th-century British prime minister*

> A man without religion or spiritual vision is like a captain who finds himself in the midst of an uncharted sea, without compass, rudder and steering wheel. He never knows where he is, which way he is going, and where he is going to land.
>
> —*William J. H. Boetcker*

EXHIBIT 1-1
A Sociological Perspective on Modernization, Cultural Change, and Traditional Values

THE STUDY

Sixty-five countries covering 75 percent of the world's population, executed in three waves: 1981–82; 1990–91; and 1995–98. Average of 1400 respondents per country.

KEY FINDING

1. Three Country Clusters
   - *Pre-industrial societies:* Lifestyles influenced by geography (seasons, storm, droughts, floods, soils, rains). Male domination, authoritarian societies, family life important and parental authority, strong emphasis on religion, highly nationalistic; anti-free-trade, social conformity
   - *Industrial societies:* Mankind dominates environment, more gender emancipation, less emphasis on parental authority and family cohesion, religiosity less evident, less nationalistic, pro-free-trade, increased individualism
   - *Post–industrial societies:* More self expression, emphasis on communicating and processing information, increases in wealth and welfare states shifts emphasis to individual well-being and quality of life, environmental protection important

2. Influence of Religion
   - Cultural heritage: 8 major cultural zones: Western Christianity, Orthodox, Islam, Confucian, Japanese, Hindu, African, Latin American
   - Religious traditions appear to have enduring impacts on societal value systems.
   - Religiously mixed societies heavily influenced by national cultures (Germany: Protestantism and Catholicism; India: Hindu and Muslims; Nigeria: Christian and Muslim)
   - Protestant societies scored highest on interpersonal trust, tolerance, and well-being.
   - Strongly religious societies tended to be nationalistic; respectful of authority; low tolerances for abortion, homosexuality, and divorce.
   - In most advanced societies (16/20), there were decreases in church attendance BUT increases in spiritual concerns (Where did we come from? Where are we going? Why are we here?). Religion in the U.S. is as important as in many industrializing societies.

3. Some General Conclusions
   - Societal value systems are significantly influenced by economic development.
   - Evidence suggests that as societies develop economically, their cultures tend to shift in predictable directions, regardless of cultural heritage.
   - Predictable changes include: occupational specialization; increasing levels of affluence and income; changes in gender roles, attitudes toward authority and sexual norms; broader political participation ("less easily led publics").

Source: Adapted from Ronald Inglehart and Wayne E. Baker, "Modernization, Cultural Change and the Persistence of Traditional Values," *American Sociological Review* 65, 1 (February, 2000): 19–51.

Geography is a known quantity to companies competing in their national markets. It warrants little analysis or commentary. Then, too, in advanced markets, technology overcomes many geographic obstacles (bridges, tunnels, irrigation systems), and there are few obstacles to adjusting products and services to prevailing climatic conditions. But as business people evaluate new markets, geography, climate, and topography (the study of terrains, land surfaces) become major elements in market analysis. Geographic resource availability (minerals, agriculture) is a key shaper of national development. Topography and climate influence target markets (where populations reside), distribution (how to reach and service customers), and, in a more general sense, attitudes toward life (e.g., in severe climates or harsh terrains, where "mother nature" determines life's outcomes).

History's contribution to world business is often underestimated by business people whose major orientations are to the present and the future. Yet it is difficult to understand country markets without appreciating how national histories have shaped current political, economic, and cultural circumstances. Historical analysis, with its emphasis on how the past influences the present, is a key tool in interpreting and anticipating market behaviors and trends.

> When I want to understand what is happening today, I decide what will happen tomorrow; I look back. A page of history is worth a volume of logic.
>
> —*Oliver Wendell Holmes, 19th-century U.S. author*

GLOBALIZATION: HISTORIC BACKGROUND

Definition and Components

The globalization movement is the trend toward increasing interdependencies among world markets and the diffusion of new ideas, technologies, products, services, and lifestyles through international markets. Globalization comprises two components: *modernization* involves the upgrading of technologies and living standards that occur as ideas, products, and services diffuse through world markets. The second component, *westernization,* involves the emulation of lifestyles and behaviors of Western societies, most notably those of North America and Western Europe. From a nation-state perspective, most countries desire modernization, but not all have been keen to adopt the materialistic trappings and competitive behaviors associated with westernization. From a company perspective, many firms seek to take advantage of globalization trends to standardize output as they extend their wares into the world marketplace. Exhibit 1-2 highlights key characteristics and controversies associated with globalization, modernization, and westernization. While globalization has been occurring since world business began thousands of years ago, its effects have become more pronounced with the technological developments of the twentieth century, most notably after 1945 and again after the 1980s.

> Globalization is really another name for the dominant role of the United States.
>
> —*Henry Kissinger, former U.S. Secretary of State*

The evolution of world business and globalization has occurred through three discernible eras: the Exploration Era to 1500; the Colonization Era spanning 1500–1900; and the Era of the International Corporation, from 1900 to

EXHIBIT 1-2
Modernization, Westernization, and Americanization

Transfers of technology and foreign intrusions into national cultures have been occurring for hundreds of years. Starting with the European colonization movement of the sixteenth century, and proceeding through the industrial revolutions of the eighteenth and nineteenth centuries, the spread of technology has jumpstarted modernization movements in many countries as scientific and technological advances have upgraded national lifestyles and aided efficient resource use.

In contrast, westernization can be defined as the inculcation of (mainly) U.S. and European values on national cultures. As major international traders throughout the twentieth century, U.S. and European influences on other nations' lifestyles has been extensive, and as U.S. power has increased, so "Americanization" has become synonymous with westernization. Hollywood movies dominate the world market with 70 percent market share in the European Union and over 50 percent of the Japanese market. U.S. franchises and brands proliferate the global landscape (the "McDonald's" and "Coca-Cola" culture). British music, French

> Up to the 20th century, it was Western Europe trying to dominate world culture. In the 20th century, it was the turn of the USSR and the communist movement to try to be the dominant global philosophy. Now it's the U.S.'s and Hollywood's turn.
>
> —*Anonymous*

cuisine, and Italian fashions have established reputations worldwide, and in many developing countries, European language use is a lasting legacy from their colonial pasts.

Americanization in particular has been resisted in many parts of the world. Both Canada and the EU have turned to cultural protectionism to shield their cultures from Americanization. In 1998, nineteen European, African, and Latin American countries (not the U.S.) met to discuss some international rules to protect national cultures from

> Look back along the endless corridors of time and you will see that four things have built civilization: the spirit of religion, the spirit of creative art, the spirit of research, and the spirit of business enterprise.
>
> —*Neil Carothers*

the present. Throughout history, innovation and technology have been decisive influences in extending commerce across national boundaries and diffusing new ideas through world markets (see Figure 1.3).

The Exploration Era to 1500

The history of business dates back to prehistoric times. Villages formed to allow early divisions of labor to provide goods and services for communities. As expertise accumulated in the production of goods, infrastructures (mainly roads) were built to link communities and local markets evolved into regional markets, attracting increased varieties of merchants and manufacturers. As regional markets took shape, so road and transportation systems developed to link major commercial centers, and national markets for products emerged. The ancient civilizations in Latin America (the Incas, Mayas, and Aztecs), Egypt (the pharaohs, pyramids), Western Europe (the Romans), and

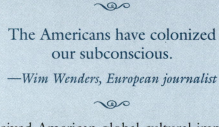

The Americans have colonized our subconscious.

—*Wim Wenders, European journalist*

perceived American global cultural imperialism. In developing markets in particular, local knowledge, cultures, and systems have lost ground to the "global monoculture." Westernization and Americanization challenge national cultures as they:

- Undermine religious values, the cornerstones of many traditional societies, with materialistic orientations. The U.S. is known as the "great Satan" in many Islamic nations.

- Encourage individualism at the expense of family, community, and national allegiances.

- Challenge social class structures based on hereditary privilege (family name, pedigree, aristocracies) and substitute competitive social-class systems based on income and wealth (yuppies, nouveau riche).

But westernization and Americanization are not the only shows in town. Other national cultures have impacted the west. For example, Asian cuisines (Indian, Chinese, Japanese, Thai, Korean) have been well received in Western Europe and North America. Japanese management practices have had significant influences on European and U.S. businesses; and Islamic, Hindu, Buddhist, and other religions have increasing followings in the West. As commerce lubricates cross-border flows of products, lifestyles, and philosophies, so global citizens have more alternatives from which to choose their ideal cultural mix. Perhaps sadly, these changes are occurring at the expense of national cultures.

Sources: Anonymous, "Culture Wars," *Economist* (September 12, 1998): 97–99; Craig Turner, "Countries discuss their concerns about US effects on global culture," *Denver Post* (Colorado: July 8, 1998): A16; and John Stackhouse, "Artisans drowning in global monoculture," *The Globe and Mail*, Canada: Thomson, (October 31, 1998): C16.

Asia (India and China) illustrate mankind's early efforts to innovate and use technology to upgrade standards of living. But, for the most part, advances in technologies and living standards rarely extended beyond national frontiers. As commerce extended throughout countries, merchants began to look to foreign markets for trading opportunities, and so the seeds of international business were sewn. In its early years, international commerce was limited to the reliability of seafaring ships, and land routes were popular. From the sixth century B.C., the Silk Road, running from the Middle East to China, was a major commercial conduit carrying artifacts, metals, and semi-precious stones across Asia, as well as new ideas such as Buddhism and, later, Islam. Still later, the Romans demonstrated the importance of supply routes as they managed an empire stretching from Britain across Europe to reach East Asia and North Africa. Trade routes were established and roads built to equip its armies; a common currency (the Dinarius) was used to lubricate commercial dealings.

Major steps forward occurred in the twelfth and thirteen centuries as compasses for navigational use, advances in sails and rigging, and hinged rudders

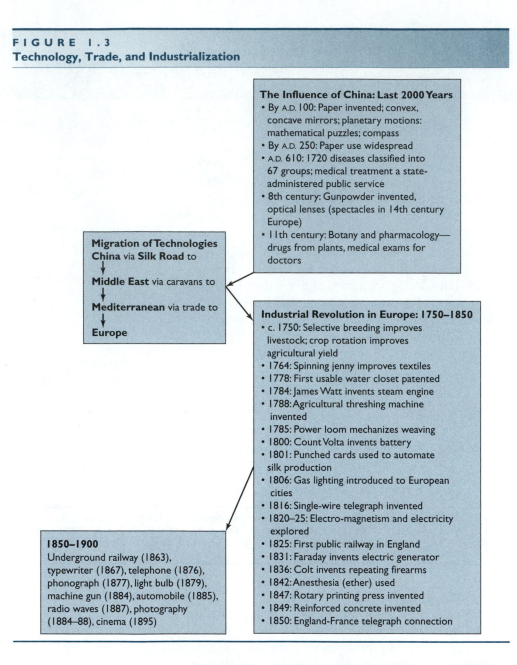

FIGURE 1.3
Technology, Trade, and Industrialization

The Influence of China: Last 2000 Years
- By A.D. 100: Paper invented; convex, concave mirrors; planetary motions: mathematical puzzles; compass
- By A.D. 250: Paper use widespread
- A.D. 610: 1720 diseases classified into 67 groups; medical treatment a state-administered public service
- 8th century: Gunpowder invented, optical lenses (spectacles in 14th century Europe)
- 11th century: Botany and pharmacology—drugs from plants, medical exams for doctors

Migration of Technologies
China via **Silk Road** to
↓
Middle East via caravans to
↓
Mediterranean via trade to
↓
Europe

Industrial Revolution in Europe: 1750–1850
- c. 1750: Selective breeding improves livestock; crop rotation improves agricultural yield
- 1764: Spinning jenny improves textiles
- 1778: First usable water closet patented
- 1784: James Watt invents steam engine
- 1788: Agricultural threshing machine invented
- 1785: Power loom mechanizes weaving
- 1800: Count Volta invents battery
- 1801: Punched cards used to automate silk production
- 1806: Gas lighting introduced to European cities
- 1816: Single-wire telegraph invented
- 1820–25: Electro-magnetism and electricity explored
- 1825: First public railway in England
- 1831: Faraday invents electric generator
- 1836: Colt invents repeating firearms
- 1842: Anesthesia (ether) used
- 1847: Rotary printing press invented
- 1849: Reinforced concrete invented
- 1850: England-France telegraph connection

1850–1900
Underground railway (1863), typewriter (1867), telephone (1876), phonograph (1877), light bulb (1879), machine gun (1884), automobile (1885), radio waves (1887), photography (1884–88), cinema (1895)

revolutionized ocean travel. Italian explorer Marco Polo reached China by the late thirteen century. Vasco de Gama, a Portuguese navigator, circumnavigated the South American Cape to reach India in 1498, and Columbus officially discovered the Americas in 1492. To replenish ships and to provide bases for further exploration, trading outposts were established. As the commercial potential of the Americas and Asia unfolded, regular trading routes were established. To finance transcontinental trade, new corporate forms emerged in Italy and later in Europe, such as joint stock companies. Intercontinental trade prospered until nationalistic concerns took over and European countries saw merit in taking political control of the new foreign markets.[4]

1500–1900: The Colonial Era

The colonial era saw military conquests, colonization, and the advent of regular international trade taking technologies to other nations as the major European powers competed to establish empires in the Americas, Africa, and Asia. Foreign influences were magnified through *diffusion catalysts*: ideas, philosophies, and technical innovations that increased the speed, efficiency, and effectiveness of the movements of ideas and goods between and within nations. These diffusion catalysts included:[5]

The development of mega languages: For ideas and technologies to travel, there had to be common means of communication between markets. In early times, these included Latin and Mandarin Chinese. In later years, the use of English and European languages facilitated the transfer of ideas and technologies among countries.

Advances in arms and military capabilities: The advent of the cannon and firearms gave colonizing powers significant advantages over local populations and enabled those powers to subdue and maintain control of their colonies with limited manpower and resources.

Writing and printing technologies extended the spread of knowledge beyond personal experiences and oral transmissions. "Potted" knowledge, in the form of books, brought about a broadening of individual knowledge bases. Formal education systems, emphasizing literacy and technical skills, led to a wider dissemination of skills via schools, guilds, and universities. Knowledge became increasingly mobile and transferable.

Transportation innovations: The steam engine revolutionized industry and travel with its applications to factories (1781), ships (1783), rail (1803–29), and buses (1824). The steam engine brought international markets closer together and provided access to remote corners of large national markets. As the colonizing powers took these innovations to foreign markets, the transportation of goods over wider areas created regional and national markets for merchandise.

The industrial revolution in England between 1750 and 1830 brought about vast changes in productive capabilities. Though cast iron and steel had been used in India and China between 500–300 B.C. and in Scandinavia around A.D. 800, its use for industrial equipment dates from Abraham Darby's coke-based smelting processes in England during the industrial revolution. Similarly, knitting machines capable of 1000 stitches per minute revolutionized the textile industry, as did Jethro Tull's mechanical seed drill for agriculture. Finally, Michael Faraday's electric generator laid the foundations for the widespread use of electricity as an industrial energy source.

Advances in communications complemented transportation innovations. The nineteenth century saw the advent of the electronic telegraph and the telephone. Both facilitated information flows between and within national markets and aided market supply and demand mechanisms. These factors, along with national print media, gave the world a connectivity it had never before experienced.

> Gutenberg made everyone a reader. Xerox made everyone a publisher.
>
> —*Marshall McLuhan, 20th-century Canadian author*

> The industrial age had to wait centuries until people in Scotland watched their kettles boil and so invented the steam engine.
>
> —*Alfred North Whitehead, 19th–20th-century English philosopher*

> Thomas Edison did not invent the first talking machine. He invented the first one you could turn off.
>
> —*Herbert V. Prochnow*

Retail establishments were important diffusion catalysts as they gave the general public access to new products, services, and ideas and facilitated the acceptance of new lifestyles and philosophies.

These diffusion catalysts facilitated the expansion of world business over the centuries, but are relevant today as developing nations confront communication, literacy, and infrastructure problems associated with industrialization. Table 1.1 sets out some of the major technological innovations that influenced the development of world business. Note that many early innovations came out of Asia (and China in particular). It was left to the Europeans to "reinvent" many innovations and diffuse them regionally and into world markets through their colonization efforts of the fifteenth to twentieth centuries.

T A B L E 1 . 1
Perspective on Technological Developments

Diffusion Catalyst Technologies

A. Transportation
- 5000 B.C.: Sailing ships appear in Middle East/Mediterranean
- 1050 B.C.: Primitive compass developed in China
- A.D. 1125: Compass developed for navigational use in China
- 1200: Hinged ship rudders appear
- 1500: Galleon ship developed by Spanish for ocean travel
- 1769: James Watt patents the steam engine. Applications to factories (1781), ships (1783), rail (1803–29), buses (1824)
- 1815: McAdam uses crushed rock for permanent road surfacing and building
- 1852: First flight of a dirigible
- 1859: Drilling of first commercial oil well in Pennsylvania, U.S.
- 1870s–1880s: Continuous ignition combustion engine invented
- 1903: Wright brothers fly first heavier-than-air craft in North Carolina
- 1880s–1890s: Automobiles with internal combustion engines by Carl Benz and Gottlieb Daimler in Germany
- 1930: Frank Whittle invents jet engine, first jet aircraft flies in Germany 1939
- 1936: British Broadcasting Corporation begins television broadcasting
- 1957: Soviets launch first satellite into space, 1962 U.S. satellite Telstar is the first commercial communications satellite
- 1960s: Internet technologies developed in U.S.; commercialized 1990s

B. Printing/Writing
- 150 B.C.: First paper made by Chinese
- A.D. 600: Chinese develop woodblock printing
- A.D. 740: First printed newspaper in China
- 1050: Chinese print using movable type
- 1423: Wood block print used in Europe
- 1438: Gutenberg invents offset printing press; rotary press 1796 in Germany, unotype in U.S. 1880s

C. Key Industrial Technologies
- 500 B.C.: Steel smelted in India
- 300 B.C.: Cast iron invented in China
- A.D. 790: Scandinavians use blast furnaces to make cast iron
- c. 1590: Simple knitting machine developed in England (1000 stitches/minute)
- 1701: Englishman Jethro Tull develops first mechanical seed drill
- c. 1750: Iron smelting with coke developed in England
- 1831: Michael Faraday builds first electric generator
- 1908: Henry Ford introduces the Model T, mass production assembly line 1913
- 1930: First large-scale analog computer is built
- 1959: IBM introduces second-generation computer using transistors
- 1968: Control Data and NCR use integrated circuits in third-generation computers

D. Time Awareness
- 800 B.C.: Egyptians develop sun dials with 6 time divisions
- 500 B.C.: Greeks and Chinese use sundials
- A.D. 725: Earliest known mechanical clock
- 1335: Italians build first European mechanical clock
- 1656: Huygens builds accurate pendulum clock (Dutch)

E. Communications
- 1831: Electric telegraph built by Wheatstore and Fothergill
- 1844: Samuel Morse introduces first practical telegraph service
- 1876: Alexander Graham Bell patents the telephone
- 1895: First commercial movie projector developed in France
- 1897: Marconi achieves radio transmissions over long distances
- 1900: Wall-mounted telephone introduced with separate mouth piece and earpieces
- Radiotelephony: 1915: Trans-Atlantic voice communication, U.S. to France; 1926: first trans-Atlantic conversation
- 1923: Iconoscope, first electronic television camera tube is patented
- 1926: *The Jazz Singer* is the first talking motion picture
- 1985: Optical fiber technologies used, 300,000 telephone calls over one line

1900–Today: The Era of the Modern International Corporation

By the end of the nineteenth century, much of the world had been explored and colonized. While foreign influences had introduced new technologies and lifestyles into the developing world, there had been some notable early backlashes, especially in the Americas, with U.S. independence in 1776 and Latin America's between 1810 and 1824. As the twentieth century unfolded, independence movements gained momentum in Africa, the Middle East, and Asia.

1900–1945: Company Internationalization But the next globalization wave was waiting in the wings, and companies began to replace countries as the major catalysts of economic and cultural change. A Belgian company established the first foreign subsidiary in Prussia (today's Germany) in 1837. Commensurate with their overseas interests, most European investments up to 1945 were colonies-based.[6] As a result of their industrialization and colonization efforts then, Western Europe was the center of world business at the turn of the century. In recognition of this trend, Japanese trading companies, such as Mitsui, and the Yokohama Specie Bank had set up offices in Western Europe in the 1880s, as did numerous Japanese shipping and insurance companies.[7] U.S. companies such as NCR and IBM also established European presences in the thriving regional market. European companies such as Unilever, British Petroleum, Royal Dutch Shell, Siemens, BASF, Bayer, Hoechst, and Nestle all had foreign manufacturing plants by 1890.[8] However, the 1914–18 war, the Great Depression of the 1920s and 1930s, and the 1939–45 war all contributed to a curtailment of international activities until after 1945.

Nevertheless, this was an era of continued change. In the transportation sector, increasing use of aircraft for personal and industrial uses meant additional options for companies serving foreign markets, and the automobile transformed personal and industrial transportation. Television also made its debut in 1936. These advances set the scene for rapid international growth in the post-1945 era.

1945–1980: Era of Increasing International Competition It was not until the 1950s that corporations began to reassert themselves in international markets. The U.S., whose economy had suffered least in the 1939–45 war, was the first to reinitiate foreign investments, and during the 1950s and 1960s U.S. firms established secure footholds in Canada and in the reemerging Western European economy. The 1960s and 1970s saw the revitalization and expansion of Japanese and European firms in the international marketplace as market blocs, such as the European Economic Community (today's European Union) and free trade movements, increased the number of opportunities in the worldwide marketplace. During this period, the cold war political rivalry between the U.S. and the USSR dampened commercial prospects.

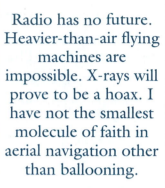

Radio has no future. Heavier-than-air flying machines are impossible. X-rays will prove to be a hoax. I have not the smallest molecule of faith in aerial navigation other than ballooning.

—*Lord Kelvin, 19th-century British scientist and president, Royal Society*

THE GLOBAL WEB

For an excellent look at twentieth century economic history see Commanding Heights at www.pbs.org/wgbh/commandingheights. Includes: Key events of the twentieth century with some short online videos; Economic development histories of 41 nations; 150 people who shaped twentieth century history, some with video footage. Ideas: Includes videos (1) Battle of Ideas: Markets vs. Governments: 2:05 minutes; (2) First Era of Globalization: 2:08 minutes; (3) Bretton Woods Conference: 1:53 minutes.

THE GLOBALIZATION ERA SINCE 1980

During the 1980s, the world marketplace changed yet again. The collapse of communism and the industrialization of developing markets led to significant increases in global commerce. The internationalization of North American, Western European, and Japanese firms had contributed to an upsurge of commercial activities in the developing world, and, by the 1990s, developing market competitors were entering world markets. These competitors included Petroleos de Venezuela; Daewoo, Samsung, Hyundai, LG Group (all Korean); Cemex, Gruma (Mexico); and Petroles Brasileiro, Vale do Rio Doce, Cervejaria Brahma (Brazil). As the 1990s drew to a close, companies from China, Argentina, Philippines, South Africa, Malaysia, Singapore, and India were internationalizing and heightening competition in the world marketplace.

With the new millennium, international corporations were on their ways to becoming true global commercial empires. By 2002, 64,000 international companies had about 870,000 foreign subsidiaries in world markets. These subsidiaries employed about 53 million people, and their sales totaled over $18 trillion, almost half the world's $40+ trillion GDP. Of these, about 90 percent were from North America, Western Europe, and Japan.[9] Table 1.2 shows the world's top 25 international corporations by sales.

- U.S. companies accounted for over 20 percent of foreign direct investment in world markets. In terms of sales, they had nine of the top 25 international corporations (with one German–U.S. firm—DaimlerChrysler), but five out of the top 10 companies.

- Western European firms, long established in colonial markets and in the European Union, had over $3.7 trillion of foreign direct investments in world markets (over 50 percent of the world total). Heading the list was world #4 DaimlerChrysler, with Royal Dutch Shell, BP, Total-Fina-Elf, Volkswagon, E.On, Carrefour, Royal Ahold, and RWE Group rounding out the European presence in the top 25 list. Most have major dependencies on world markets, with about 50 percent of world sales outside of their home markets. Note, however, that sales dependencies on foreign markets are but one indicator of corporate globalization measures. Others, such as percentages of foreign-based assets and foreign employees, are examined in our Chapter 8 discussion of globalization measures.

- Japanese firms occupied seven spots in the top 25 list. Perhaps surprisingly, Japan had "only" $331 billion of direct investments in world markets. Their trading company presence is notable, with Mitsui and Mitsubishi having presences outside their domestic market. Outside of these firms, the Japanese have had major impacts in automobiles (Toyota, Honda) and electronics (Hitachi, Matsushita, and Sony).

- From an industry perspective, four industry categories stand out—petroleum, automobiles, electronics, and distribution (trading companies and retail)—all have five entries in the top 25 listing.

TABLE 1.2
World's 25 Largest Corporations: Ranked by Sales 2001 ($m)

	Company	Country	Industry	Total Sales	Foreign Sales	% Foreign
1	Wal-Mart	U.S.	Retailing	217,799	35,485	16.3
2	Exxonmobil	U.S.	Petroleum	209,417	145,814	69.6
3	General Motors	U.S.	Motor Vehicles	177,260	45,256	25.5
4	BP	U.K.	Petroleum	175,389	141,225	80.5
5	Ford	U.S.	Motor Vehicles	162,412	52,983	32.6
6	Daimler-ObrChrysler	German/U.S.	Motor Vehicles	137,051	43,556	31.8
7	Royal Dutch Shell	U.K.-Dutch	Petroleum	135,211	72,952	53.9
8	General Electric	U.S.	Electronical	125,913	39,914	31.7
9	Toyota	Japan	Motor Vehicles	108,808	59,880	55.0
10	Chevron-Texaco	U.S.	Petroleum	104,409	57,673	55.2
11	Mitsubishi	Japan	Trading	100,553	15,821	15.7
12	Mitsui	Japan	Trading	96,174	25,553	26.6
13	Total-Fina-Elf	France	Petroleum	94,418	74,647	79.1
14	Philip Morris	U.S.	Consumer goods	89,924	33,924	37.7
15	IBM	U.S.	Electrical	85,866	50,651	59.0
16	Volkswagen	Germany	Motor Vehicles	79,376	57,426	72.3
17	E.On	Germany	Utilities	71,419	22,744	31.8
18	Verizon	U.S.	Telecommunication	67,190	2,541	3.8
19	Carrefour	France	Retailing	62,294	31,513	50.6
20	Hitachi	Japan	Electronics	60,753	14,130	23.3
21	Royal Ahold	Netherlands	Retailing	59,701	40,150	67.3
22	RWE Group	Germany	Utilities	58,039	23,151	39.9
23	Sony	Japan	Electronics	57,795	38,605	66.8
24	Honda	Japan	Motor Vehicles	55,955	40,088	71.6
25	Matsushita	Japan	Electronics	52,263	26,815	51.3

Source: Adapted from "World's Top 100 Transnational Corporations" *World Investment Report 2003* (New York: United Nations): 187–88.

The Major Catalysts of Post-1980 Globalization

International Trade The world has moved irrevocably toward free trade since 1945 through the efforts of the General Agreement on Tariffs and Trade (GATT, a United Nations agency) until 1995, and, since that time, through GATT's replacement, the World Trade Organization. The results have been dramatic. Since 1945, tariffs have fallen from an average of over 40 percent for industrial goods to less than 4 percent. World trade expanded from $2 trillion in 1980 to about $8 trillion in 2002. The expansion of world trade has been aided by the UN's International Monetary Fund (IMF), which monitors and coordinates foreign-exchange rate values among nations and provides aid to countries with international payment problems. Increasingly efficient air and ocean transportation systems have also aided international trade expansion.

Trade Blocs For some countries, the worldwide liberalization of trade and commerce did not occur fast enough, and countries got together to form trade blocs to facilitate commercial interactions among members. The European Economic Community (now the European Union) was formed in 1957. Since then, trade

> The merchant has no country.
>
> —*Thomas Jefferson, 18th–19th-century U.S. president*

blocs have been formed in North America (North American Free Trade Area), South America (the Mercosur and Andean Pact groups), Asia, and Africa.

Foreign Direct Investments (FDI) These occur when international companies make investments in factories, plants, and machinery in non-domestic markets. As firms have increased their international commitments, FDI has grown from $615 billion in 1980 to over $7.1 trillion in 2002. Nation states, recognizing the economic stimulus FDI provides, have increasingly worked to make their economies more attractive to international corporate investors. Throughout history, there have been three major reasons for international business expansion. In early times (sixteenth through twentieth centuries), explorers looked for new *resources* (often gold, silver, mineral deposits). Then, as countries began to develop, business people began to regard distant nations as *markets* (the colonial era). Finally, as free trade movements took hold after 1945, *efficiency-seeking* companies looked to overseas markets as manufacturing sites to lower global costs of doing business. Today all three major motives (resource-seekers, market-seekers, efficiency-seekers) are reasons why firms invest abroad.[10]

> The selfish spirit of commerce knows no country, and feels no passion or principles but that of gain.
>
> *—Thomas Jefferson, 18th–19th-century, U.S. president*

Global Movements Towards Capitalism The demise of communism in the 1980s and 1990s left little competition to capitalism as the world's dominant economic and political philosophy. Since that time, Latin America, Eastern Europe, and Asia have slowly opened up their markets and become active participants in the global marketplace. Within national markets, former government-owned industrial monopolies such as airlines, telecommunications, energy, and utilities have been sold back into the private sector (privatization) and their markets deregulated to allow companies to compete for market share and profits.

> Global communications are one of the most important contemporary manifestations of Western power . . . the extent to which global communications are dominated by the West is . . . a major source of resentment and hostility of non-Western peoples against the West.
>
> *—Samuel P. Huntington, political scientist*

Technology and Global Media The advent of satellite, computer, and Internet technologies has transformed worldwide communications and facilitated information flows between nations, companies, and individuals. At the nation-state level, it has become increasingly difficult for countries to isolate their citizens from outside influences, and consumers worldwide have begun to enjoy the benefits of the international marketplace. Companies now have superior abilities to coordinate activities, products, and strategies across markets, and individuals have increased access to new ideas, philosophies, products, and lifestyles. Note, though, that many traditional barriers to world business—literacy, language problems—still affect the spread of international electronic (E) commerce (see Casette 1-2).

Globalization and the Developing World

Up to 1985, the Triad nations of North America, Western Europe, and Japan were dominant in world commerce, and are still today major providers of global capital. But, as developing markets opened up to trade and investments, so new ideas and technologies began to contribute to economic and cultural change. Trade and investments brought many new (and affordable) products to developing nations. The advent of global media made information more readily available to developing nation publics that, coupled with moves toward democratization, have made politicians more accountable to their electors.[11]

But the diffusion of technologies and consequent modernization processes have barely impacted many emerging markets, where large percentages of national populations still reside in agriculturally based rural areas, largely untouched by modernization trends. As the World Bank notes:

- About 1.2 billion people live on less than $1 a day. This number has increased, not decreased, over the last decade. About 2.8 billion live on less than $2 a day.

- Underweight children number over 150 million.

- The average income of the twenty richest countries was 15 times that of the twenty poorest countries in 1960. It is now 30 times the average of the twenty poorest countries.

- The world population reached 6 billion in 2000 and is set to reach over 7 billion by 2015. Most of these increases will occur in the developing world.

- In the U.S. from 1990 to 1998, eight women died in childbirth for every 100,000 live births. In Eritrea and the Central African Republic, this number was 1000.

- Average life expectancies in many African nations have fallen from over 60 years to below 40 years because of AIDS. Over 95 percent of AIDS victims are in the developing world.

- In 1998, about one quarter of 3.4 billion adults in the developing world were illiterate, and females were twice as likely to be illiterate as males (18 percent versus 33 percent).

- The poorest 40 percent of the 15–19 years age group of the populations of India, Pakistan, Mali, and Benin averaged 0 years of schooling.

- In the developing world, 90 percent of sewage was discharged into rivers, lakes, and coastal waterways without any treatment.[12]

Development has proceeded unevenly in the developing world for two reasons. First, some countries (such as Chile, Brazil, Malaysia, South Korea) have made greater efforts to open their economies up to international trade and foreign influences and have benefited from technology transfers to create new jobs and opportunities. Other countries have remained isolated and made less economic progress. Second, the diffusion process within many countries has been hindered by geographic, political, and cultural factors that have slowed the impact of modernization processes. The slow diffusion of new ideas and technologies has limited opportunities to evaluate alternative lifestyles and philosophies prevalent in the world economy.

> A hungry man is not a free man.
>
> —*Adlai Stevenson, 20th-century U.S. diplomat*

> Lack of money is the root of all evil.
>
> —*George Bernard Shaw, 19th–20th-century British playwright*

> There are two kinds of fools. One says: "This is old, therefore it is good." The other says: "This is new, therefore it is better."
>
> —*William R. Inge*

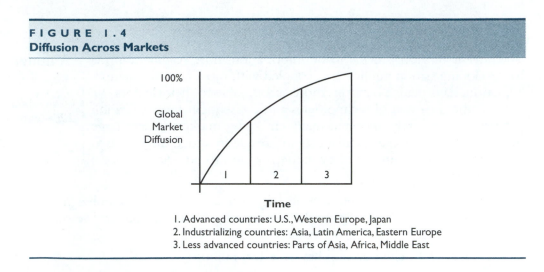

FIGURE 1.4
Diffusion Across Markets

Time

1. Advanced countries: U.S., Western Europe, Japan
2. Industrializing countries: Asia, Latin America, Eastern Europe
3. Less advanced countries: Parts of Asia, Africa, Middle East

Reasons for Developmental Differences: The Diffusion Process in International Business

Developmental differences among and within nations demonstrate that technologies and ideas diffuse at variable rates throughout world markets. Not surprisingly, this affects the extent to which companies can leverage technologies, products, and services across markets. The diffusion of innovations occurs at two levels: between markets and within markets. Figures 1.4 and 1.5 illustrate these processes.

The International Diffusion Process In Figure 1.4, the diffusion process begins in advanced markets like the U.S., Japan, and Western Europe. These are the headquarters of major international corporations. The competitiveness of these markets, and their high levels of education and affluence have constantly stimulated the development of new products and technologies.[13] As corporations see commercial opportunities in foreign markets, new products and technologies are transferred into other industrialized countries through export sales and overseas manufacturing in foreign affiliates. Over time, and through exports and foreign direct investments, products and technologies diffuse into developing countries and throughout world markets.[14]

The Diffusion Process in National Markets Within individual countries, the diffusion process usually begins in urban centers (see Figure 1.5). In industrializing countries in particular, major metropolitan areas are the seats of government, have developed infrastructures (power grids, telecommunications, road, rail systems, airports) and contain concentrations of economically significant customers. This has made cities ideal springboards for the diffusion of new products and technologies in emerging markets. Over time, and just as they did in medieval Europe, infrastructures develop, general levels of education and affluence rise, and innovations spread outside of towns into semi-urban areas (where rural migrants settle) and eventually into rural markets. As successive

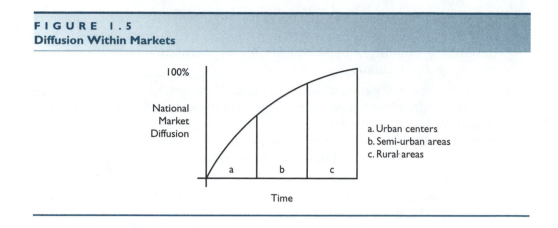

FIGURE 1.5
Diffusion Within Markets

waves of technologies and products diffuse, so modernization and industrialization take hold. In developed markets, this process has already occurred. Urban-rural differences in affluence and education levels are minimal, and established infrastructures facilitate speedy diffusions of new ideas, products, and services.

Many factors affect the rates at which new ideas and technologies diffuse through world markets, including:

- *Country openness to external influences:* The diffusion of technologies and new ideas into country markets is affected by national interactions with the outside world. In some cases, a country's geographic position can effectively isolate it from outside influences (for example, China and Japan up to the late nineteenth century). In other cases, countries take steps to protect national industries and cultures from international influences (for example, through trade and investment restrictions), essentially limiting their abilities to benefit from other countries' innovations. Middle Eastern and some Asian economies have been apprehensive about the importation of Western lifestyles that they perceive as disruptive to their national cultures.

- *The importance of education and literacy:* Use and adoption of technologies requires educated personnel. Ineffective national education systems are problematic for three reasons. First, they hinder national abilities to invent and be at the cutting edge of industry innovations. Second, the number and caliber of technical and educated personnel affects countries' abilities to adopt and use technologies for national development. Third, poorly educated consumers are less able to appreciate and adopt new ideas and technologies.

    Literary rates also affect diffusion rates for new ideas, as consumer education is limited to personal experiences and local interactions. While the

> The crossroads of trade are the meeting place of ideas, the attrition ground of rival custom and beliefs; diversities beget conflict, comparison, thought; superstitions cancel each other, and reason begins.
>
> —*Will Durant, 20th-century U.S. historian*

growth of broadcast media such as radio and television can offset illiteracy problems, the combination of low literacy rates and poverty, particularly in developing countries, limits educational opportunities and exposures to new ideas and technologies.

- *The importance of national infrastructures:* How quickly new ideas and innovations spread within countries depends on the degree of national infrastructure development (roads, energy grids, transportation systems, water facilities). The ease with which nations can develop infrastructures to link communities and populations in turn is influenced by country size, national resources, topographies, and climates.

- *Effects of national ethnic and linguistic compositions:* Cultural and linguistic differences between countries affect the ease with which nations can communicate and do business with each other. Similarly, within nations, cultural heterogeneity (i.e., many different ethnic and language groups) slows the diffusions of new ideas, products, and technologies. Conversely, single language and culturally homogeneous nations have fewer obstacles in diffusing new technologies and ideas.

- *How disruptive innovations are on national lifestyles.*[15] The rate of innovation diffusion depends on how different products and services are and how customers perceive the costs and benefits of the innovation. Innovations must get around two sets of obstacles to diffuse effectively throughout world markets. First, when they cross country borders, they must overcome national differences in culture and development, and, second, when they are rolled out into rural areas, particularly in developing markets, where differences in urban-rural cultures must be negotiated. For example, introducing a new brand of toothpaste into developing country towns and cities is a minor innovation. Rolling out toothpaste into rural markets is a different matter and may involve disrupting traditional dental-hygiene patterns (for example, in India where charcoal commonly is used in rural areas to clean teeth).

> Innovators are inevitably controversial.
>
> —*Eva Le Gallienne, U.S. film director*

Cumulatively, the introduction of new products, technologies, and business methods continue to have major impacts on national cultures and mindsets. While many are welcomed, some are not. When introducing new products and technologies into foreign markets, international corporations must take account of diffusion processes in their choice of strategies.

Diffusion Effects on Strategy Formulation and Implementation

Historically, countries have developed at varying rates and in different ways. They have different resource bases, climates, topographies, languages, values, attitudes, and behaviors. In the competitive world marketplace, the challenge for international business executives is to recognize what aspects of business strategy can be transferred to other markets with few or no adaptations (a standardized or global strategy to take advantage of customer similarities) and what aspects need to be adapted to facilitate customer acceptance and use (an adaptive or multi-domestic strategy). The links between traditional-modern societies and strategy formulation and implementation are shown in Figure 1.6.

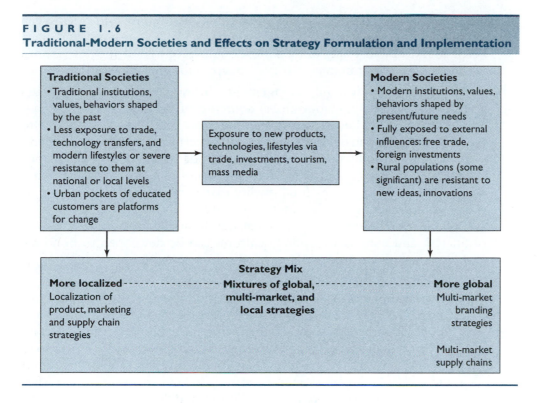

FIGURE 1.6
Traditional-Modern Societies and Effects on Strategy Formulation and Implementation

Traditional Societies
- Traditional institutions, values, behaviors shaped by the past
- Less exposure to trade, technology transfers, and modern lifestyles or severe resistance to them at national or local levels
- Urban pockets of educated customers are platforms for change

Exposure to new products, technologies, lifestyles via trade, investments, tourism, mass media

Modern Societies
- Modern institutions, values, behaviors shaped by present/future needs
- Fully exposed to external influences: free trade, foreign investments
- Rural populations (some significant) are resistant to new ideas, innovations

Strategy Mix

More localized - - - - - - - - - - - - - - - - **Mixtures of global,** - - - - - - - - - - - - - - - - **More global**
Localization of product, marketing and supply chain strategies   **multi-market, and local strategies**   Multi-market branding strategies

Multi-market supply chains

The Arguments for Standardized Strategies The temptation to standardize products has never been stronger. Global customer awareness and appreciation of new products and technologies has never been higher. International media, trade, the Internet, and the increasing presence of international corporations in world markets have homogenized tastes to the point that customer similarities across markets have outstripped national differences. The constant sharing of technologies, goods, and services among developed markets in particular has reduced (but not eliminated) many national differences in customer prefer- ences. This globalization trend has encouraged firms to standardize products and services across markets.[16]

International companies have taken advantage of the globalization trend by transferring products, services, and technologies abroad. Initial product roll- outs are usually to developed countries with similar demand patterns (e.g., North America and Western Europe). While companies make some adaptations (voltage changes for electronic goods, right/left hand drives and minor stylistic changes for autos, labeling changes for consumer products), essentially prod- ucts and services are similar from market to market. This is a *global or multi- market standardization strategy.* Also, in urban parts of developing markets, outside of translations and language differences, customer tastes are similar to those in developed markets as modernization trends have taken hold. Global and multi-market strategies have a number of advantages. These include:

- Global, regional or multi-market rollouts of new products maximize their competitive impact. Opportunities exist to transfer products and brand images across markets, and policies regarding distribution and pricing can be standardized to varying degrees. Carlsberg beer is brewed and marketed identically in thirty-one countries, and Hollywood movies go into world markets with minimal changes (except dubbing and subtitles).

- Supply-chain activities and management philosophies can be integrated across nations. This includes global sourcing of products, raw materials, and components. Manufacturing methods can be transferred abroad to capitalize on home-market efficiencies and expertise. Toyota routinely employs Japanese production methods and standards in its overseas plants. Where foreign-market infrastructures and conditions are favorable, management processes, such as total quality management, just-in-time supply chains, reengineering can be assessed for use. Worldwide R and D efforts and globally orchestrated new-product development processes can be coordinated, and common corporate cultures can be developed to bond together managements from different countries and cultures.

<blockquote>
To change and to improve are two different things.

—*German proverb*
</blockquote>

<blockquote>
God, grant me the serenity to accept the things I cannot change, the courage to change the things I can, and the wisdom to know the difference.

—*Reinhold Niebuhr, 20th-century U.S. theologian*
</blockquote>

The Arguments for Localized Strategies Foreign markets and customers have not been equally receptive to cross-border influences and trends. Hundreds and thousands of years of national culture continuity breed habits and behaviors that are not easily set aside. Where local markets retain their traditional national cultures, modern products and technologies are slow to be assimilated (for example, in the Middle East and Asia where national cultures are deeply rooted). This occurs where protectionist tendencies are present, where local traditions are strong enough to resist the diffusion of modern technologies, and where business acumen dictates that localization strategies are optimal. In such markets, national tastes are less influenced by global trends and international firms must cater to local needs in order to be successful. This involves taking full account of national cultures, values, and behaviors. Localization strategies become key competitive tools as international firms compete not only against other worldwide companies but also against national competitors with superior knowledge of local customs and behaviors. But while completely localized strategies are tempting options, they are not the answers for most international companies for three reasons. First, localized approaches are expensive and time-consuming, as top-to-bottom assessments of customer needs are necessary for each new market. Second, localized strategies often do not differentiate corporate output from that of local rivals. Third, they do not take advantage of the international company's worldwide experience and scale economies—often key reasons firms have been successful in world markets in the first place. In many situations, however, business strategies must be adapted and localized to optimize their appeals. Localization strategies include the following:

- Adapting imported product ideas and custom-building goods and services so they can maximize their appeal to national tastes. Television networks such as the U.S.'s MTV and Asia's Star TV have recognized that customizing programming to national tastes is a major key to marketplace success.

- Use of country-oriented manufacturing techniques (for example, more labor intensive production processes), local sources of supply, and adherence to local management styles and supply-chain relations. Hankook Tire, a global top 5 tire manufacturer, deliberately gives its foreign subsidiaries decision-making autonomy to respond quickly to local market needs.[17]

- Adoption of localized marketing strategies, with advertising and promotional strategies oriented toward national and local values and major adaptations to local distribution and pricing habits. In China, McDonald's and Kentucky Fried Chicken both adorned their restaurants with Spring Festival decorations to maximize local appeal, while Coca Cola printed cartoon snakes on bottles to celebrate the year of the snake.[18]

Historically, standardization and adaptation have been viewed as opposite strategies. In reality, companies tend to standardize some aspects of their strategies (for example, building global or multi-market brands) and adapt other aspects of their operations (manufacturing methods, promotions, distribution). Also, wherever firms have foreign-market facilities, executives must adapt to local cultures in face-to-face dealings and comply with local laws and customs with respect to human resources, manufacturing, and distribution. The globalization/localization mix varies by industry, company, and market. It is management's task is to ensure that foreign operations have the appropriate global-local mixes for their situations.

WORLD BUSINESS TOPICS AND THE ORGANIZATION OF THIS TEXT

This text is organized into thirteen chapters under three sectional headings: (1) The globalization process, history, causes, and effects are examined in the first three chapters to give students background concerning how world business has affected and continues to affect global institutions, behaviors, and values through transfers of technologies, products, services, and lifestyles. (2) Chapters 3 through 6 cover analyses of the world marketplace at the regional, individual, and industry levels. (3) The remaining chapters (7–13) look at company strategies: international planning (Chapter 7), corporate globalization strategies (8–9), global and multi-market strategies (10–11), and localization strategies (12–13). What follows are details of individual chapters.

Part 1: World Business—The Globalization Process

Our world business journey has begun in Chapter 1 with a review of the two major challenges facing global executives: (1) the challenge of diversity as managers appreciate the variability of world markets and (2) the challenge of implementing strategies in a perpetually changing marketplace.

The process of understanding international markets begins with an appreciation of how the world economy has evolved over time. History shapes nations, their behaviors, values, and attitudes. The globalization process is not

TABLE 1.3
Text Layout: World Business: Globalization, Analysis, and Strategy

Globalization

Chapter 1: The World Business Challenge: Importance of globalization, historic background, diffusion through world markets and effect on strategy

Chapter 2: Globalization and Worldwide Infrastructure Development: Examines public (United Nations) and private sector forces affecting the globalization movement

Chapter 3: Globalization, Technology Transfers, Economic Development, and Cultural Change: Reviews technology transfers and their effects on political, economic, cultural institutions, and impacts on interpersonal relations, individual behaviors, and business practices

Strong Globalization Effects

Weak Globalization Effects

Analysis

Chapter 4: Geopolitical Analyses of Regional Markets: Examines the geographic and historic forces shaping economic development and behaviors at the regional level

Chapter 5: Analyses of National Markets: Evaluates key factors in the analysis of individual markets

Chapter 6: Analyzing Global Industries and Competitors: Looks at how companies analyze global demand, supply chains and rivals

Strategy

Chapter 7: International Strategic Planning and Marketing Screening: Examines corporate, competitive, and market factors affecting allocations of company resources

Internationalization and Globalization Strategies
Chapter 8: Internationalization and Globalization Processes: Reviews how firms change their internal processes as they internationalize and then link their international operations to provide global synergies

Chapter 9: Market Entry and Servicing Strategies: The various ways firms can service foreign markets, along with the pros and cons of individual market entry methods, are assessed

Global and Multi-Market Strategies
Chapter 10: Global, Regional, and Multi-Market Strategies: Discusses the formulations and implementation of global, regional, and multi-market strategies, and competition strategies—whether to compete against them or cooperate with them

Chapter 11: Global and Multi-Market Supply Chains: Evaluates how supply chains are integrated globally or over multiple markets, and the reason underlying the outsourcing of supply chain functions

Localization Strategies
Chapter 12: Managing Intercultural Differences: Looks at human relations aspects of localization strategies, including high-low context differences, the reasons for cultural differences, and conducting face-to-face negotiations

Chapter 13: Managing Local Stakeholders and Supply Chains: Reviews how local stakeholders should be be managed, and the intricacies of managing local supply chains

new, though the pace of its progress increased significantly toward the end of the twentieth century. The effects of this process, with the constant diffusion of technologies, processes, and lifestyles through world and national markets, are examined, along with its effects on global and local strategy formulation and implementation.

Chapter 2 examines the forces contributing to the globalization movement. The effects of public institutions, such as the UN, are evaluated from an international-business perspective, and the effects of specialized UN agencies are assessed. Private sector contributions are reviewed, including the impacts of global media, international retailers, transportation, and information technology catalysts on globalization. Also discussed are the effects of economic and political integrations (e.g., the European Union and other trade blocs) and the impact of privatization and deregulation trends on industries and nation-states.

Chapter 3 looks at globalization effects, with technology transfers as key inputs to country development, and the transitions from traditional to modern societies. Changes in political institutions (e.g., from autocratic to democratic systems) and economic institutions (from centralized production and distribution to capitalist systems) are examined, along with changes in social and cultural institutions (e.g., social class, family units, religiosity) and the reshaping of personal values. Paralleling these societal changes, developmental changes in industry, corporate, management, marketing, and consumer behaviors are documented.

Part 2: World Business Analysis

Analyses of world markets include a look at the development of regional markets, analyses of national markets, and a process for examining industries and competitors in their global contexts.

Chapter 4 examines regional issues. The effects of geography and history on regional commercial and cultural development are examined in their North American, Latin American, Western, Eastern European, Middle Eastern, African, and Asian contexts. These analyses provide insights as to why regions developed at different rates and why differences exist among regional behavior patterns. These insights are building blocks for the analyses of individual markets presented in Chapter 5 and include evaluations of historic, geographic, political, economic, and cultural factors affecting commercial operations within individual countries.

Having completed their environmental analyses, companies turn their attentions to industry activities, competitors, and deciding which markets present the best opportunities for commercial development. Chapter 6 looks at how industries are analyzed on a worldwide scale to determine where to sell and produce their products and services. Included are analyses of competitor actions and key factors in corporate situation, strategy, and resource deployment analysis.

Part 3: World Business Strategies

Firms use a variety of strategies to enter and penetrate international markets. The strategy-making process begins as industry and company analyses are brought into the corporate planning process. This is described in Chapter 7. In this most important of the management processes, corporate missions, assets, and competencies are reviewed and businesses and market strengths and weaknesses are assessed.

From these evaluations, companies prepare to internationalize their operations or, if they are seasoned campaigners, integrate their activities globally. These processes, described in Chapter 8, ensure that firms have the appropriate organizations and managerial talent to cope with the rigors of extending businesses over increasing numbers of markets and to ensure that personnel, corporate processes, and organizational structures are matched to industry, business, and market needs.

Once internal analyses are complete, firms review and evaluate their choices of market entry and servicing strategies. These options are presented in Chapter 9, along with the factors determining the use of specific strategies.

Firms compete in world markets with two basic strategies. In countries where the globalization process has taken root, markets and customers tend to be similar and countries have few restrictions to trade and commerce. In these cases, companies can extend products and services (with often minor changes) either worldwide or into multiple markets. These strategies are described in Chapter 10, as are competitor strategies: whether firms should compete against or form alliances with regional and national rivals in world markets.

Similarly, where markets are open, firms can link supply chain operations and take advantage of individual countries' resources and expertise. This process, detailed in Chapter 11, sets out the principles involved in operation global and multi-market supply chains. Supplier-manufacturer linkages, international manufacturing systems, and distribution strategies are set out, and market linkage mechanisms are reviewed. Finally, the outsourcing option is discussed, including the pros and cons of allowing third parties to handle supply-chain functions.

Finally, because all firms must ultimately manage their markets at the grass-roots level, localization strategies are set out in Chapters 12 and 13. In Chapter 12, the managing of intercultural differences is examined first from a conceptual perspective, then from a face-to-face vantage point as intercultural negotiating strategies are discussed. In Chapter 13, the management of local supply chains is discussed: what managers must do to build insider relations, manage suppliers and local manufacturing operations, and recalibrate their marketing strategies to suit local needs. Finally, because management styles usually need to be adapted to ensure the smooth-running of internal operations, the characteristics of North American, Latin American, Western, Eastern European, Asian, and African styles of management are set out and insights presented regarding their historic and cultural underpinnings.

KEY POINTS

- World business is the performing of commercial activities to promote the sale of goods and services across national boundaries. Major beneficiaries of these activities include countries, companies, and consumers.

- The world business challenge is to use tools from political science, anthropology, economic development, sociology, religious studies, geography, and history to understand the diversity and change inherent in world markets.

- The globalization movement is the trend toward increasing interdependencies among world markets and the diffusion of new ideas, technologies, products, services, and lifestyles through international markets. It comprises modernization and westernization processes. Historically, globalization has evolved over three eras: the Exploration Era to 1500, the Colonization Era from 1500–1900, and the Era of the International Corporation from 1900 onward.

- Modern corporations date from the nineteenth century, but their major growth period was in the post-1945 era, with U.S., European, and Japanese companies taking the lead. From about 1980, international trade, trade blocs, foreign direct investment, trends towards global capitalism, and global media accelerated the globalization movement.

- The globalization movement involves the diffusion process of new technologies and products across markets. It starts with developed countries and moves over time into developing markets. The rural parts of developing countries are the last to benefit from modernization processes, and populations in these areas lag behind those in urban and semi-urban areas. Education, literacy rates, country openness to external influences, national infrastructures, and ethnic and linguistic compositions affect diffusion rates in developing markets, as does the type of product innovation.

- The diffusion process affects strategy formulation and implementation, with standardized strategies more likely in developed markets. Greater degrees of adaptation are likely in developing markets less exposed to modernization processes.

ENDNOTES

1. This equates linguistic groups with cultural groups, as each language propagates a distinct cultural perspective of the world.

2. World Bank, *Entering the 21st Century: World Development Report 2000* (London: Oxford University Press, 2000), 45.

3. Ibid., 47.

4. Kenneth Pomeranz, "Roots of the Modern Corporations," *World Trade* (May 1996): 88–90.

5. Based on Jared Diamond, *Guns, Gems and Steel: The Fates of Human Societies* (New York: W. W. Norton 1998); and Peter R. Dickson, "Understanding the Trade Winds: The Global Evolution of Production, Consumption and the Internet," *Journal of Consumer Research* 27.1 (June 2000): 115–122.

6. Lawrence G. Franko, *The European Multinationals* (Stamford, Conn.: Greylock Publishers), 1976.

7. Mark Mason, "The origins and evolution of Japanese direct investment in Europe," *Business History Review Autumn* (1992): 435–45.

8. Franko.

9. United Nations, *World Investment Report* (New York, 2003): 23.

10. United Nations, *World Investment Report 1998* (New York: United Nations 1998): 91.

11. Pete Engardio and Catherine Belton, "Global Capitalism: Can it be made to work better?" *Business Week* (November 6, 2000): 72–76.

12. Source: www.worldbank.org/poverty/quiz.

13. Michael E. Porter, "The Competitive Advantage of Nations," *Harvard Business Review* 68, 2 (March–April 1990): 73–94.

14. This is the International Product Life Cycle thesis originally advocated by Raymond Vernon, "International Investment and International Trade in the Life Cycle," *Quarterly Journal of Economics* (May 1966): 190–207.

15. This section based on Everett M. Rogers, *Diffusion of Innovations,* Fourth Edition (New York: Free Press, 1995), 204–51.

16. Theodore Levitt, "The Globalization of Markets," *Harvard Business Review* 61, 3 (May–June 1983): 92–102.

17. Anonymous, "Global strategy sends tire profits rolling," *Business Korea* (January 2000): 55–56.

18. Anonymous, "Foreign Businesses Make Money Out of Chinese Tradition," *Asiainfo Daily China News* (February 8): 1.

CASETTE 1-1
The September 11 Tragedy: An International Business Perspective

The events of September 11, 2001, when Muslim fundamentalists hijacked four U.S. civil aircraft and flew three into the twin World Trade Towers in New York and the Pentagon, and the fourth into the ground in Pennsylvania, were tragic. Overall, about 3000 people lost their lives in the worst act of terrorism in modern history. Instantaneously, much of the world united behind the U.S., condemned the act, and set about identifying the perpetrators. Very quickly, the U.S. and its allies identified Osama bin Laden and the al Qaeda organization as the responsible party, and took steps to isolate the group. Bin Laden himself, the estranged son of a powerful Saudi Arabian family, was already known as the prime suspect behind the bombing of the USS *Cole* in the Yemen and the two U.S. embassies in Kenya and Tanzania. Soon U.S. citizens were finding out what the Europeans had known for decades: that it was almost impossible to defend against terrorism without massive curtailing of individual rights that countries like the U.S. had spent generations building up.

Yet throughout the worldwide media coverage, little had been said about one key question. Why did it happen? The primary concerns were not so much about lax or ineffectual safety procedures at airports and on airplanes, but about who could hate the U.S. that much to make such acts of terrorism feasible. What U.S. behaviors or policies had so angered Islamic fundamentalists that the September 11 bombings became an outlet for their frustrations? To understand the motives for such acts is not to condone them, but rather to avoid future escalations from other like-minded groups. Two explanations have been forthcoming. One concerns U.S. handling of the Israel-Palestinian problem. The other is more wide-ranging and looks at the globalization/westernization process and their effects on world cultures.

The Palestinian Question
The problems of the Middle East date back hundreds and thousands of years, but we begin in the early twentieth century, when the Arabian Peninsula was, with some exceptions, mainly inhabited by wandering Bedouin tribesmen and caravans. The Turkish Ottoman Empire had dominated the region for centuries, but was finally overturned during World War I,

and the Balfour Declaration in 1917 established the principle of independent states for Israel and the Palestinians. However, it was not until the 1930s and 1940s that a formalized system of independent nation-states was established. Saudi Arabia became a country in 1932, Jordan in 1946, Syria in 1945, Lebanon in 1946, Israel in 1948, Yemen in 1967. Prior to that time, the cultural bonds of language (Arabic) and religion (Islam) linked the Arabian Peninsula peoples. Today, those bonds are still apparent and are epitomized by the old Arab proverb: "I against my brothers; I and my brothers against my cousins; I, my brothers and cousins against the world." When one Arabic Muslim was harmed, other Arabs and Muslims felt the pain.

The current Israel-Palestinian problem had its origins in 1948 when the division of the Palestine into Israeli and Palestinian states produced immediate conflicts that escalated into regional conflicts in 1967, 1973, and 1982. Problems centered around U.S.-backed Israeli occupation from 1967 of the Palestinian-dominated areas of the Golan Heights (on Israel's northeastern border), the West Bank (to the east), and Gaza in the southwestern portion of the Palestine. While Gaza established some autonomy in the late 1990s, conflicts between Israel and the Palestinians continued into the new millennium. In 2001, continued Israeli incursions into the West Bank had produced continued conflicts, despite U.S. and Western efforts to broker peaceful solutions through negotiations. U.S.-supplied Israeli forces were proving superior, with Palestinian fatalities outstripping Israeli deaths by a 3 to 1 margin. The Arab and Islamic peoples around the world rallied around the Palestinian cause. The historic bonds of language, culture, and religion are not easy to erase, and the U.S.'s backing of Israel was perceived, rightly or wrongly, as anti-Arab and anti-Islam.

The Globalization Era

The globalization era has its roots in the 1980s and 1990s, decades of tumultuous change in the world economy. The fall of communism over this period gave capitalism a virtual monopoly of world economic philosophies. The economic liberalizations occurring in Latin America, Eastern Europe, and Asia were testament to the new era of global capitalism. The parallel spread of democracies brought new economic and political empowerment to increasing numbers of nations. International commerce was extending its influ-

ence across the world. The forces of globalization, aided by the World Trade Organization, had expanded international trade from $2 trillion in 1980 to $4 trillion in 1994, and to almost $6 trillion at the turn of the millennium. Foreign direct investments in factories, plants, and machinery, barely $1/2 trillion in 1980, had risen to over $2 1/2 trillion in 1995 and to $7.1 trillion in 2002, as international corporations spread their commercial tentacles into all corners of the globe. This had been foreseen in 1983, when Harvard Business Professor Theodore Levitt had noted: "A powerful force drives the world toward a converging commonality, and that force is technology. It has proletarianized communication, transport, and travel. It has made isolated places and impoverished peoples eager for modernity's allurements" (page 92).

But not everyone has been eager to sample "modernity's allurements." Indeed, many societies had shied away from the conveniences and comforts of modernization. They viewed new products, technologies, and lifestyles as form of cultural imperialism. Westernization, with its emphasis on the accumulation of material possessions and competitive lifestyles, became an anathema to peoples steeped in religious philosophies and traditional lifestyles. Preserving national cultures became difficult in the face of competitive political democracies and market-forces capitalism. Institutions such as the extended family and traditional social-class systems came under pressure as countries industrialized. Most importantly for religion-based societies (such as the Islamic nations), industrialization and modernization were perceived as distracting individuals away from spiritual ideals toward commercial pursuits. Historically, the Christian religions had been able to reconcile religious and commercial goals with, for example, "the Protestant work ethic." However, for many religions and peoples of the world, the spiritual and commercial paths were irreconcilable. For one to gain, the other must lose. Movements against modernization and westernization, featuring groups such as the al Qaeda movement, became prominent as opposition mounted to the globalization movement.

The importance of religion in the world is undeniable. Islam has over one billion followers, as does Hinduism. A further one billion people (mainly in Asia and mainland China), have had their lives shaped by Confucianism. The West's understanding of these religions and philosophies tends to be minimal, yet they are pervasive influences on their followers' lives. The influence of Protestantism and Catholicism on daily lives in the West is not extensive, and this has caused many to underestimate religious influences in other societies. For example, in agricultural societies, religion and benevolent deities are key factors in communities' fights for survival.

Then there are the modernization and westernization forces that increasingly intrude into traditional societies. Leading the cultural intrusions into foreign lifestyles have been two major forces: international corporations and global media. U.S. companies occupy five of the top 10 positions in corporate rankings by assets worldwide, and twelve of the top 50. They are often the most visible of the world's leading corporations, accounting for about two-thirds of global brands. The top 100 control over $2 trillion in assets globally. Yet this only represents one-eighth of all foreign-based assets worldwide. The influence of these companies on the global cultural landscape has been enormous, as have the effects of capitalistic-inspired profit motives, efficiency orientations, and management and marketing methods that affect national lifestyles, especially in developing countries.

Global media have revolutionized the transfers of cultural images among countries through television, radio, and the Internet. The BBC, Vivendi, and Bertelsmann have carried European values and lifestyles into foreign markets. U.S. media influences include Disney, MTV, CNN, cartoon networks, and, of course, Hollywood. Many of these target and influence youth audiences worldwide, pulling them away from national cultures toward Western lifestyles. As they do, they leave lasting impressions of the U.S. and North America.

The impacts of modern products, media, and technologies have not been positive for many peoples, with the result that many groups have coalesced under the anti-global banner. The religious right in the U.S. actively campaigns against mass media focuses on violence, crime, and sex. Attacks against McDonald's in France, India, and other parts of the world are signals of an underlying resistance to Western and U.S. intrusions into national cultures. Canadian restrictions on U.S. media activities within their national borders have occurred because of fears of cultural imperialism. The Battle in Seattle and other protest movements against the World Bank and the IMF demonstrate that not everyone in the developed world is enamored with global capitalism. Finally, there are many peoples in the developing world, and in Islamic countries in particular, that link Western influences with crime, immorality, and sex and are anxious to keep such influences out of their lives. The U.S., as the world leader of capitalism and westernization, has become the lightning rod for the evils of the world and is known in strict Islamic societies as "the Great Satan."

Modernization through globalization may be inevitable, but how countries and companies use their influence in the world is controllable. The forces of modernization must be tempered by sensitivities to national cultures that have been built up over hundreds and thousands of years. This requires knowledge and understanding of world cultures, especially in the front lines of international business practice. Business people ignorant of world cultures and business practices risk not only losing contracts and sales, but also compromising the integrity of the country they represent.

Questions

1. How do other countries view the U.S. (positives and negatives)? How do you think those views were formed?

2. What do you think are the differences between modernization and westernization?

3. What do you think caused the September 11, 2001, attacks? Why?

4. How much international business should students have as part of their business education? Put a percentage on the extent of international business content, and justify it.

CASETTE 1-2
The Internet: Revolutionizing International Business? Or Not?

The Internet, since its 1990s commercial introduction, has had major impacts on business. It has lubricated communication within companies, between companies, and built bridges via company web sites to anyone with a computer with Internet capabilities. Electronic (E) commerce has improved corporate supply chains by allowing suppliers, distributors, and customers to coordinate with manufacturers to produce appropriate goods and get them to where they are needed. The Internet's 24-hour capability allows business people to communicate easily across vast geographic distances and time zones to enhance business efficiencies. As importantly, the Internet allows global access to worldwide news and events and gives isolated groups forums for their ideas. This democratization of world communications without the selectivity and censoring effects associated with international broadcast and print media has become a potent influence on world cultures.

But the world is still comprised of nations with their own languages and cultural idiosyncrasies. As such, there are still a multitude of national differences to be overcome before the Internet and E-commerce can reach its full potential. For example, the Internet relies on computer ownership or access. This limits its effects to countries and individuals affluent enough to afford them. Then, too, the Internet's reliance on national telecommunication and energy infrastructures limits its reach, particularly in developing countries.

On the plus side, the Internet currently reaches many English-speaking populations in North America, Western Europe, and former British colonies around the world. This is important, given that North America and the U.K. account for over $2.5 trillion of the world's $7.1 trillion in foreign direct investments. Also, as language web site capabilities are expanded to include the major European languages, so worldwide coverage continues to increase.

But while the Internet facilitates communications among managers and companies, its use in propagating commerce worldwide still faces many of the traditional obstacles to commerce. Export-import regulations, customs, tariffs, currencies, transportation, and taxes must all be negotiated before Internet transactions can be consummated. Slowly, the services to complement online transactions are being made available. Financial institutions are starting to offer currency translation and conversion services (e.g., CDNow, VeriSign, SurePay), and companies are starting to offer services such as myCustoms to facilitate trade documentation, customs, and taxation functions.

Transactions among international corporations and their subsidiaries are already being overcome. The chemicals industry, one of the more global sectors, is setting the pace. Dow Chemical, BASF, Bayer, and Shell have all set up web sites and extranets to link key customers worldwide, and already generate 5–10 percent of world sales via E-commerce.

Penetrating consumer markets presents some of the greatest challenges to companies seeking to gain advantages from the E-commerce trend. In 1999, the U.S. accounted for over 60 percent of the $130 billion of Internet spending and 45 percent of online users. The U.S.'s share is projected to fall to 45 percent of an estimated $1.6 trillion market by 2003 and to about 25 percent by 2005. The Asia-Pacific region and Latin America are projected to total over 40 percent of online consumers by 2005.

How firms react to the new Internet world will undoubtedly affect their competitive standing over the next decade. Initial surveys suggest that two-thirds of U.S. companies are not well-prepared for the global online marketplace. Some are preparing multilingual web sites, especially in Western Europe. A major challenge for all firms is to incorporate languages with non-Roman alphabets, such as Russian, Arabic, Chinese, Japanese, and Korean into their corporate web sites, yet this is already underway. Even when ready, these web sites must be maintained and requisite support services provided, including financing and web site maintenance expertise. For consumer-based E-commerce, payment methods rely heavily on credit cards, and these entail credit checks and other fraud-preventing measures, many of which are not universally available. As markets become more competitive, locally appealing web sites become key issues, and while English language web sites are adequate for major developed markets, their appeal rapidly subsides as market penetration levels reach less-educated consumers in non-English-speaking countries. Then, too, the appeal of products and services marketed from a central home-market location diminishes as competition increases and customers start to prefer offerings oriented to their national cultures. Firms within in-market presences will have advantages in local appeal, rapid service, and consumer confidence.

Questions

1. Discuss the diffusion process as it is likely to affect E-commerce. How will the diffusion rates for business-to-business differ from that of business-to-consumer? Why?

2. What are the key success factors affecting the spread of E-commerce worldwide? Which do you think is the most important, and why?

3. What sort of innovation is the Internet (a congruent, continuous, dynamically continuous, or discontinuous innovation)?

Sources: D'Amico, Esther. "Global E-commerce." *Chemical Week* (Sept. 26, 2001): 24–29, and "Wanted: A multilingual Web presence" (Sept. 26, 2001): 20–30. Prince, C. J. "US lags on globalization." *Chief Executive* (March 2001): 12–13. Borck, James R. "Currency conversion, fraud prevention are hurdles to successful global commerce." *InfoWorld* (Feb. 5, 2001): 55–58. Lessin, Robert. "Shifting Internet geo-centers: Will you lose your balance?" *Chief Executive* (Feb. 2001): D11–D13. Gareiss, Dawn. "Business on the Worldwide Web." *Informationweek* (December 11, 2000): 69–78.

Chapter Two

Globalization and Worldwide Infrastructure Development

∽

"WITH A LITTLE HELP FROM MY FRIENDS": THE GLOBALIZATION OF THE AIR EXPRESS INDUSTRY

The international air express industry has become one of the great beneficiaries and enablers of today's globalizing economy. Electronic commerce, shorter product cycles, just-in-time manufacturing, global sourcing and selling have caused many industries to behave like the fashion industry. No one wants obsolete stock and technology has made hi-tech products such as semiconductors and medical equipment the "new perishables." Ninety percent of the world's GNP has become accessible by express transportation within 48 hours.

The international air express industry evolved to serve the needs of the global economy. Federal Express (FedEx) employs more than 145,000 employees, more than 600 aircraft, and 42,000 vehicles to service its 3 million pieces-per-day market. Brussels-based DHL has a network covering more than 220 countries, employs more than 60,000 people, and has a 40 percent global share of the business—double FedEx's share. Both companies have invested heavily in information systems that allow customers to track their deliveries en route. Both firms have literally taken over corporate supply chains and are primary movers of companies' components, raw materials and final products.[1]

But none of this would be possible without the globalization forces that have shaped the world economy of the 1980s and 1990s.

- *United Nations agencies have facilitated the globalization process. Among those contributing to the internationalization of the air express industry are: the World Trade Organization that has brought down barriers to global movements in products and services, the International Civil Aviation Authority that coordinates national efforts to move people and goods globally, the International Monetary Fund that facilitates money exchanges among nations, the World Bank that upgrades country transportation and energy delivery systems, the International Telecommunications Union that coordinates satellite-based transfers of data and information among the world's nations.*
- *Deregulation and privatization trends have forced the transportation and telecommunications industries to shed their national monopoly statuses and become fierce and innovative competitors in the global marketplace.*
- *The formation of trade blocs such as the European Union and the North American Free Trade Area have encouraged firms to think and trade internationally.*

Clearly, the global economy could not emerge without a lot of help. Nations and companies cannot internationalize without an umbrella of global rules and conventions to facilitate movements of goods and services. One function of the United Nations is to provide this umbrella through specialized agencies that contribute to world infrastructure development and support the globalization movement. They provide necessary global linkages among nations that enable corporations to participate in the international marketplace.

Hence, in this chapter you will learn:

- How the United Nations contributes to world infrastructure development through its specialized agencies, such as the ITU, ICAO, UPU, IMO (physical and transportations infrastructures); UNCITRAL, WIPO, WTO and the International Court of Justice (legal infrastructures); IMF (financial infrastructures); and World Bank (country infrastructures).
- The role of the private sector in developing global distribution (through international retailers); information dissemination via the Internet, IT technologies, and global media; and physical distribution through developments in the shipping and airline industries.
- The development of trade blocs to facilitate commerce among country groupings, different types of trade blocs, and how the European Union has set the pace in trade-bloc development.
- The influence of privatization and deregulation programs in extending infrastructure industries, such as airlines, financial services, energy, and utilities, beyond national borders and contributing to development in other nations; and how, at the country level, privatization has contributed to corporate efficiencies in former state-dominated economies.
- How world infrastructure development has facilitated the growth of global commerce and the spread of international corporations.

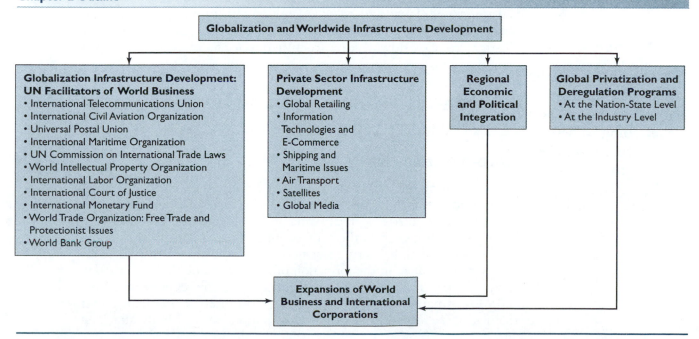

FIGURE 2.1
Chapter 2 Outline

INTRODUCTION

The world marketplace has undergone dramatic changes since 1945 and especially since the mid-1980s. The seeds of change were sown in 1945 as countries, conscious of the need to promote global interdependencies, established the United Nations. Under the UN umbrella, a number of specialized agencies were created to oversee and integrate public infrastructures on a worldwide scale (see Figure 2.2). These organizations established guidelines to regulate and coordinate national and international infrastructures on a worldwide scale, including telecommunications, aviation, mail, shipping, trade, trade law, intellectual property rights, and labor rights.

But world commerce was slow to develop as countries (especially in Western Europe and Japan) focused on rebuilding their economies in the post-war period, and world attention was diverted with the U.S.–USSR political rivalry (the cold war). Some countries, impatient with the rate of development, formed their own economic blocs to liberalize trade and facilitate commercial growth.

The global economy became more of a reality after the mid-1980s as East-West political tensions diminished with the breakup of the USSR and worldwide movements toward privatization and democratization. The global economy, previously comprising the Triad Nations of North America, Western Europe, and Japan, opened up to include 4 billion people in Latin America, Eastern Europe, and Asia. In addition, trade blocs emerged as countries began to integrate economically and politically, particularly in the Americas, Asia, and Europe. The global village started to become a reality as earth-shrinking technologies provided linkages among nations, enabling companies to integrate their international operations and allowing customers worldwide to become familiar with modern products and lifestyles. As part of this process, the UN and its agencies were key instigators of worldwide infrastructure development in the post-1945 period.

GLOBAL INFRASTRUCTURE DEVELOPMENT: UN FACILITATORS OF WORLD BUSINESS

United Nations Background

World commerce and international dependencies have increased throughout the twentieth century. At the turn of the century, the number of countries participating in world commerce numbered about sixty. But even in the early twentieth century, it was becoming obvious that a global forum was necessary to tackle worldwide problems and issues. This resulted in the formation of the League of Nations in 1919. Unfortunately, this organization floundered in the economic depression of the 1920s and 1930s as nations were forced to focus on internal problems rather than external liaisons. However, the principle of a supranational body attacking

> To write off the United Nations' achievements because of its inability to maintain world peace . . . would be like writing off medical science because it has not yet found a cure for cancer.
>
> —*George Bush, U.S. president, 1988–92*

> The League of Nations is a declaration of love without the promise of marriage.
>
> —*Admiral von Tirpitz, German diplomat*

> This organization [the United Nations] is created to prevent you from going to hell. It isn't created to take you to heaven.
>
> —*Henry Cabot Lodge, U.S. diplomat*

FIGURE 2.2
UN Agencies and Global Infrastructure Development

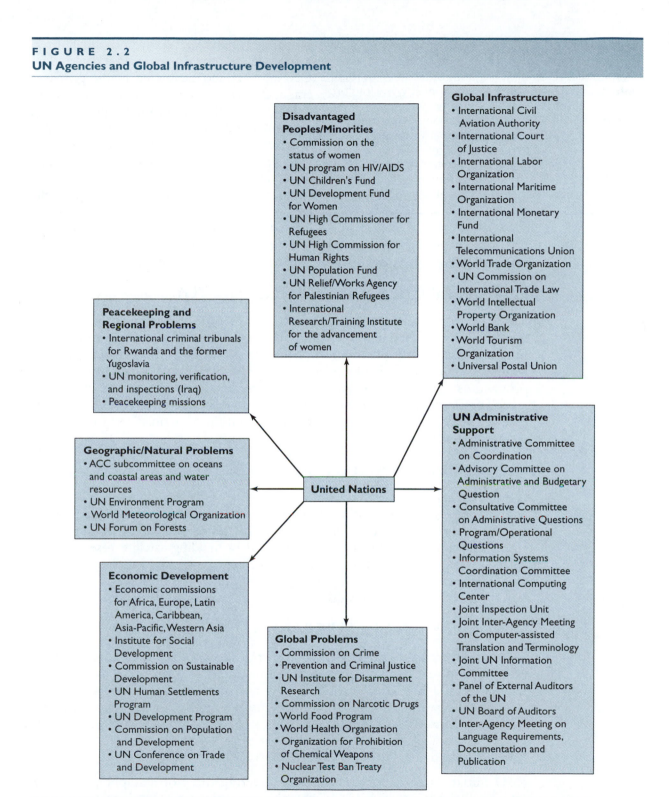

Global Infrastructure
- International Civil Aviation Authority
- International Court of Justice
- International Labor Organization
- International Maritime Organization
- International Monetary Fund
- International Telecommunications Union
- World Trade Organization
- UN Commission on International Trade Law
- World Intellectual Property Organization
- World Bank
- World Tourism Organization
- Universal Postal Union

Disadvantaged Peoples/Minorities
- Commission on the status of women
- UN program on HIV/AIDS
- UN Children's Fund
- UN Development Fund for Women
- UN High Commissioner for Refugees
- UN High Commission for Human Rights
- UN Population Fund
- UN Relief/Works Agency for Palestinian Refugees
- International Research/Training Institute for the advancement of women

Peacekeeping and Regional Problems
- International criminal tribunals for Rwanda and the former Yugoslavia
- UN monitoring, verification, and inspections (Iraq)
- Peacekeeping missions

Geographic/Natural Problems
- ACC subcommittee on oceans and coastal areas and water resources
- UN Environment Program
- World Meteorological Organization
- UN Forum on Forests

United Nations

UN Administrative Support
- Administrative Committee on Coordination
- Advisory Committee on Administrative and Budgetary Question
- Consultative Committee on Administrative Questions
- Program/Operational Questions
- Information Systems Coordination Committee
- International Computing Center
- Joint Inspection Unit
- Joint Inter-Agency Meeting on Computer-assisted Translation and Terminology
- Joint UN Information Committee
- Panel of External Auditors of the UN
- UN Board of Auditors
- Inter-Agency Meeting on Language Requirements, Documentation and Publication

Economic Development
- Economic commissions for Africa, Europe, Latin America, Caribbean, Asia-Pacific, Western Asia
- Institute for Social Development
- Commission on Sustainable Development
- UN Human Settlements Program
- UN Development Program
- Commission on Population and Development
- UN Conference on Trade and Development

Global Problems
- Commission on Crime
- Prevention and Criminal Justice
- UN Institute for Disarmament Research
- Commission on Narcotic Drugs
- World Food Program
- World Health Organization
- Organization for Prohibition of Chemical Weapons
- Nuclear Test Ban Treaty Organization

Source: Adapted from www.un.org.

THE GLOBAL WEB

International Telecommunications Union at www.itu.org
International Civil Aviation Authority at www.icao.org
Universal Postal Union at www.upu.int
International Maritime Organization at www.imo.org
UN Commission on International Trade Laws at www.uncitral.org
World Intellectual Property Organization at www.wipo.org
International Labor Organization at www.ilo.org
International Court of Justice at www.icj-cij.org

global problems survived, and the United Nations came into existence after 1945. The UN survived and prospered in the post-war era, and today it comprises more than eighty affiliated agencies monitoring and reporting on global problems and activities. Figure 2.2 shows the array of services and programs offered by the UN under seven major groupings. Of particular interest to international business people are those UN agencies facilitating world trade and investments (highlighted at the top right hand corner of Figure 2.2). These agencies have been major facilitators of world commerce and international business by providing infrastructure liaisons among nations.

International Telecommunications Union (ITU)

The ITU is a worldwide organization coordinating government and private sector initiatives in global telecommunications networks and services. Other functions include the harmonization of national telecommunications policies, including equipment standardization across borders, protocols, and operating procedures. The ITU allocates radio frequencies for shipping and airlines to avoid interference and conflicts. The ITU also has direct effects on the broadcast and telecommunications sectors in its granting of permissions for communications (telephone, TV, radio) satellites.

International Civil Aviation Organization (ICAO)

ICAO has 188 member countries and promotes uniform standards for aircraft landing procedures, and cockpit-to-ground communications; it coordinates policies for airport security (e.g., baggage screening, bomb detection). Its current focuses are primarily on flight-safety issues and in building satellite-based surveillance systems to aid aircraft navigation and safety in an era of increasing air traffic. ICAO activities have become increasingly important as privatization and deregulation trends have added competitive cost pressures to airlines' strategic agendas.

Universal Postal Union (UPU)

The UPU was first established in 1874 by the Treaty of Berne to coordinate international postal service activities. It became a UN agency in 1948. Presently the UPU has 189 country members, and its lead office in Berne acts as the international clearinghouse for the settlement of accounts among national postal administrations.

International Maritime Organization (IMO)

IMO initiates international regulations covering the global shipping industry. Its overall aim is to promote "safer shipping and cleaner oceans" among its 156 member-states. Recent initiatives have included the Global Maritime Distress and Safety System to augment existing safety systems for ships in distress, crew training standards, double-hull protection for tankers, and compensation systems for affected parties following maritime disasters, such as environmental pollution.

UN Commission on International Trade Laws (UNCITRAL)

UNCITRAL deals with trade administration issues such as rights and obligations of shippers, carriers, and co-signers; international payment systems (letters of credit terms and, increasingly, electronic payment transfers); and international contracts between importers and exporters. Current issues concern the acceptability of electronic trade document movement and container cargo liabilities.

World Intellectual Property Organization (WIPO)

WIPO deals with the promotion and protection of intellectual properties. This organization has two branches: *industrial properties,* covering inventions and trademark designs, and *copyrights* such as those pertaining to literary, musical, artistic, photographic, and audiovisual works. WIPO's 2002 Patent Cooperation Treaty allows patents to be registered in any or all of its 122 members countries. However, enforcement is at the nation-state level. WIPO also helps countries set up their own legal frameworks and systems for dealing with intellectual property issues.

International Labor Organization (ILO)

ILO was originally established in 1919 as part of the League of Nations (the forerunner of the UN), but it was brought under the UN umbrella in 1946. Its functions include formulating and monitoring international labor rights, such as the right to organize unions, abolition of forced labor, equality of opportunity and treatment, and work conditions. It also provides assistance in formulating and drawing up national employment policies, labor laws, social security systems, and safety and health rules.

International Court of Justice

Situated at the Hague (Netherlands), the International Court of Justice arbitrates and settles legal disputes among nations. While not directly affecting day-to-day business operations, the Court oversees international political disputes that affect political and commercial relations among nations. Frontier disputes, maritime boundaries (e.g., fisheries disputes between Spain and Canada) terrorist activities (e.g., Lockerbie disaster: Libya vs. U.K.), and economic rights are among the issues dealt with by the Court. Additionally, the Court tries individuals accused of "crimes against humanity." Currently, these include genocides such as the ethnic cleansing policies in Bosnia-Herzegovina and the Hutu-Tutsi pogroms (slaughters) in Rwanda and Burundi in the mid 1990s.

Financial Infrastructures: International Monetary Fund

Whenever countries interact commercially, foreign-exchange rates (the prices of currencies in terms of other currencies) usually determine the value of goods and services to be exchanged. Exchange

> The purpose of law is to prevent the strong from always having their own way.
>
> —*Ovid, Greek philosopher*

> Nationalism and internationalism! Both must stand together or the human race will be utterly destroyed. We shall never be able to destroy nationalism and we shall never be able to live without internationalism.
>
> —*Linus R. Fike*

rates are the financial linkages among nations. Because of the U.S.'s position in world business, and the dollar's key role in lubricating global commerce, most exchange rates are expressed in foreign currency units per U.S. dollar and are to be found in the *Wall Street Journal*, the *Financial Times*, and major business-related publications (e.g., 130 Japanese yen per dollar or 1,400,000 Turkish lire per dollar). A few are stated in dollars per foreign currency unit (e.g., £1 sterling = $1.40).

Establishing Foreign Exchange Rate Values: A Historic Perspective The need for an orderly system of exchange rates has been apparent since international trade and exchanges began thousands of years ago. In Roman times, the dinarius (a forerunner of today's euro) was the unit of account used throughout the Roman Empire. In medieval times, gold and silver were mainly used for international trade, along with barter systems. Gold maintained its position as the benchmark of value for goods exchanged between countries, and up to the early twentieth century, national currencies were assessed in terms of gold. For example, the U.S. dollar was worth 23 grains of gold; the pound sterling was 113 grains, and this yielded an exchange rate of $4.91 per pound sterling. Gold backed up national currencies issues, and international accounts between nations were settled through gold movements into and out of country deposits. This was the Gold Standard era, which survived the 1914–18 war but which fell apart during the Great Depression of the 1920s and 1930s.

Increasing trade and international transactions made a new system of exchange rates necessary, and, at Bretton Woods in 1944, a new set of exchange-rate arrangements was devised. The system was still gold-based, with one ounce of gold valued at $35. With the gold-dollar connection as the stabilizing influence, other countries pegged their currencies to the U.S. dollar. International transactions and trade increased steadily throughout the 1950s and 1960s, but mounting pressures on the dollar and the gold-dollar relationship caused the Bretton Woods system to fall apart in the early 1970s. Mounting pressures on national exchange rates were noticeable during the 1960s as country economies overheated. Inflation resulted, and as domestic prices rose, governments devalued their currencies against the dollar (i.e., they officially increased the number of national currency units per U.S. dollar) to remain competitive in the international marketplace. As other currencies went down in value, the dollar became overvalued, making it difficult for American businesses to remain competitive as their export prices rose in international markets. At the same time, import prices to the U.S. went down, resulting in persistent balance of trade deficits (where imports exceed exports). These trade deficits, coupled with significant dollar outlays for other reasons (significant military presences abroad and the Vietnam War), resulted in major dollar outflows to overseas-based banks. Foreign banks and traders used the surplus dollars in two ways. First, they were used to finance trade and investments where local currencies were unacceptable (inconvertible). Second, until 1971, dollars could still be exchanged for gold at $35 per ounce. Many countries took advantage of bargain gold prices, and the U.S. experienced major decreases in its gold reserves. In 1971, President Nixon closed the gold window, and 1971–73 saw the birth of a new international monetary system based on non-gold-backed fixed and floating exchange rates. Under the system, minor trading currencies were pegged (fixed) to a single mainstream currency (such as the dollar or the French franc) or to a currency basket (a mix of currencies with whom a country customarily traded). The currencies of major trading nations were often floated, and their values fluctuated according to market demand and supply. In 1999, the international monetary system (the system of exchange rate relationships) was reassessed, and currencies were placed in eight groupings.[2]

The 1999 International Monetary System The international monetary system is the set of exchange-rate arrangements governing relative prices of one currency against another. Exchange rates are critical in assessing the values of goods, services, or assets entering the international marketplace. The major managerial concern is how movements in exchange-rate values affect those transactions, and the exchange-rate regime under which currencies fall affects their variability. Our eight exchange-rate arrangements are ordered according to their degree of flexibility, from those that experience little or no movement in currency value to those whose values can fluctuate considerably over time (see Table 2.1).

> The dollar has become like a hydrant at an international convention of dogs.
>
> —*Eliot Janeway, U.S. writer*

1. *Exchange arrangements with no separate legal tenders.* Forty countries either use another nation's currency as legal tender or share a common currency.
   - *Another currency as legal tender:* Smaller nations having strong commercial ties with major trading countries can opt to use that nation's currency as legal tender. The Marshall Islands, Micronesia, Palau, and Panama all use the U.S. dollar; San Marino employs the Italian lire, while Kiribati uses the Australian dollar. In 2000, Ecuador became the largest country to adopt a foreign currency (the dollar) as its own when the sucre became a casualty of the country's deteriorating economic conditions.

   > Throughout most of the 20th century, nations were distinguished through two things: their own flag and their own currency.
   >
   > —*Anonymous*

   - Trading groups can use a *common external currency* to facilitate commerce among trading partners. The East Caribbean Common Union (ECCU) uses the East Caribbean dollar. This is issued over six sovereign states by the East Caribbean Central Bank. Individual governments have no power over currency values that have been maintained at 2.7 Caribbean dollars per U.S. dollar for over two decades, and foreign-exchange issues are based on a strict currency board operation (described on the following page). The West African Economic and Monetary Union and the Central African Economic and Monetary Community—all former French colonies—use the CFA franc. Backed up by the treasury of former colonial ruler France, the CFA franc is pegged at 656 francs per euro. Future plans include extending the currency to internal use by 2004.[3]
   - *Currency created for multi-country use:* The euro, introduced in 1999 and brought into general circulation in 2002, was created to replace the European Union's national currencies for internal and external use. This currency is discussed further as part of European integration.

TABLE 2.1
International Monetary System: Exchange Rates Arrangements Among Nations

	Another currency as legal tender	East Caribbean Currency Union	CFA Franc Zone West African Economic and Monetary Union	CFA Franc Zone Central African Economic and Monetary Community	Euro Area
Exchange arrangements with no separate legal tender (40)	Ecuador El Salvador Kiribati Marshall Islands Micronesia Palau Panama San Marino	Antigua and Barbuda Dominica Grenada St. Kitts and Nevis St. Lucia St. Vincent and the Grenadines	Benin Burkina Faso Ivory Coast Guinea-Bissau Mali Niger Senegal Togo	Cameroon C. African Rep. Chad Rep. of Congo Equatorial Guinea Gabon	Austria Belgium Finland France Germany Greece Ireland Italy Luxembourg Netherlands Portugal Spain
Currency board arrangements (8)	Argentina Bosnia and Herzegovina Brunei Bulgaria Hong Kong Djibouti Estonia Lithuania				

	Against a single currency (30)	Single currency (continued)	Against a composite (10)		
Other conventional fixed peg arrangements (40)	Aruba Bahamas Bahrain Bangladesh Barbados Belize Bhutan Cape Verde China PR Comoros Iran Jordan Lebanon Lesotho	Macedonia FYR Malaysia Maldives Namibia Nepal Netherlands Antilles Oman Qatar Saudi Arabia Sudan Suriname Swaziland Syria Turkmenistan United Arab Emirates Zimbabwe	Botswana Fiji Kuwait Latvia Libya Malta Morocco Samoa Seychelles Vanuatu		

	Within a cooperative arrangement (1)	Other band arrangements (4)			
Pegged exchange rates within horizontal bands (5)	Denmark	Cyprus Egypt Hungary Tonga			
Crawling pegs (4)	Bolivia Costa Rica Nicaragua Solomon Islands	Norway Pakistan Pakistan			
Exchange rates within crawling bands (5)	Belarus Israel Honduras Romania Uruguay Venezuela				

Managed floating with no pre-announced path (42)	Algeria	Norway
	Angola	Pakistan
	Angola	Paraguay
	Azerbaijan	Russian Federation
	Burundi	Rwanda
	Cambodia	Sao Tome and
	Croatia	Principe
	Dominican Rep.	Singapore
	Eritrea	Slovakia
	Ethiopia	Slovenia
	Ghana	Sri Lanka
	Guinea	Thailand
	Guatemala	Trinidad and
	Guyana	Tobago
	India	Tunisia
	Indonesia	Ukraine
	Iraq	Uzbekistan
	Jamaica	Vietnam
	Kazakhstan	Yugoslavia
	Kenya	Zambia
	Kyrgyz Rep.	
	Laos	
	Mauritania	
	Mauritius	
	Mongolia	
	Myanmar	
	Nigeria	
Independently floating (40)	Afghanistan	New Zealand
	Albania	Norway
	Armenia	Papua New Guinea
	Australia	Peru
	Brazil	Philippines
	Canada	Poland
	Chile	Sierra Leone
	Colombia	Somalia
	Congo, Dem. Rep.	South Africa
	Czech Rep.	Sweden
	Gambia	Switzerland
	Georgia	Tajikistan
	Haiti	Tanzania
	Iceland	Turkey
	Japan	Uganda
	Korea	United Kingdom
	Liberia	United States
	Madagascar	Yemen
	Malawi	
	Mexico	
	Moldova	
	Mozambique	

Source: Adapted from *International Financial Statistics* (New York: United Nations, January 2003): 2–3.

2. *Currency board arrangements* are in operation in eight countries. Under this arrangement, one country's currency is pegged to another's. For example, Bosnia-Herzegovina's convertible mark was fixed on a one-to-one basis to Germany's Deutsche mark (and is now pegged to the euro). The exchange rate is guaranteed, and there is full and free convertibility at that rate. The key element is that the country's central bank must maintain enough foreign-currency reserves to match its money supply. The advantages of this arrangement are that (1) It removes all exchange rate and convertibility risks. (2) It encourages national interest rates to stay aligned to international rates, as deviations with full convertibility invite speculative money movements. (3) Governments must follow sensible money-supply policies when increases must be matched by new foreign-exchange reserves. Currency board arrangements do limit central banks' abilities to pursue independent monetary policies (raising or lowering interest rates or money supplies to dampen down or fire up the economy). These limitations are tolerable, given the fiscal disciplines the system imposes on national public finances and the confidence it gives to those using the currency. Currency boards were popular in the 1960s when as many as thirty-eight countries used them. Their use declined until the 1990s when governments found them to be useful tools in dealing with problems of hyperinflation (Argentina, Bulgaria), market economy transitions (Bulgaria, Estonia, Lithuania), volatile terms of trade (East Caribbean dollar), and post-conflict disorders (Bosnia-Herzegovina). Most are pegged to the U.S. dollar, the euro, and the Singapore dollar.[4]

> If we don't discipline ourselves, the world will do it for us.
>
> —*William Feather, U.S. author*

3. *Fixed to a single currency or currency basket* (forty currencies). Many countries desire maximum financial certainty in commercial dealings with a major partner or partners. When currencies are pegged to one other currency, it is usually that of their major commercial partner. As Table 2.1 shows, thirty countries follow this practice, including Bhutan and Nepal (to the Indian rupee), Lesotho and Namibia (to the South African rand), and Cape Verde (to the Portuguese escudo, now the euro).

   A second option (followed by ten countries) is to peg a nation's currency to a currency basket. Currencies comprising the basket are usually that country's major trading partners, with currency weightings in proportion to their commercial importance. Currency baskets are inherently more stable than pegs against single currencies. In both cases, exchange rate deviations of +/− 1 percent of the central bank rate are tolerated.

4. *Currency pegged within a horizontal band* (five countries). Under this arrangement, currencies are pegged to other countries' currencies but are allowed a band of flexibility around a central rate. There are two arrangements. The first is a cooperative arrangement whereby Denmark pegs its currency to the euro with an allowable deviation of +/− 2¼ percent. The second arrangement has four nations pegging their currencies to (1) the Special Drawing Right (SDR) composite currency (SDRs are financial units of account made up of 39 percent U.S. dollar, 32 percent euro, 18 percent Japanese yen, and 11 percent British pound sterling) or to currency baskets of major trading

partners with variations as small as Cyprus +/− 2¼ percent; or as large as Hungary (+/− 15 percent).

5. *Crawling pegs* (four countries). Nations with consistent inflation problems are likely to use crawling-peg exchange-rate regimes, whereby currencies are regularly devalued (i.e., increasing numbers of national units per dollar or hard currency) according to government-announced inflation targets. As inflation is brought under control, the need for crawling pegs diminishes.

6. *Exchange rates within crawling bands* (six countries). Under this exchange-rate regime, governments adjust the band within which the exchange rate moves. In these cases, however (and dissimilar to the crawling peg), bands are flexible both upward and downward, making long-term currency values less easy to predict. In some cases, crawling bands are instigated prior to allowing currencies to float toward market forces-determined exchange rates. The bands give governments some latitude in responding to short-term fluctuations while maintaining control over general directions of currency values.

7. *Managed floats* allow currencies to float according to marketplace supply and demand, except that governments influence exchange-rate values through fiscal and monetary controls applied to the domestic economy. Interest-rate adjustments can attract or deter foreign capital, and taxation shifts can dampen down import demand or encourage consumer expenditures and exports. Forty-two countries currently use this arrangement.

8. *Independently floating currencies.* Increasing numbers of currencies (including all-important currencies, such as the dollar, the euro, and the yen), float independently against other world currencies, their values being determined by market supply and demand. Under this arrangement, trade, investment, and money-flows between two countries determine the exchange rate for their currencies. Developed countries like the arrangement, as governments have few responsibilities in currency support, and currency values respond to market forces and to national economic developments. Good economic news and conditions result in upward currency movements as foreign capital is attracted to the country, creating demand for it. Bad news causes outflows of capital, weakening the currency.

> A little uncertainty is good for everything.
>
> —*Henry Kissinger, former U.S. secretary of state*

Floating Currencies: Supply and Demand Basics When countries permit currency values to be determined by supply and demand, they allow all transactions between two nations to determine the exchange rate between those two countries. For example, for the U.S. dollar and Japanese yen:

1. *Dollar supply* consists of all dollar-to-yen conversions (supply of dollars leaving the U.S., creating demand for yen), including:
   • Japanese exports to the U.S. are paid for initially in U.S. dollars (dollar supply leaving the country), which are then converted into yen so that Japanese workers can be paid (and creating demand for yen).

- Japanese firms in the U.S. repatriating profits, royalties, etc., convert dollars to yen.
- U.S. tourists traveling to Japan convert dollars to yen.
- U.S. investments to Japan (in plant, machinery, investments in Japanese firms, or in Japan's financial markets) are dollar-to-yen conversions.

2. *Dollar demand* consists of yen to dollar conversions (supply of yen leaving Japan creating demand for U.S. dollars), including:
   - U.S. exports to Japan, with initial payments in yen being converted, and creating demand for U.S. dollars.
   - Japan-based U.S. companies repatriating profits, royalties, etc., back to the U.S.
   - Japanese tourists coming to the U.S.
   - Japanese investments in the U.S., including building subsidiaries, machinery imports, investments in U.S. companies or in the U.S. financial market.

In simple terms, when *aggregate demand for dollars exceeds aggregate supply* (i.e., when U.S. exports to Japan and all other yen-to-dollar conversions are greater than Japanese imports into the U.S. and all other dollar-to-yen conversions), then market forces push the number of yen per dollar upward (e.g., from 100 yen to 120 yen per dollar). This is a dollar appreciation (and a yen depreciation). The dollar is worth more yen. As a result, dollar-based U.S. exports to Japan suffer prices rises; dollar investments in Japan buy more assets (or more Japanese securities, bonds); U.S. tourists to Japan get more yen to make purchases; but repatriated profits and royalties take a hit as it takes more yen to purchase dollars.

When *aggregate supply of dollars leaving the U.S. exceeds aggregate demand* (i.e., when Japanese exports to the U.S. plus all other dollar-to-yen conversions is greater than U.S. exports to Japan plus all other yen-to-dollar conversions), market forces push the number of yen per dollar downward (e.g., from 110 yen to 90). This is a dollar depreciation (the dollar is worth fewer yen). The result is that dollar-based U.S. exports can be priced downward (and be more competitive); it takes fewer yen to buy assets and make investments in the U.S. (and more U.S. dollars to make investments in Japan); U.S. profits and royalties repatriated from Japan receive more dollars from a specified number of yen, and U.S. tourists to Japan have fewer yen to spend from their dollar-to-yen conversions.

Exchange Rate Arrangements and Currency Stability: What Management Looks For

Exchange Rates and Country Competitive Advantage Exchange rates can magnify or diminish monetary values of international business transactions between two countries. Countries with overvalued currencies (those that have "too few" foreign currency units per U.S. dollar or euro) have difficulty exporting as U.S. and European prices translate into very high prices in local markets. Similarly, firms in weak-currency countries (many national currency units per dollar or euro) have few problems establishing export markets. Indeed, many governments encourage weak currencies to enhance their export prospects (e.g., Mexico, China) and to encourage foreign direct investments (where one dollar or euro buys "more" assets denominated in local currencies). As international companies establish manufacturing facilities for export from weak currency markets, they enhance their abilities to compete worldwide on a price basis and increase sourcing options to strong currency markets.

Exchange Rate Regime and Currency Movements Companies must still contend with the uncertainty of exchange-rate movements, and the exchange-rate arrangements under which countries operate provide key insights about currency stability. For countries whose exchange rates are pegged to major currencies, commercial relationships with that major currency country are stable. However, as that major currency's value moves, so the pegged currency's exchange rate moves also against all other currencies. For example, as the dollar moves up and down against other major currencies, all countries whose exchange rates are pegged to the dollar suffer the same fluctuations as the dollar vis-à-vis other world currencies. Re-peggings of minor currencies occur when major currency values move excessively, especially upward (appreciations), as this affects country-export competitiveness.

There is more uncertainty with exchange-rate arrangements 4 (pegged rates within horizontal bands), 5 (crawling pegs), and 6 (pegged rates within crawling bands). While these are not usually major movements, managers know they must keep watchful eyes on country-trade balances and inflation rates. Adverse movements of these key indicators often result in downward shifts in exchange rates. Managed floats exhibit some degree of stability when national economies and trade positions are healthy, as governments can devote resources to maintaining reasonable exchange rates. Currencies that float independently show the least stability. For major currencies like the dollar, yen, pound sterling, and euro, business people can use exchange-rate forward markets to hedge against uncertainties over one, three, and six-month timeframes. For many developing countries, though, floating currencies are means of making their currencies convertible by allowing the international currency markets to determine realistic exchange rates. This process is now examined.

Currency Convertibility and the IMF Relatively few of the 186 currencies shown in Table 2.1 are fully convertible, that is, freely convertible both ways. For example, in much of the developing world, money can be converted from hard currencies (like dollars, pounds sterling, euros, Swiss francs, Japanese yen) into local currencies. But government restrictions exist in converting these currencies (e.g., the Gambian dalasi or the Haitian gourde) back into hard currencies (if it can be done at all). A *soft or inconvertible currency* is one that is not acceptable as a means of payment outside its country of origin. Many developing-country currencies are soft, in that when exports are sent to these nations, payment in the local currency is not acceptable. When this occurs, payment must be made in a currency that is acceptable to the exporter, usually their own or another hard currency. Developing countries obtain hard currencies through exports to hard currency countries and accumulate enough dollars, yen, pounds, or euros to pay their import bills.

The problem has often been that, especially during the early stages of industrialization, countries' import needs outstrip their abilities to earn convertible currencies through exports. When this occurs over a protracted period, countries get behind in their hard-currency payments to foreign exporters and hard-currency debts accumulate.

> Money has little value to its possessor unless it also has value to others.
>
> —*Leland Stanford, U.S. financier*

FIGURE 2.3
Hard Currency Loans

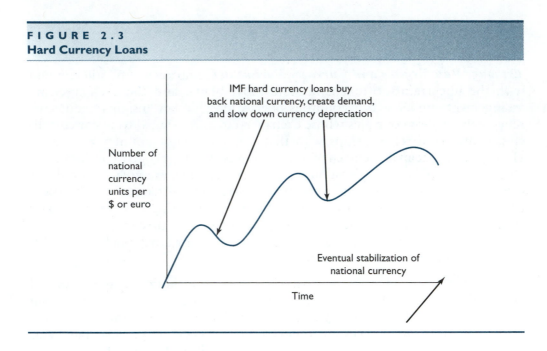

The Currency Convertibility Process Having large foreign-currency debts hinders country development because soft-currency nations can only spend what they earn in export earnings without increasing their hard-currency indebtedness (the extent of their backlog in paying import bills in hard currencies). Thus the aim of most developing countries is to make their currencies fully acceptable (i.e., two-way convertibility) in world financial markets. Achieving convertibility is a two-step process, first, establishing a realistic exchange rate acceptable in world currency markets and, second, maintaining that value for a significant time period. The first step is establishing a realistic, market-set exchange rate. This involves removing all restrictions on currency exchange and letting the forces of currency supply and demand determine a realistic exchange rate. However, once governments remove barriers to convertibility, everyone converts local currency into hard currencies, increasing the supply of local currencies leaving the country and increasing demand for hard currencies (usually the dollar or the euro). This causes a drastic weakening of the local currency, with more and more local currency units being required to buy $1 or other hard currencies. This depreciation is gradually slowed and stopped as the IMF lends the affected country sufficient hard currency to buy back and create demand for its local currency. The local currency continues to fall, but at decreasing rates, finally leveling out at a value deemed realistic by the foreign currency markets. The Asian financial crisis occurred as a number of currencies underwent this process. The Indonesian rupiah plunged from about 2,500 per dollar to about 16,500 over 1997–98. The IMF stepped in with a $43 billion loan to enable the country to buy back its currency and slow down its depreciation. In return for the loan, the IMF imposed a number of conditions, including ending special trading concessions and price controls, deregulating protected industries, and exercising fiscal discipline in government spending.[5] Two years after the crisis, the rupiah had steadied to a rate of 9,000 per U.S. dollar.

World Trade Organization (WTO)

To ensure that the world economy did not fall back into 1920s–30s isolationism, the General Agreement on Tariffs and Trade (GATT) was initiated over 1947–48 under the UN umbrella. From that time until 1994, (when it was replaced by the WTO), GATT oversaw seven rounds of multilateral trade agreements that boosted world trade from $2 trillion to $4 trillion between 1980–94.

> **THE GLOBAL WEB**
>
> World Trade Organization at <u>www.wto.org</u>

GATT's main objective was tariff reduction, and in this it was highly successful, reducing tariffs on manufactured goods from a 1945 average of 40 percent down to the year 2000 level of about 4 percent.[6] In the 1990s, as tariff concerns diminished, the emphasis switched to non-tariff barriers to international trade, and, after its creation in 1995, the WTO focused on trade in services. The WTO's major functions are to:

- Act as a forum for multilateral trade negotiations. In 1997, the WTO brokered a 69-country agreement on the liberalization of global telecommunications services.[7]

- Oversee national and regional trading policies. The EU's banana-sourcing rules came under scrutiny as the WTO ruled that current policies discriminated against the U.S. and Latin America sources.[8]

- Reduce non-tariff barriers to commerce, including rules of origin, pre-shipment inspections, trade-related investment codes, and the application of sanitary and phytosanitary regulations.

- Resolve trade disputes. The WTO has the power to sanction offenders and order compensation as authorized trade reprisals.[9] The WTO, unlike its GATT predecessor, has powers to arbitrate and to make rulings on trade disputes. Most involve free trade-protectionism issues.

> *No nation was ever ruined by trade.*
>
> —*Benjamin Franklin,*
> *18th-century U.S. statesman*

The Free Trade-Protectionism Debate Free trade has very much become associated with world development. As one has increased, so generally has the other. Yet, in particular countries and for specific industries, arguments for protectionism have been pitted against those of free trade.

Pro-free-trade arguments include:

1. *Free trade promotes global competition, which benefits consumers through increased varieties of products and lower prices.* Countries specialize and export those goods in which they have comparative advantages and import products that they produce less effectively than other nations. One ongoing debate has been whether the price advantages resulting from developing-nation cost structures are passed on to customers in developed nations in the form of lower prices, or whether developing-nation cost benefits simply result in increased margins for importing retailers or other channel intermediaries in advanced markets.

2. *The economic interdependencies of trade and global commerce make countries less likely to go to war.* One reason why the European Economic Community was formed so soon after World War II was that countries

with commercial interdependencies and regular dialogs were less likely to enter into political-military conflicts. One problem has been that commercial disputes have taken the place of military rivalries as forums for country-based competition.

3. *The uneven distribution of global resources, particularly in commodities, makes trade inevitable.* Concentrations of resources, such as oil in the Middle East, timber in South America and Asia, or gold and diamonds in South Africa, make trade inevitable as nations share resources distributed through world trade. However, commodity prices on world markets have rarely kept pace with global inflation, resulting in diminished purchasing power for developing country providers. Efforts to increase commodity prices such as oil have generally been resisted in the developed nations as inflationary, and continued low commodity prices limit developing-country industrialization efforts.

4. *Trade helps emerging economies develop through technology transfers.* The rise in world-development standards eases suffering in poor nations by contributing to their economic growth. South Korea's export-based growth strategy contributed to the raising of its GDP per capita from $87 in 1962 to over $10,000 in 1995.[10] As technology transfers have become more frequent, so more countries acquire the skills to compete worldwide. Over the long-term, these nations can become major global competitors to developed-country firms.

5. *World trade encourages efficient use of global resources.* Competition forces countries to focus on industries in which they are competitive. For example, developing nations can use their surplus workers to compete in labor-intensive industries, such as textiles. Developed countries can use their educated and skilled workforces to be manufacturing centers for technically advanced (capital intensive) goods and services such as high-tech or financial services.

6. *Global competition forces companies to become more efficient and innovative.* Many of the management philosophies and techniques of the 1990s (total quality management, reengineering, etc.) have been transferred internationally by corporations in their quests to attain competitive advantages at national-market and global levels.

7. *Trade as a source of global education has made countries and peoples increasingly aware of world events and problems.* Global media give instantaneous news coverage worldwide, educating national publics and broadening their appreciation of foreign markets. Similarly, increased product varieties educate consumers about labor-saving devices and alternative-consumption styles. A downside to this argument is that, while such products and promotions stimulate consumers toward higher standards of consumption, they also create frustrations for consumers too poor to participate fully in consumption-based societies (e.g., developing countries).

8. *Exporting creates jobs.* Estimates during the 1970s put job creation at 20,000 jobs per $1 billion in export trade. Estimates for the 1990s place this figure at about 7,000 jobs per $1 billion in exports.[11] For countries like Japan, a $100 billion trade surplus means about 700,000 additional jobs.

Protectionist/anti free-trade arguments tend to be country or industry-focused and include the following:

1. *Job loss:* Global competition through imports causes unemployment in national economies. If exporting creates 7,000 jobs per $1 billion in exports, then it can be argued that imports replace jobs at a similar rate. Thus, a U.S. trade deficit of $400 billion would be worth 2.8 million jobs if it were erased overnight.

2. *Low developing country wage rates represent unfair competition:* Industrialized countries argue that emergent-nation wage rates are too low. For example, they may not include payroll taxes (e.g., social security, unemployment benefits). Another complaint is that many countries do not adhere to established labor practices (e.g., 40 or 48-hour work weeks, five-day schedules, etc.). Developing countries have actively lobbied against low-wage arguments at the WTO, claiming that their cheap labor is a legitimate competitive advantage. They further argue that worker productivity in many industries is determined not by labor costs, but by the amount of capital backing up labor. In this case, it would be the developed nations that have "unfair" advantages. The WTO does condemn some labor practices, such as the use of child and prison labor in international trade. However, even the child-labor argument has its adherents, as in some cases, children become major financial contributors for families in dire economic circumstances. Problems occur, however, in some cases when children must work in dangerous conditions (e.g., brick-making) and endure long work hours and harsh discipline. While sweat-shop conditions are common in developing countries, they also occur in North America and Western Europe, particularly with immigrant labor.

> It is but a truism that labor is most productive where its wages are largest. Poorly paid labor is inefficient the world over.
>
> —*Henry George,*
> *19th-century U.S. economist*

3. *Infant industry argument:* Start-up industries, especially in emergent nations, often need time to build up experience and scale economies before being exposed to international competition. The automobile industries in South Korea and Brazil matured under this regimen.[12] Problems occur as industries in this situation often lack incentives to attain international competitiveness, and protection becomes difficult to remove.

4. *Strategic industry arguments:* There are some industries that governments label "strategic" and which are sheltered from international competition. In the post–1945 period, these included infrastructure industries such as mail services, telecommunications, energy (e.g., utilities), and airlines. Governments argued that such sectors should remain in the public domain for national security reasons. However, with the deescalation of East-West tensions, national security issues have become less pronounced, and many infrastructure industries have been privatized and opened up to international competition.

   However, there remain a number of sectors that national governments deem "strategic" and where some protectionism is practiced. One of these is agriculture. The EU maintains a protectionist stance on agriculture through its common agricultural policy (CAP). Under CAP, European prices are set according to the least effective producer to ensure continuous agricultural supplies. Other countries (notably the U.S.) argue that non-protected markets for agricultural produce would benefit world consumers through lower prices. While this is a valid argument, there are fears that dependencies on foreign food supplies could be disastrous in the event of crop failures, and that nations should have the right to ensure their own food supplies, even at higher prices.

Many countries, for similar reasons, prefer to maintain their own military and defense industries to prevent excessive dependence on foreign contractors. While this may result in high-priced defense systems and less-than-globally-optimal weapons, this type of protection insulates governments from political pressures that could accrue from such dependencies. Similarly, there are restrictions on trade in nuclear technologies to ensure that they do not fall into hostile hands.

> To hear the Japanese plead for free trade is like hearing the word *love* on the lips of a harlot.
>
> —*Lane Kirkland, U.S. labor leader*

5. *"Uneven playing fields":* Some countries are alleged to practice "managed trade policies," whereby governments effectively shield domestic producers from the full forces of global competition through (often) subtle non-tariff barriers. Japan has for many years maintained a significant balance of trade surpluses with the outside world and managed import-price competition through tight control of domestic distribution channels. Foreign companies and products have little choice but to distribute products through inefficient multi-layered channels that stifle price competition at the retail level. This has limited competitive options for foreign companies in the Japanese market and opened Japan up to charges of protectionism.[13] Both the EU and the U.S. have been active in pressuring Japan to secure the same access to the Japanese market as Japanese companies enjoy in North America and Western Europe.

6. *Managed trade accounts:* Countries often restrict trade to a level where export earnings in convertible currencies cover import bills. This prevents major trade-balance deficits and accumulations of hard-currency debts with the rest of the world. While this limits trade and national economic development in the short term, there are fewer pressures on national exchange-rate values, and adequate foreign-currency reserves can be maintained.

> They all come back to the same thing: we have got to decide what free and fair trade is all about, and we've got to level the playing field to be competitive. These are the gut issues.
>
> —*Lee Iacocca, former chairman, Chrysler Corporation*

7. *Free trade and economic restructuring:* Free trade has significant repercussions as resources are moved out of uncompetitive sectors into industries with secure long-term prospects. In industrialized economies, politicians recognize that unskilled labor suffers disproportionately when jobs are transferred to developing countries. While conventional economic wisdom suggests that advanced countries should export high-tech and knowledge-intensive products, retraining poorly educated and unskilled workers is a difficult task. Trends away from manufacturing employment are complemented by increases in service industries. But the hollowing out of national manufacturing sectors remains a governmental concern in maturing economies.

8. *Cultural protectionism:* Some countries restrict foreign influences (often including imports and foreign direct investments) to preserve their national cultures. Not all nations want unrestricted ac-

cess to Western products. Canada maintains curbs on U.S. "cultural imperialism" by limiting sales of U.S. textbooks, curtailing the amount of foreign content in domestic radio stations, and taxing Canadian ads in Canadian editions of U.S. magazines.[14] Similarly countries with strong national cultures (e.g., France) or profoundly religious convictions (e.g., Middle East) are skeptical of Western materialism and hype.

> *When two cultures collide is the only time when true suffering exists.*
>
> —*Hermann Hesse, German philosopher*

National Infrastructure Development: World Bank Group

UN and World Bank concerns with national infrastructure development stem from their recognition of "persistent global problems," including poverty and inadequacies in food supplies, sanitation, water, education, and physical infrastructures.

The World Bank Group is made up of five organizations that use global financial markets to provide capital for national infrastructure developments. The first loans were originally made to finance the reconstruction of Western Europe and Japan after World War II. Today the group provides loans and assistance to promote economic growth in the developing world. The details of the five organizations are provided in Exhibit 2-1. Note though that capital is raised on international money markets and that, while poorer countries (<$925 per capita) pay little by way of interest charges and have long payback periods, most World Bank activities have market-related interest rates and short grace periods before repayment begins.

THE GLOBAL WEB

World Bank Group at www.worldbank.org

PRIVATE SECTOR INFRASTRUCTURE DEVELOPMENTS

Trade liberalization and increasing investments by international corporations has led to major improvements in the coordination of corporate activities. Linkages among company subsidiaries, suppliers, production facilities, distributors, and customers have all been enhanced through improvements in transportation and communications infrastructures.

Private sector contributions to world infrastructure development include the following:

1. *Internationalization of channels* as retailers, such as Laura Ashley, Carrefour, Benetton, Wal-Mart, and Home Depot, have capitalized on global demand homogenization to go abroad in significant numbers.[15]

2. *Electronic commerce* using the Internet, international credit cards, and electronic transfers of funds have facilitated online sales, promotions to customers, and enhanced communications within international corporations.

Internally, companies have been quick to embrace the new technologies in building global communications networks. A *ComputerWorld* survey of forty-seven global companies found that thirty-five had global

THE GLOBAL WEB

Visit Wal-Mart at www.walmart.com and Carrefour at www.carrefour.com

EXHIBIT 2-1
World Bank Group: Objectives and Resources

1. International Bank for Reconstruction & Development (IBRD)
2. International Development Association (IDA)

   These two institutions are contrasted thus:

	IBRD	**IDA**
Established	1944	1960
Country targets	GNP/Capita > $925	GNP/Capita > $925
Eligibility	$1506 to $5435	
Maturity	15–20 years	35–40 years
Grace period	3–5 years	10 years
Interest rate	Variable—about 6.5%	0%, 0.75% service charge
Members	180 countries	159 countries
Funding sources	World capital markets	Government contributions, IBRD profits, earlier IDA credits
Activities 1997	141 projects totaling $14.7 billion	100 projects totaling $4.6 billion

3. International Finance Corporation (IFC): Founded 1956, 172 member countries. IFC lends directly to developing country private sectors.

4. Multilateral Investment Guarantee Agency (MIGA): Founded 1988; 141 member countries. MIGA provides guarantees to protect investors from noncommercial risks, advises governments on attracting foreign direct investments, and disseminates investment opportunity information.

5. International Center for Settlement of Investment Disputes (ICSID): Founded 1966; 127 members countries. ICSID provides arbitration and consultation services for disputes between foreign investors and host governments.

communications networks, with a further nine aiming to have their own networks by the year 2000.[16] Firms have been able to integrate supply chains from demand monitoring at retail through to purchasing, production, and distribution functions.[17] The full effects of IT technologies on supply-chain strategies are assessed in Chapter 11.

Externally, Internet effects on global commerce have been notable as E-commerce has come online. While North America accounted for two-thirds of Internet users in 1998, the non-U.S. share of E-commerce revenues was expected to increase from 11 percent in 1998 to 23 percent in 2003.[18] Worldwide web sites are expected to be major facilitators of global trade as:

- Sales orders and inquiries can be received 24 hours a day.
- Current product lines and brochures can be promoted.
- Some frustrations of international communications can be avoided. For example, miscommunications through verbal exchanges are avoided through written messages; missed telephone connections are avoided; and time can be taken to compile and compose detailed written responses.
- Communications are less affected by time differences.
- Internet remains an inexpensive means of communication.[19]

3. *Shipping developments:* Improvements in shipping have made trans-Atlantic crossing in 100 hours (as opposed to a week or more) likely in the foreseeable future.[20] Mergers have affected the shipping industry as national and regional carriers have combined to provide seamless shipping services on a global basis,[21] and intermodal alliances among airlines, shipping, and trucking firms are providing complete services across water and land.[22]

4. *Growth in international air express services* has doubled from 480,000 packages in 1992 to over 1 million deliveries per day for a growth rate of over 20 percent per year (versus rates of 7 percent for the world air-cargo industry generally). Competition among express carriers (DHL Worldwide, FedEx, UPS, and TNT/GD) has put pressures on traditional air carriers to make the industry more attractive to prospective users. So efficient have these companies become that firms like FedEx have become the logistics arms of major international corporations.[23]

5. *Satellite technology* has made global communications a reality. Recent advances have greatly expanded the variety, availability, and potential uses for satellite technology, whose costs have decreased with mass-market usage, especially in mobile communications. Lockheed Martin, Loral Space and Communications, Boeing, and TRW are current leaders in the field, though they face increasing competition from Russian and Asian companies.[24]

6. *Global media developments* proliferated over the 1990s and into the new millenium. From a broadcast perspective, global television has become a reality. CNN International carries news and current events into more than countries; the Discovery channel is broad-

Technologies that are emerging today will give us the ability to explore, convey, and to create knowledge as never before . . . if we respond with our best creative energies, we can unleash a new renaissance of discovery and learning.

—*John Scully, chairman, Apple Computer*

THE GLOBAL WEB

Visit Federal Express at www.FedEx.com and UPS at www.ups.com

The [flying] machine will eventually be fast; they will be used in sport but should not be thought of as commercial carriers.

—*Octave Chanute, 19th–20th-century French aviation pioneer*

THE GLOBAL WEB

Visit CNN International at www.cnn.com/CNNI, the British Broadcasting Corporation at www.bbc.co.uk, and Europe's *Financial Times* at www.ft.com

> The marvels—of film, radio and television— are marvels of one-way communication, which is not communication at all.
>
> *—Milton Mayer*

cast in twenty languages into 143 countries; ESPN International takes sports into 157 million households globally and in twenty languages. Broadcast media are also regional. MBC is an Arabic news and entertainment channel; AXN is an eleven country Asian entertainment network; Sony operates a Hindi-language network across India and for Indians in Western Europe; Latin America has Discovery TV networks (four channels), Fox Kids, and sports networks.[25] Print media have also expanded globally. Britain's *Financial Times* is distributed in 140 countries, *Newsweek* in 190 nations, and *Fortune* has Asian, North American, Latin American, European, and Chinese editions.

REGIONAL ECONOMIC AND POLITICAL INTEGRATION

Regional economic and political integration occurs when groups of countries put aside national differences to reduce or eliminate economic and political barriers to commerce and to bring about increased levels of competition in national marketplaces. The integration process takes time as countries adjust to their new regional marketplaces.

Degrees of Integration: Types of Trade Blocs

Typically, economic and political integration evolves through five stages.

> No society of nations . . . can benefit through mutual aid unless good will exceeds ill will, unless the spirit of cooperation surpasses antagonism, unless we all see and act as though others' welfare determines our welfare.
>
> *—Henry Ford 2nd, CEO, Ford Motor Company*

1. *Free trade areas* are first established to abolish internal tariffs among member nations while maintaining their own external tariffs against non-members. The North American Free Trade Area is at this stage.

2. *Customs unions* not only eliminate internal tariffs among member states but also instigate common external tariffs. The Latin American group, Mercosur, achieved free internal trade in 1994 and the imposition of common external tariffs by 2000.

3. *Common markets* have no internal tariffs, a common external tariff, and free movements of labor and capital among member countries. Currently, the EU is the closest to achieving common-market status, although EU-wide recognition of labor and professional credentials remains a work in progress.

4. *Full economic integration* brings member nations closer to single-market status as non-tariff barriers, such as national product standards, labeling, and product-testing requirements, are harmonized. Border controls of product movements are minimized or eliminated. Region-wide policies are established for energy and agricultural sectors, and regional laws govern corporate behaviors. The EU is the only bloc to have made significant progress in this area.

5. *Political integration* is the final stage and involves member states sacrificing national economic and political sovereignty to integrate fiscal, monetary policies and institute a common currency to replace national currencies. The EU, with its euro, established in 2002, became the first regional bloc to achieve this goal in concert with other major integration initiatives.

Formation of Economic/Political Blocs: The Evolution of the EU

Western Europe emerged from the 1939–45 World War a shadow of its former self. Yet, from this chaos emerged a determination to merge the European economies together to minimize the possibility of further political and military conflicts. To this end, talks began in 1948 about European unification. In 1951, the Treaty of Paris established the European Coal and Steel Community. Further discussions resulted in the 1957 Treaty of Rome that welded together six nations—Belgium, Netherlands, Luxembourg, France, Germany, and Italy—into the European Economic Community (EEC). In 1973, Eire (Southern Ireland), Denmark, and the United Kingdom came on board; Greece joined in 1982; Spain and Portugal in 1986; and Austria, Sweden, and Finland in 1995.

> **THE GLOBAL WEB**
>
> The official European Union website at
> www.europa.eu.int

EC '92 European Economic Integration A further step toward integration was achieved in 1992 as the European Community eliminated major non-tariff barriers and moved toward economic unification (EC '92). This involved:

*   Establishment of Europe-wide technical standards for major industries.

*   Elimination of border controls among member countries, as thirty-five pages of border and customs clearances were reduced to two pages. Electronic document transfers have further facilitated trans-border product movements.

*   Liberalization of public-procurement policies was instigated to allow non-nationals access to government contracts. However, xenophobic purchasing policies still persist, though Internet-based national bidding procedures and contract notifications have been initiated to correct the problem.[26]

*   Deregulation of the financial-services industry has heightened competition in financial markets, with banks allowed to compete in the home loans, insurance, brokerage, and securities markets, and other financial institutions able to offer banking services.

*   Privatization of telecommunications, electric, coal, gas, communications, and transportation systems was mandated.

*   EU-wide harmonization of regulatory and safety standards for many industries.

*   Liberalization of capital (short-term, long-term and stocks).

> The day will come when you, France; you, Russia; you, Italy; you, England; you, Germany—all of you nations on the continent will, without losing your distinctive qualities, blend into a . . . European fraternity.
>
> —*Victor Hugo (1802–85), French poet, novelist, dramatist*

- Free movement of labor, including EU-wide recognition of educational attainments (degrees, diplomas, professional qualifications).

- Harmonization of laws concerning intellectual property, company law, mergers and acquisitions, bankruptcies, and environmental protection.

- Harmonization of taxation policies, especially those concerning value-added taxes (VAT) and company taxation.

EC '92 Impact:[27] Economic unification created an estimated 900,000 new jobs and added 1–1.5 percent to the EU's GDP. Two sets of problems remained. First, there was a lack of consensus in key areas, such as company taxation, value-added taxes, and company law (in particular, cross-border acquisitions and European statute laws). Second, national differences remained in adoption and implementation issues, particularly in the public-procurement area.

Political Integration: Mechanisms and Single Currency Issues Four major administrative mechanisms govern the EU.

> An administration, like a machine, does not create. It carries on.
>
> —*Antoine de Saint Exupery, 19th-century French diplomat*

1. *The European Commission* is the 16,000-persons civil-service arm of the EU that proposes policies through twenty "Directorates-General" (DGs). Each DG has a portfolio of responsibilities. For example, the external relations DG handles trade policy (e.g., negotiating with the WTO) and relationships with other trade blocs (e.g., NAFTA, Mercosur). Criticisms of EU management center around the perceived excessive power of the civil-service branch against that of the European Parliament and the Council of Ministers.

2. *The European Parliament* has the authority to reject EU budgets and trade agreements with third parties, and to amend legislation. The Parliament has 626 directly elected representatives and holds twelve plenary sessions a year in Strasbourg.

3. *The Council of Ministers* are major decision makers in the EU structure. On major issues (e.g., enlargement), 70 percent majorities of the full Council are required for passage. The Council of Ministers comprises eighty-seven members, with subgroups for individual policy-making units (e.g., all Foreign Policy Ministers sit on the Foreign Affairs subcommittee). The presidency of the Council rotates twice a year.

4. *The Court of Justice* of the European Union is Luxembourg-based and interprets EU laws (EU vs. member states, country versus country, or member states vs. the EU).

A major step forward was taken in 1991 when the *Maastricht Agreement* was passed. The major proposal was for a common EU currency, though subsidiary items included cross-border police cooperation and a European defense force. Country eligibility for common currency consideration included:

- Fiscal deficits (the extent to which governments overspent their revenues) should not exceed 3 percent of total government budgets.

- Price stability: Participant price-inflation levels should not exceed 1.5 percent of the average for the best three performing states.

- Public debt should not exceed 60 percent of a country's gross national product.

- Interest rates (as measured by long-term government bonds or their equivalents) should not exceed the best three performing states' average by greater than 2 percent.

- Exchange-rate stability should be apparent for two years prior to entry.[28]

These criteria brought EU economies into convergence for the 1999–2002 transition to the euro that occurred between January 1, 1999, and January 1, 2002, with national currency units (NCUs) and euros existing side by side. National currencies were phased out by April 2002. The euro's introduction meant that national governments effectively ceded economic decisions on interest rates, money supply, and exchange rates to the EU in Brussels. The three-year transition gave companies in the euro-zone time to adapt their pricing, accounting, and financial policies to the new currency and to allow firms outside the zone time to adjust. Major adaptations include debtor–creditor payment obligations, re-denominations of contracts from NCUs to euros, making bank conversions, and reorienting invoice systems.[29]

Euro Participants and Impact Analysis Of the fifteen EU member nations, eleven opted to be charter members of the EMU: Austria, Belgium, Finland, France, Germany, Italy, Ireland, Luxembourg, Netherlands, Portugal, and Spain. Greece joined in 2001. Three countries (U.K., Sweden, and Denmark) remained outside of the euro area. Collectively in 2003, the euro group accounts for 290 million people and a GDP of over $7 trillion. The euro seems destined to join the dollar as co-leaders in world currency markets.

EU Enlargement In political terms, trade-bloc size is associated with political and economic power. The European Union has evolved from its six original members in 1957 to fifteen in 1995. But further expansion is occurring, and May, 2004, saw a further ten nations admitted: Poland, Hungary, Czech Republic, Slovakia, Malta, Cyprus, Latvia, Lithuania, Estonia, and Slovenia. This added 100 million new consumers to the EU and an additional 7 percent on the EU's GDP.[30]

As the EU adds countries, the bloc continues to expand its influence as a free-trade force in world commerce.

- In 2000, the EU signed a framework agreement with Mercosur and a free-trade agreement with Mexico, with 100 percent free trade by 2003.[31] This follows earlier European initiatives regarding a Trans-Atlantic Free Trade Area (TAFTA), involving the Americas and the EU.[32]

- The EU grants more than 70 Africa, Caribbean, and Pacific nations preferential access to EU markets.[33]

- The 1995 Barcelona Declaration called for a free-trade zone between the EU and twelve Mediterranean states in Southeastern Europe.

- A commercial partnership and cooperation agreement between the EU and Russia came into force in December 1997. The agreement sets up the intriguing prospect that, once Russia joins the WTO, its application to join the EU may not be far behind.[34]

> There is no royal road to anything; one thing at a time, and all things in succession. That which grows slowly endures.
>
> —*Josiah G. Holland*

Key Success Factors in Regional Blocs: The European Union

The European Union (EU) has been the most successful economic bloc to date, with other regional arrangements attempting to emulate that success. The major reasons for its success include the following.

Tradition of international trade: Commerce has been an active European pursuit since the Roman Empire some 2,000 years ago. Since internal trade is a primary objective of economic blocs, this commercial continuity has been a primary catalyst to integration.

Timing: Initial negotiations for a united Europe started soon after 1945, when the memories of two world wars were fresh and desires to avoid future conflicts were strong.

Outside encouragement: The United States actively encouraged European integration during the 1950s and 1960s as a buffer against the then-communist Soviet Bloc.

Geographic proximity: The geographic compactness of Western Europe facilitated trade and communication among member states.

Pressure from industrial organizations: The post-1945 technological boom saw increasing numbers of firms looking to expand their operations into international markets.

Disappearance of overseas colonies: Europe's colonizing exploits of the sixteenth to twentieth centuries came to an end as countries in Africa, the Middle East, and Asia were granted independence in the twentieth century. This left a commercial vacuum in European commercial affairs. The EU emerged to fill this void.

Political personalities: It took vision and political astuteness to advance the idea of European unity. Winston Churchill was an early advocate, and Charles de Gaulle and Jean Monnet pushed the idea from the concept stage toward reality.

Cultural similarities among European countries: While there are (and continue to be) cultural differences among the nations of Europe, they share a number of similarities. Most are at the same stage of economic development. They have similar mixed economies that combine capitalist orientations with socialist tendencies (e.g., their belief in national-welfare support systems). Further, all nations have advanced banking, economic infrastructures, and convertible currencies to support high levels of commercial and trading activities. These similarities have led to high levels of trust (but not total harmony) among EU participants.

> In Latin America, economic associations . . . reaffirm the point demonstrated most graphically by the European Union that economic integration proceeds faster and further when it is based on cultural commonality.
>
> —*Samuel P. Huntington, political scientist, Harvard University*

Other Trade Blocs: Progress and Problems

North American Free Trade Area NAFTA was formed originally in 1989 between the U.S. and Canada. Mexico joined in 1994 and has become the bloc's low-cost producer, creating about 1.75 million jobs. The U.S. lost more than 300,000 jobs since 1994 but has benefited from the economic expansion spawned by NAFTA. Mexico's addition has caused many U.S. firms to reorient their supply chain and sourcing activities from other parts of the world (e.g., Asia) to the Americas.[35] Plans are underway for a Free Trade Area of the Americas (FTAA) to integrate the thirty-four nations of North, Central, and South

America into a western hemispheric trade bloc totaling over 850 million consumers with a GDP of over $12 trillion and a total trade volume of about $3½ trillion.[36]

Mercosur is the major South American trade bloc. Originally formed in 1989 between Brazil and Argentina, Mercosur now includes Paraguay and Uruguay, with Chile and Bolivia as associate members. After achieving early successes in reducing internal tariffs and imposing a common external tariff (in 2000), Mercosur had problems in the late 1990s, as Brazil had to significantly depreciate its currency (the real), causing major problems for other bloc members, noticeably Argentina. The region's vast geographic expanse has caused problems, and the trade bloc's main priorities are to build reliable cross-border infrastructures, including roads, electricity grids, and gas pipelines.[37]

Association of Southeastern Asian Nations: ASEAN was originally formed in 1967 with Brunei, Indonesia, Philippines, Malaysia, Singapore, Thailand, Vietnam, and Burma (now Myanmar). Little progress was made initially as participating nations had poorly developed infrastructures and little to trade. Some progress was made with the 1993 formation of the ASEAN free trade area (AFTA). The future of ASEAN (and Asian trading blocs generally) lies with the integrating of regional powerhouses South Korea, Japan, and China into the region's trade bloc schemes. Japan's early twentieth-century involvements with Korea and China made both nations wary of Japanese intentions.

Asia-Pacific Economic Cooperation: The APEC group takes in twenty-one nations from both sides of the Pacific Ocean. The group's economic diversity, taking in less-affluent Asian nations along with the U.S., Japan, China, and Australia, makes agreements among group members difficult to achieve, as do variations in national economic priorities among its leading members, the U.S., Japan, and China. Geographic distance (the Pacific Ocean) and cultural distance (East-West differences) also impede coordination and integration opportunities.

African trade blocs have been historically difficult to implement. Many African nations received their national independences during the 1950s–1970s, and internal priorities have taken precedence over external trade liaisons with other countries. But as democracies and economic stability have taken hold, so trade blocs have started to flourish.

- The Common Market for Eastern and Southern Africa (COMESA) came into being in 2000 and comprises twenty countries, of which nine are active members. The bloc's aims are to remove barriers to trade and skilled labor movement by 2004 and ultimately to have a common currency by 2025. Regional conflicts are problematic, as are major inequalities in economic development (Egypt is nine times larger than Kenya, the second biggest economy). Low levels of intraregional trade, long distances between members, and poor infrastructures are additional problems to be overcome before success is possible.[38]

- *The East African Community (EAC)* comprises Kenya, Tanzania, and Uganda, with other countries awaiting entry consideration. Established in

THE GLOBAL WEB

Web sites to other trade blocs can be accessed via Yahoo at http://dir.yahoo.com/government/law/trade/international/treaties_pacts_and_agreements or key in "international trade treaties, pacts and agreement." Details on Andean Pact, ASEAN, Caricom, Central American Common Market, COMESA, EFTA, Mercosur, and NAFTA are provided.

EXHIBIT 2-2
Major Economic Blocs

Economic Bloc	Formed	Present Members	Progress/Comment
European Union (EU)	1957	France, Germany, Italy, Netherlands, Belgium, Luxembourg, U.K., Eire, Denmark, Greece, Spain, Portugal, Austria, Finland, Sweden, Poland, Hungary, Czech Republic, Slovakia, Malta, Cyprus, Latvia, Lithuania, Estonia, Slovenia	Formed from Coal & Steel Community, 1952
European Free Trade Association (EFTA)	1960	Iceland, Liechtenstein, Norway, Switzerland	Free trade area; free trade with EU in non-agricultural products
North American Free Trade Area (NAFTA)	1989	Canada, U.S., Mexico	U.S.–Canada tariffs eliminated by 1998; Mexico tariffs by 2008
Central American Integration System (SICA)	1993	Panama, Costa Rica, El Salvador, Guatemala, Honduras, Nicaragua	Revival of Central American Common Market, 1960–69
Caribbean Community and Common Market	1993	13 Caribbean nations	Caricom and other Caribbean countries formed the Association of Caribbean States
Mercosur	1988	Brazil, Argentina, Uruguay, Paraguay	Internal free trade established by 1994; common external tariffs established in 2000. Talks between EU and Mercosur.
Andean Community	1969	Bolivia, Peru, Colombia, Ecuador, Venezuela	Aim to establish free trade with Mercosur, 2004

Economic Bloc	Formed	Present Members	Progress/Comment
Association of Southeast Asian Nations (ASEAN)	1967	Brunei, Indonesia, Malaysia, Philippines, Singapore, Thailand, Vietnam, Myanmar	
ASEAN Free Trade Area (AFTA)	1993		Cambodia, Laos, negotiating entry
Asia-Pacific Economic Cooperation (APEC)	1989	21 countries, including: Australia, Brunei, Canada, China, Chile, Hong Kong, Japan, Indonesia, Malaysia, Mexico, New Zealand, Papua New Guinea, Peru, Philippines, Russia, South Korea, Singapore, Taiwan, Thailand, U.S., Vietnam	Objective is total free trade by 2010 (industrialized countries), or 2020 (all members)
Southern Africa Development Community (SADC) (formerly Southern African Development Coordination Conference)	1992, reestablished 1999	14 countries including Angola, Botswana, Malawi, Mozambique, South Africa, Zimbabwe, Seychelles, and Democratic Rep. of the Congo	South Africa the dominant economy. Free trade within zone by 2004. New investment incentives for multinationals introduced.
East African Community	1999	Kenya, Uganda, Tanzania	
Common Market for Eastern and Southern Africa (COMESA)	2000	20 members—9 active: Djibouti, Egypt, Kenya, Madagascar, Malawi, Mauritius, Sudan, Zambia, Zimbabwe	Regional conflicts and political problems plague members.

1999, these three nations have similar colonial heritages and legal systems and share a common language (Swahili). In 2001, they set up a legislative body, the East African Assembly, and established a common East African passport to facilitate free movements of labor. Current focuses include harmonizing and reducing tariffs to encourage trade, and regional infrastructure development.[39]

GLOBAL PRIVATIZATION AND DEREGULATION PROGRAMS

National Privatization and Deregulation Programs

Throughout much of the twentieth century, governments focused on building up national infrastructures and providing necessary services for citizens. For security reasons, national infrastructure industries such as airlines, utilities, and energy were state-owned. Then came the de-escalation of East-West tensions as Eastern European economies broke down and moved toward market forces economies. National security became less of a governmental concern. Global capitalist trends, coupled with cash-strapped governments made state-owned industries unnecessary expenses. The 1980s and 1990s saw major movements toward privatization as former government-owned industries were sold back into the private sector. Simultaneously, governments deregulated many of these industries so that they had to compete in their national markets and in the global marketplace. Global privatization deals rose from 700 in 1980–87 to 2,200 in 1988–93. In 1996, they totaled $85 billion,[40] and, in 1999, they topped the $145 billion mark in OECD countries.[41] Governments in Eastern Europe, Latin America, and Asia joined the rush to privatize major sectors of their economies.

But the success of privatization and deregulation movements depends on countries' and companies' abilities to adapt to the competitive global marketplace. At the nation-state level, some transitions have been traumatic. Under China's 1997 economic plan, all but 1,000 of the country's 305,000 state-owned enterprises (SOEs) were to be sold off. Inefficient firms were to be allowed to go bankrupt. To aid the transition, worker-retraining schemes, new pension plans, social services, and low-cost housing policies were enacted.[42] In South Korea, the iron rice bowl mentality (under which workers were protected and provided for by companies) was upset with the passage of a law permitting firms to lay off workers. The result was considerable civil unrest.[43]

> Some see private enterprise as a predatory target to be shot, others as a cow to be milked, but few are those who see it as a sturdy horse pulling the wagon.
>
> —*Winston S. Churchill, 20th-century British statesman*

> The issue has been the performance of capitalism against the promise of communism.
>
> —*Pual G. Hoffman, U.S. business executive*

Industry and Company Effects

For individual companies, privatization and deregulation cause internal upheavals as firms are reoriented to face marketplace realities. Exhibit 2-3 shows a contrast between SOE and privatized company mindsets. The conservative, in-

E X H I B I T   2 - 3
Reorienting SOEs to Face Marketplace Competition

	SOE Mindset	Private Sector Mindset
Marketplace competition	None	Considerable
Corporate emphasis	Maximizing production	Customer satisfaction/profit orientation
Price/Cost orientation	Low	High
Market needs	Viewed as homogeneous; no segmentation	Many heterogenous needs; multiple segments
New product development	Little emphasis	Considerable emphasis
Cost accounting	Unnecessary: state covers losses	Vital: determines profit margins
Capital financing	Provided by government	From private capital markets if projects are viable
Worker orientation	High; lifetime employment, many perks (housing, medical, recreation facilities)	Low: labor viewed as an expense
Management productivity and accountability	Not measured	Must be measured
Corporate culture	Harmonious; teamwork oriented	Competitive; individual orientation and accountability
Strategic planning	Unnecessary	A major management function
Hiring criteria	Friends, relatives, kinship	Education, qualifications
Management style	Top-down	More egalitarian

ward-looking SOE contrasts with the market-oriented, efficiency-driven privatized firm.

Within individual industries, privatization and deregulation have caused major competitive shifts. In the telecommunications sector: On January 1, 1998, the European telecommunications industry was officially deregulated. In Germany, over thirty rivals emerged to challenge Deutsche Telecom's monopoly and undercut its prices by up to 60 percent.[44]

In other industries, change has been equally dramatic. In financial markets, deregulation and information systems advances have created global opportunities for borrowers, lenders, and investors.[45] Some deregulation efforts have run into political resistance. Japan's 1998 proposed reforms of its financial sector caused Prime Minister Hashimoto's resignation.[46]

The deregulation of global infrastructures industries has prompted firms to go international. The electrical-supply sector, previously limited

> By competition the total amount of supply is increased, and this enables the consumer to buy at lower prices. Of all human powers operating on the affairs of mankind, none is greater than that of competition.
>
> *—Henry Clay*

to domestic operations, has rushed to expand service to the 2 billion people worldwide currently not on national electric grid systems.[47] Trackebel, the Belgian electric and gas giant, added 9,400 megawatts of generating power abroad to complement its 13,200 megawatt domestic capacity.[48]

WORLD INFRASTRUCTURE DEVELOPMENT AND INTERNATIONAL BUSINESS GROWTH

> The growth of big business is merely the survival of the fittest.
>
> —*John D. Rockefeller, 19th–20th-century U.S. oil magnate*

The effects of these changes have been most noticeable in world markets as economic interdependencies have risen. The United Nations, through its agencies like the IMF, the WTO, and the World Bank, laid the foundation for world commerce expansion. Other agencies, like the IMO, ICAO, ITU, and UPO, have facilitated worldwide infrastructure development, while the private sector has responded with major improvements in global transportation and communications systems. Country governments have played their parts also, sacrificing national sovereignty to join trade blocs and, through privatization and deregulation efforts, allowing more industries and national economies to compete in the world marketplace. As a result, world trade increased from about $2 trillion in 1980 to about $6 trillion in 1999.[49] Foreign direct investment flows totaled $651 billion in 2002, down though from $1.2 trillion in 2000, and total FDI stock increased to $7.1 trillion (up from $2.8 trillion in 1995).[50] International corporations are on their way to dominating world commerce. For example:

- There are 64,000 international corporations in the world with 870,000 subsidiaries. Their sales exceed $18 trillion, and their share of world GDP has grown from 17 percent in the mid–1960s to 24 percent in 1984 to 33 percent in 1995.
- Foreign affiliates (those situated outside of their country of origin) employed more than 53 million people in 2002 and accounted for a tenth of world GDP.
- Two-thirds of world trade results from internal transfers of goods and services among international corporations.
- When country GDPs are compared to corporate turnovers, 51 of the top 100 economic units are international corporations.[51]

KEY POINTS

- World economic progress has been greatly facilitated by public and private infrastructure development. The United Nations, via agencies such as ICAO, IMO, IMF, WTO, and the World Bank, have laid many of the foundations for world trade through its effects on transportation, currency exchanges, and developing country infrastructures.

- Private sector contributions to world infrastructures include more efficient transportation, global media and communications, and worldwide distribution services.

- Economic and political integration has occurred as countries have joined together in trade blocs to access each other's markets and products. The European Union has been the most successful economic bloc to date, though integration is occurring in North and Latin Americas, Africa, and Asia. Economic blocs in developing regions have been slow to develop, due to infrastructure deficiencies, political and economic instabilities, and poor diplomatic and political relations.

- The advent of market-forces capitalism worldwide has prompted national governments to privatize state-owned industries and deregulate others to make them more efficient and marketplace-responsive. This has had major effects on many industries, particularly in previously communistic economies.

ENDNOTES

1. Anonymous, "FedEx presents a unique total logistics solution," *Business Korea* (September 1999): 47–48: and Andrew Tanzer, "Warehouses that fly," *Forbes* (October 18, 1999): 120–124.

2. Much of this information can be found on the web site: http://www.imf.org.

3. Moin Siddiqi, "A Single Currency for West Africa?" *African Business* (September 2000): 16–17.

4. Charles Enoch and Anne-Marie Gulde, *Finance & Development* 35, 4 (December 1998): 40–43.

5. Maggie Ford, "Economy in need of a crisis," *Euromoney* (September 1997): 244–50; and "Piloting the Titanic," *Business Week* (January 26, 1998): 1–2.

6. Anonymous, "Border Battles," *Economist* (October 3, 1998): 6–8.

7. Marco Bronckers and Pierre LaRouche, "Telecommunications services and the World Trade Organization, *Journal of World Trade* 31.3 (June 1997): 5–48.

8. Anonymous, "Banana Row," *Economist* (May 31, 1997): 36.

9. Bruce Barnard, "The World Trade Watchdog has a big bark," *Europe* (September 1995): 28.

10. Susan Lee and Christine Foster, "The Global Hand," *Forbes* (April 21, 1997): 106.

11. Based on statistics in "Manufacturing Analytical Report Series," *Exports from Manufacturing Establishments* (U.S. Department of Commerce: Bureau of the Census, 1992, 1994).

12. John D. Daniels and Lee H. Radenbaugh, *International Business: Environments and Operations,* 5th Edition (Reading, Mass: Addison-Wesley, 1998).

13. For details, see John S. Hill, "The Japanese Business Puzzle: Or why the Japanese market is protected and likely to stay that way," *Journal of General Management* 15, 3 (Spring 1990): 20–38.

14. Joseph Weber, "Does Canadian Culture need this much protectionism?" *Business Week* (June 8, 1998): 37.

15. Brenda Sternquist, *International Retailing* (New York: Fairchild Publications, 1998).

16. Mary Brandel, "Think global, act local," *Computerworld* (March 10, 1997): 58–59.

17. Anon, "IT viewed as strategic supply chain tool," *Logistics Management* (March 1998): 34.

18. Nick Wreder, "Internet Opens Markets Abroad," *Informationweek* (November 16, 1998): 258–59.

19. Anon, "Sperka International," *Business America* (January 1998): 18.

20. Peter Bradley, "We've Only Just Begun," *Logistics Management* (January 1997): 63–64.

21. Toby B. Crooley, "New Wave of Mergers hits shipping industry," *Logistics Management* (March 1997): 107.

22. Ken Cottrill, "International Shipping at the Crossroads," *Journal of Business Strategy* (May–June 1997): 30–35.

23. Anonymous, "International Air-Express Growth Outpaces Other Airfreight Services," *Logistics Management* (March 1997): 29.

24. Krysten Jenci, "Satellites: Critical to the new global communications network," *Business America* (July 1997): 13–15.

25. "1999 Global Media Map," *Advertising Age International* (January 11, 1999).

26. "Public Procurement: An Action Program," *Business Europe* (March 25, 1998): 3.

27. Based on "The Single Market: Rhetoric versus Reality," ILT: *European Union,* Economist Intelligence Unit: 10.

28. "EMU Flies," *Business Eastern Europe* (July 6, 1998): 1.

29. "Euro Law: The Business Implications," *Business Europe* (May 6, 1998): 1–2.

30. Alex Blyth, "Analysis: EU enlargement—good or bad?" *Accountancy* (April 1, 2003): 1–3.

31. Anonymous, "Slowly, slowly," *Economist* (December 9, 1997): 34–36.

32. Anonymous, "Doing Business in Europe," *European Business Journal* 7, 4 (1995): 47–49.

33. Anonymous, "Western Europe: Economy & Trade," *Crossborder Monitor* (April 8, 1998): 3.

34. Anonymous, "Export Base for Business," *Corporate Location* (July–August 1997): 26–32.

35. Charles J. Whalen, Paul Manusson, and Geri Smith, "NAFTA's scorecard: so far, so good," *Business Week* (July 9, 2001): 54–56.

36. John S. McClenahen, "Dwarfing NAFTA," *Industry Week* (May 21, 2001): 45–48.

37. Anonymous, "Leaders: Some realism for Mercosur," *Economist* (March 31, 2001): 17–18.

38. Anonymous, "COMESA's free trade area," *Country Monitor* (November 6, 2000): 4.

39. Neil Ford, "East African Community: Will the unity hold?" *African Business* (February 2002): 20–24.

40. Claude Barfield and Douglas A Irwin, "The Future of Free Trade," *Business Economics* (April 1997): 26–31; and Ladan Mahboobi, "Recent Privatization Trends," *Financial Market Trends* (July 2000).

41. Anonymous, "Global amounts raised from privatization," *Financial Market Trends* (February 1998): 47–48.

42. Mark L. Clifford, *et al.,* "Can China reform its economy?" *Business Week* (September 29, 1997): 116–24.

43. Steven V. Brull and Katherine Kerumhyun Lee, "Why Seoul is seething," *Business Week* (January 27, 1997): 44–48.

44. Thane Peterson, Monica Larner, and Karen Anhalt, "A Heyday for Upstarts in Europe," *Business Week* (June 29, 1998): 118.

45. Edward M. Mervosh, "World-class capital access," *Industry Week* (November 17, 1997): 108–12.

46. Based on Mari Koseki, "Big Bang: A $9.6 trillion blast?" *Japan Times Weekly International Edition* (May 12, 1997): 13; and Anonymous "Leaders: Situation Normal," *Economist* (March 7, 1998): 20.

47. Anonymous, "Business: Power to the people," *Economist* (March 29, 1998): 61–63.

48. Howard Banks, "Counterattack," *Forbes* (February 24, 1997): 70–73.

49. "Directions of International Trade," *OECD* (2000): 2.

50. United Nations, *World Investment Report 2003* (New York): 23, 257.

51. Corporate Europe Observations, "The Explosive Growth of Foreign Investment," www.xs4all.nl/~ceo/mail/mmania03.html (February 1998); and *World Investment Report* (2003).

Casette 2-1
AIDS in Africa: Two Prescriptions—Any Cure?

The African continent has about 25 million of the world's 30 million AIDS sufferers. The question is not whether the problem should be tackled, but how. The United Nations and the private sector both have their ideas about how the problem should be tackled: one involves reducing AIDS transmissions from infected mothers to children via breast milk; the other using anti-AIDS drugs.

Problem #1: AIDS Transmission via Breast Milk

The facts are depressing: 3.4 million out of 3.8 million HIV-positive children were infected by their mothers. Of these, 1.1 to 1.7 million were infected through breastfeeding by HIV-positive mothers. Nelson Mandela noted that if the AIDS virus was to be stopped in Africa, the issue of mother-to-child transmission had to be dealt with "head-on." He further noted that only about 10 percent of HIV-positive pregnant women have access to medications that can save their babies from infection.

One proposed solution has been for HIV-infected mothers to use formula instead of breast milk to reduce the incidence of mother-child transmissions. To do this, the United Nations International Children's Emergency Fund (UNICEF) instituted a pilot program buying formula from a French company, Dannon subsidiary Jammet Dietetique Nouvelle S.A. Twenty-five thousand mothers in eleven African countries participated in the program. There were problems. UNICEF failed to follow its own guidelines in putting warning labels in appropriate local languages, not just English and French. A second problem was to box the formula in generic packages, making it obviously different from commercial formula, and highlighting users as HIV-positive.

In implementing the program, UNICEF refused formula donations from Wyeth-Ayerst and Nestle, both of whom would have provided the product free of charge. The donations were refused for fears that they would be used as marketing tools to gain commercial footholds in the market. UNICEF has long opposed the use of formula in developing countries, preferring instead to promote breastfeeding, which builds up babies' immune systems. A 1997 report had cited Wyeth, Nestle, and others for discouraging breastfeeding through promotional giveaways in Poland, Bangladesh, Thailand, and South Africa. UNICEF further cited a South African study suggesting that mother's milk antibodies could be effective in preventing HIV transmission.

Other problems were in implementation of a formula-based program. Only 5 percent of African women have access to their HIV status. Also, because formula lacks the antibodies of mother's milk, formula-fed infants were 4 to 6 times more likely to die of other diseases than breastfed infants. Exclusive breastfeeding was estimated to save up to 1.5 million lives a year. UNICEF's major fear was that spillover effects of a formula marketing or distribution activities would distract women from the "breast is best" philosophy. There were additional dangers of using formula in unhygienic conditions: shortages of clean water, few refrigerators for storage, shortages of soap and brushes for cleaning and sterilization purposes. Finally, supply and pricing issues were important. Africa is poor. Most mothers cannot afford cow's milk (one liter—43 cents) or commercial formula ($6 a one-pound tin).

Was UNICEF taking its distrust of commercial formula producers too far? Should formula be used at all in Africa? If yes, who should be responsible for distribution?

Problem #2: Are Private-Sector Pharmaceuticals the Answer?

A three-year confrontation came to an end when the Pharmaceutical Manufacturers Association (PMA) dropped its bid to protect anti-AIDS drugs from generic substitutions and allow other producers into the African market to stem the AIDS epidemic. Unfortunately, as one major obstacle is removed, others have risen to take its place. These include:

- Pricing problems: unrealistic exchange rates between the dollar and major African currencies made prices of anti-AIDS drug imports about $7,000 per year per person. With local production and price curbs, this could be reduced to $240 or even down to $60 a year. Unfortunately, this price is still beyond what most Africans can afford.

- Concerns have been raised about locally produced drugs not meeting required standards. Substandard drugs could promote the growth of drug-resistant AIDS viruses.

- Low-cost AIDS drugs may be diverted from the African continent and undercut manufacturer prices in other parts of the world.

- The anti-AIDS drug regimen involves taking up to thirty pills a day at specific times, some with food, some without, and some with/without water. Major supervision would be required, along with a clock-watching mentality that would be untypical of traditional African behaviors.

- Africa's health care infrastructure leaves much to be desired, not so much in urban areas as in rural parts where facilities are poor or nonexistent.

It is clear that transferring modern healthcare technologies and prescriptions into developing nations is problematic. Some advocate "prevention rather than cure" methods that condemn current AIDS sufferers in favor of longer-term prescriptions emphasizing education over drugs. Most experts acknowledge that the fate of a continent rests on the international community's ability to find both short and long-term solutions to the AIDS dilemma.

Questions

1. What do you think of UNICEF's stand on the use of formula and the role of international corporations in its supply?

2. What are the major obstacles in the way of a solution to the AIDS problem in Africa?

3. What are the respective roles of national governments, the United Nations, and the private sector in a solution? Who should take the lead? Why?

Sources: BBC News: Africa. "Mandela urges 'war' on HIV" (February 7, 2002). Carter, Tom. "Docs losing war on AIDS." *Insight on the News* (July 2, 2001): 30. Freedman, Alix M., and Stecklow, Steve. "Bottled Up: As UNICEF battles baby formula makers, African infants sicken." *Wall Street Journal* (December 5, 2000): A1, A18. Nevin, Tom. "Patent vs. patient rights." *African Business* (June 2001): 30–31. Yamey, Gavin. "The milk of human kindness." *British Medical Journal* (January 6, 2001): 57–58.

C A S E T T E   2 - 2
Free Trade for Steel? The Debate Continues

In early 2002, President George W. Bush announced a trade initiative. He imposed a new set of tariffs on imported steel, ranging from 5 to 30 percent, to protect the U.S. industry from foreign competition for a three-year period from March 2002. Countries affected were Brazil, South Korea, Japan, Taiwan, Russia, China, Australia, and the European Union. While steel industry protection was nothing new (there had been varying degrees of protection since the late 1960s), the severity of the tariffs in an extremely competitive global industry was problematic. Steel from Canada and Mexico was exempt because of the North American Free Trade Agreement.

The U.S. steel industry is an important sector of the U.S. economy, employing about 200,000 workers and servicing industries employing 12 million workers. The industry, ever since the Japanese steel invasion of the 1970s, had been in transition, with new technologies and global competitors forcing major streamlining of its activities. As a result, imports had never accounted for more than a third of U.S. consumption. The global industry as a whole reflected this trend, with employment by major world producers dropping from 2.4 million persons in 1974 to less than 900,000 in 2000. Domestically, the U.S. industry had shed two-thirds of its workforce since 1980. But as in many industries, some U.S. producers lagged behind others in introducing new technologies, such as replacing open-hearth furnaces with basic oxygen furnaces and transferring production to low-cost mini-mills that manufactured a ton of steel in under two man hours (versus the U.S. average of 3.9 man hours) and which accounted for half of U.S. steel production at the end of the millennium.

Additional problems included trade-union contracts with major legacy costs for retired steel workers and energy costs that had added $25–30 a ton onto costs for large mills during the late 1990s. Large mills in particular were under severe disadvantages. They needed 12 percent returns on capital to cover replacement costs for new capital assets, and, even in good years, their profit margins rarely exceeded 8 percent. Additionally, it could take as long as a decade to modernize obsolete facilities. As a result, the late 1990s saw over thirty steel firms apply for bankruptcy protection.

The effects of U.S. tariffs on world steel markets were pronounced. The EU immediately retaliated by placing temporary six-month tariffs of 15–26 percent on selected steel imports. EU steel imports had risen 73 percent from 15.4 million tons in 1997 to nearly 27 million tons in 2001. EU restrictions did not apply to minor developing-country steel producers. U.S. domestic steel prices increased after the imposition of tariffs. The price of hot-rolled coils rose from $240–260 per ton for first-quarter 2002 deliveries to asking prices as high as $400 per ton by quarter 3 of 2002. In the first four months of 2002, U.S. and European steel production dropped 5.3 and 4.4 percent respectively. Producers in Eastern Europe and Latin America saw their production drop 1.2 and 3.7 percent respectively as exports fell. Only Asia's steel output continued to expand under the impetus of more modern steel facilities and (as importantly) exchange rates that, since the Asian financial crisis, had depreciated and made them very low-cost competitors in world markets.

The costs to U.S. taxpayers were estimated to be about $440,000 per steel job saved, with half of each dollar of steel protection directly benefiting owners and workers. A $50 per ton steel price hike translated into a $6 billion tax on consumers. The question was: Was it worth it?

Questions

1. Explain the argument that U.S. steel would have used to persuade the government to impose steel tariffs. What do you think of the arguments?

2. Who loses when the U.S. puts tariffs on steel?

3. Explain the sequence of after-effects following the imposition of steel tariffs, i.e., the ripple effects on the world steel industry.

4. What do you think of the Canada and Mexico exemptions?

Sources: Anonymous. "New US Protectionism." *Oil & Gas Journal* (May 27, 2002): 19–20. Nagarajan, P. "American steel import policy—voodoo economics?" *Business Line Islamabad* (April 12, 2002): 1–2. Firoz, A. S. "Steel price hike driven by cuts and speculation." *Business Line Islamabad* (June 10, 2002): 1–2. Platts International Coal Report. "EU hits back at US on steel Tariffs." (April 8, 2002): 11. Barro, Robert J. "Big Steel Doesn't Need Propping Up." *Business Week* (April 1, 2002): 24. Daniel Griswold Center for Trade Policy Studies: Cato Institute. Testimony on Steel Trade Issues for House Ways and Means Committee (October 25, 1999).

CASETTE 2-3
The Battle in Seattle and the Anti-Globalization Movement

Not everyone is pleased with globalization, loosely defined as worldwide integration that facilitates cross-border movement of products, services, ideas, capital, and labor. The "battle in Seattle" in November 1999 pitted anti-globalization movements against the World Trade Organization. Similar protests against the IMF, the World Economic Forum, and G8 meetings have made UN administrators and international companies painfully aware that the global-village concept is not a panacea. Indeed, the anti-globalization movement has become an umbrella movement for many protest groups, including trade-union activists decoying developing-country labor wages and work conditions (including child labor); feminist groups protesting unequal treatment for women; groups opposing genetically modified ("Frankenstein") foods; anti big-business organizations (corporate pushiness and rampaging global brands); unequal world development, with increasing gaps between rich and poor countries; dishonest advertising; IMF and World Bank bullying of developing nations; trade protectionist groups; environmental activists. And the list goes on.

There is some legitimacy to the anti-globalization arguments. The world is converging toward a single model of democratic capitalism, and countries and individuals seem powerless to resist the movement (even if they wanted to). At the IMF, voting is in accordance with financial contributions, with the G7 (the seven most powerful industrialized countries) accounting for 45 percent of voting power. This, protesters claim, gives the major industrial powers license to push everyone else toward its brand of unfettered capitalism. The U.S.'s position is noteworthy. As perhaps the remaining superpower (both military and economic) in the world, it has a disproportionate say in what happens everywhere else. As U.S. Senator Jesse Helms is reputed to have said, "Democracy used to be a good thing, but now it has gotten into the hands of the wrong people." Politicians want eco-nomic growth, but not all the dislocations that accompany it.

Power concentrations deprive people of choice. At the UN and EU levels, decision making has indeed migrated to the supranational level, effectively depriving nations and individuals of their rights. The IMF response to the Asian financial crisis reduced millions to poverty, and many claim that it did not cure Asia of its worst ailments: crony capitalism, protected markets, political conception, and inefficient financial markets. Studies suggest no positive links between IMF interventions and increases in wealth and income. World Bank projects have only about a 40 percent success rate.

The anti-globalists had had some successes. Starbucks now offers coffee bought at "fair trade prices" that afford developing country producers a "living wage" rather than extorting the lowest prices possible. Clothing and footwear companies are monitoring their contracting companies to ensure fair wages and work conditions. And international companies are investing in local community projects to counter their profit maximizing images.

The anti-globalization movement may be, as columnist Thomas Friedman described them, "a Noah's ark of flat-earth advocates, protectionist, trade unions, and yuppies looking for their 1960s fix," but their concerns are real, and the anti-globalization movement has welded together a number of causes under one banner, taking advantage of the democratic right to be heard.

Questions
1. What is the function of the anti-globalization movement?

2. Which of their arguments do you think have merit? Why?

Sources: Brabbs, Cordelia. "Why global brands are under attack." *Marketing,* (December 9, 1999): 15–18. "Anti-capitalist protests: Angry and effective." *Economist,* (September 23, 2000): 85–87. Useem, Jerry. "There's something happening here." *Fortune,* (May 15, 2000): 232–244.

CASETTE 2-4
Working with Exchange Rates and Exchange Rate Arrangements

Review the following exchange rates and respond to the questions and situations below. (Hint: See what the exchange rate is doing against the US dollar and what exchange rate arrangement the country falls under.)

Exchange Rate/U.S.$	1999	2000	2001	2002	January 2003	March 2003	May 2003
Chad (Francs)	652	704	744	625	606	602	554
Euros/$	0.99	1.07	1.13	0.95	0.92	0.91	0.84
United Arab Emirates (Dirham)	3.6725	3.6725	3.6725	3.6725	3.6725	3.6725	3.6725
China PRC (Yuan)	8.2795	8.2774	8.2768	8.2773	8.2768	8.2772	8.2768
Costa Rica (Colones)	318	341	378	382	388	391	395
Turkey (Lira)	541,400	673,385	1,450,127	1,643,699	1,639,474	1,704,173	1,438,123
Japan (Yen)	102	115	132	120	119	120	118

1. A U.S. exporter of transportation equipment is negotiating with a distributor in Chad to sell selected lines in Cameroon, the Central African Republic, Mali, and Niger.

- What are the currency issues involved in this transaction and associated pricing issues in third party markets?

- What is the relationship between the CFA franc and the euro?

- What has happened to the CFA franc-dollar relationship between 1999 and May 2003?

- How would this affect the U.S. company's export prospects over 2003–2004? Why?

2. A U.S. company is contemplating a three-year relationship to supply products and advice to a United Arab Emirates company. Are there any financial risks associated with this arrangement?

3. A Chinese toy manufacturer has the opportunity to supply a U.S. store chain with a twelve-month supply of stuffed animals, with an average landed price of 7 yuan per piece for 1,000,000 pieces. The U.S. firm's financial vice-president notes that the U.S. is pressuring China to either float the yuan in world markets or revalue the currency 20 to 40 percent. How would this affect the imported prices? If the retail price is $1.50 per toy, how will margins be affected?

4. It was May 2003, a Friday afternoon, at Prestige Card's Costa Rican office. Carlos, the clerk, was just ready to leave for the weekend. In front of him were American James Grant's charges for his Costa Rican trip, a total of 1,115,572 colones for an extended stay and gifts. Carlos had a choice. He could translate them now at 395 colones per dollar, wait until Monday, when the rate would be 400 colones per dollar, or take his vacation next week and do it when he returned, when the creeping peg rate would probably be 410 colones per dollar. What would the effects be on James Grant's Prestige Card bill in the U.S.?

5. In 1999, large consumer-goods corporation made a $3.5 million investment in Turkey. Accountants at the head office had for some time been anxious about the Turkish lira's constant depreciation against the U.S. dollar and were balking at proposed new investments in the country where product demand remained strong. The Turkish government announced in February, 2001, that it was allowing the Turkish lira to float independently in world financial markets. Its aim was, with IMF help, to allow the currency to find a realistic, market-based exchange rate value.

- What is the current value of the initial U.S. investment in U.S. dollars terms? Should the company be alarmed? Why or why not?

- The parent company is considering not expanding the current Turkish facility and servicing the demand shortage by exports from the U.S. What do you think of this proposal?

- It was May, 2003, and the U.S. company has been wondering about what had happened to the Turkish lira between 2001 and 2003. What would your explanation be? Should the company make a new $1.5 million investment? Why or why not?

6. As the financial controller for a large industrial equipment manufacturer with major interests in Japan, you are reviewing the dollar–yen relationship 1999–May 2003.

- What is happening with the dollar–yen exchange rate?

- Japan has had a $50–60 billion trade surplus with the U.S. over these years. Does the exchange rate reflect this? Why or why not? What is happening?

- A new Japanese prime minister comes to power, promising to reform the domestic economy, and predicts the strengthening of the economy and wants an exchange rate to 135 per dollar by the end of 2003. Your exports are competing against Japanese companies with a 10 per cent margin. What would you advise?

- A Japanese company in which the U.S. firm has an equity stake has 14.5 million yen to repatriate to the U.S. Should they repatriate it now, or wait?

- The company is sending six engineers to Japan. They can go immediately or wait until the end of the year (2003). What would you advise?

Chapter Three

Globalization, Technology Transfers, Economic Development, and Cultural Change

❦

THE GREAT MIGRATION: ECONOMIC AND CULTURAL CHANGE IN CHINA

Economic and cultural change is ongoing in most of the world's developing nations. Only in fully industrialized countries does the pace of change slow. For nations in the throes of economic development, change occurs most rapidly during the industrialization process.

In China, the move from communism towards capitalism during the 1980s, 1990s, and beyond the millennium has ushered in significant change. The industrialization process, spurred on by over $400 billion of foreign direct investment, has had profound effects on the population, with over 100 million people migrating from rural villages into the sprawling urban metropolises. As they do, their lives change.

Rural lifestyles are simple, based on centuries of tradition. Most are agricultural communities, with residents living in ramshackle wooden houses, outside plumbing (if at all), and incomes averaging about $250 per person. Extended families, often numbering 10–20 people, inhabit single dwellings, and family issues are paramount. Respect is accorded to elders, and conformity to rigid social rules is expected. Tradition is revered and individual prospects are determined by family name and birthright. Under these circumstances, young people, anxious to break with rural traditions and to see what they can do, migrate to towns. There, their lifestyle changes.

Industrial urban life normally involves unskilled or low-skilled jobs, with long hours (often twelve-hour shifts or more), and highly repetitive work. Work conditions are often unsafe. Bosses are autocratic. Strikes, protests, and layoffs are common. Bureaucracy runs rife. Permits are required for work, health, and residency. Crime rates are high.

But workers are paid, often only $30 a month for twelve-hour shifts. Urban per capita incomes average over $700. Given the low costs of housing, after working for a while, migrants can afford new clothes and phones and can participate in material pop culture. If they can survive the culture shock, the talented start to progress within the industrial society, garnering higher wages for their efforts. Many, however, are disillusioned and return to the simple and predictable life in the countryside.[1]

China's great rural-urban migration underscores the major changes that occur as countries industrialize. Its 1.3 billion population has acted as a magnet attracting large international companies. The jobs generated by these firms, the massive government-sponsored privatization program, and the country's increased participation in international trade have prompted yearly growth levels of 6–8 percent. But China is only one of many nations with major development initiatives underway. About three-quarters of the world's countries are experiencing economic and cultural change, some more rapidly than others. Understanding the dynamics of this process, and its effects on institutions, groups, individuals, industries, and companies, is the subject of this chapter.

In this chapter you will learn:

- The definition of economic development, along with the resource bases needed to advance national economic agendas.
- How international corporations affect national cultures, both positively and negatively.
- The ways that political, economic, and cultural institutions change with development, along with effects on social and individual behaviors.
- The diffusion of modern behaviors in national economies and how behaviors differ among urban, semi-urban, and rural sectors in developed and developing nations.
- The developmental process as it affects industry development, business, and consumer behaviors.
- How countries change as they move from traditional pre-industrial societies through industrialization/modernization processes to postindustrial societies and then eventually become integrated into regional and global economies.
- Why some nations are not industrialized: obstacles to economic development accruing to the industrialization process, geographic, ethnic/linguistic impediments, and institutional resistance to change.

INTRODUCTION

In this chapter, the twin issues of cultural diversity and change are tackled. Economic and cultural diversity among world markets occurs as some countries develop quickly and others at much slower rates. Cultural change occurs as countries develop economically.

THE ECONOMIC DEVELOPMENT PROCESS

Economic development is the progress countries make in living standards as they experience positive economic growth and the changes occurring in societal and cultural institutions and values as nations move toward more advanced stages of industrialization. Countries, with few exceptions, desire economic development. It demonstrates human progress, and more pragmatically, it keeps politicians in power, companies busy, and consumers (and voters) optimistic about the future. But it also entails significant change. Division of labor and specialization deliver gains in economic efficiency. As affluence rises, economically enfranchised peoples look for political enfranchisement, and democracies take hold. Major changes occur as new economic and political institutions develop, with movements from traditional, noncompetitive institutions (villages, communistic economies, autarchies) to competition-based capitalistic economies and democratic institutions. As societies change, religious, family, social class, educational bodies, and gender orientations come under pressure, and there are major changes in individual values, attitudes, and behaviors.[2]

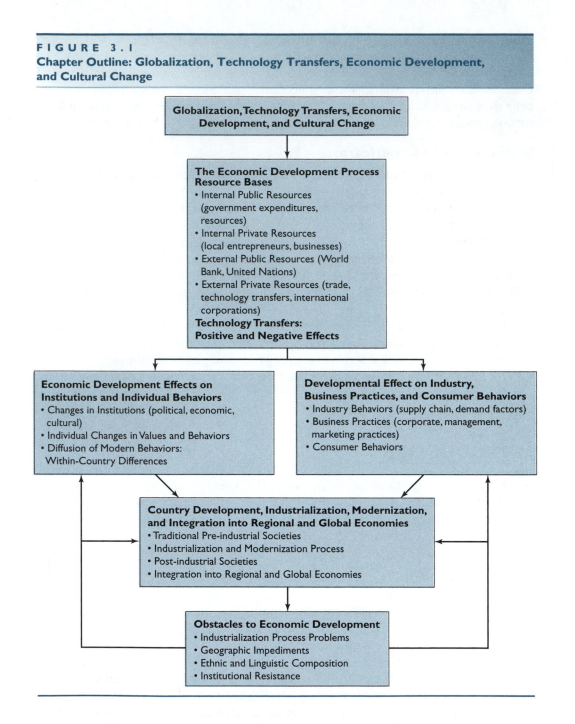

F I G U R E   3 . 1
Chapter Outline: Globalization, Technology Transfers, Economic Development, and Cultural Change

Resource Bases for Industrialization

To develop, countries need resources. These come from internal and external sources and from public and private institutions (see Figure 3.1).

Internal public resources include government investments to create infrastructures (roads, rails, airlines, water, communication systems, and so on) and to deliver essential services (education, defense, etc.). Countries at early stages of development have limited tax bases and must allocate expenditures carefully.

Internal private resources, comprising local businesspeople and entrepreneurs, are the second source of developmental funds. In many emerging nations, particularly in the Middle East, Latin America, and Asia, private sources of capital (stock markets, banks) are not well developed. As a result, socially prominent families with extensive land holdings take the lead in leveraging their resources into the industrial sector.

External public resources include supranational institutions, such as the United Nations and its many agencies. As noted in Chapter 2, the World Bank, and the IMF in particular, play prominent roles in national infrastructure development and in financing international trade needs.

External private resources, comprising international corporations, are the fourth source of development resources. They provide technology transfers through trade, contractual agreements (licensing, franchising), and investments.

For rapid economic development to occur, all four sectors (public–private, internal–external) must contribute resources. In this chapter, our emphasis is on the impact of international corporations on economic development. Through trade, investments, and other technology transfers, international corporations make significant impacts on host-country economies and cultures. Most major international companies are from developed countries and are proven international performers with world-class technologies and products. Most national governments welcome them, as they contribute to economic development without drawing upon limited government resources. In addition, international corporations are catalysts to economic development that foster change in a variety of ways. However, their commercial interests do not always coincide with those of nation states.

Technology Transfers: Positive and Negative Effects

International trade, investments, and global media have opened up world markets to a variety of modernizing influences. Through technology transfers, foreign firms have significant positive and negative effects on institutions, behaviors, and business practices. These are laid out in Table 3.1. In general terms, technology transfers occur as corporations enter new markets with products, technologies, lifestyles, and business methods developed in their home and other international markets. Technology transfers first impact urban segments of developing countries where there are developed infrastructures and pockets of economically significant customers (expatriates, local business people, government officials, civil servants, etc.). As media become commercialized and distribution channels are built into rural areas, greater proportions of developing country populations come into contact with modernization influences. Positive effects occur as societies are exposed to broad varieties of products that make lives easier. Convenience products, such as packaged foods, and consumer durables, such as refrigerators, radios, televisions, and cookers, impact consumer lifestyles in positive ways. New technologies in manufacturing and distribution make products cheaper and provide employment opportunities for local populations.

> That significant differences exist between modern and traditional cultures is beyond dispute . . . out what about a world in which all societies were traditional? This world existed a few hundred years ago.
>
> *—Samuel P. Huntington, Harvard University political scientist*

> The increased interaction among societies may not generate a common culture but it does facilitate the transfer of techniques, inventions and practices from one society to another with a speed and to a degree that were impossible in even the recent past.
>
> *—Samuel P. Huntington, Harvard University political scientist*

TABLE 3.1
Positive and Negative Effects of Technology Transfers

Technology Transfer	Positive	Negative
Product sales (Consumer)	Upgrades consumption know how/consumer education	Affordable only to affluent segments
Product sales (Industrial)	Upgrades production process technologies, technician/engineering skills, lowers per unit production costs/prices	Displaces workers with more intensive use of capital
Licensing, technology agreements; corporate R and D efforts	Broadens, elevates technology bases and workforce vocational and scientific skills	
Banking and financial institutions	Mobilizes savings to create investment markets for public/private sector stock-market capital, consumer/installment credit for individuals and business	Only the wealthy benefit in the short term and leads to power concentrations; possible unwanted foreign influences encouraging buyers to purchase goods beyond their means
Local procurement of materials and components	Stimulus for private enterprise/local initiatives	Easier for other foreign firms to meet procurement quality requirements
Establishment of wholesale/retail distribution systems	Creates distribution infrastructure/expertise, increases customer exposures to modern goods and services	Foreign control over distribution, consumer exposed to products that are beyond their means to purchase
Worker training in technologies and production know how	Upgrades labor skills and vocational bases	For a minority only, majority have insufficient education
Management training in organizational know how/methods	Increased managerial education and efficiency	Only educated elites benefit
Financial and accounting skills	Planning and budgetary control	

It was naïve of the 19th century optimists to expect paradise from technology—and it is equally naïve of 20th century pessimists to make technology the scapegoat for such old shortcomings as man's blindness, cruelty, immaturity, greed and sinful pride.

—*Peter F. Drucker,*
management consultant
and author

Labor and management skills are upgraded. Local firms pick up contracts to supply materials and components to international firms. Financial institutions mobilize capital markets to link savings and investment opportunities, and consumers gain access to high-priced products through credit financing packages.

Not all technology transfers have positive effects. In the short term, modern products are accessible only to the affluent elites. Commercial advertising also stimulates demand among poor consumers, causing frustration. Increased competition in local marketplaces causes dislocations as indigenous companies find themselves unable to compete against international competitors, and local workers are disadvantaged because of their lack of education and workplace skills.

ECONOMIC DEVELOPMENT EFFECTS ON INSTITUTIONS AND BEHAVIORS

As public and private resources impact national economies, they have major impacts on countries' institutions and individuals. Institutions comprise organized, goal-directed groups of people who influence behavior patterns in political, economic, and social settings. Governments, political parties, religious bodies, companies, and families are major institutions

TABLE 3.2
Modernization and Cultural Change in Political, Economic, and Social Institutions and Behaviors

Institutions	Traditional	Modern
Political Institutions	Autarchy (dictatorships, presidents for life, chiefs, kings, shahs)	Democracy: multiparty systems
Economic Institutions		
Economic System	Centralized (self-sufficient villages; communist economies)	Decentralized (market forces)
Community orientation	High	Low
Population base	Rural	Urban
Production base	Agricultural	Industrial
Economic power base	Land ownership	Stocks/shares
Cultural Institutions		
Family unit	Extended	Nuclear
Gender orientation	Patriarchal	Emancipated
Religiosity	High	Low
Education system	Informal	Formal
Social class: criteria	Hereditary	Wealth
Social class: mobility	Seniority/education	Income
Linguistic and ethnic backgrounds	Multilingual/many ethnic groups, often isolated	Linguistic homogeneity, infrastructures develop to link communities and promote homogeneity
Social Behaviors		
Societal tendencies	Conformist	Individualistic
Control mechanisms	Religious/social	Legal

Source: John S. Hill. "Modern-Traditional Behaviors: Anthropological Insights into Global Business Behaviors." *Journal of Transnational Management Development* 5, 3 (2000): 3–21.

affecting individual behaviors. For countries to modernize, not only must institutions change (for example, from centrally controlled economies to economies controlled by market forces), but the values and behaviors of its citizens must change also.

Changes in Institutions

Table 3.2 shows the basic types of institutional change. Some institutional changes occur quickly, such as political coups d'etat. Others evolve slowly, such as changes from agricultural to industrial-based economies. Where change occurs slowly, traditional institutions and behaviors remain (often in rural areas) for a long time in otherwise modernizing societies.

Changes in political institutions occur as economies modernize and populations become more educated. Autocracies ruled by single absolute leaders (such as monarch, shahs, tribal chieftains, or dictators) over time give way to democratic institutions and elected assemblies. In the early 1970s, less than one-third of the world's countries were democracies. By the late 1990s, this number had risen to over 60 percent.[3] Often, as intermediate states between authoritarian and democratic situations, there are single-party democracies (such as the PRI in Mexico that ruled for seventy-one years until it was deposed in 2000 or the Liberal Democrat Party in Japan) or single ruler democracies (such

> Democracy is the worst form of government except for all the others that have been tried.
>
> —*Winston S. Churchill, 20th-century British statesman*

as President Suharto until his 1998 resignation). In these cases, political opposi-tions take time to become effective and make democracies workable institutions.

Changes in economic institutions are of five types:

Economic system changes: Centralized production of goods and services (as in self-sufficient tribal communities or the dismantled state-controlled economies of Eastern Europe) is replaced by market-forces economies as devel-opment occurs. The shift to supply-and-demand-based market systems requires reliable infrastructures to distribute mass-manufactured goods over wide mar-ket areas. Communications (such as telephones, mail, and computers) must be developed to relay market information between suppliers, producers, retailers, and consumers, and promotional infrastructures such as commercial media de-velop to facilitate information flows to customers.

Community orientation changes: Paralleling the changes from production to market-force-oriented systems, there are differences in how output is dis-tributed (*community orientation* in Table 3.2). In tribal and communist econ-omy situations, there are high community orientations and output is evenly distributed without regard to age, gender or infirmities. Under market-forces systems, community orientation decreases sig-nificantly and rewards are distributed according to individuals' eco-nomic contributions. The less people contribute (the old, the sick, the disadvantaged), the fewer the resources to which they are enti-tled. In developing countries, extended-family-and-kin systems sub-sidize non-contributors as nations industrialize. In developed coun-tries (such as Western Europe), extensive social-welfare systems shield disadvantaged peoples. In the U.S., the emphasis has been on making non-contributors into contributors (e.g., moving welfare re-cipients back into employment situations).

Rural to urban, agricultural to industrial, and *economic power base shifts* occur as the industrialization process progresses. Popula-tion shifts from rural areas to towns takes place as economies shift from agricultural to industrial bases. The preoccupation with land ownership as the power base in traditional societies gives way as in-dustrial societies place emphases on stocks/share ownership. These changes occurred first in Britain from 1750–1850 and spread rapidly to continental Europe over that same period. In the U.S., 1870–1920 marked the major move to urban, industrialized nation status. In the post-1945 era, Latin America, Eastern Europe, and Asia have experienced these shifts as they have industrialized.

Changes in cultural institutions: As societies modernize and more people migrate to towns, traditional cultural institutions come under pressure to adapt to the needs of the newly industrializing economies.

Extended family systems, comprising all relatives by blood and by marriage, break down as urbanization movements pull the younger generations toward towns to become members of industrializing so-cieties. Smaller nuclear families, made up of just parents and children, become the staple family unit. Not having to provide for other rela-tives affords smaller family units more discretionary income for lux-ury goods.

Hereditary and seniority social systems dominate traditional soci-eties, with family name and "pedigrees" determining individual fu-

From each according to his ability, to each according to his needs.
—*Karl Marx, 19th-century German philosopher and cofounder of communism*

The nail that sticks up gets hammered down.
—*Japanese proverb*

A man can't get rich if he takes proper care of his family.
—*Navajo proverb*

tures, and seniority (accumulated wisdom) being accorded special status. These systems break down in fast-moving urban environments, and economic criteria, such as wealth and income (which measure individuals' economic contributions to society), become dominant measures of self-worth and success.

Gender orientations change as women formally enter the workforce. The economic contributions made by women during industrialization push patriarchal (male-dominated) tendencies aside in favor of more emancipated, egalitarian attitudes.

Religiosity: Traditional agrarian-based societies tend to have strong religious bases. The uncertainty surrounding intemperate climates and successful harvests result in heavy reliance on supernatural deities for economic success. As a result, religiosity tends to be at a high level. As individuals become part of industrializing societies, success becomes dependent on personal efforts rather than religious deities. Religious orientations, therefore, tend to weaken in industrial settings. The Western nations were the first to separate religious and secular activities during the industrialization process. This diverted national and individual energies away from the sole pursuit of religious activities toward commercial objectives.[4]

Education systems: Industrialization involves the application of science and technology to commerce, and educational systems need reorienting as modernization occurs and marketplaces become knowledge-intensive. Informal education systems emphasizing "learning by doing," demonstrations, word-of-mouth, and learning by observation and imitation (e.g., apprenticeships) give way to more formal, academic systems. Formal academic institutions and learning are set apart from daily activities and are teacher-oriented. In many countries, formal and informal systems exist side-by-side. For example, within corporations, human resource managers must constantly evaluate formal education credentials (such as MBAs) against informal credentials ("experience").

Cultural homogenization—the melting pot society: Cultural change occurs as fragmented multilingual and multiethnic groups are brought together in the industrialization process. Often over generations or hundreds of years, linguistic and ethnic differences become reconciled, and national cultures emerge. This long process is illustrated in Figure 3.2. Where industrialization processes are slow, close contacts between ethnic groups can cause major problems (e.g., African tribal politics, the 1990s upheavals in the old Yugoslavian states).

Social behaviors: The move from community-based rural systems to large-scale urban societies affects social behaviors. Traditional societies tend to be conformist as group members adhere to societal norms laid out in religious and social conventions. In many religions (e.g., Islam, Buddhism, Hinduism), social and religious duties are often indistinguishable. Behaviors are less tradition-bound in fast-paced industrial societies, individualism replaces conformism, and societies move from being "we-centered" to "me-centered." Religion, a centerpiece of rural and traditional societies, declines in importance. The complexities of the modern industrial state, coupled with increasing competitiveness, make legal frameworks necessary to govern behaviors.

> Whatever women do they must do twice as well as men to be thought half as good. Luckily, this is not difficult.
>
> *—Charlotte Whitton, mayor of Ottawa, Canada*

> I never let my schooling interfere with my education.
>
> *—Mark Twain, 19th-century U.S. writer*

> A nation is a totality of men united through communality of fate into a community of character.
>
> *—Otto Bauer*

> If you are wrapped up in yourself, you are overdressed.
>
> *—Kate Halverson, U.S. journalist*

FIGURE 3.2
The Melting Pot Society and the Evolution of Languages, Dialects in National Economic Development

Low	Economic Development		High

True multilingual societies	Emergence of common languages	Dominant languages	Single national language (either colonial or dominant ethnic language)
Society comprises many isolated rural groups, each with their own language/dialect	• Colonial languages (English, Spanish, French, etc.) • A few dominant ethnic/linguistic groups • Still many minority languages and dialects	• Colonial languages used in urban centers and commerce • Dominant national language emerges • Rural languages and dialects die out or combine into regional groupings	• Used in everyday activities and commerce nationwide. • Regional accents and dialectic differences still apparent (France, Spain, U.K.-Welsh; Gaelic) • Isolated ethnic groups in rural areas (U.S.: 500 native American languages, Latin America, Asia)
Africa: Cameroon (200 languages/dialects): Sudan (400+), Ethiopia (70+), Gabon (50), Chad (200), Rep. of Congo (40+)	Afghanistan (40% Pashtun, 12+ major ethnic groups), French North and West Africa (Algeria, Morocco), Ghana (5 major languages, 100 ethnic groups), Ivory Coast (4 regional and 80+ ethnic groups)	Eastern Europe: Russian with 100 ethnic groups, Georgia, China, South Africa, Egypt	USA, Western Europe, Japan

> In cities, no one is quiet but many are lonely; in the country, people are quiet but few are lonely.
>
> —*Geoffrey Francis Fisher*

> Competition brings out the best in products and the worst in people.
>
> —*David Sarnoff, founder RCA Corporation*

Individual Changes in Values and Behaviors

As migrants move into urban surroundings, they become immersed into modern society. The competitive nature of urban life contrasts vividly with cooperative rural environments, and individual values and behaviors change as migrants assimilate modern values. These changes are shown in Table 3.3.

Interpersonal behaviors change as insider-outsider distinctions, so easy to maintain in traditional societies, break down in urban settings. Similarly, less time is spent on social formalities in fast-paced industrial societies. This causes trust levels to diminish as competitive pressures increase in the labor market (competing for jobs), and the work situation (internal tensions in meeting company and individual goals) and socially (as old social ties are replaced by new social networks).

Individual values are reshaped in the rural-to-urban move. Preoccupations with the past/present are gradually replaced by present-future orientations. Time becomes a resource to be used efficiently, and change, once viewed with suspicion, becomes an accepted part of life. Individuals start to believe in their ability to shape their destinies rather than passively accepting what happens to them (fatalism). As a result, they move from being risk avoiders to risk managers (that is, they start to evaluate positive and negative tradeoffs in risky behaviors such as moving, jobs, locations, or making big purchases). Over time, parochial mindsets become broadened as mass-media exposure brings national and international issues to the fore. As environmental awareness in-

TABLE 3.3
Modernization and Cultural Change: Individual Values and Behaviors

Individual Values/Behaviors	Traditional	Modern
Interpersonal Behaviors		
Insider-Outsider Distinctions	High	Low
Social formality	High	Low
Trust	High	Low
Individual Values		
Temporal orientation	Past/present	Present/future
Time consciousness (efficiency orientation)	Less	More
Attitude towards change/innovation	Viewed with suspicion	Accepted and encouraged
Attitude toward risk	Risk avoider	Risk-manager
Self-help tendency	Life is preordained (fatalistic: *que sera, sera; inshallah*)	Individuals influence events (master of own destiny)
Difference of opinions	Disliked	Tolerated
Breadth of interest in outside events	Narrow/parochial	Broad/international

Source: Adapted from John S. Hill. "Modern-Traditional Behaviors: Anthropological Insights into Global Business Behaviors." *Journal of Transnational Management Development* 5, 3 (2000): 3–21.

creases, individuals develop tolerances for different opinions, conformist attitudes erode, and individualistic behaviors become prominent.

How Individuals Adapt to Industrializing Societies: The "Rat Race" Emulation Cycle[5] Many societies have been exposed to new technologies, lifestyles, and modernizing influences, but not all have been able to sustain their development efforts.

One key to sustaining development has been the emulation cycle that describes changes in individual attitudes during the industrialization process. Ragnar Nurkse first noted the emulation of Western lifestyle patterns as modernization influences with his "demonstration effect": "When people come into contact with superior goods or superior patterns of consumption, with new articles or new ways of meeting old wants, they are apt to feel after a while a certain restlessness and dissatisfaction. Their knowledge is extended, their imagination stimulated; new desires are aroused, the propensity to consume is shifted upwards . . . New wants . . . can be important as an incentive, making people work harder and produce more."[6]

This process is diagrammed as the *Emulation Cycle* in Figure 3.3. The process begins with individuals recognizing the limitations of traditional societies where birthright (hereditary criteria) and seniority determine social positions, and that migration to towns allows them to determine their own destinies in industrializing urban centers where economic criteria are used to chart social progress (*1* in Figure 3.3). As workers find jobs, they take on an industrial work ethic *(2),* and their wages allow new consumption habits to form *(3)*. As time passes, their commitment to the industrial society increases *(4)* and,

Wealth is like seawater; the more we drink, the thirstier we become, and the same is true of fame.

—*Arthur Schopenhauer, 19th-century German philosopher*

The longer I live the more keenly I feel that whatever was good enough for our fathers is not good enough for us.

—*Oscar Wilde, 19th–20th-century Irish poet and playwright*

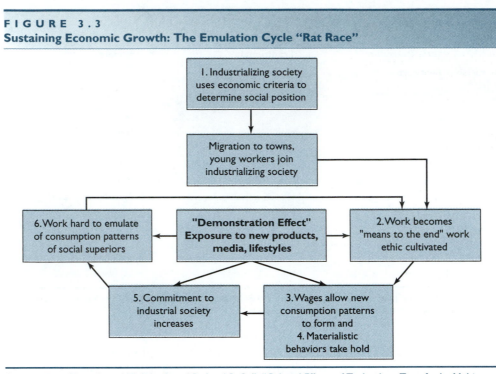

FIGURE 3.3
Sustaining Economic Growth: The Emulation Cycle "Rat Race"

Source: Based loosely on Hill, John S. and Richard R. Still. "Cultural Effects of Technology Transfer by Multinational Corporations in Lesser-Developed Countries." *Columbia Journal of World Business* 15 (Summer 1980): 40–51.

stimulated by constant exposures to affluent urban lifestyles, migrants acquire acquisitive (materialistic) tendencies that reinforce their commitments to the *money-society.* Emulation of social superiors and the acquisition of material possessions become the primary factor motivating commitment to the industrializing society *(5),* and working harder to achieve greater social status becomes the norm *(6).* This process is immortalized in U.S. folklore as "the American dream," and the constant striving to emulate social superiors is a characteristic in many developed and developing markets.

Material success, epitomized in "yuppie" middle-class lifestyles, has become a benchmark of national economic progress. In the emerging regions of Asia, Latin America, and Eastern Europe, the creation of strong middle-class movements has become a primary indicator of economic development.

The Diffusion of Modern Behaviors: Within-Country Behaviors and the Flexible Stereotype

As noted in Chapter 1, modern behaviors take time to diffuse through international and national markets. Within nations, modern behaviors take root in urban areas and gradually diffuse out into rural parts. This process takes time (often generations) and means that, even in modern societies like the United States, there are population pockets that are still modernizing (e.g., the South, Midwest U.S.,

> Advertising and its related arts thus help develop the kind of man the goals of the industrial empire require—one that reliably spends his income and works reliably because he is always in need of more.
>
> —*John Kenneth Galbraith, U.S. economist*

and rural towns), and segments, more isolated from modern influences, that remain steeped in tradition (e.g., native American communities). Similarly, in developing countries, most populations are rural and are highly traditional, though significant numbers of people migrate out of traditional rural areas to become part of the industrializing society. In urban areas, there are government officials, expatriates, local entrepreneurs, and salaried professionals that have adopted modern behaviors and have been fully absorbed into the industrializing society. The flexible stereotype, illustrated in Figure 3.4, conceptually illustrates the proportions of modern-traditional behaviors found in modern and traditional societies. These proportions vary by country. For example, cultural impediments have resulted in industrialized nations of Western Europe and Japan still maintaining some or many traditional behaviors. For example, both maintain elements of hereditary social classes, and Japan's Liberal Democrat Party has dominated democratic processes since 1945.

In economic development terms, two institutions in particular have major effects on societal and individual behaviors. These are political institutions (from autocracies to democracies) and economic institutions (as economies move from small, self-sufficient units to become market-forces-based societies). In both cases, the movements are from noncompetitive institutions (autarchies and village economies) to competition-based societies (democracies where political processes are competitive and marketplaces where companies and individuals compete). As countries move toward democracies and capitalist economies, competition becomes an increasingly important influence on their daily lives and on individual behaviors.

> [In] the most brilliant societies and civilizations . . . the interplay of town and country can never be underestimated. In no society have all regions and all parts of the population developed equally. Under-development is common in mountain areas or patches of poverty off the beaten track of modern communications—genuinely primitive societies, true "cultures" in the midst of a civilization.
>
> —*Fernand Braudel, 20th-century French historian*

DEVELOPMENTAL EFFECTS ON INDUSTRY, BUSINESS PRACTICES, AND CONSUMERS

As international businesses become regular features of national economies, they influence, and are influenced by, industry environments, prevailing business practices, and consumers. As most corporations are from developed countries, they must recognize and adapt to local conditions, particularly in industrializing countries. At the same time, through technology transfers, they exert significant influences on local industry practices, management styles, and consumer behaviors.

Developmental Effects on Industry Behaviors

Most world markets are less-than-fully industrialized. In emerging markets, variable market conditions affect supply-chain and market-demand levels in particular industries. Table 3.4 shows how developmental differences affect industry activities and growth rates.

Supply chain development involves the orderly integration of suppliers, manufacturing and distribution functions, many of which are affected by market development levels.

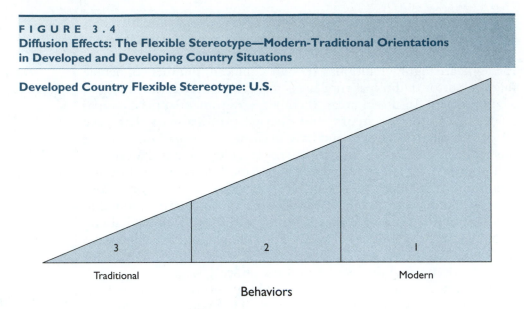

FIGURE 3.4
Diffusion Effects: The Flexible Stereotype—Modern-Traditional Orientations in Developed and Developing Country Situations

Developed Country Flexible Stereotype: U.S.

1. Majority behaviors are modern. Competitive marketplaces and political environments (e.g., elections); urban populations large corporations, nuclear families, emancipated gender roles, low religiosity, income-based "yuppie" lifestyles; untrusting, legalistic. Individualistic tendencies; informal social relations; efficiency-oriented, risk-takers; broad minded and tolerant mindsets.

2. Part modern–part traditional behaviors; Southern, Midwest U.S.

3. Traditional segments: Highly rural parts of the U.S., native Americans

Developing Country Flexible Stereotype

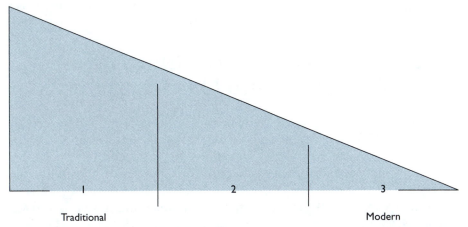

1. Majority behaviors are traditional; rural lifestyles are dominant; political processes not competitive (little, no opposition to political leaders); village economies; land owners dominant; small scale businesses; uncompetitive product markets; non-profit-maximization-oriented; cooperative, community orientation; extended families; patriarchal-oriented; high religiosity; little emphasis on formal education; family pedigree important; multilingual/ethnic societies; conformist behavior; highly religious, many social rules. Insider-outsider distinctions made; many social formalities; trust-oriented; conservative societies; conformist; narrow, parochial interests.

2. Rural-to-urban migrants: traditional/modern segments

3. Modern-urban segments: governments, expatriates, civil servants, entrepreneurs

Source: John S. Hill. "Modern-Traditional Behaviors: Anthropological Insights into Global Business Behaviors." *Journal of Transnational Management Development* 5, 3 (2000): 3–21.

T A B L E   3 . 4
Long-term Developmental Drivers of Industry Change

	COUNTRY DEVELOPMENT LEVEL		
Supply Chain Factors	**Low**	**High**	**Impact**
Import restrictions (free trade/protectionist tendencies)	More restrictions	Fewer	Affects importation of machinery, equipment, raw materials, components
Availability/Cost of labor	Surplus/low cost	Scarcity/high cost	Manufacturing location and process: labor vs. capital intensiveness, substitution of capital for labor (CIM;CAD-CAM)
Physical infrastructure (roads, ports, communications)	Poor	Advanced	Affects product distribution and urban-rural communications
Financial infrastructure (banking system, financial institutions)	Less developed	More developed	Affects accounts receivable/accounts payable Ability to raise capital locally
Societal infrastructure (social security, retirement systems, unemployment benefits, etc.)	Undeveloped	Developed	Affects human resources benefits packages, cost of manufacturing
Education system	Lower level	Higher level	Affects pool of managerial and technical talent
Government intervention in economy (economic priorities, development agendas)	High	Low	Affects company discretion in strategy-setting and implementation
Demand Factors			
Level of market affluence (e.g., GNP per capita; existence of middle class, etc.)	Low	High	Level of demand
Aggregate national demand	Undersupply	Oversupply	Oversupply conditions creates market competition and tailoring of corporate output
Materialism level	Lower	Higher	Materialism levels affected by religion (e.g., Hinduism, Buddhism, Islam can de-emphasize material possessions). Social class affects materialism and economic aspirations (economic possessions less important than family pedigree, seniority in determining social status
Existence of media/commercial media (TVs, radio, print)	Low	High	Affects demand stimulation capabilities
Rate of urbanization/migration to cities	Lower	Higher	Affects location of demand (urban-rural)
Attitudes toward change	More negative	More positive	Affected by religious values and institutions. Buddhism, Hinduism, and Islam emphasize spiritual rather than commercial values rather than commercial values
International catalysts to demand. Imports of modern products; transplanted multinationals, executives via technology transfers. Acculturation of Western/modern lifestyles	Less	More	Stimulates demand via exposure to western or modern lifestyles ("Demonstration Effect")
Cultural homogeneity of domestic demand (existence of multiple languages, different religions and ethnic groups)	Less	More	Cultural/ethnic heterogeneity slows diffusion of modern/western lifestyles

National trade policies affect company abilities to import vital machinery, equipment, components, and raw material supplies. This can be problematic in developing markets as governments restrict imports to conserve foreign exchange or to manage their trade balances. As countries become prolific traders, their currencies become convertible, and protectionist policies give way to free-trade orientations. Joining international bodies, such as the World Trade Organization (WTO) and the International Monetary Fund (IMF), are key steps in becoming fully fledged members of the international trading community.

Local labor costs and availability affects industry development and cost structures. Developing countries usually have cheap labor and attract labor-intensive industries, such as textiles or assembly operations. As they industrialize, wage rates rise, and affected industries must either substitute capital for labor or move to countries further down the development scale. Companies in Taiwan, Hong Kong, Singapore, and other parts of Asia have transferred labor-intensive assets into China to maintain cost advantages.

Infrastructure development affects industry cost structures.

1. Physical infrastructures (roads, utilities, telecommunications, etc.) affect company abilities to source materials, distribute products, and deliver promotions. Initially, developing-nation infrastructures are well-developed in urban areas, but major problems exist in reaching rural populations.

2. Financial infrastructure development affects payment mechanisms (accounts payable and receivable), whether capital can be raised locally, and the availability of consumer credit. International banks and financial institutions play key roles in financial infrastructure development.

3. Social infrastructure development affects cost structures and human-resource administration. Countries with undeveloped national social security/retirement systems have fewer payroll taxes and government deductions. Consequently, they have cost advantages over advanced countries that have complex social welfare systems and where employer contributions to state-sponsored support programs are significant (e.g., Western Europe).

4. Educational infrastructures provide managerial and technical talent. Where there are shortfalls, corporate-development programs or expatriate transfers can be costly supplements to corporate costs.

5. Government services and influence over national economies are important factors where infrastructure contracts and economic development plans provide firms with significant sales opportunities. Where industries contribute to national development (e.g., agriculture, high tech), governmental encouragement and incentives can be obtained.

Demand factors affect industry growth rates and patterns. Market development brings increased varieties of products and services and more knowledgeable customers. In economies where aggregate supplies of goods and services are at low levels *(under-supply economies)*, the focus is on production and distribution, with competitive pricing, promotions, and wide product assortments less evident. As industrialization occurs, supply capabilities outstrip demand, competition increases, and companies must spend more time on strategy and on tailoring corporate outputs to meet customers needs (the "marketing concept").

Materialism and market demand development: The development of materialistic attitudes in national populations is an important demand catalyst in the consumer product sector. For demand to take off, consumers must want "the better life." Worldwide, religion and social-class factors retard or promote consumer-product demand. Religions such as Islam, Buddhism, and Hinduism often emphasize religious and spiritual priorities ahead of commercial or materialist orientations. Similarly, rigid social-class systems stressing heredity criteria (i.e., family name or pedigree) or seniority make conspicuous-consumption products and materialism less important indicators of

One illusion is that you can industrialize a country by building factories. You don't. You industrialize it by building markets.

—*Paul Hoffman,*
U.S. business executive

social status. In many countries then, religious and social obstacles have slowed the development of aggregate demand and economic growth.[7] In other nations, however, religion and social class precipitate development. In the United States for example, the Protestant work ethic and social-class systems that emphasize income or wealth have encouraged materialistic orientations.

Media communications environments affect corporate abilities to stimulate market demand. While television, radio, and print are present in most national economies, their use for commercial advertising depends on national government orientations toward demand stimulation. The United States is highly market-oriented and has a relatively liberal advertising and promotions environment. Western European countries are more regulated, and, despite media-privatization tendencies, there is still some governmental ownership and control, particularly of broadcast media. Governments in developing markets have proceeded more cautiously. Many are wary of over-stimulating demand among less-sophisticated consumers and prefer low-key forms of promotion. This can inhibit companies with aggressive marketing instincts.

Rural to urban population movements in developing markets affect national demand patterns. Companies have two options in industrializing countries. First, they can locate in towns and wait for urbanization trends to bring customers to them. Second, they can pioneer product and brand awareness in rural sectors to build up future demand.[8] When this occurs, international companies become change agents as they actively influence customers and expose them to modern products and marketing techniques.

Cultural diversity affects demand stimulation activities through its effects on promotions. Cultural homogeneity (i.e., one or few languages, ethnic groups) simplifies countrywide communication and speeds up the diffusion of new ideas, technologies, and lifestyles. Ethnic and linguistic fragmentation slows economic progress as companies must overcome problems associated with cultural diversity and multiethnic societies. Literacy problems also add to the complexity of the communications process.

Developmental Effects on Business Practices

Corporate Behaviors As companies move out of traditional into modern modes of operation, corporate motives and behaviors must change to accommodate increased marketplace competition. This process is particularly noticeable in today's Latin American, Eastern European, and Asian economies. As Table 3.5 shows, corporate management and marketing behaviors change as market areas expand and increased production and sales bring heavy division of labor. Output, the traditional goal of small-scale operations and self-sufficient societies, gives way to profit orientations, as firms must attract external sources of capital (e.g., banks or equity) and demonstrate abilities to repay loans or issue dividends.

Corporate cultures, formerly cooperative, become internally competitive as some organizations see internal competition for resources as contributing to corporate efficiencies. Note though that in some parts of the world, notably Japan and parts of Western Europe, companies have consciously opted to avoid overly confrontational

Consumption is the sole end purpose of all production.

—*Adam Smith, 18th-century Scottish economist*

Profitability is the sovereign criterion of the enterprise.

—*Peter F. Drucker, U.S. management consultant and author*

TABLE 3.5
Traditional-Modern Shifts in Corporate Behaviors and Management Styles

Corporate Behaviors	Traditional	Modern
Size of operation	Small scale	Large scale
Division of labor	Low	High
Corporate objective	Output maximization	Profit maximization
Corporate culture	Harmonious	Competitive
Management Styles	**Autocratic**	**Participative**
Decision making		
Decision-making level	Top-down	Bottom-up
Subordinate involvement in decision making	None	Fully involved
Goal setting		
Goal-setting mechanism	Orders issued	Group consensus
Covert resistance to goals	Strong	Little
Responsibility for goal achievement	Top level	At all levels
Leadership style		
Confidence in subordinates	None	Complete
Subordinate ideas sought and used	Rarely	Always
Motivation methods	Fears, threats, punishments	Rewards, involvement
Communication		
Major information flows	Downward	Down, up, sideways
Superior knowledge of subordinate problems	Little	Extensive
Management-worker interactions	Little, with fear, distrust	Extensive, much trust and confidence
Career progression		
Evaluation criteria	Seniority, loyalty	Merit
Measurement method	Subjective	Objective

> If you command wisely, you'll be obeyed cheerfully.
>
> —*Thomas Fuller, 17th–18th-century author*

> Cooperation is spelled with two letters—WE.
>
> —*George M. Verity, U.S. industrialist*

and conflict-oriented management styles. In line with their less-competitive cultures, their firms see teamwork (cooperation) and synergies as the keys to corporate success. Japanese management in particular has endeavored to preserve its team approaches (with job rotation, management and quality circles) and still regards market share and employment maximization as major corporate objectives. Interestingly, team approaches increased in popularity in the 1990s, with Western and North American firms in particular recognizing the problems associated with competitive internal environments.

Management Styles Country development brings increases in educational levels and more opportunities for firms to allow employee participation in corporate decision-making activities. This enables companies to move away from autocratic management styles and tap the creative energies of employees through participative decision making. Table 3.5 illustrates the changes that occur as firms open up their management styles.

Decision making becomes less top-down, and employee involvement in corporate strategy making increases. Information flows are enhanced within companies as higher-caliber employees and computerization allows increased employee participation in decision making.

Goal setting and planning become more democratic as business units, country managers, and employees participate in the process. Teamwork and collegiality become the means through which plans are devised and implemented.

Leadership styles change to encourage and solicit participation at all organizational levels. "Softer" management styles are encouraged, and autocratic "do as I say" leaders become less effective.

Motivation methods change to reflect the new orientation. "Carrot and stick" means of employee motivation give way to involvement and reward methods.

Management-worker interactions change. Traditional antagonisms between managers and workers erode as trade unions are integrated into corporate decision-making activities. In some cases, governmental intervention is the catalyst to action (as with the 1970s German codetermination legislation that mandated management-worker boards or the EU 1998 version to cover European-based multinationals). At the same time, though, work rules change. Objective merit-based criteria replace subjective and seniority-oriented criteria for individual assessments, and worker longevity is not guaranteed as marketplace competition makes job tenure an unworkable proposition.

Note that movements toward modern, participative management styles have never been uniform. In developed markets, management styles vary by industry. In knowledge-intensive industries (consulting, hi-tech), modern participative styles work best among professionally qualified, experienced colleagues. In industries with wide disparities in employee skills (e.g., labor-intensive industries), traditional management styles are the norm, with untrusting corporate cultures, strong top-down decision-making styles, and antagonistic worker-management relations.

Country histories and national characteristics also affect management styles. Countries with strong left-wing orientations (e.g., France) make smooth management-worker relations less likely. Similarly, nations with long histories of social distinctions (e.g., Latin America, Asia) often strive to maintain social distinctions in the workplace, with clearly defined corporate hierarchies. How managers recognize and respond to these challenges is examined in Chapter 13 (local supply chain management).

Developmental Effects on Marketing Practices While marketing is a universal function in all countries, countries at different stages of development require corporate adjustments in strategic approaches. Table 3.6 depicts major differences in traditional and modern marketing environments. One major difference between less and more-developed markets relates to aggregate supply-and-demand conditions. Developing markets are often in undersupply situations, as production and distribution systems are inadequate to make manufactured output widely available. Customers are relatively unsophisticated, especially outside of urban centers. This makes promotions less critical (except to announce product availability) and competitive pricing less necessary. Underdeveloped infrastructures hinder accessibility to rural segments, and, in ethnically and linguistically diverse societies, the combination of cultural diversity and low discretionary incomes slow down product diffusion and distribution into

> There is a homely adage that runs: speak softly and carry a big stick.
>
> —*Theodore Roosevelt, 20th-century U.S. president*

> Marketing is the delivery of a standard of living.
>
> —*Paul Mazur, U.S. investment banker*

TABLE 3.6
Traditional-Modern Differences in Marketing Practices

	Market	Development
	Less	**More**
Aggregate supply, vis-à-vis demand	Undersupply	Oversupply
Market segmentation based on	Ethnic/geographic criteria in rural areas	Income, demographics, and psychographics criteria (activities, interest, opinions)
Product rollouts	Urban to semi-urban to rural	Nationally
Product lines	Limited	Extensive
Promotions	Mainly in urban centers	National media
Pricing	Retail price maintenance in urban areas, barter and haggling in rural areas	Competitive tool
Distribution	Geographically-based wholesalers and retailers, general product assortments	Product specialization with dealers/distributors, wholesalers/retailers
Marketing emphasis	Physical distribution	Demand creation; tailoring of products, information-based targeting and product planning
Market research	Complicated by literacy problems, many ethnic groups, undeveloped infrastructures (mails, telephone) and unfamiliarity with market research methods	Market research not normally a problem

Source: Based on Hill, John S. "Targeting Promotions in Lesser-Developed Countries." *Journal of Advertising* (1984); and Cateora, Philip R. *International Marketing,* 9th Edition (Chicago: Richard D. Irwin, 1996), 235.

these areas. Companies adjust to developing market conditions by slow rollouts of products from towns into semi-urban areas (where migrant populations live) and then into rural parts. Under these conditions, distribution is simple, with wholesalers and retailers having geographic monopolies and carrying broad product assortments. Local retailers, despite little competition, are community-oriented, and price gouging for maximum margins rarely occurs.

> Few people at the beginning of the 19th-century needed an adman to tell them what they wanted.
>
> —*John Kenneth Galbraith, U.S. economist*

As development occurs and more firms enter the marketplace, competitive pressures increase for companies. Enhanced distribution systems make goods and services more widely available. Oversupply situations develop, competition increases, and producers start to adopt the marketing concept and tailor-marketing mixes to the needs of customers. Corporate product lines expand as new customer needs become apparent. Increased use is made of manufacturing economies and products are distributed nationally as distribution systems develop. Competition increases, making large-scale promotions (either through mass media or via personal selling) necessary to maintain market shares. Deeper and broader product lines cause channel specialization as distributors and retailers cater to the needs of discriminating customers. Price competition increases, and corporate sales fluctuations become common. This puts pressures on firms to adjust labor needs according to sales levels, and problems occur as lifetime employment policies are threatened in favor of cost-cutting labor layoffs. Market research and data-based information systems enable managers to exercise increased control over corporate activities.

TABLE 3.7
Traditional-Modern Changes in Consumer Habits and Behaviors

Consumer Habits/Behaviors	Traditional	Modern
Purchasing roles	Female dominant on day-to-day items, male dominant on big-ticket items	Joint decision making on most products and services
Sources of information	Personal sources	Commercial sources
Branding	Not important in product choice (waste of resources)	Important in discriminating among products
Labor-saving products	Unimportant, adversely considered (home cooking is best)	Very important
Product purchasing and retail habit	Mostly at local stores	Mostly at mass merchandisers (supermarkets, department stores)
Merchandising (advertising, point-of-purchase displays, "specials")	Unimportant	Very important
Packaging	Wasteful, excessive, not important	Important
Means of purchase	Money	Credit/debit cards

Source: Medina, Jose F. *The Impact of Modernization on Developing Nation Consumption Patterns—The Case of Mexico,* Ph.D. Dissertation (University of Alabama, 1989). Used with author's permission.

Developmental Effects on Consumer Behavior

As consumers become experienced, their consumption patterns change.[9] They come into contact with mass retailers, branded products, mass-media promotions, and greater varieties of outlets and products. New marketing methods and institutions pressure traditional consumption behaviors. Table 3.7 summarizes adjustments consumers make to new shopping and consumption habits.

Purchasing roles change as families acquire more purchasing power and buy more products. Instead of males making most purchasing decisions, women become more involved in day-to-day decisions (for food items) and in big-ticket decisions (such as refrigerators and stoves). With more women working outside of the home, husbands often become involved in day-to-day shopping decisions.

Sources of information change as consumers become increasingly exposed to mass media. Commercial media become primary sources of purchasing information for products and brands, and personal sources of information diminish in importance.

Branding, unimportant in traditional societies, becomes necessary as manufacturers seek to differentiate similar products. Initially, product variety and multiple sizes confuse traditional consumers, but, as they become more experienced, they become more discriminating purchasers of products and services.

Labor-saving consumer-durable products (such as refrigerators, stoves, and microwave ovens) and non-durable items (such as canned goods, dried "instant" foods, and frozen products) gain in importance as the number of working women increases. These goods change shopping habits and consumption patterns as shopping and food preparation times are reduced. Women then have increased options to become wage earners. Traditional homemakers have less

I sleep so much better at night knowing that America is protected from thin pickles and fast ketchup.

—Orrin Hatch,
U.S. politician

need for labor-saving gadgets and generally regard daily shopping and home-cooked meals as superior to commercially prepared foods.

Retail outlet options increase and consumption patterns change as consumers start shopping at supermarkets, department stores, and specialty shops. Increased ownership of refrigerators and cars makes one-stop shopping feasible. Fewer trips are made to local stores, and socializing in shopping becomes less important.

Merchandising and packaging, basic components of modern retailing, are no longer viewed as superfluous. While traditional consumers see in-store promotions, displays, and prepackaged products as expensive and unnecessary, modern consumers view merchandising and package displays as useful information sources.

Means of purchase change as financial infrastructures, such as banks, develop, and consumers become sophisticated. Credit/debit cards come into common use, and cash purchases become less frequent.

COUNTRY DEVELOPMENT, INDUSTRIALIZATION, MODERNIZATION, AND INTEGRATION INTO THE REGIONAL AND GLOBAL ECONOMIES

Having outlined the institutional and behavioral changes occurring in the development process, we now integrate them at the nation-state level as countries go through four discernible stages in their move from traditional societies through to integration into regional and global economies (see Table 3.8).

Stage 1: Traditional Pre-industrial Societies

Traditional societies dominated world markets just a few decades ago. Today they are dying out as technology transfers and modernization diffuse through world markets, though many are still to be found in rural parts of Africa, Asia, and Latin America and in remote parts of industrialized economies (e.g., Eskimos and other native populations in North America). These communities often have centralized, communistic systems, self-sufficient to a degree but with increasing involvements with the outside world. They are agricultural or hunting communities, either independent or often living under feudal conditions (see Pakistan in Casette 3-2). Many maintain their own unique languages or dialects that can effectively hinder their involvement in local regional or national economies. Their economies produce only essential goods and services. Their communities have social hierarchies based on hereditary criteria *(influential families)* and on seniority systems that equate wisdom with accumulated experiences.

Stage 2: Industrialization and Modernization Processes

Industrialization and modernization are occurring in almost all nations. The process begins as towns develop and infrastructure linkages among communities provide means for regional, and then national, exchanges of goods and services. This process is gradual and often occurs over decades or generations.

TABLE 3.8
The Industrialization, Modernization, and Globalization Process

	Traditional Pre-industrial Societies	Industrialization–Modernization Process	Postindustrial Economies	Regional and Global Economies
Market Mechanisms				
Market system	Centralized, communistic	Market-forces system takes hold with some degree of government involvement	Mature capitalist economy	Regional trade blocs and global trade
Market demand	Local, self-sufficient communities	Regional, then national, markets develop	International	Worldwide
Major sector	Agricultural	Industrial	Service	According to national expertise and resources
Physical infrastructure	None needed	Roads, rail, air transportation systems develop		Regional and global road, rail, and air systems develop
Communications infrastructure	Personal	Spread of telephone, television, radio, print media	All media and computer and Internet linkages	Development of regional and global media capabilities
Social infrastructures and support systems	The extended family	Development of national health, pensions, unemployment, and education systems	Managed trade-offs among government-sponsored services	
Financial infrastructures	None	Development of regional and national banks and financial institutions to manage increasingly complex markets and to link savings and investments	Financial services market becomes a major sector	Financial institutions go global to establish a worldwide financial infrastructure
Means of exchange	None	Barter and money systems develop into national currencies	Money and credit	Regional currencies (e.g., euro)
Political/Cultural Factors				
Political system	Autarchy: chiefs, kings, sheiks, emirs, dictators, presidents-for-life	Moves toward democracies and single/multiple party systems	Mature, highly competitive democracies	Regional political bodies (e.g., EU), with guidance from world bodies (e.g., the United Nations)
Cultural-ethnic-linguistic composition	Heterogeneous, many local communities, languages, dialects	Increased interactions result in cultural melting-pot effect and development of a national culture	National cultures become influenced by regional and world influences	Development of regional cultural identities (European, Latin American, Asian)
Social class hierarchies based on:	Hereditary, seniority criteria	Hereditary, seniority, and income	Income and wealth	
Commercial and Corporate Activities				
National aggregate supply and demand (S and D)	Under-supply economies D>S	Supply technologies develop so that S = D	Supply capabilities outstrip demand S>D	International competition intensifies
Corporate orientation	Production orientation	Selling orientation	Marketing orientation	Marketing and competitive orientation
Product/service variety	Basic	Increasing	Extensive	Saturated
Company size	None	Small-medium	Large	Extremely large
Division of labor and management orientation	Little-generalist	Factory and management specialization	Extreme specialization, emphasis on coordination	International division of labor and cross-border coordination
Corporate objective	Output maximization	Output, sales, and profit	Profit	

Transportation and communication facilities are put into place, enabling market-forces-systems to function. As isolated communities interact over time, a "melting-pot effect" occurs, and local cultures blend into regional and, ultimately, national cultures (a very lengthy process that usually takes centuries). As internal markets develop, national currencies come into use, and financial institutions provide capital for industrial expansion. Government priorities are on infrastructure development (roads, rail, telecommunications, etc.) and on providing basic services to facilitate development of the economy (education, health, social-service systems). As widespread economic participation in the industrialization process occurs, many countries move toward political participation, and democracies are put into place. Companies grow as infrastructure development makes regional and then national distribution feasible, promoting scale economies and heavy division of labor in manufacturing and management. Efficiencies increase as companies pursue output, sales, and profit goals.

Stage 3: Postindustrial Economies

As national economies mature, they continue to evolve. In North America, Japan, and Western Europe, increasing global involvements cause a "hollowing out" of national manufacturing bases as firms move production offshore where the Internet revolution facilitates the coordination of corporate empires. Service sectors come to dominate the economy and many (e.g., those in the financial sector) take their expertise into overseas markets. At this stage, most nations have established democratic systems, and their global connections make them increasingly susceptible to regional and global influences. Technology and exposures to global competition make their companies formidable players in the world economy, and their extensive foreign investments give them competitive leverage in international markets.

Stage 4: Regionally and Globally Involved Societies

The globalization process continues as countries seek to establish trade blocs among neighboring nations and participate more fully in the global economy. Companies take advantage of their technological, manufacturing, and marketing expertise to become major players in non-domestic markets, their globalization efforts aided by developments of regional and global infrastructures. Corporate division of labor places manufacturing in countries that present the best cost-quality returns. Recognition of national interdependencies promotes regional currencies and regional political bodies. UN agencies, such as the IMF and the WTO, continue to provide individual countries with guidelines to become part of the global marketplace.

Some Conclusions

Movements from traditional societies to industrialization and beyond to postindustrial and global economies occur over decades and generations, but do not always occur sequentially. Developing economies in Latin America, Asia, and Africa have not waited until the completion of their industrialization processes to form trade blocs or to participate as fully as possible in global commerce. Similarly, political and cultural institutions often behind lag commercial sector developments. Indeed, these institutions can impede industrialization and modernization efforts. These obstacles are now examined.

OBSTACLES TO ECONOMIC DEVELOPMENT

All countries would be developed if impediments did not exist. Four types of obstacles impede economic development: (1) those associated with the industrialization process, (2) geographic impediments, (3) ethnic/linguistic obstacles, and (4) institutional resistance to change. International executives must be aware of these impediments, as they also affect commercial development.

Industrialization Process Impediments

There are three major problems associated with the industrialization process itself.

Population migration problems: First, as has happened in most developing countries, the influx of rural migrants into urban areas occurs too rapidly for easy absorption into the workforce. This results in shanty dwellings on the outskirts of urban areas. Most developing-country urban centers have semi-urban townships located 3–10 miles outside of city centers (e.g., Mexico City; Buenos Aires, Argentina; Djakarta, Indonesia; Bangkok, Thailand; Manila, Philippines). These areas, though natural outcomes of the industrialization process, cause infrastructure problems as authorities lag in extending urban amenities outside of towns. They can also be centers of civil unrest as migrating ethnic groups, formerly isolated in rural communities, are placed in close proximity to each other. Some melting-pot effects occur as ethnic groups mix together and cultural differences erode, drawing peoples toward national cultural unity, though identifications with ethnic groups often continue for generations.

Worker frustration: Even when workers find jobs, generally they are not the hoped-for, high-paid jobs, because most migrants are uneducated and qualify only for unskilled work. Although some can upgrade their skills by on-the-job training, most migrants remain in unskilled jobs. As increasing numbers of rural migrants compete for places in the urban workforce, pay levels stay at or near subsistence levels. But at the same time, television and other media expose migrants to modern lifestyles. Frustration mounts, and violence, alcohol, drug abuse, and vandalism often result.

Worker adjustment problems: The regimented discipline of the factory system creates worker adjustment problems. The cooperative efforts of village economies contrast with regimented factory routines and discipline, with extensive division of labor, workplace rules, and penalties for noncompliance. Morale can also be hurt by long work hours and poor working conditions.

> Specialization and organization are the basis of human progress.
>
> —*Charlotte Perkins Gilman, U.S. author*

Geographic Impediments

Resource Impediments Countries need two types of resources for industrial development. First, they need *renewable resources,* such as crops and other agricultural resources. A good climate (no extreme temperatures, tropical rains, or severe droughts) is essential for orderly transitions from agricultural to industrial economies, and the loss of farm populations in rural-to-urban migrations must be offset by mechanized farming processes. However, many countries do not have the temperate climates that produce consistent crops year after year. African countries, most recently Ethiopia and the Sudan, find it difficult to sustain good harvests. A second resource impediment is *lack of nonrenewable resources,* such as coal, energy, and minerals such as iron. Where nations lack these resources, they either develop very slowly or procure them through international trade. Some adapt. For example, South America uses its water resources to generate about 90 percent of its electricity needs.

Geographic Location Where a country is located on the world map can affect development. For example, country latitude (how far north or south it is) affects climate, with extremely hot or cold climates affecting work patterns (how long or hard individuals can physically work) and infrastructure development (the ease with which roads, rails, electric grids can be put into place).

Geographic location also affects access to trading routes. Landlocked nations (e.g., Africa) can be disadvantaged, and island states either become highly trade-oriented (e.g., Britain, Japan) or commercially isolated (e.g., Pacific islands). Nations with island configurations like Indonesia and the Philippines can also be difficult to coordinate, both industrially and economically.

Ethnic and Linguistic Composition

Ethnic and linguistic composition can be major obstacles to industrialization. In the colonial era, many national boundaries were determined by political or military events, with little regard for cultural groupings. Many of the world's lesser-developed countries are multilingual, while most advanced countries are predominately single-language. For multilingual countries to industrialize, there must be common means of communication to facilitate the manufacture and distribution of products and services. At the company level, communication is essential in order to coordinate corporate activities. For example, South African mines generally are worked by single tribal and ethnic groups to facilitate coordination. On the national level, in India and elsewhere in many parts of the world, former colonial languages are used, for example, Spanish and Portuguese in Latin America, French, English, and German in Africa, and English in Asia. In some countries, various dialects are blended into a common language. In the Democratic Republic of the Congo (formerly Zaire), a hundred or so local dialects have been reduced to four major dialects.[10] In other countries, the dialect of the dominant cultural group becomes a national tongue (Mandarin in China, Shona in Zimbabwe).

Institutional Resistance to Change

All societies have political, economic, and cultural power bases. In developing countries, modernization and cultural change threaten traditional institutions and power structures. Almost inevitably, these power structures oppose cultural change. Also, cultural inertia pulls people back to traditional ways when economic development disappoints.

Political Resistance Traditional political power bases are undermined as countries move from autocracies and dictatorships and toward democratic styles of government. As a result, incumbent leaders resist political reform. Indonesia, for many years a nominal democracy, had problems ousting President Suharto in 1998, even in the face of serious economic prob-

> *Civilization exists by geological consent, subject to change.*
>
> —*Will Durant, U.S. historian*

> *A common western assumption that cultural diversity is a historical curiosity being rapidly eroded by the growth of a common, western-oriented Anglophone culture . . . is simply not true.*
>
> —*Sir Michael Howard, British diplomat*

> *If you want to make enemies, try to change something.*
>
> —*Woodrow Wilson, 20th-century U.S. president*

lems precipitated by the Asian financial crisis. Similarly, in Russia, the left-wing Parliament (the Duma) has consistently resisted Russian reform efforts. Most countries today have political groups representing traditional and antibusiness interests.

Economic Resistance The change from centrally controlled to market-force based economies creates problems for consumers. In Eastern Europe, unrealistic state-supported prices that had been stable for decades rose and created discontent, resulting in antireform sentiments. Similarly, national companies in privileged positions (e.g., state-owned enterprises or those owned by powerful families or economic groups) can apply pressures to resist reforming the economy or opening it up to foreign competition. This resistance occurs not only in developing economies but also in mature markets like Germany or Japan.

Cultural Resistance Cultural Resistance occurs at many levels. *Religious resistance* has been most noticeable in traditional societies, such as those of the Middle East and some parts of Africa and Asia. In these areas, religious values stress conformity and family cohesiveness and emphasize continuity with past traditions. This weakens motives for the individual economic advancement and make individuals reluctant to cast aside traditional ways to emphasize personal, rather than family or community, development. Westernization is also perceived as a threat to core religious values, as materialism and preoccupations with personal advancement threaten religion as the dominant theme in individuals' lives. Islamic fundamentalists have long sought to insulate followers from excessive Western influences.

Education systems can either resist or encourage change. Where national educational systems emphasize science and technology (e.g., Korea, Germany, France, Russia) appropriately trained workforces exist to promote economic development. Where education is oriented toward the humanities (religion, history, literature, and so on), not only are there shortfalls in science and technology skills, but national cultures become preoccupied with the past rather than the future. In Islamic societies, Madrases (religious schools) place their primary educational emphasis on the Qur'ān, the primary Muslim text.

Rigid class systems make development difficult. Where family pedigree determines personal status (as in much of Latin America and Asia), individual motivations to excel economically are diminished. Similarly, where seniority systems are evident, merit is less important than longevity (time in job) and loyalty.

Ethnic or tribal divisions can continue to cause problems, even when national identities and democratic processes have been established. Africa's problems have been typical, with much political unrest following the national independence movements of the 1960s. In the mid-1990s, of the forty-two mainland states in sub-Saharan Africa, thirty had held democratic elections, and only four military rulers remained. Nevertheless, these young democracies have been deemed fragile because of their lack of ethnic unity.[11]

> The reasonable man adapts himself to the world; the unreasonable one persists in trying to adapt the world to himself. Therefore, all progress depends on the unreasonable man.
>
> —*George Bernard Shaw, 20th-century British playwright*

> The religious resurgence throughout the world is a reaction against secularism, moral relativism and self-indulgence, and a reaffirmation of the values of order, discipline, work, mutual help and human solidarity.
>
> —*Samuel P. Huntington, Harvard University political scientist*

> If you think education is expensive, try ignorance.
>
> —*Derek Bok, president, Harvard University*

KEY POINTS

- Economic development comprises positive economic growth and entails changes in a country's political, economic, and cultural institutions and in individual values, attitudes, and behaviors. Economic development also affects industry behaviors (supply chain and demand), management, marketing practices, and consumer behaviors.

- Economic development requires resources from public and private sectors, both internal (national governments, businesses), and external (the United Nations, international corporations).

- Technology transfers by international corporations comprise manufacturing technologies, management organization, and marketing know-how. Such transfers have both positive and negative effects on national cultures.

- Major institutional changes brought about by modernization are movements toward democracies and market-forces economies. Other cultural changes affect family systems, social classes, gender roles, religious orientations, and education systems. Culturally, heterogeneous societies are molded over generations into unified national cultures.

- Changes in individual values and behaviors occur as insider-outsider distinctions fall, efficiency orientations are instilled, and people become more risk-oriented, tolerant, and individualistic. These changes take time to diffuse in national markets, and pockets of traditional behaviors remain, especially in rural sectors of developed and especially developing economies.

- Development is sustained as individuals become part of the industrialized societies, earning money and emulating urban-consumption patterns.

- Industry development is affected by supply-chain factors (trade policies, labor costs, and infrastructure availability) and by demand factors (materialistic attitudes, mass-media development and availability, population movements, and cultural diversity).

- Corporate behaviors alter as divisions of labor, corporate culture changes, and profit motives become necessary to compete in market-forces-based economies.

- Management styles move from autocratic to participative as education levels rise, information system use becomes widespread, and market orientations make speedy decision making and internal cooperation necessary for profitable operations.

- Marketing practices are transformed as mass distribution and increasingly competitive marketplaces call for wider product assortments, media advertising, and market feedback.

- Consumer behaviors alter as purchasing habits change and are influences by corporate promotional efforts. Branding and packaging become important, and credit cards, labor-saving products, and services affect household consumption patterns.

- Country development, industrialization, modernization, and integration into regional and global economies occur as nations progress from traditional preindustrial societies through industrialization to postindustrial societies, and then begin to integrate their economies into regional and global settings, using trade blocs and UN agencies. Many developing nations leapfrog some developmental stages to participate in regional and global commerce.

- Country development is slowed by impediments in the industrialization process and by geographic, political, economic, and cultural resistance factors.

ENDNOTES

1. Dexter Roberts, "The Great Migration," *Business Week* (December 18, 2000): 176–88.

2. John S. Hill, "Modern-Traditional Behaviors: Anthropological Insights into Global Business Behaviors," *Journal of Transnational Management Development* 5, 3 (2000): 3–21.

3. World Bank, *World Development Report* 1999–2000: (Oxford University Press, 2000): 8–9.

4. David S. Landes, *The Wealth and Poverty of Nations: Why Some Are So Rich and Some Are So Poor* (New York: W. W. Norton, 1998).

5. From John S. Hill and Richard R. Still, "Cultural Effects of Technology Transfer by Multinational Corporations in Lesser Developed Countries," *Columbia Journal of World Business* (Summer 1980): 40–52.

6. Ragnar Nurkse, *Problems of Capital Formation in Underdeveloped Countries* (New York: Oxford University Press, 1953), 58–59, 63.

7. Vern Terpstra and Kenneth David, *The Cultural Environment of International Business* 3rd Edition, (Cincinnati, Ohio: Southwestern Publishing Co., 1991), chapter 4.

8. Miriam Jordan, "In Rural India, Video Vans Sell Toothpaste and Shampoo," *Wall Street Journal* (January 10, 1996): B1.

9. Adapted from Jose F. Medina, *The Impact of Modernization on Developing Nations Consumption Patterns: The Case of Mexico,* Ph.D. Dissertation (University of Alabama, 1989).

10. Vern Terpstra and Kenneth David, *Cultural Environment of International Business,* 3rd Edition (Cincinnati, Ohio: Southwestern Publishing, 1991), 27.

11. "Guns and Votes," *Economist* (June 29, 1996): 41.

Casette 3-1
Transitioning to the Market Economy: The Case of Eastern Europe

Since the 1989 fall of the Berlin Wall, the 1991 breaking up of the USSR and the advent of *perestroika* (restructuring) and *glasnost* during the 1980s and 1990s, Eastern Europe has been making the transition from communist to capitalist economies. Such change has not been easy. Shaking off seventy years of communism meant changing institutions, values and behaviors in a big way. Some of the problems Central and Eastern Europe have experienced are:

- Significant inflation as price levels adjusted to marketplace realities. Price rises of 50+ percent have not been unusual. With such inflation, interest rates have been high and inhibited local investments.

- Unemployment levels have risen as state-owned businesses have been closed down and downsized to realistic levels. Current unemployment levels range from 6½ percent (Czech Republic) to 17 percent (Croatia).

- At the company level, some state-owned enterprises (SOEs) have been successfully restructured. In doing so, their organizational structures have become flatter and less hierarchical. Profit centers, Western-style balance sheets, and financial reporting systems have been introduced along with new emphases on marketing and distribution. The task of modernizing is monumental, and so is the cost. Estimates put the cost of modernizing all 18,000 Russian SOEs at about $200 billion. Undeveloped capital markets and high interest rates make internal financing difficult, and there has been insufficient foreign company interest to make a real difference. For example, most of Romania's 5500 SOEs are technologically obsolete and financially insolvent.

- Motivation is a key issue in the move toward capitalistic behaviors. Rewarding individuals according to their contributions prompts workers to innovate, be productive, and work hard. This contrasts to communistic principles of pay being unrelated to performance.

- Governmental influences over business have historically been chaotic, with onerous taxation and accounting requirements, long waits for licenses and planning permissions, complex tax procedures, and multiple levels of approvals needed for new business projects.

- Corporate adjustments in making decisions according to market signals, producing what customers want and distributing widely to give products sales exposure.

- Sets of regulations to govern corporate behaviors in the emerging private sector, especially with regard to property ownership—company formation, contract enforcement, labor conditions, and so on.

- Priorities given to development of national infrastructures, including mail, telephones, faxes, and e-mails. Included in this is achieving sustainability in agriculture and agribusiness with improved production techniques (seeds, fertilizers, planting, harvesting), distribution (transportation, storage, refrigeration), processing (canning, freezing), and retail sales.

But as institutions change slowly, individuals adapt, and, in Central Europe and Russia, entrepreneurs and consumers are pushing to provide the rudiments of middle-class consumption. In Russia, local entrepreneurs own their own retail establishments, hotels, and computer software companies. Lawyers, accountants, and the white-collar professionals are slowly creating a viable middle class, along with the growth in professional managerial ranks at the big multinationals and major national companies. Russia's middle class accounts for between 10–20 percent of the nation's 145 million population and provides about a third of the country's $220 billion in GDP. However, at the other end of the spectrum, about one-third of Russians have slipped below the official poverty line.

In Central Europe, especially in the Czech Republic, Hungary, and Poland, the middle-class push has been more dramatic. With inflation down, banks and savings institutions have developed to provide a capital market for business use. Hypermarkets and malls are springing up. Advertising, once a luxury, has become a corporate necessity as companies compete for increased consumer discretionary income. Unlike

Russia, international companies, such as Germany's supermarket giant Metro, Sweden's Ikea and Ericsson, the U.S.'s Citibank, Coca Cola, Nike, and consumer firms Procter & Gamble and Unilever, have all moved into Central Europe and propelled its economy toward Western consumption levels. In consumer goods in particular, though, local companies have provided severe competition. Many Eastern European consumers still like low prices and are wary of the hype, expensive packaging, and high-profile brands westernization provides.

Questions

1. What problems has Eastern Europe faced in converting from communist to capitalist economies? What problems need to be tackled first, and why?

2. Track the traditional-to-modern movements in institutions and behaviors. What is promoting change—institutions or individuals?

3. Why is Central Europe apparently more successful in making the transition than Russia?

Sources: Behrman, Jack, and Dennis Rondinelli. "The transition to market-oriented economies in Central and Eastern Europe." *European Business Journal* 12: 2 (2000): 87–99. **Starobin, Paul, and Olga Kravchenko. "Russia's Middle Class."** *Business Week* (October 16, 2000): 78–84 **Woodruff, David, et al. "Ready to shop until they drop."** *Business Week* (June 22, 1998): 104–13.

Casette 3-2
Tradition and Modernization in Developing Pakistan

Pakistan became an independent nation at the same time as India in 1947, but the 140-million-person Islamic country has essentially been ruled since that time by three sections of the ruling class: the military, the civilian bureaucracy, and the feudal landlords. The military ruled from 1958 to 1969 when Pakistan was at the forefront of the cold-war rivalry between the U.S. and the USSR. Ali Bhutto then came to power via democratic processes but was deposed by the military in 1977 by General Zia, who executed Bhutto and returned Pakistan to the rule of fundamentalist Islamic law for a further decade. After Zia's death in a plane crash, elections were held, and Ali Bhutto's daughter Benizir was returned to power. Though part of the feudal-landlord elite, Benizir Bhutto was Western-educated. Her two administrations during the 1980s and 1990s were plagued and were ended by allegations of corruption. Another of the feudal-landlord elite, Nawaz Sharif, came to power but was deposed, again by allegations of corruption, in 2000, and another military ruler, General Mushariff, came to power.

The feudal landlords *(waderas)* of Pakistan reign supreme in the country's authority structure. Numbering about 5000, their major power base is land. Together with tribal leaders, they hold 126 out of 207 seats in the National Assembly, the main elected body. In Benizir Bhutto's last administration (1993–96), seventeen out of thirty-nine cabinet posts went to the *waderas,* and while they control only a quarter of the land, their power base is extensive. In addition to their land holdings and political power bases, *waderas* are often *pirs,* hereditary religious leaders with as many as 20,000 disciples who believe them to have unique spiritual powers. Many also oversee *jirgas,* or local courts. These bodies adjudicate disputes and even murder cases and are preferred by local people over civil courts. In their landowning capacities, *waderas* sublet their land for cultivation to *haris* (sharecroppers). Under the *batai* system, they split the crops equally with landlords. Landowners even have their own jails for transgressors. Not surprisingly, rural productivity is low. Land-reform legislation has been steadily resisted, and, in 1997, 4 million tons of agricultural produce had to be imported to avoid famine. National literacy rates are below 40 percent. This compares to nearly 70 percent for developing countries generally. Education accounts for just 2 percent of GNP and is dwarfed by military expenditures.

The seeds of social and economic change have been sewn. Democratic institutions are in place, though the dominant rural vote reinforces the *waderas*. About 35 percent of the population is now urbanized, up from 17 percent in 1950, though towns' political power in the National Assembly is limited.

Pakistan's political situation is not unique in Asia. The Nehru-Gandhi family dynasty has ruled India for all but nine of its 50+ years of independence. In neighboring Bangladesh, Prime Minister Sheckh Hasina is the daughter of a ruling dynasty. Indonesia's President Megawati is the daughter of President Sukarno, the founder of the independent state of Indonesia. Sri Lanka's and Burma's political power bases are also hereditary-based. Nepal and Bhutan have hereditary monarchies. All survive because of the strong feudal, tribal and hierarchical social structures of their countries, where power resides in individuals rather than in democratic processes and the rules of law.

Questions

1. What are the major power bases in Pakistan? Which do you think is the most powerful, and why? How are these power bases different from what is found in modern countries?

2. Use Chapter 3 materials and concepts to identify what changes in economic and social institutions must occur for economic development to be successful.

3. What sorts of obstacles does Pakistan face in its economic development? How can it overcome them?

Sources: Elliott, John. "In Asia, the Dynasties still rule." *New Statesman* (November 8, 1999): 22–24. Islam, Shada and Mirpur Khas. "Lords of Misrule." *Far Eastern Economic Review* (May 20, 1999): 22–26. Khan, Tariq Amin. "Economy, Society and the State in Pakistan." *Contemporary South Asia* 9, 2 (July 2000): 181–95.

CASE 1

Globalization and the Middle East

❦

In today's global economy, North America, Western Europe, and Japan dominate. But 1,000 years or so ago, it was Asia (excluding Japan) that accounted for two-thirds of world GDP, with Africa weighing in at about 12 percent of GDP. This state of affairs did not change appreciably over the next 500 years. By 1500, Asia still accounted for more than 60 percent of world production, and Europe had just 18 percent. Included in this total was Southwest Asia, today's Middle East. During medieval times and earlier, the Middle East was a world leader. Its medicine, mathematics, chemistry, astrology, and philosophy were the envy of the world, and the Silk Road linking the region to Asia was the major trade route in the world. Rice, sugar cane, cotton, watermelons, artichokes, oranges, tea, coffee, and metals came from Asia and Africa.

The world changed after 1500 as European sea power and military prowess exerted itself. While the Turkish Ottoman Empire continued as a diminishing world power until the twentieth century, the Middle East languished until the discovery and popularity of oil gave the region a new lease on life in the rapidly industrializing world. But it came at a cost. As world demand for oil continued to rise, oil price hikes from the 1970s onward placed a new emphasis on Middle Eastern stability. Internal regional conflicts became important to global commerce. The Palestinian-Israeli conflicts that began with the granting of Israeli statehood in 1947 escalated with the 1967 occupation of the West Bank, the Golan Heights, and Gaza, and with the continued U.S. support for Israel. Iraqi imperialism led to wars against Iran (1980–88), the invasion of Kuwait (1990–91), and the country's eventual occupation in 2003 by a U.S.-led military force.

Throughout the 1990s, tensions continued to rise between the West (and the U.S. in particular) and Islam, the dominant Middle Eastern religion. The 9/11 catastrophe, in which 3000 U.S. citizens were killed in a terrorist attack on the U.S. mainland in 2001, highlighted the philosophical chasm between the West and the Middle Eastern perspectives on the world.

Globalization

Eduardo Aninat, Deputy Managing Director of the IMF, has defined globalization as the process through which the increasingly free flow of ideas, people, goods, services, and capital leads to the integration of economies and societies. Successive waves of globalization, particularly from the thirteenth century onward have resulted in the expansion of world trade, the diffusion of technology, extensive migrations of peoples, and the cross-fertilizations of diverse cultures. Generally, participating countries have prospered. But the dominance of Western corporations has resulted in not just the modernization of nations, but also in the importation of Western values, philosophies, and lifestyles (westernization). These include democratic institutions, free market principles, and increasing emphases on commercial and material activities over other societal priorities.

GLOBALIZATION AND CHRISTIANITY The Christian nations of North America and Western Europe are well-developed. Many have identified the Protestant work ethic and frugal lifestyles as key factors in capitalism's development. Nevertheless, globalization and capitalist principles clash with some Christian ideals. For example:

- The "love thy neighbor as yourself" principle dovetails better with collectivist ideals that stress community orientations (communism) than with the individualistic orientations of Western societies.

- "Thou shalt not covet thy neighbor's goods" (the Tenth Commandment) is at odds with the materialistic, acquisitive nature of capitalistic societies. In economic theory, Duesenberry's permanent income hypothesis (1949) posits that emulation of social superiors is a motivational force driving consumption in advanced societies. In developing countries, Nurkse's Demonstration Effect (1953) and Hill and Still's Emulation Cycle (1980) all attest to the power of "coveting thy neighbor's goods" in stimulating consumption in emerging markets. In popular parlance, *the rat race* also signals the use of material possessions in determining individuals' positions in modern economic societies.

- The profit maximization principle can be equated with greed (Enron, for example).

- Sunday (the Christian Sabbath—Lord's day) is not a day of rest for most retailers—Third Commandment—"Keep holy the Sabbath").

- The kingdom of God is not a democracy.

In popular culture, television and Hollywood influences cultivate unrest, and soap operas routinely violate the Sixth and Ninth Commandments ("Thou shalt not commit adultery" and "Thou shalt not covet thy neighbor's spouse"). Crime-based dramas are often violence-based ("Thou shalt not kill") or robbery-based ("Thou shalt not steal"). According to Miller, Govil, McMurria, and Maxwell (2001), U.S. popular culture is highly exportable and was valued at $31 billion worldwide. The Hollywood influence is particularly notable, accounting for ownership of between 40 and 90 percent of the movies shown in most countries.

Hollywood's portrayal of U.S. lifestyles ("where the men are tall, the women good-looking, and the children are all above average") has always been controversial. Glitz, glamour, affluence, and sex have often been prominent features of the Hollywood product. But, as its wares are distributed into foreign markets, problems arise when non-U.S. audiences equate screen images with reality; distorted views of the U.S. then cause major image problems. In parts of the Middle East, for example, U.S. lifestyles are associated with greed, violence, and promiscuity, and the U.S. becomes "the Great Satan." Despite some leveling of the playing field via "good" media, such as CNN and the Discovery channel, poor images (such as MTV) dominate foreign mindsets. This tends to be the case especially in Islamic societies, such as those in the Middle East.

Middle Eastern Culture: Islam

Islam is the newest of the major world religions, having been established in the seventh century A.D. Like Judaism, Islam is descended from Abraham, whose second wife, Hagar, bore Ishmael. After Abraham's first wife unexpectedly gave birth to Isaac, Hagar and Ishmael were banished to what became Mecca. Their descendants included the prophet Muhammad who founded the Islamic religion in A.D. 610 when he got "the call" from Allah (God). Over twelve years, Muhammad challenged the area's existing polytheistic religion with his teaching of a single omnipotent god and castigated the licentiousness and inequalities endemic in other religions. In 622, opposition to his teachings forced him to migrate to Yathrib (later Medina), where he unified the major tribes and became a political leader and statesman. After defeating the Meccans in battle, he succeeded in unifying Arabia under the Islamic banner before dying in A.D. 632.

Islam spread rapidly. By 700, Muhammad's successors had conquered much of today's Middle East, North Africa, and parts of Spain. The Qur'ān, dictated directly to Muhammad by the angel Gabriel over twenty-three years, became the centerpiece of the Islamic faith. Over time, via the Silk Road commercial linkages, Islam spread to parts of Asia, where its single-god philosophy and egalitarian orientation garnered much support, particu-larly in Northern India (today's Pakistan and Bangladesh) and in Southeast Asia (today's Indonesia). Islam's advantages over other religions were significant enough that many of these regions have retained their Muslim allegiances to the present day.

Islamic teachings and philosophy are based around the Qur'ān and the Hadith, the thoughts, sayings, and teachings of the Prophet Muhammad. Islamic duties center around the five pillars of faith: recognition of Allah as the only God, prayer five times a day, alms to the poor (2 percent of wealth), observance of Ramadan as the holy month, and the pilgrimage to Mecca. Islam's influence over its adherents is extensive; it is truly a lifestyle religion and is the dominant philosophy underlying political, legal, social, and educational institutions.

POLITICAL INFLUENCE In contrast to Christianity, in particular, there are no real distinctions between the religious and the political ("Render unto Caesar the things that are Caesar's, and unto God the things which are God's"—Matthew 22:21). In Islam, the reverse is true. Political and religious institutions are intertwined as classical theocracies. There is a Muslim saying, often attributed to the Prophet: "Islam and the government are twin brothers. One cannot thrive without the other. Islam is the foundation, and government the guardian. What has no foundation, collapses; what has no guardian, perishes" (Lewis 1995: 149). Lewis further notes (p. 155) that the egalitarian principles of Islam militate against elite aristocracies. Historically, however, the evolution of Islamic societies has been based on leadership institutions such as kings, shahs, and emirs. The Prophet himself was a sovereign ruler of Medina, and historic precedents of the period (700–1900), were toward European-style sovereign-based states. The autocratic nature of Middle Eastern tribal-based societies was also a powerful force for the centralization of political power. More recently, Sunni jurists have legitimized the political-religious connection, "with God as the source of sovereignty, of legitimacy, and of law, and the ruler as his instrument and representative . . . the shadow of God on earth" (Lewis 1995: 224–25).

The advent of democratic forces is, therefore, an anathema to the hereditary rulers of the Middle East who have governed the region for centuries. In the West, autocracies are associated with corruption and self-interests. In the Middle East, most people view their hereditary heads of state as benevolent leaders serving the needs of their people according to Islamic principles. As in many parts of Asia, benevolent, stable autocracies are viewed as preferable to volatile democratic systems where powerful lobbies and pressure groups use financial contributions to distort the political process. In essence, both sides popularize the corruptive elements of each other's systems.

LEGAL INFLUENCE: ISLAMIC LAW "SHARIA" There are four sources of Islamic law: the Qur'ān as the direct expression of divine will, the Hadith (the teachings of the Prophet himself), the Ijma (the consensus interpretation), and the Qiyas (decision areas over which the Qur'ān did not offer clear instruction). What is clear is that the Sharia covered all aspects of Muslim life—public, private, communal, and personal. Many, such as the provisions relating to marriage, divorce, property, and inheritance, have been woven into a normative code of law. Those that have evolved through historical interpretation are customs, but carry the weight of precedent.

There are two sides to Islamic law—civil and criminal. Land, family, and money disputes are usually settled through jirgas (local courts). In Nigeria, for example, such courts arbitrate local disputes. People represent themselves. Judges are local landowners or tribal elders. They dispense justice in rough but rapid fashion, usually on the same day. This contrasts with colonial-style formal courts, which are expensive, time-consuming, and perceived to be corrupt. Problems arise, however, in criminal cases, where traditional punishments are meted out for drinking alcohol (flogging), theft (amputation), and sexual crimes, such as adultery (where death by stoning is an option). In Gaza, for example, massive fines or physical punishments are typical options. In Nigeria and Pakistan, human rights organizations have long protested death by stoning punishments handed down to women convicted of adultery and "honor killings" of women accused of sexual improprieties, such as illicit relationships. By Western standards, such punishments are draconian. But strict interpretations of Islamic law have little tolerance for noncompliant citizens.

In Christianity, mankind has free will to commit sins (a choice between doing right or wrong). Judgment on the balance sheet for rights and wrongs for individuals is at death, with heaven and hell as the alternative consequences. In Hinduism and Buddhism, positive karma (actions) must exceed negative karma to make progress on the path toward enlightenment. In Islam, there is no such latitude. There is only one way—the right way, which is in accordance with God's law. The rationale for such strictness is that Islamic law came directly from God, through the Qur'ān and the Hadith. Western law, by contrast, is viewed as largely man-made. Hence, for example, apostasy, the renouncing of Allah, is punishable by death.

INFLUENCE ON SOCIAL BEHAVIORS Islamic law not only dictates the relationship between mankind and God, it also extends to the maintenance of community order and integrity and regulates personal and community behaviors through five classifications of behaviors: those that are required (e.g., prayer requirements), those that are recommended (e.g., forgiveness of debt), those where there are no rulings, those that are discouraged (e.g., polygamy), and those that are forbidden (e.g., usury, eating of pork, drinking of alcohol, apostasy—denial of God). The Qur'ān and the Hadith lay out the Islamic conception of the virtuous life: living modestly; being charitable and truthful; refraining from mockery, gambling, fortune-telling, and falsehoods; helping orphans; and giving true weight in commerce.

INFLUENCE ON EDUCATION Much education in Islamic societies is done through madrasas, or religion schools. Created in the eleventh century, these schools have dominated the Islamic world for centuries. Funded through zakat, the obligatory giving of alms to charitable causes, these religion-based schools focus mainly on the Qur'ān and are free to students. In Pakistan, there were over 10,000 madrasas in 2001, with over a million students enrolled. This compared to 1.9 million enrolled in primary schools. It is estimated that about 6 million (mainly poorer) Muslims attend these schools worldwide, with twice that number attending maktabs or kuttabs—small Qur'ān-based schools attached to mosques. All teach religion-based education. Few are militant, but all emphasize that Western ways and modernity compromise Islamic teachings and lifestyles. The result is that, as Haqqani (2002, p. 64) notes: "The Muslim world is divided between the rich and powerful who are aligned with the West and the impoverished masses who turn to religion in the absence of adequate means of livelihood."

However, it has to be noted that both Turkey and Indonesia are managing to industrialize while maintaining their Islamic principles, though both face significant religious oppositions within their borders.

Middle Eastern Internal Problems

As in all parts of the emerging world, there are issues associated with economic development and the preservation of local traditions. In the Middle East, these are:

- Freedom of the press: Insulating the Arab world from globalizing influences has meant extreme limitations on the popular press. A *Newsweek* survey (October 15, 2001, p. 37) showed that of the seventeen major countries comprising the Arab world in the Middle East and North Africa, only three (Kuwait, Morocco, and Jordan) had some degree of freedom of the press. The remaining countries were heavily restricted.

- Education—the knowledge deficit: While the Arab world has consistently out-spent other developing countries on education, its emphasis has been on secondary and university education. Key areas such as primary education and vocational training have been neglected, and this has resulted in a poorly trained labor force and significant unemployment among young Arabs. In Saudi Arabia, for example, unemployment stands at 27 percent for 20–24 year olds. Primary school deficiencies, especially outside urban areas, have resulted in regional literacy levels that increased only slightly over 1980–95, with illiteracy rates at about 50 percent for women. This, along with the region's inability to attract non-petroleum-based industry, has caused many to be educated in the madrasas, or religion schools.

- Military expenditures: The potential for regional conflict has caused significant expenditures on arms and defense. The Middle East spends a greater proportion of its GDP on arms than any other region in the world. Over 1980–95 this amounted to over $420 billion. The reasons for this include the presence of an armed Israel, and until 2003, a potentially hostile Iraq.

- Falling standards of prosperity: Saudi Arabia, the leading oil producer at 9 million barrels a day, has seen its per capita income fall from $23,294 in 1980 to $8,711 in 2002.

- Population concerns: Since 1950, the Middle East's population has risen from less than 100 million to over 350 million people. This has placed major pressures on national pension schemes. Saudi Arabia, for example, expects its senior citizen ranks to swell from about 1 million in 2000 to over 7 million by 2050. Health-care facilities are also under major pressures for expansion. Only sub-Saharan Africa's annual population growth of 4.12 percent eclipses the Middle East's at 2.79 percent. The lack of employment opportunities has been a major cause of resentment for the region's young people, causing many to seek refuge in religious idealism.

- Politics and democratic status are variable.

  1. Bahrain has a monarchy and in 2001 adopted a charter for a democratic body.

  2. Iran has a president, a prime minister, a 290-seat parliament, though a 24-person Council of Guardians approves candidates and laws.

  3. Iraq is moving toward democratic status in 2004 under U.S. supervision.

  4. Jordan has a monarchy, a senate appointed by the king, and deputies from major clans.

  5. Kuwait has a monarchy.

  6. Lebanon has a president (Christian), a Sunni prime minister, a Shiá speaker, and a 128-seat parliament with equal Muslim and Christian representation.

  7. Oman has a monarchy (sultanate), state council is appointed, and a 110-seat lower house advises the sultan.

  8. Qatar has a monarchy (emirate) which take advice from citizens but appoints the Council of Ministers and the judiciary.

  9. Saudi Arabia has a monarch who appoints the Council of Ministers and a Consultative Council.

  10. Syria is a republic and has a president and a 250-seat legislature, "People's Council."

  11. United Arab Emirates is a federation of emirates.

  12. Yemen has a president and a 301-member legislature.

Western Economic Interests in the Middle East: Oil

Oil's importance to the world economy probably began with the British navy's conversion from coal to oil-based engines in the first part of the twentieth century in order to gain speed advantages over military rivals. From that time, demand continued to rise, and with it the Middle East's stature in world affairs. Oil price hikes over 1973–74 (from $3 to $13 a barrel), 1978–79 (up to $40+ a barrel), and 1990–91 resulted in global downturns in aggregate demand. Depressed prices also cause problems. When they dipped precipitously in the late 1980s to below $10 a barrel, chaos resulted as high-cost producers were forced to shut down operations to avoid major losses.

Today, oil's importance in the world has not diminished. It powers 57 percent of the world's boats, airlines, and autos, up from 42 percent in the early 1990s. But oil revenues over the years have not resulted in regional affluence. In 1999, the GDPs of the twenty-two Arab nations were $531 billion, less than that of Spain. The Middle East accounts for just 28 percent of current world production but generates less than 2 percent of world GDP. But oil remains a power base. The region still controls 63 percent of the world's reserves. Saudi Arabia provides 11 percent of the world's production, controls a quarter of global reserves, and is a key player in price setting. Oil provides 90 percent of the nation's exports, a third of its GDP, and 75 percent of government revenues. It continues to be the world's low-cost producer at about $1.50 a barrel, and this importance continues to give the region and Saudi Arabia considerable leverage in world affairs.

Middle Eastern involvement extends beyond oil to include natural gas, making the region a key player in global energy policies of the future. The Middle East contains the world's second-largest gas reserves (after the former USSR) with around 1,855 trillion cubic feet (52.5 trillion cubic meters), with Iran, Qatar, Saudi Arabia, and the

UAE having the second- to fifth-largest reserves globally. Global demand for natural gas is expected to double from 84 trillion cubic feet to 162 from 1999–2020. The combination of oil and gas enhances regional prospects for the foreseeable future. Individual nations profile as follows:

- Saudi Arabia has 260 billion barrels of oil reserves, with a possible 1 trillion barrels deemed ultimately retrievable. Gas reserves are at about 200 trillion cubic feet.

- Iraq has 112 billion barrels of oil reserves, with future prospects of about 220 billion barrels. Gas reserves are at about 110 trillion cubic feet.

- Kuwait has an estimated 94 billion of oil reserves (about 9 percent of the world total). Gas production is minor at about 290 billion cubic feet.

- Oman has 5.5 billion barrels of oil reserves and gas reserves of 29 trillion cubic feet.

- Qatar has 13.2 billion barrels of oil reserves and 380 trillion cubic feet of gas.

- United Arab Emirates has oil reserves of 98 billion barrels and has the world's fifth-largest reserves of natural gas.

Religion and Politics: Western Interventions in the Middle East

The establishment of Islam from the seventh century and its consequent expansion throughout the Middle East and North Africa gave the region a distinct commercial identity. From the eighth to the twelfth centuries, a market- and money-based economy was established, and the region prospered as the "Golden Age of Islam." Its progress was interrupted with the crusades as a series of Western expeditions, beginning at the end of the eleventh century, set out to recapture Christian holy places from Islamic rulers. Five major crusades followed, with spasmodic conflicts over the next 200 years until Western influence in the region died away in the thirteenth century.

From the sixteenth century onward, the Turkish Ottoman Empire asserted itself and remained the dominant regional power into the twentieth century. During the nineteenth century, however, the Middle East again became important. The building and opening up of the Suez Canal in 1869 gave empire-minded Europeans easier access to India and Asia. Britain established colonial presences in Oman, Bahrain, Kuwait, and Yemen in the nineteenth century and in Egypt, Iraq, and Jordan in the twentieth century, and France in Egypt, Syria and Lebanon.

Throughout the twentieth century, the Middle Eastern nations gradually became independent. It was over 1947–48 that a critical regional event occurred—the establishment by UN mandate of the State of Israel. Pushed heavily by the United States and Britain, this move produced immediate and ongoing conflicts with other Middle Eastern states, resulting in wars in 1948, 1967, and 1973. The 1967 war, in particular, was significant, as Israel—with U.S. military technology and financial assistance—seized control of the Golan Heights, Gaza, and the West Bank. This also included control over the al-Aqsa mosque in Jerusalem, the third-most holy site in Islam (after Mecca and Medina). Despite United Nations resolutions 242 and 338 requiring Israel to withdraw, these areas remain under Israeli control to the present day. The Arab nations, wary of U.S. military support for Israel, maintained their support of the Palestinian people. It was this support that prompted the region to use its power over oil prices to pressure the Western powers to seek a solution to the Palestinian question in 1974. None was forthcoming.

The other major conflicts involving Middle Eastern nations have concerned Iraq. The holy war between Iran and Iraq took place over 1980–88. At this time the West, and the U.S. in particular, supported Iraq. Military support, including chemical and biological weapons, was supplied to Iraq. Then, with a failing economy, Iraq's leader, Saddam Hussein attacked Kuwait in 1990, only to be driven out by a UN military force in 1991. Relations between the West and the Middle East simmered throughout the 1990s as Israel continued its occupation of territories gained in 1967. The 9/11 terrorist attack on the U.S. raised tensions again in the region, and allegations concerning weapons of mass destruction and human rights violations led to a U.S.-led force occupying Iraq in 2003.

The Future?

Major questions remain about globalization, particularly in the Middle Eastern context. Within even the developed nations, the increase in competitiveness from the adoption of democratic and capitalistic principles adds to individual uncertainties and insecurities, especially in the workplace. In developing countries, globalization's intrusions into national cultures tend to be unavoidable—reducing country options in cultural development and putting religious institutions and personal faiths under considerable pressures. Do nation states have the power to resist? Or do they fall as dominoes under the powerful globalization movement?

Questions

1. What are the major contrasts between the political and cultural institutions of the Middle East and those of the Western world. Which do you think is the most important? Why?

2. Is Christianity incompatible with democratic and capitalistic principles? If so, why have democracies and market-forces societies flourished in Western Europe and North America?

3. If oil is such a major energy source for the global economy, why is the Middle East not more prosperous?

4. Of the internal problems facing the Middle East, which do you consider to be the most important? Why?

5. Is Islam fundamentally incompatible with globalization?

6. Review Western interventions in the Middle East. What do you conclude?

Sources: Townsend, David. "The balance of power." *Petroleum Economist* (Nov. 2001): 21–27. Henry, Clement. "A clash of civilizations." *Harvard International Review* 25:1 (Spring 2003): 60–65. Lightman, Alex. "Responding to the critics of globalization." *Chief Executive* (Dec. 2001): 62–64. Martin, Josh. "The population time bomb." *Middle East* (Nov. 2003): 6–12. Bahgat, Gawdat. "The new Middle East: The Gulf Monarchies and Israel." *The Journal of Social, Political, and Economic Studies* 28:2 (Summer 2003): 123–35. Haqqani, Hussain. "Islam's Medieval Outposts." *Foreign Affairs* (Nov.–Dec. 2002): 58–64. Braudel, Fernand. *A History of Civilizations.* New York: Penguin. 1993. Roberts, J. M. *History of the World.* New York. Penguin Putnam. 1998. Lewis, Bernard. *The Middle East.* New York. Touchstone. 1995. Smith, Huston. *The World's Religions.* HarperSanFrancisco. 1998. "Why do they hate us: What to do." *Newsweek* (October 15, 2001). McRae, Hamish. "1000 years of globalization." *Organization for Economic Cooperation and Development: The OECD Observer* (Sept. 2001): 51–52. Aninat, Eduardo. "Surmounting the challenges of globalization." *Finance and Development* 39:1 (March 2002): 4–8. Duesenberry, James. *Income, Savings, and the Theory of Consumer Behavior.* Cambridge, Mass. Harvard University Press. 1949. Nurkse, Ragnar. *Problems in Capital Formation in Underdeveloped Countries.* New York. Cambridge University Press. 1953. Hill, John S., and Richard R. Still. "Cultural Effects of Technology Transfer by Multinational Corporations in Lesser Developed Countries." *Columbia Journal of World Business* (Summer 1980): 40–51. Miller, Toby, Nitin Govil, John McMurria, Richard Maxwell. *Global Hollywood.* London. BFI Publishing. 2001.

CASE 2

Královopolská: Managing the Transition to a Market Economy

Introduction

In early 1996, Zdenek Pánek, the general director of Královopolská, reviewed his predecessor's words in the company's 1992 annual report.[1]

> Management intends to concentrate its efforts on the long-term development of the company, to increase productivity to a level that is five times its current status by 1997, to increase the value of the company by 30% every year, and to pay dividends to its shareholders starting in 1994.

Pánek smiled. So much had changed since these words were written, just three years ago. Goals to become more productive and pay dividends were typical for many Czech companies immediately following the "Velvet Revolution" of 1989.[2] Královopolská was making the transition from central planning to market economy fairly successfully; it was among the top-third of large Czech companies in business performance, Pánek thought. But after declining profits in 1992, the company reported losses in 1993 and 1994. Profits returned in 1995, but they were small (3 percent of assets), and the company's gross margin from production was negative. Pánek knew that Královopolská had to focus its business strategy, but he was not sure how. It was critical to answer this question now because the management team he headed had just purchased 51 percent of Královopolská via a leveraged buyout. Pánek was not only the president, but now also an owner.

The Company and Its Business

Královopolská was a medium-sized producer of industrial equipment for a diverse range of end users. The company was located in Brno, the second-largest city in the Czech Republic (population 400,000 in 1990), about 200 km (120 miles) southeast of Prague. Sales revenue in 1994 was 3,508 million korunas (Kc)—about $122 million, and employment was 3,400.

Královopolská was established in 1889 at Královo Pole (King's Field) on a greenfield site as a machinery works, first making railway carriages and storage tanks and soon adding steam boilers, woodworking machinery, and cranes. Employment was 300 to 400 people in the nineteenth century. The company's production program did not change throughout the World War I and II periods. Czechoslovakia's post-World War II government nationalized Královopolská in 1945 and enlarged it by combining six facilities with the original plant in 1948. The company stopped producing railway carriages but added chemical plant equipment during the first five-year plan imposed by the communist government beginning in 1949. The company's product lines were expanded in 1958 with the addition of steel structures and in 1961 with water-treatment plant equipment.

In 1958, the Czechoslovak government consolidated the country's chemical and food-processing industries. Královopolská manufactured equipment for the industries and, in addition, was given responsibility for directing and controlling the activities of other enterprises in the industries, including two research-and-development institutes, a design-engineering firm, and a construction firm. Seven years later, in 1965, Královopolská lost its central role and its independent status when the government reorganized the chemical and food-equipment industries and placed the enterprises under the control of CHEPOS (a type of holding company whose acronym comes from the Czech words for chemical [chemicky], food [potrava], and machinery [strojirna]). Královopolská regained its independence from CHEPOS in 1988 but remained primarily an equipment manufacturer.

During 1958–65, as the head of the Czechoslovak chemical and food equipment industries, Královopolská developed the capability to manage turnkey projects—to design, engineer, manufacture, deliver, install, and service entire water-treatment and chemical manufacturing facilities in cooperation with other enterprises. The turnkey business diminished substantially in 1965. A small turnkey operation, later known as the RIA Division, survived. (RIA stands for Realizace Investicních Akcí, translated literally as "Realization of Investment Activities," but more meaningfully rendered in the company's reports as "Comprehensive Plant Equipment Delivery.")

At the time of the Velvet Revolution, Královopolská primarily manufactured equipment for the chemical industry, which accounted for half its production volume. Nuclear power stations purchased about another quarter of its output, and water-treatment plant equipment, cranes, and steel structures each accounted for less than 10 percent of Královopolská's production.

Privatization

Centrally planned economies in Eastern and Central Europe with communist governments functioned very differently from market economies. Central planning business methods may have been well-adapted to that system, but they were not suitable for firms in market economies. Companies in Eastern and Central Europe had to adjust when central planning ended, and Královopolská was no exception. (Features of business under central planning are detailed in Exhibit 1.) The first order of business after the Velvet Revolution was to privatize the economy.[3]

Královopolská's management urged the Ministry of Privatization to support early privatization of the company because, "we wanted to be free of the state method of management as soon as possible," according to one manager. Initial privatization for Královopolská occurred in May 1992, during the first wave of voucher privatization. About 30 percent of the company's 1,004,000 shares were sold to individuals and investment funds (the shares began trading one year later). The National Property Fund (NPF), the state agency that held shares pending the completion of privatization, retained 66 percent of the shares. The legal status of the company changed from that of state plant (s.p.) to joint stock company (a.s.).

In March 1995 a partnership called KENOP, created by Pánek and six other managers from Královopolská, bought shares from the NPF to create a 51 percent stake to complete privatization. (Individuals held 22 percent and investment funds held the remaining 27 percent of the company's shares.)

Business Conditions During the Transition

The transition from central planning to a market economy caused many hardships and brought severe challenges to all Czech companies. Macroeconomic conditions made business difficult. Real gross domestic product in Czechoslovakia dropped by 26 percent between the Velvet Revolution and 1993, and industrial production fell by 44 percent, thus reducing demand for the company's products from the domestic market. In 1991, the government allowed the market to set prices, and inflation soared to 58 percent. Short-term financing was scarce, and nominal interest rates were around 14–15 percent in 1991–93. The government devalued the currency from Kc 15 per U.S. dollar to about Kc 29 per U.S. dollar in 1991 and pegged the exchange rate to the German mark and U.S. dollar with 60–40 weights (see Table 1).

EXPORT MARKETS Královopolská was a relatively low-cost producer. Low labor wages outweighed low labor productivity. At the same time, Královopolská had a reputation as a manufacturer of good, serviceable products. The company won medals at industry fairs in Brno, despite the fact that the central planners had authorized no significant investment in technology or equipment during the twenty years prior to the Velvet Revolution. Královopolská produced equipment that met the prevailing specifications in the East. Nevertheless, the combination of price and quality gave Královopolská a potential advantage in international markets because it could underprice Western producers (by about 10–15 percent, some managers estimated) and make affordable products for developing countries.

In 1989, Královopolská earned three-quarters of its revenue from exports, and, of that total, about 70 percent came from business with the Soviet Union and Iraq. In August 1990, the United Nations embargo against Iraq stopped those exports, and, in August 1991, the Soviet Union collapsed and went into a steep economic decline. Královopolská's exports dropped sharply to 9 percent of sales in 1991 and 16 percent in 1992. A recovery to 48 percent of sales in 1993 was partly illusory because Slovakia became a separate country in January 1993, and thus formerly domestic sales became export sales.

Through this period, some of Královopolská's exports to Russia continued, despite that country's economic hardship, because the products were furnaces and replacement parts for oil refineries, which Russia needed to generate its own hard-currency exports. Russia continued to buy these products from Královopolská and paid for them in U.S. dollars. Exports to Russia accounted for about 10 percent of Královopolská's production volume in 1993.

The company found it difficult to develop new export business. Like many large Czech firms, Královopolská did not own or control its distribution channels, so it had few direct relationships with customers. Before the revolution, 50 percent of its exports were handled through one state trading company, Technoexport. The other half was exported indirectly via the engineering firms that actually constructed power plants, chemical plants, and water-treatment facilities.

Other factors made export development difficult as well. Much of Western Europe was in the midst of recession in the early 1990s, and West European technical standards were different from those that Královopolská followed. In some cases, price was less important than established relationships with customers, where Královopolská was at a disadvantage because it had very little Western business experience. In some developing countries, on the other hand, the problem was national political and economic instability. Královopolská developed new export business in Iran, accounting for about a quarter of all exports in 1993, but this business encountered its own problems—the Iranian government defaulted on payments in 1994. Other business was developed in Syria, Egypt, and Iraq.

DOMESTIC MARKET Similar to other Czech firms, Královopolská had been a monopoly producer in most of its domestic businesses, including chemical equipment, industrial cranes, and water-treatment plant equipment. However, its domestic monopoly in water-treatment facilities eroded after the Revolution as new privatized firms entered the business. In addition, water-treatment equipment was readily available outside the Czech Republic and could be imported after the revolution.

Nevertheless, the water-treatment plant business was of special interest to Královopolská. During the previous forty years, municipal and industrial water-treatment systems were seldom improved. Roughly half of all city water supplies were below standard in water quality, according to a government study. A new effort to reduce environmental pollution and improve water quality led to government regulations and investments in water-purification and sewage-treatment facilities, effectively expanding one of Královopolská's markets. Growth in this business helped to counter declines from the depressed chemical and nuclear power industries and contributed to increased revenues for the RIA division especially.

Financial Results

Královopolská posted better financial results than many other companies in the 1991–93 transition years, though the firm was not without its troubles (see Table 2). Revenue decreased in 1990 and 1991, and the high rate of price inflation in 1991 meant that revenue in real terms declined about 40 percent in that year. However, revenue went up both in nominal and real terms in 1992 and 1993, counter to the trend in the economy as a whole. Královopolská was profitable throughout the transition period until 1993, when it incurred a loss of Kc 103 million (about $3.5 million). This loss was largely a result of a first-time charge for reserves of Kc 180 million. Its loss of Kc 54 million in 1994 was partly the result of little new business booked in 1992 and 1993 and partly due to more changes in financial reporting to bring accounting standards in line with Western financial reporting methods. Sales were up substantially in 1995, with a small profit of Kc 162 million.

Czech companies faced a serious financial threat during the transition due to the lack of trade credit. The Czech government followed a conservative fiscal and monetary policy from 1991 onward, resulting in tight credit and high nominal interest rates. In the absence of a functioning banking system, and lacking trade credit from banks, firms financed sales to customers by simply not paying their bills from suppliers, creating huge balances of both accounts payable and receivable. The sum of all receivables in the Czech Republic was Kc 200 billion ($7 billion) in 1993.

Královopolská was in relatively good shape during this period because it managed to keep its receivables under control (which also helped its position with banks). Receivables exceeded payables in 1989 and 1990, but not after that. Královopolská managers attacked the receivables problem vigorously, sending its sales force to customers to work out swaps of receivables, sometimes in three-way trades facilitated by the Ministry of Finance or assisted by consultants from Brno Technical University, who provided computer tracking. As a result, Královopolská's receivables were less than payables in the critical years 1991–93, thus easing its cash flow problem and reducing its need for bank credit to cover receivables.

It was almost impossible for firms to obtain long-term loans. Komercni Banka (Commercial Bank), Královopolská's bank, "is very good if we don't ask for anything," said finance director, Jirí Cupák, in 1993. "Getting credit is very difficult. We need 100 percent collateral for loans. This is new for us. It is uncomfortable. Before the revolution it was no problem to pay off loans. Now we have trouble. Sometimes we are late. We only get one-year loans now."

However, Královopolská was more fortunate than other companies. It was able to obtain short-term credit because, according to one manager, "We pay our interest." The Czech government was cooperating with Královopolská in long-term financing and trade credit for major export business, notably equipment for the aluminum refinery on which Iran later defaulted.

When asked about the effect of his country's economic condition on Královopolská in 1993, Zdenek Pánek said, "I cannot change the economic conditions. If I want to cross a dirty river I either have to build a bridge or jump in and swim." He knew he could not "clean the river" himself, so he had to find another way to the other side and was likely to get a bit muddied in the process.

Management's Actions During the Transition

After initial privatization in 1992, Královopolská changed its top management, which acted quickly to reorganize the company, to try to instill a new corporate culture, to improve technology and quality, and to develop new markets.

THE MANAGERS Královopolská managers reported that even before the Velvet Revolution, people were promoted more on the basis of merit than party membership. Technical qualifications were always more important than political favor. In this way Královopolská was different from the central planning norm. After the revolution, political history was not a major factor in top management succession. Former Communist Party officials left the company, but technically qualified rank-and-file party members stayed. None of the new top managers was old enough to have been deeply involved in the failed Prague Spring of 1968 or the reprisals that followed it. The average age of the eleven top managers in 1992 was only 43.

Karel Jelínek was chairman of the board, a position the company established in 1992. He simultaneously served as the company's strategy director. Jelínek was the only top manager after privatization who was also a top manager in 1989, when he was production director (before that he was the company's technical director). He was also unusual by being just over 50 years old in 1993. Together, Pánek and Jelínek, who was technically educated, ran Královopolská.

The board appointed Zdenek Pánek to be the new general manager in July 1992 after initial privatization (his predecessor had served just 1 1/2 years and then left the company). Pánek, 37, was the director of the RIA division at the time, but was not in top management of the company when the Velvet Revolution occurred. Pánek was unusual because he was trained in economics rather than engineering. Before he headed the RIA division, he was a field sales engineer. Pánek had no Western-style management training and spoke neither German nor English. However, he mandated that all top managers learn English in company-provided classes (although he himself did not do so). Pánek had a keen sense of the importance of customers' needs and of the necessity to change the corporate culture to one that rewarded quality, customer orientation, financial performance, and initiative rather than longevity or party membership.

The rest of the management team was composed of engineers who had devoted their entire working life to Královopolská. Vladimír Relich was typical. He was educated at Brno Technical University in engineering. He started at Královopolská as a designer, then became head of a department (chemical equipment), then head of all design, then head of central product development, and finally technical director and a member of top management in 1992.

ORGANIZATIONAL STRUCTURE Královopolská was organized by function until 1991, like most Czech firms. The functional departments were production, technical, economy, commercial, personnel, and training. The economy function under central planning involved record-keeping for cash, production, and wages. Královopolská eliminated this function in 1991 and created instead a finance function. The former commercial function was remade and renamed as the strategy function (headed by Jelínek), and a marketing function, for which there was no need before, was added.

The company reorganized in 1991 into six product divisions: (1) Water, Wood, and Light Chemical Equipment, (2) Heavy Chemical Equipment, (3) Specialty (Nuclear) Chemical Equipment, (4) Cranes and Steel Structures, (5) Metallurgy, and (6) RIA. The first three of these divisions manufactured tanks and pipes for sale to engineering and construction firms. RIA was a small engineering and construction firm for water treatment plants, purchasing some of its product from the Water, Wood, and Light Chemical Equipment division.

In 1992, three more functions were added to the organization: quality assurance, information systems, and legal. Also in 1992 after initial privatization, Královopolská created an inside board of directors, to whom the general manager was responsible, and an outside advisory board, consistent with Czech law.

The RIA division became the largest division in terms of revenue generated from external customers by 1993 (other divisions sold some of their output to RIA so that the reckoning of division size in terms of revenue understates the size of the other divisions in terms of volume (Figuire 1).

In 1994, the first three product divisions, distinguished primarily by the technical aspects of their products (e.g., size and specifications) and their end use (e.g., petrochemical plants, water-treatment plants, or nuclear-power stations) were combined into one division. The intent was to eliminate unproductive interdivisional competition, combine similar technologies and production processes, make all divisions into strategic business units with decentralized profit responsibility, and move further away from technologically determined collections of products to a customer focus.

NEW MARKET DEVELOPMENT Královopolská made progress in new market development and marketing after 1991. The company's objectives were to build business relationships with large Czech chemical and construction companies, to create new distribution channels for export business independent of its former export trading company, and to focus on West European markets for both export and joint venture opportunities, while also maintaining its trade links with Russia.

The company succeeded in setting up a joint venture with seven other Czech companies for trading with Russia, and it established country-level trading entities in Slovakia, Poland, and Italy. However, gaining new customers, especially in new markets, was difficult in this industry because most relationships between equipment makers and customers were long-standing. Attractive brochures and new, modern logos for each division made a good impression, nevertheless.

QUALITY INITIATIVES AND COMPETITIVENESS Quality, customer-orientation, and competitiveness became the mantra of top management. Královopolská started a company-wide quality assurance program in 1992 and obtained ISO 9000 and other relevant certifications by the end of 1994. The technical director, Vladimír Relich, said, "Our products were always high quality, but they did not meet West European standards. Now we have certificates of quality according to West European standards. Our products are higher in quality than Italian products." The company produced glossy brochures with eye-catching graphics that illustrated Královopolská's commitment to quality, including language about the firm's trust in its employees to demonstrate Královopolská's commitment to quality in every interaction with customers.

Relich conducted an international competitive analysis of every Královopolská product in 1993 and 1994, including the products' technical specifications, quality, price, and perceptions of customer service. Competitors included companies from France, Italy, and Germany. The competitive analysis yielded six categories of products: those that were excellent (7 percent), competitive (44 percent), needed innovation (11 percent), needed a price decrease (21 percent), needed marketing support (7 percent), and were not competitive (11 percent). The competitive analysis served as an important guide for investment and divestment decisions during 1994 and 1995.

RESEARCH AND TECHNOLOGY Before the change in governments, Královopolská obtained research and development services centrally from the CHEPOS organization, as was usual in centrally planned economies. However, the breakup of CHEPOS during privatization meant that its R and D unit began competing with Královopolská, so Královopolská began to build its own R and D capability through alliances with universities and technical colleges and through a newly created internal R and D group. This was inevitably going to be a slow process, according to Relich.

"We need to buy or license technology," said Relich. "It is an acute problem. We need a partner who does not need a return right away." While no such licensing deal occurred immediately, Královopolská did in fact make commercial agreements with firms in Austria and Finland for long-term purchases of high-technology components by Královopolská that would enable it to make, sell, and deliver new products.

CORPORATE CULTURE Královopolská's managers identified the company's culture as a persistent challenge. The history of the firm favored manufacturing. "Production was king," said one manager. "Management tries now to put sales on top and production next. We are still learning to make what the customer wants." He went on to say, "Our main problem is not on-time delivery. The problems are inside the company—deciding that one contract is more important than another and writing a contract that we can fulfill."

Karel Jelínek, speaking in 1994, discussed the difficulty Královopolská was having in changing the corporate culture from one that focused on following orders to one that focused on customers, quality, and initiative.

> We are trying to change the corporate culture, and have been trying hard for three years. The easy thing is to write it down. The hard thing is to persuade the people so that they are convinced about the company. We want our customers to feel the corporate culture from every employee. This is the basis of a market-based approach. We introduced a motivation system. It is too early to show results. People don't like to take responsibility for their own decisions. They expect other signatures on decisions [an attitude left over from the communist era]. We are trying to find people who are not afraid of big decisions. I like people who make me lose sleep because of the possible bad results of their decisions. I prefer these people to those who wait for my approval.

Královopolská was attempting to create a new corporate culture in several ways. In addition to public statements by the general manager and the chairman of the board, Královopolská used management training, competitive analyses, merit-based performance appraisal, and incentive pay (with "disappointing results so far," said one manager in 1994) to create a more customer-, quality-, and performance-oriented climate. Pánek's observations in 1993 illustrate the challenge.

> All of top management went through training to use human and democratic elements of management. But these management techniques can't be applied completely. We need order. To make order we use a direct system which is supported by control. The old system was disorder.
>
> We want a new organizational culture in our new company. The new culture is presented on video. Each meeting of managers begins with the video. They see the video until order is there. In the worst cases they work on Saturdays seeing the video. After three Saturdays it is okay because even the worst cases don't want to come in for a fourth Saturday.

Pánek's frustration with the pace of change echoed Jelínek's:

The hardest problem is changing the people. In one year we worked out all of our quality control manuals with detailed descriptions about quality and activities. Now we fight the human factor. Even though we describe the changes in detail, people don't behave that way. They go back to the old system in which they were raised. We change people with pressure.

Královopolská also needed to create an awareness of costs, prices, profits, and financial discipline. Cupák noted, "We have a problem with management internally—with financial controls. They [financial controls] are good discipline but managers don't like them." Královopolská created a company bank to stimulate accountability and competition among divisions for corporate resources. Each division was required to show a profit or run the risk of being sold.

Královopolská steadily reduced its employment during the five years after the Velvet Revolution, from 5,469 in 1989 to about 3,250 at the end of 1994. Top management planned to reduce employment by about 400 people per year for at least two more years.

Strategic Options

During the transition, Královopolská top management sought to determine a clear strategy of development for the company with the objective of creating an added value very close to the value usual in the prosperous companies in the developed European countries. When Pánek became general manager in 1992, his first effort was to create a genuine business plan. Working with people from the Consulting Institute of the Prague School of Economics, top managers addressed a number of key issues, among them the objectives of the company, its strategy, and its structure. At this early stage, top management agreed to focus on quality, customer orientation, and improved discipline and motivation among employees. "We will increase productivity by 15 percent, decrease costs by 10 percent, increase efficiency by 10 percent, and extend our business into new markets," said Pánek.

Královopolská managers remembered and used a gem of Czech management wisdom from the 1930s that predated the central planning era. It is written in *Královopolská Strojírna Brno 1992,* a company document, and it refers to the famous Czech industrialist, Tomas Bat'a:

> We follow the well-known—and nearly forgotten but today often repeated Czech saying: "Our customer, our master."

Pánek's emphasis on "order" and incentive pay was also part of the Bat'a philosophy.

Královopolská undertook business transformation largely without the help of Western consultants. Pánek believed that Western consultants were too interested in the consultant's way of doing things and not familiar enough with Czech business practices, circumstances, and culture to be of much use. One bad early experience with a German consulting firm that delivered a product (for DM 38,000) that was little more than copies of publicly available documents supported his point of view. "Consultants," he said, "don't respect Czech management. They forget that we did not just jump down from the trees." He added, "We think, therefore we are." His allusion to philosophy in this statement was his way of emphasizing the cultural sophistication and intellect of Czech managers.

Pánek elaborated his view of consultants. While admitting that Královopolská needed help with financial management and business strategy, he did not want to hire consultants. "I would prefer that no one give us company-to-company advice. If someone wants to share the risk with us they should become our employee and solve problems together."

He also was determined not to use foreign trade companies as had been the practice prior to the revolution. Instead, he wanted his own sales people.

> The goal of the new business policy is to build up a high quality sales network of our own people in the Czech Republic. Also outside the Czech Republic. In this region [Western Europe] we don't know the markets and don't have enough qualified people. Our philosophy is our employees will become qualified. We will hire people from abroad rather than consultants. We will pay them in their currency.

Exactly how Královopolská could best achieve its business objectives was yet to be determined in 1995. Two questions needed to be resolved: What should the company's main business be? On what basis could the company best compete?

The company's long history, pride in Czech management, and skepticism of Western advice indicated that it should try to remain independent and evolve its current lines of business. Exports to Russia could be expected to continue, although they were not very large. Progress was being made in developing new business in the Middle East, where Královopolská's products and prices were well-suited, and where it had some experience from central planning times, although this business was unstable.

Domestically, Královopolská was lucky that one of its businesses, water-treatment plant equipment, was in a growth industry. The Czech government adopted a policy of extending long-term, low-interest loans to municipalities to help them finance improved water treatment facilities. Laws passed in 1992 mandated ecologically conscious water systems that adhered to environmental regulations and required Czech company participation. Company managers projected an expenditure of Kc 16 billion (about $575 million) on municipal water treatment projects in the Czech and Slovak Republics over the five-year period 1993–98.

One of the options that especially interested Pánek and Jelínek was to develop vigorously the RIA division and become a full-service engineering company that would design, engineer, manufacture, and build complete projects, especially water treatment projects with which RIA already had some experience. Both industrial waste water treatment and purification of drinking water would be included. The RIA division was small in employment (only 280 employees in mid-1993), marginally profitable (Kc 16 million in 1992, amounting to about 3 percent of its sales), but already fast-growing. Pánek thought a reasonable goal for the RIA division was that it should account for 70 percent of total company revenue by 1997; in 1995 it reached two-thirds.

However, Pánek believed that Czech investment in water-treatment facilities would begin to decrease in a few years, and he recognized the value in turnkey capability for chemical plants and steel construction. To this end, Královopolská established a small chemical engineering group reporting directly to Jelínek in 1994 and a small engineering capability in the cranes division at the same time. Relich, when asked about the company of the future, said,

> We will be in all our businesses [in the next five years], but we must change the base of our divisions. I hope the new chemical engineering department will be a separate division and will support production in the shops by getting orders and work in the field [within five years]. We will operate as an engineering company with a majority of the company moving toward turnkey projects in cranes, water, and chemical plants. We will start with small projects and learn for bigger projects, step by step. Technology know how has to be purchased because it is owned by big American and German companies.

The RIA division purchased many of its components from the other divisions. About 30 percent of the Chemical and Ecological division's output went to RIA. In early 1995, the RIA division opened every job to outside suppliers for bids. "Every RIA job is contested for suppliers. When the internal price is competitive, our division will get the job. Now RIA buys more products from other companies than from our division," said one manager.

However, the RIA division faced growing competition for the water-treatment business from former state-owned enterprises that now also were privatized and restructured. One of the competitors was Sigma Engineering in Olomouc (a large town near Brno), which was strong in industrial waste water treatment, the forecasted fastest growing market segment. Sigma also posed a threat to RIA internationally because it had a good foreign sales unit and an international network left over from its role as a hard-currency earner before 1989. Another competitor was Vitkovice in Ostrava (a steel town near Poland), which was expert in small water-treatment plant projects for villages of 1,200 or fewer inhabitants, a segment in which Královopolská acknowledged it was less efficient and less experienced. However, Vitkovice relied on outside installers and thus did not do complete turnkey projects. Three other potential competitors, Kunst, Eko, and Fontana, were created in 1992 out of a larger former state plant but they were hampered by quality problems with their biological water treatment products. Because they were new, they did not have the name recognition and reputation that Královopolská had.

Numerous engineering and manufacturing firms were potential competitors in Western Europe. For example, Královopolská benchmarked itself against forty firms that manufactured equipment for water treatment plants, among them English firms (A.G. Tapsell, Ltd.; Contra-Shear Development, Ltd.; Jones Attwood, Ltd.; Kee Services, Ltd.; and Three Star Environmental Engineering, Ltd), German firms (Durr GmbH, Eisenbau Heilbronn GmbH, Fischtechnik GmbH, Handke Stengelin GmbH, Kary GmbH, Preussag Hoell GmbH, and Windolf AG, among others), and Dutch firms (Hubert Stavoren BV, Kopcke Industrie BV, and Landustrie Maschinenfabrik BV).

Královopolská needed newer technology than it had if it was to be up to world standards, and, like all Czech companies, it needed capital for plant modernization. For these reasons Královopolská explored a foreign partnership. A joint venture between the RIA division and a West European partner was sought to improve access to West European markets that otherwise were proving difficult to enter.

Discussions took place in 1993 with a French firm in which the RIA division was especially interested. The business of the proposed joint venture would be to build water treatment facilities in the Czech Republic. The French company was interested in the venture because it needed a Czech partner to satisfy government requirements for domestic participation. Královopolská saw the joint venture as a means for obtaining technology—the French firm would license its technology to the joint venture—and capital. Technology included not only physical processes and hardware, but also management techniques such as cost accounting. Capital was needed for investment in new plant and equipment. In addition, Královopolská's Chemical and Ecological division might be able to sell its products to the French parent. The risk of doing business with the French firm was that it allowed easy access to the potentially large Czech and Slovak markets—possibly trading away future business for current business. In the end, the two firms failed to reach an agreement. Though revenue for the joint venture was projected to grow rapidly, profits were expected to be too small and too far in the future for the French firm.

When the management buyout occurred in January 1995, the company's financial situation captured more of Pánek's attention than ever before. Cash flow and debt repayment had to become priorities. The company was the collateral for the bank loan used for the purchase. More profitable business was needed soon. When asked about the future, one top manager said,

> Královopolská is among the top third of all Czech companies. Our products are competitive. We have good equipment and well-trained people. The future is relatively good for us, but the next two years are important for us. It is necessary to change people's minds. The highest level people have changed, but it is necessary to go to the lowest level. We will change the base of our business. We want to become an engineering company. Results from turnkey projects will be two times higher in five years. We will buy parts from outside Královopolská. The result will be a more competitive environment within our own divisions.

Pánek reviewed Královopolská's position in mid-1995. He knew he would have to harness Královopolská's resources quickly to return to profitability, but he was not sure what his priorities should be. How would the domestic and international environments change in the near future? What opportunities and threats would those changes present to the firm? What resources and capabilities did Královopolská possess now or need to develop for the future? What were the firm's strengths and weaknesses? Should the firm emphasize a particular product line? Should business development efforts focus on the domestic Czech market, on Western Europe, on Eastern Europe, or on the developing countries? What additional internal organizational and cultural changes would be needed? Pánek was sure only that a specific business plan concerning how to proceed next was vital to Královopolská's future success.

Questions

1. Track the evolution of Kralovopolska's business interests from 1945 onward. What were the key events?

2. What were the key changes in the Czechoslovak and Czech economies during and after the Velvet Revolution? What were the consequences of these changes at the company level?

3. What mindset changes were necessary to compete in the new Czech economy? Why was Kralovopolska having a tough time instituting change?

4. What were the strengths, weaknesses of Kralovopolska? And what opportunities and threats faced them? What strategy options do they have?

Notes

1. Case by Karen L. Newman and Stanley D. Nollen of Georgetown University. It appeared in the *Case Research Journal* 16:3–4 (Summer–Fall 1996). Reproduced with permission.

2. The Velvet Revolution occurred in the late November and early December of 1989 in Czechoslovakia, a few months after the fall of the Berlin wall. The name *Velvet Revolution* comes from the fact that the existing communist government resigned without bloodshed after massive peaceful demonstrations in Prague, giving way to a democracy almost overnight. The first post-communist government was led by Václav Havel, a playwright who had been imprisoned under the former regime for his political views. Havel, though inexperienced in government, was a strong symbol of the moral underpinnings of the Velvet Revolution and the future for Czechoslovakia.

3. The Czech economy was the most state-owned of all Soviet bloc countries (97 percent of industry was state-owned). However, the Czech Republic had a history of capitalism. Between World Wars I and II, it was among the ten largest economies in the world. Privatization of large state-owned enterprises began in 1992. In some cases, foreign companies bought Czech firms in deals brokered by the government (e.g., Volkswagen bought Skoda), or foreign companies established joint ventures with Czech companies [e.g., ABB, the Swiss-Swedish multinational, and První Brnenska Strojírna (PBS) created a new 67%–33% joint venture company from part of the formerly state-owned PBS]). However, the largest share of Czech industry was privatized by vouchers. Because the government wanted to privatize industry quickly, but Czech citizens had insufficient funds to buy companies, enterprises were practically given away. Each citizen could buy a voucher book for Kc 1,000, which was about one week's pay for the average industrial worker at that time. Vouchers could be spent on shares of stock in companies or sold to investment funds that purchased shares. Between 1992 and 1995, the vast majority of large firms were privatized via this voucher method.

EXHIBIT 1
Business Under Central Planning

The Czechoslovak economy was nearly totally state-owned, and mostly closed to trade and investment with the West from 1946 until the end of 1989. Most industries had only a few large enterprises, and in many instances they were monopoly producers of individual products. This meant that enterprises were typically very big (relative to the size of the market) and specialized in the production of just one product or a narrow product line. Enterprises in an industry were typically combined under a single "konzern" such as CHEPOS. The needs of the Soviet Union shaped the production program of many enterprises.

Producers in centrally planned economies typically were only manufacturing plants (an enterprise was termed a *statni podnik* or state plant). They were producers, but they did not do other business functions such as marketing and finance. Distribution and sales were handled by separate state-owned trading companies, research and development was either centralized or assigned to a separate enterprise, and capital investment decisions were made by the state. Banks disbursed funds and collected "profits" but did not make lending decisions. There were no capital markets.

The goal of the firm that all managers understood was to meet the production plan set by the central ministry. Successful managers were those who could skillfully negotiate a favorable plan and who knew how to produce the required quantity. Another goal imposed on firms by the state was to provide employment for everyone. There was little concern about costs, prices, money, or profits.

Most managers were technically trained, and all top managers were necessarily members of the Communist Party; selection depended on political as well as business considerations.

Enterprises were centralized and hierarchical and typically had a functional organizational structure in which the production function was the biggest and most important. Other functions usually included a technical function, a commercial function (this was mainly order-filling and shipping), an economy function (mainly financial record-keeping), a personnel function, and others depending on the company's type of business.

Large enterprises during the socialist era typically provided a wide range of housing, recreation, education, and medical services to their employees. For example, Královopolská had 579 flats (apartments) for workers and a "staff quarters building" with 478 beds (later to become the company hotel), four recreation centers, a youth pioneer camp, and a heated swimming pool near the factory (open to townspeople as well), three kindergartens and one nursery that could accommodate all employees' children, a clinic located within the plant area staffed by thirteen full-time and five part-time medical doctors, and two kitchens that prepared hot meals for all three shifts, served in ten dining rooms on the grounds.

TABLE 1
Economic Conditions in Czechoslovakia, 1989–1995

Variable	1989	1990	1991	1992	1993[a]	1994[a]	1995[a]
Gross domestic product, real %	0.7[b]	−3.5	−15.0	−7.1	−0.9	2.6	4.6
Industrial production, real %	0.9	−3.7	−23.1	−12.4	−5.3	2.3	9.0
Consumer price inflation, %	1.4	10.0	57.8	11.5	20.8	10.0	8.9
Interest rate, %[c]	5.5	6.2	15.4	13.9	14.1	13.1	12.8
Exchange rate, Kc/US$, annual average	15.1	18.0	29.5	28.3	29.3	28.8	26.3
Unemployment rate, %	na	0.3	6.8	7.7	3.5	3.2	3.0

[a]Czech Republic only
[b]Net material product
[c]Lending rate to state enterprises

TABLE 2
Královopolská's Selected Income Statement Data, 1989–1995 (Kc million current)

	1989	1990	1991	1992	1993	1994	1995
Revenue							
Sales of products and services to external customers	1826	1737	1560	1915	2430	2304[a]	3143
Other revenue	1	8	82	114	155	1204	1041
Total revenue	1827	1745	1642	2029	2585	3508[a]	4184
Costs							
Cost of purchased inputs and services	na	na	1145	1360	994	1987[a]	2105
Labor, depreciation, reserves of which: wages	448		459	461	731	1018	1072
		244	263	261	322	327	311
Change in inventory and work in process	−132	153	−438	−97	710	−169	617
Total costs of production	na	na	1166	1724	2435	2836[a]	3794
Other costs	na	na	270	104	253	723	226
Total costs	1788	1625	1436	1828	2688	3559[a]	4022
Profits							
Gross margin from production (Sales of products less costs of production)	na	na	394	191	−5	−532	−651
Profits before taxes (total revenue less total costs)	39	120	204	201	−103	−51	162

[a]Data for 1994 include internal sales of one division to another, and costs of purchased inputs by one division from another; therefore, these figures cannot be compared to 1993 or earlier data. However, profit figures are comparable.

Other revenue includes sale of fixed assets, penalties received, and interest from financial investments. Reserves were first set aside in 1993 for plant and equipment repair and upgrades in the amount of Kc 180 million. Change in inventory and work-in-process appears in the revenue section of the income statement in the company's annual reports as is the German custom; we have moved it to the costs section. Other costs include costs of selling fixed assets, penalties paid, gifts, write-off of accounts receivable, interest paid on loans, and exchange rate losses.

Source: Královopolská *Annual Reports* for 1992–95.

FIGURE I
Revenue of Královopolská Divisions (Kc million current)

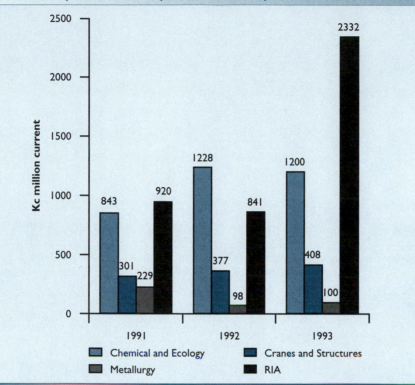

Source: Královopolská *Annual Reports.* Division-level data not available after 1993.

Chemical and Ecology Division (formed in 1994 by consolidation of three former divisions)

Water, Wood, and Light Chemical Division: Tanks, tubes, filters, pumps, evaporators, agitators, furnaces, and other small equipment for water-treatment plants, wood-working machinery, and light chemical industries

Heavy Chemical Division: Tanks, towers, reactors, heat exchanges, hydrogenerators, extractors, autoclaves, steam reformers, and other large scale equipment for the chemical and petrochemical industries

Special Chemical (Nuclear) Division: Special purpose, highly engineered steel, alloy, and plastic equipment for nuclear-power stations and water-treatment plants

Cranes and Steel Structures Division

Bridge cranes, gantry cranes, special cranes, steel buildings, and road and railway bridges for industrial and commercial applications designed in accordance with customers' requirements and erected on-site

Metallurgy Division

Production of tubes, elbows, castings, forgings, steel and alloy ingots, and annealing, tempering, and surface treatment of metallurgic products for the chemical and other industries

RIA Division

Design, engineering, production, delivery, installation, commissioning, and maintenance of complete water treatment, chemical, and nuclear plants as turnkey jobs

PART TWO

World Business Analysis

Competing in world markets requires careful preparation and analysis. Part 1 examined the forces shaping the global marketplace. As noted, the influence of globalization, modernization, and westernization are variable. This section starts with an assessment of how regional geography and history have shaped economic development and influenced regional cultures. Their effects are assessed in Chapter 4. From regional evaluations come national market analyses (detailed in Chapter 5) as executives zero in on key countries for in-depth assessments. This process involves looking at national histories, geographies, current political, economic, and international positions and reviews of commercial environments.

Finally, because many industries and competitors in today's markets tend to be global or regional, their activities need to be monitored and assessed. This includes evaluations of global, regional, and national demands and assessments made of supply-chain activities. These topics are examined in Chapter 6. These analyses provide key inputs into the international planning and market screening processes described in Chapter 7, as well as the strategy-crafting activities outlined in Chapters 8 through 13.

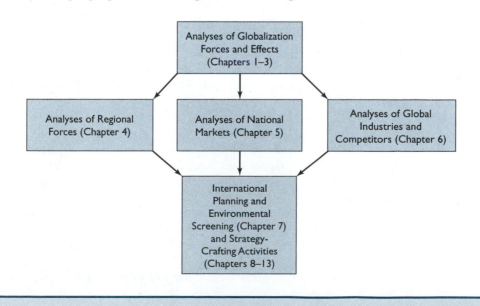

Chapter Four

Geopolitical Analyses of Regional Markets

∿

THE NEW WORLD ORDER

The fall of communism in the late 1980s and early 1990s prompted much new thinking about the post-cold war world. Enter Samuel P. Huntington. In his Clash of Civilizations and the Remaking of World Order, Huntington sets out the seven (or eight, including Africa) civilizations that are set to dominate world culture and politics in the 1990s and beyond.[1]

Western civilization includes the Catholic and Protestant cultures of Western Europe, North America, Australia, and New Zealand and promotes the ideas of individualism, liberalism, human rights, equality, the rule of law, democracy, free markets, and the separation of church and state. So pervasive are these ideas that a "West versus the Rest" mentality influences economic progress worldwide and has resulted in returns to grassroots cultures: "Asianization," "Hinduization," and re-Islamization. Noted anthropologist Harry Triandis concluded that: "the values that are most important in the West are least important worldwide."

Latin American civilization, despite its geographic ties to the Western hemisphere, evolved from its European immigrant roots differently to North America, becoming more authoritarian, adopting a different religion (Catholicism), and incorporating native American ways into its regional culture.

Slavic Orthodox civilization includes Russia, Greece, and other Eastern European countries with Orthodox traditions. While geographically close to Western Europe, religious, ethnic divisions, and ultimately political differences caused major divergences.

African civilization, especially south of the Sahara, has retained its many cultural identities despite the long presences of colonial powers, though today there are appearances of the establishment of an African identity.

Islamic civilization has a religion-based identity whose philosophies and lifestyles have caused frictions with Christianity (from the crusades onward, and currently in Africa), Orthodox Serbs in the Balkans, Judaism in Israel, Hindus in India, Buddhists in Burma, and Catholics in the Philippines. Given this history, Huntington correctly forecasted continued conflicts in the later 1990s.

Japanese civilization, despite owing much to its Chinese origins, has managed to preserve its Asian cultural identity while becoming a world economic power to rival the West.
Hindu civilization has religion as its centerpiece; this religion defines many aspects of Indian and Sri Lanka societies.

The Chinese-Confucian civilization has influenced mainland China and had significant impacts on mainstream Asian culture.

These eight civilizations are differentiated by history, language, culture, tradition, and religion. They are, as Huntington notes, "the product of centuries. They will not soon disappear."

How and why regions develop is the theme of this chapter. Executives are interested in regional development for a number of reasons, including the following.

1. As indicated in Huntington's assessments, regions delineate major cultural differences among world markets. Evaluating such differences provides key inputs into the viability of regional strategies.
2. Regional geographies and histories also affect the commercial development of individual countries within those regions, for example, the extent to which nations trade with adjoining countries or have formed political bodies to aid their economic development. These intra-regional commonalities also enhance the viability of region-based strategies.
3. Such studies give managers valuable background for assessing individual markets in their regional contexts (see Chapter 5).

For simplicity's sake, the world is divided into six regions. Western civilization is divided into its North American and Western European components; Latin America and the Slavic nations of Eastern Europe have their own sections; Islamic and African civilizations are discussed under Middle East/Africa; the Japanese, Hindu, and Chinese Confucian civilizations are examined in their Asian context.

Hence, in this chapter you will learn:

- An overview of world regions is presented to illustrate the uneven nature of regional development in the worldwide context and the economic supremacy of North America, Western Europe, and Japan.
- Regional profiles are presented of North America, Latin America, Western Europe, Eastern Europe, Africa and the Middle East, and Asia to summarize major geographic characteristics, historical and cultural perspectives, and commercial developments. These geopolitical profiles provide insights to link past histories to current situations and provide backgrounds to evaluate present-day market potentials and problems.

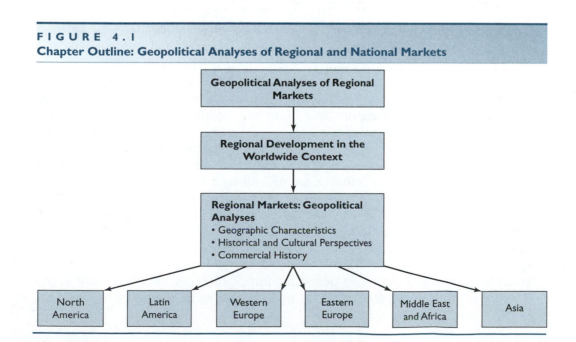

FIGURE 4.1
Chapter Outline: Geopolitical Analyses of Regional and National Markets

INTRODUCTION: THE IMPORTANCE OF GEOPOLITICAL STUDIES

Geopolitical studies relate a region's geographic circumstances and history to its economic development and present day-situation. Its importance stems from the need to understand how a region evolved and what factors influenced that evolution. For business people, this provides valuable background for:

- Recognizing what historic factors have impacted regional development and giving insights into the regional forces affecting economic and cultural development of nations within the regional grouping.

- Understanding regional and national ethnic and linguistic compositions: Africa, for example, has over 2500 ethnic groups. Cameroon, Chad, Ghana, Nigeria, the Sudan, and Tanzania all have over 100 ethnic groups. This affects regional efforts to integrate economically and politically and national efforts to unite economically and culturally.[2]

- Understanding how climates and topography can affect communications and infrastructure development. Climatic variability affects food production. Good topographies with few major geographic obstacles facilitate road, rail, and telecommunications infrastructures. Poor topographies are significant hindrances to economic development. Climate and geography determine not only access to resources but also how easily new technologies, ideas, and lifestyles diffuse through regions and nations. Natural barriers such as mountain ranges, deserts, and oceans can isolate countries and limit learning potential.[3]

REGIONAL DEVELOPMENT IN THE WORLDWIDE CONTEXT

The world has more that 230 countries and more than 6 billion people. Of these countries, fewer than forty-five nations are fully industrialized and are mainly to be found in North America and Western Europe. Many others are at various stages of economic development. Throughout Eastern Europe, Latin America, the Middle East, Africa, and Asia, only Japan stands out economically, although South Korea, Taiwan, Singapore, and China have emerged as Asian powerhouses.

Most of the world's countries, then, are in the process of industrializing. But development is slow, and major differences still exist between the developed and developing worlds with respect to industrial output and the populations that output must support. Some of the differences are shown in Table 4.1.

North America, Western Europe, and Australasia (Australia and New Zealand) together account for over 59 percent of the world's gross domestic product (32.1 percent, 26 percent, and 1.3 percent, respectively), but they have less than 13 percent of the world's population. At the other end of the spectrum, Latin America, Middle East, Africa, and Asia account for just over one-third of world gross domestic product (36.8 percent, but only about 25 percent without Japan), but these regions have more than 80 percent of the world's population (more than 4 billion people).

T A B L E   4 . 1
World and Regional Analyses: Gross Domestic Products and Populations

	2002 Gross Domestic Product ($bn)	2002 Average GDP per Capita	Range per Capita	POPULATION ESTIMATES AND PROJECTIONS (MILLIONS)		
				2002	2010	2020
Africa	$1,144	$1,410	$90 (Ethiopia) to	811	1,009	1,230
	3.3%		$3,782 (Mauritius)	13.1%		
Middle East	$858	$1,963	$434 (Yemen) to	214	N/A	N/A
	2.5%		$19,628 (UAE)	3.5%		
Asia	$7,743	$2,425	$175 (Myanmar) to	3,534	4,075	4,495
	22.2%		$30,990 (Japan)	57.2%		
North America	$11,186	$35,143	$23,620 (Canada) to	300	330	358
	32.1%		$36,440 (U.S.)	4.8%		
Latin America	$3,076	$3,353	$429 (Haiti) to	529	583	642
	8.8%		$16,497 (Bahamas)	8.6%		
Western Europe	$9,065	$23,215	$2,700 (Turkey) to	457	523	521
	26.0%		$42,300 (Norway)	7.4%		
Eastern Europe	$1,343	$4,634	$185 (Tajikistan) to	310	320	330
	3.8%		$11,031 (Slovenia)	5.0%		
Australasia	$469	$19,833	$14,730 (NZ) to	23	33	37
	1.3%		$22,090 (Australia)	0.4%		
Totals	$34,884			6,178	6,862	7,601
	100%			100%		

Source: Adapted from "Indicators of Market Size," *Country Monitor*, (December 23, 2002): 1–12; *OECD Observer* (Paris, December 2002); World Economic Outlook Database (September 2003) at www.imf.org; and *World Almanac* 2001 (Mahwah, N.J.: World Almanac Books, 2002), 838–39.

Population projections in Table 4.1 suggest that this situation is not likely to change much before 2020. Africa and Asia, in particular, show steep increases in population. Their excess labor supply situations make them attractive to international corporations as manufacturing sites, especially for labor-intensive operations. They also represent significant potential for long-term market growth. Industrially advanced countries are attractive because of their immediate market potential, their educated populations, and their advanced technologies.

It is apparent that the world's major regions—North America, Latin America, Western Europe, Eastern Europe, the Middle East, Africa, and Asia—have developed unevenly, but why? In the following section, we look at the geographic and historical shapers of regional development and the major factors influencing commercial development.

NORTH AMERICA

Geographic Characteristics

North America, for the purposes of this book, consists of the United States and Canada (see Figure 4.2). Although Mexico and the Central American countries are geographically part of North America, their culture and history make them part of Latin America.

F I G U R E   4 . 2
North America

Geographically, Canada and the United States extend from the frozen Arctic south to the semitropical states of Florida, Texas, and California. In terms of area, Canada is the second largest country in the world (smaller than Russia but larger than China), and the U.S. is the fourth-largest nation. The two countries share a 3,000-mile border, and, because of the rigorous climate in northern Canada, almost 80 percent of Canadians live within 100 miles of the U.S. border. It has abundant raw materials and is the world's second-largest gold and uranium producer. Canada ranks third-largest in silver and fourth in copper, and it has good supplies of nickel, zinc, lead, potash, and wood-related products.[4] The United States has abundant supplies of coal and petroleum (though it has less than 1/20 of world oil reserves) and is well-stocked in sulfur, phosphates, lead, and aluminum. Massive twentieth-century exploitations of iron ore deposits depleted U.S. stocks, and the iron and steel industry now depends on Canadian and imported ores.

Historical and Cultural Perspectives

Prior to colonization in the fifteenth and sixteenth centuries, North America was inhabited solely by Indian tribes and Inuit. Although Columbus "discovered" what is now the United States in 1492, serious colonization did not begin until the seventeenth century, with the landing of the Mayflower in 1620. From that time on, the continent attracted immigrants of many nationalities—French, English, Scots, Irish, Dutch, Scandinavian, Belgian, Polish, Russian, German, Czech, Italian, and Greek, among others. Despite the influx of many northern and central European immigrants, the Anglo-Saxon culture, with English as the primary language, emerged as the dominant cultural force that, along with an absence of major geographic obstacles, facilitated national unification efforts. Protestant settlements set early precedents in religious orientations, and the Protestant work ethic emerged as a key factor promoting economic development. From this melting pot emerged the United States that eventually liberated itself from the British in 1776. The Civil War of 1861–65 further unified the country, and the abolition of slavery established an egalitarian ethos that was to become a cornerstone of the new republic.

> Of course, America had often been discovered before, but it had always been hushed up.
>
> —*Oscar Wilde, 19th-century Irish playwright*

The 1823 Monroe Doctrine asserting national sovereignty confirmed U.S. independence from Europe, and a benevolent climate facilitated population growth from 4 million Europeans in 1790 to 24 million by 1850. Immigration continued to be a key factor in North American growth, with 33 million Europeans establishing themselves in the U.S. between 1820 and 1950.[5] Their immigrant status and willingness to explore the new continent (particularly after the gold rush to California) confirmed the pioneering attitudes of the new North-American settlers. The new immigrants' willingness to set up their own self-supporting communities and survive in often hostile environments contributed to current U.S. values of self-reliance and individualism. Privilege and hereditary rights, the cornerstones of English society, were superceded by a work ethic that made economic contributions the primary measures of societal status.

> How is it that we hear the loudest yelps for liberty among the drivers of slaves?
>
> —*Samuel Johnson, 18th-century English author*

The ethnic composition of the United States reflects its history. It includes around 1.5 million native Americans, and about 30 million each of Hispanics and African Americans. Its economy, the strongest in the world, is based largely on the principles of competition and free trade. The United States accounts for approximately 5 percent of the world's population, but it is responsible for over a quarter of the world's gross domestic product (GDP). The nation's 280 million consumers have an average income of over $35,000 per person, making the United States the world's largest national mass market. Its currency, the dollar, is widely used and accepted around the world in commercial transactions of every description.

> When the whites came, we had the land and they had the bibles. Now they have the land and we have the bibles.
>
> —*Chief Dan George, 20th-century Squeamish chief*

The French were the first to colonize part of Atlantic Canada in 1604, while the British came in 1755. Today, these two groups comprise Canada's major ethnic segments. About one-fourth of Canada's 30 million population are French-speaking and live mainly in the province of Quebec. Differences between French-speaking and English-speaking Canadians have resulted in movements to separate Quebec from Canada.

Commercial History

Early North American settlements were agriculturally based. Northern areas focused on shipbuilding, fisheries, grains, and spirits. Mid and southern regions grew rice, tobacco, and cotton and harvested timber. As international demand for cotton increased, the southern states established the plantation method of mass-market cultivation. This required labor, so 5 million slaves were imported from Africa by 1860. This occurred at a time when European nations were backing away from the slavery concept.[6]

The 1840s discovery of gold in the western hinterlands prompted renewed interest in the region, and the nation slowly began to unite. The region's geographically benign environment permitted the first trans-U.S. railroad to be opened in 1869, and by 1900 the telegraph was providing transcontinental communications.

America is like a gigantic boiler. Once the fuse is lighted under it, there is no limit to the power it can generate.

—Winston S. Churchill, 20th-century British statesman

The U.S. industrial revolution occurred between 1870 and 1920. By 1914, U.S. output exceeded that of Britain, France, and Germany combined. By the 1920s, it produced 40 percent of the world's coal and half its manufactured goods. Economic progress was halted with the 1929 stock market crash that signaled the onset of the Great Depression.[7]

Compared to Western Europe and Japan, the U.S. emerged from World War II in good economic condition, and as these economies were rebuilt, U.S. companies reigned supreme in international markets during the 1950s and 1960s. By the 1970s, Japanese and European firms were successfully challenging U.S. supremacy. But U.S. commitments to foreign markets remained strong, and by 2002, U.S. foreign direct investments (FDI) accounted for $1.5 trillion out of a world total of over $7.1 trillion. Canada's $273 billion placed the North American contribution to the world economy at $1.77 trillion.[8]

The U.S. has always had a close commercial relationship with Canada, with these two countries constituting the world's largest bilateral trading relationship. To cement economic relations, the United States and Canada signed a North American Free Trade Agreement (NAFTA) in 1988. The aim of this agreement was to gradually remove barriers to trade and investment for most industrial, agricultural, and service sectors. In 1994, Mexico joined NAFTA. In the 1990s, the thirty-four nations of the Americas (North, South, and Central) began discussions to establish a Free Trade Agreement of the Americas (FTAA) by 2005, the eventual aim being to establish a western hemispheric free trade area by that date.

With the United States as the world's largest industrial economy, the country's affluent mass market makes it a magnet for exporters. In 2002, the U.S. trade deficit (how far import values exceed export values) stood at over $400 billion. Of this, the NAFTA countries (Canada and Mexico), Japan, and China PRC each exported over $50 billion more to the U.S. than they imported from the U.S. These trade imbalances have been a source of commercial and political friction between the U.S. and these nations.

LATIN AMERICA

Geographic Characteristics

Latin America encompasses Mexico, the countries of Central America, the island states of the Caribbean, and South America (see Figure 4.3). While geographically and economically, Mexico is part of North America, culturally and historically it is associated with Latin America.

Climatically, much of Latin America is affected by its proximity to the equator. Central America, the Caribbean, and northern South America have predominantly subtropical climates. The countries to the south (e.g., Argentina, parts of Brazil and Chile) are more varied. Argentina is mainly temperate, but its northern regions (such as Chaco) are hot and humid, while its southern parts (such as Patagonia) are on the cold side (subantarctic). Brazil is subtropical in the north and center but temperate in the south and east. Chile, which runs nearly 4,000 miles along South America's west coast, is subtropical in the north and subantarctic in the south.

Topographically, South America is similar to those parts of Asia that are on the same latitude. Earthquakes are common. Much of the area is made up of rain forests (Brazil of over 60 percent rain forest, Bolivia, 40 percent). There are also some very fertile lands, and coffee, cocoa, corn, and livestock are principal exports from these regions.[9]

South America has considerable natural resources. Chile is a world-class producer of copper, which is extracted from the mineral-rich Andes Mountains. Bolivia is a major source of tin, zinc, and silver; and Peru is an important source of silver and copper. Venezuela and Mexico are oil producers, as is Colombia, which also produces 90 percent of the world's emeralds and has the largest coal reserves in Latin America.[10]

> You can divide the countries of the world into two types—the ones that have all the oil and the ones that do not. We have oil.
>
> —*Jose Lopez Portillo, ex-president of Mexico*

Historical and Cultural Perspectives

Many Latin American countries had Indian civilizations predating the arrival of European settlers in the fifteenth and sixteenth centuries. The Mayas in Guatemala and Mexico, the Aztecs in Mexico, and the Incas in Peru and adjacent areas all had advanced forms of social and economic organization many years before the European conquests. Only the Aztecs survived to meet the colonialists of the sixteenth century.

Modern Latin American history dates from the early 1500s, when the Spanish colonized most of the region and the Portuguese occupied Brazil. It remained under Spanish and Portuguese rule for over 300 years. Independence was won from 1810 to 1824, when the Revolt of the Colonies occurred against Spain—Mexico, Honduras, Peru, Panama, Nicaragua, Venezuela, and Colombia in 1821;

> When asked by anthropologists what the Indians called America before the white man came, the Indian said simply "Ours."
>
> —*Vine Deloria, U.S. author*

FIGURE 4.3
Latin America

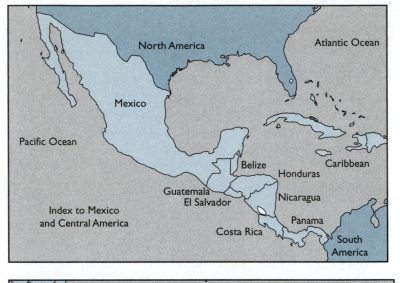

Ecuador in 1822; Costa Rica in 1824; and Bolivia in 1825. Brazil became independent from Portugal in 1822.

After independence, there were opportunities to form a U.S.-style of government for Latin America. A number of factors militated against Latin American unification. Geography was a factor. Sheer size, rapid rain-forest growth, and rough mountain terrain made region-wide linkages difficult. Social ethnic problems were evident as Spanish/Portuguese populations were slow to integrate with native Indian groups. Traditions of self-government were not present, and the Catholic Church emerged as a major landowner with political power.[11]

The Southern European influence on Central and South America is evident in language (with the adoption of Portuguese in Brazil and Spanish elsewhere), religion (with Roman Catholicism being imported), and social class, with Southern European hereditary class systems being adopted. Ethnically, Latin Americans are mixed. Many are descendents of the Spanish and Portuguese conquerors, but there are large groups of native Indian peoples, mixed groups of Indian and white ancestry (called *mestizos*), and blacks. Many dialects are spoken; Guatemala, for instance, has more than twenty.[12]

U.S. interest in Latin America increased in the early twentieth century when it helped Cuba become independent, took effective control of Puerto Rico, and intervened militarily in Mexico and Nicaragua. During this time, the U.S. became a major provider of foreign capital to the region. By the 1930s, this was reversed as President Roosevelt's "good neighbor" policies mandated noninterference in Latin American affairs. This was to continue until the 1960s and 1970s when Soviet influences caused a rethink in U.S. policies.

Commercial History

Of the early Latin American civilizations, the Incas (who occupied today's Ecuador and Chile) were the most advanced. They built more than 10,000 miles of roads, kept records, and had village-based communities. Light industry in precious metals was encouraged, though all output and facilities were centrally controlled.[13]

Early interest in the region was spawned with the discovery of silver at Potosi, and the Spanish mined more than 16,000 tons by 1650. South America continued to be the primary source of European silver well into the nineteenth century. Other commodities, nitrates, oil, and minerals were also discovered, and Argentina's agricultural potential was exploited as refrigerator ships made the nation's meat supplies available to world markets in the 1880s.[14]

In the seventeenth century, tobacco, hardwood, and coffee crops became extensively cultivated in the Caribbean and Brazil. Lacking indigenous labor to work plantations, landowners imported slaves from Africa to both North and South America. The sixteenth to the nineteenth centuries saw close to 10 million slaves transplanted into the Americas.[15] Commodities and agriculture continued to be the region's primary industries well into the twentieth century.

The collapse of the global economy in the 1930s caused civil unrest throughout the region. Military coups occurred to maintain order, and foreign company expropriations were common up to and through the 1970s. Problems continued during this time as protected economies contributed to major inflationary problems, with annual price increases often in the hundreds or

> *Those who make peaceful revolution impossible make violent revolution inevitable.*
>
> —*John F. Kennedy, U.S. president*

thousands of percents. Latin American currencies at that time were not accepted in the world marketplace, and excessive imports resulted in major hard-currency debts (backlogs) owed to the industrialized nations.

In the 1980s, privatization and movements toward market blocs followed the democratization trends and opened up Latin markets to trade and investment. The year 1993 saw the Central American Common Market replaced by the System of Central American Integration (Honduras, El Salvador, Guatemala, and Nicaragua, with Panama joining in 1996). This consolidated the regionalization of Latin American trade that started with Mercosur in 1988 (Brazil and Argentina, with Paraguay and Uruguay joining in 1991) and the 1992 rejuvenation of the Andean Pact Bloc (Colombia, Venezuela, Ecuador, Peru, and Bolivia). In 1994, the free-trade movement continued with the FTAA move to establish a western hemispheric free trade area by 2005.[16] By 2003, Mexico had signed a free-trade agreement with the European Union, and talks between Mercosur and the EU had been initiated to establish the beginnings of a pan-Atlantic free-trade area.[17] Privatization trends have also been apparent throughout much of Latin America. Airlines, banking, energy, metals, public works, and telecommunications have been among the many industries being moved into the private sector.

WESTERN EUROPE

Geographic Characteristics

Western Europe extends from the Scandinavian countries of the north (which are on the same latitude and have similar weather patterns as Alaska) to the Mediterranean coastlines of Spain, France, and Italy (see Figure 4.4). From west to east, the region extends from Iceland (Greenland is Danish but has only 55,000 people over a huge, largely frozen area) to the borders of Poland, the Czech and Slovak Republics, Hungary, and Yugoslavia (now Serbia and Montenegro). The major economic powers of Western Europe—the United Kingdom, France, and Germany—have temperate climates, with moderate winters (by Scandinavian standards) and warm (60–70 degrees Fahrenheit) rather than hot summers (unlike the southern United States and North and Central Africa, where temperatures are typically in the range of 80–90 degrees Fahrenheit). Historically, Western Europe's clement conditions have encouraged the year-round pursuit of economic activities. The extensive coastlines and geographic compactness of the region aided early trade and development efforts and facilitated the establishment of commercial infrastructures.

Today, for the most part, Western European countries are highly developed and heavily urbanized, with up to 60 percent of populations concentrated around major urban areas. Public transportation systems (buses, subways, trains) are common within cities, and there are extensive train and bus networks between urban areas. The region's geographic compactness facilitates international travel and commerce and contributes greatly to the interrelatedness of European economies.

Historical and Cultural Perspectives

An early unification of Europe was brought about by the Romans who, in the 500 years from about 100 B.C. to A.D. 400, established an empire spreading over western and central Europe, parts of the Middle East, and the northern

Europe

1. Slovenia
2. Croatia
3. Bosnia-Herzegovina
4. Yugoslavia
5. Albania
6. Macedonia
7. Greece
8. Estonia
9. Latvia
10. Lithuania
11. Russia
12. Belarus
13. Moldova
14. Romania
15. Bulgaria
16. Hungary
17. Austria
18. Czech Republic
19. Slovak Republic
20. Poland
21. Denmark
22. Netherlands
23. Belgium
24. Luxembourg
25. Germany
26. Switzerland
27. Italy
28. France
29. Andorra
30. Spain
31. Portugal

Africa

1. Western Sahara
2. Senegal
3. Gambia
4. Guinea-Bissau
5. Guinea
6. Sierra Leone
7. Liberia
8. Ivory Coast
9. Burkina Faso
10. Ghana
11. Togo
12. Benin
13. Cameroon
14. Equatorial Guinea
15. Gabon
16. Congo
17. Central African Republic
18. Rwanda
19. Burundi

* United Arab Emirates

> We adore titles and heredities in our hearts, and ridicule them with our mouths.
>
> —*Mark Twain, 19th–20th-century U.S. writer*

> We want to draw a line below which we will not allow persons to live and labor, yet above which they may compete with all the strength of their manhood. We want free competition upwards; we decline to have free competition downwards.
>
> —*Winston S. Churchill, 20th-century British statesman*

> The art of [European] taxation consists of plucking the goose so as to get the most feathers with the least hissing.
>
> —*Jean-Baptiste Colbert, 17th-century French finance minister*

African coast from Egypt in the east to Morocco in the west. However, the overthrow of the Romans by tribes from the east in the fifth century caused chaos throughout much of the region. Not until the eleventh century did economic stability emerge through a form of political organization known as feudalism, in which kings gave lands to loyal vassals, who then formed a military aristocracy. Monarchies and aristocracies laid the basis for a hereditary social-class system, the vestiges of which are still apparent in European society today.

Western Europe's colonizing activities of the sixteenth through nineteenth centuries established the region as the political and economic leaders worldwide. Its supremacy in maritime technologies enabled Britain, France, Spain, Portugal, and Holland to extend their influence across the globe. Their military technologies (firearms, cannon) allowed them to dominate larger countries that had inferior technologies. Trade was an important part of their colonizing activities. From the Americas came tobacco, maize, potatoes, and tomatoes. Silk and spices were imported from China and India respectively, and tea and coffee came from China and Africa.

Britain was the first country to industrialize (between 1750 and 1830), with iron, steel, steam power, electricity, and the factory system playing key roles in its economic growth. From the British lead, technology and economic growth spread to the continent (France, Germany, Belgium, and the Netherlands) during the nineteenth century and, through their colonizing activities, to the world's other continents. Economic progress was interrupted during World War I (1914–18) and World War II (1939–45). With the development of atomic weaponry and rivalry between the superpowers, the United States and the Soviet Union, Western Europe's political role in the world declined, though it is enjoying a rejuvenation as the European Union.

The 1930s economic slump left its mark on European society and politics. Until that time, the region had been the bastion of world capitalism. However, the widespread misery caused by the Great Depression caused European politicians to rethink their economic and social policies. The 1940s and 1950s saw many European countries becoming mixed economies, with some governmental ownership of key industries (e.g., utilities, energy, transportation, telecommunications) and extensive welfare-state provisions to protect citizens during economic downturns. The 1990s movement toward a more competitive European market saw many of the nationalized industries being sold into the private sector, and the number of economies in social-welfare systems increased.

To pay for Western Europe's mixed economy, personal tax rates are high compared to those of non-European countries. High personal income taxes are the norm in many of the leading European economies, including the Netherlands, Spain, Italy, and Germany. But, in return, Western Europeans enjoy extensive public transportation systems (e.g., rail and buses, many of them subsidized), free medical and hospital facilities and mostly free education, including the university level.

From a cultural perspective, Western Europeans continue to maintain national distinctions, but there are sufficient similarities in their historical backgrounds and economic circumstances to give meaning to the term *European*. Fifteen of the nineteen Western European countries have per capita gross domestic products of more than $15,000.

Europe's feudal history and its heredity monarchies and aristocracies have contributed to the maintaining of a social-class system based mainly on lineage ("family pedigree"). Europeans are born into specific social classes and generally stay there unless they are recognized for significant educational or professional achievements. Otherwise, social mobility (the ease in moving between social classes) is limited.

Politically, Europe is more left-wing than the United States. European politics are complex. Many countries have multiparty systems, including left-wing socialist parties (left of center but not communist). Socialists favor high government involvement in industry and high taxes to finance broad social-welfare programs. Right-wing conservative parties favor low taxes, low government involvement in the economy, and less-extensive welfare programs. The diversity of European political interests results in many national governments being formed from multiparty coalitions (for example, Switzerland, Italy, and Germany).

> They who say that all men are equal speak an undoubted truth, if they mean that all have an equal right to liberty, to their property, and to their protection of the laws. But they are mistaken if they think men are equal in their station and employments, since they are not so by their talents.
>
> —*Voltaire, 18th-century French philosopher*

Commercial History

The Romans were the first economic unifiers of Europe, building roads, formalizing trade routes, making region-wide laws, and establishing a common currency (the dinarius). After that time, a thousand years elapsed before international commerce reestablished itself. Europe's geography, its extensive coastlines and geographic compactness, made the region a "natural" for international trade. Also, with its food needs taken care of by regular harvests, commercial objectives could be pursued without major distractions. The Italians were early international pioneers. They were using bills of exchange in the thirteenth century, and, by the fourteenth century, they were bringing back gold from (what is today) Mali and trading in Asia.

By the fifteenth century, superior rigging (sails), rudders, compasses, and maps enabled ships to sail longer distances. Within a century, Ferdinand Magellan of Spain and Francis Drake of England had circumnavigated the globe, and the rush to colonize the world had begun. During the next three-hundred years, Europeans colonized the Americas, Africa, the Middle East, and parts of Asia. Trade ensued, and European society benefited from introductions of rice, potatoes, tobacco, coffee, tea, and sugar. As time passed, colonized nations got new technologies, medicines (and some new diseases to go with them), sanitation systems, foods, agricultural techniques, hospitals, schools and education (often by missionaries).[18]

In the seventeenth century, British, German, Belgian, and Dutch banking systems had caught up with the Italians, and paper monies, checks, and joint stock companies were common. By the middle of the eighteenth century, Europeans were establishing trading posts, ports, forts, and military bases worldwide.

The sun never sets on the British Empire because God would never trust an Englishman in the dark.

—*Anonymous*

At this point, Britain began to move to the forefront of colonial and trading activities. Backed by a powerful navy, British commercial interests became the primary drivers of foreign policy. By the end of the eighteenth century, a world trading system could be said to exist. Its continued development meant that by the early twentieth century, Europeans could get rubber from Asia, teak from Burma, oil from Persia, and bountiful commodities from all over the world.

By the 1914 outbreak of the First World War, London was the center of world commerce. The sterling bill of exchange was the primary lubricant of world trade, and currencies were valued in gold. Britain was the world's dominant trader and a major exporter of capital to the Americas. Limited liability companies, banks, commodity and stock exchanges were spreading around the world. European innovations, such as the steam engine and the petroleum engine, were revolutionizing the transportation of goods through automobiles and steam-driven trains and ships.

The two World Wars decimated European industry and made de-colonization inevitable. To compensate for its post-1945 loss of colonies and to ensure that Europeans would never again go to war with one another, Western Europe began to integrate economically. In 1952, the Coal and Steel Community was founded. In 1957, the Treaty of Rome established economic blueprints for a "United States of Europe," known as the European Economic Community (EEC). Signatories to the initial agreement were France, West Germany, Italy, the Netherlands, Belgium, and Luxembourg.

Not long afterward, in 1960, the European Free Trade Association (EFTA) was founded in Stockholm. EFTA's intentions were to abolish trade tariffs between member countries (Austria, Iceland, Norway, Portugal, Sweden, Switzerland, Finland, Ireland, Denmark, and the United Kingdom). In 1973, the United Kingdom, Denmark, and Ireland joined the European Economic Community. Greece joined the European Community (EC, formerly known as the EEC) in 1982, and Spain and Portugal were added in 1986. In 1995, Sweden, Austria, and Finland entered what became the European Union.

The next step in European unification was the abolition of nontariff barriers within the EC. This was largely achieved in 1992 as national industry standards were largely harmonized and barriers to the Europe-wide movements of products, labor, and capital were removed. In 1994 came the Maastricht Agreement, by which the European Community was renamed the European Union. Target dates were set for a common currency (the euro) in 1999 and for further joint political involvement on a European scale (e.g., common foreign and security policies).

European multinationals have long been active in world markets and currently account for about half of the world's $7.1 trillion of foreign direct investment. Unilever is one of the world's largest manufacturers of consumer goods. Shell (a Dutch-British concern) is cur-

There have been many definitions of hell, but for the English the best definition is that it is a place where the Germans are the police, the Swedish are the comedians, the Italians are the defense force, Frenchmen dig the roads, the Belgians are the pop singers, the Spanish run the railways, the Turks cook the food, the Irish are the waiters, the Greeks run the government, and the common language is Dutch.

—*David Frost and Antony Jay English, authors*

rently the biggest gasoline retailer in the United States. Many European companies have global brand names and reputations, including the Dutch electronics giant Philips; Britain's Rolls Royce; Germany's BMW, Mercedes, Porsche, and Volkswagen; Sweden's Saab and Volvo cars and Ericsson electronics; Finland's Nokia; Swiss-owned Nestle and Hoffman-Laroche; and Germany's chemicals giant Bayer (the aspirin-chemical conglomerate), Hoeschst, and BASF.

The trend toward privatization (i.e., turning over government-controlled industries such as telecommunications to private ownership) and deregulation (permitting industries to compete openly against one another) picked up pace during the 1990s. Between 1990 and 2002, privatization sell-offs totaled $675 billion, with Britain leading the way, lowering public ownership stakes from 12 percent of GDP to about 2 percent. In continental Europe, the rate of privatization has been less impressive. The sheer sizes of government-controlled industries have made companies such as Deutsche Telekom and France Telecom difficult to privatize. As a result, twenty-four of Europe's largest companies by market capitalization retain some government ownership. The French government, for example, still owns over 50 percent of France Telecom and Air France and retains a 25 percent stake in auto manufacturer Renault.[19] Deregulation has brought about increased competition in Europe's insurance, telephone services, and energy sectors as companies previously sheltered as national monopolies began to compete nationally and internationally.

Eastern Europe

Geographic Characteristics

Eastern Europe, for the purpose of this book, includes the Central European countries of Poland, the Czech and Slovak Republics, Hungary, the Balkan countries, Russia, and the other states of the former Soviet Union (see Figure 4.5). Its northern shores touch the Arctic Circle. The largest part of the region comprises the states of the former Soviet Union, which together take up one-sixth of the world's land mass, span eleven time zones, and are about two-and-one-half times larger than the United States.

Throughout its history, Russia, the strongest of these states, tried to maintain control over this vast geographic expanse. A major coordination problem has been the inhospitable climate of large parts of the region, which varies from subarctic temperatures in the north to desert-like temperatures in the south. Only the western and southern borders of Russia are free from long, severe winters. Hungary, Poland, and the Balkans all enjoy moderate climates, but northwestern Russia bordering Finland is on the same latitude as Alaska and has similar severe weather.

Russia and the other former Soviet states are well-endowed with natural resources. Russia, for example, has natural gas, coal, gold, oil, diamonds, copper, silver, and lead. Azerbaijan's economy is based on oil and natural-gas production, as is Kazakhstan's. Only the region's inability to sustain agricultural output (because of climatic problems) prevented it from being self-sufficient in resources.

FIGURE 4.5
Eastern Europe in Its Global Context

Europe

1. Slovenia
2. Croatia
3. Bosnia-Herzegovina
4. Yugoslavia
5. Albania
6. Macedonia
7. Greece
8. Estonia
9. Latvia
10. Lithuania
11. Russia
12. Belarus
13. Moldova
14. Romania
15. Bulgaria
16. Hungary
17. Austria
18. Czech Republic
19. Slovak Republic
20. Poland
21. Denmark
22. Netherlands
23. Belgium
24. Luxembourg
25. Germany
26. Switzerland
27. Italy
28. France
29. Andorra
30. Spain
31. Portugal

Africa

1. Western Sahara
2. Senegal
3. Gambia
4. Guinea-Bissau
5. Guinea
6. Sierra Leone
7. Liberia
8. Ivory Coast
9. Burkina Faso
10. Ghana
11. Togo
12. Benin
13. Cameroon
14. Equatorial Guinea
15. Gabon
16. Congo
17. Central African Republic
18. Rwanda
19. Burundi

* United Arab Emirates

Historical and Cultural Perspectives

Much of Eastern Europe's post-1500 history is tied to Russia, whose vast geographic size and military power have been dominant shapers of regional development. Its size and tempestuous climate made industrialization difficult. Early attempts to modernize were made by Peter the Great (1672–1725). But Russia's feudal system, with the czar at its center, assured that its citizens remained in serfdom until the twentieth century. Some change occurred as Czar Alexander II undertook key economic and governmental reforms. But agricultural output remained at inadequate levels. What food and products the nation could manufacture could not be distributed, due to inadequate infrastructures. Much of it ended up at the Imperial Court in Moscow. This created much discontent among the population at large and ultimately led to the Russian Revolution of 1917–18. Engineered by Vladimir Ilyich Ulyanov, known as Lenin, and Leon Trotsky, the revolution caused the downfall of Czar Nicholas II. Lenin ruled the USSR until his death in 1924.

World War I and the revolution decimated Russian society and industry, and it was not until 1927 that Russia regained its 1914 levels of production and prosperity. Joseph Stalin, who succeeded Lenin, was ruthless in eliminating opposition. Millions were executed or died in labor camps during the Great Purge of 1936–38.

The USSR was pulled into World War II in 1941 when, despite Stalin having signed a nonaggression pact with Adolf Hitler, the Germans attacked Russia. This resulted in the "Unholy Alliance" among the United States, Britain, and the USSR, which eventually forced Germany to capitulate in 1945.

The postwar boundaries of Eastern Europe, or the Eastern Bloc, as it was called, were determined in 1945 at the Yalta Conference by Franklin D. Roosevelt, Winston Churchill, and Joseph Stalin. This arrangement culminated in an "Iron Curtain" separation of Eastern and Western Europe and led to communist influence over Romania, Bulgaria, Poland, Hungary, Czechoslovakia, Yugoslavia, Albania, and East Germany. In the postwar period, U.S.–Soviet tensions increased as both countries used their global influence to encourage noncommitted countries to adopt capitalistic or communistic philosophies. The wars in Korea, Vietnam, Nicaragua, and Afghanistan all grew out of East-West conflicts over economic and political philosophies. The cold war between the United States and the USSR continued until the breakup of the Soviet Union in 1991.

After years of government control and repression, the seeds of reform in the Soviet Union were sewn in 1985 when three aging Soviet ex-revolutionaries (Andropov, Chernenko, and Brezhev) died within the space of three years and Mikhail Gorbachev emerged as the Soviet leader. Intent on reform, Gorbachev initiated restructuring of the Soviet economy *(perestroika),* which reduced governmental interference in economic matters and allowed greater freedom of expression *(glasnost).* Censorship was almost eliminated, and, in 1989, elections were held. *Perestroika* and *glasnost* spread to most other Eastern Bloc countries. Poland and Hungary both held elections in 1989 and began to transform their state-controlled economies to allow more capitalist influences. East Germany

> *Communism never came to power in a country that was not disrupted by war or corruption, or both.*
>
> —*John F. Kennedy, U.S. president*

> *A single death is a tragedy, a million deaths is a statistic.*
>
> —*Joseph Stalin, Russian leader, 1924–53*

> We have slain a large (Soviet) dragon, but now we must live in a jungle filled with a bewildering variety of poisonous snakes, and in many ways the dragon was easier to keep track of.
>
> —*R. James Woolsey, ex-director, U.S. Central Intelligence Agency*

and West Germany were reunited in July 1990. The 1990s saw the countries of Central and Eastern Europe implement democratic reforms, free up prices, cut back state subsidies to industry, and privatize state enterprises. Results have been mixed, but the seeds of capitalism appear to have been sewn.

In Russia, Gorbachev's reforms encouraged expression of the great cultural diversity present in the Soviet Union. The USSR comprised more than 100 ethnic groups, speaking eighty different languages and writing in five different alphabets. The Russians were the dominant ethnic group, with 140 million out of 270 million people.[20] In 1991, a new order was created. The provinces within Russia came together (after considerable turmoil in some regions, notably Chechnya) to become the Russian Federation. The former USSR, minus Latvia, Lithuania, and Estonia, reconstituted itself as the Commonwealth of Independent States (CIS) in 1992. In 1998, Tajikistan was invited to join the CIS-4 customs union comprising Russia, Belarus, Kazakhstan, and the Kyrgyz Republic.[21]

Commercial History

Peter the Great started the gargantuan task of modernizing Russia. He cultivated experts and shipwrights, and modernized administrative systems and the army. Technical schools were established, and European standards and manners were adopted. Advantage was taken of iron ore deposits and gun foundries, built, as factories increased from 100 to 3000 during his reign.[22] Unfortunately, this modernization impetus was not maintained after Peter's death in 1725, and Russia lapsed back into feudalism. Russia's backwardness became apparent as its navy suffered a major defeat at the hands of the Japanese in 1905.

World War I and the 1917–18 Communist Revolution transformed Russia. Joseph Stalin succeeded Lenin in 1924. He collectivized agriculture (i.e., he placed all private farms under public ownership) and initiated comprehensive industrialization programs. By the late 1930s, 80 percent of Russian production came from plants established since 1928.[23]

Communism prospered with Stalin's consolidation of neighboring territories into the Union of Soviet Socialist Republics, and with further additions from the 1945 Yalta Conference. The next four decades saw East-West tensions rise with the cold war between the U.S. and the USSR. The advent of Gorbachev's *perestroika* after the mid 1980s established a platform for the economic restructuring of Eastern Europe.

> I cannot forecast to you the action of Russia. It is a riddle wrapped in a mystery inside an enigma.
>
> —*Winston S. Churchill, 20th-century British statesman*

With democratic processes, *glasnost,* and *perestroika* as the driving forces, the economic reform of Eastern Europe established momentum. In 1992, Hungary, Poland, and the Czech and Slovak Republics signed a Central European Free Trade Agreement (CEFTA), covering industrial and agricultural products and drawing together 85 million consumers. This agreement set the stage for these countries' applications to join the EU. Additionally, Estonia, Latvia, Lithuania, Slovenia, Bulgaria, and Romania also applied for EU membership and eventually joined in May 2004.

Further Eastern-Western European negotiations have moved the two regions toward a united Europe. In 1994, partnership agreements were also concluded to normalize trade relations between the EU, Russia, and the Ukraine.[24]

Privatization of former state-owned businesses has been brisk, with an estimated $200 billion of assets returned to private shareholders. These assets currently account for 55 percent of regional GDP. Privatization methods have included sales to strategic owners (foreign companies, or grouping firms in the same industries to gain scale economies and synergies), insider buyouts to managers and workers (in Russia and Slovenia), financial intermediaries to market and manage privatized portfolios (in the Czech Republic, Slovakia, and Poland), and voucher schemes (in Moldova, Belarus, Romania, and Bulgaria).[25]

Operating conditions remain difficult for international companies in Eastern Europe. These include fluctuating economic fortunes, deficient physical infrastructures (which affect distribution and logistics), lack of commercial legal infrastructures (affecting contract enforceability, for example), and crime problems (hooliganism, pilfering from work, corrupt bureaucracies, and racketeering/extortion). Backlashes to market reforms, uncertainties over political succession and cabinet reshuffles, and a 1998 run on the ruble eroded confidence in Russia's investment prospects. However, 1999–2001 saw an economic resurgence as $8 billion of foreign direct investment was injected into the Russian economy.[26]

> When money speaks,
> the truth keeps silent.
> —*Russian proverb*

Nevertheless, companies have been attracted to Eastern Europe for a number of reasons. The accession of many former Iron Curtain countries into the EU in 2004 has made them attractive propositions for international firms. In Russia, foreign companies, such as British American Tobacco, Mercedes, and Sun Interbrew (a joint venture between Interbrew of Belgium and India's Sun Brewing), are slowly moving beyond Moscow and St. Petersburg to establish distribution in urban centers throughout the region. Danone (France), Ehrman (Germany), and Campina (Netherlands) have built plants to service the growing milk and dairy markets. Avon (U.S.) and Oriflame (Sweden) have done the same in the cosmetics sector to challenge market-leader Estee Lauder (France).[27]

MIDDLE EAST AND AFRICA

Geographic Characteristics

The Middle East Geographically, the Middle East is comprised of countries between the Mediterranean and Afghanistan (see Figure 4.6). Culturally, the term includes the North African countries from Morocco to Egypt, because they, like the Middle Eastern countries, are also predominantly Muslim. Turkey is also considered part of the Middle East, although it is militarily allied with Western Europe.

Much of the Middle East has a harsh desert climate. In Saudi Arabia, daytime temperatures often reach 130 degrees Fahrenheit. The flat rock surfaces that dominate Arabian landscapes often are too hot to touch, but, in winter, freezing

FIGURE 4.6
Middle East and Africa in Their Global Contexts

Europe

1. Slovenia
2. Croatia
3. Bosnia-Herzegovina
4. Yugoslavia
5. Albania
6. Macedonia
7. Greece
8. Estonia
9. Latvia
10. Lithuania
11. Russia
12. Belarus
13. Moldova
14. Romania
15. Bulgaria
16. Hungary
17. Austria
18. Czech Republic
19. Slovak Republic
20. Poland
21. Denmark
22. Netherlands
23. Belgium
24. Luxembourg
25. Germany
26. Switzerland
27. Italy
28. France
29. Andorra
30. Spain
31. Portugal

Africa

1. Western Sahara
2. Senegal
3. Gambia
4. Guinea-Bissau
5. Guinea
6. Sierra Leone
7. Liberia
8. Ivory Coast
9. Burkina Faso
10. Ghana
11. Togo
12. Benin
13. Cameroon
14. Equatorial Guinea
15. Gabon
16. Congo
17. Central African Republic
18. Rwanda
19. Burundi

* United Arab Emirates

temperatures are normal at night. In most of the Middle East, rainfall is low (except in Yemen, whose mountains catch the Indian monsoons and receive around twenty inches of rain per year). Hence, obtaining sufficient water for drinking and crop irrigation has been an important objective of most Middle Eastern states. Egypt has the River Nile; others (e.g., Saudi Arabia, Kuwait, and United Arab Emirates) have plans for national irrigation systems, including dams for rivers and desalination plants to take the salt out of seawater.[28]

Poor in water resources, the Middle East is rich in petroleum—the region contains about 60 percent of the world's oil reserves. During the 1980s, in oil-producing Arab countries, a gallon of gasoline sold for the U.S. equivalent of 20 cents, but the price of a gallon of bottled drinking water was $2.40.[29]

> Climate has much to do with cheerfulness, but nourishing food, a good digestion, and good health much more.
>
> —*Alexander Rhodes*

Africa Africa's size and proximity to the equator are dominant factors in the region's development. Similar to South America, its climate is hot and humid, and its dense tropical vegetation has inhibited regional infrastructure development. These factors have limited Africa's abilities to establish internal communications and markets and made the diffusions of modern technologies difficult. Of the 50-plus countries in Africa, only the Republic of South Africa is reasonably well-developed. One persistent problem over much of Africa has been inconsistent crop-raising climates. Droughts, poor crop-growing soils, soil erosion, and poor management of available agricultural land have resulted in inconsistent food supplies. Famines in Ethiopia, the Sudan, and neighboring countries have been regular occurrences.

Africa, however, has other resources. In northern Africa (i.e., Africa north of the Sahara), there is oil in Libya, Morocco, and Algeria. In central and southern Africa, there are diamonds, copper, and other valuable minerals. These resources, discovered in the nineteenth and early twentieth centuries, prompted the European colonization of Africa.

> In understanding Black Africa, geography is more important than history. The geographic context is not all that matters, but it is the most significant.
>
> —*Fernand Braudel, 20th-century French historian*

Historical and Cultural Perspectives

The Middle East and North Africa While Europe was immersed in the "Dark Ages" of the first millennium, the Middle East and North Africa prospered. Its mathematicians invented trigonometry and algebra. Its scientists were at the forefront of innovations in astronomy, optics, chemistry, pharmacy, and medicine. United by its language (Arabic) and religion (Islam), Middle Eastern military prowess and culture spread from the seventh century to include North Africa and parts of both Asia and Europe. From the fourteenth to the early twentieth century, the Turkish-based Ottoman Empire consolidated these gains and was a key player in world politics until 1918.[30]

During the nineteenth and twentieth centuries, the Arabian Peninsula and North Africa were under the influence of Britain and France, whose interests in the region were colonial and oil-based. Table 4.2 shows the duration of foreign domination and current political characteristics. The Turkish Ottoman Empire, the previous occupier, had its interests curtailed during the 1914–18 war as Arab insurgents, lead by T. E. Lawrence (Lawrence of Arabia) fought for their independence. It was not until the 1920s and 1930s that nation-states were

TABLE 4.2
Foreign Domination of the Middle East and North Africa

Country	Foreign Domination	Forms of Government	Political Bodies
Algeria	France 1848–1962	Democratic Republic, socialist oriented	Two houses: 3 major parties
Bahrain	Britain 1861–1971	Monarchy (emirate) capitalist oriented	2001 charter for a democratic body; no political parties
Egypt	Britain 1914–22	Arab Republic	454-person elected People's Assembly main body
Iran		Islamic Republic: 290-seat Parliament	24-person Council of Guardians approve candidates and laws
Iraq	Britain 1924–32	Republic socialist oriented	2; 1 represented
Israel	Britain 1923–48	State with prime minister as head of government	Knesset is the parliament, 120 members elected
Jordan	Britain 1923–46	Monarchy	Senate appointed by the king; deputies are tribal dominated
Kuwait	Britain 1899–1961	Monarchy (sheikhdom), state capitalist	None
Lebanon	France 1923–46	Republic: President is always Christian; prime minister is Sunni Muslim; speaker is Shia	128-seat Parliament has equal seats for Christians and Muslims
Libya	Italy 1912–47	Republic (military), socialist oriented	1
Morocco	France 1912–56	Constitutional monarchy has broad powers	270-person upper house; 325-person lower house
Oman	Britain 1853–1951	Monarchy (sultanate)	State Council is appointed; 110-member elected lower house advises Sultan
Qatar	Britain 1916–71	Monarchy (emirate)	Emir consults citizens; appoints council of ministers and judiciary
Saudi Arabia		Monarchy advised by Council of Ministers; 14 regional emirs	90 appointed members of Consultative Council
Sudan	Britain 1898–1946	Republic: Head of state elected; political "groups" legalized 1999	360-seat National Assembly suspended (2003); 1 party
Syria	France 1923–46	Republic: President and 3 VPs	250-seat legislature "People's Council"—essentially 1 party
Tunisia	France 1881–1956	Republic: President, prime minister, council of ministers	182-seat Chamber of Deputies elected
UAE	Britain 1853–1971	Federation of emirates, state capitalist	None
Yemen Republic	Britain 1893–1967	Republic: President and 301-member legislature	Villages, towns ruled through sheiks—local tribal leaders

Sources: Tuma, Elias H. *Economic and Political Change in the Middle East,* (Palo Alto: Pacific Books, Publishers, 1987). *Culture Grams 2003.* (Utah: Brigham Young University).

formed. Egypt became independent in 1922 and Saudi Arabia in 1932, and Persia became Iran in 1935. The establishment of separate Israeli and Palestinian states, advocated originally under the Balfour Declaration in 1917, was not implemented until 1948, when the United Nations (with U.S. and British backing) divided Palestine (as it was then known) into Jewish and Arab states. In 1948, the state of Israel was officially created. Since then, numerous disputes have occurred over the establishment of an independent Palestinian homeland, and a number of conflicts have ensued (notably in 1967 and 1973).

A lack of economic progress after 1945 caused major frustrations in the region. Soviet infiltration into Arabic politics produced a pan-Arabic Socialist philosophy known as Baathism, and cold-war conflicts resulted, with the U.S. and its Western allies supporting Israel. Tensions persisted between Israel and the Arab states, despite a U.S. initiated peace accord between Egypt and Israel in 1979. As cold-war tensions diminished in the 1980s and 1990s, further attempts have been made to heal Arab-Israeli rifts.

More recently, the creation of the state of Gaza has given the Palestinians a homeland. Tensions are still high over Gaza's statehood status and over the Golan Heights and West Bank territories, lands seized by Israel during the 1967 war.

Though Middle Eastern countries had fewer problems making the transition to independence, in part due to some degree of cultural uniformity in language (Arabic) and religion (Islam), there remain major problem areas in both the Middle East and North Africa. In the Middle East, religious tensions between the Sunnis and Shi'ites (both factions within the Islamic, or Muslim, religion) contributed to the 1980–88 Iraq-Iran war. In Lebanon, religious struggles between Christian groups (to whom the French gave majority political power in 1946) and the numerically superior Palestinian-Muslim groups resulted in decades of civil war, particularly in the Lebanese capital of Beirut. Elections were held in 1996, and some political stability was achieved.[31]

> I against my brothers; I and my brothers against my cousins; I, my brothers and my cousins against the world.
>
> —*Arab proverb*

In 1990, tensions escalated again when Saddam Hussein of Iraq invaded neighboring Kuwait. Oil prices rose, and a United Nations force was dispatched to evict the Iraqis and to protect Saudi Arabia. As with the earlier Middle Eastern conflicts of 1973–74 and 1978–79, the rise in oil prices proved highly disruptive to the world economy, prompting global slowdowns in industrial activities. An ensuing conflict saw a U.S.-led coalition force depose Saddam Hussein in 2003.

Emerging modernization and westernization trends in the Middle East and North Africa have been met with resistance from fundamentalist Islamic groups. Turkey, Algeria, Afghanistan, Pakistan, Iran, Libya, Bahrain, and Sudan are among the countries most affected by the resurgence of extremist philosophies favoring strict interpretations of Muslim doctrines.

Africa From the sixteenth to the nineteenth centuries, Africa's contribution to the world economy was as a source of slaves, especially to the Americas. Inhospitable climates and terrain prevented penetration into the interior, so most early settlements were coastal. The situation changed in the 1870s as medicine began to master tropical diseases and steamships made internal exploration possible. The 1869 opening of the Suez Canal along with gold and mineral discoveries resulted in increased attention from the European colonial powers. The "scramble for Africa" finally abated with the 1884 Berlin Conference that partitioned Africa according to British, French, Belgian, Portuguese, and German interests (see Figure 4.7). De-colonization came mainly in the 1950s and 1960s. By 1961, twenty-four nations were independent. Many had major internal problems after independence. Between 1957–84, there were twelve major conflicts and thirteen head-of-state assassinations.[32]

FIGURE 4.7
Foreign Domination of Colonial Africa

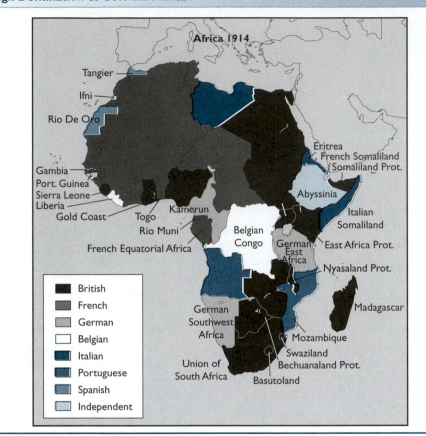

Africa 1914

Tangier
Ifni
Rio De Oro
Gambia
Port. Guinea
Sierra Leone
Liberia
Gold Coast
Togo
Rio Muni
French Equatorial Africa
Kamerun
Belgian Congo
German East Africa
Eritrea
French Somaliland
Somaliland Prot.
Abyssinia
Italian Somaliland
East Africa Prot.
Nyasaland Prot.
Madagascar
German Southwest Africa
Union of South Africa
Basutoland
Swaziland
Bechuanaland Prot.
Mozambique

- British
- French
- German
- Belgian
- Italian
- Portuguese
- Spanish
- Independent

Source: *The World Almanac and Book of Facts,* 1991 edition, © Pharos Books 1990, New York, NY 10166.

Today, democratic institutions are slowly emerging in Africa, where countries historically have been run by one-party governments and presidents-for-life. Many of Africa's political problems relate to its ethnic fragmentation. The Democratic Republic of the Congo (formerly Zaire), for example, has more than 200 cultural groups, and South Africa has over twenty major tribal groupings. In many countries, such as Nigeria, voting trends have tended to be along tribal rather than political party lines. African countries after independence showed considerable political instability. Figure 4.8 shows dates of African independence and principal coups d'etat (political and military takeovers).

Democratic institutions have taken hold in sub-Saharan Africa, though many are fragile. Of the forty-two mainland states in the region, only four had military rulers in 1996, with thirty having had elections. Still, in many African countries, political instability is apparent. The major concern in the new millenium has been the AIDS virus, with over 20 million affected within the region, amounting to over two-thirds of the global total.

FIGURE 4.8
Africa: Independence Dates and Principal Coups d'état

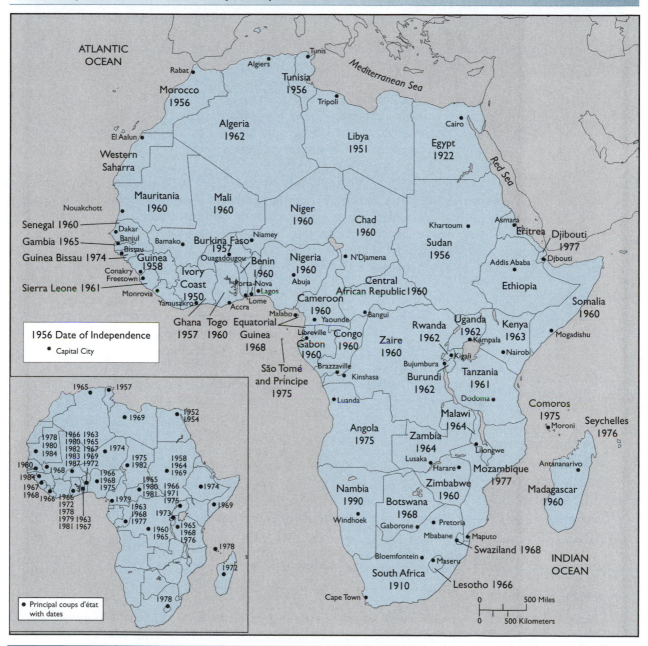

Commercial History

The Middle East Prior to the discovery of the Americas, the Middle East was a center of world commerce. Its geographic position, straddling the Far East, Europe, and Africa, gave it a pivotal position in international trade for close to a thousand years. Middle Eastern merchants sent Sudanese gold and black slaves to the Mediterranean; silk, pepper, spices, and pearls to Europe; and European products to Asia. Its transcontinental caravans, often consisting of five thousand to six thousand camels, each carrying 300 kilograms of merchandise, were complemented with complex credit and payment schemes. Only the onset of large ocean-going ships in Europe stunted further progress of its capitalistic system and resulted in a commercial downturn that was to last until the late nineteenth century.[33]

From the 1870s to 1918, agricultural produce was the major Middle Eastern export, mainly to Europe. After that time, British and French interest in the region increased as oil became a major commodity in world markets. British interests in particular were prompted by naval use of oil over coal to give its ships speed advantages over other navies.

The 1930s depression devastated Middle Eastern economies with major declines in raw material and commodity prices. In the Gulf area, major concessions were granted to international oil companies. Many of these were rescinded after 1945 as oil industries were nationalized to control their exploitation. Foreign influences diminished also as nationals took control of other commercial interests. Import substitution plans were enacted with protectionist trade policies. It was not until the 1970s, after significant investments in social welfare and heavy industry, that the Middle Eastern economies began to open up to the outside world. The 1980s and 1990s have seen privatization movements take hold, most notably in Turkey and Egypt.[34]

Since the 1950s, oil has been dominant in the Middle Eastern economies. The formation of the Organization of Petroleum Exporting Countries (OPEC) occurred after oil company attempts to reduce government income from that commodity. From that time, efforts to maintain oil revenues have been top national and regional priorities. Regional stability has important effects on oil prices. Arab-Israeli conflicts contributed to the 1973–74 oil crisis; the Iran-Iraq war figured strongly in 1979–80 oil price increases, and Iraq's invasion of Kuwait caused oil price escalations.

Africa Regional economic progress has been slowed by ongoing internal conflicts and deflated world prices for commodity exports. Undeveloped infrastructures (ports, roads, rails, energy grids, telecommunications) have continued to be major impediments to regional developments. Some progress is notable at national and regional levels. South Africa has made steady economic gains after its first free elections in 1994. Trade blocs are being formed. The Common Market for Eastern and Southern Africa (COMESA) is a twenty-one-country grouping with $5 billion in intra-bloc commerce in 1999. The group is working toward full free trade and common

> For my sins, I worked with the Nigerians when they became independent. I told them what they needed was a late 18th century English mechanic who could design a better hoe. They asked me: "Is that what they do at MIT?" I said no, of course not. They said, "We are going to do what they do at MIT! Anything else is second class."
>
> —*Peter Drucker,*
> *U.S. author and consultant*

external tariffs by 2005.[35] Similarly, the South African Development Community (SADC) was founded in 1992. This fourteen-country grouping's aim is total free trade by 2004. Currently, its intra-regional trade is $7.2 billion.[36]

ASIA

Geographic Characteristics

Asia, for the purposes of this book, begins with Afghanistan and continues east to Japan. It extends from Mongolia in the north through the countries of South and East Asia, including the island states of Indonesia and the Philippines. Rounding out the Asian group are the Pacific Islands and the mainly English-speaking nations of Australia and New Zealand (see Figure 4.9).

Geographically, Asia is large, scattered, and diverse, ranging from the world's third-largest nation, the People's Republic of China (which has 1.3 billion of the world's 6+ billion population), down to the small states of Brunei and Singapore. In between, there is India (with one-sixth of the world's population, over 1 billion people) and the sprawling countries of Indonesia and the Philippines (which comprise more that 13,000 and 7,000 islands respectively).

Asia has varied climates. Indonesia, for example, whose islands stretch more than 3,000 miles, is very wet in its western parts and arid in its eastern parts. The three inner islands of Java, Bali, and Lombok (where most of the country's 170 million people reside) have some of the most fertile soils in the world. Thailand, Malaysia, Indonesia, and many other areas of southern Asia have tropical rain forest as their major vegetation, with monsoons (heavy rains) occurring daily for six months of the year. In these areas, wet rice cultivation is the major agricultural pursuit. Parts of Asia along the Pacific are volcanic and subject to earthquakes. Japan, for example, averaged two earth tremors a day somewhere in the country during the late 1980s.

> Simply to see [Asia] in all its immensity is already to go halfway to understanding its strange destiny and civilizations.
>
> —*Fernand Braudel, 20th-century French historian*

Historical and Cultural Perspectives

Much of Asia's history and development was shaped in early times by religion and in the nineteenth and twentieth centuries by colonization. The early histories of China, India, and Japan illustrate the influence of religious and political factors on regional development. In China, Confucius was a major influence on Chinese government and society for nearly 2000 years. He advocated the principles of order in society, respect for tradition, good form, regular behaviors, moral obligations, and discharge of duties. Along with Mo Tzu, (who advocated altruistic behaviors toward fellow man), Lao Tse (whose Taoistic teachings included simplicity and passivity), and Buddhist philosophies, the principles underlying Chinese (and Asian) cultures were established early and continue to shape present-day Chinese and Asian behaviors.[37]

> If you are planning for one year, grow rice. If you are planning for 20 years, grow trees. If you are planning for centuries, grow men.
>
> —*Chinese proverb*

In India, the Gupta dynasty, starting about A.D. 320, sparked major literary and intellectual achievements that evolved after A.D. 600 into the Hindu religion. The caste system of occupation-based divisions in society can be traced

FIGURE 4.9
Asia in Its Global Context

Europe

1. Slovenia
2. Croatia
3. Bosnia-Herzegovina
4. Yugoslavia
5. Albania
6. Macedonia
7. Greece
8. Estonia
9. Latvia
10. Lithuania
11. Russia
12. Belarus
13. Moldova
14. Romania
15. Bulgaria
16. Hungary
17. Austria
18. Czech Republic
19. Slovak Republic
20. Poland
21. Denmark
22. Netherlands
23. Belgium
24. Luxembourg
25. Germany
26. Switzerland
27. Italy
28. France
29. Andorra
30. Spain
31. Portugal

Africa

1. Western Sahara
2. Senegal
3. Gambia
4. Guinea-Bissau
5. Guinea
6. Sierra Leone
7. Liberia
8. Ivory Coast
9. Burkina Faso
10. Ghana
11. Togo
12. Benin
13. Cameroon
14. Equatorial Guinea
15. Gabon
16. Congo
17. Central African Republic
18. Rwanda
19. Burundi

* United Arab Emirates

from this period, as can the philosophy of *samsara* (the endless cycle of birth, life, death and rebirth). These early influences were critical, as the Hindu religion has been noted as emphasizing the limits of human actions rather than its potential for development.[38] India's modern history dates from its involvement in eighteenth-century European colonization. Robert Clive took Bengal in 1757 and opened up India to British influences that were to last for the next 190 years.

In Japan's case, island status insulated the country from outside influences until the mid-nineteenth century. Until that time, the major shapers of Japanese behaviors had been Confucianism, Taoism, and Buddhism, which had fused with precepts from the native Kami cult to produce the primary Japanese religion, Shinto. Shinto's tenets include community rather than individual orientations, loyalty toward groups, and sets of deities, rites, and obligations. In 1868, the Meiji Restoration brought a renewed emphasis on the emperor as a religious deity, and Japanese nationalism (and imperialism) became a part of "State Shinto" that was to last until 1947.[39]

Early trade and commerce aided the spread of religion in Asia. Buddhism traveled through central Asian trading routes to China and Japan. Islam migrated to Indonesia from the Middle East, and the Spanish introduced Catholicism into the Philippines.

Today's Asia comprises a diverse set of religions, some of which have contributed to political frictions. India is a Hindu state, but it borders Pakistan to the northwest and Bangladesh to the northeast, both Muslim countries. Both were formerly part of India. Recognition of religious differences led to the creation of West and East Pakistan as Muslim states at India's independence in 1947. East Pakistan became Bangladesh in 1971. Religious problems have persisted in India's northern Kashmir region that has a majority Muslim population. Other problems are apparent in Sri Lanka (the island formerly called Ceylon, off southern India), where conflicts exist between the Tamils (Hindus who make up 18 percent of the population) and the majority Singhalese, who are Buddhists. Religious tensions also exist in Malaysia between Malay Muslims and the descendents of Chinese immigrants, who are largely Buddhist.

Much of Asia, like Africa and the Middle East, was colonized by Europeans between the sixteenth and nineteenth centuries. Only Thailand (formerly Siam) was never occupied. The saying, "The sun never sets over the British Empire" originated during the nineteenth century when Britain ruled India (until 1947), Malaysia (until 1957), and Singapore (until 1965). Australia and New Zealand were also under British influence as part of the British Commonwealth of Nations. The Netherlands ruled Indonesia until 1949. The Philippines, after 300 years of Spanish rule and forty-eight years of U.S. rule, gained its independence in 1946. The seeds of Asian independence had been sewn in the 1920s and 1930s, with anti-imperialist insurrections in China, French Indochina (today's Vietnam), Indonesia, and India.

Asia's response to colonization was mixed. Since the twelfth century, Japan had been essentially ruled through a military aristocracy, the shoguns. In the sixteenth century, when other Asian nations were being colonized, Japan elected to use its island status to insulate itself from Western influences, superior military technologies, and Christianity. This geographic isolation resulted

> One must become as humble as the dust before he can discover the truth.
>
> —*Mahatma Gandhi 20th-century Indian leader*

in an inward-looking society, and, anthropologically, Japan had been (and still is) one of the world's purest racial groups. It was not until 1853, when the U.S.'s Admiral Perry ventured into Tokyo Bay, that Japanese eyes were opened to the outside world. The power of the shoguns was broken down after the 1868 Meiji Restoration, the power of the emperor was restored and radical change ensued. Industrialization, a railway infrastructure, and military modernization (of the army and the navy by the Germans and British respectively) began to shape the new Japan. A Western calendar was adopted, and a bicameral parliament was operational by 1879.[40] The 1905 defeat of the Russian navy, the 1910 annexation of Korea, and the 1930s "creeping" invasion of China gave vent to Japanese imperialistic aspirations. Japan's defeat in World War II prompted a reorientation of national energies toward the commercial arena.

China, up to and including the early part of the nineteenth century, shunned external intervention and displayed indifference to European products and lifestyles.[41] It was only through the Opium Wars of 1839–42 that the country was opened up to Western trade and influences. Chinese opposition to Western encroachment culminated in a xenophobic backlash in 1900 known as the Boxer Rebellion. From that time, China experienced significant and continuous change. Ruled by successive imperial dynasties until 1911, China was governed from 1911 until 1925 by Dr. Sun Yat-Sen, a Western-educated physician who choreographed the downfall of the emperor. In the 1920s, civil wars among China's many warlords created national disunity, and, in the resulting struggle, Chiang Kai-Shek came to power. The 1930s were characterized by a "creeping" Japanese invasion until Japan formally invaded China in 1937. Chiang fought alongside the British and Americans against the Chinese communists led by Mao Tse Tung, who overthrew Chiang in 1949. Chiang and his Chinese nationalists fled to the island of Formosa to establish their own Republic of China—Taiwan.

Over the next twenty-five years, Mao collectivized industry and agriculture on a massive scale. Mao died in 1976, and, after a brief period of rule by the "Gang of Four" (which included Mao's widow), Deng Xiao Peng took over in 1981. In 1985, he initiated reforms aimed at returning China to a more market-oriented economic system.[42]

Another element of Asian cultural diversity is language. India alone has fifteen major languages and hundreds of dialectic variations of Hindi, its principal language. China has dozens of regional and local dialects. Indonesia has more than 250 languages and dialects, while the Philippines has more than thirty.

Australia and New Zealand, in the South Pacific, were originally inhabited by native peoples, the Aborigines and Maoris, respectively. Both countries became part of the British Empire after Captain James Cook claimed them in 1769–70. Australia was a penal colony until the mid-nineteenth century, when gold discoveries in the state of Victoria accelerated immigration by free citizens in the 1850s. New Zealand was one of the first nations to create a comprehensive welfare state in 1898. In both nations there were conflicts between natives and the British settlers.

Both countries are sparsely populated. Australia has about 20 million people, and New Zealand has less than 4 million. Both economies have substantial agricultural bases of livestock and crops, which are exported. Australia also has many natural resources, including iron ore, petroleum, natural gas, coal, and gemstones.[43]

Commercial History

Asia from the fifteenth century was a source of silks and spices, but was largely disinterested in European products and lifestyles. The Chinese invented the magnetic compass and gunpowder and could cast iron 1500 years before the Europeans. But China lacked colonial ambitions, possibly due to its geographic size, its relative isolation, and a pride in its Confucian traditions and order.[44] The 1839–42 Opium Wars opened the country up to trade, and British and French commercial influences were apparent until the fall of the Imperial Dynasty in 1911. From that time, civil war, world war, and communistic influences stunted economic progress. After 1949, Mao collectivized industry and agriculture. As the end of the cold war approached, Deng Xiao Peng initiated economic reforms aimed at returning China to a more market-oriented system. By the late 1980s, China was the second-largest coal producer and the fourth-biggest steel producer in the world, and trade per capita had risen 25 times since 1950.[45]

Japan's industrial dynamism dominated Asia for the first four decades of the twentieth century, during which the country became a major steel producer and a world munitions center. Coal and textile industries flourished, though Japan lacked critical non-agricultural resources, most notably oil.

The post-1945 economic rebuilding of Japan paid off as the country impacted world markets, especially after the 1960s. An insulated (and some would argue, protected) domestic market gave Japanese producers economic and financial bases to innovate and attack international markets. Today, Japanese firms such as Toyota, Nissan, Mitsubishi, Toshiba, Sharp, Panasonic, and Canon are household names worldwide, and Japanese management methods such as just-in-time, total quality management, consensus decision making, market share orientations, and company (rather than industry) based trade unions have been scrutinized and selectively adopted by leading Western companies.

India was a heavily protected economy until 1991, when Rajiv Ghandi began to open national doors to foreign direct investment and trade. Slowly, India has begun the task of modernization and building competitive positions in high-tech industries, using its considerable math, science, and engineering manpower bases.

Asian economic growth in the latter half of the twentieth century was powered first by Japan, then by South Korea, Hong Kong, Singapore, and Taiwan. More recently, China, India, Malaysia, Thailand, Indonesia, and the Philippines have joined the Asian economic resurgence. Only the Asian Financial Crisis of 1997–99 slowed down regional development as affected countries followed International Monetary Fund suggestions to reform their economies and make their currencies convertible.

Trading blocs have taken on new importance as Asian countries have pushed toward increased commercial interdependence. As noted in Chapter 2, the Association of Southeast Asia Nations (ASEAN), the Asia-Pacific Cooperation group (APEC), and on a smaller scale, an Australian-New Zealand free trade area have all contributed to the development of what is arguably the world's most dynamic region.

> As opposed to the nations in the West, Asia is a growing market. By the year 2000, two thirds of the world's consumers will live around the edge of the Pacific Rim.
>
> —*Christopher Mill, vice-president, Saatchi & Saatchi*

GEOPOLITICS AND STRATEGY

The analysis of regional geographies and histories gives business people key insights into how markets develop and affects interactions among peoples and nations.

North America is highly developed and a world leader in branding, information technologies, and supply chains. Despite its size, a benevolent climate and topography (by world standards) facilitated infrastructure development (essential for a market-forces-based economy) and historical circumstances complemented this with an outgoing, capitalist mentality. The result has been a highly successful market-forces economy.

Latin America's size and proximity to the equator have made regional infrastructures and market-forces economies difficult to implement for much of its history. 1990s improvements in transportation, communication, and energy networks—both regionally and nationally—are contributing to improved corporate supply chains and regional supply chains. Historically, the common Spanish-Portuguese-Latin background has contributed to the formation of trade blocs for nations and to regional branding strategies for companies.

Western Europe's geographic compactness, coastal outlines, and temperate climate resulted in the region becoming an early and prolific trader. Its maritime and military technologies gave Western Europe decisive advantages in colonizing much of the world, and many nations still bear the cultural imprints of that period. The region's early industrial prowess gave it a world leadership role in commerce that has continued to the present day. The formation of the EU consolidated Western Europe's political and economic position, and, despite its multilingual heritage, firms have been successful in implementing regional branding and supply-chain strategies.

Eastern Europe's size and latitude has historically made regional infrastructures and market-based economies hard to execute. As a result, autocratic and communistic systems were perhaps inevitable outcomes. Today, the region is benefiting from resource exploitation (oil, minerals) and the Eastern movements of Western firms and technologies, though Russia's size and climate remain formidable obstacles to technology diffusions and supply chains.

The Middle East was a center of world commerce until the Europe-to-Asia camel-based Silk Road was overtaken by Europe's maritime advances. A decisive moment in history was the region's adoption of the Islamic faith that has subsequently dominated Middle-Eastern lifestyles and behaviors. The region was rejuvenated as it became the center of the oil industry in the twentieth century. Regional unrest has effectively impeded full-scale exploitation of its oil wealth and cultural commonalities (the Islamic faith and the Arabic language).

Africa's vast size and proximity to the equator, like Latin America, have been problematic in installing the infrastructures needed for development and establishing supply-demand economies. As a result, the geographic barriers among ethnic groups have been slow to subside, and diffusions of modernizing technologies have been impeded. The culturally heterogeneous nature of African society, particularly in the south, has been maintained and ethnic affiliations have been slow to erode as democratic processes and national identities struggle to become established. The region's raw-material resources attracted Europe's attentions in the nineteenth century and continue to contribute to world commodity markets. Africa generally, however, has not yet become an attractive investment site, except for raw-material exploitation.

Asia's size, climatic vicissitudes, and ethnic and religious diversity successfully resisted Western colonial influences until the nineteenth century, and today the region retains its many cultural identities. Since the 1970s, Asia's population has made it attractive as a major market and improvements in world infrastructures have improved its accessibility as a center of global manufacturing. These two factors make Asia arguably the most dynamic of the regional markets. The region's long history and varied cultural make-up make localization strategies optimal, though some Westernization is occurring.

The roles of geography and history are to provide background and to illustrate how world business and the forces of globalization have shaped regions and countries. The impact of global and regional forces also lay the groundwork for understanding the cultural and developmental underpinnings of national cultures—the topic we examine next.

KEY POINTS

- Geopolitical studies are important to international business people as they provide key insights into regional and national development and valuable background in understanding current policies and problems.

- A review of world markets and economic development shows major disparities among regions, with North America and Western Europe having progressed significantly more than other parts of the world.

- North American development progressed out of European colonization, with religious freedom and nonhereditary social-class systems as hallmarks of the new American society. Pioneering and westward exploration contributed to societal characteristics of self-reliance and individualism.

- Latin America was colonized by the Spanish and the Portuguese at about the same time as North America, and their cultural imprints—language, religion, and a hereditary social-class system—are still apparent today. Independence occurred between 1810 and 1824. Instability characterized the next 150 years until major movements toward democratization and market-forces economies during the 1980s and 1990s.

- Western Europe's compact geography and temperate climate significantly aided the region's industrialization and trading efforts, and historic monarchies and feudal background laid the foundations of a hereditary social-class system. European colonization gave the region worldwide influence up to the mid-twentieth century. World wars and common historical heritages formed the basis for today's economic and political integration.

- Eastern Europe's geographic size and climate significantly shaped its development. Russian influence through the communist revolution of 1917–18 and the Yalta agreement was a major influence on world politics up to the 1980s, when democratization and market-forces economies reshaped regional destinies.

- Middle East and African development was greatly influenced by geographic size, climate, and natural resource deposits. Both regions were heavily affected by European colonizing efforts. Present-day development has been hindered by politics and religion (Middle East), and by ethnic compositions (Africa).

- Like the Americas, the Middle East, and Africa, Asia's modern history has been influenced through European colonizing activities. Ethnic, cultural, and religious diversity is apparent over much of Asia and has affected regional development. Japan has historically been the dominant regional power, though China's economic ascendancy has altered the regional political and economic balance.

- Geography and history are prime shapers of regional and national cultures. Geographic size, climate, and topography affect commercial interactions within markets and with the outside world. History records how peoples have responded to their geographic and environmental circumstances and provides key insights into current cultures and behaviors.

ENDNOTES

1. Samuel P. Huntington, *The Clash of Civilizations and the Remaking of World Order* (New York: Simon & Schuster, 1996); and Huntington, "The Clash of Civilizations," *Foreign Affairs* 72, 3 (Summer 1993): 22–40.

2. For an excellent reference on national ethnic groups, see David Levinson, *Ethnic Groups Worldwide* (Phoenix, Ariz.: Oryx Press, 1998).

3. Jared Diamond, *Guns, Germs and Steel: Fates of Human Societies* (New York: W. W. Norton, 1998).

4. *Culturgram: Canada* (Provo: Utah, Brigham Young University, 2001).

5. J. M. Roberts, *History of the World* (London: Penguin Books, 1997), 744, 769.

6. Ibid., 629–32.

7. Ibid., 765, 879.

8. *World Investment Report 2003* (New York: United Nations, 2003): p. 262.

9. *Culturgrams: Bolivia, Costa Rica, Mexico, Honduras, Peru, Panama, Nicaragua, and Ecuador* (Provo, Utah: Brigham Young University, 2002).

10. *Culturgrams: Chile, Bolivia, Peru, Venezuela and Colombia* (Provo, Utah: Brigham Young University, 2002).

11. Roberts, 772–74.

12. *Culturgram: Guatemala* (Provo, Utah: Brigham Young University, 2001).

13. Roberts, 470.

14. Roberts., 619, 774.

15. Roberts., 624, 644.

16. Steven Pearlstein, "Free Trade Zone for the Western Hemisphere moves forward," *Washington Post* (November 5, 1999): E-3.

17. Julian M. Weiss, "Mercosur on the road to recovery," *World Trade* (February 2000): 26–30.

18. Roberts, 761.

19. Anonymous, "Coming Home to Roost—Privatization in Europe," *Economist* (June 29, 2002): 63–65.

20. *The Soviet Union* (Alexandria, Va.: Time-Life Books), 1985.

21. "Russia/CIS: Trade Tics," *Crossborder Monitor* (May 6, 1998): 4.

22. Roberts, 597–600.

23. Roberts, 875.

24. Alice Enders and Ronald J. Wonnacott, "The Liberalization of East-West European Trade: Hubs, Spokes and Further Complications," *World Economy* (May 1996): 253–72.

25. Cheryl W. Gray, "In Search of Owners: Privatization and Corporate Governance in Transition Economies," *World Bank Research Observer* (August 1996): 179–97.

26. *World Investment Report* (2002): 305.

27. "Solid Foundation," *Business Eastern Europe* (March 3, 2003): 5; Simon Pirani, "Get your juices running," *Business Eastern Europe* (March 25, 2002): 4; and Jason Bush, "The fewer the better," *Business Eastern Europe* (June 3, 2002): 4.

28. *Arabian Peninsula* (Alexandria Va.: Time-Life Books, 1986), 100–104.

29. Ibid., 100.

30. Fernand Braudel, *A History of Civilizations* (New York: Penguin Books, 1993), Chapter 6; and Bernard Lewis, *The Middle East* (New York: Touchstone Books, 1995).

31. "Investment in Lebanon: Garden or Jungle?" *Crossborder Monitor* (October 30, 1996): 1, 8.

32. Roberts, 1029.

33. Fernand Braudel, *A History of Civilizations* (New York: Penguin Books, 1993), chapter 5.

34. Roger Owen and Sevket Pamuk, *A History of Middle Eastern Economies in the Twentieth Century* (London: I. B. Tauris, 1998).

35. Anonymous, "Major Trading Bloc Takes Shape," *South China Morning Post* (July 23, 2000): 7.

36. Anonymous, "Prospects for SADC's Free Trade Area," *Country Monitor* (August 21, 2000): 1.

37. Roberts, 139–42.

38. Roberts, 414–18.

39. John Breen, "Shinto," in Peter B. Clarke, *The World's Religions* (New York: Reader's Digest, 1993).

40. Roberts, 811–14.

41. David S. Landes, *Revolutions in Time* (Cambridge, Mass: Harvard University Press, 1983).

42. *China* (Alexandria, Va.: Time-Life Books, 1989), 93–94, 145–46.

43. *Culturegrams: Australia, New Zealand* (Provo, Utah: Brigham Young University, 2001).

44. Roberts, 442, 447–48.

45. Roberts, 1065.

C A S E T T E   4 - 1
The Effects of Geography and History on Regional Development

∽

Review the contents of this chapter. What have been the key geographic and historic factors shaping development in each region? Identify the positive and negative factors for each region, and indicate how you think they have impacted regional cultures and behaviors. Form conclusions about (a) the similarities and differences between North American (U.S. and Canada) and Latin American development. Why were there differences in their development rates? (b) North America and Western Europe developed faster than other regions. Why do you think this occurred?

C A S E T T E   4 - 2
Oil and the Middle East

∽

The Short-Term Problem: Oil Prices and the World Economy

When Iraq's Saddam Hussein marched his armies into Kuwait on August 2, 1990, starting the Gulf War, the world held its breath. Although the Middle East (especially Saudi Arabia) produced only about 40 percent of the world's oil, the region contained almost 60 percent of world reserves. Regional turmoil and instability had contributed to the 1973–74 quadrupling of oil prices (from $3 to $13 per barrel) and to the 1979–80 rise from $13 to $40 per barrel. In 1973, war between Egypt and Syria against Israel led to other countries taking sides with the United States and the Netherlands against the Arabs and caused OPEC to limit the sales of oil supplies to certain countries. The price of oil rose and stayed high.

In 1979, after the fall of the Shah of Iran, the Ayatollah Ruolla Khomeini came to power and initiated a "holy war" against Iraq. The United States' previous support of the shah had resulted in the holding hostage of over fifty Americans for more than a year (1980–81).

Oil prices fell in the early 1980s and went down as low as $10 a barrel. Slowly, they rose to $18 a barrel in 1989. The overall reduction in oil prices over the decade damped down worldwide inflation and encouraged nations (especially the United States) to expand economically.

In the wake of Iraq's invasion of Kuwait in 1990, oil prices moved inexorably up past the $30-per-barrel mark in August 1990, and world stock markets panicked. In the United States, the Dow Jones average fell 200 points in four days. Japan's Nikkei stock average fell 3383 points, or 11 percent of its total value. In 1973–74, the oil price spiral had soaked up about 2 percent of developed countries' gross national products. Inflation doubled from 7 to 14 percent. There followed a period of general price rises and economic stagnation, which came to be known as "stagflation." In 1979–80, world inflation rates, having barely recovered from the 1973–74 war, doubled again, this time from 8 to 14 percent.

But the world was better prepared in 1990. The 1974–74 and 1979–80 price hikes had caused some nations to rethink their energy-related policies, and many new measures and policies had been adopted, including:

- Smaller, more fuel-efficient cars became more widely available, courtesy mainly of the Japanese. American manufacturers, with the exception of the Ford Escort, were slow to build and market compact and subcompact cars.

- Offshore drilling gave the oil and gas industries new energy sources.

- European governments encouraged the upgrading of their public transportation systems. High-speed trains began to compete with auto and airline companies. Governments also discouraged private transportation by continued heavy taxing of petroleum. Petrol prices of $3 to $4 a gallon were not uncommon in Western Europe.

Japan's approach was to make more efficient use of its oil imports. It has been said that if Americans used oil as efficiently as the Japanese, they would need only 9.2 million barrels per day instead of the 16.6 million actually consumed. The United States accounts for over one-fourth of the world's 61-million-barrel daily consumption.

Long-Term Problems: Reducing Tensions in the Middle East

As 400,000 American troops moved into Saudi Arabia as part of the United Nations force in the Gulf War of 1991, it became apparent that, over the long term, some new approaches were needed to ensure stability in this economically vital region. Some of the problems that needed to be addressed were the following:

1. Were $18-per-barrel oil prices sufficient to sustain a modernization program in the Middle Eastern countries? Just before his invasion of Kuwait, Saddam Hussein had demanded $25 per barrel. This price would have helped Iraq's $70 billion external debt. Oil prices had averaged about $18 from 1986–90. At an average of 3 percent inflation worldwide, what should the price be in 2002 if the purchasing power of oil producing countries was to be maintained?

2. Should the United States and the United Nations continue to support feudal monarchies, such as Saudi Arabia's, while encouraging democracies elsewhere in the world (e.g., in Latin America and Eastern Europe)? Even the most ardent supporters of Middle Eastern monarchies would admit that oil revenue dispersals were the prerogative of just a few people.

3. Israel's position in the Middle East needed to be clarified. While President Carter's Camp David Accords in 1979 were a start (it was the first-ever peace treaty between an Arabic state—Egypt—and Israel), there needed to be a permanent solution, especially with respect to the Occupied Territories taken and held by Israel since the 1967 War. The position of the Palestinian peoples, essentially stateless since 1948, needed attention, especially with respect to Gaza, the West Bank, and the Golan Heights.

4. While the Middle East was mainly Muslim, there were ongoing rivalries between the more moderate Sunni Muslims and the more militant fundamentalist Shi'ites. Saudi Arabia, Kuwait, and Iraq are mainly Sunni; Iran is Shi'ite. All Arabic countries contained pockets of fundamentalist Muslims favoring strict interpretations of their holy book, the Qur'ān (or Koran).

5. The Middle East had generally resisted outside attempts to change its traditional lifestyle. The region generally welcomed modernization in the form of hospitals, roads, and new infrastructures. But it had resisted the intrusion of Western lifestyles and consumption orientations, which it regarded as morally corrosive through its depictions of crime, sex, and violence. The amount of economic and social change that could be introduced was therefore limited, making it difficult for Middle Eastern countries to keep pace in a rapidly developing world.

Nations Versus Technologies

As the 1990s drew to a close, the world, having experienced global recessions after each of the oil price hikes, had been using technology to bring oil exploration costs down by over 60 percent, find new oil fields, and tap higher percentages of oil finds. Platform technologies made deep, sea oil available, and oil became cheaper than bottled water. But oil consumption was also on the rise. Auto production was bringing cars to wider segments of world consumers. Gas-guzzling SUVs became the most popular autos in the U.S.—and, despite the development of electronic and hybrid cars, no reductions in oil demand were in sight.

But Saudi Arabia, the world's low-cost oil producer at $1.50 a barrel, was still in control. Producing 8 million barrels a day (much of it going to the U.S., the world's prominent consumer), and with a quarter of the world's reserve (260 billion barrels), the kingdom still had a major say in world oil prices. Then, too, the oil companies were happy: Exxon-Mobil, BP, and Shell made profits of $17.7 bn, $14.2 bn, and $13.1 bn respectively in 2000.

Questions

1. Do you think the 1990 oil price hike affected the world as much as the price rises of 1973–74 or 1979–80? Support your conclusions.

2. Do you think Americans could have done more during the 1980s to reduce their reliance on oil? If your answer is yes, think about what would have happened if European- or Japanese-style solutions had been applied in the United States.

3. Discuss each of the five long-term problems. For each, identify a solution, and consider its consequences.

4. What are the strategic consequences of the new oil technologies? Are they likely to unseat Saudi Arabia as the major influence on world oil prices?

Sources: Adelman, M. A. "The 1990 Oil Shock Is Like the Others" *The Energy Journal* 11:4 (1990): 1–44. Verleger, Jr., Philip K. "Understanding the 1990 Oil Crisis." *The Energy Journal* 11:4 (1990): 15–34. Coy, Peter, Gary McWilliams, and John Rossant. "The New Economics of Oil." *Business Week,* (Nov 3, 1997): 140–54. Wrampelmeier, Brooks, "The Oil Kingdom at 100: Petroleum Policymaking in Saudi Arabia," *Middle East Policy* 8, 1 (March, 2001): 163–67.

Chapter Five

Analyses of National Markets

⟶⟵

INTERNATIONAL RETAILERS DOING THEIR HOMEWORK

Anytime international firms enter new markets, they must do their homework. Companies that don't face all sorts of costly and unpleasant surprises. Take international retailers, for example; they must deal with the full quota of foreign obstacles as they assemble store delivery systems and product mixes to appeal to local consumers.

Geography is important. U.S. retailers used to North American conditions must often downsize stores to accommodate smaller foreign sites. This has affected mass retailers in France, as well as KFC franchises in Japan. K-Mart had to site its Singapore stores in high-rent mall locations, considerably raising its fixed costs.

Legal and regulatory constraints must be assessed. In predominantly English-speaking Canada, Quebec requires French labeling and advertising. In Europe, EU franchisees receive more legal protection than elsewhere, causing control problems for companies like McDonald's.

Financial infrastructures vary, as do consumer payment means. In France, carte bleu *debit cards are popular, but non-French cash registers often do not accept this form of payment.*

Cost structures are affected by minimum wage levels that are $4–5 in the U.S. but rise to $10+ in France.

Even when stores are set up and ready to operate, they must have done enough market research to understand consumers. Restaurant menus and décor must be acceptable. Store layouts must be logical. Clothing must fit. For women, form-fitting garments that are popular in southern Europe don't work in Northern Europe. And smaller garment sizes are needed in Mediterranean Europe and Asia.

Once global and regional analyses are complete, managers are in positions to analyze individual markets in which they have special interests. For international companies entering new markets, there are no excuses for not knowing all about local operating conditions and customer tastes. Early mistakes make critically bad first impressions. Getting it right (or close to right) gets new businesses off to good starts.[1]

FIGURE 5.1
Chapter Outline: National Markets Analysis

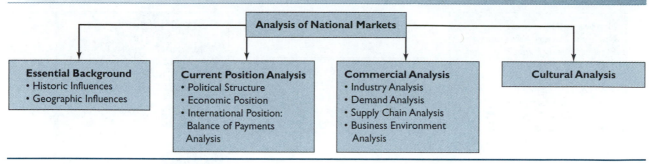

Hence, in this chapter you will learn:

- How the study of a country's history helps managers understand national political and cultural environments.
- The importance of geographic factors, such as country location, climate, resources, and topography, in national development, and how such factors aid assessments of infrastructure facilities, such as energy sources, transportation, and communication systems.
- The importance of political, economic, and international analyses in evaluating current political and economic circumstances and how balance of payments analyses help managers understand country interactions with the world economy.
- The ways that firms dissect commercial environments with analyses of national industries (market size, structure, characteristics), market demand (customers, segments, market profiles), supply-chain considerations (suppliers, manufacturing-site decision making), and business environments, including financial aspects and legal infrastructures (ownership restrictions, intellectual property rules, consumer and environmental laws).
- Finally, a look at the sorts of factors used to give managers overviews of national cultures, including country backgrounds, interpersonal relations, lifestyles, and general attitudes.

THE GLOBAL WEB

There are many excellent sources of country data, including:
www.countryreports.org
www.cia.gov/cia/publications/factbook
www.countrywatch.com
The Library of Congress Country Studies at:
http://lcweb2.loc.gov/frd/cs/

INTRODUCTION

Understanding national markets begins with examinations of countries' historical and geographic characteristics to gain insights into their political, economic, and cultural heritages. These analyses (summarized in Figure 5.2) give managers the background to assess current conditions and commercial situations

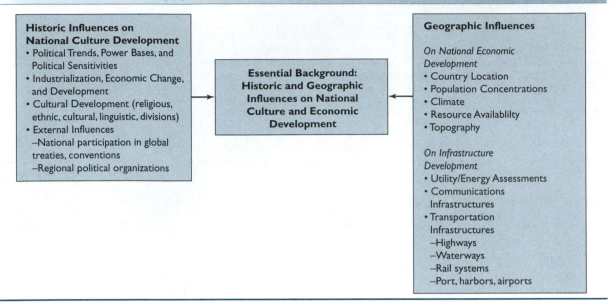

FIGURE 5.2
Overview of Historic and Geographic Influences on National Culture and Economic Development

and yield key insights as to how nations developed and the power bases underpinning current political, economic, and cultural structures.

ESSENTIAL BACKGROUND

Historical Influences on National Culture Development

History is a primary shaper of national cultures. It records how countries have responded to internal frictions and external pressures and influences, including the following.

> Study history. . . . In history lie all the secrets of statecraft.
>
> —*Winston S. Churchill, 20th-century British statesman*

Political Trends, Power Bases, and Sensitivities As countries industrialize and develop national identities, political institutions and power bases evolve. Initially (and in many developing nations today), hereditary monarchies and feudal institutions based on aristocracies and land ownership provided political leadership. As industrialization occurred, these powerful families or groups leveraged their resources and landowning interests into commercial companies, enabling them to maintain their leadership positions in the political and economic arenas. These family-based interests are still major factors in Latin America, Asia, the Middle East, and, to a lesser extent, Western Europe.

But as development occurs, populations become educated and political democracies start to emerge. In many countries, key personalities emerge to engineer political and economic change (for example, Nelson Mandela in South Africa, Deng Xiou Peng in China, and Mikel Gorbachev in the former USSR). Once these changes occur, the old power bases slowly erode, democracies take root, and political power diffuses to the national citizenry.

FIGURE 5.3
Business Sector Compositions and Economic Development

Low ————————— Economic Development ————————— High

Percentages employed in each sector	Agricultural Economy	Industrial Economy	Service Economy
	80%+ employed in agricultural or food gathering sector	Gradual mechanization of agriculture as urban-rural population shifts occur	Agribusiness develops
			Mechanization and automation transforms manufacturing.
		Urban factory systems take root. Infrastructures develop and regional/national markets appear.	Majority employment in service sectors (U.S.—80% in service sector)
	Minority in manufacturing tools, implements	Service sector develops—retailing, banks, etc.	

Industrialization, Economic Change, and Development The industrial revolutions that transformed Western Europe and North America between the eighteenth and twentieth centuries now affect many emerging nations. The transitions from agricultural to industrial to service economies are natural evolutions, but these evolutions cause major dislocations as national populations adjust to perpetually changing economic sectors. Agricultural-industrial-service sector breakdowns are key indicators of economic development. Countries with heavy agricultural emphases tend to be at the lower stages of development, while dominant service sectors indicate maturing economies. Figure 5.3 shows the evolution of the agricultural, industrial, and service sectors as nations develop. The job of national governments is to provide educational and social-welfare systems to support the technological and labor needs of the marketplace and the legal frameworks to regulate the increasingly complex and competitive economy.

How governments and countries respond to these challenges and how well these changes are accepted are primary determinants of the business and economic climates that international firms must face. Excessive change and major economic dislocations can result in voter backlashes and reactionary political movements away from market capitalism toward communist, socialist, labor, or social democratic parties. Brazil's election of the left-wing leader Lula in 2002 was such a movement.

THE GLOBAL WEB

For country developmental statistics (highest to lowest, greatest to least) and for geography, people, economy, communications, transportation, and military, see: www.globastat.com

Cultural Development National cultures may be relatively homogeneous, with few differences among country citizens. Common languages and religions and few or no differences among ethnic groups are key homogenizing factors. This tends to be the case in many developed nations, and such homogenizing influences

should be catalogued and understood. At the other end of the spectrum, many countries, particularly in the developing world, have many ethnic, cultural, and linguistic differences that must be evaluated. Historically, invasions, wars, and politics have typically determined country borders and ethnic compositions within nations. Today, linguistic and cultural diversity within nations are causes of ethnic rivalries and civil unrest (e.g., ethnic rivalries in Africa and religious problems in India). Such diversities and conflicts affect political stability. Management's task is to assess how such problems affect operations, both short-term (impacts on day-to-day operations) and over the long-term.

External Influences on Country Behaviors Three sets of external factors influence national behaviors: (1) memberships of international organizations, (2) memberships of regional organizations, and (3) past histories with individual nations.

National participation and membership in global treaties and conventions: This includes memberships of UN organizations such as the IMF, the WTO, the World Bank, IMO, ICAO, and so on. These memberships show the extent of national participation in the world economy and country acceptance of global conventions covering world commerce. China's entry into the WTO in 2001 was important, as will be Russia's when it occurs. Similarly, not being signatories to international protocols, treaties on environmentalism, human rights, intellectual property rights, etc. signals non-accountabilities toward global conventions (for example, the U.S.'s opting out of the Kyoto Agreement on Global Warming).

Participation in regional political organizations: Many parts of the world have political bodies to address regional issues. In the western hemisphere, there is the Organization of American States (OAS); in Africa there is the Organization of African Unity (OAU). In other cases, economic issues dominate, and trade bloc organizations such as the EU or ASEAN move nations toward regional disciplines based on commercial as well as political interests.

Historic events and national rivalries: A country's past inevitably impacts present-day relations. Some historic animosities are relatively short-lived (e.g., Germany in Europe). Others go back decades or centuries and still linger in national memories (e.g., China and Taiwan, Korean and Chinese attitudes toward Japan, Northern versus Southern Ireland). Colonial influences continue to be controversial throughout the Americas, Africa, and Asia. Protagonists claim that European colonization contributed to country development by establishing basic infrastructures, opening up trade routes, and exposing developing nations to alternative lifestyles. Antagonists have branded colonizers as exploiters of countries' natural resources and destroyers of local cultures. Unfavorable foreign interventions have left their marks on national cultures through distrust of foreigners and xenophobic tendencies (e.g., Middle East, Africa, and Asia).

In summary, the more managers know about national histories, the better they can appreciate and understand present-day behaviors, values, and attitudes and the more likely they are to implement effective strategies within national markets.

Geographic Influences on National Culture Development

Country geography has two major impacts on corporate strategies. First, just as geography has impacted regional cultures and development (especially in the Middle East, Africa and Asia), so it affects culture and development at the national level. Second, geographic characteristics are major influences on national infrastructure development and affect business and supply-chain operations within markets.

Geographic Influences on National Development These include country location (the physical location of a nation on the world map), population concentrations within countries, climate, resource availability, and topography.

Country location affects political, trade relationships, the exchange of ideas, and cultural interactions. Proximity to oceans and sea-based trade historically has facilitated or limited exposures to international commerce. Much of Western Europe's early development came from the spread of industrial technologies via trade. The proximity of Latin America to the U.S. and Asia to Japan has encouraged commercial interactions and technology transfers. The opposite is also true. The relative isolation of China and Japan from Western influences throughout much of the twentieth century contributed to the maintenance of traditional cultures.

Climate affects human behaviors and country development. Adverse (i.e., excessively hot or cold) climates affect population concentrations (where people choose to live: 80 percent of Canada's population lives in the southern-most part of the country), agricultural pursuits (types of crops and regularity of harvests), and how long people can work (e.g., siestas in Latin America). In harsh environmental conditions (e.g., monsoon, desert conditions), the dominance of Mother Nature can adversely affect national and individual mindsets, resulting in fatalistic attitudes toward life in general and inabilities to progress economically. For example, Central America's climatic fluctuations (e.g., 1997–98 flooding effects of El Niño were followed by drought and crop failures in 2000) have dulled regional attitudes toward economic progress.

International companies can use their expertise and technologies to adapt to or nullify the effects of extreme climates. For example, genetically modified seeds have been used to bolster crop yields in countries such as Pakistan to counter adverse climatic conditions. Also, product redesigns, customized logistics networks for distribution, and recognition of seasonal-demand variations for clothes, food, etc. are all ways that managers work around climatic extremes.

Population concentrations and ethnic compositions affect market demand and where manufacturing and physical distribution resources are sited. Populations and ethnic concentrations, the residue of history, must be mapped out for target marketing purposes. For example, Indonesia's 200 million people are divided into 250 distinct ethnic groups, although 60 percent of the national population lives on Java, one of the 13,000 islands comprising the nation. While Nigeria's 250 ethnic groups are spread out over 90 million people, four groups dominate: the Hausa and the Fulani in the north, the Yorubas in the southwest, and

Civilization exists by geological consent, subject to change without notice.

—*Will Durant,
U.S. historian*

Why would we have different races if God meant us to be alike and associate with each other?

—*Lester G. Maddox,
southern U.S. politician
of the segregationist era*

the Ibos in the southeast. Knowledge of ethnic groupings aids the tailoring of marketing strategies (e.g., literacy and linguistic needs for brand names, labeling, and promotions).

Resources facilitate economic development and trade. Countries need three types of resources to develop effectively. First, they need regular harvests to ensure adequate food supplies. Where food production is limited to specific areas, nationwide distribution facilities are necessary (not easy in geographically large nations such as Russia). Second, countries need energy supplies, such as coal, oil, or hydroelectric power, to aid industrialization. Energy sources must be both available and accessible. National governments often use international corporations to tap petroleum, natural gas, coal, nuclear, or other energy sources and to build energy infrastructures for national distribution. Third, nations need access to iron and mineral deposits for industrial development. International firms are often either key providers of extraction technologies or have the necessary contacts for global procurement.

Topography deals with the surface features of countries and often impacts language and cultural divisions. Globally, topography dictates population movements and settlements. Three-quarters of the Earth's surface has sparse populations due to extreme cold (Arctic and sub-arctic areas), lack of moisture (desert and dry grassland), steep slopes and high altitude (rugged highlands), and the multiple problems of a tropical forest that inhibit fixed settlements (excessive heat, moisture, dense forestation, and infertile soils, e.g., Latin America, Asia).[2] At the country level, mountain ranges form natural divisions within countries, most notably in Switzerland where they effectively divide German, French, Italian, and Romansh cultures. In Colombia, the Andes separate four regions, each with its own languages, dialects, and discernable climates.

Geographic Influences on Infrastructure Development For most industrialized countries, infrastructure analyses are unnecessary. Energy grids are established, as are water, sanitation facilities, and transportation systems (seaports, airports, roads). But with increasing emphases on developing markets, infrastructure facilities cannot be taken for granted. In these markets, companies must thoroughly evaluate national infrastructures, including:

Utility and energy assessments include water, sewer amenities, energy generation systems (power station locations, etc.), and energy grids to determine what proportions of populations receive electricity and gas amenities. For example, only 5–10 percent of Uganda's 22 million residents have electricity. Energy costs are also important considerations in factory designs (what energy sources are most cost-effective) and for consumers (for example, gasoline taxes in Western Europe that promote public transportation use).

Communication infrastructures need careful review as they affect corporate communications systems within markets, contacts with other countries, and corporate promotional efforts within markets. In the telecommunications area, the number of telephones, telephone units per 1000 population, and technological level (e.g., older analog systems vs. fiber-optic technology) should be evaluated. Increasingly today, wire-based grids have become less necessary for voice communications, with wireless cell phones now capable of transmitting and receiving voice and data inputs and with abilities to reach remote parts of emerging markets.

Radio and TV station availability and the degree of government ownership of media are important indicators of mass-media potential. Other media options (newspapers, magazines, direct-mail possibilities) are essential for products with mass-media dependencies (e.g., consumer products).

Transportation infrastructures include road networks (major highways down to dirt roads), rail systems, ports, airports, waterways, and bus systems.

- National highway systems vary enormously within countries. For most countries, links between urban centers are well-developed, as are connections with coastal areas. Countries with large land-masses (e.g., Russia, African countries) tend to be most variable, given the resources required to complete national highway systems. It must be remembered that it was not until the 1950s and 1960s that national highway systems were built in the U.S. and Western Europe. Natural impediments to transportation, such as climate and topography, are influential factors here, as are flooding, earthquakes, and hostile terrains.

- Waterways were major means of goods transportation prior to the industrial revolutions in North America and Europe, and are still important in many nations today. In North America, the Great Lakes–St. Lawrence and Mississippi waterways are still important trade corridors, as is the Rhine in Western and Central Europe. In South America, the Amazon River is an important commercial waterway. In India and Pakistan respectively, the Ganges and the Indus Rivers are important commercial conduits, and in China, the Yangste River is a major arterial waterway linking the Chinese interior with the commercially developed coastal areas.

- Rail systems are important where commodities or bulk shipments are necessary (e.g., chemicals, autos, industrial equipment). Most nations have rail systems, though their efficacy is variable. Railways are well-developed in Western Europe where they provide competition to road systems in moving goods among urban centers. As competition among transportation modes has intensified, so government-owned rail systems have been privatized and streamlined in many parts of the world, including China, Mexico, Philippines, Botswana, Ukraine, and Korea.

- Port, harbor, and airport locations must be mapped out and assessed. Port facilities are evaluated for their deepwater capabilities (i.e., abilities to service major freight-carrying fleets) and freight-loading/unloading facilities (degree of mechanization, equipment, labor efficiencies, etc.). Airport locations and proximity to commercial centers and major population groups are also evaluated, along with available facilities. For example, Afghanistan has forty-four airports, of which eleven have paved runways. Of these, three have runways over 3000 meters.[3]

There are three things that make a nation great and prosperous— a fertile soil, busy workshops, and easy conveyance for men and commodities.

—Francis Bacon, 16th–17th-century English philosopher

Ride the tributaries to the sea.

—Arabian proverb

Table 5.1 shows an example of how key historical and geographic factors have influenced China's development. Further discussion of the Chinese economy and general situation can also be found in Casette 5-3.

TABLE 5.1
Geographic and Historic Analysis of China

Geographic Factors	Effects
• Third largest nation in the world; 3.7 million square miles; 2000 miles east-west	• Hard to coordinate though north-south Grand Canal 7th century A.D. 1100 miles and defend (Great Wall 3800 miles long); isolationist tendencies
• Four Chinas: (1) Agricultural China, (2) Treeless plains, (3) Desert China (Gobi), (4) Ice-capped China	• Rice growing south; grain production in north; population concentrations in northeast and southern China. 950 million farmers make agriculture a "sensitive" industry
• Rivers dominate early transportation (Yellow, Yangste and West Rivers)	• River transportation still a major form of internal transportation

Historic Factors	Effects
• 4000 years of continuous culture and language, philosophy, writing, painting	• Pride in China and ethnocentrism; disdain for inferior "outsiders"
• Innovators • Iron Foundry 800 B.C. • Printing A.D. 105 • Compass 1st century A.D. • Astronomy 2nd century A.D. • Ink 3rd century A.D. • Wood block printing 8th century A.D. • Gunpowder 9th century A.D. • Moveable type A.D. 1050 • Leaders in crossbows, wheelbarrows, porcelain, mechanical clocks • 15th century Junk galleys 400 feet long, 4 decks • 1405–40: 36 countries visited.	• Lack of imperial interest in colonization, trade because little to learn from other cultures at that time. Foreign travel only confirmed Chinese cultural superiority.
• Imperial Dynasty: Emperor absolute ruler	• Respect for social hierarchies; social class differences
• Teachings of Confucius • Contentment with station in life • Importance of tradition • Obedience to authority • Rules, rites, etiquette in regular life • Responsibilities to family and society	• "Striving" "trying" inappropriate • Still apparent today • Harmony, conflict avoidance important • Deeply respectful and sincere in personal relationships • For 1,400 years (A.D. 600–present) knowledge of Confucian classics prerequisite for government posts
• Lao Zi: Taoism	• Rejection of self assertiveness, competitiveness • Live with nature • Encourage selflessness, cleanliness, emotional calm • Avoid desire, revulsion, grief, joy, anger—wasted emotions
• 19th–20th centuries: Conflicts with outsiders • 1839–42, 1st Opium War: Lost • 1856–60, 2nd Opium War: Lost • 1884–85, French Conflict: Lost • 1894–95 Japanese Conflict: Lost	• Chinese discontent with foreign influences • 1900 Boxer Rebellion • 1911 Overthrow of Imperial Dynasty—1200 years of rule by emperor ended by Dr. Sun Yat-sen
• 1925: Dr. Sun Yat-sen dies	• Civil war between Chinese Nationalists and Communists/regional warlords
• 1930s: Japanese invasion and atrocities (e.g., Rape of Nanking)	• Distrust of Japanese
• 1949: Nationalists beaten by communists—go to island of Formosa and establish Taiwan ROC; Mao Tse Tung comes to power	• Ongoing tensions between China–Taiwan; China officially becomes a communist state
• 1950s: Economy stabilized, landed gentry/Lords destroyed	• Destroyed old aristocracies and archaic economic institutions
• 1960s: Great Leap Forward: Industrialization efforts fail; universities, schools closed, Red Guard brutality; disrespect for elders	• Disillusionment mounts with communism; USSR–China disagreements; attacks on schools and education considered "Un-Chinese"
• 1976: Mao Tse Tung, Chou En Lai die	• Communism loses founding fathers; loses impetus
• 1981: Deng Xiou Peng and moderates gain control • 1982: New constitution: More personal freedom, room for individual initiatives • 1985: Younger generation replaces old guard • 1989: Tiannemen Square massacre • 1997: Major restructuring of Chinese economy, emphasizing capitalistic methods • 1999: Deng Xiou Peng dies • 2001: China admitted to World Trade Organization	• Ongoing internal struggles between old line communists and new generation of market forces-oriented politicians • Gradual introduction of market forces-based principles and entry into the global economy

Sources: Compiled from: *Library of Nations: China.* (Alexandria, Va.: Time-Life Books, 1985). Roberts, J. M. *History of the World.* (London: Penguin Books, 1997). *Timetables of History.* (New York: Random House, 1996). Smith, Huston. *The World's Religions.* (San Francisco: Harper Collins Books, 1998).

CURRENT POSITION ANALYSIS

Once historic and geographic factors have been reviewed, managers turn their attentions to present-day conditions. This involves examining a country's current political, economic, and international positions (see Table 5.2).

The Current Political Situation

Business people cannot know too much about how political systems work within nations and what factors drive policy decisions. Corporate analyses of political structures usually include the following elements.

Political System While 60 percent of nations have functioning democratic systems, others retain high degrees of authoritarianism in their political systems. Plus many democratic systems have retained authoritarian characteristics, for example, when one party is reelected most or all of the time. Examples include the PRI party that ruled Mexico for seventy-one years (until 2000), the Liberal Democrat Party in Japan that has held office continually since 1945, and various family political dynasties that have dominated Asian and Middle Eastern politics over generations (e.g., Egypt, Indonesia, India, Pakistan, Bangladesh).

> No man is good enough to govern another man without the other's consent.
>
> —*Abraham Lincoln, 19th-century U.S. president*

Parliamentary Assemblies In addition to presidents and political figureheads, most democracies have elected assemblies. Many, like the United States and Japan, have two chambers of representatives. In Japan's case, there is the powerful House of Representatives, numbering 500 members who are elected to four-year terms, and the 252-member House of Counselors who are elected to six-year terms.[4]

Key Political Parties Profiling major parties and political philosophies provide insights into political and economic policy formulation. In most democracies, there are right-wing parties that represent pro-business interests (e.g., the Conservative and Republican Parties in the U.K. and U.S.); and those that support broader interests (e.g., Labour and Democrat Parties in those same countries). Where governments are formed out of coalitions, managers must assess how robust (or fragile) the coalition is. Late 1990s elections in India put the Bharatiya Janata Party (BJP) into power with the leading voice in a 15–20 party coalition government.[5]

Political Risk, Elections, and the Likelihood of Political Change These are important topics for international executives, particularly where there are major philosophical differences among political parties. While general methods of political and environmental risk assessments a laid out in Chapter 7, four specific analyses are necessary for in-depth country evaluations.

Internal frictions heighten the probability of political change. In countries with major ethnic or religious differences, rivalries among diverse groups create political and civil discontent. For example, the breakup of Yugoslavia in the mid-1990s resulted in political turmoil in Bosnia-Herzegovina as rival Serbian, Croatian and Muslim groups sought to maintain their ethnic identities. In South Africa, rival tribal groups have contributed to upsurges in violent crime,[6] and religion

> There is no more evil thing in this world than race prejudice . . . It justifies and holds together more baseness, cruelty and abomination than any other sort of error in the world.
>
> —*H. G. Wells, 19th–20th-century English author*

TABLE 5.2
Effects of Political, Economic, and International Factors on Business Activities

Political, Economic, and International Factors	Significance for Business
Political Factors	
• Political system: Authoritarian to multi-party democratic system; political history	Gives insights as to political risk of doing business (pro or anti-business); likelihood of political change due to elections, internal frictions, external influences, economic, political problems
• Parliamentary assemblies: Elections for head of state, national assemblies e.g. every 2, 4, or 6 years.	
• Key political parties: Philosophies, key issues	The greater the policy differences among parties, the greater the changes in governmental changes.
Economic Changes	

1. Comparative Economic Analysis: Against regional rivals
  • GDP size
  • GDP/Capita
  • GDP growth
  • Inflation
  • Trade balance
  • Foreign debt
  • Currency situation
	Relative attractiveness of regional markets; regional differences/similarities among affluence levels, growth potential; government trade policies (free trade/protectionist)

2. Country Economic Analyses (over time)
  General Economic Indicators
  • GDP size and GDP/Capita
  • Public sector finances (government income/expenditures, deficits, overall debt)
  • Inflation and price movements (wholesale, consumer, general), money supply (usually M2)
  • Wage movements, unemployment
	Market size and affluence indicator
	Responsible government economic management
	
	Problematic if high, rising
	
	General indicators of economic well-being

Private Sector Performance
  • Public versus private consumption
  • Splits between agriculture, industry and service sectors
 	
  • Private sector analysis: Key industries: construction, retail sales, and stock market activity
	Extent of governmental influence on the economy
	Indicators of level of economic and sector development
	
	Key indicators of economic growth, activity, and consumption levels

3. International Economic and Trade Policy • Membership of WTO, trade blocs, international trading agreements	Key shaper of national trade policies and indicator of free-trade orientations
International Position	
• Exchange rate regime and national currency trends/movements	Currency stability over time

• Balance of payments analysis
  −Balance of trade position
  −Balance of payments on current account
	Competitiveness of country as a manufacturing base
	Persistent deficits indicate increased likelihood of depreciating currency or governmental action

−Investment flows (inflows, outflows, foreign direct investments, portfolio investments, money flows)	Attractiveness as an investment site
• Foreign debt situation: External (hard currency) debt; debt-service ratio (% export earnings that go toward debt repayment)	Problems when high % export earnings to service ratio
• Foreign currency reserves (foreign exchange, gold, SDRs)—measured by number of months of import coverage	Low reserves are warning signs for currencies

continues to be a divisive factor in countries as different as Northern Ireland and India.

External influences from the global political and economic marketplace impact country politics. Privatization movements in the former communist-controlled countries of Eastern Europe have produced backlashes where the benefits of market-forces-based economies have been slow to benefit national electorates. In 2002, China, South Korea, and other Asian countries experienced major labor unrest as privatization reforms produced layoffs and became major threats to the "iron rice bowl" philosophy of job security and permanent employment.

Economic problems often cause political change, and political risk analysts routinely include key economic indicators alongside political assessments. Downturns in economic growth limit job creation and affect politically sensitive unemployment statistics. Inflation erodes consumer purchasing power. National trade performance is monitored as exports create jobs, while imports are perceived as taking them away (and promoting protectionist tendencies). Severe trade imbalances between exports and imports indicate needs for foreign-exchange rate adjustments.

Political problems to be addressed over the short and medium-term are sources of internal unrest. Conflicts over government-funding priorities are common, including welfare and benefit-support levels (Western Europe), investment priorities (labor or capital-intensive industries), taxation levels ("no new taxes") and government-expenditures plans. The relative strengths of pro and anti-business factions affect developments in company laws; intellectual property rights; environmental, competition, and taxation policies; issues in foreign trade, currencies; and capital markets; human resource legislation; and, increasingly these days, factors affecting electronic commerce.

The Current Economic Position

Comparative Economic Analyses It is difficult and dangerous to review national economic performance in isolation. A first step, therefore, is to assess country economic performance in its regional context. Casette 5-2 examines Brazil's economic performance in its Latin American context. GDP size, per capita, inflation rates, and trade performance are assessed for individual and surrounding markets to assess their relative performance. Such evaluations not only help economic assessments, they also provide indicators of business potential for company products in neighboring markets. Where trade blocs are in operation, these analyses aid corporate assessments of regional investment prospects and potentials for cross-border branding and manufacturing scale economies.

> The only good budget is a balanced budget.
>
> —*Adam Smith,*
> *18th-century economist*

Country-specific economic analyses focus on three areas.

1. *General economic indicators* must be assessed.

    - GDP size and GDP per capita must be evaluated over time to evaluate trends in market affluence. Other key indicators include economic growth and unemployment rates.

    - Public-sector finances are also subject to scrutiny: whether government income and expenditures are in balance and (if not) how public finance deficits are managed. Stable public finances breed political

> Think of the inflation spiral as a giant corkscrew . . . and think of yourself as the cork.
>
> —*Bert Lance, former U.S. budget director*

stability, stable economic growth, and international confidence in national currency values.

- Inflation indicators are important in emerging markets where aggregate supply-and-demand imbalances cause price fluctuations during industrialization. For example, triple-digit inflation plagued Turkey's economic performance throughout the 1990s as successive governments battled to contain price increases.[7] Inflation can be monitored in three ways: (1) at general, retail, or wholesale levels, (2) through upward shifts in wages levels, and (3) through money supply indicators. Chaotic increases in M2 money supply (currency, demand deposits, and government bills) are causes for concern. Inflationary tendencies have major adverse effects on economic performance, economic policy, political stability, and foreign exchange rates, particularly in less-stable, emerging market contexts.

2. *Private-sector performance* shows how specific industries and sectors are performing.

- Splits between public and private expenditures show the extent of government influence in the national economy.

- Divisions between agriculture, industry, and services show the extent of development, with basic economies having extensive agrarian interests and mature countries having heavy service components.

- Other useful indicators include construction statistics (key indicators of economic growth), retail sales (as yardsticks of consumer demand), and stock market activity (as general indicators of business confidence levels). Managers should examine as broad an array of economic indicators as possible and supplement statistical data with expert economic analyses.

3. *International economic and trade policies* affect tariff levels and country trading policies. For example, Egypt, a member of the WTO, has most-favored trading relationships with the U.S. and Israel (meaning that trade with these nations is "normal"). It signed an agreement to phase in free trade with the EU by 2012. Egypt is a member of the nineteen-state Arab Common Market to be established by 2007, the twenty-one-state Common Market of Eastern and Southern Africa (COMESA), and the Islamic Group of Eight to establish a free-trade area across the Middle East and parts of Asia.[8]

The Current International Position

Analyzing Country Balance of Payments How nations interact financially with the rest of the world is examined through balance-of-payments analyses. The balance of payments of a country, simply stated, is an "accounting record of all economic transactions between residents of that nation and foreign residents during some specific time (usually a year)." The International Monetary Fund (IMF) standard balance-of-payments presentation has three sections: (1) current accounts, (2) capital account, and (3) reserves. Table 5.3 summarizes key concepts in balance of payments analysis.

TABLE 5.3
Balance of Payments Digest: Definitions and Impacts on National Economies and Companies

Balance of Payments Components	Country/Company Effects
Balance of Payments on Current Account	
Merchandise Trade Balance	*Country Effects:* Persistent negative trade balances may result in government devaluations of national currencies, or allowing national currencies to depreciate in value according to market forces (more national currency units per dollar/euro/yen.
Merchandise exports—merchandise imports	
Inflows/Credits: Payments to country for exports	
Outflows/Debits: Payments by country for imports	*Company Effects:* Persistent negative trade balances can result in governments offering export incentives and/or placing restrictions on imports (tariffs, quotas, etc.)
Exports > Imports: Trade balance surplus	
Imports > Exports: Trade balance deficit	
Trade in Services (freight, insurance, shipping)	Country restrictions on carriers: e.g., exports or imports must use domestic carriers
Inflows/Credits: Payments by foreigners to national service providers	
Outflows/Debits: Payments by national firms to foreign service providers	
Income (corporate profits, individuals repatriating income or salaries)	Where outflows of profits or income are deemed excessive/disruptive, restrictions may be applied or taxes placed on dividend, royalty, or profit repatriations
Inflows/Credits: Foreign subsidiary profits or expatriates repatriating income or salaries	
Outflows/Debits: Foreign profits or salaries made in the domestic market repatriated out of the country to home market.	
Unrequited (one-time) Payments	Government aid may have "strings" attached requiring contracts to go to home market contractors or be used for specific purposes
(government aid, foreign military expenditures, embassy expenditures, etc.)	
Capital Account	
Capital Equipment Account	
Inflows/Credits: Payments made by foreign companies in the domestic market for capital equipment purchases	
Outflows/Debits: Equipment purchases made by national firms in foreign markets	
Direct Investments: In factories and plant	Inflows show the attractiveness of the national economy/market to foreign investors as a manufacturing site.
Inflows/Credits: Foreign investments in the national economy	
Outflows/Debits: National companies making investments in foreign markets	Outflows demonstrate national company interest in producing in foreign markets. May show diminishing competitiveness of the national market as a manufacturing or export site
Portfolio Investments are investments made in companies without the intent of outright ownership or control (e.g. < 10 percent control or buying shares through stock markets)	Inflows occur during economic growth periods ("boom times"), as national economies and stock markets demonstrate growth and superior returns.
Inflows/credits are foreign investments in the national stock markets	
Outflows/Debits are investments in foreign stock markets	Outflows occur during economic downturns/recessions or as political risk factors increase (strikes, wars, civil unrest)
Monetary Transactions comprise money movements among international financial institutions to take advantage of exchange rate and interest rate differences	Financial flows among countries very much influenced by national interest rates and government monetary policies. Governments may increase national interest rates to attract foreign capital or prevent "capital flight" out of countries due to economic slowdowns. Low national interest rates on government bonds/certificates of deposit discourage buildups of foreign "speculative" capital.
Inflows/Credits: Foreign money movements into domestic financial markets and institutions	
Outflows/Debits: Domestic money movements into foreign financial markets or institutions	
Net Errors and Omissions are items not included under other headings or unaccounted financial flows or money movements	
Overall Balance of Payments	Overall surpluses on balance of payments mean that incoming payments exceed outgoing payments. This may result in excess demand for the home currency and pressures for currency appreciation (fewer national currency units per euro/dollar/yen).
Balance of payments on current account + capital account + net errors and omissions	
	Overall deficits mean that currency outflows (supply) exceed inflows (demand), resulting in pressures for currency depreciation (more national currency units per dollar/euro/yen).

1. The balance of payments on current account consists of four parts.

   - *The merchandise trade balance* is the first component and comprises manufacturing exports and imports and goods for processing. When country product exports exceed imports, the nation has a balance of trade surplus. When it imports more than it exports, it has a trade deficit. Generally, the crude trade balance (as it is known) is an important indicator of a country's manufacturing competitiveness in international trade.

   - *The goods and services balance* is the second part of the current account and includes not only merchandise exports ("credits," or "inflows" of money) and imports ("debits," or "outflows" of money) but also freight, insurance, and shipping charges (paid out by a country's residents [debits] or received by its residents [credits]). These two sectors combined comprise the goods and services account.

   - *The income account* is the third component. This is made up of outflows and inflows of corporate profits and individual earnings from the resident country to foreign sources (outflows, or debits) and profit and income repatriations from foreign-based companies and individuals back into the resident country (inflows, or credits). For example, worker remittances comprise 24 and 20 percent respectively of Nicaraguan and Indian GDPs.[9] The goods, services, and income balance shows the net inflows/outflows resulting from these activities.

   - *Unrequited (one-time) transfers* are the fourth current account component. They include transfers by foreign governments into the resident country (inflows, or credits) and resident government transfers out of the country (outflows, or debits). Together, these four items comprise the balance of payments on current account.

2. The balance of payments on capital account consists of outflows and inflows of capital, mainly for investment purposes. Note that capital items are often labeled "assets" and "liabilities." Outgoing investments are capital outflows, which then become "assets" in foreign markets. Incoming investments are inflows but represent foreign "liabilities" in capital accounts. There are five parts.

   - *The capital account n.i.e.* is the first component and comprises payments for fixed assets such as machinery and equipment. Credit items are foreign companies bringing equipment into the resident country. Debit payments are money outflows as resident firms send machinery into foreign markets.

   - *Direct investments* in factories with plant and machinery is the second part. Incoming direct investments by foreigners are credits (inflows), and country resident investments made abroad are debits, or outflows.

   - *Portfolio investments* comprise purchases of corporate securities, bonds, or equities. These include minority holdings in individual companies (share purchases—less than 10 percent—without the intent to participate in the company's management), stock market

> One of the funny things about the stock market is that every time one man buys, another sells, and both think they are astute.
>
> —*William Feather, 20th-century U.S. author*

investments made by residents in foreign markets (outflows, or debits), and those made by foreigners in the resident country (inflows, or credits).

- *Financial derivatives* comprise the fourth component. These are financial instruments that transfer risks in foreign exchange, equities, interest rates, and commodity prices among financial intermediaries in more than one market. That is, financial institutions in more than one nation share foreign exchange or other risks in return for a share of the risk premium (the price of insuring the risk).

- *Other investments* are the fifth part. They include currency transactions from monetary authorities (e.g., the IMF) and the government; deposits and loans made among international banks; and investment inflows/outflows, often trade credits. Payments made into the resident country are inflows, or credits, and outflows (debits) are from resident-nation financial institutions into foreign markets.

The financial account comprises direct investments, portfolio investments, financial derivatives, and other investments.

Net errors and omissions are items that do not fall under mainstream balance of payments headings. The balance of payments on current account (trade + services + income + current transfers) plus the capital account n.i.e. (machinery and equipment transactions) plus financial accounts (direct, portfolio investment, financial derivatives, and other investments) plus net errors and omissions comprise the *overall balance of payments*. Positive balances of trade signify net inflows of monies ("surpluses"); negative numbers indicate net money outflows ("deficits").

3. Reserves and related items accounts show how balance-of-payments surpluses are used (generally they are added to foreign convertible currency reserves) or how deficits are financed (usually by decreases in convertible currency reserves). Where deficits are significant and continuous, "exceptional financing" packages are used, usually comprising IMF loans.

How Managers Use Balance-of-Payments Data

Balance-of-payments accounts show a country's financial interactions with the rest of the world. Table 5.4 shows the U.S. balance of payments and what conclusions can be drawn from them regarding its international situation. As well as being general indicators of a country's international well-being, they also provide a number of other useful indicators.

Merchandise Trade Balance: Imports and Exports In many, particularly developing countries, merchandise trade tends to be the most important component of the national balance of payments. Persistent balance-of-trade deficits (imports > exports) invite governments to (a) limit imports through protectionist measures (tariffs, non-tariff barriers, quotas), (b) encourage exports (e.g., making them value-added tax exempt as in the EU, or making export activities prerequisites for direct investment permissions), (c) devalue home currencies to make export prices more competitive and limit the price effectiveness of imports. Maintaining exports is important as developing market governments use convertible foreign exchange to finance imports and economic growth.

TABLE 5.4
The U.S. Balance of Payments, 1995–2001

U.S. Balance/Payments	1995	1996	1997	1998	1999	2000	2001
Goods: Exports fob	577.05	614.02	680.33	672..38	686.28	774.64	721.75
Goods: Imports fob	−749.38	−803.12	−876.51	−917.12	−1029.9	−1224.4	−1145.9
Trade Balance	−172.33	−189.10	−196.18	−244.74	−343.70	−449.79	−424.23
Services: Credit	217.46	238.17	254.70	260.28	270.90	289.63	276.28
Services: Debit	−141.50	−150.91	−166.28	−182.53	−189.47	−218.52	210.35
Goods/Serv. Balance	−96.37	−101.84	−107.76	−166.99	−262.27	−378.68	−358.30
Income: Credit	211.54	225.86	260.58	259.40	290.56	353.03	283.76
Income: Debit	−186.92	−201.77	−240.39	−251.76	−272.39	−331.22	−269.39
Gds/Serv/Inc Balance	−71.75	−77.75	−87.57	−159.35	−244.10	−356.87	−343.93
Current transfers: Credit	7.68	8.89	8.49	9.19	9.57	10.65	10.47
Current transfers: Debit	−41.75	−48.98	−49.28	−53.69	−58.33	−64.08	−59.94
B/P on Current Account	−105.82	−117.84	−128.36	−203.85	−292.86	−410.30	−393.40
Capital Account							
Capital account: n.i.e.	0.37	0.69	0.35	0.70	−3.39	0.84	0.83
Capital account: Credit	0.67	0.69	0.35	0.70	0.60	0.84	0.83
Capital account: Debit	−0.3	0	0	0	−3.99	0	0
Financial account n.i.e.	95.94	130.52	220.16	70.60	256.11	409.81	386.79
Direct investment abroad	−98.78	−91.88	−104.82	−142.64	−188.91	−178.29	−127.84
FDI: Home market	57.80	86.52	105.59	179.03	289.44	307.74	130.80
Portfolio invest: Assets	−122.51	−149.83	−118.98	−136.13	−128.44	−127.50	−94.66
Equity securities	−65.41	−82.85	−57.58	−101.28	−114.31	−103.64	−106.81
Debt securities	−57.1	−66.98	−61.4	−34.85	−14.13	−23.86	12.16
Portfolio invest: Liabilities	210.36	332.78	333.11	187.58	285.59	419.90	426.06
Equity securities	16.53	11.06	67.04	41.96	112.29	193.51	121.42
Debt securities	193.83	321.72	266.07	145.62	173.30	226.39	304.64
Financial deriv's: Assets	0	0	0	0	0	0	0
Financial deriv's: Liabilities	0	0	0	0	0	0	0
Other investment assets	−121.38	−178.90	−262.83	−74.21	−169.00	−300.40	−143.54
Monetary authorities	0	0	0	0	0	0	0
General government	−0.98	−1.00	0.06	−0.42	2.75	−0.94	−0.48
Banks	−75.11	−91.56	−141.13	−35.58	−76.27	−148.66	−128.70
Other sectors	−45.29	−86.34	−121.76	−38.21	−95.48	−150.80	−14.36
Other investment liabilities	170.45	131.83	268.09	56.97	167.43	288.36	195.97
Monetary authorities	46.73	56.88	−18.86	6.89	24.59	−6.70	35.10
General government	0.9	0.73	−2.70	−3.26	−0.85	−0.48	−4.35
Banks	64.19	22.19	171.32	30.27	67.19	122.72	80.39
Other sectors	58.63	52.03	118.33	23.07	76.50	172.82	84.83
Net errors & omissions	19.26	−20.04	−91.13	139.29	31.41	−0.05	10.71
OVERALL BALANCE	9.75	−6.67	1.02	6.74	−8.73	0.30	4.93
Reserves and related items	−9.75	6.67	−1.02	−6.74	8.73	−0.30	−4.93
Reserve assets	−9.75	6.67	−1.02	−6.73	8.73	−0.30	−4.93
Fund credit and loans	0	0	0	0	0	0	0
Exceptional financing	0	0	0	0	0	0	0

Analysis

1. The overall balance of payments shows two minor deficits (1996, 1999) and five minor surpluses. This suggests that against world currency generally, the U.S. dollar should be quite stable. The deficits on current account (goods, services, income, and transfers) are offset by major inflows of investments on the capital account.

2. The trade balance (export minus imports) shows increasing deficits over 1995–2000, with a lessened deficit for 2001. This reflects a steady deterioration in the U.S.'s position as a world manufacturing and export base. Exports over 1995–2001 show a 25 percent increase, while imports increased by 52.8 percent. It also demonstrates U.S. appetites for foreign-sourced products (e.g., autos, retail consumer goods).

3. Balance on goods and services is negative, but less so than the crude trade balance, reflecting U.S. service credits in shipping, insurance, and other services. Similarly, incoming incomes from U.S. companies and personnel overseas are greater than outgoings from the U.S., bringing the goods, services, and income deficit down overall.

4. The financial account (direct investments, portfolio investments, financial derivatives, and other investments) shows major capital inflows into the U.S. economy (especially 1999–2001 when they offset the current account deficit). Closer examination shows that:

   • Traditionally, the U.S. has invested more in overseas markets than other countries do in the U.S. From 1998 onward though, this trend is reversing itself, with foreigners finding the U.S. economy more attractive than U.S. firms find foreign markets.

   • More striking is the portfolio investments made in U.S. equity and other debt securities, with non-U.S. investors injecting three-to-four times the amounts that U.S. investors are investing in foreign stock markets. This reflects the relative attractiveness of the U.S. economy and stock market over this period. Interestingly, U.S. investors are more likely to invest in foreign equity markets than in debt securities. Foreign investors prefer U.S. bonds, debentures, notes, and other debt instruments over stock market equity options.

   • The "Other investment" figure shows the increasing importance of international money movements—transactions in currencies, bank deposits, loans, and trade credits. Banks are particularly active in transferring monies into and out of the U.S. economy. Other sectors (mainly comprising trade credits) are also increasing in importance as U.S. trade expands and trade credits become an competitive tool in the global marketplace.

Conclusion: The adverse trade accounts are being offset by capital inflows, providing steady influences on the value of the dollar against world currency. Questions remain over what happens to the U.S. dollar if/when the U.S. economy and capital market suffers an economic downturn or becomes less attractive to foreign capital. If this occurs, capital inflows would fall, and the U.S.'s adverse trade and current account balance would cause a significant balance-of-payments deficit, resulting in a likely depreciation of the U.S. dollar.

Services Where nations have significant deficits on items like shipping, insurance, etc., they are prone to enact laws requiring foreign firms to use domestic shipping for exports or imports or to use local companies as insurance carriers.

Investments Few countries today restrict outgoing or incoming investments. Occasionally, however, during economic crises such as the 1997–99 Asian financial crisis, governments restrict outgoing capital ("capital flight") to stabilize national currencies.

Balance-of-Payments Effects on Currency Values Where nations allow their currencies to float according to market supply and demand, home-country exchange rates are affected by their balance-of-payments situations. National balance-of-payment figures show currency inflows (demands for the home currency) and currency outflows (supplies of home currency going out and demand for foreign currencies). Where countries have overall *balance-of-payments surpluses,* demand for the home currency (foreign currency conversions into the home currency) is greater than supply (home currencies leaving the country to be converted into foreign currencies). Overall, this means that the domestic currency should appreciate against world currencies (i.e., more foreign currency units per domestic currency unit). *Balance-of-payments deficits* indicate that more domestic currency is leaving the country than is being demanded. Consequently, the home currency should depreciate (i.e., fewer foreign currency units per domestic unit).

> Inflation is the one form of taxation that can be imposed without legislation.
>
> —*Milton Friedman, U.S. economist*

Inflation Rate Effects on Balances of Payments and Currency Values

Where price rises are excessive (i.e., above those in the international economy generally), exports and imports become less competitive, and governments are prone to devalue their currencies (i.e., increasing the number of national currency units per dollar/euro/yen). Where imports are essential and nonresponsive to upward-price movements, further inflation can result. At the same time, severe inflation makes international companies wary of making investments and may result in capital flight as domestic residents seek to preserve purchasing power by converting assets and monies into strong currencies, such as the dollar and euro. From a practical standpoint, managers can expect national currencies to depreciate in proportion to the rise in domestic prices (i.e., a 25 percent inflation rate is likely to result in a 25 percent devaluation of the currency).

COMMERCIAL ANALYSIS

Once analyses of past and current political and economic conditions are complete, managers must evaluate industry and operating conditions within markets. This involves commercial assessments of national industry structures, demand analyses, and supply-chain issues, and analyses of business environment factors, including financial elements (capital markets, taxation, and currency issues) and legal infrastructures.

Industry Analysis

While global industry analyses focus on worldwide consumption, production, major players, and trends, analyses of individual markets are in-depth assessments of industry size, growth rates, market structures, and sector characteristics. International and national industry associations, trade magazines, web sites, and news services are useful sources for compiling industry and corporate business profiles.[10] Assessments should include the following elements.

1. Market size, growth rate; principal segments
2. Market structure

   - Number of firms and sizes
   - National competitors—global, regional, national and local firms
   - Industry concentration—percent total output of largest companies
   - Industry profitability
   - Primary competitive platforms (e.g., low-cost vs. differentiation options)
   - Pace of technological and marketplace change—technologies, customer preferences
   - Key success factors—what it takes to become a market leader
   - Degree of vertical integration (e.g., ownership levels of suppliers and channels)
   - Industry characteristics—scale economy effects in manufacturing (e.g., costs) and in marketing (advertising, selling, R and D, new product development costs)

The industry situation directly impacts how firms choose to service and compete in individual markets. In particular, market size, growth rates, and competitive intensity are key factors in market entry and servicing options (discussed fully in Chapter 9).

Demand Analysis: Customer and Marketing Considerations

Customer Concentrations Customers are focal points of corporate marketing efforts. As such, the starting point for demand analyses are geographic concentrations of customers. For consumer-goods firms, towns and urban concentrations are important because: (a) Developed and many developing countries have high urban populations. (b) Urban consumers tend to be affluent and better educated. (c) Towns tend to have superior infrastructures, particularly in developing nations. For industrial companies, industry clusters often develop in particular areas, reflecting skilled-labor availability (Silicon Valley) or raw-material availability (extractive industries, glass-making, chemicals).

> There is only one valid definition of business purpose: to create a customer.
>
> —*Peter Drucker,*
> *U.S. business author and consultant*

Customer Segmentation Issues Firms normally go to great lengths to profile national, regional, and local populations with respect to income, occupation, education, and other demographic and lifestyle (attitudes, interests, and opinions) factors. In India, for example, Hindustan Lever profiles villages, including dialects, education levels, religions, literacy rates, even the number of bank balances above specific levels.[11] Where profiles are similar to those in other markets, product and service transfers from those markets (the basis of global and multi-market strategies) can be contemplated. Product-and-service-mix options include transferring product or service concepts from home markets or from other subsidiaries (e.g., from other Asian affiliates for a new Asian start-up). Where significant variations exist in customer profiles (affluence, education, the presence of multiple ethnic or language groups, or differences in religious affiliations), firms are careful about product and service transfers and may customize their marketing approaches. This may involve major adaptations to product or service transfers or creating new items for use in the market. In most cases, market research and customer testing is necessary.

THE GLOBAL WEB

For some listings of market research firms worldwide, regionally, and by country, and linkages see:
www.imriresearch.com

Marketing Research Services Many firms outsource data-gathering activities, particularly in unfamiliar markets, to locally based companies that are aware of the problems associated with doing market research in their locales. These include unusual social class categories (such as the U.K.'s A-E lifestyle classifications), unreliable government statistics, data collection problems (focus-group usefulness, obtaining reliable samples of consumers, uncooperative respondents, telephone-research biases, mailing-list problems, etc.). Fortunately, market research organizations have become increasingly global, often following major clients into foreign markets. Two of the largest are U.S. firms, A. C. Nielsen (forty-five countries and 78 percent foreign

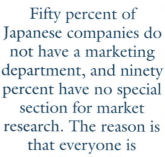

> Fifty percent of Japanese companies do not have a marketing department, and ninety percent have no special section for market research. The reason is that everyone is considered to be a marketing specialist.
>
> —*Hiroyuki Takeuchi,*
> *U.S. educator and business writer*

revenue) and IMS International (seventy-four countries, 64 percent foreign revenue). Other top 10 global research organizations are European (U.K.'s Research International and Taylor Nelson Sofres, France's SOFRES Group, and Germany's GFK Holding AG). All have twenty to thirty foreign locations and receive about half their revenues from foreign operations.[12] Some of the services they offer include brand-image measurement and tracking, advertising research (messages, pretests, post-tests), new product testing, customer satisfaction and relationship measures, attitudinal/lifestyle research, media exposure data and expenditures, and consumer panels.

Supply Chain Analyses

Supplier Considerations Availability and quality of local suppliers determine what can be sourced within the market and what must be sourced internationally. Where there are problems with in-market suppliers, options include (a) upgrading local suppliers through training programs, (b) acquiring and managing local suppliers, (c) and encouraging foreign suppliers to invest locally. Other factors affecting localized supply chain are discussed in Chapter 13. Where international sourcing looks likely, national trade policies are examined (including balance-of-trade and payments situations), along with any problems involved in obtaining timely supplies (including infrastructure facilities, especially for just-in-time manufacturing). Tariff and non-tariff barriers must be assessed. Discussions with importers can alert companies to non-tariff barriers, such as special product designs or quality requirements, government subsidies to local industries, variations in customs valuations, administrative delays (e.g., product inspections procedures), or xenophobic buying habits (e.g., "Buy American" laws in some U.S. states or requirements that imports should be carried on domestic ships or airlines).[13] Discussions of global and multi-market sourcing strategies are continued in Chapter 11.

Manufacturing Investment and Site-Location Decisions This involves evaluating many factors, including the following.

Investment permissions: Many nations, particularly in the developing world, require approvals from one or more government ministries. In Malaysia, for example, investment approvals must be obtained from the Malaysian Industrial Development Authority. This body screens potential investments to ensure a suitable fit with national industrial development goals, a process that normally takes six weeks to two months. Well-planned proposals include job creation opportunities, estimates of sales and profits, raw material and component needs (locally sourced or imported), and export contributions.[14]

Investment incentives: Many governments are keen to direct new investments to specific parts of the country and offer location incentives. For investments sited in underdeveloped parts, Egypt provides regional incentives, including profit tax exemptions for ten or twenty years, free land, and government-supplied infrastructures (e.g., road, energy, water supplies).[15] Within the European Union, EU project assistance varies according to whether areas are classified as backward, in long-term industrial decline, or in need of economic diversification away from agricultural pursuits. Incentives also vary with company size, with large firms receiving the fewest benefits.[16]

Industry-specific incentives encourage development in individual sectors. Peru's priority sectors include basic foodstuffs, medicines,

> Where money talks, there are few interruptions.
>
> —*Herbert V. Prochnow*

and industrial machinery. Additionally, mining, gas, and oil industries can qualify for tax exemptions, credits, and foreign-exchange allowances.[17]

Where countries wish to promote export, re-export, or product-processing bases, they establish foreign trade zones (FTZs). These are specially designated customs-free areas where companies can assemble, store, package, and otherwise process goods without being subject to national tariffs, duties, quotas, and permits. Products remain unaffected by customs laws unless they are sold within the country where the FTZ is located. Hungary has 150 such FTZs.

Infrastructure connections: However, despite the generosity of government regional incentives, firms must be assured that locations will meet operational requirements, including access to energy needs and good communications infrastructures, (roads, rails, air, sea, and telecommunications facilities). Other infrastructure factors include ready access to raw materials, suppliers, or customers.

Labor quality and availability are key issues in deciding where to manufacture. Supplies of skilled and unskilled labor are essential for many industries. The quality of national educational infrastructures is important. General education levels and the availability of trade and vocational colleges affect the supply of skilled labor. Likewise, the quality of college and university educations affects supplies of managers (e.g., business schools) and technical personnel (engineers, scientists).

Labor laws and their enforcement affect management relations and corporate cost structures. Most nations have labor laws, such as Mexico's 1969 Federal Labor Law that covers labor contracts, wages, hours of work, legal holidays, paid vacations, trade union rights and regulations, strikes, dismissal procedures, and compensation. Within these general codes and laws, specific issues are given prominence, such as health and safety codes; collective bargaining rules (who may strike and who may not) and rules for arbitration; minimum wages and fringe benefits (which in Mexico add 70–100 percent to base payroll expenses); workweek lengths, shift work, and maternity-leave benefits (Mexico allows twelve weeks of maternity leave and additional benefits); rules and rights of part-time and temporary labor; employment termination; and employment of foreigners.[18]

Information technology and E-commerce issues: Supply-chain coordination has become a key issue for international firms, and managers today routinely evaluate the status of IT development within nations as it affects supply-chain coordination (with suppliers, distributors), sales (the extent to which transactions can be conducted directly with consumers), and internal coordination (corporate Internet communications). While E-commerce is well-developed in the industrialized nations, there is considerable variability in developing countries, where infrastructure deficiencies and poverty are key obstacles. Mexico's Internet-ready computer ownership doubled between 2000–2002 to 5½ million users under the impetus of an ambitious national program named E-Mexico[19]; in Pakistan's case, poor infrastructure, limited computer use, and a state-owned telecommunications monopoly has slowed E-commerce development.[20]

Cost chain considerations: Cost chains are financial breakdowns for supply-chain activities and include supplier costs, labor, manufacturing and distribution costs, capital depreciation, and taxes affecting customer prices. Of these,

> Labor is the great producer of wealth; it moves all other causes.
>
> —*Daniel Webster,*
> *19th-century U.S. statesman*

> It is only when they go wrong that computers remind you how powerful they are.
>
> –*Clive James,*
> *British journalist*

firms have least influence over labor, depreciation, and taxation costs, as these tend to be market or government-controlled.

- Wage rates are normally subject to national minimums and are market-determined above that level. In Peru, the minimum wage in 2000 was 410 Ns (Nuevo Sol [about $120]) per month. Industry variations were from 650 Ns per month for retailing to about 4000 Ns in the mining sector. Additional wage differences relate to skill status (blue collar, unskilled, semi-skilled, skilled), white collar (graduates, junior, senior management).[21] Additional costs accrue with social security, pension, and payroll taxes that can add 20–100 percent onto basic wage and salary rates.

- Depreciation allowances: Most countries operate on straight-line (i.e., non-variable) methods for various asset types. Egyptian rates are 2–5 percent for buildings; 10–15 percent for plant and machinery, 6–15 percent for furniture and fixtures, and 12.5–20 percent for office and accounting machinery.[22]

- Value added, sales, and excise taxes: Many nations have value-added taxes that are assessed on monetary value added in the manufacturing process (as in the EU, where it averages about 15 percent), general sales taxes assessed at point of purchase (often with many exemptions for foods, medicines, etc.), and special excise taxes that are levied on specific sectors such as alcohol, tobacco, and petroleum.

Business Environment Analyses

Outside of industry, demand, and supply-chain factors, two other areas require expert analysis: financial aspects and legal infrastructures.

Financial Aspects: Capital Markets, Taxation Policies, and Currency Issues *National capital markets* need evaluating to ensure access to local capital. While many international companies prefer to fund their own subsidiaries to maintain control and minimize local shareholder interference, there are times when raising capital locally is the preferred option. The pros and cons of international versus local financing are fully discussed in Chapter 8 (Internationalization and Globalization). Where local long-term financing is used, national stock markets must be evaluated, or where these prove deficient, other financing options can be contemplated. Medium and short-term capital needs are more likely to be locally sourced. Medium-term funds are used for projects such as additional facilities (e.g., warehouses or financing special research projects). Short-term capital is necessary to finance inventories, exports, and the like. In both cases, local banking facilities and cost of capital factors weigh heavily in financing decisions.

Corporate taxation and taxes affecting international operations: Most nations tax profits (exceptions include island states such as Bermuda or the Cayman Islands). Most often these are in the 30–40 percent range (Peru's base rate is 30 percent, Mexico's 35 percent, and Egypt's 32 percent). Some countries, to attract investment, grant international firms "tax holidays" (partial or complete exemption from taxation) for specific time periods. Other taxes that must

> You cannot take a whiff of "Free Enterprise" or a "Way of Life" and start a factory with it. To start a factory and provide jobs, you have to have money—capital.
>
> *–Eric A. Johnston,*
> *former president,*
> *U.S. Chamber of Commerce*

be factored in for international companies include those on profit remittances, capital loans, royalties, and fees. Taxes on royalties and fees differ by country. Withholding taxes up to 30 percent are common in Latin America, but in most countries, there are few or no restrictions. Mexican authorities routinely scrutinize "excessive" transfers to ensure that no advantage is being taken of legal allowances, and the Chinese government varies its taxes on royalties and fees to encourage technology transfers in specific industries.

Currency considerations: National currency values and behaviors are key issues for international firms as they affect foreign sourcing abilities; export potential; asset valuations for corporate balance sheets; repatriation of profits, fees, royalties and the like. Two prime issues top management's currency concerns. The first is currency convertibility—whether the country's currency is tradable/acceptable outside of its national borders. Where national currencies are "soft" (i.e., inconvertible/unacceptable), international companies must often generate hard/convertible currencies—often through exports—to help money repatriation efforts. Where nations have persistent balance-of-payment problems, excessive imports, rapidly depreciating currencies, or major capital outflows, restrictions on currencies are likely.

The second issue is currency value. Movements in currency values depend on what exchange-rate arrangement the country uses (common currency, currency board, fixed rates, managed or freely floating—see Chapter 2). Stable exchange rates facilitate planning with regard to trade, investments, asset valuations, and money movements in and out of countries. But, as is often the case with developing nations, depreciating exchange rates (i.e., increasing numbers of national currency units per dollar or euro) are often "normal". Depreciating exchange rates aid exports, make imports more expensive, and force in-market subsidiaries to earn increasing profits locally to generate respectable incomes for parent companies. In general, depreciating exchange rates complicate financial planning for international firms.

Legal Infrastructures   Legal infrastructures define permissible behaviors for international companies and cover a wide range of business areas. Some of these are the following.

Industry ownership limitations: Most countries have industry sectors that are "off-limits" to foreigners or that restrict foreign participation to joint ventures. In Singapore's case, telecom share purchases were restricted until recent privatization movements, as were holdings in financial institutions (such as banks and brokerage firms).[23] In India, the Foreign Investment Protection Board (FIPB) reviews foreign investments in numerous sectors. In some industries (e.g., insurance, print media, brokerage firms), investments are prohibited. In other cases, investments are permitted, but foreign ownership is restricted (20 percent for banks, 49 percent for cable television systems).[24]

Monopoly and anti-trust laws: In many countries and regions, governments are wary of the abilities of international firms to build powerful marketplace positions, and most have laws in place to limit monopoly-threatening strategies. In the European Union, the Directorate-General for Competition is the antitrust enforcement agency. Assisted by national bodies (including the U.S.'s antitrust commission), this agency has the power to investigate mergers that have the

> In this world nothing can be said to be certain, except death and taxes.
>
> *–Benjamin Franklin, 18th-century U.S. statesman*

> Laws are not invented; they grow out of circumstances.
>
> *—Azarias*

potential to limit competition within the EU. In Thailand, the 1995 Takeover Code requires firms to inform the Thai Securities and Exchange Commission of intentions to purchase over 25 percent of a company's shares and to notify all relevant parties.[25]

Intellectual property laws are important for high-tech firms and companies wishing to maintain control over brand names, logos, manufacturing processes, and the like in foreign markets, as "pirating" and counterfeiting are problematic in many countries. In Yugoslavia, the counterfeiting of videos, CDs, and athletic wear was pervasive in the late 1990s,[26] and pirated computer software accounts for about 70 percent of the markets in the Middle East, Africa, and Latin America.[27]

Protection for intellectual property can occur at the supra-national or, more frequently, at the national level. At the multi-country level, for example, there is the European Patent Convention (EPC), established 1978. The EPC does not grant Europe-wide patents. Rather, it grants a bundle of national patents that differ according to each contracting country's laws. While the EU's eventual aim to have region-wide patent protection under a harmonized law, progress toward this goal has been sporadic. Already a number of EU directives have been issued covering semiconductors, computer programs, medical products, authors' rights, and databases.[28]

Most companies rely on national laws for protection of intellectual property rights. This simplifies registration and gives firms accountability through national legal systems. Problems occur in countries where (1) legal systems are not sufficiently developed to include meaningful intellectual property protection laws; (2) laws are in place, but enforcement is problematic due to ineffective policing or corruption; (3) judicial systems are slow, corrupt, or subject to manipulation (e.g., xenophobic tendencies).

China's situation is typical among many industrializing countries. While the nation is a signatory to the major global patent conventions and has constantly amended its intellectual property laws since the early 1980s, significant problems exist in its enforcement policies. Between 80–90 percent of software is pirated, and computer and video-game piracy accounted for over $1.3 billion in industry sales. In addition, consumer products such as infant cereals have encountered increasing incidences of trademark violations.[29]

Consumer protection laws: Almost all nations have laws protecting consumers against unscrupulous business practices. These cover product/service warranties and performance guarantees, truth-in-advertising legislation (what is or is not deceptive advertising); restrictions on sales promotions; rules on predatory pricing; distributor contracts, rights, and obligations.

Environmental laws cover many areas. In the Czech Republic, major efforts have been made to upgrade environmental protection to conform to EU standards. Particular attention has been paid to air, water, and soil-pollution standards, to waste recycling, sewage treatment, water pollution from agricultural pesticides, and to the draining of industrial waste into waterways—all identified as problem areas.[30] Heavy industry, such as metal smelting and manufacture, and chemicals are particularly affected by national environmental policies.

Local company organization: When firms establish subsidiaries, they must conform to local statutes concerning organization and shareholder/owner responsibilities. Taiwan's

THE GLOBAL WEB

An excellent website is www.globalroadwarrior.com Go to "Select Country" where you will find lots of country details. To focus on culture, go to "business culture." There is also a section on "the business woman."

laws are typical and have four basic formats: (1) the unlimited company, where at least two shareholders have unlimited liability for its obligations, (2) the unlimited company where some shareholders have limited liability, (3) limited share companies whose owners' liabilities are limited to the proportion of shares they own, and (4) limited companies whose owners are liable only to the extent of the capital they contribute. These different formats vary according to the capital requirements, board-of-director appointments and duties, financial disclosure, voting rights, dividend payment preferences, and other criteria.[31]

CULTURAL ANALYSIS

All countries tend to develop differently, and cultural differences, particularly at the national levels, continue to be important. As national cultures are too numerous for exhaustive categorizations, managers can obtain good overviews of national cultures through specialist sources (e.g., Brigham Young's *Culturegram* Series). These guides include:

- *General national backgrounds* include land size, climate, history, economy, government, education, population, religion, language, and health system details.

- *Interpersonal relations* include the importance of the family unit, dating and marriage customs, personal appearance (how casual, fashionable, formal), visiting formalities (punctuality, gift-giving), greetings (degree of formality, handshakes, embraces, bows, physical space), eating habits (use of hands, utensils, finishing/leaving food, compliments about food, when to begin eating), tipping (whether to tip, how much), attitudes and behaviors to the opposite gender and children (appropriate greetings), and gestures and body language (hand movements, use of right hand in the Middle East, pointing, sole of foot, whistling, winking, public displays of affection).

> Culture is not just an ornament; it is the expression of a nation's character, and at the same time it is a powerful instrument to mold character.
>
> —*Somerset Maugham, 19th–20th-century English novelist*

- *Lifestyles* cover eating in/out, recreational habits (national sports, movie and TV watching habits, dance, concerts), diet (major meats, food groups, taboo foods, specialty items, degree of spiciness), recreational refreshments (alcohol, tea, coffee, etc.), business hours (siestas).

- *General attitudes* are important, particularly those toward family, friends; punctuality, modesty, humility, surprises, embarrassment, degree of materialism, fatalistic or go-getter attitudes, religiosity, social classes, ethnic identities, cleanliness, and male-female relations (degree of chauvinism).

KEY POINTS

- Thorough examinations of national markets entail reviewing background information on country history and geography; assessing the current political, economic, and international situations; and evaluating its commercial environment and national culture.

- Historic background traces national political development and economic change (including industrialization processes). It also includes national country profiles, internal divisions, ethnic, religious and cultural conflicts; and how external factors such as global, regional institutions, and national rivalries moderate national policies.

- How geographic factors such as country location, climate, population concentrations, resources, and topography affect national development; and how geography affects infrastructure development (utilities, energy, communications, and transportation).

- Managers then examine the current political, economic, and international situations. Political analyses include political systems, assemblies, party and personality profiles, and the factors that contribute to political risk and the likelihood of political change.

- National economic positions should be assessed in their regional context first and then through examinations of economic indicators, private sectors, and memberships of international organizations.

- Analyses of country balance of payments show how nations are performing in international trade in products and services, income flows, and government money movements on the current account, and country investment inflows and outflows in machinery, direct investments, portfolio investments, and money movements. Merchandise trade balances are indicators of future trade policies, and overall balances of payments indicate pressures on national currencies to appreciate or depreciate against world currencies.

- Commercial analyses comprise examinations of national industry conditions and evaluations of national demand (customers, segments), supply-chain factors, including supplier considerations and various influences on manufacturing site selection such as investment permissions, incentives, infrastructure availability, labor, information technologies, and cost-chain considerations.

- Business environment analyses review general factors affecting operations in foreign markets, including financial elements (capital markets, taxation, and currencies), and national legal infrastructures (limits on ownership, antitrust laws, and legal regulations on intellectual property, consumer protection, environment, and local company organization).

- Cultural analyses look at national backgrounds and behaviors, including interpersonal relations, lifestyles, and general attitudes.

ENDNOTES

1. John C. Koopman, "Successful global retailers: A rare breed," *The Canadian Manager* 25, 1 (Spring 2000): 22–24.

2. Wheeler and Kostbade, 50.

3. *CIA World Factbook* (Washington, D.C.: 1998).

4. "Political Structures," *Business Asia* (March 23, 1998): 15.

5. "India: No end to inertia," *Business Asia* (March 23, 1998): 18.

6. Kathy Chenault and Stan Crock, "A Nation under siege," *Business Week* (September 30, 1996): 54.

7. Anonymous, "Turkey," *OECD Economic Outlook* (December 1998): 120–21.

8. *Country Commerce: Egypt* (New York: EIU, 2001) 14.

9. Moises Naim, "The new diaspora," *Foreign Policy* (July–August, 2002): 95–6.

10. Based on Arthur A. Thompson Jr. and A. J. Strickland, *Strategic Management,* 11th Edition (Boston: Irwin-McGraw-Hill, 1999), chapter 3.

11. Rekha Balu, "Strategic Innovation: Hindustan Lever," *Fast Company* 47 (June, 2001): 120–36.

12. Jack Honomichl, "Research growth knows no boundaries," *Marketing News* (August 17, 1998): H2–H4.

13. "Register of United States barriers to trade," *External Affairs and International Trade: Canada* (April, 1992).

14. *Country Commerce: Malaysia* (New York: EIU, 2001), 14.

15. *Country Commerce: Egypt* (New York: EIU, 2001), 20–22.

16. *Country Commerce: European Union* (New York: EIU, 2001), 18–19.

17. *Country Commerce: Peru* (New York: EIU, 2001), 19.

18. *Country Commerce: Mexico* (New York: EIU, 2001), 38–42.

19. *Ibid.* 49.

20. *Country Commerce: Pakistan* (New York: EIU, 2001), 37.

21. *Country Commerce: Peru* (New York: EIU, 2001), 33–34.

22. *Country Commerce: Egypt* (New York: EIU, 2001), 32.

23. *ILT: Singapore* (1997), 11–12.

24. *ILT: India* (1997), 17–18.

25. *ILT: Thailand* (1996), 32.

26. "Eastern Europe," *Crossborder Monitor* (November 26, 1997), 3.

27. Peggy E. Chaudhry and Michael G Walsh, "Intellectual Property Rights: Changing Levels of Protection under GATT, NAFTA and the EU," *Columbia Journal of World Business* 30:2 (Summer, 1995): 80–92.

28. *Country Commerce: European Union* (New York: Economist Intelligence Unit, 2001), 19–26.

29. *Country Commerce: China:* (New York: Economist Intelligence Unit, 2001), 42–51.

30. *Country Commerce: Czech Republic* (New York: Economist Intelligence Unit, 2001), 14–15.

31. *Country Commerce: Taiwan* (New York: EIU, 2001), 20.

C A S E T T E   5 - 1

The Japanese Economy—Historic Perspectives and Current Situation

Japan, the "land of the rising sun" (named after Amaterasu, the sun goddess) has, in common with other Asian nations, a long and proud history dating from 600 B.C. Its emperors, starting with Jimmu (a direct descendant of Amaterasu) at that time, have remained constitutional figureheads to the present day with Akihito. The shoguns (feudal lords) dominated the country until the late nineteenth century when the emperor regained effective control after the Meiji Restoration in 1868.

Japan's geography can be said to have contributed to its national culture and development. Asia's geographic distance from the West ensured that European influences on Japanese culture were muted during the sixteenth–nineteenth century colonization period, and shogun actions in expelling all foreigners from the country in the seventeenth century contributed to Japan's isolation. The country's island status further insulated Japan until the U.S.'s Commodore Perry reengaged the nation's attentions with the Western economy in 1853. After that time, Japan slowly began a modernization process that led to its establishment as a world power in the early twentieth century. The country's folk-based Shinto religion was reoriented to emphasize the nation state ("State Shinto"), and a unified patriotic Japan began to assert itself. Imperial aspirations led to occupations of Korea and China during the first part of the century and subsequently to the country's ill-fated participation in World War II.

After 1945 and a brief occupation by U.S. military forces, Japan emerged with a new constitution. Its post-war focus on economic development paid off with rapid industrialization and modernization. The country's lack of natural resources (coal had been its major energy source until the early twentieth century), and lack of cultivatable land (only 11 percent) had caused major dependencies on imports to sustain its economic prosperity. This led to a sustained drive to export that exists to the present day. Its trading companies, founded in the sixteenth century, became export powerhouses, and the 1970s to 1990s saw Japan emerge as the world's second-largest free-market economy.

However, the 1990s saw a gradual reversing of Japanese economic fortunes. As world markets opened up under the impetus of global capitalism, Japan's market became embroiled with accusations of protectionism and a closed market mentality. The Liberal Democratic Party, which had monopolized Japanese politics since 1945, came under external pressures to open up the domestic economy to the full forces of international competition. Successive LDP leaders tried to institute reforms to break up the country's traditional keiretzus—the interlocking ownership patterns that insulated industrial conglomerates from open competition and made them less accountable to profit-seeking shareholders. Government finances went into disarray as public spending to jump-start the economy failed, and inadequate revenues caused embarrassing budget deficits. Ultra-low interest rates lowered operating costs for companies whose capital structures were debt, not equity-based, but resulted in slim margins for financial institutions. A few bad debts, and some financial institutions showed severe losses. The Asian Iron Rice Bowl tradition of full employment came under pressure as unemployment rose from under 3 percent to 5.3 percent in 2002.

But global skeptics will have their say. Japan, they claim, is not in that bad economic shape. Its unemployment rate is similar to the U.S. and significantly below European levels. The country's trade performance continues to be very positive. If Japan has economic woes, the argument goes, they are self-inflicted.

Questions

1. Review Japan's geography and brief history. Japan has been profiled as ethnocentric (feelings of home country superiority) and nationalistic; protectionist, xenophobic and very wary of westernization; very export-oriented; and a culture characterized by social distinctions and deferential respect for superiors. What factors do you think have contributed to this profile?

2. Below are some current statistics on the Japanese economy. What is your assessment?

Comparative Economic Indicators: 2001

Economic Indicator	Japan	U.S.	Germany	China
GDP (US$ bn.)	4,133	10,206	1,878	1,179
GDP/head (US$)	32,464	35,888	22,885	926
Inflation (%)	−0.7	2.8	2.5	0.7
Current Account Balance (US$ bn.)	90.7	−409.8	−2.7	20.9
Merchandise Exports ($ bn.)	381.8	723.3	568.2	265.8
Merchandise imports ($ bn.)	312.0	1,147.5	502.8	233.8
Foreign Trade (% GDP)	16.8	18.3	57.0	42.4

Selected Economic Indicators: 1998–2001

Economic Indicator	1998	1999	2000	2001
GDP per capita ($ at PPP*)	24,572	25,036	26,058	26,480
GDP (% real change per year)	−1.04	0.67	2.24	−0.46
Government Expenditures (% GDP)	15.64	16.18	16.70	17.53
Household consumer expenditures (bn. yen)	286,946	288,764	287,231	283,652
Public (government) debt (% GDP)	103.0	115.3	122.9	136.7
Consumer Prices (% change per annum)	0.66	−0.34	−0.67	−0.73
Unemployment (%)	4.11	4.68	4.72	5.03
Interest Rate % (CDs)	0.27	0.12	0.07	0.06
Exchange Rate: yen/$	115.6	102.2	114.9	131.8
Foreign Exchange Reserves ($ bn.)	203,215	277,708	347,212	387,727

***GDP/capita at PPP (purchasing power parity)** rate is a measurement of per-head income levels adjusted for differences in international price levels. A straight conversion from yen to dollars (as with the comparative economic indicators figures) shows $32,464 per capita for Japan. But Japan's price levels are significantly above those of the U.S. When account is taken of these differences and adjustments made, a figure of $26,480 becomes the figure in directly comparing the affluence levels of Japan and the U.S. In other cases (and especially with developing nations that have had severely depreciated exchange rates), the reverse is true, and adjustments for purchasing power parity cause an upward movement in relative affluence. That is, the GDP/capita conversion at current exchange rates do not reflect the true purchasing power of the domestic currency (it considerably underestimates it), and that country's citizens have more purchasing power per head than is indicated by a straight conversion at existing exchange rates.

3. Evaluate Japan's balance of payments. What do you see?

Japan Bal. of Payments	1994	1996	1998	1999	2000	2001
Goods: Exports fob	385.7	400.28	374.04	403.69	459.51	383.59
Goods Imports fob	−241.51	−316.72	−251.66	−280.37	−342.8	−313.38
Trade Balance	144.19	83.56	122.39	123.32	116.72	70.21
Services: Credit	58.3	67.72	62.41	61	69.24	64.52
Services: Debit	−106.36	−129.96	−111.83	−115.16	−116.86	−108.25
Goods/Serv. Balance	96.13	21.32	72.97	69.16	69.09	26.48
Income: Credit	155.19	225.1	209.58	188.27	206.94	103.09
Income: Debit	−114.96	−171.55	−153.01	−138.43	−149.31	−33.87
Gds./Serv/Inc. Balance	136.36	74.88	129.54	119	126.71	95.7
Current transfers: Credit	1.83	6.04	5.53	6.21	7.38	6.15
Current transfers: Debit	−7.94	−15.04	−14.37	−18.35	−17.81	−14.06
B/P on Current Account	130.26	65.88	120.7	106.87	116.88	87.8
Capital Account						
Capital account: n.i.e.	−1.85	−3.29	−14.45	−16.47	−9.26	−2.87
Capital account: Credit	0	1.22	1.57	0.75	0.78	0.99
Capital account: Debit	−1.85	−4.51	−16.02	−17.21	−10.04	−3.86
Financial account: n.i.e.	−85.11	−28.1	−116.76	−31.11	−75.54	−48.16
Direct investment abroad	−18.09	−23.44	−24.62	−22.27	−31.53	−38.5
FDI in home market	0.91	0.2	3.27	12.31	8.23	6.19
Portfolio invest.: Assets	−91.97	−100.62	−95.24	−154.41	−83.36	−106.79
Equity securities	−14	−8.18	−14	−32.4	−19.72	−11.78
Debt securities	−77.97	−92.44	−81.24	−122.01	−63.64	−95.51
Portfolio invest: Liabilities	64.53	66.81	56.06	126.93	47.39	60.5
Equity securities	48.95	49.46	16.11	103.89	−1.29	39.1
Debt securities	15.58	17.35	39.95	23.04	48.67	21.4
Financial derivs.: Assets	0.43	−13.96	−18.49	−12.43	−3	102.79
Financial derivs.: Liabilities	−0.2	6.63	17.64	17.53	1.1	−101.4
Other investment assets	−35.12	5.22	37.94	266.34	−4.15	46.59
Monetary authorities	0	0	0	0	0	0
General government	−8.76	−5.28	−15.5	−11.56	−1.89	−3.95
Banks	−10.67	75.56	54.14	239.4	36.51	15.59
Other sectors	−15.69	−65.07	−0.7	38.5	−38.77	34.95
Other investment liabilities	−5.6	31.07	−93.33	−265.12	−10.21	−17.55
Monetary authorities	0	0	0	0	0	0
General government	−2	−2.13	−1.3	0.55	−0.93	7.01
Banks	4.87	−9.06	−23.75	−189.16	28.22	4.99
Other sectors	−8.47	42.26	−68.28	−76.5	−37.49	−29.54
Net errors & omissions	−18.03	0.64	4.36	16.97	16.87	3.72
OVERALL BALANCE	25.27	35.14	−6.16	76.26	48.95	40.49
Reserves & related items	−25.27	−35.14	6.16	−76.26	−48.95	−40.49
Reserve assets	−25.27	−35.14	6.16	−76.26	−48.95	−40.49
Fund credit and loans	0	0	0	0	0	0
Exceptional financing	0	0	0	0	0	0

CASETTE 5-2
Looking at Brazil in Its Latin American Context

~❧~

You are an executive in a large consumer goods corporation that is looking at entering the Latin American market. Brazil looks to be a prime market, but as part of your preliminary examination of the region, you are reviewing some basic statistics about the major nations in the region. Your assistant has brought you the following data.

Comparative Economic Indicators, 2001

	Brazil	Argentina	Mexico	Venezuela
Population (million)	176	37	100	24
GDP ($ bn)	1,340	453	920.0	146
GDP per head ($)	7,400	12,000	9,000	6,200
Consumer price inflation (%)	7.7	4.0	6.5	13.0
Unemployment (%)	6.4	25.0	3 (urban)	14.0
Economic growth (%)	1.9	–4.6	–0.3	3.2
Gov't revenues ($bn.)	100.6	44	136	26.4
Gov't expenditures	91.6	48	140	27
Export of goods ($ bn)	57.8	26.5	159.0	32.8
Import of goods ($ bn)	57.7	23.8	168.0	14.7
External debt ($ bn)	251	155.0	191.0	34.0
Exchange rate/$	2.36 reals	1.0 pesos	9.34 pesos	699 bolivars
GDP by sector (%)				
Agriculture	9	6	5	5
Industry	32	28	26	24
Services	59	66	69	71

Specific Economic Indicators

Brazil	2001	2000	1999	1998
GDP per capita (ppp)	7,510	7,308	6,905	6,765
GDP real growth %	1.50	4.50	0.79	0.22
Inflation (general prices)%	6.84	7.04	4.86	3.20
Household consumer expenditures (m. reals)	712,300	658,726	597,418	566,192
Government finances (m. reals)				
Revenue	272,110	235,062	158,751	
Expenditures	283,752	247,252	163,652	
Balance (%)	–4.3	–5.2	–3.1	
Public sector debt % GDP	55.8	51.8	53.6	42.2
Money supply (m. reals)				
M1 (currency plus demand deposits)	83,707	74,352	62,744	50,707
M2 (M1 +government bonds/bills)	321,612	283,785	274,770	254,965
M3 (M2 + savings deposits)	625,057	556,577	468,728	376,015
M4 (M3 + time deposits)	756,181	652,093	551,092	459,308
Interest rates—CDs %	17.86	17.20	26.02	28.00
Labor force				
Total (m)			79.3	76.9
Unemployment rate%	6.23	7.14	7.56	7.6

	2001	2000	1999	1998
Global trade/investment				
Exports ($m fob)	58,224	55,087	48,011	51,136
Imports ($m fob)	55,579	55,783	49,272	57,739
Balance ($m)	2,645	−696	−1,261	−6,603
Current account	−23,211	−24,632	−25,400	−33,829
Financial account ($m)	20,079	29,369	8,056	20,063
Of which: portfolio investment	873	8,646	3,542	19,013
Direct investment	22,636	32,779	28,576	31,913
Overall balance of payments	−3,418	7,980	−16,765	−16,302
Exchange Rate/$	2.32	1.95	1.79	1.21
Foreign exchange reserves ($m)	35,729	32,488	34,786	42,578

4. How does Brazil look in its Latin American context?

5. How would you assess Brazil's economic performance?

6. How would you assess its balance of payments situation?

Sources: IMF, *International Financial Statistics* (January, 2003); www.economist.com/countries/Brazil; Business Risk Services (2002).

CASETTE 5-3
Comparing Market Profiles for the U.S., Brazil, and China

You are a Europe-wide manufacturer of earthmoving equipment contemplating international expansion; you have narrowed your initial choices down to the U.S., Brazil, and China. Your assistant has prepared general market profiles for these three countries. Critique these profiles.

- What are the major similarities among these markets?
- What are the major differences?
- What other information would you require in preparing a preliminary report on these countries?

Market Factor	U.S.	Brazil	China
Background	Became independent in 1776; civil war 1861–65; very large, steady growth economy	Became independent in 1822 after 3 centuries of Portuguese rule; largest country in South America; vast natural resources and large labor pool	One of world's first civilizations; controlled by emperors until 1911; civil/international strife until 1949 when became communist until capitalist reforms in 1980s
Total area (square kilometers)	9,372,558	8,511,965	9,596,960
Climate	Varies from frozen tundra in the north (Alaska) to semitropical in the south. Much of U.S. is temperate and ideal for agriculture	Mostly tropical, temperate in south	Diverse: tropical in south, subarctic in north
Terrain	Mountainous in the west giving way to vast central plains that merge with the hills and low mountain ranges of the east	65% forests	Much of China covered by mountains and desert; populations live in east, where agriculture is productive

Market Factor	U.S.	Brazil	China
Natural resources	Coal, copper, lead, phosphates, uranium, bauxite, gold, iron, mercury, zinc, silver, potash, petroleum, natural gas, timber	Bauxite, gold, iron ore, manganese, nickel, phosphates, platinum, tin, uranium, petroleum, hydropower, timber	Coal, iron ore, petroleum, natural gas, mercury, tin, tungsten, many other minerals, much hydroelectric potential
Land use: Arable	19%	5%	10%
Permanent crops	0%	1%	0%
Permanent pastures	25%	22%	43%
Forests, woodlands	30%	58%	14%
Environmental Issues	Air pollution, acid rain, largest emitter of carbon dioxide	Deforestation of Amazon Basin, air/water pollution in urban areas, land degradation/pollution caused by mining	Air pollution, acid rain, water shortages and pollution, deforestation, soil erosion, desertification
Population (millions)	278	160	1,273
Infant mortality: Deaths/1000 live births	6.76	36.96	28.08
Life Expectancy (years)	77	63	72
Fertility: Children/woman	2.06	2.09	1.82
Ethnic groups	White 83%; African American 12.4%; Asian 3.3%; native American 0.8%	White (European ancestry) 55%; mixed races 38%; black 6%; 200,000 indigenous peoples	Han Chinese 92%
Religions	Protestant 56%; Roman Catholic 28%	Roman Catholic	Confucian, Taoist, Buddhist
Literacy	97%	83%	82%
Languages	English-spoken; 1/7 speaks non-English language in the home; native Americans speak a vast variety of languages and dialects	Portuguese mainly spoken; 100+ native languages	70% speak Mandarin; regional dialects: Wu (Shanghai); Cantonese; Kejia; local dialects in central/southern China
Government	Federal Republic: 50 states	Federal Republic: 26 states	Communist state: 23 provinces, 5 autonomous regions
Elections	President/Vice-president every four years	President/Vice-president every 4 years	President/Vice-president elected by National Congress every 5 years
Legislative branch	Senate 100 seats, 6-year terms; House of Representatives, 435 seats, 2-year terms	National Congress, 81 seats, 8-year terms; Chamber of Deputies, 513 seats, 4-year terms	National Congress, 2979 members elected/nominated by municipal, regional, and people's congresses
Political parties	Two major parties	11 major parties	One main party: Chinese Communist party
Pressure groups	Numerous	Catholic Church, landless workers, labor unions	Few/none internally; international pressure groups (e.g., human rights)
Economy (general)	$10 trillion economy; largest and most powerful in world	High inflation up to 1994, when "Real Plan" was implemented	Quadrupling of economy since 1978; second largest recipient of foreign direct investment globally (including Hong Kong); world's second-largest economy (GDP)
General affluence (GDP per capita)	$36,200	$6500	$3600
Inflation	3.4%	6%	0.4%
Economic growth	5%	4.5%	8%
Government budget	Surplus, but problems	Balanced	N/A
Economic sectors (%)			
Agriculture	2%	9%	50%
Industry	18	29%	24%
Services	80%	62%	26%
Income distribution			
% below poverty level	12.9%	17.4%	10%
Consumption of top 10%	30.5%	47%	30.4%
Balance of payments	$450 billion trade deficit (imports > exports)	Current account deficits countered by surpluses on capital account	Exports > imports and significant capital inflows from foreign direct investments

Market Factor	U.S.	Brazil	China
Currency	US$ one of the strongest currencies in the world	Real: 1.005 per $ in 1996 to 1.954/$ in 2001	Yuan very steady at 8.27 per US$
Military expenditures	$276 billion (3.2% GDP)	$13.4 billion (1.9% GDP)	$12.66 billion (1.2% GDP)
Infrastructure			
Energy: Electricity	3.678 trillion kWh; 70% from fossil fuels	337.44 billion kWh; 90+% from hydroelectric sources	1.173 trillion kWh; 80% fossil fuels and 19% hydroelectric sources
Telephone: Lines	194 million	17 million	135 million
Cellular	69 million	4.4 million	65 million
Radio stations	10,000	1600 (mainly AM)	650
Radios	575 million	71 million	417 million
Television stations	1500+	138	3240 (?).
Televisions	219 million	36.5	400 million
Internet users	148 million	8.65	22 million
Railways (kilometers)	225,750km	30,539km	67,524km
Highways (million kilometers)	6.3m kms. (90% paved)	1.98m kms (10% paved)	1.4m kms (20% paved)
Waterways (kilometers)	41,009 km	50,000 km	110,000 km
Airports (number)	14720	3264	489
Paved runways	5174	570	324
Paved over 3047 meters	182	5	27

Chapter Six

Analyzing Global Industries and Competitors

❦

YAMAHA'S GLOBAL MARKET ANALYSIS

When Yamaha Motorcycles plots global strategy, the company starts by analyzing world market trends in the industry. In its latest three-year plan (covering 2002–2005), Yamaha anticipated a 16 percent increase in global market size to 30.18 million units by 2005. Regional analyses indicated that North American unit sales would increase 14 percent to 930,000, European sales to decrease by 4 percent to 2 million units, and Japanese sales to grow by 10 percent to 850,000 motorcycles. While these were mainly positive trends, the major market growth was in Asia, where market sizes were due to rise by over 20 percent to top 24 million units. Not surprisingly, the company targeted the region for its major strategic push. The Chinese market, at half the Asian total, was the focal point for company attentions. In 2002, Yamaha sold just 50,000 units. This was to be upped to 440,000 motorcycles by 2005. A market and competitor analysis suggested that motorcycles priced at 80,000 yen or less (less than $1000) would work, though sales networks would need to be expanded inland away from the coastal areas. To minimize costs both in China and worldwide, the company would need to slash costs by 30 percent. To achieve this, joint ventures were contemplated with selected Chinese motorcycle manufacturers. The big push in Asia was the key component in a plan to attain 20 percent of the global market by 2010.[1]

As industries and firms globalize, so managements must increasingly analyze industries and competitors on a worldwide basis. This occurs because corporate resources are never plentiful and must be allocated to take advantage of new market opportunities and to counter moves of global rivals. Yamaha's approach to world market analysis tends to be typical of how international corporations look at global markets—analyzing world and regional trends and then zeroing in on key markets and calculating what it takes to compete against rivals. Complementing the global industry analysis are assessments of competitors. Together, these assessments lay the groundwork for realistic sales goals and expected market shares in specific regions and critical markets. From our lead-in scenario, Yamaha would use its global and regional analyses to devise its market and competitive strategies and allocate its resources to achieve its objectives.

Hence, in this chapter, you will learn:

- How industries look on a worldwide basis. This includes estimates of industry demand, supply chains, structures, financial benchmarks, and industry change drivers. For trade-oriented industries, export prospects need evaluating.

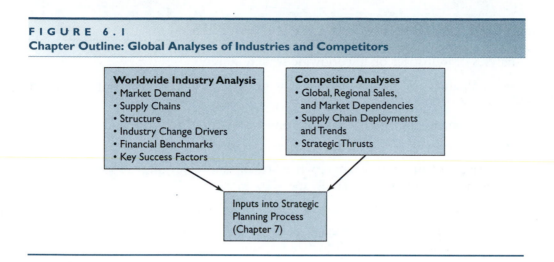

FIGURE 6.1
Chapter Outline: Global Analyses of Industries and Competitors

- How global rivals are positioned in worldwide markets; their corporate missions, strategic intents, core competencies; the distribution of their worldwide sales, major product lines, and their efforts to streamline supply chain operations; strategic emphases (products, markets, operations).

INTRODUCTION

Once managements have a basic understanding of the global and regional forces impacting the international marketplace, they can focus on how these forces affect global aspects of their industries and competitors. The strategic usefulness of these analyses is outlined Table 6.1.

TABLE 6.1
Strategic Significance of Global Industry and Competitor Analyses

Market Opportunity Analyses	Strategic Significance
• Industry Consumption and Production Patterns	
—Global consumption patterns	Investment and manufacturing capacity planning
—Regional/country consumption levels	Market targets, regional/country investment plans
—Import penetration levels	Market entry strategy (e.g., import or invest)
—Regional/country production levels	Regional and country centers of manufacturing expertise and technological competence
—Country export orientation	Countries that are competitive in the international marketplace
• Global Trade Analyses	
—Export market analysis	Identify major export markets from a given country production base
—Import market analysis	Identify major supply sources into particular markets
Industry and Competitor Analyses	
—Global Industry Analysis	Industry characteristics, players, demand drivers, supply chain influences, financial performance benchmarks, key success factors
—Global Competitor Analysis	Strategic orientation; global, regional sales; profits, margins; resource deployments

WORLDWIDE INDUSTRY ANALYSIS

Analyses of industries on a worldwide scale requires:

- Evaluations of market demand at worldwide, regional, and country market levels

- Assessments of supply-chain options for procurement and manufacturing

- Industry structure—the major players in world markets

- Drivers of industry change: what present and emerging trends are affecting the global industry landscape

- Financial benchmarks to assess market prospects

- Key success factors impacting industry performance: what firms must do to contend for industry leadership positions

There is a world market for about five computers.

—*Thomas J. Watson, founder IBM Corporation (1943 estimate)*

I don't set trends. I just find out what they are and follow them.

—*Dick Clark, U.S. music industry executive*

Ability is nothing without opportunity.

—*Napoleon Bonaparte, French general and emperor*

Evaluations of Worldwide Market Demand

Industry demand can be assessed from two perspectives. First, for mature global companies with extensive international operations, consumption patterns must be evaluated on worldwide, regional, and individual market bases. This information provides inputs for deciding where to allot resources such as distribution facilities and determining where marketing resources should be allocated. Second, for those servicing markets from home-country bases, export prospects need evaluating.

Global industry demand shows worldwide sector demand over time and is a key input into future investment decisions. Table 6.2 shows statistics for the machine tool industry. From this overview, a number of key points emerge.

- First, the machine tool industry suffers fluctuations on a worldwide scale. The 20–25 percent downturns in the early 1990s resulted from the post-Gulf-war global slump. Recovery was evident over the 1995–97 period, though a slump was again evident over 2000–2. Such fluctuations have major impacts on manufacturing capacity management and resource allocation planning.

- Second, the global demand schedule is further refined by breakdowns by region. For machine tools, regional demand was concentrated in Western Europe, Asia, and North America, with minor contributions from Eastern Europe and Latin America.

- Third, account can be taken of individual markets, with Japan and China in particular showing buoyant demand for 2002.

- Finally, Asia's machine-tool consumption is being matched with increased regional production, though Japan's over-production ($6+ billion manufacturing versus $3+ billion consumption) is countered with China's under-production ($5+ billion consumption versus $3+ billion production). Western Europe, with Germany ahead, maintains its world leadership position in regional production.

TABLE 6.2
Global Consumption and Production Trends: Machine Tool Industry

Global Consumption Analyses

- Global consumption patterns: Top 34 markets ($m)

1992	1993	1995	1997	2000	2002
34337	25950	35937	34524	35320	29,856

- 2002 regional consumption

Western Europe $12.7bn	North America $4.2bn
Eastern Europe $594mn	Latin America $602mn
Japan $3.44bn	Other Asia $8.3bn

- Top 5 consuming markets (2002)

China	Germany	Japan	USA	Italy
$5.7bn	$4.8bn	$3.4bn	$3.3bn	$2.9bn

Global Production Patterns

- Regional production (2002)

Western Europe	Japan	North America	Other Asia	Eastern Europe	Latin America
50.8%	20.5%	7.4%	18.7%	1.6%	1.0%

- Major country producers (2002)

Germany	Japan	Italy	China	USA
$6.7bn	$6.4bn	$3.8bn	$3.0bn	1.9bn

Sources: UNIDO. *World Industry Report.* (United Nations: Washington, D.C., 1994). 1998 World Machine Tool Output and Consumption Survey. *Metalworking Insiders' Report.* (New York: Gardner Publications, Jan. 29, 1998). www.gardnerweb.com

Data on worldwide industry demand can be obtained from industry associations, web sites, and professional industry analyst services (such as the Economist Intelligence Unit, Standard and Poors).

Export market demand: With about $6 trillion of international trade occurring worldwide, exporting is a primary strategy for servicing foreign markets. As such, locating export markets is an important task. For firms just starting out in international business, exporting is a good way to test their products internationally and gain experience in serving foreign markets. For large international companies, exporting is a convenient way to service markets either from the home base or from foreign-based subsidiaries. In both cases, national trade statistics show what countries can be serviced from a particular (usually home) market. All major countries maintain export statistics to monitor their external positions and to maintain compliance with international bodies, such as the WTO. Finding export markets involves using national trade statistics and, for market contacts, foreign-company directories and web sites. In the U.S.'s case, the Department of Commerce's International Trade Administration maintains a national trade database (NTDB). Subscribers use its U.S. Exports by Commodity to locate suitable export markets.

THE GLOBAL WEB

The U.S.'s National Trade Data Base can be accessed at: www.usatradeonline.gov. This is a subscriber or fee-based site.

Locating export opportunities requires statistics showing product category exports by country. The first step is to locate the appropriate product category. Table 6.3 shows the Harmonized System (HS) product classification that most

TABLE 6.3
Deriving Harmonized System Product Codes: Computers and Components

	Section	Product Categories
1	Live animals; animal products	1–5
2	Vegetable products	6–14
3	Animal or vegetable fats and oils	15
4	Prepared foodstuffs; beverages, spirits, tobacco and manufactured tobacco substitutes	16–24
5	Mineral products; salt, sulphur, ores, minerals, fuels, oil	25–27
6	Chemical or allied industries products	28–38
7	Plastics and rubbers and articles thereof	39–40
8	Raw hides, skins, leather, saddlery, travel goods, handbags	41–43
9	Wood and wooden articles; cork, manufactures of straw	44–46
10	Woodpulp, paperboard	47–49
11	Textiles, textile products	50–63
12	Footwear, headgear, umbrellas	64–67
13	Articles of stone, plaster, ceramic products, glassware	68–70
14	Pearls, precious stones, metals	71
15	Base metals and articles	72–83
16	8471 Computers & components	84–85
17	Vehicles, aircraft, transportation equipment	86–89
18	Optical, photographic equipment; surgical/medical instruments; clocks, watches	90–92
19	Arms and ammunition	93
20	Miscellaneous manufactured articles (bedding, furniture, prefab buildings)	94–96
21	Works of art, antiques	97
22	Special classifications	98–99

countries use for international trade statistics. Let's look at the procedure to look for export markets for computers. Find the HS number (HS 8471) and then access the NTDB Export by Commodity listings. Listings of computer exports by country can be found there (Table 6.4). The NTDB lists exports by market size for 2000–2. Note the overall fall-off in U.S. exports over this period and the lead positions of Canada and Mexico as the U.S.'s NAFTA partners. These can be further grouped to show markets by size (large, medium, and small) and by market condition (expanding, constant, declining). Alternate analyses can be organized by area (Latin America, Western, Eastern Europe, Africa, Asia, etc.) to assess regional prospects. These statistics show what country markets can be effectively serviced from (in this case) the United States.

A supplemental source can be used to find major import markets. The *United Nations Trade Data Yearbook* (Volume 2) shows imports and exports by broad product sectors. Note that this source uses a different product classification (the standard international trade classification—SITC). In this case, use SITC data for a broader classification—automatic data processing equipment. A summary of the data is shown in Table 6.5. This gives managers three additional types of information. First, they scrutinize importing countries to identify markets that are major importers, but not necessarily from their home market (in this case the U.S.). These

THE GLOBAL WEB

International trade in Coarse Grains Market can be viewed at www.fas.usda.gov/grain/circular/2002/05-02/cgra_txt.htm.
Go to the coarse grains table to identify major exporters and importers of world grains by country.

TABLE 6.4
Top 25 U.S. Annual Exports of Automatic Data Process Machines
(H.S. Code 8471)

(Ranked by FAS value, U.S. $ millions)

Country	2000	2001	2002
World	30,929	27,324	21,803
Canada	6,130	5,057	4,767
Mexico	2,628	2,864	2,721
Japan	2,877	2,541	1,779
Netherlands	2,269	2,109	1,457
United Kingdom	2,208	1,978	1,388
Germany	1,282	1,117	965
Hong Kong	1,227	1,250	800
China	941	949	738
South Korea	1,477	811	694
Singapore	1,204	923	660
Australia	661	594	424
Brazil	905	761	423
Taiwan	606	545	416
France	593	505	414
Ireland	810	647	411
Malaysia	413	407	370
India	259	246	255
Colombia	191	228	216
Chile	241	193	187
Israel	335	303	186
Italy	237	196	174
Paraguay	127	117	170
Belgium	193	219	136
Thailand	146	139	135
Venezuela	204	219	110

Source: *World Trade Atlas* (2003).

are likely targets for future exporting efforts. Second, the regional U.S. export profile can be matched against UN trade data regional import profiles. Geographic strengths and weaknesses of U.S. exporters could then be identified (those where U.S. exports do well against those where they fair poorly). Finally, executives would look at major exporting nations to assess international competitors. As a computer exporter, they would be gratified to see the U.S. at the top of major exporting countries. Note that comparability of statistics is rarely perfect. Different product classification schemes make exact comparisons difficult. Nevertheless, they are useful indicators.

Assessing Industry Supply Chains

Once industry demand has been quantified, executive attentions turn to supply-chain issues. In part, some downstream decisions (e.g., distribution) are determined by market demand. Similarly, market size and growth are major influences on manufacturing-site decisions. However, there remain important decisions about sourcing and manufacturing sites.

T A B L E   6 . 5
Using United Nations Trade Data
Imports/Exports: Automatic Data Processing Machines SITC 752

Area Imports	1999 $ millions	2000 $ millions	2001 $ millions	Value % 2001
World	191,429	211,663	192,223	100
Africa	1,538	1,526	1,684	0.9
Americas	63,100	71,712	62,755	32.6
—North America	57,302	64,771	55,069	28.6
—South America	5,269	6,335	7,047	3.7
—Central America	233	279	278	0.1
Asia	33,850	44,314	41,624	21.7
—Middle East	1,616	2,014	1,715	0.9
European Union	81,207	81,974	74,245	38.6
Central Europe	2,551	2,724	3,410	1.8
Former USSR	483	554	804	0.4
Australia/NZ	3,473	3,762	2,990	1.6
Country Imports (top 20)				
United States	50,115	57,064	48,492	
Germany	17,430	16,892	15,842	
United Kingdom	15,586	16,742	14,255	
Netherlands	15,635	14,923	14,177	
Japan	12,514	17,459	15,038	
France	8,920	9,393	8,054	
Canada	7,142	7,662	6,561	
Singapore	5,257	6,363	5,423	
China/Hong Kong	5,613	6,258	6,448	
Ireland	4,579	4,986	4,535	
Italy	4,965	5,163	4,523	
China	3,253	4,516	4,981	
Switzerland	3,488	3,503	3,105	
Australia	2,965	3,255	2,495	
Mexico	2,507	3,291	4,224	
Spain	2,694	2,905	2,858	
South Korea	2,265	3,814	3,039	
Sweden	2,263	2,087	1,719	
Belgium	3,522	3,690	3,394	
Denmark	1,496	1,550	1,261	
Country Exporters (top 5)				
United States	26,714	30,929	27,386	
Singapore	19,784	19,424	16,532	
Japan	14,472	14,850	12,643	
Netherlands	15,428	15,187	16,081	
United Kingdom	13,920	13,807	12,237	

Source: *United Nations Trade Data,* Volume 2 (United Nations: New York, 2002): 360–361.

TABLE 6.6
Top 25 U.S. Annual Imports of Cellular Phones

(HS Code 8525.20.90.70—Cellular Radio Phones)
(Ranked by FAS value, U.S. $ millions)

Country	2000	2001	2002
World	6,069	8,452	9,455
South Korea	2,694	4,049	4,164
China	280	614	1,443
Mexico	1,693	2,118	1,404
Brazil	231	634	913
Japan	640	425	680
Malaysia	191	213	394
Philippines	1	57	151
Germany	32	65	119
Singapore	58	101	41
Sweden	80	41	33
Finland	6	23	29
Taiwan	4	8	22
Denmark	1	13	16
Thailand	0	0	10
Ireland	1	22	7
United Kingdom	123	52	6
Argentina	1	1	6
Canada	18	3	3
Norway	2	1	1
France	2	2	1
Hong Kong	1	1	1
Italy	1	1	1
Indonesia	0	0	1
Netherlands	0	1	1
Switzerland	0	0	1

Source: *World Trade Atlas* (2003).

Locating import sources of supply uses the same databases as the exporting analyses, except that (in the U.S. case) Imports by Commodity is used to find major country importers into the U.S. A breakdown of cellular-phone importers is shown in Table 6.6. Note the massive growth in imports generally, the position of South Korea as the primary import provider, and the surge of cellular imports from China. These statistics can be crossed-matched with the UN Trade Data list of major exporting nations to identify countries that are prolific exporters in world markets but have yet to impact the U.S. market. The next stage is to use industry and country directories and web sites to locate prospective export customers or foreign sources of supply.

There are limitations of country-based analyses of imports and exports. For example, international corporations are major traders worldwide. Some distortions occur because many exports and imports take place between operating units of international corporations.

Manufacturing site assessment is important in many industries where countries build up expertise in particular sectors. Natural resources, technical expertise,

---

TABLE 6.7
Global Profile: Communications Equipment Industry

(Voice, data network equipment; telephones, etc.)

Market Size/Growth	**Market Size 2001 $264bn** Growth was expected to be negative in 2002.
Industry Structure/Dominant Players	Two major sectors: Wireline equipment suppliers • Alcatel (France), Siemens (Germany), Japan: Fujitsu, NEC; North America: Lucent Technologies (U.S.) Nortel (Canadian) Wireless equipment suppliers • Lucent Technologies, Motorola (U.S.); Nokia (Finland); Ericsson (Sweden). Two segments: wireless infrastructure (Ericsson leads 30% market share), and handsets (Nokia leads with 36% market share and Motorola at 14.4%)
Global Demand Drivers	• Wireless handsets and systems growth: 1999: 480 m. subscribers worldwide; 2000: 700 m.; 2001: 900 m; 2003 forecast 1.3 billion. Cellular penetration worldwide varies from #1 Luxembourg at 96.7% to #39 USA at 44.4%; worldwide wireless penetration up from 12.3% in 2000 to 15.6% in 2001 • Technologies being built into handsets: paging, call waiting, call messaging, E-mail, fax, caller ID, Internet, and imaging (camera phones expected to overtake digital cameras by 2007) • 60 countries deregulate their communications service industries 1997–2002 • WTO Telecommunications Agreement liberalizing global communications markets • Global development potential: India 1.86 lines/100 people vs. Developed Countries 60 lines/100 people • Internet potential and convergence of voice/data networks
Global Supply/ Supply Chain Factors	• Technologies: Movement from analog to digital technologies, copper to fiber-optics transmission lines, from wire line to wireless technologies • Downsizing of workforces in 2002 • Battle over technical standards: notably European vs. U.S. companies • Mega mergers/alliances among major corporations, but Sony Ericsson Mobile Communications failed to live up to expectations
Financial/ Profitability Benchmarks	• Major infrastructure network producers average 40–45% gross margins • Other segments (e.g., wireless handsets) are competitive with annual 10–15% decreases in prices
Present/Future Key Success Factors	1. Relationships with major telephone companies 2. Scale economies 3. Superior R and D (e.g., Lucent 3.5 patents every 24 hours)

Source: "Communications Equipment." *Standard & Poor's Industry Surveys.* (January 2003). www.wow-com.com. www.itu.org.

and the availability of skilled labor pools give individual nations aptitudes in specific industries. For example, the U.S. leads the world in computer software, Germany in high performance autos and chemicals, Japan in consumer electronics, Switzerland and the U.S. in banking, and Italy in footwear and fashions.[2] While many technologies are transferable into the international marketplace, having production sites in lead markets keeps companies on the cutting edge of industry developments. As such, worldwide production analyses are useful inputs into manufacturing resource allocation decisions. In the machine tool Table 6.2, note that Germany and Japan have major expertise in this area, ahead of the Italy, China, and the U.S. These analyses also highlight up-and-coming producers and can be useful in identifying (for example) lower-cost manufacturing sites.

Industry Structure

Dominant firms can be identified in most industries. As Table 6.7 shows, the telecommunications equipment sector comprises European companies (Alcatel in France, Ericsson in Sweden, Siemens in Germany, and Nokia in Finland),

TABLE 6.8
Global Profile: Household Non-Durables Industry

(Household products; personal care products)

Market Size/Growth	**Size $120 billion**
Industry Structure	"Big 2 + others" • Unilever (Anglo-Dutch—$46.1 billion 2001 sales) • Procter & Gamble (U.S.—$40.2 billion 2002 sales) • Kimberley-Clark (U.S.—$14.5 billion 2001 sales) • L'Oreal (France—$12.2 billion 2001 sales) • Colgate-Palmolive (U.S.—$9.4 billion 2001 sales) Big 2 dominate 2/3 of global market
Global Demand Drivers	• Global demand is slow as world economy recovers from 9/11 tragedy, but corporate commitments to global expansion into emerging markets (low usage rates and growing economies). Latin America and Asia viewed as best long-term prospects, but mature economies must not be neglected. • Economic development is the key in emerging markets as growth, urbanization, and improvements in social conditions lead to upturns in consumption of basic household products • Globalization is favoring worldwide branding strategies. As a result, companies are restructuring into global product divisions to facilitate product launches, global brand strategy (e.g., P & G: 7 global business units; Gillette, six global business units; Unilever emphasis on 400 strategic brands). • Price sensitivity for private brands (developed markets) and products for lower income consumers (emergent markets)
Global Supply/Supply Chain Factors	• Countering increases in retailer power (e.g., Wal-Mart, Carrefour) • 2002 raw material prices are steady or decreasing over 2001. Represent 70% on cost of goods but 50% of retail price • Building of distribution relationships and outlets critical as market coverage expands, particularly in developing markets • Maintaining new product flows to be a unique formula, revised ingredients, packaging innovations, and responses to consumer changes
Financial/Profitability Benchmarks	• High margins and return on equity of 15%+; return on assets 11% • As firms increase their foreign operations, exchange rate values affect profit returns. Weaker home currencies inflate foreign earnings, and stronger currencies weaken overseas effects on corporate profits.
Present/Future Key Success Factors	• Overcoming emergent nation problems: trade barriers, local manufacturing, cultural obstacles, undeveloped infrastructures (distribution, media) • Acquisitions are crucial for market growth for local contacts, local brands, and distribution. • Taking brands global; leveraging brand power

Source: Howard Choe. "Household Non-durables." *Industry Surveys.* (Standard & Poor's, 2002). www.unilever.com. www.pg.com.

Japanese firms (Fujitsu and NEC), and North American companies (Lucent and Motorola—both U.S., and Nortel—Canadian). These top 10 firms make up almost two-thirds of world sales. Similar dominance is apparent in the household non-durable sector (Table 6.8) with Unilever (UK), Procter & Gamble and Colgate-Palmolive (both U.S.). Industry structures are becoming more global as mergers and acquisitions, particularly among major players ("mega-mergers") are increasingly impacting industry competitive landscapes.

THE GLOBAL WEB

Review the importance and changing structure of the world auto industry in the late 1990s at: http://people.hofstra.edu/geotrans/eng/chlen/conclen/carproduction96.html.

Drivers of Industry Change

To maintain competitiveness within their sector, firms must be acutely aware of what factors drive industry change. On a general level, political economic, societal, and technological changes are potent drivers of world-wide industry change through their effects on global demand structures and supply chains. At the individual industry level, dominant change drivers must be identified. In the telecommunications sector, economic slowdowns, deregulation, and technological drivers are major factors affecting industry demand and supply chains (see Table 6.7). In the household non-durables industry (Table 6.8), while supply-chain issues are important, they are subordinate to factors affecting global demand, and, in this industry, the impact of the post-9/11 slowdown and the importance of emerging markets are apparent, as is the impact of globalization on branding and corporate strategies.

But, on a general level, managers must screen a multitude of drivers to identify those critical to their industry, as change-causing factors vary over time and across markets and regions. These include:

Politics: the conduct of public affairs for private advantage.

—*Ambrose Bierce,
19th–20th-century
U.S. writer*

Political Trends Political trends include global, regional, and national trends.

Global political trends include:

- Efforts by UN agencies, such as the WTO and IMF, to improve worldwide infrastructures and payments mechanisms. This results in increased trading and investment opportunities and heightened competition between and within markets. The UN also pushes for global industry standards in telecommunications (through the International Telecommunications Union), pharmaceuticals (through the World Health Organization), and other sectors.

- Increasing numbers of nations are adopting democratic institutions that, while favorable in the long term, often produce short-term political disruptions as transitions take place, particularly in emerging markets.

- Movements toward market forces economies in Latin America, Asia, and Eastern Europe affect the global economy as markets are opened up, though occasionally with disruptive spillover effects (e.g., the Asian financial crisis).

Regional political trends include developments within and toward trade-bloc status. As regional trading blocs move toward intra-regional free trade, needs for country-based organizational structures diminish and pan-regional strategies become strategic options (e.g., regional strategies and supply chains).

At the *nation-state level,* elections and changes in political and economic agendas are constant sources of political uncertainty. Pro-business governments are generally favored, although autocratic governments are tolerated where they provide stable operating environments (e.g., China PRC). How firms monitor country-level risks is evaluated in the next chapter.

Economic Trends Economic trends must be evaluated at global, regional, and nation-state levels. *Global economic growth* has major effects on international businesses, as in many industries, aggregate sales vary according to global demand (e.g., in the machine tool example above, in industrial sectors such as semiconductors, and in consumer durables).

Regional economic growth levels are important as firms allocate resources among worldwide operations. For example, Gross Domestic Product forecasts for 2004 were for 4.1 percent global growth, with regional rates varying from 1.9 percent (Western Europe) to 4.7 and 6.5 percent for Middle East/North Africa and developing Asia respectively.[3]

National economic growth rate forecasts are important as companies determine national sales goals and finalize plans for manufacturing capacity and demand management for individual countries. National inflation rates are also routinely monitored as they affect cost structures (as wages and material prices increase) and for their effects on governmental policies. Excessive inflation for example, usually causes governments to deflate economies (causing downturns in national demand) and result in national currency realignments. In the short-term, currency devaluations present firms with export opportunities and make acquisitions cheaper for foreign firms. Over the long-term, however, inflationary tendencies are destabilizing, causing economic and political upheavals.

Societal Trends International firms have advantages in being able to monitor customer behavior over many markets and to move deftly to get ahead of prevailing trends. Some examples:

National industrialization efforts create demand for industrial products such as financial services, power-generating equipment, and construction equipment, and consumer products such as convenience foods (canned, frozen foods), clothes (for professionals, fashion), consumer durables (such as autos, ovens, refrigerators, TVs, etc.). As countries develop, demand is created in numerous industry sectors, including:

- Education: books, magazines, computer literacy
- Healthcare: medical equipment, pharmaceuticals; fitness equipment
- Increasing varieties of consumer products, brands
- Labor-saving products as women enter the work force

Societal priorities: At the regional and individual country levels, national governments push other issues onto corporate agendas, such as:

- Conservation issues: environmental protection (global warming), recycling, environmentally friendly manufacturing processes (ISO 14000)
- Concern for underprivileged peoples, minorities, and communities: use of philanthropy to build corporate image, viewing local communities as stakeholders, not taking excessive advantage of low wage rates in developing countries (e.g., SA 8000: Social Accountability Guidelines for international corporations)

> I believe that economists put decimal points in their forecasts to show they have a sense of humor.
>
> —*William E. Simon, former U.S. Secretary of the Treasury*

> The uprisings of 1789 cost Louis XVI some prerogatives, but four years later a valueless currency cost him his head. Germany's inflation of the 1920s laid the foundation upon which Hitler built. Indeed, runaway inflation is the goal of revolutionaries. The maxim of that apostle of revolution Lenin was "Debauch the currency!"
>
> —*Edgar M. Queeny*

- Increasing consumer mobility: As national and international infrastructures improve and affluence levels rise, governments push international companies to provide amenities for citizens, including auto ownership, travel services, financial services, and cheap air travel.

- National infrastructure development and technological upgrades: International firms have abilities to enhance national infrastructures and import technologies to enhance consumer knowledge (the Internet, CNN), consumer purchasing (telephone/Internet orders, next-day deliveries), industrial processes (JIT manufacturing), online banking/financial services. Some technology imports can be controversial. For example, genetically modified crops and animals have spurred national debates on the morality of disrupting natural biological processes.

Technological Trends The effects of technology on worldwide behaviors were notable over the 1990s, with the Internet and international media heightening popular appreciation of global events and providing corporations with efficient means of coordinating far-flung corporate empires. Technology has had far-reaching effects on societies and businesses. Societal effects include impacts on:

- *Religion:* As technology has modernized countries and provided consumers with increased product varieties, new media, alternative viewpoints, and new activities, there have been two religion-related consequences. First, as predicted in the anthropological field, religiosity has declined in importance as consumers have come to rely on technology rather than benevolent deities for their well-being. At the other end of the spectrum, modernization pressures have produced notable backlashes, ranging from movements against genetically modified ("Frankenstein") foods to wholesale rejections of Western technologies, most notably from fundamentalist Muslim groups.

- *Demographics:* As medical technologies have improved, so human longevity has been enhanced. From 1960 to 2000, world population doubled to 6 billion, and projections point to a total of 9 billion people by 2050.[4] Pressures on medical services, national pension systems, and social welfare are projected to be acute, particularly in North America, Western Europe, and Japan.

- *Education:* The Internet continues to make vast knowledge bases available to increasing numbers of people electronically. The diffusion of knowledge is occurring at faster rates, making proprietary technologies and ideas more difficult to maintain. At the consumer level, exposures to new lifestyles and behaviors are slowly educating individuals out of parochial perspectives into broader, more tolerant mindsets.

- *Popular culture:* The advent of international media and modern consumption styles has made global icons out of products (Coca Cola), movies and movie stars, sports (soccer, basketball, American football, the Olympic Games), fashions, and many other areas. The intrusion of modern popular culture into national cultures has been welcomed in many countries but rejected in others. As noted in Chapter 1, "westernization" is not for everyone.

Technology is transforming the ways companies do business, what products they offer, and how they communicate both internally and externally (e.g., with customers and with other supply-chain members). Some examples:

- *Internet technologies* have given the public access to companies via their web sites. Corporate activities have become accessible, with web sites providing free public relations and promotions for products, corporate achievements, and technologies.

- *Customer access:* Direct access has enabled firms to personalize customer relationships and, in some cases, build and sell tailor-make products. Custom-configured PCs by Dell, autos by Toyota, and printers by Lexmark are on the vanguard of a personalized competitive advantage.[5]

- *Supply chains* have been tightened up as distributors and suppliers have technological interfaces with manufacturers to speed along the production process. Cisco computers uses Internet linkages to coordinate its thirty-seven-factory outsourcing system. Suppliers make all components and perform 90 percent of subassembly work and 55 percent of final assembly. In some cases, Cisco employees have no contact at all with products or parts before they reach the final customer.[6] Internet relationships have made asset ownership less necessary for product manufacture and sale. Similarly, industry web sites for raw material and component sourcing have enabled firms in chemicals and auto parts to access worldwide suppliers instantaneously.

- *Global market access* via web sites has given small companies new opportunities to trade in the worldwide marketplace. Global transactions have been facilitated through international credit cards, reliable international deliveries, and lower trade barriers. Similarly, services such as banking, education, consulting, retailing, and gambling have become globally accessible via the Internet.[7]

- *Corporate human resource* needs have changed. The Internet and technology-based competition have made international corporations sensitive to attracting and retaining the best technical talent. Corporate mindsets have slowly shifted from emphases on capital investments to buildups of intellectual capital.[8] This trend is particularly noticeable in developing markets, as shortages of educated personnel have delayed participation in worldwide markets and corporate supply chains.

- *The Intranet,* the corporate Internet—has made information and data increasingly accessible within companies. More efficient data management has enabled firms to reduce headcounts, flatten their organizations, and quicken decision-making processes to keep pace with the web-based global marketplace.

- *Global financial resource availability:* Internet technologies have had profound effects on global capital markets. International lenders and borrowers can be brought together instantaneously. Credit references can be easily checked. Banks such as Citicorps

> These men of the technostructure are the new and universal priesthood. Their religion is business success; their test of virtue is growth and profit. Their bible is the computer printout; their communion bench is the committee room. The sales force carries their message to the world, and a message is what it is often called.
>
> —*John Kenneth Galbraith, U.S. economist*

> The real danger is not that computers will begin to think like men, but that men will begin to think like computers.
>
> —*Sydney J. Harris, U.S. journalist*

Without a yardstick there is no measurement. And without measurement there is no control.

—*Pravin M. Shah, Indian management*

The toughest thing about success is that you've got to keep on being a success.

—*Irving Berlin, U.S. composer*

and HSBC can leverage their global reach to get the best returns on capital and low lending rates. These advances have made information technologies key competitive advantages in the global finance arena.

Financial Benchmarks

Financial performance remains an important external and internal indicator of industry attractiveness and competitiveness. Outside of the company, profitability and return-on-investment benchmarks either attract or discourage the financial community as it evaluates alternative industries as potential investment outlets. Internally, financial benchmarks are used to assess company performance against industry standards and to evaluate the contributions of individual businesses and product lines to overall corporate performance.

Key Success Factors

Key success factors (KSFs) are the strategic expertise, competencies, resources, and competitive capabilities that companies must possess to survive and prosper in their industry environments.[9] In the telecommunications industry, relationships with major telephone companies, securing operating scale economies, and maintaining strong R and D programs are key success factors. For non-durable firms, penetrating emerging markets and leveraging brands globally are major factors in building and maintaining competitive positions in world markets.

GLOBAL COMPETITOR ANALYSES

Global competitor analysis occurs at three major levels: worldwide overviews, the regional market level, and the national market level. The aim of these analyses is to provide insights into rivals' strategies to enable companies to:

- *Outwit* rivals by detecting marketplace changes more quickly than competitors, anticipating rival moves in the competitive arena, and mobilizing far-flung corporate resources to react faster to marketplace and competitor changes.

- *Outmaneuver* rivals by being the first to introduce new products and technologies, dominating major channels of distribution, and establishing key relationships with suppliers and major stakeholders (e.g., financial community, labor force, press relations).

- *Outperform* rivals in terms of new product development, market share, customer-satisfaction levels, and corporate reputation.[10]

A primary task in competitive analysis is to gain strategic overviews of major competitors, their aims, their aspirations, and how they are performing worldwide. Preliminary insights into company strategy can be obtained by examining mission statements, strategic intents, and core competencies.

Internal Assessments

Corporate missions provide overviews of corporate priorities in terms of products, markets, technology, and corporate culture. For example, Unilever's corporate purpose is "to meet the every-day needs of people everywhere—to anticipate aspirations of our consumers and customers and to respond creatively and competitively with branded products and services which raise the quality of life."[11]

Strategic intents relate to long-term competitive aspirations. They are more action-oriented than mission statements and relate more directly to competitive positions. Typical strategic intents are to be the market leader in key product areas or technology, become a best-cost producer (i.e., achieving the best combination of cost, product reliability, and overall product value), or attain lead market positioning globally, regionally, or in specific markets.[12]

Core competencies are articulations of what companies do better than others—their acknowledged expertise areas vis-à-vis the rest of the industry. Sony's core competency is its ability to translate technological expertise into innovative new products; Microsoft's is its hard-driving approach to software innovation; Jaguar autos are renowned for their performance and styling expertise. Such competencies are established over long time periods and are the basis for competitive advantages in specific product lines. Examination of mission statements, strategic intents, and core competencies give managements key insights into rivals' products, expertise, and competitive objectives.

> I have studied the enemy all my life. I have read the memoirs of his generals and his leaders. I have even read his philosophers and listened to his music. I have studies in detail the accounts of every damned one of his battles. I know exactly how he will react under any given set of circumstances. And he hasn't the slightest idea of what I'm going to do. So when the time comes, I'm going to whip the hell out of him.
>
> —*George S. Patton, U.S. army general*

External Assessments: Analyzing Competitor Operations

Total sales and regional breakdowns show current revenue streams of competitors and regional sales dependencies. As Table 6.9 shows, Unilever sales are only slightly ahead of Procter & Gamble's. Both companies are heavily dependent on their home markets—Unilever on Europe and P & G on North America. Unilever's foreign sales have greater reach and penetration over emerging markets than their North American rival.

Global demand analyses show recent sales trends in specific regions and product areas, as well as how they contribute to overall corporate performance. Table 6.9 shows both Unilever and Procter & Gamble emphasizing their global brands and reducing their focuses on marginal brands and businesses. In large corporations, these analyses are taken several steps further. A framework for analyzing major competitors is shown in Figure 6.2. Sales, market shares, competitor strengths, weaknesses, and recent developments (new resource deployments, etc.) are principal tools of analysis. A similar framework can be used to analyze individual competitors within regions (Figure 6.3).

Supply-chain strategies show the efforts firms are making to streamline purchasing, manufacturing, and distribution activities on a worldwide basis. As Table 6.9 shows, both Unilever and Colgate Palmolive are tightening up their

TABLE 6.9
Competitive Profiles: Unilever and Procter & Gamble

	Unilever (2002)	Procter & Gamble
Total Sales	48.8 billion euros	$43.4 billion (2003)
Global Coverage	188 countries	160 countries
Regional Sales		
Europe	40%	27%
North America	26%	55%
Latin America	11%	8%
Africa/Middle East	7%	10%
Asia-Pacific	16%	
Global Demand	Europe: sales up 3% with significant contributions from Central/Eastern Europe North America: sales up 1% but divestitures cause 5% downturn Africa/Middle East sales ↑ 9% Asia-Pacific sales ↑ 2% Latin America sales ↑ 12%, but affected by currency fluctuations Global advertising a key to demand stimulation: company budgets (pounds sterling) 2001 (4,514 million) to 2003 (4852 million) Brand focus: cut from 1600 brands in 2000 to 400 by 2004 Unilever corporate logo put on major brands 2002 Innovation centers for product groups Harmonized market research across regions	Organization 2005 restructuring into 7 worldwide business units: • Fabrics and homecare • Food-beverages • Feminine hygiene • Beauty care • Tissues and towels • Baby care • Healthcare P & G focus on brands with $500+ million potential in global sales Media strategies emphasis on transfers among regions to get the most out of the $3.6 billion global advertising outlays
Supply Chain Strategies	Internet-based information systems link communications among worldwide affiliates Global buying system for technology purchases. Manufacturing plants to be cut from 380 to 150; 25,000 jobs cut 2000 reorganization into two divisions: Food and non-foods each under geographic organization	Global ERP system to link operations in 130 countries driven by product demand rather than forecasts Suppliers: Electronic bids for company business through reverse auctions Web-based ordering systems and supplier tracking of orders to 300 plants worldwide Retailing: Efficient Consumer Response initiatives; electronic catalogs and close relations with large retailers like Wal-Mart
Strategic Thrusts	75% of food business in Europe in North America "a striking mismatch between Unilever's with sales and the growth markets of developing countries." Greater focus on developing world	Excessive reliance on North America to be addressed More localization to be introduced into foreign marketing (fears of over-globalization)

Sources: Web sites www.unilever.com and www.colgate.com, Beck, Ernest. "Unilever to cut 25,000 jobs, close factories." *Wall Street Journal* (February 23, 2000): 1. Bureau and press reports.

purchasing organizations and are emphasizing coordination efforts among worldwide units. A key element in supply-chain analysis is to map out competitor supply chains. This involves plotting R and D facilities, key raw material and component sources, manufacturing and assembly operations, and distribution centers worldwide. A framework for global supply-chain mapping is shown in Figure 6.4.

Strategic initiative analyses highlight management priorities in market expansion efforts. Both Unilever and Procter & Gamble's concerns center around exploiting the market potentials in emerging markets and reducing their reliance on mature markets. Both companies were also intent on leveraging their global branding skills though P & G were wary of over-globalizing and were reemphasizing localization strategies.

FIGURE 6.2
Global/Regional Analysis of Principal Competitors

	COMPETITOR			
	A	**B**	**C**	**'N'**
Western Europe Sales Market Share Competitor Strengths Competitor Weaknesses Recent Developments				
North America Sales Market Share Competitor Strengths Competitor Weaknesses Recent Developments				
Asia Sales Market Share Competitor Strengths Competitor Weaknesses Recent Developments				
Eastern Europe **Africa/Middle East** **Latin America** **Etc.**				

FIGURE 6.3
Intra-regional Analyses of Individual Competitors

Competitor A

Western Europe	Sales	Market Share	Facilities	Strategic Emphasis
UK				
France				
Germany*				
Italy				
Belgium/Lux				
Spain				
Sweden				
Norway				
Etc.				

*Indicates competitor A home market

FIGURE 6.4
Geographic Evaluation of Competition

Framework for analyzing competitor supply chains

	North America	Latin America	Western Europe	Eastern Europe	Middle East	Africa	Asia
R and D Laboratories							
Raw Material Sourcing							
Component Sourcing and Manufacture							
Assembly Operations							
Distribution Facilities							
Marketing and Sales							

Source: Adapted from Charles W. Hofer and Terry P. Haller. "Globalscan: A Way to Better International Assessments." *Journal of Business Strategy* 2 (Fall, 1980): 53.

USING MARKET OPPORTUNITY AND COMPETITIVE ANALYSES TO CRAFT GLOBAL STRATEGIES

Global industry and trade analyses show which countries represent the best market opportunities. Supply-chain analyses show where materials can be procured and products effectively manufactured. Competitor analyses indicate geographic strengths and weaknesses of individual rivals. From these analyses, management can craft strategies that capitalize on, first, market size and growth tendencies and, second, on competitor strengths and weaknesses.

Market Selection Strategies

Managements of large international companies routinely monitor market sizes and growth rates in over 150 national markets. Obviously (as indicated in Table 6.10), large and medium-sized growth markets are always attractive propositions, and companies compete to build up resources in these regions (such as Asia or Latin America) and countries such as China, India, and Brazil. Similarly, large stable markets, such as North America and Western Europe, are good investment sites for most industries. It is not surprising, therefore, that these areas continue to attract the lion's share of foreign direct investments. But managements maintain positive outlooks in small-growth markets, medium-sized stable markets, and large declining markets, as they know that markets grow under the right economic conditions and with the right marketing strategies. The same can be said for smaller markets, where patience is the

TABLE 6.10
Market Size/Growth and Investment Priorities

Market Size/Growth	Growth	Stable	Declining
Large	1	2	3
Medium	4	5	6
Small	7	8	9

Top Investment Priorities: 1, 2, and 4
Moderate Investment Priorities: 7, 5, and 3
Low Investment Priorities: 6, 8, and 9

key to demand development. Only where there are adverse political and/or economic circumstances (such as civil unrest or severe governmental mismanagement of the economy) do managers consider market withdrawal or disinvestments strategies.

Other factors weigh on management minds as they craft their market selections strategies. Smaller companies, especially exporters, may want to avoid head-to-head competition with industry leaders and emphasize markets where larger rivals are not present or have few assets (e.g., building presences in smaller Latin American markets, but not in Brazil or Argentina). Similarly, they may emphasize particular market groupings (e.g., Eastern Europe, or Southeast Asia) where they can focus their resources to become a viable regional competitor. In these cases, competitor actions are critical inputs into resource allocation decisions. These are now examined. Company considerations and market conditions, the other major inputs, are examined in the next chapter.

THE GLOBAL WEB

Global auto production of light vehicles can be found at: www.esmauto.com. Go to File Downloads and to Global Light Vehicle Production Forecast summaries by region/manufacturer, and by region and country. These are by manufacturer.

Competitive Effects on Strategic Decision Making

Successful companies, global or domestic, must not only satisfy customers but out-compete market rivals. Analyses of key global and regional rivals help the formulation of effective competitive strategies. This has become important because the large international companies are active in most or all major markets (e.g., soft drinks, autos, computers). Careful monitoring of their resource commitments and market positions are crucial in deciding where and how to compete in the international marketplace.

Where market rivals are strong, market challengers must be careful how they attack them. Few global firms are strong everywhere. Regional and national market weaknesses become attack options, as do under-performing business divisions and product lines. Where home-market dominance underwrites international operations, disruptive tactics by foreign rivals in the home market can undermine the global competitor (as Fuji did to Kodak: see Chapter 9).

All strategy depends on competition.

—*Bruce D. Henderson, founder, Boston Consulting Group*

The underdog in many products . . . can pick and choose where it wants to hit the giant; the giant by contrast, must defend itself everywhere.

—*George H. Lesch, former president, Colgate-Palmolive*

Where smaller competitors lack the global reach or resources to challenge market leaders, they can use acquisitions, joint ventures, or global alliances to attain the critical size needed to compete (e.g., airline alliances).

Finally, where global firms face weaker competitors (global, regional, or national), they can use superior brand names, corporate reputations, cost structures, and technologies to carve out competitive advantages. Where they want "instant" market presences, or where local advantages are important (output customization, distribution, local connections), they can use superior financial resources and reputations to make acquisitions, joint ventures, or alliances work to give them insider advantages.

Where competitor supply chains are mapped out, firms can imitate (and nullify) competitive advantages in materials or component procurement (for example, by acquiring or taking ownership stakes in leading suppliers). They can decide how best to configure their international production arrangements (globally, regionally, or nationally configured manufacturing systems). Finally, they can locate their distribution and customer servicing centers to optimize cost and customer service objectives. These strategic initiatives are summarized in Table 6.11.

Even where companies are performing well worldwide, complete overviews of industries, competitors, and markets are key tools in effective decision making.

T A B L E   6 . 1 1
Global Industry and Competitor Analysis Inputs into Strategy-Crafting and Decision Making

Competitor Profile	Strategic/Competitive Options	Text Coverage

Strong Global Competitor	• Attack selectively: products, regions, markets where rival is less dominant
	• Disrupt competitor in key markets (e.g., home market)
	• Build critical mass in world markets through acquisitions, joint ventures, global alliances
		Details in:
		  Chapter 8 (Globalization)
		  Chapter 9 (Global and Multi-Market Strategies)
		  Chapter 10 (Market Entry and Servicing Strategies)

Weaker Global Competitor	• Attack head-to-head using superior resources and competitive advantages (brand names, quality, costs, technologies) • Acquire competitor • Identify competitor weaknesses and attack selectively	
Regional/National Competitors	• Attack using superior resource bases: corporate reputation, brands, technologies, scale economies • Build local presences via investments or through acquisitions/alliances with (a) major regional competitor and/or (b) major national competitors	
Supply Chain Initiatives		
Suppliers	• Locate best suppliers—globally, regionally, nationally: acquire ownership stakes, lock into long-term contracts, or maintain flexibility with multiple suppliers.	Chapter 11: Global and Multi-Market Supply Chain Management
Manufacturing Strategy	• Identify best options: (a) Worldwide manufacturing for scale economies (b) Regional manufacturing for best combination of scale economies and customization for regional preferences (c) National manufacturing for country-based customization	
Distribution Centers/Customer Servicing	• Locate for best combinations of cost and customer service	

KEY POINTS

- Analyzing industries on a worldwide scale has become essential as companies and industry sectors have expanded their global presences throughout international markets.

- Worldwide industry analyses starts with evaluations of worldwide and regional market demand and demand within individual countries. Also, because international trade is an important component of global demand, export market demand should be assessed using national and international trade statistics.

- Industry supply chains can be analyzed to examine international sources of supply via import trade statistics and to evaluate national expertise in manufacturing.

- Industry structure analyses show who the leading companies are in particular sectors. Firms can then isolate individual rivals for in-depth competitor analysis.

- Industry change drivers should be examined, including trends in global, regional, and national political environments and economic, societal and technological trends.

- Finally, for worldwide industry analyses, financial benchmarks are sought to provide guidelines for corporate assessment of business divisions and subsidiaries and key success factors established to focus corporate efforts on "what they must do well" to be successful in their industry.

- Analyses of global competitors include internal assessments of rivals' corporate missions, strategic intents, and core competencies and external evaluations of global and regional revenue streams, trends, supply-chain strategies, and strategic initiatives. Market opportunity and competitor analyses can be used as the bases for market diversification moves and competitive strategies against key rivals.

ENDNOTES

1. Anonymous, "Yamaha Motor aims to boost global motorcycle market share," *Jiji Press English News Service* (Tokyo, April 9, 2002).

2. Michael E. Porter, "The Competitive Advantage of Nations," *Harvard Business Review* 68, 2 (March–April, 1990): 73–93.

3. International Monetary Fund, *World Economic Outlook* (Washington, D.C.: September, 2003): 2.

4. Peter Coy, "The 'little emperors' can save the world's aging population," *Business Week* (August 30, 1999): 140–42.

5. Otis Port, "Customers move into the driver's seat," *Business Week* (Oct. 4, 1999): 103–6.

6. *Ibid.* 106.

7. Michael J. Mandel, "The Internet Economy: The World's Next Growth Engine," *Business Week* (Oct. 4, 1999): 72–77.

8. John Byrne, "The Search for the Young and Gifted," *Business Week* (Oct. 4, 1999): 112.

9. Arthur A. Thompson Jr. and A. J. Strickland, *Strategic Management: Concepts and Cases,* 11th Edition (Boston: Irwin McGraw-Hill, 1999): 95–96.

10. From Liam Fahey, *Competitors* (New York, John Wiley, 1999): chapter 1.

11. From *www.unilever.com.*

12. Lynda Gratton, "Implementing a Strategic Vision—Key Factors for Success," *Long Range Planning* 29 (1996): 290–303.

Casette 6-1
Global Change and the Wine Industry

"Dom Perignon '53, please." James Bond might be at home with the elite European wines, but he would be one of a dying breed of connoisseurs who "know" wines. While France, Italy, and Spain continue to produce top-quality vintages, upstart winemakers in North America, South Africa, Australia, and New Zealand and other European producers are emerging to challenge the traditionally strong Mediterranean triad. As global affluence increases, greater proportions of consumers are accessing the increasing varieties of wines available in the international marketplace. At the retail level, global retailers (and supermarkets in particular) are challenging liquor stores and wine specialists as the top outlets for purchase. Fewer consumers appreciate the differences between the top wines and the less-than-$15 per bottle segment.

To be sure, no one really challenges France as the top quality producer. From Roman times, the country has been the quality producer, and even today, twelve of the thirteen three-star vineyards ("the very best wine money can buy") are in France (the other being in Portugal). Yet globalization is causing major dislocations in the industry, and the top three national producers (and France in particular) have come under increasing pressures to adapt to the new wine-drinking market. The structure of the industry shows France with 689 producers, North America with 549, Australia 239, South Africa 133, New Zealand 92, Spain 87, South America 83, Britain 80, and Portugal 38. France also dominates the 2½-star wines with 28 producers against the rest of the world's 15. Only when the quality level reaches 2 stars is there any real competition to France, where North America's 26 producers, Australia's 20, and South Africa's 19 get close to the French total of 33.

Global Production of Wines by Country

Table 1 shows the top 20 major national producers of wines. The clear supremacy of Italy, France, and Spain is notable, yet a number of countries are beginning to challenge the leaders. Wine as an agricultural product suffers from the volatility associated with the sector. Poor weather conditions affect crop yields and quality, as do exceptionally fine conditions that produce "gluts."

World totals are for all 62 of the major global producers.

Global Consumption of Wines by Country

Table 2 shows the top 20 wine-consuming nations in thousands of hectoliters, along with historic consumption trends.

World totals include all 66 major wine-consuming countries.

TABLE 1
World Wine Production by Country (thousands of in thousands of hectoliters)

2000 Country Rank	2000	1999	1998
1. France	57,541	60,435	52,671
2. Italy	51,620	56,454	54,188
3. Spain	41,692	33,723	31,175
4. United States	23,300	19,050	20,504
5. Argentina	12,538	15,888	12,673
6. Germany	9,852	12,123	10,834
7. Australia	8,064	8,511	7,415
8. South Africa	6,949	7,968	7,703
9. Portugal	6,694	7,859	3,750
10. Chile	6,419	4,807	5,475
11. China	5,750	5,200	3,550
12. Romania	5,456	6,054	5,002
13. Brazil	3,704	3,190	2,782
14. Greece	3,558	3,680	3,826
15. Hungary	3,000	3,339	4,334
16. Russia	2,903	2,093	2,180
17. Moldova	2,402	1,332	1,700
18. Austria	2,338	2,803	2,703
19. Bulgaria	2,099	2,026	2,129
20. Croatia	2,094	2,094	2,277
World total	275,892	277,171	256,399

Source: Office International de la Vigne as presented at www.wineinstitute.org

TABLE 2

2000 Country Rank	2000	1999	1998	Average 1996–1999
1. France	34,500	35,400	36,330	35,506
2. Italy	30,800	31,200	31,840	32,147
3. United States	21,200	20,938	20,748	20,343
4. Germany	19,565	19,751	18,970	19,106
5. Spain	13,843	15,000	14,793	14,710
6. Argentina	12,443	12,567	12,683	13,001
7. United Kingdom	9,146	8,757	8,290	8,176
8. China	5,535	5,535	3,940	3,983
9. Russia	5,500	5,500	5,500	5,675
10. Romania	5,215	5,823	4,430	5,838
11. Portugal	5,020	4,980	5,055	5,265
12. South Africa	3,893	3,953	3,867	3,975
13. Australia	3,889	3,726	3,644	3,532
14. Brazil	3,205	2,963	2,552	2,613
15. Japan	3,100	3,100	3,200	2,698
16. Chile	2,972	2,853	2,713	2,445
17. Switzerland	2,958	2,946	2,914	2,923
18. Greece	2,747	2,868	2,927	2,833
19. Netherlands	2,700	2,518	2,200	2,294
20. Austria	2,400	2,500	2,500	2,536
World Total	219,833	221,388	219,946	219,908

Source: Office International de la Vigna et du Vin as presented by www.wineinstitute.org

Consumption Potential Indicators

Wine consumption per capita is a useful indicator of market potential, especially when analyzed by country population size. Figure 1 shows this analysis.

Industry Supply Chain Developments

Capacity Planning In the U.S., California producers doubled their production of Chardonnays and Cabernet Sauvignon and tripled their Merlot-producing capacities between 1996 and 2000. Australian output expanded by 40,000 hectors, and the EU supplies of premium quality grapes were expected to increase by 15 percent by 2003. South Africa, Argentina, and Eastern Europe were also engaged in industry and ca-

pacity upgrades to make them more competitive in the international marketplace.

Changing Industry Structure Of the ten largest wine companies, only one is French. Bordeaux alone has about 20,000 different producers, many with their own brands and distinctive characteristics. In contrast, three Australian producers dominate that nation's market.

Branding Australian and U.S. producers simplified their product lines according to grape origin: Merlot, Cabernet Sauvignon, Chardonnay, etc. The French maintained their geographic origin names (numbering over 450) despite major differences in quality within

FIGURE 1

Charting Wine Consumption Per Capita by Country Population

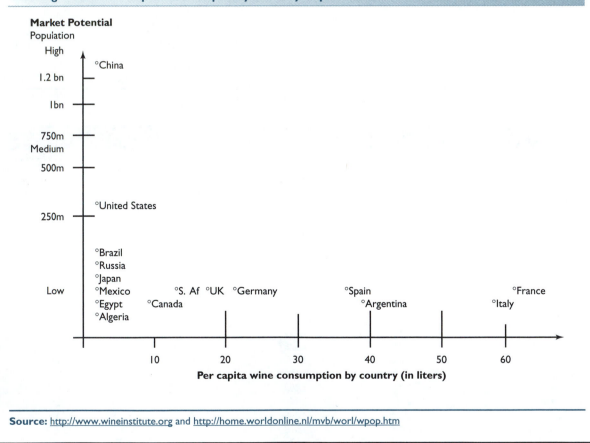

Source: http://www.wineinstitute.org and http://home.worldonline.nl/mvb/worl/wpop.htm

origin name designation. Grape origin commonality gave non-French producers flexibility in sourcing materials—a luxury not possible under the French system. Non-French producers were aiming to create consistent-quality world brands. The French were aiming to maintain their unique brand images.

The New Competition While the old-world European wine producers were being pressured by the new-world producers (U.S., Australia, South Africa, Argentina, etc.), new entrants were lining up, including Eastern European nations, such as Armenia and Georgia, and other Latin American producers, such as Brazil and Mexico. These countries tended to be low-cost producers because of low wages, weak currencies, and plentiful grape supplies due to steady hot climates. This contrasted to the unpredictable weather and variable vintages of European producers.

Changing Consumer Tastes Younger wine drinkers were finding some traditional European wines to be too acidic and were turning to the fruitier tastes in North American, Australian, and South African wines. The fruity orientation was being augmented with natural flavorings such as peach and berries and was attracting new consumers.

Marketing Orientation The large wineries, such as Gallo and Mondavi, were engaging in major marketing and promotional programs using film stars and sports people to broaden consumer appeal for their products. Big marketing budgets were being allocated to promote sales and heighten consumer awareness about the pleasures of wine drinking and some health benefits of red wines in particular.

Distribution Changes The industry was increasingly moving toward a bi-polar distribution system, emphasizing either specialty outlets (wine shops, liquor stores, wine clubs) or mass distribution through supermarkets and mass merchandisers that were able to squeeze producer margins.

Strategic Orientations The large wine producers were scanning global markets for acquisitions to access new markets and add to their supply capabilities. In Europe, Mildara Blass purchased major wine clubs in the Netherlands and Germany to increase their exposure among heavy wine drinkers.

Questions

1. Examine the structure of the global wine industry and the tables of global wine statistics. What conclusions do you draw from the figures presented? What implications do the figures have for wine industry executives?

2. Review the trends present in the industry's supply chain. What implications do you see for the sector as a whole?

3. You have been brought in to advise (a) the French wine industry and/or (b) the Australian wine industry about what strategies to follow. What would you advise, and why?

Sources: www.wineinstitute.org. United Nations: Food and Agriculture Organization. Rachman, Gideon. "Christmas survey: Glug, glug, glut." *Economist* (December 18, 1999): 103–5. Echikson, William, et al. "Wine War." *Business Week* (September 3, 2001): 54–60. Anonymous. "Trouble ahead for the global wine industry." *Grocer* (February 27, 1999): 57–58.

CASETTE 6-2
The Airbus–Boeing Global Rivalry

Airbus and Boeing currently dominate the world aircraft-production market. Their rivalry is intense. Below are profiles of the two companies.

	Boeing	Airbus
Corporate Missions, Strategic Intents and Core Competencies	• Corporate philosophies emphasize 8 values: leadership, integrity, qualities, customer satisfaction, teamwork, participative decision making, corporate citizenship, and shareholder value • Core competencies are detailed customer knowledge and focus; large scale systems integration; lean, efficient design and production system	• Market orientation: listening to airlines, passengers and pilots • Operating philosophy guided by: 1. Anticipating market needs 2. Common operating systems among products 3. Innovation 4. Passenger comfort

Global Market Demand
- World airline fleets to double 2000–19 to 31,755 aircraft
- Growth rates 5.2% p.a. to 2010 and 4.6% to 2020
- Regional demand: North America 35%; Europe 30% (mature markets); Asia-Pacific 24%; 11% for Latin America, Middle East, and Africa
- Demand segments: Small aircraft 65% global demand, 20% medium sized aircraft, 15% large aircraft

	Boeing	Airbus
Product Lines	Six families of jetliners 717,737,747,757,767,777 and the Boeing Business Jet	Three families of aircraft with 15 aircraft products each focusing on an identifiable market niche
New Product Development	• One new plane (777) in last 20 years; focus on modifying existing aircraft to suit customer present and future needs • Work on Sonic cruiser underway for high speed, high altitude aircraft. Possible entry date: 2008	Development of new A3XX to carry over 550 passengers with possible sleeping, shower, and shopping facilities. Competitive advantages include 49% more floor space, 35% more seating, 10–15% more range. First flight scheduled for 2004 and deliveries in 2006. Problems include high costs and break even orders; airport landing facilities.
Supply Chain Issues	• Established Global Airline inventory network; positioned to be the complete supplier of parts to airlines (e.g., British Airways) • Consolidation of aluminum requirements to 5 mills	• Use of SAP software system to link and service all suppliers and airlines with company • Worldwide distribution centers in Frankfurt, Hamburg (Germany), U.S., Singapore, and China • Common cockpits among aircraft to facilitate and reduce aircrew and pilot training times and easier flight operations. • Technology: "fly by wire" technology which uses electronic signals to respond to pilot controls (Boeing uses cables and hydraulic systems.)
Strategic Thrusts	• 1997 merger with McDonnell-Douglas • Using buy backs of older aircraft to maintain Singapore Airlines as a Boeing customer • Working with China to provide technical and operating support	• Emphasis on key Boeing accounts, e.g., Minyan prayer service offered to El Al Israeli airlines broke Boeing monopoly • India whose airfleet is projected to double to 2020 • Strengthening of ties with Chinese and Japanese firms for aircraft parts • Development of 2000 A3XX suppliers in Western and Eastern Europe, U.S., and Asia

Global Marketplace Issues
- Safety issues and the UN's International Civil Aviation Authority
- Privatization and deregulation issues increasing airline competition, reducing operating margins and increasing needs for cost effective aircraft operations
- Environmental impacts of increased pollution from aircraft engines
- U.S. and EU handling of China's human rights controversy may determine sales in the PRC

Airbus was steadily increasing its sales as the 1990s drew to a close. The company outsold Boeing 2 to 1 in 1999 and was positioning itself to capture 55–60% of the global market on a consistent basis.

Questions

1. Compare the Airbus-Boeing orientations as indicated in their missions, strategic intents, and core competencies. What conclusions would you draw?

2. What are the key competitive battlegrounds for Boeing and Airbus from product and market perspectives?

3. Airbus was criticized for borrowing $2.1 billion from the French, UK, German, and Spanish governments in development loans. Airbus responded by noting that Boeing's defense, NASA contracts and tax deferments on exports from the U.S. government, amounted to between $30–40 billion in financial support. What do you think?

4. Web sites and secondary sources are often used in this type of research. What are the advantages and disadvantages of such resources, and how can they affect competitor analyses?

Sources: Holmes, Stanley. "Battle looms over aircraft subsidies." *Europe* (November, 1999): 20–21. Holmes, Stanley. "Why Airbus is outselling Boeing lately." *Seattle Times Aerospace Reporter* (October 31, 1999). Jones Newswires. "Flying High." *www.interactive.wsj.com* (September 25, 2000).Web site, WWW.boeing.com. Web site, WWW.airbus.com. Web site, *www.tourismfutureintl.com.*

Chapter Seven

International Strategic Planning and Market Screening

❦

GLOBAL PLANNING IN THE CHEMICAL INDUSTRY

When three medium-sized European firms—Elf Atochem, Petrofina, and Total Chimie—combined their assets to form Atofina, they became the fifth largest chemical company in the world, and their planning processes took on a global dimension. First Atofina looked at its prime businesses. Its petrochemicals and commodity plastics comprised 38 percent of its $17 billion turnover, intermediates and specialty polymers 26 percent, and specialties (e.g., agricultural foodstuffs) 36 percent. To streamline its activities, the company sold its metal and aviation unit ($100 million in sales), its oleochemicat group (about $200 million in sales), and was looking to unload a further $1 billion in assets to focus on its mainstream businesses. Geographically, 63 percent of sales were in slow growth markets of Europe, and the company realized that it needed to focus on North America's huge market, and in the fast-growing markets of Latin America, the Middle East, and Asia. In North America, Atofina's emphasis was on building up its polyethylene and propylene businesses, and to increase access to key specialty chemical users in the automotive, construction, and electronics sectors. In Asia and the Middle East, the company had few assets and was looking to expand through investment opportunities.[1]

Almost all companies are planners. In the chemical industry, like many other asset-intensive industries (e.g., autos, metals, industrial equipment), planning is all-important when production capacity expansions take years to execute and carry heavy penalties for failure. As a result, global planning efforts occupy much of top management's time. Assets are scarce, and businesses not contributing to the firm's international effectiveness are likely to be discontinued in favor of mainstream businesses. Geographic strategies must be mapped out for global effectiveness and focused to achieve global balance across industries and regions. Planning processes must therefore systematically evaluate corporate performance from business and market perspectives and come up with viable objectives and strategies to guide future operations worldwide.

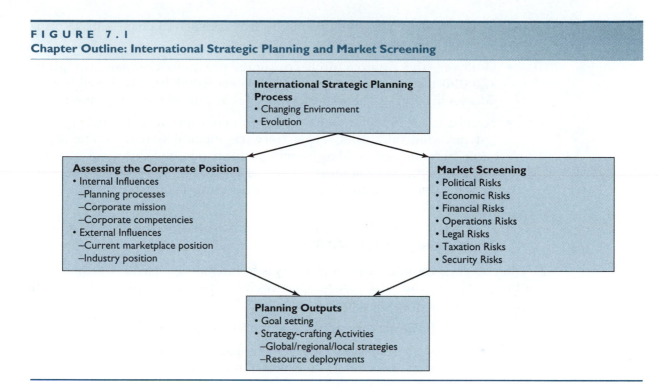

FIGURE 7.1
Chapter Outline: International Strategic Planning and Market Screening

International Strategic Planning Process
• Changing Environment
• Evolution

Assessing the Corporate Position
• Internal Influences
 –Planning processes
 –Corporate mission
 –Corporate competencies
• External Influences
 –Current marketplace position
 –Industry position

Market Screening
• Political Risks
• Economic Risks
• Financial Risks
• Operations Risks
• Legal Risks
• Taxation Risks
• Security Risks

Planning Outputs
• Goal setting
• Strategy-crafting Activities
 –Global/regional/local strategies
 –Resource deployments

Hence, in this chapter, you will learn:

• How the international planning process is defined, how the complexity of world-wide planning has increased since 1945, and the ways companies have modified planning processes to respond to heightening competition in world markets
• How international firms assess their internal orientations and their external marketplace situations
• The formulation of international plans at the national, regional, and global levels, and the process of global resource allocation
• The screening criteria international companies use to evaluate worldwide markets on a comparative basis, including emerging countries

INTRODUCTION: THE INTERNATIONAL PLANNING PROCESS

International strategic planning is the process through which worldwide companies evaluate past results, assess their corporate strengths and weaknesses, and map out future resource allocation and strategies based on marketplace opportunities and threats. The organizational complexity of international corporations and the geographically far-flung nature of their commercial empires make planning a complex process to manage. For example:

- Unilever, the Anglo-Dutch consumer products company, employs 270,000 people worldwide, and sells over 1000 brands through subsidiaries in eighty-eight countries and sales in a further seventy nations.

- Toshiba is a $45 billion corporation with eight product divisions (power systems, semiconductors, display services, medical systems, home appliances, elevator and building systems, information and industrial systems, and digital media equipment). These are managed over 100 foreign subsidiaries, including thirty-nine manufacturing facilities outside of the Japanese home market.

- IBM has worldwide revenues of over $80 billion and employs over 290,000 people making 40,000 products.

The challenge for international planners is to interactively blend together head office, regional, and subsidiary perspectives into a cohesive global plan. At each level, management's task is to:

- Evaluate the firm's current position and its strengths and weaknesses

- Assess how environmental factors will impact corporate strategies and performance over the short (1 to 3 years), medium (3 to 5 years) and long-term planning horizons

- Identify key strategic objectives to be attained and performance benchmarks to ascertain progress

General guidelines are established to unify strategic approaches at the worldwide, regional, and local levels. This process is illustrated in Figure 7.1.

The Changing Environment of International Planning: Historical Perspectives

Strategic-planning roles and philosophies have changed significantly since 1945 as companies have internationalized their operations and integrated them on a worldwide basis.[2] In the 1950s and early 1960s, international planning was a centralized activity. Many countries were rebuilding their economies, and planning activities were production-oriented. Firms focused on determining required manufacturing levels, expected revenues, and resources needed to deliver products into an under-supplied marketplace. Little "strategy" was necessary, and planning centered on budgets and outputs.

The situation changed during the 1960s and 1970s as European and Japanese firms entered the world marketplace and competition heated up. Tools for assessing competitive strengths, weaknesses, and marketplace situation were developed (e.g., the GE matrix and the Boston Consulting Group's competitive position matrix). Strategies were formulated to counter rivals' activities. Planning staffs grew as firms addressed the issues of escalating international competition and rapid geographic and business diversifications. This trend continued

> The trouble with our times is that the future is not what it used to be.
>
> *—Paul Valery,*
> *19th–20th-century French*
> *poet and philosopher*

during the 1980s as the global marketplace expanded away from the Triad countries of North America, Western Europe, and Japan to include big emerging markets in Latin America, Eastern Europe, and Asia.

As the 1990s progressed, heightened competition caused companies to reorient strategies based on scale economies back toward customizing output to suit individual countries and segments. In Western companies, this has led to the decentralization of planning activities to product divisions and national subsidiaries. Central-planning departments were cut, and country subsidiaries were encouraged to "get close to their customers." Head offices took on new roles emphasizing coordination among divisions and subsidiaries and monitoring global competitor activities.

The Evolution of the International Corporate Planning Processes

International planning processes vary in complexity according to the degree of strategic analysis involved in the planning process. For example, Japanese planning processes have historically emphasized budgetary mechanisms, while American firms have tended to incorporate a wider variety of strategic elements into their plans.[3] To help people understand the evolution of planning processes, four stages of corporate planning development have been identified.[4]

1. *Financial planning:* In this phase, organizations set budgets and costs, and revenue and profits are forecasted, usually for the year ahead. Companies know which product lines are profitable, and limits are placed on all expenditures. Because of the limited time horizon, little emphasis is given to market developments, except as they affected sales or profits.

2. *Long-term (forecast-based) planning:* Statistical techniques are used to forecast up to three or five years ahead for sales, costs, and profits. Assumptions are laid out concerning the circumstances under which such forecasts should be accurate. Longer-range planning enables firms to use broader sets of evaluative benchmarks, including productivity improvements, capacity utilization, and financial control objectives. Planning is still primarily set out in financial terms.

3. *Environmental planning* brings in formal evaluations of external developments, with economic, socio-demographic, and technological trends influencing corporate and industry sales projections. Competitor strategies are analyzed, and formal account taken of governmental policies as they affect infrastructures, social security, and environmental protection legislation.

4. *Integrative strategic planning* includes strengths-weaknesses-opportunities-threats analyses and orients them toward strategic issues leading to sustainable competitive advantages. The planning process becomes broader and involves more people. "What if" scenarios are addressed. Stakeholder participation is encouraged in the planning process to keep employees,

> We should all be concerned with the future because we will have to spend the rest of our lives there.
>
> —*Charles F. Kettering, 19th–20th-century U.S. engineer and inventor*

> The art of prophecy is very difficult, especially with respect to the future.
>
> —*Mark Twain, 19th-century U.S. author*

suppliers, and distributors informed about marketplace developments, and to encourage entrepreneurial initiatives.

ASSESSING THE CORPORATE POSITION

The first task for international planners is to take stock of the corporation's current position. This includes evaluations of internal environments (corporate missions and core competencies) and assessments of marketplace performance (individual businesses and sales by region and by country market). External assessments include industry and competitive performance measures discussed in the last chapter.

Internal Assessments

Effective planning occurs when firms have definite ideas about where they want to be and what has enabled them to get where they are. To this end, mission statements and reviews of core competencies guide company efforts and provide continuity between past and future planning efforts.

The Corporate Mission The corporate mission is "a statement of vision, or ambition that defines success and establishes the ground rules by which success is achieved for a particular company or institution; the articulation of management's intent regarding the future of an organization, expressed in aspirational terms."[5]

Most mission statements, particularly those of international corporations, are broad-based and encompass one or more of the following features:[6]

* Description of the business in terms of customers, products, and services and geographic locations

* Strategic intent: the corporation's long-term goals, often stated in competitive or performance terms ("to be a/the global leader in . . .")

* Perceived organizational strengths: These list the marketplace and internal advantages that have led to organizational success and include brand names, customer satisfaction levels, technology, corporate culture, quality orientation, and supply-chain assets (dedicated suppliers, distributors, etc.).

* Strategic elements such as how organizational strengths are being leveraged in the marketplace to make progress toward long-term goals

* Organizational values describing key elements of corporate cultures and how they contribute to organizational performance

Exhibit 7-1 provides some examples of mission statements of some major corporations. Corporate mission statements provide a focal point for company priorities and activities. They emphasize what firms should strive for (goals), the audiences they should strive to please (e.g., major stakeholders who can influence company performance), and what lasting impact firms should have on society at large. Mission statements influence corporate culture ("the way we do things around here") and company values. The challenge for international cor-

He who knows others is clever; he who knows himself is enlightened.

—Lao-Tzu, 6th-century B.C. Chinese philosopher

Always remember that this whole thing was started by a mouse.

—Walt Disney, U.S. film producer

EXHIBIT 7-1

Mission Statements of Major International Corporations

While some organizations have mission statements embracing all five characteristics, many emphasize just one or two.* Some examples of different types of mission orientations:

- Shareholder Orientations—Nike: To maximize profits to the shareholders through products and services that enrich people's lives

- Stakeholder Orientation—BP: To give the best possible return to all BP's stakeholders: our shareholders, our customers, our employees, our suppliers, and our neighbors

- Competitive Orientation—Gillette: To achieve or enhance clear leadership worldwide in the existing or new core consumer product categories in which we choose to compete

- Internal Employee Orientation: The Seven Spirits of Matsushita—Spirit of: service thought industry, fairness, harmony and cooperation, striving for progress, courtesy and humility, accord with natural law, and gratitude

- Societal Orientation—Rhone-Poulenc: To use innovations in the areas of life science and chemistry to create products and services that make people's lives better

- Customer Orientation—Apple Computer: To help people transform the way they work, learn, and communicate by providing exceptional personal computing products and innovative customer services

- Quality Orientation—Wendy's International: To deliver total quality

- Community Orientation—Abbott Laboratories: To improve lives worldwide by providing cost-effective healthcare products and services. And we do so through much more than our products. Abbott makes a difference in the community, through programs, through donations, through people.

*Most examples taken from Haschak, Paul G. *Corporate Statements.* Jefferson, N.C., and London: McFarland & Company, 1998.

---

porations is to make mission statements relevant to employees and stakeholders worldwide. For example, it is not difficult for North Americans to appreciate stockholder and competitive orientations. The U.S. is the bastion of global capitalism—money and corporate rivalries are the cornerstones of their economic system. However, corporate materialism is less appreciated in Western Europe and in emergent nations, where profit-making is only one of many corporate priorities. Similarly, European stakeholder capitalism, with its broader obligations, has its skeptics as Western European firms invest in the U.S.

Assessing Corporate Competencies The major strength of international corporations is their ability to transfer winning strategies and management processes across national markets. International companies are successful when they can develop core competencies for use on a worldwide basis. Core competencies are bundles of organizational skills and corporate assets that produce winning marketplace formulas. They have three characteristics: they contribute to perceived customer benefits, are difficult for competitors to imitate, and can be leveraged over a variety of markets.[7] For international corporations, there are three major types of competencies.[8]

1. *Superior technological know-how and product innovation:* Companies such as Microsoft, Intel, Ciba-Geigy, Merck, Canon, and Toshiba have successfully leveraged their world-class expertise and technologies into innovative products that few rivals can match in the worldwide marketplace.

2. *Reliable processes* that produce consistent, efficient quality products and services in world markets: Examples include Beckton-Dickinson's ability to manufacture low-cost but high-quality medical products; the Toyota Production System that consistently manufactures high-quality, reliable automobiles; Citicorps financial services network that provides a multitude of banking services, anywhere, anytime, in any currency, without delays; and FedEx, whose worldwide delivery service has secured the company a global reputation for reliability.

3. *Close external relationships with suppliers, regulators, professional organizations, distributors, and especially customers:* Consumer-goods firms, such as Unilever, Proctor & Gamble, and Nestle, have established reputations worldwide for their customer orientations, and industrial companies, such as Lockheed-Martin in the aerospace defense business and Siemens in the capital equipment field, have capitalized on their external relationships to build world-class corporate reputations.

While a logical strategy, transferring corporate competencies among international markets is easier said than done. As noted in Chapter 1, the diffusing of modern technologies, products, and ideas through world markets takes time, and national cultures can be highly resistant to change. The competitive imperative makes international firms impatient, and one weakness of international corporations has been their failure to take full account of national market differences as they leverage products and services across foreign markets. The most successful international businesses have been adept at building sufficient flexibility into worldwide operations to appeal to local tastes. Asea-Brown-Boveri (the Swedish-Swiss industrial conglomerate), Unilever (the Anglo-Dutch consumer products firm), IBM, and Toshiba have demonstrated this ability.

External Assessments: The Marketplace Situation

The end product of planning is the allocating of corporate resources across markets, businesses, and product lines. The front end of planning, therefore, involves evaluating corporate performance from a strategic business unit (SBU) and from a geographic perspective. The managerial aim is to identify those SBUs and geographic regions where the company is strong and those where corporate performance is weak. The key dimensions to assess are:

- Contributions to group financial performance
- Competitive positions on a regional and market basis

SBU Evaluation Companies routinely divide their businesses or product lines into strategic business units. The U.S. company GE has eleven business divisions worldwide. The first step is to identify SBUs that contribute positively to group performance (i.e., the above- and below-average financial performers) and those that are competitive within their industry sectors (above- and below-average performers in their respective industries; for example, GE customarily requires its SBUs to be in the top 2 in their industry sectors). Figure 7.2 shows a hypothetical international firm with eight SBUs, with contributions to group-performance and industry-performance levels graphed against each other.

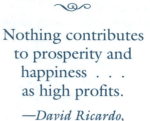

Nothing contributes to prosperity and happiness . . . as high profits.

—David Ricardo, 19th-century economist

- Obviously SBU2 and SBU3 are "winners"—above average performers in their industries and excellent contributors to group profits.

- SBUs 1 and 4 contribute strongly to group profits but lag industry competitors in financial performance. These SBUs would be benchmarked against industry rivals to determine how to improve competitive performance levels.

- SBUs 5 and 8 are competitively placed within their industries, earning above-average ROIs (return-on-investments) in their respective sectors but nonetheless pull down the group ROI average.

- SBUs 6 and 7 are prime candidates for divestiture. They lag industry ROIs in their respective sectors and are drags on group performance.

FIGURE 7.2
Group Assessments of SBUs
Contribution to the Group and Performance in Their Industry

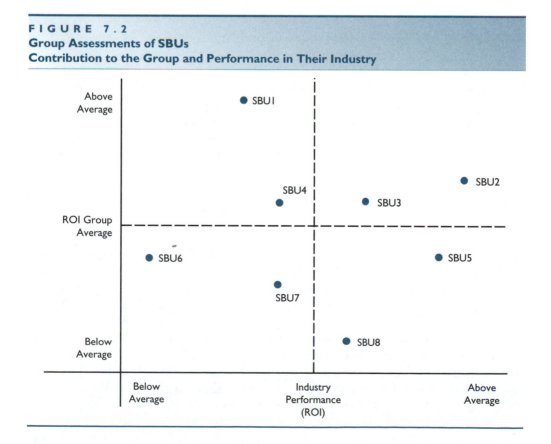

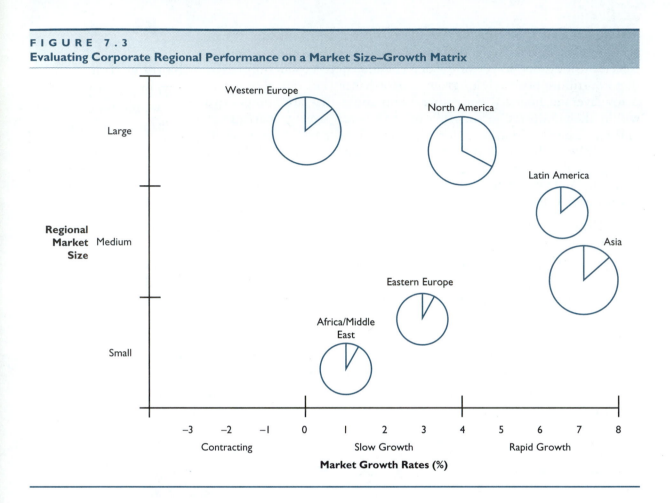

In under-performing units, top-to-bottom analyses would be performed to evaluate their historical sales performances, future prospects, and strategic usefulness (e.g., as a supplier to other SBUs). External factors affecting SBU performance would be assessed (e.g., downturns in key markets, guerilla attacks by major rivals). Both internal and external factors would be evaluated and strategic alternatives laid out (continue on present course, add/subtract resources, restructure, downsize, form a new management team, sell the unit, etc.). In consumer-goods industries, company brands are also often evaluated as SBUs and decisions made about their future viability.

Worldwide/Regional Evaluations The assessment of geographic strategies is a key element in deciding where to allocate corporate resources on a worldwide basis. The process begins with plotting regional corporate performances on market size–market growth matrix. Figure 7.3 illustrates how this is done.

The relative size of each regional circle indicates the proportion of corporate sales emanating from that region (the larger the circle, the greater the proportion of company sales occurring there). In Figure 7.3, Western Europe and North America account for major proportions of worldwide sales. The pie-shaped wedges indicate the company's market share (greater in Western Europe and North America). The horizontal axis shows regional growth rates for individual regions (the highest rates being in Latin America and Asia). From a resource allocation perspective, management would draw a number of conclusions; for example:

- Slow growth in Western Europe would likely result in increasingly competitive markets. Sales gains would come primarily at the expense of rivals, from cost-cutting measures to squeeze more profits from existing sales, or from acquisitions.

- The company's position in North America is solid, with a dominant market share in a moderately expanding market.

- Corporate sales might be aggressively pursued in the Latin American and Asian regions to take advantage of expanding markets.

- The African, Middle East, and Eastern European regions show slow growth in relatively small markets. Proceeding with caution would be appropriate strategies in these areas.

Regional/Country Assessments Managing similar product lines across regions and markets has become increasingly important for international corporations, especially as free trade and technology transfers facilitate comparisons among country subsidiaries. Executives can consolidate data from national subsidiaries into regional and worldwide contexts, giving them "bird's eye views" of critical yardsticks such as market share, sales, costs, and margins. Table 7.1 shows the framework for such a consolidation. From these analyses, executives can:

- Identify subsidiaries and regions with successful track records (e.g., those with superior market shares, nationally and regionally). The strategies of these affiliates can then be scrutinized to isolate key success factors that could be used in other countries as "best practices transfers."

- Compare and contrast cost structures across markets to identify the most efficient and cost-effective national producers. Follow-up studies to examine supply-chain characteristics of best/worst producers can be used to identify optimal practices and to promote cross-border exchanges of ideas and techniques.

Note that cross-market comparisons involve exchange-rate translations among currencies. Sales, costs, margins, and market-size statistics are meaningful only when exchange rates are both realistic and stable. Countries with depreciating exchange rates (i.e., increasing numbers of local currency units per dollar or euro or yen) give deceptive results. Market sizes and sales turnovers diminish in value, as do costs, as currencies depreciate in value. As product prices fall, there are opportunities for low-cost exports to other markets. Where local production relies on imported components and materials, costs escalate as import prices rise.

Assessing Subsidiary Contributions to Group Performance Subsidiary performance within product or regional SBUs must also be evaluated to identify above-average contributors to SBU profitability and those SBUs that are competitive in

TABLE 7.1
Product Division Analysis Across Countries and Regions

	HISTORIC ANALYSIS			CURRENT
REGION A	2001	2002	2003	2004
National Subsidiary #1 Market Share Sales Costs				
Gross Margins				
National Subsidiary #2 Market Share Sales Costs				
Gross Margins				
National Subsidiary "n" Market Share Sales Costs				
Gross Margins				
Region A Consolidated Market Share Sales Costs				
Gross Margins				
Region B Consolidated				
Region "N" Consolidated				
Worldwide Consolidated Market Share Sales Costs				
Gross Margins				

their national markets. Again, return-on-investments (ROIs) are key initial measures. Figure 7.4 plots subsidiary performance within a global product division (above- and below-average contributions to SBU ROI) and measures of national market competitiveness (where subsidiary ROI stands vis-à-vis national competitors).

- Subsidiaries in the upper-right hand quadrant (above-average SBU ROIs and above average performers in their national industries—China, France, U.S.) are "stars." They would be scrutinized to evaluate whether their strategies or internal procedures are transferable to under-performing units.

- The German, Argentinian, and Brazilian affiliates are competitive in their national markets (as illustrated by their above-average national industry ROIs), but are a drag on group ROI. Reasons for low national industry ROIs would be reviewed. For example, these affiliates may have significantly more local rivals within their markets than other affiliates, effectively pulling national profit levels down. Or there may be other factors at work (e.g., a national economic downturn).

- Taiwan ROC, Belgium-Luxembourg, and Sweden are above-average contributors to SBU overall results, but lag rivals within their national mar-

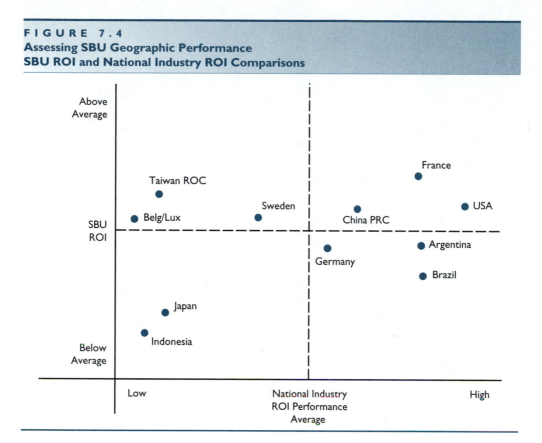

FIGURE 7.4
Assessing SBU Geographic Performance
SBU ROI and National Industry ROI Comparisons

kets. A competitive analysis against in-market rivals might suggest where improvements can be made.

- Japan and Indonesia are sub-par performers, both within the group and in their national markets. Determination must be made about whether this is due to severe competition, ill-advised strategies, poor strategy implementation, or other factors. Competitive benchmarking, market and competitive strategy evaluations, and assessments of internal operations would be mandated prior to decisions about possible divestiture moves.

Individual Subsidiary Analysis Once management has assessed the relative performance of its subsidiaries, executive attention can be focused on factors contributing to success and failure at the national market level. Two analyses contribute to this determination: an examination of the affiliate's product lines, and how the subsidiary stacks up against major national competitors along key competitive dimensions.

Market share/momentum analyses plot product performance against market performance to ascertain which products are under-performing market trends (and losing market-share momentum) and those that are outperforming market trends (i.e., gaining market-share momentum). As Figure 7.5 shows, company sales growth is plotted on the horizontal axis and market growth on the vertical axis, with circle size being proportional to sales. The 45-degree diagonal line shows where sales growth is proportional to market share growth.

FIGURE 7.5
Share/Momentum Chart for a Consumer Goods Subsidiary

Global, regional brands (local brands are Brand 1, 2, etc.)

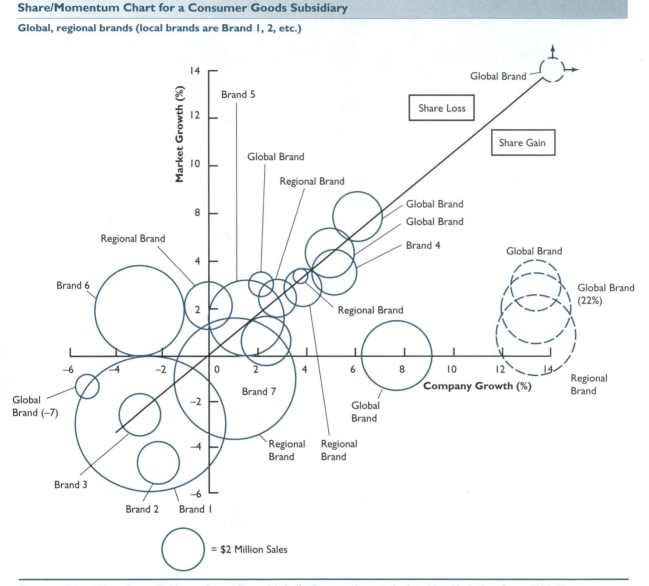

Sources: Adapted from Bogue III, Marcus C., and Elwood S. Buffa. *Corporate Strategic Analysis*. New York: Free Press, 1986, 19.

Product lines to the left of the line show relative market share loss (i.e., where product-sales-growth is less than market-sales growth) and need corrective action. Products to the right are outperforming the market (gaining in market-share momentum), and analyses should be geared toward what strategies are working, and why. From this analysis, over- and under-performing product lines can be identified, along with their relative contributions to sales goals. Notice in Figure 7.5 the contributions of the regional and global brands that are out-performing the market in the right quadrant and the relatively poor performances of some local brands in the lower-left quadrant. Remember also that market share/momentum analyses only summarize product-mix perfor-

FIGURE 7.6
Plotting Subsidiary Performance (A) Against Key National Competitors (B & C)

Marketing Profile

Product line	Broad	A B _____ C	Narrow
Pricing strategy	Premium pricing	C A _____ B	Competitive pricing
Distribution	Intensive	___ B Selective ___ A C	Exclusive
Distribution ownership	Company owned	A C _____ B	Independent distributors
Sales force	Company sales force	AC _____ B	Third-party representation
Sales force size	Large	_____ C A B	Small
Advertising/PR budget	Large	C B _____ A	Small
Advertising approach	Intensive	_____ C B A	Selective

Competitive Profile

Service levels	High	A ___ C ___ B	Low
Customer satisfaction levels	High	___ A ___ C B	Low
Product quality levels	High	___ A C ___ B	Low
R and D levels (% sales)	Above	C A At the industry average B	Below
—Industry average			
New product development (compared to industry average)	Above	C A At the industry average B	Below
Manufacturing costs (compared to industry average)	Below Average	B ___ Average ___ A ___ C	Above average
Manufacturing process technology	State of the art	C B ___ Average A ___	Older technologies

mance. More complete explanations involve market research and/or competitive analyses, such as the one outlined below.

Competitive benchmarking profiles the characteristics and strategies of rival companies and their performances along key competitive dimensions (see Figure 7.6). Note the division between market and competitive profiles. Market profiles of competitors list their key characteristics and strategic approaches to the marketplace. They can be obtained from roundtable discussions among executives (e.g., sales forces). Competitor profile data can be obtained from secondary sources (e.g., industry associations) or from competitive benchmarking surveys. As individual rivals are plotted along each dimension, management can discern key differences in strategies among competitors and can devise ways to differentiate their strategic approaches.

As can be noted from Figure 7.6, subsidiary A has the broadest product line and controls its own sales force and distribution. Competitor C is more of a niche player with narrow product lines, focused distribution, and more of a reliance on advertising/PR in its promotional efforts. Its competitive profile gives company A leadership status for service, customer satisfaction, and quality levels in this group. Company A's disadvantages vis-à-vis rivals B and C are in R and D and new product development (though A is distinctly superior to company B). Of concern are product costs and manufacturing technologies that are below average for the industry.

FIGURE 7.7
Plotting Geographic Strengths and Weaknesses in Sales and Production Deployments

	Global Sales	Corporate Sales	Global Production	Corporate Production
North America	35%	53%	40%	65%
Western Europe	21%	11%	25%	10%
Eastern Europe	6%	2%	3%	0%
Middle East/Africa	3%	0%	2%	0%
Latin America	15%	15%	10%	15%
Asia	20%	19%	20%	10%

External Assessments: Corporate and Industry Resource Deployments

Industry behaviors are important reference points for individual firms, and company-industry comparisons of worldwide resource deployments give key insights for strategic decision makers. International corporations are rarely well positioned in all major and emerging markets within their industry. For example, many international firms hold leading positions in their home and regional markets (e.g., a German company in Germany and in Western Europe). Using information derived from the global industry analysis, corporate sales and manufacturing can be mapped against global industry consumption and production patterns to provide insights for market expansion strategies and the siting of manufacturing and other facilities.

As can be seen in Figure 7.7, the firm's sales position is North America-oriented, with 53 percent of sales in that region, against 35 percent for the industry as a whole. Proportionately, corporate sales are under-represented in Western Europe, Eastern Europe, and Africa/Middle East, although the latter two regions account for only 9 percent of global sales. The firm is well-positioned in Latin America and Asia, with corporate sales being roughly proportional to regional sales.

From a production standpoint, the company's position is Americas-oriented, with North and Latin America accounting for 80 percent of corporate production (65 and 15 percent respectively), against 50 percent for the industry as a whole (40 + 10 percent). The firm is under-positioned in the rest of the world, with 20 percent of manufacturing assets in Western Europe and Asia, against 50 percent for the industry as a whole.

Note that other factors influence manufacturing-site location decisions. In high-tech industries, for example, companies prefer to maximize production in particular markets to obtain scale economies or to be stimulated by the market's competitive conditions. In more locally oriented sectors, where national preferences are more of a consideration (e.g., in consumer packaged goods), firms may prefer to even out corporate manufacturing allocations in accordance with global industry trends.

FORMULATION OF STRATEGIC PLANS

Once management has assessed the current situation and evaluated competitors and environmental trends, it is time to formulate plans for the future. For most international corporations, planning is done with 3 to 5 year projections into the future. The process involves making assumptions about economic growth at the global, regional, and national levels; judgments about market environmental factors and how they affect industry growth rates; and assessments of how rival strategies impact corporate sales and market share. The role of senior management is to evaluate current and future plans against past performances and expected future conditions. We look at this process from the subsidiary and regional/divisional perspectives.

> Long range planning does not deal with future decisions, but with the future of present decisions.
>
> —*Peter F. Drucker, 20th-century U.S. management consultant and author*

Subsidiary-Level Planning

Planning at the subsidiary level starts with historic analyses of product line sales, costs, and margins being projected into the future (see Table 7.2). To place results into perspective, market-size, growth, and market-share trends are taken into account. This is followed by managerial assessments concerning the effectiveness of past strategies, what competitors have been doing, and what factors have been influential in containing costs (manufacturing-process improvements, supplier relations, raw material and component costs). These figures provide necessary backgrounds for future projections and rationales for strategies over the projected planning period. Equally important are the environmental factors underlying marketplace conditions. The rate of national economic growth is a major underlying determinant of industry-growth patterns, and future sales projections are based on assumptions about national economic policies and the political situation that drives them. Political assessments are made based on the party in power, its economic and political philosophy, and the likelihood of changes and their effects.

Integrating National Plans into Regional and Global Strategies

Once subsidiary managements have completed their preliminary forecasts, discussions are held with regional and/or head-office executives to put these plans into regional or global contexts. Differences in opinions about strategies and goals are resolved, and mutually acceptable goals are established for periods ranging from one year (short-term) to 3–5 years (medium-range plans). In these plans, critical assumptions are laid out (economic-growth rates, industry-market sizes, key competitor responses, etc.) and major strategic decisions are outlined. Table 7.3 illustrates the consolidation process. From these consolidations, corporate goals, strategies, and policies can be outlined at the appropriate levels (subsidiary, regional, product division, global), and appropriate control mechanisms can be put into place.

TABLE 7.2
Subsidiary-Level Planning with 3-Year Projections

	HISTORIC			CURRENT	PROJECTIONS		
	2001	2002	2003	2004	2005	2006	2007
Product Line 1							
Sales							
Costs							
Gross Margins							
Expenses							
Net Margin							
Market Size							
Market Growth							
Market Share							
Strategy: Summary of goals set, achieved; key success factors; what worked; what didn't					Strategies to be pursued and rationale		
Competitor Actions: Activity levels; degree of disruption; counter moves					Probable competitor strategies and reactions to our strategies		
Supply Chain: Changes in raw material, components, costs, suppliers, technology process improvements; distribution					Anticipated changes in supply-chain activities		
Product Line 2							
Sales							
Costs							
Gross Margins							
Expenses							
Net Margin							
Market Size							
Market Growth							
Market Share							
Strategy:							
Competitor Actions:							
Supply Chain:							
Product Line "n"							
Sales							
Costs							
Gross Margins							
Expenses							
Net Margin							
Market Size							
Market Growth							
Market Share							
Strategy: Competitor Actions: Supply Chain: Environmental Factors • Economic growth rate • Inflation • Exchange rates • Political situation	Historic data recorded to provide background information to judge present conditions and future trends				Future projections and how changes in growth rates, etc., can affect the industry situation; and political environment predictions (parties in power, likely changes, etc.).		

TABLE 7.3
Integrating Subsidiary Forecasts into Regional Plans

| Region "A" | Market Size | Market Growth | | Current Sales | Forecasted Sales/Market Share | | | Critical Strategy Elements/ Goals | Key Environmental Assumptions | Likely Competitive Reaction/ Strategy |
		Last 3 Years	Next 3 Years		+1 Year	+2 Year	+3 Year			
Subsidiary 1										
2										
"n"										
Region A Plans										
Region B Plans										
Region "n" Plans										
Consolidated Worldwide Plans										

Setting Objectives For many firms (particularly in the U.S. and increasingly in Western European corporations) financial objectives are emphasized and employee behaviors are oriented to satisfying shareholders and the expectations of the financial community—the primary providers of new capital needs. Increasingly though, while financial goals have great relevance at senior management levels, they have proven to be inadequate motivators at middle and lower organizational levels, as employees find it difficult to relate financial objectives to daily activities. Other problems with financial goals include:

- Lack of linkages between financial goals and the competitive strategies needed to achieve them

- Many factors affect financial performance. Fortuitous circumstances can mask inept strategy-making, and superior strategies do not always produce outstanding results, particularly in highly competitive markets.

- Behaviors within firms require a number of yardsticks to assess internal activities and steer them toward superior performance. This is the essence of the four-component balanced scoreboard.[9]

Financial perspectives are traditional business measures that show how firms look to shareholders and the financial community. They track profitability, growth goals, and progress toward shareholder value improvements. Further refinements include survival yardsticks (measured by cash flow), success indicators (divisional progress toward sales and profit goals), and prosperity (market shares and returns on equity).

Customer perspectives refer to how companies look to their customers; they are measured by:

- Lead times: how long it takes to fulfill customer orders : new product development times

- Quality levels: number of defects and product returns, on-time deliveries (customer-defined)

> If you don't know where you're going, you'll end up somewhere else.
>
> —*Yogi Berra, U.S. baseball coach and sage*

- Performance/service levels: number of preferred-supplier positions held, shares of key account purchases, customer-satisfaction levels (ordering, delivery scheduling, payments, inspections, handling defects, etc.)

Internal perspectives refers to how firms are adapting their organizations and procedures to maintain and improve cycle times, quality levels, product/service costs, technological capabilities, and employee skill levels. Corporate information systems are key elements alerting management when deviations occur.

Innovation and learning perspectives assess organizational learning and improvement efforts. These yardsticks track customer satisfaction and internal business-process improvements over time. For example, in industries where new product flows are critical, the process tracks new-product success rates, time lags getting products to market, percentages of sales from new products over specific time periods (e.g., 3M's goal of 30 percent sales revenues from products launched over a four-year period[10]).

The key advantages of the balanced scorecard are that:

- Goals and measures are looked at *as a package,* giving management more complete pictures of corporate performance.

- Goals and measures can be custom-built to suit corporate needs.

- Goals and measures relate to marketplace, competitive needs, and employees' daily activities.

> I don't know any CEO who doesn't love numbers.
>
> —*Jeffrey Silverman, CEO, U.S. company Ply Gem Industries*

Corporate Goals and Feedback "Even the best laid plans go awry" sums up the situation many companies face when goals are not met. One study found that at the corporate level, 55 percent of firms went back and reformulated both objectives and strategies; 24 percent revamped strategies but maintained their original goals; 15 percent adjusted their goals but maintained their original strategies; and the few remaining companies maintained both original goals and strategies.[11]

At subsidiary levels, when supply-chain goals are not met (dips in quality control, service levels, lengthy new product development times, etc.), local managements get the interested parties together to solve the problem. If this does not work, regional or head-office help is sought and experts brought in from other parts of the company.

> It is a bad plan that admits no modification.
>
> —*Publilius Syrus, 1st-century B.C. Latin writer of mimes*

The Benefits of Well-Executed Planning Processes

There are definite external and internal benefits when companies are diligent in their planning processes.

External Benefits: Good Resource Deployment Decisions Once management has evaluated corporate performance, market trends, and projections and set goals, decisions about resource deployments must be finalized and market priorities established. A good starting point is to map out current resource allocations and prioritize them according to market attractiveness criteria (usually market-size and market-growth rates). Figure 7.8 illustrates the process for the Asian division of a hypothetical international corporation. Current deployments show

FIGURE 7.8
Plotting Company Resource Deployments on a Market Size–Growth Matrix

(e.g., Asia)

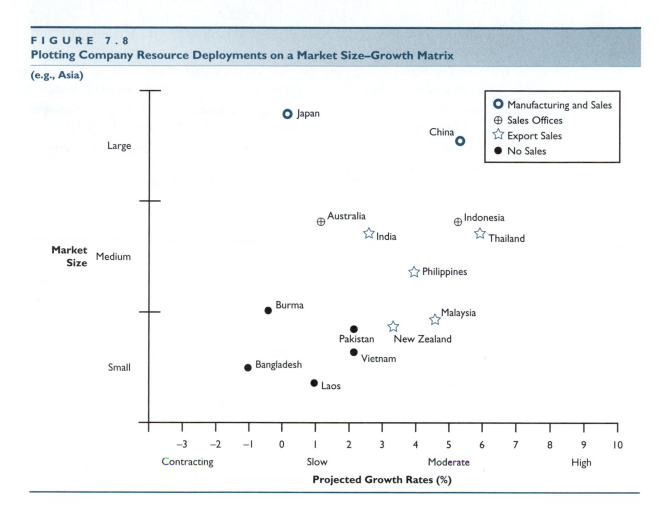

that this company has manufacturing/converting and sales facilities in Japan and China and corporate sales subsidiaries in Australia and Indonesia. Additionally, corporate sales are made in India, Thailand, Philippines, Malaysia, and New Zealand. Reviewing the situation, management has a number of options:

- Expand manufacturing in the rapid-growth China PRC market.

- Consider adding corporate sales offices in Thailand, India, and possibly the Philippines to gain insights into these markets. If prospects look promising, manufacturing/converting operations might be added if sales volumes can support such investments.

- Evaluate market prospects in Pakistan and Vietnam and consider appointing import/distributors. Burma (Myanmar) might be considered, pending a move away from its 1990s military junta to a democratic form of government.

Internal Benefits Internal benefits of a well-executed international planning process include:

- Defining the strategic direction of the corporation. Corporate-mission statements, core-competency definitions, and business-unit analyses guide

R and D priorities, business-unit portfolio adjustments, and mergers and acquisition strategies.

- Providing insights into competitor strategies and how best to compete against industry rivals globally, regionally, or on a national-market basis.

- Systematic incorporation of political, economic, societal, and technological industry-change drivers into global, regional, and national strategies.

- Concise guidance for geographic strategies and international resource commitments: which regions and countries to emphasize and, based on market potential and country risk assessments, what sorts of commitments should be made.

- Providing direction at the subsidiary level by identifying performance criteria for product lines and by benchmarking competitor strengths and weaknesses.

Most importantly, planning processes help identify what strategies are effective in the international marketplace, and, along with competitor analyses, suggest new strategic options for management consideration.

MARKET SCREENING AND RISK ASSESSMENTS

> To get profit without risk, experience without danger, and reward without work is as impossible as it is to live without being born.
>
> —*A. P. Gouthey*

Once managements have assessed past and present company performances and looked at future opportunities within its industry, they must assess the relative risks of operating in different countries. This involves evaluating country risks on a comparative basis (i.e., using the same criteria), and, for individual markets, to gain critical insights about how to operate and manage risk in those countries. This is a daunting task. More than 200 national markets proliferate the global landscape, of which about 150 are economically significant (i.e., excluding island states, etc.), and of which about sixty are mainstream markets with significant business potential. Initially, most firms use data from commercial vendors of business-risk information. Seven types of risk are usually assessed: political, economic, operational, financial, legal, taxation, and security factors.

Political Risks

Most companies focus first on political risks because governments are major influences on national economic performance, exchange rates, and legal, taxation, and security systems. Governmental change, through elections or other means, often signals new directions in national policies.

Country governance systems vary in broad terms from full, mature stable democratic systems to nations engulfed in civil or international strife with little or no political direction. Primary causes of political risk are:

- Fractionalization of the political spectrum (multiple parties or political power groups)

- Numerous linguistic, ethnic, religious factions (Middle East, Africa, Asia)

- Restrictive means of retaining power (dictatorships)

- Evidence of xenophobia, nepotism, corruption
- Poor social conditions (e.g., uneven distributions of wealth)
- Existence of radical, especially leftist, political movements

Symptoms of political risk include civil conflicts (strikes, demonstrations), destabilizing elements (assassinations, kidnappings, guerilla movements), ethnic rivalries (e.g., Africa, Asia), religious conflicts (among Muslim factions [e.g., Sunni and Shi'ite groups], between religions [Muslim-Hindu in India], wars (the breakup of the former Yugoslavia and the Democratic Republic of the Congo, Angola, Sudan in Africa), and so on.

Economic problems occur as development and economic restructuring causes high unemployment or lack of job-creation capabilities. Economic change and industrialization causes population shifts (rural to urban), the opening up of countries to market-force-based competition (e.g., the Asian financial crisis), and significant disruptions as social and cultural changes accompany economic growth. Additional problems occur as high inflation rates erode consumer purchasing power and push economies into downward spirals.

Whenever nations experience problems, the likelihood of governmental change increases. From a commercial perspective, some changes are positive as pro-business governments come to power with mandates to reduce trade barriers and investment restrictions and to facilitate money transfers into and out of the country. In other cases, antibusiness governments gain power, and trade protection, investment restrictions, and limits on financial transfers occur. Monitoring political events over perhaps 150 countries is a difficult task for even the largest of international corporations. Hence, many subscribe to commercial services that monitor and analyze political risk. Political Risk Services, a company based in New York, provides abbreviated and in-depth political coverage of major markets, coverage that shows which political party (or leader) is in power, the extent of political turmoil, who is likely to be in power in eighteen months and in five years. Prospects for foreign investments (e.g., restrictions, ownership questions), trade (tariffs, taxes, import restrictions), and financial transfers (hard currency availability, foreign exchange restrictions) are evaluated. Key economic indicators (inflation, economic growth, trade balances) are monitored, and expert commentaries provide in-depth coverage for individual markets.

> There are risks and costs to a program of action. But they are far less than the long-range risks and costs of comfortable inaction.
>
> —*John F. Kennedy, 20th-century U.S. president*

Economic Risks

Economic-risk assessment involves evaluating the stability, openness, and market forces-orientations of national economies. Advanced capitalistic countries with stable economic-performance indicators and convertible currencies rate highly. Closed economies suffering major economic fluctuations (e.g., hyperinflationary environments) are rated poorly. The greatest economic risks relate to political mismanagement of the economy and include persistent government budget deficits (overspending), inflationary tendencies (over-stimulating the economy, or printing too much money), excessive or corruptive influences in financial or product markets (e.g., nepotism, or protectionism), and so on.

Financial and Foreign Currency Risks

These measure a country's ability to meet its foreign financial obligations. That is, the likelihood that convertible currencies are available for the importation of goods, materials, or profit repatriation needs. One company, Business Risk Services (BRS), uses four factors in this evaluation.

1. Legal frameworks for profit, dividend, fees, and capital repatriation are evaluated: as written and as practiced.

2. Balance-of-payments analysis, as currency movements into and out of a country determine its ability to generate foreign exchange. Trade, current account, and capital accounts are scrutinized to evaluate trends. Key factors are the crude trade balance (exports–imports) and the current account performance (trade inflows [imports], outflows [exports], service inflows and outflows, profit and personal-incomes flows, and government-oriented flows). Net outflows are assessed negatively, and inflows are positively graded. Then, capital flows (foreign direct investments, portfolio investments, and other capital flows) are assessed. Net inflows are evaluated positively and outflows assessed negatively. Overall surpluses (financial inflows) are good indicators as foreign exchange accumulates. Negative financial outflows (balance of payments deficits) are more problematic in developing nations that lack financial reserves and large, strong economies.

3. International reserves are countries' stocks of foreign currencies accumulated from (1) exports and capital inflows, and (2) gold holdings—both normally held at the IMF. Countries holding plentiful reserves of hard currency (dollars, yen, euros, etc.) receive high ratings. Those with few hard-currency reserves get lesser ratings. Country gold holdings are assessed alongside convertible currency positions to give overall evaluations of nations' abilities to meet import bills.

4. Foreign-debt assessments are evaluations of foreign debt relative to country gross domestic product, with creditor nations receiving the highest rating. Also included are foreign-debt obligations in relation to hard currencies earned through exports.

Operations Risks

Operations environmental risks are those associated with day-to-day managements of foreign enterprises. BRS includes evaluations of:

- Political policy continuity, whether governmental changes have major effects on national policies
- Attitudes toward foreign investors and profits
- Degree of nationalization (i.e., government ownership of economic assets)
- Bureaucratic delays: corruption, bribes
- Use and enforceability of contracts
- Labor cost and availability, including inclusiveness or exclusiveness of education opportunities

- Availability of professional services and contractors
- Quality and cost of local communications
- Infrastructure availability: roads, rail, water systems; energy sources
- Caliber of local managers, partners
- Financial institutions and the availability of short, medium, and long-term financing

Legal Risks

Legal risks are important where companies rely heavily on contracts (e.g., military, industrial, commodity markets) and when legal recourse may be necessary (e.g., counterfeit goods, medical or pharmaceutical products or processes). Legal risks vary from nations with clear, mature, and nonarbitrary legal systems to those where judicial and enforcement systems are politically influenced, arbitrary, incoherent, and unclear; and where civil and constitutional liberties are nonexistent.

Taxation Risks

Companies that move financial assets, money, products, and components extensively throughout world markets are aware of needs to satisfy national tax authorities. Taxation risks vary from those with well-developed and equitable tax frameworks with clear dispute-resolution mechanisms to those where taxation systems are highly inequitable and arbitrarily implemented.

Security Risks

For firms that depend on expatriates in their managements of local subsidiaries, personal security must be evaluated. Low levels of crime, little or no terrorism, and freedom to demonstrate are associated with low-risk nations. Civil strife, ethnic tensions, high crime rates, kidnapping risks are problematic in some countries (e.g., Colombia, Peru, South Africa), making them poor risks for personal security.

Business Risk Evaluation Methodologies

As managers review market-risk assessments, they should be aware of how such evaluations are derived. To illustrate differences in risk-research methodologies, two commercial services, Business Risk Services (BRS) and World Markets Online (WMO) are contrasted.

Markets Covered BRS covers about fifty markets; WMO takes in about 150 countries.

Business Risks Evaluated BRS assesses fifteen factors in its operations-risk index and weights them differentially (e.g., policy continuity has a 3 weighting, economic growth and currency convertibility a 2.5, professional contractors 0.5) to add up to 25. A permanent panel of +/- 105 experts then rate country conditions from 0 (unacceptable conditions) to 4 (superior conditions) to total 100, the perfect operating environment. Similar procedures are used in BRS's political-risk index (ten factors) and its R factor (four factors). The summation of these three factors results in

> Take calculated risks. That is quite different from being rash.
>
> —*George S. Patton, general, U.S. army, World War II*

an aggregate score that is converted into a profit-opportunity recommendation (POR). These vary from 1A to 1C (investment quality markets) through to 2A–2C (trade, technology, and assistance contracts), 3A–3B (trade only), to 4A (no business transactions). All risk and POR scores are projected for 1 and 5 years into the future, and historical data is presented.

WMO provides measures of six dimensions: political, economic, legal, tax, operations, and security. Each dimension is rated in each market on a 1 to 5 rating, with 1 representing minimal risk and 5 being prohibitive risk. The sum and average of all six dimensions yields an overall assessment of country risk, varying from 1.00–1.99 (insignificant to low risk) to 4.00–5.00 (very high to extreme risk). For individual market evaluations, political and economic risks are weighted at 25 percent each, legal and tax risks at 15 percent, and operational and security risks at 10 percent.

Using Commercial Risk Assessment Services Risk services such as BRS and WMO are useful for three reasons. First, they are excellent indicators of overall market conditions. Second, they allow countries to be compared using the same criteria. Third, they are useful in identifying potential problem areas that need further investigation. For example, low scores on bureaucracy or negative attributes toward foreign direct investment should invite further research to ascertain effects on business strategies. Similarly, low scores on civil unrest or excessive ethnic or religious should trigger further evaluations of these problems.

There are three major drawbacks to general market assessments. First, they are complete evaluations of country markets, and, as such, are more suited to foreign direct-investment projects. Firms wishing to trade or to license products need only assess specific aspects of environmental analyses (e.g., currency payments affecting trade or contract enforceability for franchise or licensing agreements).

Second, assessments focusing on environmental factors often gloss over cultural aspects of doing business. Separate evaluations of cultural environments are needed to identify necessary business protocols—the importance of relationships, religious impact on commerce, social class hierarchies, etc.

Third, individual industries have specific needs in their market evaluations, and generalized assessments have limited uses under these circumstances.

Special Case: Evaluating Emerging Markets

The importance of emerging markets and their rapid rate of change poses difficulties for business people evaluating market potential in these countries. As such, emerging country assessments emphasize many developmental characteristics that get lost in broader evaluations.[12] Markets to which these criteria apply include "big emerging markets" (BEMs) such as: China, Hong Kong, Taiwan, Indonesia, Malaysia, Philippine, Singapore, Thailand, Brunei, Vietnam, India, South Korea, Argentina, Mexico, Brazil, Turkey, South Africa, Chile, Venezuela, Greece, Israel, Portugal, Czech Republic, Hungary, and Russia.

THE GLOBAL WEB

For an updated evaluation of emerging market listings, visit:
http://globaledge.msu.edu/ibrd/marketpot.asp.
Which markets are labeled "the best" and "the worst" according to the Michigan State criteria?

One approach to estimating emerging market attractiveness has been to evaluate BEMs on seven weighted criteria. These are:

1. *Market size:* measured by country populations (20 percent weighting)

2. *Market growth rate:* average industry growth rate (15 percent weighting)

3. *Market intensity:* measured by

   - GNP per capita

   - Personal consumption expenditures per capita: purchases by households and private nonprofit institutions per capita (15 percent weighting)

4. *Market consumption capacity:* the proportion of the populations earning 20–80 percent of a nation's income, i.e., a measure of middle-class consumption excluding the extremely rich and poor segments. In 2003, Hungary, Czech Republic, and South Korea were the top three; Chile, Brazil, and South Africa were the worst rated on this dimension. (10 percent weighting)

5. *Commercial infrastructure:* measured in equal portions by telephone lines per capita, paved road density, trucks and buses per capita, population per retail outlet, and percentage color TV ownership. 2003 rating placed Hong Kong, Singapore, and South Korea at the top; Peru, Indonesia, and Egypt were the bottom three. (10 percent weighting)

6. *Economic freedom:* measured by Heritage Foundation estimates of trade and taxation policies, government consumption of economic output, monetary and banking policies, capital flows and foreign investment, wage and price controls, property rights, regulatory policy, and black market activity. Chile, Hong Kong, and the Czech Republic had the most freedom on these measures in 2003; Russia, Egypt, and China were the most restrictive. (10 percent weighting)

7. *Market receptivity:* measured by growth rates in U.S. exports to the country (60 percent) and per capita consumption of U.S. imports (40 percent). Singapore, Hong Kong, and Malaysia headed this list in 2003, while Brazil, India, and Argentina were the last three ranked. (20 percent weighting overall)

> If you dip your arm into the pickle pot, let it be up to the elbow.
>
> —*Malay proverb*

Scores on the various dimensions are standardized to 1–100 scores with higher scores indicating more favorable market conditions. The seven scores are then weighted and finalized into an Overall Market Opportunity Index (OMOI). In 2003, the top five markets were: Hong Kong, Singapore, South Korea, Israel, and China. The bottom five nations were the Philippines, South Africa, Venezuela, Argentina, and Colombia.

Note that these market potential indicators are U.S.-oriented and focus on emergent market characteristics. As with all aggregate measures, there are limitations. Political risk factors in particular are downplayed, except for the economic freedom measure. Also, industry factors, local demand, cheap factors of production would need to be added into the market assessment equation, as would financial considerations, such as currency convertibility. Nevertheless, the more factors that enter management's market evaluations, the more balanced the overall assessment.

Long-Term Planning: Scenario Analyses

For most industries, 3 to 5 year planning horizons are fine. But, for some companies, these time frames are too short to capture major environmental trends affecting long-term industry investments. In such cases, scenario planning is a useful management tool. Scenarios are, according to leading exponent Shell International, "stories that describe different versions of the future."[13] It is estimated that over half of the largest European and North American companies use various forms of scenario planning to support their long-range planning efforts, where their aim is to broaden executive perspectives of factors affecting long-term industry and market development.[14] The Shell Oil Company first pioneered scenario analysis in the 1970s, when it was instrumental in helping the European oil giant navigate the turbulent oil markets of that decade. Today's applications of scenario analysis are concerned with industry and market development.

> Plan ahead. It wasn't raining when Noah built the ark.
>
> —*Richard Cushing*

Industry Scenarios   In industry sectors subject to major environmental changes, scenarios help managers understand long-term market changes and the factors promoting them. Shell Oil's prognostications to 2025 yielded two scenarios. The first, *Business Class,* projects global capitalism as the dominant movement with relatively unfettered access to world markets. Under this scenario, energy trends are an evolutionary progression from coal and oil to gas and other renewable forms of energy (e.g., fuel cell technologies), with major growth in international pipelines. Growth in natural gas was forecasted at between 80 and 100+ percent to 2025. The second scenario, labeled *Prism,* envisaged a slowing of globalization tendencies, with regional and national security issues being prominent. Under these circumstances, cross-border gas pipeline development would be hindered and oil would remain the dominant fuel.[15]

Scenario analyses can be used in a variety of situations. Electrolux used scenario planning to evaluate the effects of the environmental "green" movement on appliance use and consumption. Nestle envisaged a world without chocolate, and the UK water industry examined different outcomes under industry deregulation.

While there are no dominant methodologies for scenario development, there are systematic methods of assessing past and current trends. These involve reviewing developments over the past decade in a number of areas: changes in customer bases, products, technologies, competitors, environments, demographics, governmental (de)regulations, and geopolitical events (e.g.,

> The executive of the future will be rated by his ability to anticipate his problems rather than to meet them as they come.
>
> —*Howard Coonley, U.S. executive*

formation of trade blocs, etc.) and projecting these changes into the future. This helps industries identify key change drivers and evaluate their impacts on market development.[16]

Market Scenarios Market scenarios help firms anticipate developments in individual countries or regions. A mid-1990s scenario analysis of China in 2010 by seventy experts identified five alternative paths of development. These were:

1. *Muddling through:* Ongoing struggles between proreform and antireform groups result in erratic government policies and continuing instability.

2. *Asian power:* China becomes a major regional power, somewhat at the expense of Japan. Both compete vigorously for world markets, resulting in worldwide trade restrictions against Asian goods. Chinese military and economic power causes major rethinks in Japanese commercial and military policies.

3. *Fragmentation:* Differing developmental levels result in Chinese regions competing against each other. The power of the Chinese central government diminishes and hurts the country's political position in the world. A regional confederation becomes the dominant system of government.

4. *Shutting the doors:* China's economic growth falters and unemployment soars. Movements back toward state-owned enterprises result in protectionist outlooks and crackdowns on foreign firms, causing downturns in international company interests.

5. *Global powerhouse:* China's economy becomes diversified with labor- and skill-intensive industries blossoming. Infrastructure growth results in more even economic development, and middle-income consumers contribute to further economic growth. Democratic institutions take root at local and regional levels, making national elections a future possibility.[17]

Scenario analyses provide important inputs to long-range planning efforts. Perhaps their most important contribution is to encourage executives to think creatively outside of the corporate confines of sales and profits. Scenario analyses allow managers to factor broader ranges of variables into their strategic management processes. For example, the 1980s fall of communism, the global slowdowns due to oil market disruptions, the Asian financial crisis, and global terrorism caught unawares all but a few firms. Scenario analyses sharpen managerial abilities to anticipate and prepare for unforeseen eventualities.

KEY POINTS

- International strategic planning is the process through which worldwide companies evaluate past results, assess their corporate strengths and weaknesses, and map out future resource allocations and strategies, based on marketplace opportunities and threats. Planning has become increasingly important since 1945 as worldwide competition has increased, and more complex as more variables have been factored into the process.

- Internal assessments include evaluations of corporate missions (what the company is, where it wants to be), and its competencies (what it is good at). External assessments look at how the international company is performing in its various businesses (SBUs) and at the firm's geographic performance worldwide, regionally, and in specific country markets. Contributions to group performance are monitored (above- or below-average performers), along with assessments of competitive performance against market rivals. Subsidiaries evaluate current product-line performances (market share/momentum analyses) and benchmark themselves against market competitors. Many firms benchmark their resource deployments against those of their industry to provide external reference points for strategic decision making.

- Formulation of strategic plans usually starts at the subsidiary level and includes historic analyses of sales, costs, market sizes, shares, as well as strategy summaries and supply-chain developments for all products, with projections for 3 to 5 year periods. These are then consolidated into regional and global strategies and plans.

- Goal setting includes financial perspectives (ROIs, shareholder value) and increasingly customer perspectives (customer fulfillment, quality, etc.), internal perspectives (technological capabilities, employee skills), and innovation/learning perspectives (improvements over time).

- Resource deployment decisions take in investment/divestment decisions in specific businesses and markets.

- Prior to investment decisions, companies screen markets to gain preliminary assessments of political, economic, operational, financial, legal, taxation, and security risks. Most often, firms use commercial vendors of business risk information for this purpose. Because of the special status of emerging markets, additional data sources may be used.

ENDNOTES

1. Robert Westervelt, "Atofina expands outside Europe," *Chemical Week* (June 15, 2001): 37, 39.

2. This section is based loosely on Tamara J. Erickson, "The Evolution of Strategic Planning," *Business International* (New York: Global Strategic Planning, 1991): 1–9.

3. "Global Strategic Planning," *Business International Corporation* (New York, 1991).

4. Based on Philip Waalewijn and Peter Segaar, "Strategic Management: The key to profitability in small companies," *Long Range Planning* 26: 2 (1993): 24–30.

5. Geoffrey J. Nightingale in Timothy R. V. Foster, "101 Great Mission Statements" (London: Kogan Page Ltd., 1995), 19.

6. Ferdinand de Bakker, "The Elements of a Mission Statement" in Foster, *op cit.,* chapter 3.

7. C. K. Prahalad and G. Hamel, "The Core Competence of the Corporation," *Harvard Business Review* 68, 3 (May–June 1990): 79–91.

8. Based on B. Mascarenhas, A. Baveja, and M. Jamil, "Dynamics of core competencies in leading multinational companies," *California Management Review* 40:4 (Summer 1998): 117–32; and William L. Shanklin and David Griffith, "Crafting Strategies for Global Marketing in the New Millenium," *Business Horizons* (Sept.–Oct. 1996): 11–16.

9. Robert S. Kaplan and David P. Norton, "The Balanced Scorecard—Measures that drive performance," *Harvard Business Review* 69.1 (Jan.–Feb. 1992): 71—79.

10. Shawn Tully, "Why go for stretch targets," *Fortune* (Nov. 14, 1994): 145–48.

11. Myung-Su Chae and John S. Hill, "The Hazards of Strategic Planning for Global Markets," *Long Range Planning* 29:6 (1996): 880–96.

12. This section is based on S. Tamer Cavusgil, "Measuring the potential of emerging markets: and indexing approach," *Business Horizons* (Jan.–Feb. 1997): 87–91.

13. Peter Bartram, "Prophet Making," *Director* 54: 12 (July 2001): 76–79.

14. R. Phelps, C. Chan, and S. C. Kapsalis, "Does scenario planning affect performance? Two exploratory case studies," *Journal of Business Research* 51: 3 (March 2001): 223–32.

15. "Energy Outlook: Shell maps out possible scenarios," *Petroleum Outlook* (December 2001):39–40.

16. Bartram, *op. cit.*

17. Doug Randall, Piero Telesio, "China: Five scenarios for managing risks," *Planning Review* 23: 1 (Jan.–Feb. 1995): 30–40.

CASETTE 7-1
Strategic Planning at Benetton

The Benetton tale began in the 1960s in Italy, when Luciano and Guiliana Benetton began producing colorful sweaters in Treviso. Their hand-knitted output was strikingly successful. Ten years later, they built a factory in Ponzano, and in 1968 they opened a store for their sweaters in Paris, France. Today, Benetton is a $2 billion company with 7000 stores in 120 countries. They are heavily European, with over 70 percent of sales from that region, with the remainder coming equally from the Americas (mainly North America) and other regions. Its major business is its fashion lines for men, women, and children ("The United Colors of Benetton") that accounts for over 60 percent of worldwide sales. Its current businesses consist of:

United Colors of Benetton: Fashion wear, but also includes watches and perfumes (from Europe); diapers (nappies) from the U.S.; condoms (from Japan); golf/sports bags and equipment

Playlife: Sportswear

Sisley: Denim garments styled according to latest trends

Rollerblade: Global leader in the rollerblade market

Nordica: World leader in ski boots

Killer Loop: Mainly high-tech snowboarding and snow equipment

Prince: A world leader in tennis racquets

Benetton's initial successes were in its fashion garment area, where its highly efficient supply chain was linked to its retail stores worldwide and was able to predict and capitalize on the color-conscious fashion market much faster than other producers. The Benetton name and Italy's strong fashion image helped to propel the company to international stardom. The company also became renowned for its controversial advertising featuring an AIDS victim and his family, a dead Bosnian fighter in a blood-soaked T-shirt, an oil-smeared seabird, a nun kissing a priest, and a black woman nursing a white baby. The latest effort, using interviews with death-row inmates in North Carolina, U.S., was equally controversial.

Benetton's trademark efficiency is still apparent, with a major computer network linking its nine factories worldwide with its distributors and retailers. Its trademark supply system was reproduced at Benetton Hungary, where the firm coordinated contractors in seven countries for output into Eastern Europe. But the company has had its dark moments. Its 600 subcontractors are nonunionized. In 1997, a Sicilian subcontractor, Bronte Jeans, was investigated by the trade unions after workforce wages were halved, and allegations that there were illegal dismissals of women after marriage. In 1998, a Turkish subcontractor was found to be using child labor (aged 11–13 years old), and Romanian workers were said to work about 250 hours a month to reach their manufacturing targets and receive the basic wage.

But its innovative "try anything" corporate culture has not lost its spark. The company has seventy licenses with international companies outside of the apparel field to produce perfumes, cosmetics, diapers/nappies, golf clubs, plates, fluorescent hair dyes, autos (the Renault Benetton Twingo), and colorful telephone pagers. Benetton was the first Western retailer into Eastern Europe, and its joint venture, Benetton Korea, hopes not only to take advantage of the country's low costs to supply the premium-priced Japanese market, but also to be first into the North Korean market.

Questions

1. Write a mission statement for Benetton that captures the essence of the firm's corporate culture, its target markets, and its approach to the marketplace.

2. What are Benetton's core competencies? What makes them special?

3. Review the company's product and market strategies. What are they doing, and what other products might work for them?

Sources: www.benetton.com. Camuffo, Analdo, Pietro Romano, and Adrea Vinelli. "Back to the Future: Benetton transforms its global network." *MIT Sloan Management Review* 43:1 (Fall 2001): 46–52. Brabbs, Cordelia. "Which of these ads sells jumpers?" *Marketing* (January 22, 2000). McEvoy, Chris. "The SGB interview: Dennis Shafer." *Sporting Goods Business* (March 8, 1999): 28–29.

⤙⤚

Wal-Mart began its international push in earnest during the 1990s. In the decade that followed, the company achieved retail leadership positions in Canada and Mexico. Its international division has become the second biggest in the company, with international sales at $32 billion, comprising one-sixth of company turnover. While its profit-to-sales ratio lags, the retailer's 1100 stores in nine countries yielded $1.1 billion in profits.

To be sure, Wal-Mart made some mistakes in its early days, but the company is slowly moving down the learning curve and figuring out when to transfer and use its U.S. expertise and when to defer to local managerial experience and adapt to existing market conditions. As the company gains in foreign market experience, its top managers are getting clearer ideas about how to evaluate international markets that will be at the forefront of corporate strategy in the forthcoming decades.

In the Latin American market, Wal-Mart in 2001 had a dozen supercenter stores in Argentina and 20 units in Brazil. Its global rival, France's Carrefour, had 22 hypermarkets and 340 other stores in Argentina, and 74 hypermarkets and 115 supermarkets in Brazil. The company has been in Brazil and Argentina for thirty-five and twenty years respectively. For Wal-Mart, Latin America was a learning experience as it learned how to operate in an inflationary environment and how to cope with changing governments, variable economic policies, and fluctuating exchange rates. While Latin American affluence levels generally are at the upper end of developing market levels, the mass market is still at the lower income levels. Given the retailing industry's competitive landscape, Wal-Mart's strategic focus has shifted from large urban metropolises to smaller urban centers with populations of about 500,000 or more.

In Asia, Wal-Mart has focused on China, where it had 19 units by mid-2002, and South Korea. Retail prospects in China look good, with sales expected to reach over $700 billion by 2008. In China, the company was encouraged to set up in the eight special economic zones on the coast that house over 50 million consumers. For space and real-estate cost reasons, Wall-Mart operates multilevel units (the opposite of its home market), going up to nine stories in Korea, and carries about 25,000 stock-keeping-units (SKUs)—about half a typical U.S. supercenter store. Most of its Chinese customers use motorcycles or bicycles to reach the store, and "fresh" meats include live fish, frogs, and snakes, and barbequed pigeons. Chinese consumers shop more frequently than most, often on a daily basis, but in smaller quantities (about one-fifth of the average U.S. Wal-Mart shopper). As a result, Chinese stores are high-traffic. In the more affluent Korean market, cars are used, refrigeration is widespread, and consumption patterns are similar to those in the U.S. Commentators see Korea as a rapid-expansion market for Wal-Mart, and store numbers are expected to reach 50–60 units by 2007. But Asia's development record makes the region an attractive market, and China and Korea in particular have been targeted by Carrefour, UK retailer Tesco, and Germany's Metro.

Wal-Mart's ventures into the highly competitive retail market of Western Europe have also been learning experiences, as the region is home to fourteen of the world's hypermarket retailers. In Germany, Wal-Mart bought the 21-unit Wertkauf chain in 1997 and the 74-unit Interspar group in 1998. There was resistance: from vendors who did not take to Wal-Mart's centralized warehouse system, from German managers who resented English-only-speaking U.S. executives telling them how to run things, and from the German Cartel Office that objected to Wal-Mart's everyday low-pricing philosophy that priced staple food products below cost. In Britain, the firm's takeover of ASDA was less controversial. Wal-Mart gave local managers freedom to run the businesses their way, but gave ASDA stores access to its global purchasing system, and better technology for tracking store sales and inventories. Dialogs were two-way also. ASDA's efficient food replenishment system was brought back to the U.S. for implementation, as were some product lines and management methods.

Question

You are Wal-Mart's new advisor on screening for new retail markets. From your international business knowledge and Wal-Mart's experiences in Latin America, Asia, and Western Europe, prepare a list of factors and information you would use for screening potential retail markets. For each, say why it is important.

Sources: Troy, Mike. "The world's largest retailer." *Chain Store Age* (June 2001): 47–49. "Another adaptation of the rural strategy." *Discount Store News* (October 1999): 89. "Asian Aspiration." *Chain Store Age* (June 2001): 66–67. Zellner, Wendy, et al. "How well does Wal-Mart travel?" *Business Week* (September 3, 2001): 82–84. "A great wall worth hurdling." *Discount Store News* (October 1999): 91, 167. "Wal-Mart's other America." *Chain Store Age* (June 2001): 64–65.

CASSETTE 7-3
Managing Risk in Emerging Markets

There are risks attached to all business ventures, even in domestic situations where managers are thoroughly familiar with customers and markets. In home markets, executives use their experience, supplemented by research to counter these risks.

It is not so different in international markets. The more managers know about country markets, the better able they are to manage the risks associated with them. International companies are present in virtually all world markets, even those classified as high risk. If industry competitors or other international firms are present in high-risk markets, the signal is that such country risks are manageable. The task of international managers, therefore, is to understand risks, but not to be afraid of them. The role of commercial risk evaluators is to identify what risks are present. The role of the manager is to manage them.

> Unless you enter the lion's den, you cannot take the cubs.
>
> —*Japanese proverb*

For example, managers looking at Central and Eastern Europe have noted major differences in political risk within the region. With that in mind, most firms have opted for Hungary, Poland, and the Czech Republic, and these nations had garnered $20 billion, $36 billion, and $21 billion of foreign direct investment respectively, a major factor being those countries' impending entry into the European Union. In 2001, Business Risk Services evaluated their weaknesses as: Czech Republic—economic growth and currency convertibility; Hungary—bureaucracy, labor cost/productivity, and professional services; Poland—bureaucracy and communication/transportation infrastructures. All three scored poorly on financial markets, such as short-term credit and long-term loans and venture capital. Politically, all three scored low on political structure (many different parties), mentality

(xenophobia, nepotism, nationalism, corruption), and radical political groups. However, *Euromoney* reports suggest that given their historic circumstances, their political progress has been significant, and while there are some economic problems (infrastructure, lack of entrepreneurs), there was little evidence of significant economic risks.

Russia too has slowly emerged as a more attractive market for investments. Business Risk Services noted numerous operating and political weaknesses for the former communist superpower (xenophobia, degree of nationalization, inflation, infrastructure, capital markets, left-wing orientations of the Dumas Parliament, etc). Recent problems stemmed from the currency crash of 1998, when Russia caught the Asian financial "flu" and saw its currency depreciate from 7 rubles per dollar to 27. Many international firms left or put their expansion plans on hold, especially in the financial sector. But many foreign financial concerns stayed on as Russian banks took a battering, with some going belly-up. One of them, Bank Austria Creditanstalt, used the crisis to cement relations with its corporate clients and provide high-quality links with foreign markets through its multilingual services. The bank also built up its relationships with the emerging Russian middle classes, investing their savings, opening new branches in Moscow, and delivering new products such as Visa debit cards, ATMs, and telebanking.

For some countries, solving one major problem is the key. In Brazil's case, the introduction of a new currency, the real, in 1994, and a massive economic austerity program were the keys to prosperity. Inflation dropped from 2500 percent in 1993 to 4 percent in 1997. But Brazil has always been a market to test a company's patience. Stock market volatility, trade restrictions, corruption, and bureaucracy have all been ongoing concerns. As a result, despite everything, international companies have flocked to Brazil, with foreign direct investments rising from $42 billion in 1995 to $164 billion in 1999 to $$198 billion in 2000. The Brazilian government during this period has been stable under the watchful eye of the Real-Plan creator, President Cardozo, and the country's progress has been the mainstay of the Mercosur trading bloc.

Mineral-rich Africa includes many countries labeled as "high risk." Risks multiply when mining firms joint-venture with governments. Where governments are democratic and honest, there are few problems. When governments are undemocratic, or unstable, problems accrue. Political instability often goes hand-in-hand with economic, legal, and personal security problems. Economic mismanagement and government budget deficits and inflation have been common occurrences. Infrastructure problems, with power supply restrictions, fuel shortages, corrupt officials, and import restrictions, became part of everyday life. To counter and manage these sorts of problems, dependable and influential local representatives became essential.

Personal security is a problem in over seventy countries, according to the U.S. government, and of these, over thirty have civil wars or rebel groups that can threaten expatriates or international company facilities. Firms in Algeria spend 8–9 percent of budgets on security (fences, guards, security systems). In Colombia, this figure is 4–6 percent. Expatriate houses in Lagos, Nigeria, or Johannesburg, South Africa, often resemble stockades. Companies must often tutor executives in safety codes: how to deal with car-jackers (cooperate, don't make sudden moves, etc.), defensive driving (lock doors, vary routes), and even pre-rape counseling for female expatriates in Africa. Other basic measures to bolster security include:

- The projecting of favorable corporate images, with proactive public relations and participation in local community projects and affairs

- Checking out local business people surreptitiously to avoid those associated with crime, e.g., the Russian Mafia

- In bribery situations, insisting that "someone else" makes the decision, and never going to such meetings alone

- Using home-market or international standards for environmental policies

- Protecting employees and offering above-average wages and work conditions

- Using local subcontractors, suitably supervised, for delicate operations

In today's Internet world, corporate information technology (IT) systems have become security issues for foreign-based corporate affiliates. Normal security measures, such as encryption codes, must often be registered with national governments. This allows governments to "look in" or steal corporate information. Countries such as Russia and others in Asia openly acknowledge that they steal business information, and in South America there are problems with internal espionage or embezzlement. These sorts of problems easily intimidate inexperienced firms, but seasoned companies take many precautionary measures: running extensive background checks on new employees, providing extensive training, building internal "walls" among departments, and instituting stringent security precautions, including biometric access (fingerprints, retinal checks) to sensitive areas and periodic security sweeps by experts. In addition, many use couriers to move sensitive data and documents.

Ultimately, the adaptable and careful international corporation can operate almost anywhere in reasonable safety. But sensitivity to market conditions and knowledge of the local culture are prerequisites for successful risk management.

Questions

1. Why do firms operate in high-risk countries? (Give specific examples.)

2. What sorts of risks are uncontrollable? Why?

3. You are traveling to a country (a) with a reputation for kidnapping rich international executives, (b) where business activities often have criminal connections, and (c) that has active guerilla movements. What precautions would you take and why?

Sources: Ramcharran, Harri. "Foreign direct investments in Central and Eastern Europe: An analysis of regulatory and country risk factors." *American Business Review* 18:2 (June 2000): 1–8. Franz, Michael P. "Success, despite a national crisis." *Euromoney* (September 1999): 6–7. Wallace, David J. "The future in Brazil." *World Trade* 12:2 (February 1999): 42–46; "Business in difficult places: Risky returns," *The Economist* (May 2000): 85–88. Radcliff, Deborah. "Volatile states." *Computerworld* (October 22, 2001): 32–33.

CASE 3

IBCA, Ltd.[1]

*I*t was a summer day in 1997. Ex-British Royal Navy fighter pilot Robin Monro-Davies, gazed thoughtfully at the bright sunshine outside his office window. As the managing director of IBCA, Ltd., an international credit rating agency, he faced several challenges ahead.

> The external challenge is the competitive market . . . we're competing with people much bigger than ourselves. The internal challenge is the management of a small company with a tremendous spread of offices. I'd think it is highly unusual for a firm of 200 people to have 12 overseas offices.

IBCA, Ltd. was Europe's leading credit rating agency with offices in the major financial centres of London, New York, and Tokyo, as well as in Singapore, Hong Kong, Argentina, Brazil, South Africa, and Australia. Its main competitors were the market leaders in the international credit rating industry—Standard & Poors and Moody's, the "bigger people" that Monro-Davis referred to.

Basically, a rating agency's business was to rate debt issued by banks, corporations, or even governments wanting to borrow in the international capital markets. Regulatory bodies in a number of countries required debt (e.g., corporate and government bonds, and asset- or mortgage-backed securities) to be rated by an authorized rating agency before it could be sold to investors in their countries. A rating enabled regulators and investors to know how likely a borrower was to default on the debt. Rating agencies provided this information by assigning risk to debt issues with letter grades—AAA, AA, BBB, and so on. Ratings determined the cost of borrowing; the higher the rating, the lower the cost and vice versa. Although ratings were required by regulators, many borrowers, especially credit-worthy ones, actually found it advantageous to be rated, as a good rating could reduce their costs of funds. As financial markets became internationalized and increasingly deregulated, borrowers had become more sophisticated in their borrowing activities. They no longer limited their borrowing to domestic capital markets but also sought funds overseas. All this had led to the growth of the international credit rating industry. IBCA had grown rapidly in recent years in line with the growth and globalization of capital markets.

Robin Monro-Davies had been with the IBCA since its inception in 1978. In 1968, after ten years in the British Royal Navy, Monro-Davies left to pursue a graduate business degree at the Massachusetts Institute of Technology (MIT). After graduating from MIT, he worked as a credit analyst in Wall Street and, later, for Fox-Pitt Kelton, a brokerage firm. In 1978, Fox-Pitt Kelton started IBCA, with Monro-Davies being involved in its founding. In the late 1980s Monro-Davies became involved solely with IBCA, although retaining his ties to FPK. The inherent conflict of interest between IBCA and FPK eventually led to FPK selling IBCA. Monro-Davies sold out his share in FPK to concentrate on IBCA. Fourteen years after it was founded, IBCA was acquired by the French investment company, *Centenaire Blanzy*. A new entity, IBCA Groupe S.A., was established as the holding company for IBCA Limited. Monro-Davies remained as Managing Director and actively ran the firm from his London office.

As the firm grew, Monro-Davies found that he was unable to be as involved in the firm's operations as he was before. The total number of employees was 158, having increased from 110 in 1995. The London office was the largest, with staff strength of eighty-two, followed by its South African and New York offices with fifteen and fourteen employees, respectively. IBCA opened a Hong Kong office in early 1997, after having set up one in Singapore in 1996. "What I'd like is six key managers under me, six key guys between 35 and 45 who are great. That's what we've not got . . . those people should be doing a lot of what comes up to me." Turnover among senior staff is low. Recently, however, a long-time senior analyst who had also been much involved in the administration of the London office resigned to join another firm.

The Credit Ratings Industry

In the credit rating industry, two firms dominated in the U.S. and worldwide: Moody's Investors Service (Moody's) and Standard and Poor's (S & P). Both had revenues of approximately $400 million.[2] Other major players included Fitch Investors Service, Duff and Phelps Credit Rating Company, and IBCA, with approximately $65 million, $53 million, and $30 million in revenues, respectively. The revenue of Thomson BankWatch, the smallest of the players, was not known. The relative rankings of these players by market share had not changed over the last five years.

Some rating agencies were boutique agencies specializing in banking and insurance industries. For example, AM Best company specialized in rating the claims-paying ability of insurance companies. IBCA had started out rating only banks but had since moved on to rating insurance companies, corporations ("corporates"), and countries ("sovereigns"), while Thomson had largely remained with rating only banks. Although the larger rating agencies also rated bank and insurance companies, the specialists dominated in terms of market share in the industries they rated. Thomson, for instance, was the world's largest bank rating agency, rating over 1000 financial institutions in more than eighty-five countries. It rated twice as many banks in the U.S. and 30–40 percent more banks in Asia than IBCA did. IBCA did not rate the smallest banks, preferring instead to cover the larger banks in greater detail. On average, an IBCA bank analyst rated half as many banks as a Thomson analyst.

Fitch and Duff & Phelps rated many more structured finance issues than S & P and Moody's. Fitch had grown substantially from forty-three employees and less than $3 million in revenues in 1989 to 300 employees and over $65 million in 1996, after having been acquired by new investors in 1996. Fitch's growth had largely been in the U.S. market, as it had little international presence. Duff had over 240 employees with affiliates either in operation or awaiting final regulatory approval in North and South America, Europe, Asia, and Africa. The range of capital issues rated by the major rating agencies is listed in Table 1.

In the last several years, however, the "once-sleepy" agencies had begun to be more aggressive in their marketing tactics, particularly among the largest four players. Overseas, S & P had substantially increased its international presence with an aggressive acquisition and affiliation strategy. It had opened a number of offices worldwide; in Asia, S & P had tied up with Asian rating agencies. Moody's, on the other hand, had decided as a matter of policy against linking up with Asian rating agencies.

In addition, several countries had their own rating agencies: Australian Ratings,[3] Canadian Bond Rating Service, Dominion Bond Rating Service (Canada), Japan Bond Research Institute, Japan Credit Rating Agency, Nippon Investors Services, Agence d'Evaluation Financiere,[3] Thai Rating and Information Service (TRIS), and Rating Agency Malaysia (RAM). Many governments, particularly in Southeast Asia, preferred to have their own rating agencies, rather than having foreign rating agencies, such as IBCA, Moody's, and S & P, assess the credit-worthiness of their institutions. Hence, agencies such as RAM in Malaysia, TRIS in Thailand, PEFINDO in Indonesia and CIBI in the Philippines had been created. IBCA had been engaged by RAM to train its analysts and had a 5 percent equity stake in RAM. In Indonesia, IBCA had been paid a fee for helping the local agency, PEFINDO, set up its operations. (S & P had been involved in the setting up of Thailand's TRIS.) At present, these rating agencies were protected from competition in their local markets. However, because Southeast Asian nations were signatories to the World Trade Organization, they would have to liberalize their financial-services industry over time.

Commercial and investment banks also carried out credit analysis. Commercial banks constantly evaluated the creditworthiness of foreign banks with which they had trade-financing relationships through a specialized department called *correspondent banking*. For example, a U.S. commerical bank which had to settle a trade transaction on behalf of a U.S. business would want to be certain, before transferring money to a foreign bank, that the foreign bank was not fraudulent. Or it might want to

TABLE 1
Market Coverage

Rating Agency	Scope of Coverage
IBCA	Financial institutions, insurance companies, and corporations worldwide; sovereign countries
Thomson Bank Watch	Financial institutions worldwide
Fitch	Public and private fixed income securities, securitized ratings in the U.S.
Duff and Phelps	Corporate debt securities sold by U.S. and foreign-based corporations, securitized ratings, insurance companies
Standard & Poor's	Comprehensive—covers all entities listed above and more
Moody's	Comprehensive—covers all entities listed above and more

determine whether the foreign bank would settle obligations promptly. A commercial bank often dealt with hundreds of international banks, some of which were very small. Its correspondent banking department, on its own, might not be able to evaluate satisfactorily all the international banks. As a result, many commercial banks outsourced their evaluation work by using a rating agency such as IBCA or Thomson. IBCA's earliest subscribers were, in fact, correspondent banking departments of international banks.

In investment banks, credit analysis was done to back up a bank origination work, that is, putting together research that would price the issue, as well as introduce it to investors. Investment banks were big providers of business to rating agencies, as an issue required a rating before it could be sold to investors. Outside the U.S., credit research had not been significant in investment houses until perhaps five years ago, and that only in Europe. Notes Joseph Biernat, director of global credit research at Deutsche Morgan Grenfell, "London is where New York was fifteen years ago. Asia is further behind it, and it's impossible to hire people there." The net result was that rating agencies, which had traditionally been the training ground for credit analysts, had seen more of their analysts enticed away by investment banks.

Market Presence

IBCA was present in the following markets: North America, Europe, Asia, Latin America, and South Africa. It was the only foreign rating agency to be recognized by the Securities and Exchange Commission (SEC) in the U.S. as a Nationally Recognised Statistical Rating Organisation (NRSRO). The SEC required U.S. investors (e.g., pension funds, mutual funds, and financial institutions) to buy securities that had been rated by an NRSRO-designated rating agency. Without such a designation, securities or issues rated by a rating agency could not be bought by U.S. investors, who made up a large source of funds for many international debt issuers. Thus, many borrowers who planned to tap the U.S. capital market had to get an NRSRO-designated rating agency to rate their debt issues. All of the four major U.S. players—Moody's, S & P, Fitch, and Duff & Phelps—were NRSROs. IBCA and Thomson BankWatch were designated NRSROs for a restricted set of securities, namely, banks and financial institutions. There were no formal criteria for obtaining an NRSRO designation, and many non-U.S. rating agencies had complained that their applications for an NRSRO designation had been in limbo for many years.

In Europe, IBCA faced keen competition from Moody's and S & P, particularly in corporate ratings. Although IBCA was Europe's leading international rating agency, any European company that wanted to raise capital in the U.S. had to have its issue rated by an NRSRO rating agency. Europe, in particular Eastern Europe and Russia, would continue to provide significant opportunities for rating agencies. In the long-term, however, the Latin American and Asian markets were the markets with the most growth potential. IBCA had been expanding aggressively in both regions in recent years. For Monro-Davis, an issue was whether to continue expanding in an ad hoc fashion in Asia and Latin America or to emphasize one region over the other.

ASIA The so-called "tiger" economies of South Korea, Taiwan, Hong Kong, and Singapore grew an average of 6.8 percent in 1992–96, while growth in the Southeast Asian nations of Indonesia, Thailand, and Malaysia averaged 8 percent. Economic growth for 1997–2001 was forecasted to average 6.8 percent for the "tiger" economies and 7.4 percent for the three Southeast Asian countries. China had grown 12.1 percent in the last five years and was projected to grow 8.8 percent for the next five years (Table 2). The sheer size of the growth figures of these countries made them very attractive investment opportunities, yet, from the perspective of rating agencies, the picture was a little more complex. Monro-Davies explained,

> In the classic model, people place money with banks; banks lend money to companies. Banks are the providers of credit; they also are the rating agencies. It is the banks who decide who to lend their money to. The next one up is the disintermediated model. Somebody, typically an investment banker, comes along and asks, why do you bother to put your money in a bank; why don't you lend direct to a company? However, the investment banker's interest is in completing the transaction, so the investor would now have to look for an independent source to advise on the quality of the credit. That's how you get rating agencies axiomatically.
>
> The growth potential for rating agencies is the disintermediated market. So, when I talk about the growth of the market, one has to say, is it a disintermediated market or is it likely to become one? There are lots of areas in Asia that are growing dramatically, but for rating agencies, it's not interesting. It's not established debt market. You don't know the rules of law, you don't know this or that. We are an information service. Our business only gets going if you have a well-structured market.

To assess whether disintermediation was likely to occur, most analysts looked to see if the trends and fundamentals that existed in the U.S. would also occur in that market. If they did, then disintermediation was likely to occur. According to Monro-Davies, "It doesn't mean that today, if I put up an office in Taiwan I would make any money." IBCA would have to tie its expansion to this natural market phenomenon of debt issuance. "To do so," he continued, "you firstly have to have a product. Can you analyze the Far East or Latin America from London? No, you can't. You have to set up overseas offices. So what we've done in Asia in the last eighteen months is to establish in Singapore, Hong Kong, Brisbane, Tokyo. That's the base. Now we feed people into it. It's a very risky strategy having lots of tiny offices. As a businessman, I'd like to have all our offices with ten people plus."

To Monro-Davies, it was important to be clear what one meant when talking about the Asian market:

> There's Japan, which clearly is huge and will reinternationalize very soon, and then you've got the rest—the fast-growth countries which in reality are mostly quite small. The most interesting area outside Japan has got to be Indonesia because it's big. Doesn't matter how exciting Singapore is, it's small. You need a mass, but Japan's not exciting at the moment at all, but it will change. Hong Kong's great, but China . . . ? I just don't know. You've got a billion people and it's growing at 10 percent, it's got to be exciting. But how we make money out of China in the rating business or how disintermediated markets develop is not clear at all.

The expansion of IBCA's offices in Asia meant that IBCA could cover banks in Asia close up rather than at arms' length. The Singapore office covered Singapore, Malaysia, and Indonesia, while the Brisbane office covered Australia, Thailand, and the Philippines. Japanese banks were covered by IBCA's Tokyo office, while the Hong Kong office covered Hong Kong, China, and, to some extent, South Korea.

David Marshall, IBCA's head of Asia, was based in the Hong Kong office. Marshall, a graduate of Oxford University and fluent in Japanese, joined IBCA in 1987 after working for a leading Japanese trading company. A director of IBCA, he had been responsible for IBCA's rating work on Japanese banks and was now involved in developing IBCA's rating business in Asia. He described the difficulty of doing ratings in China:

> You need quite clear and strict accounting standards so you can rely on financial statements that companies issue, and China hasn't really got that. You also need a clear legal system so you know when you buy an asset, you own the asset, you can sell it, and you or somebody can foreclose on the bond if the company doesn't pay. Again that's not at all clear in China. Even more important, in any

rational capital market, the finances available to those who are able to pay and willing to pay is in part determined by the credit ratings as to who is able to borrow. In China, it doesn't work like that. The borrowing is done on the basis of government decisions, essentially, not really on the needs of the companies or on their ability to repay. At the moment, I don't think it's going to be very meaningful for us to assign ratings to companies issuing bonds in China. The bonds are being issued because the government has told the companies to do so. Of course, it's all going to change. It's shifting from that situation to a free-market situation in which borrowing is done on a rational basis.

Nevertheless, Marshall thought that such change would be a difficult process. China had set up local rating agencies, although, according to Marshall, "They're not doing very much at the moment. They are adding a stamp on a decision that's already been made by the State Planning Commission." IBCA as well as its competitors had explored setting up offices in China but the Chinese authorities were not keen to give licenses to foreign companies. Marshall continued,

> The only possibility we have is to link up with a local company to do a joint venture and employ some senior person who has good connections as the Chairman of the joint venture. We do know the experience of foreign joint ventures in China is not a happy one. It's easy to put money in, it's not so easy to get profits out. So we're a little cautious about that but like a lot of companies, China is so exciting for the long-term I guess we're prepared to take a risk for a modest amount of money to invest in a joint venture there.

Until about two years ago, IBCA had devoted very little of its resources to Asia. What had changed in the last two years was that management recognized that the firm had to be there to compete not just with Moody's and S & P but also Thomson. Marshall believed,

> We have to have a comprehensive, a global rating coverage of banks. So we have to be there. We've invested, we have increased our offices in Asia, and got more people there. Secondly, it's attractive in its own right. We can actually produce a product in Asian bank ratings which we can then sell; it should be a profitable business and give rise to rating fees coming in from those banks, enabling expansion to take place.

IBCA's strategy for Asia was to do bank ratings wherever possible. Marshall also felt that it was important to be in corporate ratings. However, he concluded,

We don't have a clear strategy on that at the moment. We're looking at hiring some people, specialists in corporate ratings essentially to do marketing, to try to develop relationships with potential clients. We would see how that develops in one or two years. If there are encouraging signs, we'd put more resources into that and try to develop the business. If there weren't encouraging signs, we'd have to give up and that would be rather sad. We'd have to find some way to develop an Asian corporate rating even if it is quite limited at first. We have to do more marketing, restructured finance, asset-backed securities, rating mortgage-backed bonds. Again, we need to hire more specialists, probably in the Australasia region. It's really a marketing effort in the next two years to get our name better known and develop more business. It's going to be tough for us to do this, but that's what we need to do.

Like IBCA, S&P and Moody's had expanded their coverage of Asia in the last few years. Marshall assessed IBCA's current position in relation to these two major competitors as well as the market opportunities in Asia:

China is important but the bulk of our business is Japan. Strangely enough, our growth prospects are probably quite limited there because it's a very difficult market. Moody's and S & P are strong there, and there are also three Japanese rating agencies. We'd have to cover Japanese corporates. We'd have to hire huge teams of people and send them out to analyze Sony and Hitachi and Sharp. Moody's, S & P and the Japanese agencies are doing it, and it's probably not profitable for us to be doing that. But still it's an important base to do bank ratings in Japan.

Where is the growth in Asia taking place? . . . We do credit ratings, so we rate borrowers, people who want to borrow money. Who wants to borrow the money? It's really not the Japanese—they are big investors now. They are lending the money. So are the Koreans, increasingly. The development is more from Thailand, Indonesia, Malaysia, and other developing countries where companies are borrowing a lot of money to finance their development. So there are quite a lot of opportunities in credit ratings in those countries. They do have local rating agencies in Thailand, Indonesia, and Malaysia, which are competitors to us, as are Moody's and S & P. Those countries where we see demand coming, we see companies coming to us to ask us to rate them. Though all those countries will be important, it'll be fairly slow growth over several years.

Where we've had a bit of a jumpstart is in Hong Kong where the Hong Kong Monetary Authority has introduced regulation which in effect makes it very attractive for companies, particularly local banks, to get a rating from a group of four or five rating agencies of which we are one. Because of this regulation, we've had a number of companies come to us in Hong Kong to ask for ratings, so that's led to significant growth in the rating business in Hong Kong. That's the reason why we established an office in Hong Kong.

One of the challenges faced by IBCA in Asia was that S & P and Moody's were better known in Asia. Both companies had been in existence a lot longer than IBCA. Moody's first bond ratings were published in 1909 in the U.S. while S & P first assigned corporate ratings to U.S. companies in 1923. Marshall offered his view of IBCA's strengths which it could leverage on:

The strengths we have are fortunately twofold. The first is banks. We are very well-known as a highly regarded and professional rating agency with a special expertise in rating banks, and that is known worldwide. So if we do go to banks in Korea, for example, they know us, they know people use our ratings, and they know it will be quite useful for them to get a rating from our company. So even if we take a long time to get into other products in Asia, at least the banking market gives us a foothold we can use to establish our name.

Secondly, our sovereign team which has been very successful and which we're all very pleased about. They've attracted a lot of attention and have attained a very high profile and are very highly regarded. Worldwide, it is increasingly clear that after Moody's and S & P, we are the third international rating agency.

LATIN AMERICA IBCA had been present in Latin America a lot longer than in Asia, over fifteen years. It had offices in Chile, Argentina, Brazil, and Venezuela. IBCA's head of Latin America was Charles Prescott, a Gibraltarn by birth and a chartered accountant by training. Prescott had been a board member since 1985 and was responsible for IBCA's rating activities in Latin America.

Overall, Latin America was now in a more favorable position than at any time since its debt crisis in the '80s to borrow long-term from international capital markets. Political and economic reforms as well as foreign investment inflows had made the region attractive to investors. Nonetheless, debt service burdens were high with the big

TABLE 2
Growth Rates: Asia and Latin America

	GDP Growth (annual ave. %) 1992–96	GDP Growth (annual ave. %) 1997–2001
Asia		
China	12.1	8.8
South Korea	7.0	6.5
Taiwan	6.3	6.0
Hong Kong	5.4	5.2
Singapore	8.5	6.4
Indonesia	7.3	8.2
Thailand	8.1	6.2
Malaysia	8.6	7.8
Latin America		
Brazil	3.3	4.1
Mexico	1.1	3.7
Argentina	4.3	4.1
Colombia	4.4	3.3
Chile	7.4	6.3
Venezuela	1.3	3.7
Peru	5.4	4.8

risk being a sharp rise in U.S. interest rates in the medium-term. Another big risk was that a crisis of confidence in Brazil, which had a very large fiscal deficit and faced a politically uncertain future (due to impending elections in 1997), could unsettle the whole region. Latin America's forecasted growth for 1997–2001 is listed in Table 2.

As credit risk was an issue for investors in an emerging market like Latin America, investors depended on rating agencies to provide them with information regarding the riskworthiness of companies and institutions. More importantly for a rating agency like IBCA, government regulations in many Latin American countries requiring that companies and institutions be rated meant that there was a natural business in ratings (which may not exist in some other markets where such regulations were absent). But whether the Latin American market was at a more developed stage in terms of growth potential than the Asian market was not clear. According to Monro-Davies,

> My intuition is that the Latin market is a bit more developed for growth, but if you say, give me the data, I can't. But Latin Americans are more used to funding themselves in the U.S. market. It's more natural for them to do so. So I think there may be more rating business in Latin America than in Asia, excluding Japan.

IBCA first started covering Latin America in the late 1970s. After all the countries defaulted in the Latin American crisis in the 1980s, there was a drop in demand from investors for Latin American ratings. However, IBCA stayed on in those countries they had been present in, viz., Brazil and Venezuela, because it felt that sooner or later, business would pick up. But that took quite a while. Charles Prescott described the development of IBCA's Latin American presence, as well as the difficulty in doing ratings in the region:

> Roughly five years ago, investors became much more interested and were asking for information on ratings. We found that it was very difficult to do ratings because these markets were very volatile. Economic plans in Brazil would be implemented, inflation would hit 1,000% p.a. and then fall to −5% p.a. over 3 months and then the plan would collapse and inflation would rise again. We felt that we could do a visit, and we could do due diligence, but 3 months later we just didn't know if anything we were told was true. The whole scenario had changed. Many of our clients were phoning up and asking what was happening. Although we knew more than them, we weren't satisfied or comfortable with the knowledge that we had.

> All this coincided with the Chilean government deciding to privatize their pension funds. What they did was to say that everybody in the family had to put 13% into a pension fund that was to be administered privately. However, pension funds could only invest in rated paper. As a result, there was a number of rating agencies authorized and that meant that the rating industry took off. Chile did very well; over time, many Latin American countries copied that, with the exception of Brazil.

Although local rating agencies had been authorized in a number of Latin American countries, few of the agencies had the expertise or experience of setting up a rating agency. Some, like the Argentinian rating agency, went to IBCA for help. Prescott recalled,

> Now I think they had been to S & P and Moody's but S & P and Moody's weren't interested because they were very small and S & P and Moody's possibly had better things to do. For us, it was interesting because it fitted in with what we wanted to do. We had come to the conclusion that we didn't want to do unsolicited ratings because it was difficult enough when it was solicited; if you didn't have the cooperation of management it was even harder. The situation was interesting because it gave us

the opportunity—for an amount that was not very large to invest in—to have a local rating agency there to inform us as to what was happening. We would have an option to buy control in the agency after a number of years.

This arrangement suited IBCA, and it was willing to pay a bit more for the local rating agency in the future should it prove profitable. It also gave IBCA some time to get to know the people in the local rating agency, something that Prescott felt was very important. He stated,

> None of these agencies we had helped to set up were IBCA—they all had different names. We were happy for the agencies to say IBCA had a minority stake. We helped them with our methodology, but it was their ratings.

> We own 100% of the local rating agency in Argentina, are just in the process of buying the local rating agency in Chile, have affiliates in Peru and Venezuela. We set up in Brazil by ourselves. We're likely to go into Colombia because in all these countries, the same thing is happening—there is a demand for rating agencies to go in. Some are too small, say Bolivia and Uruguay; there is just not enough business to set up a local agency.

> Gradually, we have built up quite a large network of offices. We have 400 ratings in Latin America, which probably makes us the biggest or one of the biggest in Latin America. What we have to do now is to consolidate what we have and make it known to the world that we have this substantial presence.

Acquiring local agencies had advantages and disadvantages. "You get a certain force there—bigger, but they may have to be retrained to meet international standards," said Monro-Davis. The challenge was one of corporate culture. Charles Prescott explained,

> Most of the emphasis in these local agencies is different from IBCA's. In Latin America, the corporate business is stronger than the bank business. Seventy-five percent of what we do is in corporates, as opposed to the rest of IBCA which is very much in banks. In some regards, it's a big complement because IBCA's bank rating business is doing very well, and if we have a strong corporate rating business, it makes us more balanced. But it also means sometimes it's harder to integrate because the local agencies have a different view than we have.

The result was that the local agencies, which formed IBCA's network of Latin American subsidiaries and affiliates, wrote rating reports oriented toward local needs, while IBCA's reports were written for the global investor. As part of IBCA's network, the rating reports by IBCA's subsidiaries/affiliates needed to be oriented toward the global market. In that regard, their methodologies needed to be upgraded to meet international standards. Another difference in culture resulted from the type of clients the local affiliates had. Their clients, primarily local companies required by government regulations to be rated, would pay the subsidiaries/affiliates a fee for rating them. The subsidiaries/affiliates were very much fee-based businesses. Said Prescott,

> IBCA historically has had fees but also subscribers who buy our services. We communicate with them, send comments out, and give our opinions. Therefore, we have to change the way the subsidiaries and affiliates think in this respect. Not only is it important for the quality of the product, but also if we are going to be present in these countries in the next five or ten years, this idea of a rating agency being obligatory has to change. The rating has got to be useful in the market; otherwise, what's the point of IBCA being there?

IBCA's expansion strategy in Latin America was in contrast to that in Asia. Sam Chin, a Malaysian educated at Vassar College and New York University, who had recently set up IBCA's Singapore office said,

> In Asia we had to build up our offices from scratch as it was not possible to buy up local agencies or have majority equity stakes in them. Although it has made our expansion in Asia more demanding, a positive result is that we are able to keep consistency of our rating system and establish levels of quality control that are equivalent to those we have in Europe.

IBCA's competitors had recently been active in Latin America. Charles Prescott described their moves:

> S & P and Fitch are making associations with other rating agencies, and, in fact, in Argentina, they have bought one out. I expect similar things in other countries. Moody's is not there. Moody's does it from New York, and always has. There is no evidence they are buying up companies. S & P has got associations in Chile and Brazil and has become bigger in the past one and a half to two years. Duff and Phelps has also done something similar to us. I'd say they are as big as us or perhaps slightly smaller than us but they have followed a similar strategy pretty much from the beginning. We were first, they were second there.

Although he was not completely certain, Prescott thought that the difference in strategy between Duff & Phelps and IBCA was that Duff & Phelps was perhaps more willing to lend their name to the local affiliates in Latin America than IBCA. "We don't give the name unless we have total management control."

Products

IBCA produced and sold credit reports ("publications") on more than 400 financial institutions worldwide and 100 corporations in Europe. IBCA had 1,500 subscribers in the investment communities worldwide. IBCA also obtained revenues ("rating fees") from institutions that issued commercial papers such as bonds. These institutions paid to be rated because a creditworthy institution could lower its costs of funds by obtaining a strong rating. However, not all institutions wanted to be rated, much less pay for the rating. Nevertheless, a number of such institutions were rated because rating agencies' clients asked for information about them. These unsolicited ratings relied solely on publicly available data about the company, industry, and economy; they were not supplemented with a visit to the business, interviews with top management, and private information about the institution's plans, budgets, and information.

In Asia, the number of solicited ratings was low. Businesses tended to turn to the equity rather than the debt market to raise capital. According to Sam Chin,

> The tradition of paying to be rated just isn't here. Creditors[4] are not as demanding. In Asia, say, an Indonesian firm wants to issue bonds to raise funds, it goes to an investment bank. The investment bank sells the company's bonds to investors and provides implicitly a credit rating because the bank indicates what rate of return the investor should expect from this Indonesian institution. This is a conflict of interest—after all the person selling the instrument should not be involved in rating it. Ratings should be independent. This certainly would not be accepted in the West. Investors, or rather the authorities, would not allow investment banks to rate issues they are selling. Now, part of the problem in Asia is that there isn't enough rating agencies, or rating agencies have not established themselves firmly enough in Asia. Therefore, they are just not available to rate all the issues. So quite a bit of paper in Asia is not rated by international rating agencies. In some countries, such as Indonesia, where you have a local agency, the local agency is totally swamped, so there is quite a bit of paper floating around constantly being issued which is not rated even by a local rating

agency, so investors are totally dependent on the investment banks for their credit analysis. Now, as far as local rating agencies go, they do not have much credibility with the international investment community. Local rating agencies exist because they are required by local regulators and they are protected, that is, foreign rating agencies are not allowed to rate local issues. So what that means is that international investors are rather skeptical about these ratings.

IBCA also rated the foreign currency debt of sovereign governments. IBCA covered over thirty countries and hoped to be on par with S & P's coverage in a year to two. The sovereign ratings had been the most successful of IBCA's nonbank ratings (the others being insurance and corporate ratings).

Table 3 shows IBCA's revenues from 1979 to 1996 as well as the distribution of revenues among the firm's three product categories: publications, rating fees, and database. The database contained information on 10,000 banks worldwide and came with software to do analysis, comparison, and presentation of data. It did not contain credit analysis done by IBCA. Although revenues had increased, costs had also increased, while margins had remained static. In 1996, revenues came from the following geographical regions: 50.7 percent from the U.S. and Europe, 19.3 percent from the U.S., and 30 percent from the rest of the world (Table 4).

The Credit Rating Process

In preparing a rating, the rating agency's analyst(s) would first review a company's reports and published figures to determine what additional information was needed from the company. The analyst then met with the company's senior management to discuss the company's financial position, earning trends, operating practices, competitive standing, future prospects, the economic environment, and any other issues that might affect the company's credit assessment. The analyst would keep in contact with the company for interim figures and any internal or external developments that might affect his/her assessments. They also monitored economic factors or trends that might affect the company's credit standing. A draft report was then sent to the company for review to ensure accuracy of information and that no confidential data was included. This also gave the company being rated a chance to respond to the review. In the case of IBCA, the final report was then reviewed by a Rating Committee made up of the analysts who wrote the report, one or more senior analysts and other staff members covering similar institutions. The Rating Committee's purpose was to try to maintain objectivity in the ratings, as well as consistency on a global

TABLE 3
IBCA's Revenues and Revenue Distribution

	1978	1985	1990	1991	1992	1993	1994	1995	1996
Sales (£)[1]	20,000	1,553,377	3,659,842	4,268,768	5,767,856	7,911,862	10,102,492	12,291,540	14,271,766
Other Income	0	79,543	265,909	221,305	197,476	122,790	113,843	201,736	235,767
Pre Tax Profit	0	739,465[2]	899,201	897,594	396,631[3]	1,438,118	2,144,712	2,936,380	3,177,228
Staff	3	23	43	51	69	75	95	120	158
Offices	1	2	4	5	6	8	9	9	9
New Offices	London	New York	Malaysia	Spain	France	South Africa	Australia	Chile	Venezuela
Investments			Japan			Argentina		Pakistan	
			Brazil					Peru	
								Singapore	
New Activities			Corporate Ratings				Sovereign Ratings		Securitization
									Insurance Ratio
Database	0	0	342,994	424,084	501,611	610,464	814,405	1,259,936	1,783,970
Publications	20,000	1,553,377	3,078,588	3,368,379	3,863,440	4,602,076	5,195,373	5,647,740	5,894,240
Rating Fees	0		238,260	476,305	1,402,805	2,699,322	4,092,714	5,383,864	6,593,556
Total Sales	20,000	1,553,377	3,659,842	4,268,768	5,767,856	7,911,862	10,102,492	12,291,540	14,271,766

[1]All figures in £
[2]To begin with, FPK absorbed many of IBCA's costs so profits were overstated. By 1990 all costs were correctly allocated.
[3]Profits dropped because of merger.

TABLE 4
IBCA's Turnover by Geographical Market (%)

	1996	1995	1994
U.K.	17.5	19.4	24.0
Western Europe	32.8	35.0	29.0
North America	19.3	21.1	26.0
Rest of the World	30.0	24.5	21.0

basis. After the Rating Committee assigned a rating, the company would be notified and the ratings made public through the financial press and international wire services, such as Reuters and PR Newswire, and on trading screens such as Bloomberg and Telerate. The rating reports could differ substantially in length. Moody's ratings were accompanied by a one-page summary; S & P's reports averaged four pages, while IBCA's averaged eight pages.

Although this process was typical of well-developed markets, the credit analyst was called upon to do more investigative work in certain markets where much of the bond issue was not rated and where corporate disclosure was poor. According to Chris Francis, head of fixed-income credit research at Merrill Lynch in Hong Kong, "A lot of the companies have a tight ownership through a series of holding companies, and a credit researcher has to do much more than study cashflows and debt ratios. He needs to know what are the resources and reputation of the people in charge."

IBCA staff believed the quality of their rating reports was very high. Monro-Davies said,

> Although it is always difficult to provide firm evidence, I remain certain that our emphasis on producing high quality research is paying off although it does take time and money . . . What we have to do is continue to keep this emphasis on quality and make sure that quality relates not only to our analytical product but also to the service that we provide clients. The only way we can compete effectively with the much larger companies that dominate this field is by constantly emphasizing and reemphasising the service aspect of our business.

One way in which IBCA hoped to improve subscriber service was to put more resources into meeting clients' demands for visits, something which S & P and Moody's do. IBCA was looking into harnessing teleconferencing technology so that it could make virtual visits.

The Future

When asked about IBCA's goals, Monro-Davies replied,

> In the long-term, the question is what is going to happen in the rating business? Can we continue by ourselves or should we merge, take over or be taken over? That's the most fundamental issue. That relates to the issue of how big the nature of the ratings market, how many companies are going to exist. It's a highly oligopolized industry. If we remain independent, we'd have to invest a lot to maintain growth, so the goal is to be a global rating agency. In the short-term, I'd say, "Just running the business, keeping quite a difficult group, and continuing to grow."

Questions

1. What factors are contributing to the globalization of the credit ratings industry?

2. What are the strengths, weaknesses, opportunities, and threats facing IBCA? What would you conclude?

3. Do a side-by-side analysis of Asia and Latin America. Include (a) a general geographic and cultural overview (chapter 4), (b) their respective economic profiles, (c) an assessment of the credit ratings industry, the competition, and IBCA's position. What conclusions would you draw?

4. The Asian financial crisis occurred 1997–99. What do you think its effects would be on the financial ratings industry over the short-term (1997–99), and the longer-term (1999 onward)?

5. The euro was introduced as an accounting currency in 1999 and as a paper currency in 2002. How would this affect IBCA and the financial ratings industry?

6. What do you think of IBCA's situation? Can the company survive on its own? What options does it have?

Notes

1. By Gaik Eng Lim, National University of Singapore. This case was first published in the *Case Research Journal* (Spring 1999); 27–54. Reproduced with permission.

2. All figures in U.S. dollars unless otherwise stated.

3. Now owned by S & P.

4. Creditors or investors tend to be institutional (e.g., pension funds, mutual funds, financial institutions, corporations, and governments) rather than retail or individual investors.

APPENDIX 1
Profile: Asia

	Hong Kong	China	S. Korea	Indonesia	Thailand	Singapore	Malaysia	Philippines	Australia
Population (in millions)	6.1	1220.2	44.9	197.5	58.2	3.3	20.1	67.8	17.9
GDP	142.0	745.0	435.0	190.0	160.0	80.0	78.0	72.0	338.0
Origins of GDP									
• Agriculture	10.0%	20.5%	6.5%	17.2%	10.9%	20.0%	13.6%	21.7%	8.0%
• Industry of which	16.0%	49.2%	44.0%	40.4%	9.5%	37.1%	44.9%	32.2%	23.4%
—Manufacturing	8.8%	. . .	29.9%	24.3%	30.2%	28.0%	33.1%	23.0%	17.2%
• Services	83.9%	30.3%	49.5%	42.4%	49.6%	62.7%	41.5%	46.1%	68.6%
Components of GDP									
• Private consumption	60.2%	46.2%	52.9%	56.0%	54.5%	41.7%	49.8%	74.1%	62.4%
• Public consumption	8.8%	12.8%	10.4%	8.2%	9.7%	9.3%	12.7%	8.9%	17.2%
• Investment	34.6%	34.7%	37.1%	37.8%	42.9%	34.9%	40.7%	22.3%	20.9%
• Exports less imports	−3.4%	2.5%	1.0%	2.0%	−6.9%	15.6%	−3.3%	−6.9%	0.4%

(continued)

APPENDIX 1
Profile: Asia—Continued

	Hong Kong	China	S.Korea	Indonesia	Thailand	Singapore	Malaysia	Philippines	Australia
Consumer Price Inflation									
1996	6.0%	8.3%	5.0%	7.9%	6.0%	1.7%	3.5%	8.4%	2.6%
Avg. Annual Inflation									
1989–1996	9.1%	11.3%	6.3%	8.8%	5.2%	2.5%	3.8%	10.8%	3.7%
Balance of Payments, Reserves, & Debt									
• Current account balance	−4.9	1.6	−8.3	−7.0	−13.6	15.1	−4.1	−2.0	−19.2
• Capital account balance	. . .	38.7	16.7	10.4	21.9	−6.9	1.5	5.3	13.7
• Overall balance	. . .	22.5	7.0	1.6	7.2	8.6	−3.2	1.2	0.4
• Level of reserves	57.2	80.3	32.8	14.9	36.9	68.7	24.7	7.8	15.0
• Foreign debt	18.9	118.1	74.6	107.8	56.8	5.5	34.4	39.4	
—as a % of GDP	13.5%	17.5%	16.4%	56.9%	34.9%	10.0%	42.6%	51.5%	
• Debt service	2.3	15.1	10.6	16.4	7.5	0.6	6.5	5.3	
• Debt service ratio	1.1%	9.9%	7.0%	30.9%	10.2%	0.6%	7.8%	16.4%	

APPENDIX 2
Profile: Latin America*

	Argentina	Brazil	Chile	Colombia	Mexico	Peru	Venezuela
Population (in millions)	34.8	159.0	14.2	35.8	91.1	23.5	21.8
GDP	278.0	580.0	59.0	70.0	305.0	55.0	65.0
Origins of GDP							
• Agriculture	5.9%	10.7%	6.9%	20.9%	7.6%	12.2%	5.5%
• Industry of which	30.7%	42.0%	30.2%	29.2%	32.6%	39.3%	40.8%
—Manufacturing	20.2%	28.3%	16.8%	20.3%	22.6%	23.5%	16.2%
• Services	63.4%	47.3%	62.9%	49.9%	59.8%	48.5%	53.7%
Components of GDP							
• Private consumption	81.8%	65.1%	62.0%	69.1%	67.3%	73.1%	62.9%
• Public consumption	. . .	15.2%	8.8%	13.4%	10.4%	8.2%	10.2%
• Investment	18.1%	22.1%	27.3%	27.5%	19.4%	23.8%	20.2%
• Exports less imports	0.2%	−1.9%	29.3%	−10.0%	2.9%	−5.1%	6.7%
Consumer Price Inflation 1996	0.2%	15.5%	7.4%	20.8%	34.4%	11.5%	99.9%
Avg. Annual Inflation 1989–96	173.3%	746.0%	14.8%	24.8%	21.0%	289.0%	54.5%
Balance of Payments, Reserves, and Debt							
• Current account balance	−2.4	−18.1	0.2	−4.1	−0.7	−4.2	2.3
• Capital account balance	0.2	29.7	1.2	5.0	−11.8	1.9	−2.7
• Overall balance	−2.2	13.0	1.1	0.4	−15.3	−1.1	−1.0
• Level of reserves	16.0	51.5	14.9	8.2	17.0	8.7	10.7
• Foreign debt	89.7	159.1	25.7	20.9	165.7	30.8	35.8
—as a % of GDP	33.1%	24.0%	43.3%	28.2%	69.9%	54.1%	49.0%
• Debt service	9.7	22.3	5.2	3.8	23.6	1.2	4.9
• Debt service ratio	34.7%	37.9%	25.7%	25.2%	24.2%	15.3%	21.7%

*All figures in $US billions, unless otherwise stated.

Moody's Investors Service

Moody's was founded by John Moody who introduced the first bond ratings as part of his analyses of railroad investments in 1909. His Aaa-through-C symbols used to rate individual securities of U.S. railroads then have since become a world standard in assigning ratings. Moody's ratings are based on public information and assigned without the request of issuers.

In the 1970s Moody's ratings were further extended to the commercial paper market and to bank deposits. The 1970s also saw major rating agencies including Moody's begin the practice of charging issuers as well as investors for rating services. The rationale for this change was, and is, that issuers should pay for the substantial value objective ratings provided in terms of gaining access to capital markets.

Standard & Poor's Corporation

S & P's history can be traced back to 1860. It was a major publisher of financial information and research services on U.S. as well as foreign corporate and municipal debt obligations. S & P was an independent, publicly-owned corporation until 1966, when all of S & P's common stock was acquired by McGraw-Hill Inc., a major publishing company. In matters of credit analysis and ratings, S & P operated independently of McGraw-Hill.

S & P had two operating groups—S & P's Ratings Group, which conducted all ratings activities, and S & P's Information Group, which provided investment, financial, and trading information, data, and analyses, primarily on equity securities. Each group operated independently. The Ratings Group had seven offices: New York, London, Tokyo, Paris, Stockholm, Melbourne, and San Francisco. The London and Tokyo offices were opened in the mid-1980s as the ratings business expanded internationally. Additional steps to pursue a global strategy were taken in 1990 with the acquisition of Australian Ratings Pte. Ltd. (Melbourne, Australia), Insurance Solvency International Ltd. (London, England), and 50 percent of Agence D'Evaluation Financiere (Paris, France), renamed S & P-ADEF. In 1990, S & P finally acquired the remaining 50 percent interest in Nordisk Ratings AB, a rating agency in Sweden.

S & P's Ratings Group is organized into six departments, each headed by an executive managing director who reported to the President of the S & P Ratings Group. Together, S & P's President and department heads form the Executive Committee, which was responsible for the conduct of group business. The six departments were: Corporate Finance, Financial Institutions/LOC, Structured Finance, Insurance Ratings Services, Municipal Finance, and International Finance. Each department was organized by specialization, according to industry or type of issue.

Fitch Investors Service, L.P.

Established in 1913, Fitch was a full service rating agency. It rated public and private fixed-income securities of industrial corporations, financial institutions, municipalities, utilities, and sovereign and subsovereign issuers, as well as to mortgage- and asset-backed securities.

Fitch led in rating structured finance, with a 65 percent market share in both residential and commercial mortgage-backed securities and a 55 percent market share in asset-backed securities.

In 1995, Fitch opened an office in London to better service its European investors and to initiate ratings of European structured and project financings, as well as financial and industrial issuers.

In the international arena, Fitch has trained analysts from ratings agencies in Israel, Japan, and Mexico and has provided advice to the governments of emerging markets.

Fitch is a limited partnership. Approximately 70 percent of the firm is owned by the Judy Van Kampen Trust, a family trust, with the balance owned by senior Fitch executives.

Thomson Bankwatch

Established more than twenty years ago, Thomson Bankwatch was the world's largest bank rating agency providing ratings, research, and analysis on over 1000 banks in more than eighty-five countries. Thomson had over sixty credit analysts who monitored financial institutions from offices in New York, London, Hong Kong, Sydney, Kuala Lumpur, and Cyprus.

Thomson is a division of Thomson Financial Services, a major provider of financial information products, such as *American Banker* newspapers and newsletters, research, and software, to the global investment and corporate communities. Part of The Thomson Corporation, a $7.7 billion company based in Toronto, Thomson Financial Services employs nearly 4500 people in forty offices worldwide.

Duff & Phelps Credit Rating Co.

Duff & Phelps Credit Rating Company provided ratings and research on corporate, structured, and sovereign financings, as well as insurance claims paying ability.

DCR had fourteen affiliates either in operation or awaiting final regulatory approval in North America, South America, Europe, Asia, and Africa in late 1997. It coordinated its international network from offices in Chicago, New York, London, and Hong Kong. As of December 1996, it had 240 employees.

Duff & Phelps Credit Rating Co. is a spinoff of Duff & Phelps Corp. It is the only company among the major international rating agencies to be publicly listed (in the New York Stock Exchange). As such, financial information is available on this company. For the six months ended June 30, 1997, revenues increased 24 percent to $31.3 million. Net income rose 17 percent to $5 million.

CASE 4

Nestle (Ghana) Ltd.[1]

It was January 1995 and Pierre Charles had just taken up his new position of Marketing Director of Nestle's subsidiary in Ghana in West Africa. A native of Switzerland, he had never been to Africa. In fact, apart from reports that periodically crossed his desk at headquarters in Vevey, Switzerland, he was not very familiar with developing country environments. His education and work experience had all been in Switzerland. Prior to taking up the appointment, Pierre took the opportunity to review conditions in Ghana and Nestle's operations in that country. It was important that he do well in the new job, since that would enhance his career prospects in the international division.

As he reviewed the available information, Pierre was struck by how different the Ghanaian environment was from what he was used to. Economic and political conditions were like nothing he had experienced. The infrastructure for marketing was totally different. For example, it was impossible to get reliable information on such crucial factors as market shares, market segments, distributor volumes, and other market data. Conducting market research was also a major task, primarily because of deficiencies in postal and telephone systems. Yet marketing managers were expected to design effective strategies and maintain profitable positions. It appeared to him that he had to quickly adjust to this environment in order to maximize his effectiveness. Fortunately, he spoke English, the official language of Ghana, so language problems would be minimized. In particular, he had to assess the situation and, make decisions about expanding operations, maintaining competitive position, and, above all, maintaining profit margins. He did not have a whole lot of time, because competitive pressures were mounting and the economic and political situation was changing rapidly. Underlying all of this was a need to prioritize possible courses of action.

Nestle (Ghana) Operations

Nestle (Ghana) was a joint venture between Nestle S.A. (a Swiss multinational corporation) and the state-owned National Investment Bank (NIB). The joint venture was established in 1971, with Nestle S.A. owning 51 percent.

In the mid-1970s, the then ruling military government of Ghana, the National Redemption Council (NRC), pursuing an indigenization strategy, acquired 55 percent of the shares. The government of current President Rawlings reverted to a 49 percent share in 1993, held by the National Investment Bank (NIB). These changes in ownership structure reflect the country's shift from a nationalistic philosophy involving state participation in leading enterprises to a reluctant push toward privatization. Nestle was very interested in acquiring the shares held by NIB.

The company had stated capital of 1 billion cedis (about U.S. $1.05 million) and 600 employees, 350 more than normal Nestle standards in its other subsidiaries for that level of capitalization. Annual sales were currently about 25 billion cedis (about U.S.$26.3 million). The company had four main product lines: canned and powdered milk, powdered cocoa drinks, coffee, and Maggi spice cubes. It had one factory in the industrial port city of Tema, some twenty miles from the capital Accra, and this was Nestle's only milk-processing plant in West Africa. The subsidiary had been set a growth target of 5 percent in Swiss francs but had actually averaged a rate of 12 percent in recent years compared to 5 percent for Nestle worldwide.

Nestle (Ghana) was headed by a Managing Director who oversaw a three-division structure—Marketing, Production, and Finance and Administration. The Managing Director and the Plant Engineer were typically appointed by Nestle S.A. that had a management contract to run Nestle (Ghana). These appointees had usually been white expatriates. As of January 1995, the Managing Director, Director of Marketing, Sales Manager, and Plant Engineer positions were filled with white expatriates. The remaining positions were mostly filled by Ghanaians. The company had a six-member Board of Directors, four appointed by Nestle's S.A. and two appointed by the NIB. Nestle (Ghana)'s operating results for 1992–93 are shown in Table 1.

The Republic of Ghana

POLITICAL HISTORY The Republic of Ghana lay on the western coast of Africa. It had an area of 92,000 square

TABLE 1
Nestle Operating Results (billions of cedis)

	1993	1992
Sales	19.3	14.7
Operating Profit	2.7	1.9
Net Profit	2.5	1.8
Fixed Costs	4.9	3.4
Variable Costs	11.6	8.4
Total Assets	11.8	9.9
Total Equity	5.7	4.2
Liabilities (short-term)	4.0	2.2
Liabilities (medium-term)	1.8	1.7
Dividends	1.7	1.5

1993: U.S.$1 = 699.30 cedis
1992: U.S.$1 = 437.09 cedis

miles and had an estimated population of 15.5 million in 1991. The country had experienced a chequered political history since independence was gained from the British in 1957. Military regimes had run the country for twenty-one of the years since independence. The current civilian government of President Rawlings, which won the latest elections in 1992, was an offshoot of a military regime, the Provisional National Defence Council (PNDC), that overthrew the previous civilian democratic government of the People's National Party in 1981. The rule of then Flight-Lieutenant Rawlings' PNDC was characterized by suppression of human rights, including imprisonment and execution of alleged opponents. The period was also marked by many attempts to overthrow the PNDC regime. Political and ethnic tensions increased and continue currently. Even though Rawlings won the 1992 presidential election with 58 percent of the vote, a result certified by international observers despite incidents of irregularities. Other political parties refused to accept the results and boycotted the parliamentary elections. This resulted in a situation in which Rawlings and his allies won 199 out of 200 seats in the Parliament, with the remaining seat going to a political independent. Independent media consistently attacked government policies and personalities, while the state-owned media consistently supported them. Allegations of corruption and ethnic bias had been leveled against the government. Of particular concern were the upcoming 1996 presidential and parliamentary elections. The government and opposition parties had serious disagreements over revision of the voters' register and issuance of identity cards, with the latter threatening violence if the elections were not fair.

ECONOMY Ghana was in the lower tier of developing countries and classified as a Least Developed Country (LDC) by international development agencies because its per capita annual income was U.S.$400. Quite prosperous at independence, the country had declined precipitously as a result of economic mismanagement, political instability, brain drain, and corruption. The World Bank and other external donors were currently funding an Economic Recovery Program (ERP) that appeared to be pulling the economy out of the doldrums. Gross National Product (GNP) was about $7 billion or $400 per capita and growing at around 1.2 percent per annum in real terms. Gross Domestic Product was growing at about 3.2 percent in real terms. Consumer prices increased by an average of 10 percent in 1992 and 16 percent in 1993. Inflation had averaged 40 percent per annum since 1985.

Agriculture contributed about 49 percent of GDP and was growing at an annual average of 1.2 percent. Forty-nine percent of the labor force was employed in this sector. Industry (including mining, manufacturing, construction, and power) contributed 17 percent of GDP and employed 13 percent of the labor force. Industrial GDP had been growing at an annual average of 3.7 percent in recent times. While mining had shown the greatest growth (17.7 percent) in the industrial sector, manufacturing remained the largest component of the sector. It contributed 10 percent of national GDP, growing at a rate of 4.1 percent per annum, and employed 11 percent of the labor force.

Ghana had merchandise trade and balance of payments deficits in the five years prior to 1995. Principal exports were cocoa, gold, and timber, growing at 5 percent per annum. Major imports were machinery, transport equipment, basic manufactures, and petroleum. External debt was about $4.3 billion, and debt-service was equal to 30 percent of exports of goods and services.

Discussions with other Nestle managers familiar with Ghana brought out the following additional information:

- Inflation was higher than official estimates.
- Foreign exchange availability was low.
- Cedi would continue to depreciate.
- A high level of currency instability
- Very little commitment to exports
- No price controls
- Interest rates were currently high (around 30 percent) but were expected to come down to 25 percent.
- Government regulations were not very burdensome. Sales taxes, for example, had declined from 35 percent to 15 percent. Potential problems were expected though from current government attempts to implement a value-added tax (VAT).

- Money supply was expected to rise dramatically as the government launched its campaign for the 1996 election.

- Nestle had few labor problems, even though there might be general labor unrest.

Exhibit 1 provides selected statistics and information on Ghana.

The Cocoa Beverage Market

The size of Ghana's cocoa beverage market was estimated at 4,500 tons and growing slowly. It was forecast to grow at approximately 5 percent per annum through 1997. Cocoa beverages were primarily a breakfast drink. Information on market segments relating to beverage consumption was unavailable or was highly proprietary.

However, the market could be divided into three categories, based on the product.

1. The Premium Segment: Brands in this category included malt in addition to the basic cocoa powder, sugar, and milk. Leading brands were Milo, Bournvita, and Ovaltine.

2. Mass Market: Brands in this category did not contain malt, thus reducing their costs considerably. Leading brands were Chocolim, Drinking Chocolate, Richoco, and Golden Tree.

3. Institutional Market: Products aimed at this segment contained basic unsweetened cocoa powder supplied to schools, hospitals, the armed forces, etc.

NESTLE'S (GHANA) PRODUCTS Nestle's powdered cocoa drinks consisted of Milo and Chocolim. Milo came in a 450-gram tin size with twenty-four tins to a carton. Tin for making the containers was supplied by headquarters and was rapidly becoming a major cost component in the production process. Consideration was being given to the introduction of a 200-gram soft plastic pack. Chocolim was sold in a 500-gram soft plastic pack with forty packs to a carton. The two products were quite similar, with a cocoa base, added milk, and presweetened. Chocolim did not contain malt, and this made it cheaper. Sixty percent of the company's powdered beverage sales came from Milo and 40 percent from Chocolim. Milo was introduced into Ghana from another Nestle subsidiary. It was formulated by an Australian, Thomas Mayne, about sixty years ago and was extremely popular in Africa and Southeast Asia. Annual worldwide sales are 90,000 tons worth about $430m from the thirty countries where it is marketed. Chocolim was locally developed in 1981–82.

Milo was the premier brand and was targeted to the high end of the market, while Chocolim was aimed at rural areas and low-end urban segments. In terms of age, Milo was targeted toward 10–18 year olds, but with a focus on mothers as decision makers. The thrust in Nestle's strategy was to ensure high awareness of its brands and widespread distribution.

COMPETITION Finding information on competitors' activities was one of the most difficult aspects of designing marketing strategy in Ghana. Industry and brand-level data were hard to come by. Nestle managers estimated their share of the cocoa beverage market at 80 percent, based on research by a firm which tracked sales in a sample of retailers, in addition to tracking consumption. However, other observers believed Nestle's share was closer to 55 percent. Major competitors for Nestle were Bournvita and Richoco, manufactured by Cadbury (Ghana) with an estimated 20 percent–40 percent market share, and imported Ovaltine.

Originally known as Cadbury and Fry (England), Cadbury entered Ghana in 1910 to source cocoa beans for its own chocolate-making plants in England. Processing of cocoa beans started in 1963, with a cocoa-based drink introduced soon after. Cadbury (Ghana) was 100 percent owned by Cadbury Schweppes (U.K.) and had 120 employees. Of estimated 1994 sales of 4 billion cedis, 70 percent was derived from cocoa beverages and the remainder from sugar confectioneries (e.g., Hacks and Trebor) and Kwench, a fruit-flavored noncarbonated drink. Cocoa beverage capacity of Cadbury averaged 2000 tons per annum, with profit margins of about 35 percent. In 1990, Cadbury started a major diversification away from cocoa beverages and into sugar confectioneries. The company hoped to have the latter contributing 51 percent of sales by 1997. Introduction of Richoco in 1990 to exploit a gap in the lower end of the market and good relations with distributors reflected Cadbury's strong marketing skills. For example, Cadbury went to a 1 kg package for Richoco, which enabled retailers to repackage, thus increasing the latter's margins by 40 percent.

Another competitor, though on a much smaller scale, was the state-owned Cocoa Processing Company (CPC), which made Golden Tree Vitaco Instant Drinking Chocolate. CPC was strongest in the institutional market where it had a cost advantage (estimated 23 percent lower) because it supplied the basic cocoa powder to other firms. The company also made Golden Tree Chocolates, which had won numerous awards in European and Japanese competitions.

An additional category of competition came from imports, the most prominent of which was Ovaltine, marketed by NABB Brothers, a leading distributor of supermarket products. Volume of imports was low, about 2 percent of the market, and there were no statistics on brand volumes. It was believed that these imports were either smuggled or evaded taxes and could, therefore, be sold at lower prices than domestically produced brands. The major brands, their composition, packaging, and

EXHIBIT 1
Selected Information on Ghana

1. **Average Exchange Rate** (cedis per U.S.$)

1990	326.33
1991	367.83
1992	437.09
1993	699.30
1994	950.00

2. **Money Supply** ('000 million cedis at 31 December)

1990	271.64
1991	345.49
1992	525.93
1993	664.67

Average annual growth, 1980–91: 43%

3. **Cost of Living** (Consumer Price Index, Base: 1980 = 100)

	1990	1991	1992
Food	2,711	2,955	3,261
Clothing and footwear	4,371	5,052	5,488
Rent, fuel, and light	5,802	8,373	10,097
All items (incl. others)	3,575	4,219	4,644

4. Communications Media

	1989	1990	1991
Radios ('000s)	n.a.	4,000	4,150
TVs ('000s)	211	225	235
Telephones ('000s)	83	84	85

Newspapers	Circulation
Daily:	
Daily Graphic	100,000
Ghanaian Times	40,000
Pioneer	100,000
Other major:	
Chronicle	60,000
Mirror	90,000
Spectator	165,000
Standard	50,000

5. **Income Distribution** (% Share of Income)

Lowest 20%	2nd Quintile	3rd Quintile
7.0	11.3	15.8
4th Quintile	Highest 20%	Highest 10%
21.8	44.1	29.0

6. **Education**

Primary School	Secondary School	Higher Education
Student population		
1.95m (1990)	805,000 (1990)	16,350 (1981)

Government expenditure 65 billion cedis (1990) i.e., 26% of total spending

7. **Population**

	1970–75	1980–85	1989–94
Urban % of population	30.1	32.3	35.8
Urban population growth rate	2.9	4.3	4.0

Access to safe water (% of population)

Total	35	49.2	55.7
Urban	86	72	93
Rural	14	39	39

Age Profile of Population:

0–14	=	45%
15–29	=	26.4%
30–44	=	14.6%
45–59	=	8.1%
60–74	=	4.1%
75 plus	=	1.8%

Annual growth rate of population estimated at 31% for 1990–95 and 3.04% for 1995–2000

Sources: International Monetary Fund's International Financial Statistics and World Bank Tables (1995).

TABLE 2
Leading Brands and Prices
Selected Powdered Cocoa Beverages at a Leading Supermarket in Accra (January 9, 1995)

Company	Brand	Composition	Pack Size	Price (cedis)
Nestle	Milo	Malt extract, milk, sugar, cocoa powder, ethyl vanillin	200g soft pack	850
			450g can	2,400
Nestle	Chocolim	Cocoa powder, milk, sugar, vegetable fat, mineral salts, vitamins	500g soft pack	1,300
Cadbury	Bournvita	Malt extract, sugar, glucose syrup, Fat reduced cocoa, dried skimmed milk, dried egg	450g plastic jar	2,200
	Drinking Chocolate	Sugar, skimmed milk powder, cocoa flavorings	500g soft pack	1,050
	Richoco	Cocoa, sugar, milk, mineral salts	1kg soft pack	2,800
Cocoa Processing Company (CPC)	Golden Tree Vitaco Instant Drinking Chocolate	Cocoa powder, sugar, skimmed milk powder, lecithin, vanillin	350g soft pack	980
NABB Brothers	Ovaltine (Imported)	Barley and Malt extract, skimmed milk powder, whey powder, vegetable fat, sugar, sodium bicarbonate, potassium bicarbonate	200g can	2,700
			400g can	4,250
			1200g can	11,500
Unknown (Imported from France)	Petit de Jeuner		400g box	2,800
Unknown (Imported from France)	Instantane		400g plastic jar	2,800

prices are shown in Table 2. Milo was the leader in the premium category, while Golden Tree was strongest in the institutional market. Richoco was believed to lead Chocolim by about 5–10 percent market share in the mass market. Table 3 indicates available government statistics on imports. Table 4 shows domestic production of cocoa powder.

DISTRIBUTION STRUCTURE "Ghana is fast becoming a nation of shopkeepers" was a popular joke in the country, as economic liberalization had given the retail industry a very strong boost in urban areas. Most of the retail outlets were small and specialized in merchandise lines such as appliances, food and beverages, and clothing. Competition was intense; however, this had not shown up in price wars at the general retail level. Most outlets were stand-alone, and there were very few retail chains. Stores were usually of the "mom and pop" variety found in the Western world. Additional retailing institutions included itinerant street hawkers, wooden kiosks, and "container" stores made from metal shipping containers. With no zoning laws, all the retailing forms were found in business districts as well as in residential neighborhoods, making location extremely important. Nestle had 100 regular distributors nationwide and a few other irregulars. Warehouses in Accra (the capital) and Tamale (in the northern part of the country) supplied these distributors. Some of the large distributors, such as supermarkets and department stores, were supplied directly from the

TABLE 3
Imports of Cocoa Powder*

Period	Imports (CIF value in cedis)	Cedi/kg
January–May 1991	27,971,505	837.75
January–December 1992	66,379,420	1159.24
January–September 1993	15,559,184	1098.73
January–May 1994	28,920,619	3748.62

*Cocoa powder, containing added sugar or other sweetening matter

TABLE 4
Local Production of Cocoa Powder

Year	Production (kilograms)
1986	578,000
1987	665,000
1988	618,000
1989	557,000
1990	830,000
1991	1,078,000
1992	462,000
1993*	467,500

*provisional

plant at Tema. The biggest distributor was Unilever's G.B. Ollivant subsidiary. Nestle also operated its own sales outlets in three of the biggest cities (Kumasi, Takoradi, and Tamale) outside of the capital, Accra. Margins to distributors were nominally 7.5 percent, but in reality they made only 2–3 percent because of serious price undercutting among them to gain sales. Some distributors were also granted a 21-day interest-free credit on supplied goods. The large distributors typically ordered in quantities of 15–20 million cedis (about U.S.\$16,000–21,000) while the smaller ones ordered around 5 million cedis (about U.S.\$5,500). While officially Nestle did not place any restriction on its distributors carrying competing lines, unofficially, it frowned on the practice.

PROMOTION Promotion in Ghanaian industries had become quite intense as the economy was liberalized and consumer goods flooded the market. Most of the promotional wars took the form of contests and advertising in all its forms. What was not so clear were the effects of such promotions. Some argued that different companies' promotions canceled each other out, and consumers often postponed their purchases until there was a sales promotion in effect. Others argued that if a company's promotion was unique enough, it would gain an edge. The problem with the latter view was that many of these promotions were easily imitated.

For Milo, Nestle used a combination of media advertising and sales promotions targeted at the youth. In particular, sports-based promotion was emphasized. The company sponsored highly popular youth soccer leagues for children ages 10–18 years and for schools and colleges. It also sponsored tennis tournaments and a marathon race for all age groups. Another widely used sales promotion technique was wet sampling (free drinks) at the Ministry of Education Sports Department's events for school children. Total expenditure for promotion was about 150 million cedis (about U.S.\$150,800) and was estimated to grow by 10–15 percent per annum. Sixty percent of the budget went for non-media promotion, while 40 percent covered media expenditures. This was the reverse of other Nestle products. Media advertising promoted the themes of good health, growing up, and success as closely related and linked to drinking Milo. Another theme was that Milo contributed to success in sports, and success in sports contributed to success in life. As a policy, Nestle did not use sports personalities because they switched product endorsements frequently and often had short popularity spans. Rather, Nestle emphasized the use of ordinary people in its advertisements. This was despite the national and international popularity of Ghanaian stars like Azumah Nelson (world featherweight boxing champion), Abedi Pele (star midfielder in the French soccer league), and Tony Yeboah (star striker in the English soccer league). Advertising development was performed by Media Magique and Market Research Systems (MMRS) and the Advertising Design Agency (ADA), which focused on Milo.

Mass promotion in Ghana was particularly difficult, given low levels of TV and radio ownership as well as low circulation of print media. This meant that it was viable primarily in the urban areas, but the majority of people lived in rural areas. Companies had to use the more expensive sponsorship approach in the latter areas. The rural areas were also places where ethnic differences, particularly language, were most pronounced. This required the use of various languages and dialects in local sponsorship programs and activities.

PRICING Nestle's brands were sold at premiums of 5–10 percent over competitors because of its perceived better quality. With declining real incomes, products were becoming less affordable. There was also increasing price pressure from imports that were flooding the market as a result of import liberalization. Prices of the major brands in the country are shown in Table 2. Ghana had a long history of government-controlled prices for consumer goods, and it was only since the late 1980s that companies had been really free to set their own prices. As a result, people were quite sensitive to price changes and were said to have long-term negative perceptions of companies that were perceived to engage in price gouging. Such incidents also attracted negative press coverage. On the other hand, though, rapid increases in inflation and the fast falling cedi were exerting upward pressure on costs of production and reducing profit margins. Distributors, therefore, raised their prices frequently in an attempt to keep up with inflation. This often had unintended consequences on the pricing strategy of manufacturers who often had to reduce their margins to keep their products affordable.

Conclusion

As Pierre pondered all this information, he realized the complexity of the task ahead of him and wondered what his focus should be. There was increasing competition in the market; the external economic and political environment was increasingly hostile and risky, and yet there was clearly insufficient information to make decisions in the manner to which he was accustomed. A major concern was cocoa powder. Import prices were under pressure from a depreciating currency (see Table 3), and local production trends had been anything but consistent (Table 4). Pierre was used to making decisions on marketing data, the likes of which was unavailable in Ghana. While he could argue that nothing should be done until a marketing information system was put in place, reality indicated that some responses had to be made soon in order to compete effectively and maintain profitability. In the long-term, issues relating to new-product introductions, further market penetration, market data, diversification, and contingency planning would have to be addressed. Foremost in his mind was the sequence of actions to pursue. Could he put everything on hold while he launched a comprehensive marketing research effort to provide appropriate information? What if, in the meantime, Nestle's strong position was adversely affected by competition and the political/economic environment?

Questions

1. From the developed-developing country contrasts in Chapter 3, prepare a list of adjustments that Pierre Charles must make as he makes the transition from Switzerland and Swiss ways of doing things to the ways things are done in Ghana. What would be his greatest challenges?

2. Prepare an analysis of strengths, weaknesses, opportunities, and threats facing Nestle. What does it tell us?

3. Assess the cocoa products market for Nestle. What should Nestle do?

Note

1. By Franklyn A. Manu and Ven Sriram, Morgan State University. This case appeared in *Case Research Journal* (Spring 1999): 69–83. Reproduced with permission.

CASE 5

The Evolution of an Irish Multinational: Kerry Group plc[1]

*W*hat future have they on the land?" asked a leading IFA (Irish Farming Association) officer. "Will they be able to follow their fathers and grandfathers into farming?" Nobody in the attendance of well over 800 in the ballroom of Ballygarry House Hotel said "yea" or "nay" but, by their stony silence, they answered the question in their own way.

These (the small farmers of Kerry) are our people. We feel for them. They started Kerry Group, and they'll be there to see the success of the Kerry Group as it goes through, and we'll make sure of that.

—Dick O'Sullivan, head of Kerry Group's Agriculture Division)

Gazing out his window, Kerry Group Managing Director Denis Brosnan could see, past the busy streets of the provincial town of Tralee, the expanse of the Dingle Peninsula creeping out into the Atlantic Ocean. With the sun shining intermittently amid billowing clouds blowing in from the ocean, the mottled colors of the changing landscape made for a powerful and beautiful sight. But Brosnan hadn't time to be long distracted by the view, as he turned again to reviewing his notes for the first of two special general meetings of the Kerry co-op scheduled for that afternoon. As the prime architect of the crucial proposal to be voted on that day, Brosnan wanted to be certain that his case was clear and convincing.

The most controversial item on the agenda was a vote on a rule change that would allow the Co-op, an association of local County Kerry farmers then functioning as essentially a holding company, to reduce its ownership stake in Kerry Group to below 51 percent. To achieve this, a vote of 75 percent in favor of the rule change, at two consecutive meetings scheduled two weeks apart, was required. This afternoon's meeting promised to be the biggest meeting in the co-op's history, with over 2,000 members expected to pack the conference center at the Brandon Hotel. Although the proposal was expected to pass, the "no" forces had mounted an intensive, and emotional, door-to-door and telephone lobbying effort in an attempt to gain the necessary 25 percent "no" vote necessary to derail the proposal. As he prepared his opening remarks, Brosnan wondered if their ef-

forts would have any effect. Despite his confidence, he knew that when it came to Irish farming politics, there was never any such thing as a "sure thing."

Introduction

From its beginnings as a collection of small dairy cooperative societies in rural County Kerry, Ireland, in 1974, Kerry Group plc had, by 1996, grown to the status of a full-fledged multinational corporation with manufacturing operations and markets throughout the world. As a major player in the international specialty-food ingredients business (particularly in North America) and with a growing presence in consumer foods in European markets, it was well on its way to becoming a substantial global business.

Over the course of twenty-five years, sales revenue had grown to £1.2 billion (All financial amounts are stated in Irish punts [£]. In 1996, the Irish £ was valued at approximately $1.60.) and after-tax profits to £49 million. (Table 1 provides an eleven-year summary of financial results). Over 60 percent of sales revenue and 69 percent of operating profit were now sourced outside of Ireland. (Table 2 provides geographical segment data.) Most of this growth was a result of a continuous program of strategic acquisitions in North America and Europe. The Kerry Group was led by an experienced management team, most of whom had been with Kerry since its inception (as a cooperative society) in 1974. Indeed, one element often cited by the local Kerry community for the success of the group was the leadership and vision of its managing director, Denis Brosnan. In the public houses of Kerry, Brosnan was widely reputed, only partly in jest, to have the "Midas Touch." Certainly, in Kerry's first twenty-two years, serious blunders appeared to have been few. Meanwhile, its shareholders, primarily "land rich but cash poor" small farmers based in rural County Kerry, had profited over the years as the group's share price rose from .35p in 1986 to over £6.00

Background and History

THE FORMATION OF THE KERRY CO-OP The Kerry Group began business as the Kerry Co-operative Creameries (or,

TABLE 1
Eleven-Year Summary of P&L Statements

IR£1,000	1986	1987	1988	1989	1990	1991	1992	1993	1994	1995	1996
Turnover	265,242	291,289	396,721	559,551	584,099	754,931	826,737	879,975	882,697	1,199,093	1,233,253
Operating profit	11,157	11,397	17,906	31,397	31,963	42,084	46,403	50,196	55,549	85,739	90,594
Loss (Profit) on disposal of assets	(14)	65	(97)		(112)	(30)	243	10	(359)	1,685	
Interest payable and similar charges	4,842	3,223	4,987	12,229	10,854	14,753	13,889	10,991	11,578	29,726	27,876
Profit before taxation	6,329	8,109	13,016	19,168	21,221	27,361	32,271	39,195	44,330	54,328	62,718
Taxation	37	216	322	467	666	1,645	3,901	5,959	7,480	5,055	7,103
Profit after taxation	6,292	7,893	12,694	18,701	20,555	25,716	28,370	33,236	36,850	49,273	55,615
Minority interest	451	480	548	428	(305)	205	156	185			
Profit to ordinary shareholders	5,841	7,413	12,146	18,273	20,860	25,511	28,214	33,051	36,850	49,273	55,615
Dividend	819	1,152	1,497	2,281	2,746	3,355	3,527	4,057	4,608	5,456	6,268
Retained profit	5,022	6,261	10,649	15,992	18,114	22,156	24,687	28,994	32,242	43,817	49,347
Earnings per share (after goodwill)	6.01p	6.63p	9.40p	11.38p	12.60p	14.50p	15.80p	18.50p	20.50p	23.30p	26.90p
End-of-year exchange rate to US$	1.3995	1.6755	1.5075	1.5563	$1.7794	$1.7513	$1.6234	$1.4085	$1.5456	$1.6000	$1.6584

TABLE 2
Geographical Segment Data, 1994–95

Geographical Market of Origin	1994 Turnover IR£1,000	1994 Op Profit IR£1,000	1995 Turnover IR£1,000	1995 Op Profit IR£1,000
Ireland	428,153	24,447	447,212	26,353
Rest of Europe	178,474	5,186	313,522	20,554
North America	190,423	25,649	363,361	38,347
	797,050	**55,282**	**1,124,095**	**85,254**
Discontinued operations	85,647	267	74,998	485
Total	**882,697**	**55,549**	**1,199,093**	**85,739**

Geographical Market by Destination	1994 Turnover IR£1,000		1995 Turnover IR£1,000	
Ireland	247,959		255,918	
Rest of Europe	275,385		437,441	
North America	262,834		424,566	
Rest of world	10,872		6,170	
	797,050		**1,124,095**	
Discontinued operations	85,647		74,998	
Total	**882,697**		**1,199,093**	

Source: 1995 Kerry Group Annual Report

more affectionately, the Kerry Co-op). It was formed in January 1974 by the amalgamation of a number of small independent cooperative societies and milk suppliers in County Kerry, Ireland, and the purchase of the assets of the state run Dairy Disposal Board. The dairy farmer/milk suppliers of North Kerry, who now took an ownership stake in the new, larger cooperative, had owned these small cooperatives. Similarly, independent farmers from South Kerry who had supplied milk to the Dairy Disposal Board also "bought into" the new co-op. It had taken a small group of managers, all in their late 20s, about eighteen months (since mid-1972) to get the enterprise off the ground. During that time the small group, led by Denis Brosnan and his "twelve apostles," thirteen in all, worked together in cramped quarters in the parking lot of a milk processing plant owned by North Kerry Milk Products, Ltd.

> We started from a caravan [similar to a construction trailer or a camper] outside Listowel in 1972. We rented that for twenty pounds a week. Hugh Friel, myself and others, thirteen in all, we lived in that cramped space for about eighteen months.

Central to the formation of the Kerry Co-op was its acquisition of an 83 percent stake in North Kerry Milk Products Limited and its aforementioned milk processing plant, located in the 20-acre "Canon's Field" just outside of Listowel. The cost of this purchase was £1.5 million, an amount raised by the farmers of Kerry who reached into their own pockets to fund the purchase. This was accomplished through the farmer-suppliers contributing a set amount per gallon of milk supplied to the co-op over a six-year period, in return for which they received shares in the co-op (up to a maximum of 1,000 shares). Membership was open to all milk suppliers. Democratic control of the co-op was ensured by entitling all shareholders to vote (on the basis of one member, one vote) for various governing committees and, ultimately, for the Board of Directors. Fully nine thousand dairy farmers in Kerry answered the call and became co-owners of the Kerry Co-op by the time it opened its doors in January 1974. The management of the co-op quickly set about consolidating and rationalizing the various operations involved with the collection, processing, and distribution of milk, butter, and other dairy products, as well as the production of casein (a protein powder extracted from milk) for the export market.

Despite its modest beginnings, the creation of the Kerry Co-op was greeted with great anticipation in County Kerry, for the times demanded larger, more efficient, dairy organizations. Ireland's entry into the EEC in 1973 provided not only large and rich markets for Irish dairy products, but also put pressure on the national government to privatize its state-owned holdings (e.g., the quasi-government Dairy Disposal Board). Similarly, the farmers in the county, who for generations were wed to their own small, independent, but relatively inefficient cooperatives and creameries, had by now become sufficiently frustrated to see the wisdom of banding together into large and more scale-efficient cooperative ventures that could better compete with the large milk producers in the rest of the EEC. With milk prices in the EEC high and demand rising, farmers hoped that at long last their historically depressed farm incomes would rise.

THE EARLY YEARS OF THE KERRY CO-OP A cooperative can be defined as "an enterprise that is collectively owned and operated for mutual benefit." As such, the Kerry Co-op was owned by, and for the benefit of, the small farmer/milk suppliers of Kerry. This, however, did not prevent Kerry Co-op's management group from engaging in a vigorous program of expansion almost from the very beginning. This growth reflected both continuous internal expansion and a series of strategic acquisitions.

Between 1974 and 1982, the Kerry Co-op acquired various milk businesses throughout the west of Ireland, building in the process an extensive distribution system in that area. Indeed, these were halcyon days for the dairy business. Milk yields were increasing, prices were high, and EEC milk quota schemes were still in the future. With the exception of a 33 percent stake in a joint venture to manufacture packaging material with Union Camp in 1980 (an ill-fitting venture from which they soon exited), Kerry "stuck to its knitting" and remained largely anchored in its traditional dairy businesses of consumer milk, butter, and cheese and in the export market for casein. This was entirely consistent with the activities of other milk producers throughout Ireland, and Europe, at the time, except that Kerry Co-op was consistently (but not spectacularly) profitable. (See Table 3 for Kerry Co-op P&L Statements.) In 1980, however, an event occurred that clearly exposed Kerry's reliance on the vagaries of the dairy business.

THE BRUCELLOSIS "WAKE-UP CALL" AND DIVERSIFICATION In 1980, the Irish government decided to introduce a program for the eradication of brucellosis, a disease carried in cows. Given County Kerry's remote location at the extreme southwest of the country, it was decided that Kerry would serve as the pilot area in which to begin implementation of the scheme. Unfortunately, enforcement of the eradication scheme led to a substantial decline in the number of cows in the county (as herds were thinned to eliminate animals exposed to the virus). By most accounts, the productive capacity of the farmer-suppliers of the Kerry Co-op was reduced by some 20 percent. Additionally, the weather was particularly bad, even by Irish standards, further reducing milk production. Finally, major construction projects around Shannon (by the

TABLE 3
Summary of Kerry Co-operative Creameries P&L's, 1981–86

IR£1,000	1981	1982	1983	1984	1985
Turnover					
Dairy products	58,516	72,263	80,646	92,462	115,641
Foods	13,985	30,179	43,848	51,540	61,311
Agricultural trading	23,157	26,817	33,585	36,468	34,287
Total	**95,658**	**129,259**	**158,079**	**180,470**	**211,239**
Trading profit before int. & dep.	**6,417**	**9,940**	**9,948**	**11,421**	**12,330**
Interest (Net)	1,409	2,479	1,953	2,778	3,016
Depreciation (Net)	2,776	3,248	3,688	3,887	4,201
Profit before taxation	**2,232**	**4,213**	**4,307**	**4,756**	**5,113**
Taxation	0	0	0	0	0
Profit after taxation	**2,232**	**4,213**	**4,307**	**4,756**	**5,113**
Minority interest (Erie Cassein)	376	591	533	457	586
Profit attributable to Kerry Co-op	1,856	3,622	3,774	4,299	4,527
Share interest (dividends)	363	365	360	358	710
Retained profit	1,493	3,257	3,414	3,941	3,817

international airport) provided construction jobs to quite a number of smaller, more marginal dairy farmers who decided that this was an ideal time to leave the farm. As Brosnan describes it, this "war on three fronts" occurred at a particularly bad time, since the co-op's £15 million investment in new processing capacity was just coming on line. But, rather than having 50 percent more milk to process, the co-op had 20 percent less! As the firm suffered under the weight of this substantial idle capacity, profits for 1980 and 1981 declined from prior years.

It was clear to the management and, importantly, to the directors of the cooperative, that if the cooperative were to survive and thrive, it would need to reduce its reliance on dairy products by diversifying into more "value-added" activities, and away from milk processing. In the eyes of some observers, this was a "radical move" that "redirected the group beyond the geography and tradition of County Kerry." Says Brosnan, "I clearly remember stating categorically in a meeting of the Board of Directors that we will never again be dependent on manufacturing milk!" In 1982, the co-op made a major foray outside of the milk sector with the purchase of a pig-meat processing plant in Tralee (Denny's) and a meat processing plant (Duffy's) in County Carlow. It followed this up with the purchase of two additional beef-processing plants in March 1986. These plants were in serious financial trouble; one, in fact, had already been closed. Kerry Co-op reopened it only after extensive renovations.

These actions reflected the execution of Kerry's plan for diversifying its business, a strategy company official Frank Hayes called its "equation for growth."

The Board of Kerry Group Co-operative and its management realized that the future lay with strong diversified businesses capable of competing in a world market. In terms of the food sector, Kerry viewed this as a momentum toward the development of large international companies, financially strong, with a significant share of any market in which they choose to compete. A five-year corporate plan was defined and agreed to by the Board, research and development became a priority, overseas offices were opened, and the quiet search for suitable acquisitions began. Kerry was determined to become a large-scale food business and an appropriate management structure was put in place to cater for this strategy. Kerry's strategy was based on an equation for growth which read: Strategy × Capability × Capital = Sustained Profitable Growth. The organization was and indeed remains convinced that where one of the elements in this equation is missing, the result at best is zero profitable growth.

By 1986, this strategy appeared to be working, and Kerry Co-op had become one of Ireland's more successful food-processing businesses. Yet it was clear that to attain (or even to maintain) such a position, more extensive growth would be required. However, the problem was that the co-op had only two of the three required components to accelerate its growth. Certainly, it had the people, and it had the technology, but it was severely constrained by its organizational structure in its access to capital. Up to that point, the funding for acquisitions had come from both internally generated funds and debt, as well as from the farmer-shareholders of the cooperative who had answered the call to provide (a modest amount of) additional funds on several occasions. But banks were still cautious in their loans to agricultural cooperatives (where tradition had it that "farmers always paid themselves first"), and the farmer-shareholders of the cooperative were nervous about having so much of their funds invested in an illiquid investment (shares in the co-op did not trade, and there was no easy way to ascertain the value of a share; additionally, when members decided to "cash out" their co-op shares, they were typically paid out on the basis of £1 per share, with no capital appreciation). To continue on their path of strategic acquisitions, therefore, Kerry Co-op would have to tap other sources of equity capital. This would require the involvement of "outside" shareholders in the ownership and affairs of the Kerry Co-op.

A Defining Moment—The Formation of the Kerry Group

In February 1986, the Kerry Co-op took a novel and innovative step, one never before done by a cooperative organization in Ireland. It began the process of converting its enterprise into a public limited company (a plc, the equivalent of a publicly owned corporation). This conversion was accomplished in three distinct steps. First, Kerry Group (which was formed as a subsidiary of the Kerry Co-op) acquired all of the assets and property of the former Kerry Co-op in return for consideration of "B" ordinary shares in Kerry Group plc. The Kerry Co-op thus became the equivalent of an investment holding company, with no direct operational connection to the Kerry Group. It also, at this point, owned 100 percent of the share capital of Kerry Group plc. A second placing of "A" ordinary shares was accomplished by offering additional shares (totaling 10,350,000 shares) to existing shareholders in the Kerry Co-op, as well as milk suppliers and employees of the Kerry Co-op, at 35p per share. Finally, the Kerry Group choreographed an additional offering of 8,000,000 "A" ordinary shares to institutions and the general public (at 52p per share). At the end of this recapitalization scheme in July 1986, the ownership structure of the Kerry Group was 83 percent owned by the Kerry Co-op (which still existed as essentially a "holding company") and 17 percent owned by individuals and institutions (although predominantly farmer/shareholders, suppliers, and employees of the

Kerry Co-op). The stock was also listed for trading on the Dublin and London Stock Exchanges.

Although this step was overwhelmingly supported by the majority of the co-op's farmer/shareholders, it was not completely without opposition. Some farmers felt that "going public" was essentially selling out on fundamental cooperative principles. These objections, however, were overridden by (1) the necessity of the firm to have access to additional capital to maintain its growth program, (2) the fact that the shares of the firm would now have a market value and some liquidity so that farmers could begin to realize some of the appreciation in their investment and importantly, (3) the creation of a complex governance structure that provided the cooperative and its shareholders with a means to continue to exercise control over the activities of the enterprise. The articles of association for the creation of the publicly traded Kerry Group stipulated that no less than 52 percent of the shares of the enterprise were to be held by the Kerry Co-op, and that this required percentage of ownership could not be changed without a vote of at least 75 percent of the shareholders of the co-op. With this "fail-safe" provision, the farmers of Kerry could maintain control over the activities and future strategies of the Kerry Group and be protected from the rule of Dublin-based institutional investors.

The Creation of a Multinational Corporation—1986–1996

From a sales turnover of £265 million in 1986, the Kerry Group grew at an annual rate of approximately 20 percent over the next decade, to a turnover of £1.2 billion in 1996. This growth was the result of the Group's strategy of external expansion in a number of targeted business segments in the food-ingredients and consumer-foods businesses. The acquisition program is detailed in the following explanations by major business line.

KERRY INGREDIENTS The largest and most important business group in the Kerry Group's portfolio, accounting for £707 million, or 57 percent of group sales in 1996, was Kerry Ingredients, which developed and produced a wide array of food coatings, flavorings, seasonings, and other ingredients. These products are quite specialized and include such products as cheese-powder coatings for convenience foods, processed fruit preparations, clear batter coatings for french fries, and dry marinates and glazes for dessert foods.

This industry segment was among the fastest growing segments of the food industry, driven by the growth of convenience foods and the global snack markets, as well as the continued growth of food-service enterprises. As described in one Kerry publication:

> Key drivers in specialist-ingredients markets are the accelerating trends toward snacking and convenience, together with the internationalization of food markets through the global expansion of food manufacturing and foodservice companies and their mission to provide consistent high-quality prepared food products. The growth in demand for convenient foods to match modern lifestyles and for fresh natural-food products which yield higher flavor impact, ranging from savory to traditional to ethnic tastes, has led to a proliferation of new-product development, thereby providing significant growth opportunities for competent ingredient suppliers capable of delivering the requisite technologies and range of ingredient systems to service the global marketplace.

Kerry Ingredients was also extremely competitive, both in terms of firms and products. The major competitors on a global basis included McCormicks, International Flavor and Fragrance, Unilever, and Monsanto, although the industry was extremely fragmented. It was a segment that saw the introduction of literally thousands of new products each year, making R and D and process technologies key factors for success in the industry. Such

core technologies also represented a distinctive competence of Kerry Group.

Kerry's initial foray into the food-ingredients business can actually be traced back to the very beginnings of the processing facility in Listowel in 1973, where it built a processing center for the production of casein from skim milk. (A timeline of Kerry Group's investments and acquisitions can be found in Figure 1.) Casein was initially exported to North America through Erie Casein, an American firm with a minority interest in the facility. Casein is a feedstock for many food ingredients, including infant formula and other supplements. In 1984, Kerry opened its first sales office in North America, intending to build the relationships necessary to market its casein and other products directly to the food industry (rather than through Erie Casein as a middleman).

This was followed by the acquisition of a pharmaceutical plant in the United States in 1987, Kerry's first investment in manufacturing in North America. This plant, located in Jackson, Wisconsin, in the heartland of American dairy country, specialized in the coating and drying operations associated with the manufacture of various food ingredients. Nevertheless, until 1988, Kerry's North American operations were insignificant.

This abruptly changed with the Group's acquisition of Beatreme Foods in 1988. Beatreme was the premier specialty food-ingredients supplier in the U.S. and, at the time, was larger than the entire Kerry Group. Beatreme

FIGURE 1
Timeline of Investments and Acquisitions

Ingredients Business Segment

1972	Commissioning of Dairy & Specialty Ingredients facility in Listowel (Ireland)
1974	Purchase of assets of Dairy Disposal Board (Ireland)
1987	Commissioning of Jackson, WI, Facility (U.S.)
1988	Beatreme Food Ingredients (U.S.)
1990	Milac, GMBH (Germany)
1991	Eastleigh Flavours (U.K.)
	Dairyland Products (U.S.)
1992	Northlands (U.S.)
1993	Malcolm Foods (Canada)
	Research Foods (Canada)
	Tingles Ltd (U.K.)
1994	Commissioning of Kerry de Mexico Facility in Irapuato (Mexico)
	Acquisition of DCA (U.S., Canada, U.K.)
	Margetts (U.K., Poland)
1996	Ciprial S.A. (France, Italy)
	DCA–Solutech (Australia)

Consumer Foods Business Segment

1972	Commissioning of Dairy & Specialty Ingredients Facility in Listowel (Ireland)
1974	Purchase of assets of Dairy Disposal Board (Ireland)
1974–82	Purchase of Independent Dairies in Killarney, Limerick, Cork, & Galway (Ireland)
1982	Denny, Duffy Meats (Ireland)
1986	Convenience Foods (Ireland)
	Snowcream Dairies, Moate (Ireland)
1987	Denny Meats (Northern Ireland)
1988	Grove & Ballyfree Turkeys (Ireland)
	S.W.M. Chard (U.K.)
1990	A.E. Button (U.K.)
	Miller-Robirch (U.K.)
1992	Buxted Duckling (U.K.)
	Kanthoher Food Products (Ireland)
1993	Kerry Spring Water (Ireland)
1994	Commissioning of Porkmeat Products Facility in Shillelagh (Ireland)
	Mattessons Wall's (U.K.)

had been an acquisition target for some time. Indeed, there is a story, perhaps apocryphal, that back in 1984, when Kerry made its first appearance at the International Food Fair in Los Angeles, Denis Brosnan had looked across at the extensive and impressive display fielded by Beatreme and remarked that "someday we'll own that company." Kerry's chance came when Beatreme, sold off by parent company Beatrice Foods, fell into the hands of a succession of investors during the mergers-and-acquisitions craze of the 80s, with owners who were more interested in short-term profit considerations than in the long-run management of the business. Although other investors (from New Zealand) were interested in purchasing Beatreme, the Kerry Group succeeded in moving quickly to line up financing and effect the purchase. It was also not without risk, as the Kerry Group financed the acquisition primarily through debt financing, pushing its debt-to-equity ratio inordinately high. Still, the purchase of Beatreme was a critical breakthrough for the Group; they were now a major player in the largest specialty food-ingredients market in the world.

Kerry's strategic focus on the expansion of its global food-ingredients business continued with a number of smaller acquisitions in the U.S. and U.K. between 1990–93, culminating in the largest acquisition ever undertaken by the group, a £250 million takeover of DCA Food Industries, Inc. and its subsidiaries in 1994. DCA, headquartered in the United States, and its Margetts Foods subsidiary based in the U.K., were global competitors in food ingredients, with operations in five countries. These, and several smaller strategic acquisitions, placed Kerry Ingredients in the front rank of the specialty food-ingredients segment, particularly in the European and North American markets. Acquisitions were primarily funded through debt, since the requirement to maintain at least 52 percent co-op ownership in the Group effectively constrained additional equity issues.

The global food-ingredients business remained the cornerstone of the Group's growth strategy in 1996. The sector was expected to continue experiencing strong growth in the future, particularly in the emerging markets of the Pacific Rim, where the Kerry Group had little presence. The ingredients segment also represented the foundation of the group's profitability, returning approximately 72 percent of the group's total operating profit in 1995 (see Table 4 for product segment data).

KERRY FOODS The Kerry Group's second major business segment is the consumer-foods business, which constituted 39 percent of the group's sales and 27 percent of its operating profit in 1996. From its beginnings as a supplier of milk and dairy products to a few regional markets in Ireland in the early 1970s, the consumer-foods business had grown to encompass a wide array of prepared and chilled meat products (beef, pork, lamb, and poultry), snack foods, pastries, microwavable prepared food products, and flavored spring water and other juice drinks, as well as its more traditional milk and dairy products. The growth of this business segment, like that of the ingredients sector, came about through a continuing strategy of external expansion. It also represented the production and marketing of a mixture of both branded and unbranded (private or own label) products.

Although the business began, understandably, with a focus upon the domestic Irish market, it had expanded by 1996 to a major presence in the U.K. and selected markets of the European community. It should be noted that the Group's mission statement articulates its goal to be "a leading consumer foods processing and marketing organization in selected EU markets." The statement pointedly excludes reference to the consumer markets of North America and Asia.

KERRY AGRIBUSINESS The agribusiness segment of the Kerry Group is the business most directly linked to the Group's farmer/shareholders in County Kerry and to the group's heritage as an agricultural cooperative. Ironically, by 1996, this business segment had dwindled to the least important component of the Group's operations, at least

TABLE 4
Business Group Segment Data

Business Group	1994 Turnover IR£1,000	1994 Op. Profit IR£1,000	1995 Turnover IR£1,000	1995 Op. Profit IR£1,000
Kerry Ingredients	369,687	35,091	620,987	60,517
Kerry Foods	383,864	17,509	445,460	22,517
Kerry Agribusiness	43,499	2,682	57,648	2,220
	797,050	**55,282**	**1,124,095**	**85,254**
Discontinued operations	85,647	267	74,998	485
	882,697	**55,549**	**1,199,093**	**85,739**

in terms of direct sales and profits. In 1996, the agribusiness segment returned 4 percent of group sales revenue and 1 percent of operating profit.

However, the contribution of the business to the Kerry Group may be overlooked by a focus on sales and profit contributions exclusively, since the intended function of the agribusiness segment is more that of an internal service center than a profit center. Kerry Agribusiness is charged with all aspects of the Group's milk supply and assembly business. It is charged with providing various technical and advisory services to the Group's milk suppliers in the Southwest of Ireland (primarily County Kerry), operating a bulk milk-collection system consisting of a sizable fleet of computerized tankers, providing feeds, fertilizers, and other farm inputs to the Group's suppliers, and operating an animal-breeding research center and providing breeding technology and services to its suppliers. It is this division that services a host of needs of the group's Irish farmer/suppliers and represents in great measure the "old" Kerry Co-op to the rural community of Kerry.

Despite the reduced importance of this sector, however, Denis Brosnan has continued to assure farmers that they remain important to the group. Says Brosnan, "Agribusiness will still be with us for a very long time because we still look after the farmers in the Southwest of Ireland."

COMPETITIVE ENVIRONMENT The global food sector in which Kerry competed was fragmented and far-reaching, encompassing a wide range of industries and product segments. The Kerry Group itself was unique, defying easy categorization into a specific industry segment. For example, there was no one particular firm which competed "head to head" with Kerry across its entire product line. Rather, Kerry competed with particular rivals in very specific product segments, market niches, and in the case of consumer foods, a limited geographical area. Most typically, Kerry was classified under "Other Diversified Food Manufacturers," reflecting its mix of consumer goods (marketed in limited geographic markets) and food ingredients (industrial sales targeted at very specific product niches and marketed globally). Many of the firms that competed with Kerry in consumer foods were, in fact, customers of Kerry on the food ingredients side of the business.

The Kerry Group—1996

THE MANAGEMENT "TROIKA" The management at Kerry Group had been unusually stable over the years. Indeed, of the "twelve apostles" who, along with Denis Brosnan, labored in the caravan in the parking lot in 1972, ten were still with the firm nearly twenty-five years later. The trio of managers, Managing Director (MD) Denis Bros-

nan and Deputy Managing Directors (DMDs) Denis Cregan and Hugh Friel who, in the early 1970s, organized the farmers of North Kerry into a sizable and profitable cooperative organization, still led the firm in 1996 (and in identical capacities). By all accounts, these were managers with skills that complemented each other well. Brosnan was credited with a sense of strategic vision and an absolute, utter, and relentless focus on the achievement of that vision. Hugh Friel, as DMD for Finance and Administration, handled the financial elements of the many acquisitions and the relations with investors. Importantly, he orchestrated the strategic planning process that had become so intrinsic to the firm's operations. Finally, Denis Cregan, as DMD for Operations, was the man who "made things happen," particularly in the integration of newly acquired firms into the "Kerry way" of doing things.

Similarly, the Board of Directors had had only two chairmen over the course of twenty-two years. Michael Hanrahan, a local farmer from the seaside resort of Ballybunion, had been the chairman since 1980.

Still, if there is one name associated with the Kerry Group in the public eye, it is Denis Brosnan. He is the prototypical "local boy who made good." His ID card number with Kerry Group reads "employee #1," which he is, quite literally. He is also the first, and only, managing director of the organization. His roots in Kerry, and in farming, run deep:

> I am a native of Kilflynn, about five miles from Tralee. My parents, Dan and Mary, are both dead. My brother James is farming at home . . . the farm is at Fahavane on the main Tralee-Listowel road. I went to the national school in Kilflynn. We milked about 25 cows then on 130 acres, and nowadays with modern farming it could carry 100 cows. We used to, when we were very young, get a lift in the horse and cart to school when it was on its way to the creamery with milk. It was said when I was growing up that I loved farming so much that I would surely end up farming, but that was not to be.

Brosnan did B.S. and M.S. degrees in Dairy Science at University College Cork and spent several years working for Golden Vale, the largest dairy co-op in Ireland at the time. Although his tenure at Golden Vale was short, his rapid rotation into increasingly important positions clearly earmarked him as a rising young executive there. He was, in fact, even considered for the top position of general manager of the cooperative, but was apparently considered too young. Coincidentally, the movement to amalgamate the cooperatives in Kerry was in full swing at the time, and they were in need of a general manager. When the call came to return to Kerry and create a county-wide cooperative organization, he took advantage of the opportunity, although he was leaving the largest cooperative organization in Ireland (in the most productive farm region) to attempt to form what would be among the smaller ones (in one of the more hardscrabble farm regions). This decision itself may be characteristic of Brosnan, for he has acquired a reputation for taking risks. From the start, Brosnan pursued the development of Kerry's international businesses with a nearly missionary zeal, spending enormous amounts of time on the road. Yet his philosophy of business was deceptively simple:

> I always try to keep things simple. Look, there are usually only about six simple things to be done. Do those and it will work. You need money, patience, and commitment . . . if I say we are going to get to that goal, when all the advice has been given, when all the pitfalls have been pointed out, we still get there. It is the goal that has to be right.

This business philosophy has become a core element of the Kerry way of doing things. Numerous senior managers at Kerry have explained that, when being assigned a new challenge such as an acquisition or a poorly performing business, they'd come to expect a "flying visit" from Denis Brosnan which would result in a list with five or six things to be done. This simple list would serve as the "brief" for that executive until the list was fully executed. This straightforward, "can do" ethos has been indelibly imprinted upon the organization by the personality and philosophy of Denis Brosnan. He has clearly set the tone in the organization he has so dominated since its creation.

Patience is not Brosnan's strong suit. Although he is a good listener, he does not suffer fools gladly. He listens intently and actively, but he has little tolerance for those he feels are "just blowing smoke." If he has a bias, it is a bias toward action. As a leader, he has developed a knack for remaining "grounded" and connected to his roots in Kerry, even while he travels the world in search of further acquisitions or to visit existing operations. Each year, in advance of the annual meeting, he visits each of the farmers' advisory council meetings (there are eight) to talk with the farmers informally about the performance of the business and to hear from them directly about their own particular local concerns (most typically the price of milk). He still knows most of the farmer/suppliers (about 5,000 in 1996) by name.

Brosnan, however, does *not* have a reputation for telling people what they want to hear. He can be very direct.

> If I was to be remembered as an individual, I think I would like to be remembered because I was never afraid to speak the truth, regardless of the consequences. Whether I go into a hostile or a friendly audience, I never have any difficulty laying the bare facts before them. And I think I usually come away with a higher reputation than I went in with.

STRATEGIC FOCUS There is little that is confusing about the Group's strategy. First, it is clearly to be a major player in the global food-ingredients business. Second, it is to have a major position in selected consumer food markets in the U.K. and Europe. Ask any employee of any level, in any location, or any farmer/supplier, or any shareholder, and they will be able to quickly and clearly articulate this straightforward strategic agenda. Both of these foci imply continued growth through external, as opposed to primarily internal organic, expansion. As stated in the annual report:

> Kerry is committed to being a leader in its selected markets through technological creativity, total quality and superior customer service. The Group is focused on continuing to expand its presence in global food ingredients markets and on the further development of its consumer foods businesses in Europe.

ORGANIZATIONAL CULTURE Denis Brosnan described the Kerry culture, or ethos, in this way:

> We feel we have the edge being from Kerry. Maybe we are biased, but that is what we harnessed back in the early 1970s. We harnessed Kerry farmers and people to come together. And right through to 1986, when Kerry plc, Kerry farmers and workers took shares and they are all as interested in what is taking place in Mexico as perhaps the institutional shareholders. So that pride, that togetherness is still there. And long may it remain.

The Kerry Group is the largest employer of new business graduates in the county, providing opportunities for young managers to work all over the world. It is known to be a demanding place to work, with rigorous standards and a very strong work ethic. Less sympathetic wags say managers have to "sell their souls" to succeed there. But Denis Brosnan puts it differently:

> The unforgivable sin is half-doing a job, and we have a very strong ethic in Kerry, apart from how we are seen—tough or otherwise— and, that is, whatever we say we do, we'll do it, even if we have to do it to our own cost. If we are betrayed, we never forget or forgive.

Kerry employees are also expected to show singular commitment. Says Conor Keane, a local journalist who has covered the Group for many years:

> There is a Kerry way of thinking, a Kerry way of doing things. One of them is "Second Best

is not an option." If you are in a business, you are the best, or you are out, in the manure business. That's where they strive to be, the main player. It stems from part of the football code of the County. We've got to be the best!

This ethos is not limited to the firm's Irish employees. More and more, nationals from the Group's increasingly far-flung locations are being brought into the headquarters at Tralee. Says Keane:

> They have Spanish speakers who have been "Kerryized" in Tralee. They bring them over, and if they don't learn to think Kerry, they're out. And they get into the ethos. Color or creed, it doesn't matter.

The Kerry Group and Local Community

IN THE "KINGDOM" OF KERRY It is said that Ireland is composed of thirty-one counties and one kingdom; it is only the County of Kerry, in the relatively remote southwest corner of the island, that presumes to call itself a kingdom. From the Ring of Kerry with its Lakes of Killarney, to the windswept beauty of the Dingle Peninsula, to the smooth expanse of the Shannon Estuary, Kerry, the "Kingdom County," has been blessed with spectacular natural beauty. For the 120,000 souls residing in this little corner of the world, however, agriculture remains a primary economic activity, one that has shaped the culture and traditions of Kerry indelibly.

However, for all its bountiful scenery, Kerry has historically been an economically depressed area, relying on the dairy industry, tourism, and emigration. Indeed, emigration has been, until quite recently, often the only way for improving one's economic condition. For generations Kerry's youth have fled to England, the States, or even further abroad in search of employment. Jobs in Kerry were simply nonexistent, industry was nil, agriculture was in the doldrums. Such jobs as were available tended to be in the service sector, catering to the needs of the growing tourist trade. These were often unattractive, both in terms of job satisfaction and compensation, for the young, well-educated, and highly skilled workforce. The sadness of this experience is summed up in the "American Wake," the Kerry equivalent of a farewell party, given as a sendoff to the emigrant on the night before the journey to the States, or England, or Australia, or Canada. Emigration from Kerry has been among the highest of any part of Ireland, leading to a large and vocal diaspora of Kerry people around the world. The pain of emigration is seared in the soul of the people.

Yet, the economy of Kerry has revived along with the fortunes of Ireland itself during the 1990s. Ireland, with an annual growth in GDP of nearly 7.2 percent annually during the period of 1992–96, had achieved the status of the fastest growing economy in Europe, the "Celtic Tiger."

Ireland's economic buoyancy reinforces a new self-confidence. In marketing terms, Ireland is changing its homely, bucolic image into an international brand increasingly recognized in business and the arts. The changes have been tumultuous. Dublin's skyline is being transformed by new hotels and apartment blocks. Car sales are at record levels. The new affluence is evident in shops selling foreign-made luxury goods . . . . Ireland has rarely had such a benign economic climate.

As Ireland emerged from the economic doldrums, the positive spillover in County Kerry was quite pronounced. Although unemployment remained a serious issue, foreign investment in Kerry was up, housing starts and construction were booming, and there was a new air of optimism quite at odds with the dismal economic past.

COMMUNITY RELATIONS

> Since every moment of the clock
> Accumulates to form a final name,
> Since I am come of Kerry clay and rock
>
> —From the poem "My Dark Fathers"
> by Brendan Kennelly, Ballylongford,
> County Kerry

The connections between the Kerry Group and the people of County Kerry are strong and myriad and not susceptible to easy untangling. Even as the Group has grown from a simple regional milk processor to a diversified international food products company, its ties to the local community have in many ways grown deeper and more varied. Worldwide, in 1996, the firm had approximately 7,000 employees, roughly half of them in Ireland. Approximately 6,000 local farmers both supply milk to them and are shareholders in their own right through both the co-op and the publicly traded company. These "men of the soil" have made up the preponderance of Kerry Group investors and occupy all of the nonexecutive director positions on the Board of Directors. Their involvement with the Kerry Group had been continuous, direct, and influential. Said Denis Brosnan:

> The farmers are very involved there, and as management we enjoy that, and the farmers do as well. We listen to the farmers at area advisory meetings and have a pint in the pub afterward, and that keeps one's feet on the ground. We work tightly to five-year plans. So we have plans from now to the end of the decade, and that plan will take Kerry Plc around the world to be more spread out internationally.

The Kerry Group played a large role in the development of the Kerry Airport. It also has been influential in many other areas of the county's life, particularly in its many contributions to the arts and culture, as in its support of both the Kerry Museum and the National Folk Theater of Ireland, which are located across from the Group's corporate offices in Tralee. As a local politician from Listowel remarked as he dedicated a new grandstand at the racetrack:

> As the largest and most successful company in the area, it is inundated with requests for sponsorship. All are considered, and very few of merit go unaided. The fine new stand we saw on the (Listowel) race course today would not have got off the ground without their assistance. The Kerry Cultural and Literary Centre, another major project for Listowel, is indebted also to Kerry Group.

As a provider of jobs, a buyer of milk products (often at above market prices) from Kerry farmers, and the creator of substantial financial gains for its many Kerry investors, the Kerry Group has become a leader in the economic revival of Kerry. Indeed, more than a few of its farmer/shareholders have, by virtue of the conversion of their shares in the co-op to the more liquid shares in the plc, become "seriously rich," with the value of their shareholdings gleefully reported in the local newspapers.

It should be noted that, in matters affecting County Kerry, Managing Director Denis Brosnan has never been accused of keeping a low profile. Indeed, Brosnan has been a leading figure not just in his leadership of the Group, but as a prominent booster for economic development throughout Kerry. But his perspective on the economic future of the region differs markedly from past notions and has added to the discomfort of some of the small farmers in the area. He has been clear and articulate in his belief that the future of Kerry lies in tourism rather than in farming.

> I think it would be wishful thinking to imagine into the future local industries centering around the local creamery making butter or whatever. That has all gone and will never come back. . . . If we are to keep Kerry alive as a county and keep our young people there, it will come from tourism-related activity. Not out of farming.

Nor can it be said that such a perspective is Brosnan's alone. In conversations with farmers throughout the county, the predominant sense is that farming as a way of life is destined to disappear, as the seemingly inevitable machinations of the global economy demand farm enterprises of such efficiency that small farmers can never hope to meet.

The Proposal to Reduce the Cooperative's Shareholding in Kerry Group

In 1986, when the Kerry Co-op agreed to float the company on the stock market and create Kerry Group plc, it also created a complicated rule structure that stipulated that the co-op would continue to own at least 51 percent of the new public company. This, they hoped would ensure continuing farmer control of the enterprise. In the ensuing decade, however, a number of factors had surfaced which led to Kerry Group's proposal that the co-op further reduce their share:

- First, the Kerry Group's continuing rapid growth had required a high level of borrowing, since the 51 percent rule effectively limited its ability to finance further growth by issuing additional equity stakes. This, in turn, left the firm highly leveraged (or "geared"). For example, the firm's debt to equity ratios for the years 1993–95 were 71 percent, 130 percent, and 101 percent respectively.

- Second, market analysts had speculated that Kerry Group had bypassed some acquisition opportunities due to its reluctance to further increase its debt load and its inability to raise funds in the equity markets. Although the firm strenuously denied such assertions, such speculation continued.

- Finally, the farmer/owners of the cooperative, with their 51 percent stake in the Group, owned an asset that had considerable value, but had no liquidity since cooperative shares did not trade on the market. Given the position of many farmers as "land rich and cash poor," there was no pressure to provide farmer/shareholders a means to *realize* at least some portion of the gains in the value of their Kerry Co-op (and thus Kerry Group) holdings.

The proposal on the table called for the transfer of 21.4 million shares in the Group, now held by the cooperative, to be turned over directly to the co-op's shareholders. This would have the effect of (1) handing over roughly £130 million in Kerry Group shares to some 6,000 Kerry Co-op shareholders (these were all farmer/suppliers of the Group, over one hundred of whom would become millionaires overnight), (2) reducing the co-op's current share in the Group to 39 percent (from 51 percent), (3) creating a new minimum shareholding level in Kerry Group (the level below which co-op holdings cannot be allowed to drop without a "rule change") of just under 20 percent, enabling the group to issue up to 20 million new shares in the future, and finally (4) reducing the number of farmer representatives on the Kerry Group Board of Directors from fifteen to nine, with the six vacancies filled "by six people whose expertise is of major value to the plc." The Group also provided the Kerry Co-op an option to purchase the agribusiness segment (exercisable between 2001 and 2010), so that the farmers could maintain control of those assets most directly related to them in the event of a further decline in co-op ownership of the Group.

Earlier, at the annual meeting of Kerry Group, a shareholder had asked whether the reduction in shares owned by the co-op would lead to the co-op losing control of the Group. Denis Brosnan had replied, "the question of control has been raised, but its not an issue. Control is too emotional a term. I have always said that having an organization functioning well is much more important than who has 50, 40, or 30 percent."

DISSENTING VOICES Although Kerry Group management had done its homework thoroughly, believed in the proposal fully, and had communicated the proposal personally to farmers at the local Area Advisory Meetings (with little apparent objection), there *were* some who objected to the proposal. The opposition centered on philosophical rather than practical grounds and focused on the issue of continuing farmer control of the enterprise and adherence to fundamental cooperative principles.

The general concern centered on the evolution of the Group from a co-op to a plc and the continued dilution of "farmer control" of the Group. More and more, shares in the Kerry Group were controlled by "outside" shareholders, particularly large financial institutions. As one farmer who campaigned against the proposal said, "What do these institutions know, or care, of the concerns of small farmers?" Some farmers, as they watched the number of people involved with agriculture in Kerry dwindle (from 17,000 fifteen years ago to 12,000 in 1995), worried that, as the emphasis at Kerry Group changed to being a global player in food ingredients, its commitment to local farmers and, indeed, to farming as a way of life in Kerry would weaken. As Donal Hickey reported in *The Cork Examiner*:

> When co-ops changed to plc's this was a worry that bothered many farmers: would they lose control of their own enterprises to financiers who would henceforth be calling the shots? . . . Not so long ago, the Kerry Group (still referred to by farming folk as the more intimate Kerry Co-op) was regarded as the savior of dairy farmers in the widely-scattered county, but many men of the land now have grave reservations . . . .

Opponents, with more than a little hyperbole, suggested that farmers who voted for the proposal would be "selling out" the cooperative for "thirty pieces of silver." "It's just not right," said one prominent dissenter, "they are appealing to no more than people's greed." "After the deed is done, what will the farmers of Kerry have left but a few bob in the bank?" Yet the more reasoned core of such emotional objections can be found in basic cooperative principles that hold that:

- Owners are members of the cooperative, and they retain control of the enterprise. With the conversion, the cooperative members were taking their shares from the cooperative holding and becoming direct owners of the public limited company, Kerry Group. They were moving, said opponents, from "cooperators to capitalists."

- Cooperative members control equally, that is, one member–one vote. This "one member–one vote" applied to decisions involving the co-op's 51 percent stake in the plc. With the conversion, control of the plc will increasingly be based on "one share–one vote."

- Limited returns on capital. To pay a large return on invested capital is anathema to cooperative thinking . . . yet in this case, cooperative shareholders would be receiving a substantial return on their original investment in the cooperative.

Many of the objections, explicitly or not, also focused on fears concerning the future of farming in Kerry. Would Kerry Group continue to help the farmers of Kerry, even when those farmers no longer held substantial control of the enterprise?

> Many rural communities are gravely threatened by current farming trends. Townlands in remote parishes, once densely populated by growing families, are now practically deserted, with derelict homesteads and overgrown farm buildings bearing mute testimony to policies devoid of any social feelings.

Mr. Phil Healy, former president of the Kerry branch of the Irish Farmers Association, summed it up succinctly:

> The lack of confidence among many farmers is frightening, and there's a terrible fear among the smaller men that they're on the way out.

There were concerns that, as the Kerry Group matured into an increasingly large and diversified multinational firm with large blocks of shares held outside of County Kerry, the embeddedness of the group in Kerry and the strength and extent of its roots in this rural Irish county would be likely to weaken.

In the run-up to the vote, it seemed that such sentiments were very much in the minority. However, opponents suggested that few farmers in Kerry were anxious to openly cross the management of Kerry Group. They hoped that, given that the proposal would be voted on by secret ballot, enough farmers would side with them to protect their ownership of this enterprise that they had brought to life. After all, they needed only 25 percent of the vote!

THE FIRST SPECIAL GENERAL MEETING It was most uncharacteristic of Irish, and particularly Kerry, weather. Monday, July 15, was sweltering, and the Brandon Conference Center was not air-conditioned! Even more, it seemed that attendance might be higher than anticipated, for there were already traffic tie-ups outside the conference center an hour before the start of the meeting. Interestingly, their wives apparently accompanied many of the farmers. This fact alone demonstrated the serious nature of the meeting, for, as one wag at the hotel bar suggested, "The wives are there to make sure they vote the right way."

Although Brosnan remained confident that the proposal would pass, a considerable lobbying effort by those who objected to the change had taken place. Could the vote be as unpredictable as this weather? The first of the shareholders were already beginning to trickle into the conference center as Denis Brosnan, no longer lost in reverie as he gazed on Mount Brandon, reviewed his notes.

Questions

1. Summarize the historic evolution of Kerry from its early days to the present. What lessons did the company learn on the way? What factors account for the group's success?

2. Who are Kerry's stakeholders, and what is their significance? In what ways is Kerry moving from a stakeholder to a shareholder approach? What problems might it encounter in being successful?

3. Evaluate Kerry's major acquisitions and their significance. What do you think of Kerry's M&A approach to internationalization?

4. How have Kerry's core competencies changed over time?

5. If the change in ownership structure is approved, what should the key ingredients of Kerry's next five-year plan be?

Note

1. Reprinted by permission from the *Case Research Journal*. Copyright 2000 by James J. Kennelly and the North American Case Research Association. All rights reserved.

PART THREE

World Business Strategy

global (glo'bel) adj. worldwide -- glob... existence throughout the world... globalism (is em) n. a policy approach

*T*he International Planning Process described in Chapter 7 highlights businesses, products, and markets to be emphasized over a given time frame. First, however, firms must equip themselves and orchestrate their resources to enter international markets (the internationalization process) and, once established, provide linkages among foreign affiliates to enhance their competitive abilities (the globalization process). These processes are examined in Chapter 8. From there, how to enter and service individual markets is evaluated in Chapter 9. Market entry and servicing methods vary from simple strategies (such as indirect exporting through third parties) to full-scale in-market investments.

The globalization process described in Chapter 1 shows that technologies, products, services, and lifestyles diffuse through world markets at varying rates. Most international corporations are based in the developed countries of North America, Western Europe, and Japan, and the vast majority of trade and foreign direct investments occur in these regions. The continued commercial interactions among these nations have caused some homogenization of their cultures (toward modern ways and Western lifestyles) and patterns of demand. This has allowed companies to standardize some products, services, and brands across markets in global, regional, and multi-market strategies.

How firms implement these types of policies is described in Chapter 10.

The opening up of many national economies through free trade and investment policies has also given firms significant flexibility in managing their supply chains in optimal ways: sourcing components and materials from cost-effective locations, and manufacturing and distributing them to enhance their competitive positions. How companies manage their global and multi-market supply chains is examined in Chapter 11.

Countries further down the development curve—the industrializing and lesser-developed nations—have received fewer transfers of technology. Consequently their national cultures have been impacted less by modernization and westernization processes, allowing traditional institutions, behaviors, and values to continue unchallenged. As firms move into these markets, they accommodate national lifestyles by adapting to their cultural characteristics and behaviors (described in Chapter 12) and by adjusting stakeholder and supply-chain strategies to accommodate local conditions (Chapter 13).

Note that few firms follow purely global and multi-market strategies or purely localization strategies. The vast majority follow combinations of global/multi-market and local strategies. It is executive judgment that determines the optimal mix.

Chapter
Eight

Internationalization and Globalization Processes

INTERNATIONALIZATION AND GLOBALIZATION—SIMILAR BUT DIFFERENT

While food tastes remain national in most countries, world trade and investments are slowly but surely creating world markets for food products. Many firms internationalize initially through exports. Grupo Modelo, a Mexican conglomerate, is the number 9 brewer in the world, and its Corona beer brand is exported to over 150 countries. Its aim is to be a top 5 brewer and ultimately to have a stable of global brands and to produce beer in its major markets.[1]

Other companies have more complex arrangements and must integrate their sourcing, manufacturing, and marketing strategies to supply their foreign markets. Indian foods and spices are a good example. In the UK, Patak Foods sources 2700 tons of spices from foreign lands, mixes them, and exports them to over forty countries.[2]

Finally, there are the established global competitors. In the dairy-brands field, giants like Switzerland's Nestle, U.S.'s Kraft, UK-Dutch Unilever, and France's Danone do daily battle to establish market-share dominance in any one of dozens of established world markets. Their objectives are to extend their brands into new countries and leverage their production and marketing muscle across borders to achieve scale economies in operations, maximize market exposure, and build brand loyalties across markets.

All of these food companies do business in world markets. Corona beer has internationalized via exports. Patak Foods sources materials globally and then finds markets for the final products. Finally, there are the global brands of the major food producers, many of which have coordinated cross-border branding strategies. All of these firms are pushing their products into world markets, but are at different stages of the internationalization and globalization processes. The beer and Indian foods firms are internationalizing from a single market. The "biggies"—Nestle, Unilever—are already in most world markets and are in the process of integrating their branding strategies. Other companies, most notably in the auto and consumer-electronics sectors, produce in many different locations. Their aims are to globalize their output to obtain the best combinations of cost and quality. This often involves financing operations in many different parts of the world. All firms have their own motives and strategies in servicing world markets. How they do it, and why, is the subject of this chapter.

FIGURE 8.1
Chapter Outline: Internationalization and Globalization Topics

In this chapter you will learn:

- Definitions of internationalization and globalization and how they are measured; the advantages and disadvantages of going overseas
- How market, cost, competitive, and government factors drive corporate globalization, and the role of technology in facilitating the globalization process
- How firms prepare for globalization by focusing on core activities and restructuring around key core competencies, developing international leaders and managers, and how to orient corporate cultures for use outside of home markets
- Globalization effects on industry structure at the national, regional, and worldwide levels, and what adjustments firms make to tailor organizational structures and corporate cultures to market needs
- The ways that firms finance their foreign operations

INTRODUCTION: INTERNATIONALIZATION AND GLOBALIZATION

Definitions

Internationalization and *globalization* are similar terms and are often used interchangeably in the general business press. In this text, *internationalization* occurs when firms extend products and services in overseas markets, usually from their home country. *Globalization* is the process by which businesses create value by leveraging their resources and capabilities across borders; it includes the coordination of cross-border manufacturing and marketing strategies. Internationalization, then, is the first stage in the globalization process.[3]

Measuring Internationalization and Globalization

Both internationalization and globalization are measures of commitment to foreign markets. That commitment affects the structures and strategies used outside of home markets. Hence, measuring that commitment is a useful barometer of what structures and strategies are appropriate at various commitment stages.

T A B L E   8 . 1
Company and Industry Transnationality Index 2001

RANKING BY					
Transnationality Index	Foreign Assets	Corporation	Country	Industry	Transnationality Index (percent)
1	61	NTL Inc.	U.S.	Telecommunications	99.9
2	55	Thomson	Canada	Printing and Publishing	97.7
3	24	ABB	Switzerland	Machinery and Equipment	95.6
4	71	Holcim AG	Switzerland	Mineral products	92.9
5	39	Roche	Switzerland	Pharmaceuticals	91.8
6	36	Lafarge	France	Construction materials	89.7
7	28	Philips	Netherlands	Electronics	88.4
8	84	WPP Group	UK	Business Services	87.4
9	87	Pearson PLC	UK	Media	86.2
10	47	Diageo PLC	UK	Food and Beverage	85.8

Source: Excerpted from *World Investment Report 2003* (New York: United Nations, 2003): 187–88.

Internationalization is relatively easy to measure by calculating the proportion of international sales to total sales. Globalization measures are more complex and can be measured objectively or more subjectively via corporate benchmarks.

Objective Measures The United Nations Conference on Trade and Development (UNCTAD) have developed an objective "transnationality index" to measure the extent of corporate globalization. The measure is a composite of three ratios: foreign assets to total assets, foreign sales to total sales, and foreign employment to total employment. Not surprisingly, this measure favors firms with small domestic markets (e.g., Switzerland, Canada, UK) where international sales and assets can easily eclipse those in the home market. As Table 8.1 shows, the top 10 list has one company from the U.S., none from Japan, with Western European firms occupying eight of the top 10 spots. "Transnationality indexes" can also be used to measure industry globalization. Table 8.2 shows industry measures of global involvement. Note the concentrations in media, machinery, and chemicals where few firms dominate their sectors and the motor vehicle, electronics, and petroleum industries where competition is spread globally over a dozen or more companies.[4]

> The best kind of citizen and the solidest kind of enterprise is one that can look the whole world in the face.
>
> —*M. E. Tracy*

Corporate Measures of Globalization For individual companies, there are other measures of corporate globalization[5]:

1. Governance and responsibility
   - How far corporate management boards reflect the global dispersion of corporate activities, for example, how many nationalities are represented at senior-management levels. Japanese boards (with some exceptions) tend to be dominated by home-country management, whereas European top-level managements tend to be more cosmopolitan.

T A B L E   8 . 2
Industry Composition of Top 100 TNCs, 1995 and 2000

	NUMBER OF ENTRIES AND AVERAGE TNI		
Industry	**1995**	**2000**	**2000 Avg. TNI**
Media	2	3	85.4
Machinery/engineering	1	3	75.4
Petroleum/mining	14	12	70.8
Food, beverages, tobacco	12	8	70.1
Chemicals	11	3	63.4
Pharmaceuticals	6	9	61.8
Motor vehicles and parts	14	15	59.7
Metals	2	2	57.7
Retailing	—	4	57.3
Diversified	2	6	51.1
Electronics/computers	18	12	50.5
Utilities	—	5	47.8
Telecommunications	5	7	45.4
Total/Average	100	100	58.9

Source: *World Investment Report 2002* (New York: United Nations Conference on Trade and Development, 2002), 96–97.

- The extent to which industry regulators (e.g., governments, the UN) are dealt with centrally (with single policies governing all worldwide affiliates) or whether they are managed on a local (market-by-market) basis. Environmental and ethical policy issues are examples. In the chemical and pharmaceutical industries, the trend has been toward the development of global policies to meet all market needs.

2. Strategy and planning
   - For truly global companies, corporate missions, visions, and strategies are crafted with worldwide markets in mind. This works in industries where common needs can be serviced from largely standardized product lines. Alternatively, for industries that rely heavily on meeting localized needs, overly centralized marketing and planning approaches cause problems in developing competitive advantages at local levels.

   - How worldwide firms are in their partnership and alliance strategies, that is, whether they inevitably partner home-market firms or select alliance partners from any country that gives them strategic advantages.

3. Marketing orientation
   The extent to which firms can pursue global, multi-country, or localized marketing strategies depends on similarities and differences among its worldwide customers. Where similarities are pronounced, firms are more likely to standardize their marketing offerings. Where national differences are evident, companies tend to decentralize their

marketing operations to give local managers more latitude in strategy formulation. In practice, few firms follow purely global or localized strategies. Most combine elements of both approaches according to the needs of the marketplace and what strategies rivals choose to follow.

4. Manufacturing operations and technology
   * Customer and competitive factors dictate how far executives can manage assets on global, regional, or individual market bases. Where market needs are similar across major markets, scale economies can be gained through centralized manufacturing (e.g., Boeing, Airbus) or by specializing manufacturing tasks across countries and transshipping components among markets to take advantage of low factor costs or national expertise in product or component manufacture. Where marketing approaches are localized, firms are more likely to customize their supply chains.

   * Where labor-skill requirements and manufacturing costs are fairly constant across countries, there are opportunities to standardize production practices across countries. Similarly, where corporate cultures and work-related processes (such as total quality, or just-in-time operations) are key contributors to manufacturing success, major efforts are made to standardize those elements on a worldwide basis. The Toyota Production System for example, has been transferred successfully into many countries without significant losses of efficiency.

5. Research and development
   * Firms in R and D intensive industries (software, biotech, pharmaceutical, IT) must balance their efforts between global customer needs and the needs of individual regions and markets. R and D efforts are centralized when significant resources are needed to develop new products or technologies.

   * R and D efforts are geographically dispersed when companies wish to take advantage of national expertise in R and D and individual market stimuli for product innovation.
     Whatever R and D organization is in place, communications among laboratories and product divisions are essential. Many firms now emphasize projects that combine expertise and technologies across divisions and markets.

6. Organization and human resource management
   * Globalizing human-resource processes is a perpetual challenge for international executives. Recruitment and retention of the best available management talent has been highlighted as a problem area for over 80 percent of U.S. companies sampled by a Conference Board survey.[6] Firms found it difficult to standardize accountability and incentives programs across countries in the face of increasing dependencies among markets. Delivery firm DHL had problems with incentives programs because delivery revenues accrued at pickup sites, but major costs were incurred and customer satisfaction levels determined at delivery sites.

> The common facts of today are the products of yesterday's research.
>
> —*Duncan MacDonald*

- Leadership and management development are key issues for international corporations. As companies expand geographically, linkages among markets and managers grow at increasing rates. International firms have the challenge of developing executives with global coordination skills as well as managers with in-depth knowledge of individual markets.

Advantages of Internationalization and Globalization

There are many benefits that accrue from taking firms into foreign markets, including:

- *Extending successful home-market products and strategies* into new markets
- *Taking advantage of factor resources available in the worldwide marketplace:* These include cheaper or better raw materials and components, reductions in labor or processing costs, and access to new ideas and expertise.
- *Building scale economies* in sourcing, manufacturing, and marketing that reduce worldwide costs of doing business
- *Acquiring economies of scope:* As firms build up their foreign-market presences, they acquire a number of advantages from operating in multiple markets. These include the building up of foreign-market expertise and the leveraging of this expertise to build sustainable competitive advantages over global, regional, and local marketplace rivals.

Disadvantages of Internationalization and Globalization

Taking companies abroad is a task that requires time and patience, for example:

- *Significant resource allocations* are necessary, especially in the internationalization process. Resources that would otherwise be used to consolidate or build domestic market positions are instead diverted into overseas markets where payoffs tend to be long- rather than short-term oriented. For example, it took U.S. company UPS eleven years to make profits out of its European operations. The time and money spent on building a significant foreign-market presence can cause frustration among domestic shareholders of internationalizing firms as investment returns take time to materialize and stock prices become volatile.

- *Internationalization and globalization are learning processes:* Companies making pushes into foreign markets must have the requisite expertise to manage international operations. Exhibit 8-1 details the problems of U.S. company Lincoln Electric in growing its international markets. Note that the company had been operating internationally for many years, but this did not make them immune to internationalization problems. Firms that succeed internationally must be ready to adapt their products, services, and organizations. Initially, they recognize that some products and practices are transferable into foreign markets. Others are transferable, but with adaptations. Some practices just cannot be

EXHIBIT 8-1
Lincoln Electric Internationalizes

Lincoln Electric was a U.S. company founded in 1895 to manufacture arc-welding products for the North American markets. It was about a billion-dollar firm whose company culture had been built on open democratic principles (free, easy access to all management levels and open communication lines) and its fabled piecework and bonus system that made its factory workers among the highest paid in the world. Hundreds benefited from wages totaling over $50 million a year. It was a unique workplace system that resulted in high worker loyalty and very low absentee and labor turnover rates.

In the early 1990s, Lincoln decided to increase its international presence. While the firm had been in Canada, Australia, and France for decades, its international units had operated independently. By the early 1990s, foreign intrusions into the U.S. market made apparent the need for internationalization. In response, Lincoln spent $325 million on international expansion, building three greenfield plants in Japan, Venezuela, and Brazil and acquisitions in Germany, Norway, the UK, Netherlands, Spain, and Mexico. When it came to managing these operations, the company encountered a number of obstacles.

- Lincoln assumed that their piecework and bonus system was easily extendable into international markets. This proved not to be the case, especially in Western Europe. The foundation for U.S. operational excellence had been effectively neutralized by the region's socialistic attitudes.

- The assumption had been made that exporting arc-welding machines to Europe was not feasible because U.S. designs would not work and insider status was essential to penetrate the regional market.

- The company lacked managerial expertise to operate a geographically and culturally dispersed operation. Overoptimistic sales and profit forecasts and accompanying excessive expenditures made for loss after loss in international operations. A Western European economic downturn exacerbated the situation. The company retained a manufacturing orientation with the appointment of a U.S. engineering vice-president as head of European operations.

Lincoln eventually turned the situation around. A rejuvenated performance in North America enabled CEO Hastings to revamp European and global manufacturing and marketing operations. Plants in Brazil, Venezuela, and Japan were closed down. Expertise to manage international operations was brought in. The piecework incentive operation was successfully transferred into Mexican operations, despite initial cultural opposition. The firm gradually stabilized its situation.

Source: Adapted from Hastings, Donald F. "Lincoln Electric's harsh lessons from international expansion." *Harvard Business Review* 77:3 (May–June 1999): 162–78.

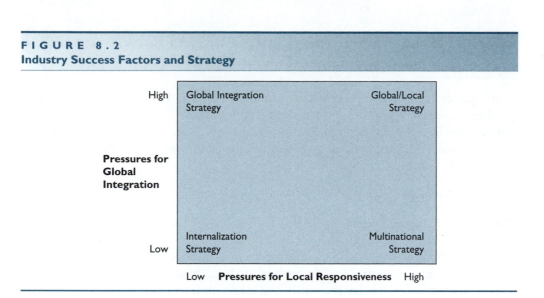

FIGURE 8.2
Industry Success Factors and Strategy

used at all. In all cases, significant learning must occur to maintain flexible and profitable operations. Initially, many executives (especially those who have not had an international business course or traveled) are overwhelmed by cultural differences. Endless variations in political, economic, legal, financial, and cultural frameworks can be intimidating. Ensuring that CEOs and senior managers are attuned to international market conditions and developments is a major corporate challenge.

Internationalization, Globalization, and Industry Strategies

How companies proceed in their internationalization and globalization strategies depends on what it takes to be successful in their industries. Prahalad and Doz developed a matrix linking industry success factors with strategy. This is shown in Figure 8.2. On the vertical axis, the pressures for global integration include linkages among product and service strategies across markets (marketing strategies) and cross-border supply-chain strategies. On the horizontal axis are pressures for local market responsiveness.

The matrix shows that when pressures for global integration are high and local responsiveness pressures are low, a globally integrated strategy is followed (cross-border branding and supply chains). Where pressures for both global integration and local responsiveness are low, internationalization strategies (usually exporting) work well. When company markets need extensive localization and there are no real pressures for global integration, multinational strategies, with localized marketing and supply chains, are appropriate. Finally, in situations requiring both integrated global strategies and degrees of local responsiveness, a global-local strategy can be implemented.[7] Note that many firms have businesses requiring different strategic orientations. Corning's businesses include electronic components and medical products that require globally integrated strategies, Corningware and laboratory products that need localizing, and TV and ophthalmic products that require degrees of both global integration and national responsiveness.[8]

DRIVERS OF CORPORATE INTERNATIONALIZATION AND GLOBALIZATION: WHY FIRMS GO ABROAD

Firms go global for many reasons, most of which can be classified under four headings: market, cost, competition, and government.[9] Additionally, information technologies have been major facilitators of globalization in streamlining international communications and coordination. Figure 8.3 summarizes these major drivers and influences.

Market Drivers

Common Customer Needs International trade and technology transfers occur as home-country products and lifestyles are transplanted into countries with similar needs or aspirations. This has resulted in increased recognition of cross-cultural segments in many industries and laid the bases for common strategies across country markets. In the food and drink industry, for example, the success of Coca-Cola, Pepsi, McDonalds, KFC, and Pizza Hut occurred because foreign customers found U.S. products to be attractive additions to their lifestyles. Common needs among business people and teenagers respectively led to the internationalization of the CNN and MTV television networks. Most importantly perhaps has been the change in managerial mindsets from focusing

FIGURE 8.3
Why Firms Go Abroad

Corporate Internationalization and Globalization Drivers

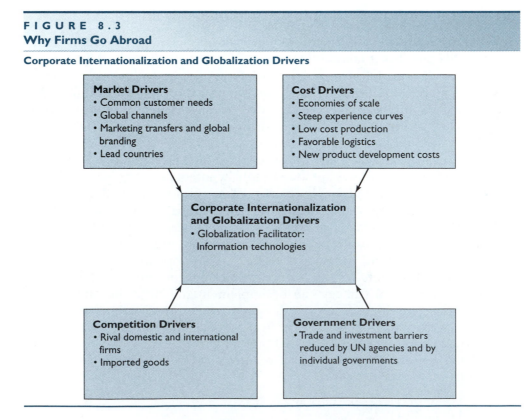

purely on customer and market differences to balanced evaluations of similarities and differences. Product and service needs are rarely *identical* from market to market, but similarities in customer needs allow executives to contemplate uniform brand images and strategies across markets. These issues are developed more fully in Chapter 10 (Global and Multi-Market Strategies).

Global Channels Global channels have emerged with free trade and as companies have gained experience in transferring products among markets. In particular, the growth of international retailers, such as Carrefour, Toys R Us, Wal-Mart, Marks & Spencer, and franchises, such as Laura Ashley, Benetton, and Blockbuster Video, have established international channels of distribution for product assortments.

Similarly, as firms have internationalized their operations, business-to-business suppliers of raw materials, components, and services have expanded their global distribution by following their users into foreign markets. Finally, as international corporations have expanded their global reach, transshipments among their subsidiaries have expanded global distribution and now account for about two-thirds of world trade.

Marketing Transfers and Global Branding International media and mobile customers have made firms aware of the advantages of global brands in foreign markets. Global approaches to brand names, packaging, and advertising have made international household names out of Coca-Cola, IBM, Toyota, Bic, Kodak, Panasonic, Bayer, Mercedes Benz, Nestle, and many other consumer goods.

Lead Countries Some countries have built up national expertise in particular product or technology sectors. Such countries are often innovation centers for the industry: Japan for consumer electronics, Switzerland for watches, U.S. for computer software. Other firms enjoy country of origin ("Made in") advantages. In the alcoholic beverage industry, Scotch Whisky, Japanese sake, British ale, German beer, Dutch liqueurs, French champagne, and Bordeaux wines all have innate "made in" advantages over competitors. Competitors can counter these advantages by, first, setting up subsidiaries or R and D posts in lead markets, second, acquiring a firm within the nation where the expertise is located, and, third, by establishing downstream control over the distribution of such products.

Cost Drivers

Economies of Scale Economies of scale are important cost determinants in many industries. For many types of steel production, major investments are necessary to set up and maintain production. In the microprocessor industry, initial investments in chip design and manufacturing technology typically exceed $1 billion. In industries where scale economies are important, plant utilization rates impact costs and investment payback periods. Significant market shares must be attained to offset initial investment costs. In the automobile industry, analysts estimate that four-million-unit per year output is necessary to support new product development, manufacturing, and distribution facilities on a worldwide scale.

Science and time and necessity have propelled us, the United States, to be the general store for the world, dealers in everything, most of all, merchants for a better way of life.

—*Lady Bird Johnson, former president's wife*

It's a fine thing to have a finger pointed at one, and hear people say: "That's the man."

—*Persius, ancient Greek philosopher*

Steep Experience Curves Firms in knowledge- and technology-intensive sectors accumulate significant expertise in their industry areas. These experience-effects are expensive to support and maintain, and leveraging this expertise into international markets is a prime motivator for global expansion. Boeing and Airbus are examples in the airline-manufacturing industry, as is Asea Brown Boveri in the power-generation field. The experience curve also has applications in the consumer-products sector. Their experiences in numerous international markets have enabled firms such as Colgate Palmolive, Unilever, and Gillette to rapidly diagnose needs in new markets and establish "first mover" advantages over rivals.

Low-Cost Production Many developing markets have vast labor pools that help reduce manufacturing costs in labor-intensive industries. However, such cost advantages can be offset by additional charges due to decreased worker productivity, poor quality control, service constraints (e.g., on time deliveries), and additional transportation costs to get products to market. As such, favorable logistics are important factors in maintaining cost advantages of offshore production.

Favorable Logistics As materials and components are increasingly transshipped among markets, additional transportation costs can be problematic. Typically, high-priced quality products are less susceptible to escalating transportation costs and deteriorations in price competitiveness. In other industries, transportation costs can undermine global cost competitiveness. Bulk items, ranging from lumber to non-specialty chemicals and plastics, have limited market areas due to excessive transportation costs.

New Product Development Costs For some industries (airlines, telecommunications, chips, pharmaceuticals), new product development costs have risen dramatically. These problems are compounded when technological advances shorten product life cycles, making investment payback and cost recovery periods ever shorter. In these cases, rapid global rollouts of new products and technologies are essential for profits to be made. For example, the new generation of semiconductor process technology, the 300mm wafer, has been priced at $3 billion. Only four companies (two U.S.—Intel and IBM, one Taiwanese, one Korean) could afford such expenditures. The projected launch date was 2002, with full cost recovery limited to three years.[10] Similarly, pharmaceutical new-product development can take up to twelve years and cost $500 million.[11]

Competition Drivers

As companies have internationalized, so competition has increased nationally, regionally, and globally. The work of GATT (to 1995) and the World Trade Organization, coupled with the formation of trading blocs, have opened up national markets to international competition through reductions in tariff and nontariff barriers. International companies are also making investments in increasing proportions of the world's markets, driving up competition to new heights. Competing with imports and other global rivals has placed increasing pressures on both domestic and international companies to be competitive in national and international markets.

Government Drivers

National governments and supranational bodies like the United Nations have played key roles in promoting free-trade policies and eliminating foreign direct-investment restrictions. In some cases, UN agencies like the IMF, World Bank, and WTO have pushed countries (such as Indonesia, South Korea, and Brazil) toward market reforms and the gradual opening up of their economies to international competition. Governments, the UN, and regional bodies like the EU have also worked to harmonize technical standards across national industries (e.g., telecommunications, airlines, computers). Governmental privatization and deregulation efforts have opened up many new industries to competition (e.g., banking, financial services, telecommunications, airlines, utilities).

In some cases, though, governmental actions and policies retard internationalization efforts. For example, many governments prefer public ownership of industries deemed vital to national security interests (utilities, banking, etc.) and limit competition in these sectors. Similarly, some governments distrust international firms because of their constant shifting of production facilities among markets, their profit maximizing motives, and their concerns about minimizing worldwide tax liabilities.

> Whenever I may be tempted to slack up and let the business run for a while under its own impetus, I picture my competitor sitting at a desk in his opposition house, thinking and thinking with the most devilish intensity and clearness, and I ask myself what I can do to be prepared for his next brilliant move.
>
> —*Gordon Selfridge, UK retailer*

A Major Globalization Facilitator: The Role of Information Technologies

Information and Internet technologies have vastly improved the ability of companies to communicate efficiently within and across national borders, greatly enhancing global coordination and facilitating cross-border flows of knowledge, information, and expertise.[12] Some examples:

> It is a luxury to be understood.
>
> —*Ralph Waldo Emerson, 19th-century U.S. poet*

- *Inter-firm linkages:* As partnerships, joint ventures, coalitions, and alliances have become commonplace in the international arena, information technologies (IT) have bonded together the constellation of enterprises that contribute to corporate output. IT technologies enable firms such as Sun Microsystems and Reebock to coordinate third-party activities so effectively that asset ownership or equity stakes in supply-chain partners have become less necessary, enabling non-essential activities to be farmed out and more corporate attention to be paid to strategic core competencies (e.g., Sun Microsystems, Nike, Reebok).

- *International new-product development* teams can pass on new-product specifications, plans, and designs among R and D centers to bring products to market more quickly. Intel, for example, has used virtual teams in this context, as has Allergan Pharmaceuticals, to design and improve products on a worldwide basis.

- *Customer responsiveness:* As supply chains linking suppliers, manufacturers, distributors, and customers have become common, so a traditional weakness of international firms—customer responsiveness—has been reduced. Electronic data interchange (EDI) linkages among retailers and producers across national borders have drastically reduced customer-response times. In the fabric industry, EDI-equipped companies take ten days to process orders against 125 days for non-EDI firms.

- *Inter-organizational systems* (IOS) are self-contained IT systems linking independent organizations, but with special provisions for reliability, data security, user privacy, and system integrity. American Hospital Supply uses IOS to link its supplier and customer networks. Singapore's TradeNet system couples government agencies, port authorities, freight forwarders, shipping firms, banks, and insurance companies with customers and immigration authorities. As a result, customs and port clearances that used to take four days can be expedited in as little as ten minutes.

- *Internet-based E-commerce* has provided companies of all sizes and nationalities with worldwide customer access with significant savings in advertising, communication, and administrative costs. E-commerce allows firms to monitor individual purchases and allows customer profiles to be developed and relationships built among companies and customers. The banking and financial services industry in particular has been revolutionized by E-commerce, with bank costs of electronic transactions anywhere in the world being one-sixth the cost of local check processing. The development of multilingual web sites and language software packages have also been major facilitators of international purchases and information transfers among markets.

- *Extranets* are Internet applications that allow designated external parties limited access to corporate information systems. These are being used in company supply chains to give suppliers and manufacturers advance notices of customer-demand shifts; they also allow customers to trace the status of orders in transit.

- *Intranets* are firewall-protected company networks that allow secure circulation of corporate information across divisions and markets. Corporate activities, programs, and data can be instantaneously transmitted to all employees. Transportation company DHL links its 20,000 employees worldwide via fifteen formal Intranet sites.

- *Groupware technology* integrates e-mails, screen sharing, group scheduling, writing, and other forms of global group communications. This facilitates global knowledge sharing and corporate learning. Groupware products such as IBM's Lotus Notes allow global teams to work on projects across countries and time zones.

- *Organizational memory systems* (OMS): Electronic systems for storing and retrieving data and documents allow managers access to archival information. The ability to track previous decisions, strategies, and results enhances corporate decision making and allows for broader inputs into planning processes.

> The computer is down. If our world needs an epitaph, and it may, could there be a better one?
>
> —*Bernard Levin, British political commentator*

IT and Internet-based systems are undoubtedly the wave of the future. They allow managers access to greater amounts of information and permit its increased dissemination. This increased transparency within companies should:

- Allow greater efficiency among supply-chain members
- Permit firms to respond rapidly to marketplace developments
- Facilitate information flows within firms, across national boundaries, and between businesses and result in enhanced corporate learning abilities
- Result in geographic boundaries, time, and language factors being less influential barriers to corporate coordination. The major corporate problems will be in the developing world where technology diffusion is slower and where (high context) cultural habits place premiums on face-to-face communications and contextual understanding of decision-making environments.

PREPARING THE COMPANY FOR INTERNATIONALIZATION AND GLOBALIZATION

Going abroad requires resources. Preparing companies for increased global commitments requires assessments of corporate and human-resource availabilities to ensure that global needs can be met without severe internal dislocations. Figure 8.4 summarizes the steps firms take in this process.

Focusing the Organization: Corporate Competencies

Globalization requires significant resources. For many corporations, this involves assessments of competencies—corporate activities and expertise that have proven international potential—and hard decisions made on activities that

FIGURE 8.4
Preparing the Company for Internationalization and Globalization

do not add value to the globalization move. For experienced firms, these evaluations are routine and occur in the planning process (see Chapter 7). For companies getting started in international markets, some of the same assessments apply. Under-performing product lines and businesses come under scrutiny. Those not contributing to corporate sales and profits and non-core business areas become candidates for divestiture to free up resources for foreign-market exploitation. Similarly, businesses unable to withstand the rigors of international competition must be critically examined. Overall, international competition causes management to focus on proven "winners" in the worldwide arena. Most often, this involves focusing on mainstream businesses with non-core operations being spun off. Occasionally though, traditional businesses are the ones that must be sacrificed. For example:

- Norwegian firm Kvaerner, whose reputation was built on shipbuilding, pulled out of the sector to focus on designing and building chemical and pharmaceutical plants, steel and aluminum factories, and oil/gas drilling installations, for which the company had global reputations. The spin-off of its thirteen shipyards became inevitable under harsh competition from Asian competitors.[13]

- Swedish-Swiss conglomerate ABB switched its organizational focus from power-generation equipment (transferred to a joint venture with Alstom of France) and rail transportation (sold to Daimler-Chrysler) to focus on faster growing and global potential-laden areas of intelligent electrical systems and services.[14]

- In the consumer-products sector, increased international competition forced Unilever to focus its efforts on 400 global and regional brands averaging 4–5 percent growth annually. The remaining 1200 brands were to be de-emphasized, cut, or sold off. Procter & Gamble pursued a similar strategy when it was found that only half of its 300 brands were building market share.[15]

Focusing the Organization: Supply Chain Restructuring

After companies have refocused their products and business units, attention is then focused on equipping corporate supply chains to compete efficiently on a worldwide basis. Initial efforts are focused on the supplier-manufacturing-distribution supply chains, and on supporting managerial infrastructures. Typical moves have been to:

- *De-layer corporate hierarchies* and push decision making down to grassroot levels as companies seek quicker decisions to take advantage of efficient Internet and information technology systems.

- *Rethink manufacturing systems* and take steps to close unproductive plants. These may occur on the domestic front (e.g., Nissan's five plant closings in Japan following its Renault merger), on a regional basis (French company Michelin cut 10 percent of its European workforce to bring costs into line with those of global rival Goodyear-Sumitomo), or on a global level (U.S. company

Johnson & Johnson closed one quarter of its plants worldwide [36 in all] to shave $300 million off its global costs).[16] Remaining manufacturing assets are then consolidated to gain scale economies and reduce regional or global production costs.

- *Reevaluate supplier relationships* to focus on a few, well-positioned providers. Marginal suppliers are discontinued and emphasis placed on those most capable of providing low-cost quality materials and components on a regional or global scale.

- *Reassess distributor capabilities* based on company needs in the global arena. For example, efforts are made to balance corporate needs to be near customers against operating economies resulting from regional and global networks.

Developing Leadership and Management Capabilities

The need to develop competent international managers and leaders increases dramatically as corporations diversify geographically into world markets.[17] U.S. firms have the most foreign direct investment of all countries. Yet, in one survey, 85 percent of Fortune 500 firms felt they had inadequate numbers of global leaders, and two-thirds thought their existing leaders needed additional skills and knowledge.

Global Leadership Characteristics

Unbridled Inquisitiveness The desire to learn and the ability to enjoy the constant stimulation and challenges presented in worldwide management is widely accepted as *the* major characteristic of successful global leaders. Constantly challenging the status quo, global leaders must rapidly adjust to new experiences and neverending change in the worldwide marketplace.

Personal Characteristics The ability to connect socially and emotionally with wide varieties of individuals is paramount. Sincerity and the ability to listen and empathize are key characteristics. Spending time with subordinates, understanding their problems, and respecting their viewpoints breed trust and goodwill, essential elements in executing strategies under adverse circumstances or uncertain conditions. Senior managers must exude integrity in their personal and professional dealings. High ethical standards and uncompromising principles add to managerial stature and their subordinates' confidence in implementing corporate policies and strategies.

> The Jack Welch of the future cannot be like me. I spent my entire career in the United States. The next head of General Electric will be someone who spent time in Bombay, in Hong Kong, in Buenos Aires. We have to send our best and brightest overseas to make sure they have the training that will allow them to become the global leaders who will make GE flourish in the future.
>
> —*Jack Welch, chairman General Electric*

Duality Duality refers to senior management's ability to appreciate global and local considerations and to balance both perspectives in making decisions that require global-local tradeoffs. These include decisions on standardization versus adaptations of marketing-mix elements, parent company modus operandi versus local subsidiary habits (e.g., management styles, labor, HR policies), and decisions on where best to locate corporate facilities (plants, assembly sites,

> To understand and be understood makes our happiness on earth.
>
> —*German proverb*

> Travel makes a wise man better but a fool worse.
>
> —*Thomas Fuller, 17th–18th-century English physician and writer*

sales, R and D subsidiaries). Global ("big picture") perspectives require enormous amounts of background data. When decisions must be made quickly, managers should instinctively know when they have sufficient information to make decisions and when additional insights are needed.

Savvy Management leaders have instinctive recognitions of strategic tradeoffs—recognizing market opportunities, realizing the importance of environmental shifts and rival reactions, and, perhaps most importantly, being able to frame these opportunities and threats within the context of organizational capabilities: what their corporations are capable of doing.

Developing Global Leaders Global leaders are part born, part made. Some individuals have innate curiosities about the world and global events, foreign-language capabilities, and heightened tolerances for nondomestic lifestyles. But organizations must groom and develop these characteristics with appropriate experiences, including:

1. *International travel* to appreciate the diversity of the corporation's international operations and local managerial perspectives on decision making. Within specific countries, getting outside of cosmopolitan urban areas is essential to experience how (in many countries) the majority of people live. Meeting with broad arrays of local nationals (not just executives or educated elites) and observing how they live, how they are educated, and how they consume (and why) are important background experiences.

2. *Global team experiences* are also essential. This includes the thought and decision processes that occur at local levels and social interactions among individuals both on and off the job.

3. *Cross-cultural training* must occur on a wide variety of corporate education topics, including international strategy formulation, implementation, organizational structure, and reporting arrangements, cross-cultural team building, and environmental analysis. Participants must include personnel from worldwide operations. Field-based team projects build contacts and networks and provide ideas for future development.

4. *Overseas assignments* are major shapers of executive development, and, most importantly, they change managerial mindsets. The steps taken to build expatriate experiences into management-development programs are examined more fully in Chapter 11 as part of the global supply-chain integration process.

Summary profiles of outstanding global leaders are shown in Exhibit 8-2. Note that primary CEO characteristics are similar across cultures: sound judgment, emotional maturity, and the ability to see and act on emerging trends.

Globalizing the Corporate Culture

What Is Corporate Culture? Corporate culture is "the way we do things around here." It is a patterned way of thinking that permeates an organization,

EXHIBIT 8-2
Global Leadership: A European Perspective

The by-products of outstanding corporate leadership are undeniable: 25 percent more revenue, 55 percent more tasks accomplished, four times as many conflicts resolved, 63 percent fewer people burned out. Business Europe noted that the following characteristics were important.

- Sound judgments about future technological and market developments

- Good communication skills to convince colleagues about the efficacies of preferred courses of action

- Creating a shared vision of where the corporation is headed

- "Emotional intelligence," self-awareness, political astuteness, and heightened capacities for self-learning

- Sound experiences base: running foreign operations, making mistakes, correcting them*

CORPORATE EXPERIENCES

- Phillips Electronics wants to develop executives who can "walk ahead" of the pack.

- British Aerospace leaders are expected to be adept at learning and adapting to change, have a wide knowledge of the industry, its participants, and its customers, and have superior understanding of strategy.

- Electrolux expects its future leaders to have experiences in a number of foreign countries and to understand what motivates different nationalities of managers.[†]

*"Focus on leadership," *Business Europe* (June 16, 1999): 1.
[†]"Leadership: Horses for courses," *Business Europe* (June 30, 1999): 4.

defines relationships, facilitates communication, and orients employee behaviors toward corporate goals. Corporate cultures include:

- *Authority structures:* how hierarchical or participative decision making is ("top-down, bottom-up")

- *Degree of organizational formality:* whether procedures are followed rigidly, how much respect is accorded to titles, or whether procedures are informal

- *Information flows:* how freely information and data move within organizations, whether information is narrowly or widely disseminated

- *Tolerance for maverick ("individual") behaviors:* Some companies encourage individual initiatives and risk-taking. In other organizations, conformism is expected and encouraged, and "rocking the boat" is frowned upon.

- *Organizational structure:* shallow organizations, with few decision-making levels, or deep hierarchies with many levels (and often bureaucratic tendencies)

> The only institutions that last a long time, do good and useful work, and are profitable, are those that are, and have been, well organized. You get the feel for this whenever you visit such a place . . . In organization there is always strength.
>
> —*George M. Adams,*
> *U.S. business consultant*

- *Organizational focus:* the extent to which corporations are inward looking (focusing on corporate needs) or outward looking (customer, marketplace, or competitive orientations)

- *Decision-making apparatus:* individual versus consensus-orientations

- *Competitive or cooperative corporate cultures:* The amount of tolerance for internal competition among employees (e.g., competing for resources, promotions, recognition), or whether teamwork is encouraged and rewarded

- *Gender orientations:* Many firms in all societies tend to be male-dominated. Chauvinistic attitudes, often imposing "glass ceilings" on women climbing the corporate ladder, take time to be broken down.

Deciding on Corporate Cultures in Foreign Markets There are no "right" or "wrong" corporate cultures for global firms. Companies that are at early stages of internationalization tend to take their home-market corporate cultures abroad. Where firms are dominant domestically (the U.S.'s General Motors or the UK's BT [formerly British Telecom]), there are dangers when they export home-market corporate cultures that are out of step with national cultures. Some examples:

- McDonalds attempts to take its corporate culture, policies, and standards into all of its overseas locations. This ensures consistency of service and output, key factors in its corporate success. But the company is careful to adapt policies, operating procedures, and menus where possible as long as corporate quality and service standards are maintained.[18]

- A global-local approach was adopted by Wal-Mart in Germany. Its company cheer "Give me a W! Give me an A! etc. Who's Number One? The Customer!" went over well. But its 10-foot rule (greeting all customers within ten feet), was less well received.

- Attempts to localize can be counterproductive. A North American oil-company partnership in Indonesia emulated local firms in having separate corporate facilities for executives and workers. An external consultant advised a breakdown to run the subsidiary in a more egalitarian way. The result was a 40 percent boost in efficiency.[19]

In general, companies have three options in molding their corporate cultures. They can maintain corporate cultures across existing markets, they can "go native" and localize to the fullest extent, or (most often) they can use the best combination of global and local approaches.

Global Standardization of Corporate Cultures The trend is toward homogenization of corporate cultures on a worldwide scale. Siemens, Nokia, and Gillette have made strenuous efforts to standardize corporate cultures in all their markets. Gillette, for example, aims to "attract, motivate and retain high performing people in all areas of our business. We will offer consumers products of the highest levels of performance for value. We will provide quality service to our customers, both internal and external, by treating them as partners, by listening, understanding their needs, responding fairly and living up to our commitments."[20]

Adapting Corporate Cultures to National Culture Influences Corporate cultures are heavily influenced by home-market national cultures. As a result, firms must understand what factors affect the corporate culture they are taking abroad. Generally, as illustrated in Figure 8.5, two key influences—societal competitive-

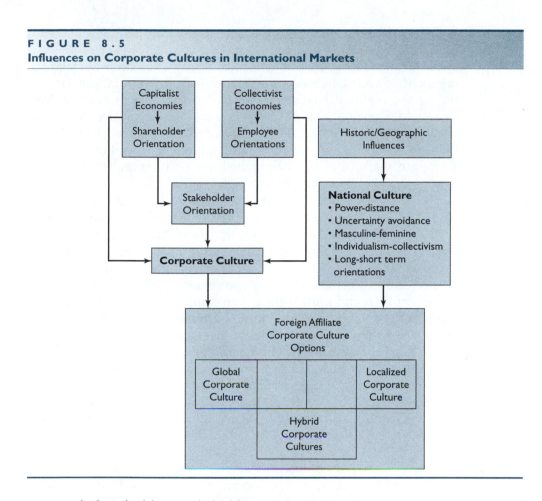

FIGURE 8.5
Influences on Corporate Cultures in International Markets

ness and shareholder- stakeholder orientation—affect home-market corporate cultures.

Societal Competitiveness The amount of competition within societies is a major influence on national behaviors. Where national behaviors are competitive, corporate cultures are likely to be so also. Competitive societies have competitive political processes (functioning democracies), economic systems (well-developed capitalist orientations), and competitive social-class systems with relatively few obstacles to social mobility. The U.S. and a number of European nations follow this model.

> Competition brings out the best in products and the worst in people.
>
> *—David Sarnoff, founder, RCA Corporation*

Less-competitive societies have one or more of the following: (1) less turbulent political systems (tribal chiefs, kings, dictators, dominant one party political systems); (2) economic systems that reduce market competition through government ownership, foreign direct-investment restrictions, or through protectionist policies (for example, to insulate domestic economies from international competition, to preserve national cultures, or to maintain full employment objectives); (3) some societies limit social competitiveness among citizens through hereditary or seniority-based social-class systems. Latin America, Middle East, Africa, and Asia all have countries with these characteristics.

> So the question is, do corporate executives, provided they stay within the law, have responsibilities in their business activities other than to make as much money for their stockholders as possible? And my answer to that is, no they do not.
>
> —*Milton Friedman, U.S. Nobel Prize-winning economist*

Shareholder-Stakeholder Orientations At the company level, corporate cultures tend to be oriented toward specific objectives or audiences. One effect of the globalization process has been to heighten competitive and shareholder orientations. U.S. corporations operating in the highly capitalist market of North America tend to have shareholder orientations: their bottom-line profit motive dominates all other considerations, and stock price valuations weigh heavily on management thinking and corporate cultures. The unification of the European market has also heightened competition and pushed firms toward shareholder orientations.

In many societies, however, capitalism and shareholder orientations are less pronounced (e.g., privately held companies, Asian corporations, family-owned businesses), and firms emphasize other objectives (market share, employment maintenance, etc.). As international firms enter foreign markets, they recognize that pure shareholder orientations are often inappropriate, as they are "guests" in those countries and must make positive impressions on governments, local businesses, and the community. Therefore, many opt for stakeholder orientations that emphasize not only external constituents such as shareholders, financial communities, government, regulators, environmental groups, consumer activists, press relations, and local communities, but also internal constituents such as suppliers, employees, distributors, and customers. Stakeholder approaches give companies flexibility in the worldwide marketplace and allow corporate cultures to be adapted to local situations.

National Culture Influences on Corporate Cultures International firms must take account of national culture influences on corporate cultures. Based on Hofstede's works, Table 8.3 shows five major factors that affect corporate cultures.

> The upper classes are . . . a nation's past; the middle class is its future.
>
> —*Ayn Rand, U.S. novelist*

1. *Power distance* refers to the extent to which strong social-class distinctions are maintained at societal and corporate levels. Countries with histories of strong social distinctions (high power distance) tend to emphasize corporate titles, protocols, and procedures. Countries with fewer social-class distinctions (e.g., the U.S.) tend to favor informal egalitarian corporate cultures. Problems arise when corporations from low power distance societies take their egalitarian principles into countries with established hierarchies where titles and protocols are accorded much respect. Note that, as societies industrialize, traditional social-class distinctions are broken down in fast-paced urban environments.

2. *Individualism/collectivism* looks at the degree to which individual or group actions are the bases for getting issues resolved. Collective societies require the needs of the group to be taken into consideration, either as part of the decision-making apparatus or with regard to outcomes (e.g., rewards, recognitions). As industrialization proceeds, individualistic behaviors and decision-making processes become more common. Corporations doing business in high- and low-individualism societies must often adjust decision-making processes and lines of communication to take account of individualism–collectivism tendencies.

T A B L E   8 . 3
National Culture Influences on Corporate Cultures

	COUNTRY EXAMPLES		
Dimension	**High**	**Low**	**Corporate Culture Effects**
Power Distance The extent to which power and status differences are accepted within national cultures	Brazil India Mexico Philippines	Scandinavia Israel	• Deep vs. shallow corporate hierarchies • Established protocols and chains of command vs. egalitarian structures • Formal vs. informal communications
Individualism vs. Collectivism Whether individual or collective action is the preferred way of dealing with issues	U.S. UK Canada Australia Netherlands	Colombia Greece Mexico Taiwan Venezuela	• Individual vs. consensus means of decision making • Rewards/accountability accrues to individuals or groups • Tolerance for individual (maverick) behaviors vs. conformism
Masculinity–Femininity Extent to which aggressive or passive behaviors dominate societal behaviors	Austria Venezuela Mexico Japan Italy	Scandinavia Thailand	• Aggressive pursuit of objectives (making things happen) vs. acceptance of prevailing conditions • Attitudes toward gender roles (strong vs. weak distinctions) • Concerns for working conditions, job satisfaction, employee participation
Uncertainty Avoidance Tolerance for uncertainty, unpredictable situations	France Greece Peru Portugal Japan	UK U.S. Scandinavia India	• Risk oriented vs. risk adverse societies • Structured, protocol-oriented organizations vs. fleet-footed, informal, fast-acting organizations • High vs. low tolerance for mistakes
Long-Term vs. Short-Term Orientations Focus on immediate needs/goals versus long-term needs/goals	Hong Kong Japan (long-term)	France Russia U.S. (short-term)	• Affects goal setting, planning frameworks, organizational accountability

Sources: Adapted from Hofstede, G. *Culture's Consequences: International Differences in Work-Related Values.* Beverly Hills, CA: Sage Publications; Jackofsky, E. F., J. W. Slocum, and S. J. McQuaid. "Cultural Values and the CEO: Alluring Companions." *Academy of Management Executive* 2, 1 (1988): 39–49.

3. *Masculine and feminine societies* differ in their tolerance levels for aggressive behaviors and their gender orientations. Masculine societies tend to maintain gender distinctions and encourage aggressive, power-based behaviors, and internal competition. Feminine societies are more collegial and less confrontational in their management styles. Gender differences are de-emphasized and human-resource issues, such as job satisfaction, collegiality, participative decision making, are corporate culture characteristics.

4. *Uncertainty avoidance* concerns the extent to which societal behaviors are risk-oriented or risk-averse. In risk-averse (high uncertainty avoidance) societies such as France and Japan, managers tend to be conservative decision makers. Procedures and protocols are followed to reduce the risk of incorrect decisions and to cover individuals if faulty decisions are made. Risk-taking societies (i.e., low uncertainty avoidance countries like the U.S. and the UK) tend to make faster decisions. Occasional mistakes are expected and forgiven.

5. *Long- versus short-term orientations:* Some societies, especially those in Asia, tend to think long-term. Others, especially firms in shareholder-oriented societies, think short-term first to maintain stock prices and corporate performance levels. Clashes between these two cultural types are common in East-West (e.g., U.S.–Japan) partnerships, especially in planning and objective setting procedures.

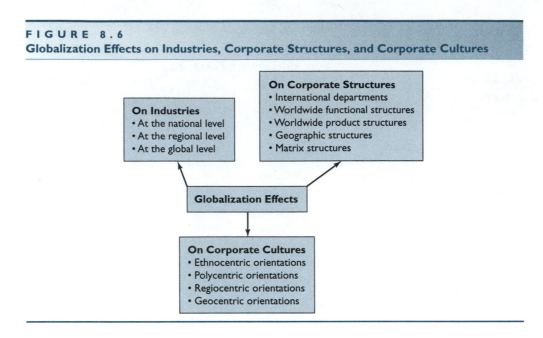

FIGURE 8.6
Globalization Effects on Industries, Corporate Structures, and Corporate Cultures

EFFECTS OF GLOBALIZATION

Corporate expansions into the worldwide marketplace can affect industry structures at national, regional, and global levels. They also cause changes in organizational structures and corporate cultures. These are summarized in Figure 8.6.

Industry Structure Effects

Industry globalization elevates the threshold of competition at national, regional, and worldwide levels.

> If you're small, you'd better be a winner.
>
> —*Billie Jean King, tennis champion*

At the national level, domestic firms have realized that they must attain critical-mass size to deal with foreign competitors. Because of time constraints, many firms have opted to achieve this through alliances, mergers, and acquisitions. In the Japanese financial services industry, Daiichi Kanyo, Fuji, and Industrial Bank of Japan merged to form the Mizuho Financial Group and to pull together their $1 trillion asset portfolios. This was followed by the 2001 consolidation of the Sanwa, Asahi, and Tokai banks. These consolidations were precipitated by an industry-wide depression and pressing needs to compete effectively against American and European banks.[21]

At the regional level, there are needs to attain regional market coverage and scale economies to compete against other global producers. Again, alliances, mergers, and acquisitions are preferred strategies. In South America, steel manufacturers have adopted two approaches. First, intraregional acquisitions among Brazilian and Argentinean firms were aimed at building scale and maintaining competitive prices. Second, local producers have entered into partnerships with international companies to upgrade technologies and gain access to worldwide distribution.[22] In the Western European chemical industry, polyolefin producers have merged to challenge North American manufacturers in global competitiveness.[23]

At the worldwide level, industry structures have been affected by a series of "mega-mergers" between large international companies. This has had the effect of reducing the number of worldwide players and setting up global rivalries among a few, well-positioned firms. Glaxo Wellcome and Smith Kline Beecham merged to create a critical mass in the pharmaceuticals industry. While attaining less than 10 percent of the worldwide market, the new firm attained lead positions in key pharmaceutical sectors. Similarly, the $9.2 billion merger of Canada's Alcan Aluminum, France's Pechiney, and Switzerland's Alusuisse-Lonza Holding had critical effects on the worldwide aluminum and metals industry.

The aims of mega-mergers are both defensive and offensive. At the national and regional levels, firms are acquired and merged, first, to provide corporate critical mass to defend home markets and to consolidate positions in regional markets. They also provide platforms to compete on a global basis, to attain global scale economies, and to obtain significant presences in all major markets and regions.

Organizational Structure Effects

For most corporations, entering foreign markets is done deliberately and incrementally, step by step, with periodic adjustments to organizational structures as worldwide involvement increases. Figure 8.7 shows a number of organizational formats companies use as their global involvement increases, starting with basic and working up to complex structures.

Most firms start off exporting products abroad. To do this efficiently, foreign-market expertise is concentrated into an *international department*. As foreign sales escalate and stabilize, marketing, then manufacturing, subsidiaries are established. Some companies then move onto a *worldwide functional structure* that gives vice-presidents of marketing, manufacturing, and other functions international responsibilities. Both organizational formats work best when companies have few products and markets.

When international sales exceed 20–30 percent of turnover, other organizational structures become appropriate. *Worldwide product structures* are used in high-tech industries to gain manufacturing scale economies and to facilitate product and technology flows throughout foreign subsidiaries. They work best when firms have broad technical product lines but service relatively few markets. *Geographic structures* are preferred where competitive advantages center around local responsiveness. Fast-moving consumer-product firms have historically favored this approach to give local managers latitude in formulating nationally based strategies. More recently, though, the homogenization of global tastes and the move toward global branding have pushed companies such as Unilever and Procter & Gamble away from geographic structures to global product divisions.

When foreign sales get close to or exceed 50 percent, *matrix structures* become an option in organizing international operations. These involve dual organizational structures (e.g., by product and by region or country) and are effective when companies have broad product lines stretching across many markets. Ideally, in a product-by-country matrix, the product structure provides cost efficiencies and technical superiority, while the geographic organization enables managers to tailor marketing mix elements (price, promotions, distribution) to meet local needs.

Matrix structures are difficult to manage because the two administrative, budgetary, and reporting systems clash as one seeks control over the other. To make matrix organizations work, companies need clear and consistent company-wide visions; effective human resource management that emphasizes worldwide recruitment, selection, and

> There is no best way of organizing a business.
>
> —*Joan Woodward, British sociologist*

> An organization chart strangles profits and stifles people.
>
> —*Robert Townsend, former president, Avis Rent-a-Car*

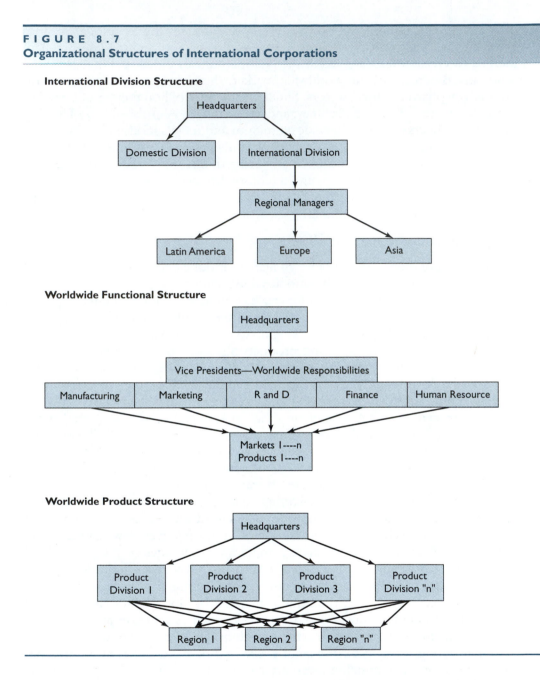

FIGURE 8.7
Organizational Structures of International Corporations

promotion policies; regular geographic rotations for key fast-track managers; and network development through meeting and management development processes. Finally, there must be worldwide policy-making bodies to coordinate product and regional strategies and to arbitrate disputes among global affiliates.[24]

Corporate Culture Effects

Companies globalize best when executives have appropriate outlooks toward world markets. There are four strategic dispositions of international companies.[25]

Ethnocentric corporate cultures emphasize home-market orientations in strategic decision making and corporate attitudes. With this orientation, product- and

Matrix Structure

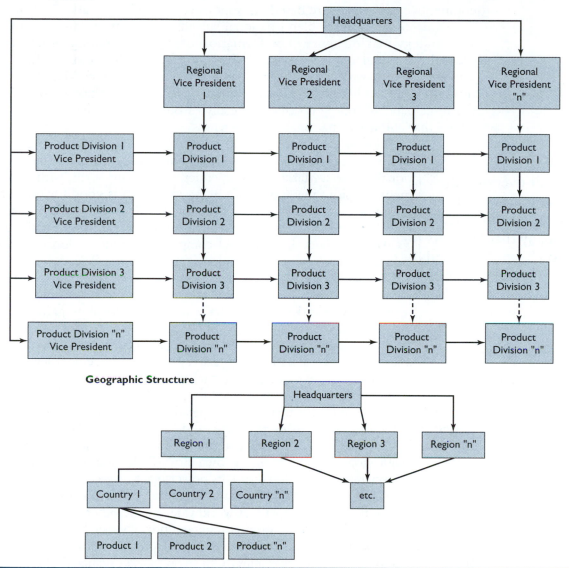

Geographic Structure

marketing-mix standardization are the norm, and foreign subsidiaries are miniature clones of the parent. Few concessions are made to foreign-market differences, and centralized decision making is usual. Many different types of companies can have this orientation, from inexperienced exporters to marketers of high-profile consumer goods such as Chanel No. 5, Louis Vuitton, Scotch Whisky, Russian caviar, Stetson cowboy hats, and French champagne. This corporate mind-set is based on the feeling of home-market superiority: the world needs their products more than they need world markets. As global involvements increase, ethnocentric behaviors become less common.

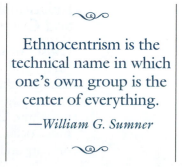

Ethnocentrism is the technical name in which one's own group is the center of everything.

—*William G. Sumner*

Polycentric operations involve complete host-country orientations, with custom-built product lines, or totally redesigned product transfers making up subsidiary lines. Organizational planning and decision making is bottom-up-oriented, and subsidiaries are locally managed. This mind-set is effective when competitive advantages are based on responsiveness to local market tastes.

Regiocentric cultures blend national subsidiaries within regions into cohesive strategy-making units. The formation of regional trading blocs has increased the popularity of regional HQs (e.g., for NAFTA and the European Union). Region-wide products and brands become feasible. Manufacturing, marketing, and other scale economies take advantage of regional commonalities in demand. Planning is done regionally through country-level strategic priorities that emphasize national responsiveness.

> Don't overlook the importance of worldwide thinking. A company that keeps its eye on Tom, Dick, and Harry is going to miss Pierre, Hans, and Yoshio.
>
> —*Al Ries chairman, Trout & Ries Advertising Agency*

Geocentric corporate cultures are totally globally-oriented, with decisions and resource allocations being made without regard to national borders. Market interdependencies are the norm, with management decisions made only on the basis of what is good for the corporation as a whole. Products are designed with global markets in mind, and the best managers attain senior positions regardless of nationality.

For very large international companies, attaining global corporate cultures is important for company unity and for focusing on global, rather than national or regional, goals. Overcoming home-market orientations and local managerial fiefdoms is not easy. Not only must resource allocation decisions be made without national prejudice, but reward systems must encourage nonnationalistic behaviors. Promoting bilingual managers, including foreign tours in corporate career patterns, and having diverse nationalities at very senior management levels are all part of the global package. The package becomes more complex for international conglomerates. Swedish-Swiss ASEA Brown-Boveri started off with a Swedish CEO but maintained its headquarters in Zurich, Switzerland. English was the official company language, and its books were kept in dollars.[26] All research and development, manufacturing, and marketing decisions are made with worldwide goals in mind. Asea-Brown-Boveri's businesses run the entire global-local spectrum. At the global end, its power-plant division competes heavily for the three or four high-voltage DC stations contracted out each year. Each bid attracts the same ten or so competitors worldwide. At the other extreme, its electrical installation and service division competes under "super local" conditions, with contracts going to companies that tailor their products best to local conditions. Most of ABB's businesses require both strong local organizations and globally cost-efficient manufacturing of parts and components.[27]

Relationships Among Strategies, Structures, and Corporate Cultures

Causes of Change In smooth-running corporations, corporate strategies, structures, and cultures are in synch. But when any one of these three elements changes, the others need to be reviewed. Usually it is marketplace change that alters strategies, with top management bringing organizational structures and cultures into line. In other situations, changes in organizational structure (such as those occurring in acquisitions and joint ventures) force adjustments in strategies or corporate cultures. Finally, when, for example, companies are performing poorly, new mind-sets are necessary, and corporate culture adjustments (often initiated by new leadership) can engender changes in structures and strategies.

Relationships Among International Strategies, Structures, and Corporate Cultures There are discernible relationships among strategies, structures, and corporate cultures as international companies increase their foreign-market commitments. Export-led global strategies can be orchestrated from the domestic market with international departments (smaller companies) or worldwide product structures (larger firms). The reliance on home-country facilities and expertise makes some ethnocentric behaviors likely. Eventually, though, the comparative advantages of offshore production and foreign-market assembly facilities force corporate reassessments of home-market dependencies, and companies like Sony, Toyota, Mercedes, and Hewlett-Packard are forced into foreign manufacturing or sourcing.

Consumer-goods industries such as food/drink, cosmetics, and household goods have historically been very customer-oriented. Hence, they have had polycentric (host market) philosophies and organized themselves on geographic bases. However, as cultural differences have diminished worldwide, regional and product-based structures have begun to replace country-oriented organizations. Cultural homogenization has also pushed regional structures toward worldwide product structures and more worldly (geocentric) orientations.

Note that companies are careful to balance product division and country-level structures. In multinational and regional structures, country-level operations are often complemented with product management teams. Similarly, export-led global strategies are often structured by product, but are complemented by geographic organizations abroad. Only in the matrix structure are the axes (often product and geographic) considered coequal (one reason why matrix organizations are conflict-oriented).

> Selling focuses on the needs of the seller; marketing on the needs of the buyer.
>
> —*Theodore Levitt, Harvard business educator*

FINANCING INTERNATIONAL AND GLOBAL OPERATIONS

As companies set up foreign operations, they must arrange financing. Two major factors influence finance sourcing: the preferred capital structure ([1] whether firms use debt financing and borrow from banks or other financial institutions or [2] if they want to use equity sources and issue shares), and whether they want to finance capital internally (from within the company) or use external sources. These are illustrated in Figure 8.8. This produces four strategic financing options, each of which has different degrees of subsidiary accountability and control.

Equity Options Using Outside Financing

International firms tend to be large and are good credit risks. This gives them access to most of the world's forty-five or so national stock exchanges. While the major exchanges are in North America, Western Europe, and Japan, stock exchanges are proliferating in Asia (Indonesia, Thailand, Hong Kong, Philippines, Malaysia, South Korea, Taiwan,

> For which of you, intending to build a tower, sitteth not down first, and counteth the cost, whether he have sufficient to finish it?
>
> —*New Testament, Bible, Luke 14:28*

FIGURE 8.8
Financing Options for Foreign Operations

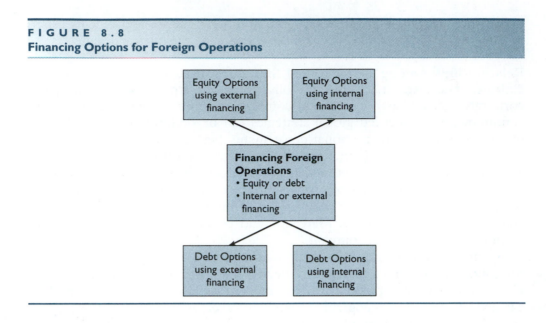

Singapore), Latin America (Mexico, Chile, Brazil, Venezuela, Colombia), and Eastern Europe (Russia, Poland, Hungary, the Czech Republic).[28] While many developing market exchanges are just getting started, they have rapidly acquired abilities to issue shares and expand the financing options for global companies. The advantages of issuing shares locally are, first, that subsidiaries tend to be perceived as local entities and not as "exploitive" foreign concerns and, second, that noncorporate entities shoulder the risks of nonperformance in the marketplace. The downsides are that (1) problems can arise in regard to profit divisions between parent companies and local shareholders, (2) company share prices are susceptible to national economic fortunes—particularly downturns, (3) subsidiaries must be sensitive to national shareholder pressures, and (4) subsidiaries can become vulnerable to takeovers.

Equity Options Using Internal Financing

International companies are uniquely structured in being able to issue equity from their parent headquarters, holding companies, regional headquarters, or from other sister subsidiaries. Crossholdings of shares among corporate affiliates are common in Japan and in Asia, but are also found in Western Europe and North America. A major advantage of this type of financing is corporate control over subsidiary operations, with minimal outside interference. Profit pressures are corporate-controlled, shielding local managements in bad times, allowing subsidiaries to focus on long-term perspectives (rather than short-term profits), and enabling them to contribute to group operations and profits rather than just the subsidiary's bottom line. Internal financing is also an effective protection against takeovers. The major problem is the lack of external pressures to be efficient and accountable to outside influences.

Debt Options Using External Financing

Borrowing capital from banks or other financial institutions occurs when (1) national stock exchanges are undeveloped (as with many developing nations) or non-functioning (as in much of Western Europe and Japan after World War II), or (2) where national interest rates have been low over long time periods (as in Asia where savings rates have been prodigiously high for a long time), or (3) when banks and companies have had long-term relationships (as in Germany, for example, or in Japan where both are part of the same keiretzu, or industrial conglomerate). The major advantage of external debt capital is that once interest payments have been made to the bank, companies have considerable discretion in formulating long-term strategies rather than having to worry about quarterly profits and shareholder prices. Japanese firms in particular benefited from being debt financed in their post-1945 expansion strategies.

There are numerous disadvantages to this form of financing. These are:

1. National economic problems (including inflation and demand downturns) can result in rising interest rates, increased costs of doing business, and possible foreclosure (or takeover) by the bank. This occurred in Russia in the mid-1990s, resulting in high ownership concentrations among Russian financial institutions (the "Robber Barons").

2. Keeping national interest rates low over long periods is difficult unless national financial markets can be shielded from international competition. Japan has managed this feat since 1945, but at tremendous cost to its citizens (who get miniscule returns on their savings), and to the financial institutions themselves, as their diminished margins make them vulnerable to small percentages of bad debts.

3. Cozy relationships between companies and banks can shield managements from marketplace realities and competitive returns on assets.

Let us be happy and live within our means, even if we have to borrow money to do it.

*—Artemus Ward,
19th-century U.S. humorist*

A banker is a fellow who lends you his umbrella when the sun is shining and wants it back the minute it begins to rains.

*—Mark Twain,
19th–20th-century
U.S. author*

Debt Options and Internal Financing

International companies have considerable resources that can be used to finance new operations. They can use capital borrowed in low interest-rate markets and lend it to affiliates in high rate markets, or they can borrow from subsidiaries anywhere in the world. Internal borrowing provides firms with considerable flexibility in financing arrangements. In particular, they can adjust interest rates and payback periods to reflect market conditions. In high-risk markets, for example, they can shorten payback periods or increase interest rates to counter adverse environmental conditions. They can vary interest rates, making them high in "soft," "easy" markets, and bringing them down in highly competitive markets where new subsidiaries come under heavy cost pressures. The downside is that it is corporate (rather than shareholder) capital that is placed at risk, and developing-nation governments often scrutinize repayment schedules to guard against "excessive" repatriations of loans and profits.

KEY POINTS

- Internationalization occurs as firms extend products and services into foreign markets. It is the initial part of the corporate globalization process by which companies create value by leveraging resources and capabilities across borders.

- As companies globalize, they must balance pressures to globally integrate their operations with pressures to localize output. Their efforts to manage these pressures are reflected in internationalization strategies, global integration strategies, multinational strategies, and global-local strategies.

- Globalization can be measured objectively through foreign percentages of assets, sales, and employment. Corporate measures take in such measures as corporate governance and responsibility, strategy and planning, marketing orientation, operations and technology, research and development, and organizational/human resource management.

- Globalization drivers can be based on market, cost, competitor, or government factors. Information technologies are major facilitators of global integration.

- Companies prepare for globalization by assessing corporate competences, supply chains, leadership capabilities, and corporate cultures.

- Globalizing corporate cultures involves defining and critically examining organizational relationships, communication patterns, and employee behaviors. Firms can attempt to standardize corporate cultures across markets or adapt them, partially or totally, to foreign markets. Societal competitiveness and shareholder-stakeholder orientations affect corporate culture transferability. Power distance, individualism-collectivism, masculine-feminine orientations, uncertainty avoidance, and short- long-term orientations are key factors affecting individual corporate culture adaptations.

- Effects of globalization must be assessed for industry structure, organizational structure, and corporate culture. Change in any one of the strategy-structure-corporate culture variables is often accompanied by adjustments to the other two elements.

- International firms have a number of options in financing their internationalization and globalization efforts. These include issuing shares, either internationally or domestically, or raising capital from banks or from other members of the corporate group.

ENDNOTES

1. Elizabeth Mora-Mass, "Mr. Modelo risin'," *Beverage World* (January 15, 2002): 11, 23.

2. Neil Bromage, "Captain Spice," *Supply Management* (March 28, 2002): 26–28.

3. From Robert Gunn, "Why CEOs are stuck on globalization," *Canadian Underwriter* (July 1999): 22–25.

4. United Nations Conference on Trade and Development, *World Investment Report 2002* (New York 2002), 96–97.

5. Based on Thomas A. Stewart, "A Way to Measure Worldwide Success," *Fortune* (March 15, 1999): 196:8.

6. Stewart, *Op. cit.*, 198.

7. Based on C. K. Prahalad and Yves L. Doz, *The Multinational Mission: Balancing Local Demands and Global Vision* (New York: Free Press, 1987).

8. C. D. Prahalad, Yves L. Doz, *The Multinational Mission* (New York: The Free Press, 1987), 24.

9. Based on George S. Yip, *Total Global Strategy* (New York: Prentice Hall Inc., 1995), chapter 2.

10. David Manners, "The Price of 300mm" *Electronic News* (Feb. 28, 2000): p. 16.

11. Karen Hsu, "Drug Economics 101: Making drugs, profits and doing some good," *Boston Globe* (October 25, 1999): F14.

12. Marie-Claude Boudreau, Karen D. Loch, Daniel Robey, Detmar Straud, "Going global: Using information technology to advance the competitiveness of the virtual transnational corporation," *Academy of Management Executive* 12.4 (Nov. 1998): 120–28.

13. Andrea Knox, "Kvaerner ASA," *Industry Week* (June 7, 1999): 36–38.

14. John S. McClenaken, "CEO of the year," *Industry Week* (Nov. 15, 1999): 42–46.

15. Helena Harvilicz, "Unilever undertakes massive restructuring," *Chemical Market Reporter* (Feb. 28, 2000): 9; and Steve Bell, "P & G forced by rivals to change old habits," *Marketing* (June 17, 1999): 15–18.

16. "Nissan to name Ghosn as its President in June," *Detroit News* (March 17, 2000): B3; Carol Matlack, "Letting some air out of Michelin," *Business Week* (Oct. 4, 1999): 58; Amy Barrett, "J & J babying itself," *Business Week* (Sept. 13, 1999): 95–97.

17. This section based on Hal B. Gregerson, Allen J. Morrison, and J. Stewart Black, "Developing leader for the global frontier," *Sloan Management Review* 40 (Fall 1998): 21–32.

18. Michael Hickins, "Irreconcilable differences," *Management Review* 87: 10 (Nov. 1998): 54–58.

19. Jenny McCune, "Exporting corporate culture," *Management Review* 88: 11 (Dec. 1999): 52–56.

20. McCune, *op. cit.*, 56.

21. Anonymous, "Japanese banks hope tie-up will revive sector," *Irish Times* (August 21, 1999): 19.

22. Corinna C. Petry, "A volatile outlook for Latin American steel," *Metal Center News* (March 1999): 38–46.

23. Marjorie Walker, "North American Petrochemicals: Staying ahead of the game," *Chemical Market Reporter* (March 22, 1999): N20–N24.

24. For elaboration, see Christopher A. Bartlett and Sumantra Ghoshal, "Matrix Management: Not a Structure, a Frame of Mind," *Harvard Business Review* (July–Aug. 1990): 138–45.

25. Based on Balaji S. Chakravarthy and Howard V. Perlmutter, "Strategic Planning for a Global Business," *Columbia Journal of World Business* (Summer 1985): 3–10.

26. "The Stateless Corporation," *Business Week* (May 14, 1990): 98–105.

27. William Taylor, "The Logic of Global Business: An Interview with ABB's Percy Barnevik," *Harvard Business Review* (March–April 1991): 91–103.

28. Meridian Securities, *World Stock Exchange Handbook* (Plano, Texas: 2001) 314–56.

CASETTE 8-1
Four Companies Go Global

For increasing numbers of firms, going global has become a corporate imperative. But as companies review the requirements for globalization, each sees a different set of challenges in orienting their firms to the dynamics of the international marketplace. Here are four examples, one each from the candy/confectionary, legal services, utility (water services), and auto industries.

ARCOR: Candy and Confectionary

Candy manufacturer ARCOR is part of Grupo ARCOR, an Argentine conglomerate that has been in business in Latin America for over five decades. For years, the company has dominated its regional market. But as competition has increased, ARCOR has placed increasing emphasis on developing its international markets to push global sales up from 37 percent of turnover to 50 percent over the 2001–6 period. The company already distributes its products to 105 countries, but it wants to increase its commitments to North America (including Mexico), Africa, the Middle East, the EU, Australia, and New Zealand.

As a major producer of hard and soft candies, ARCOR prides itself on developing and adapting its products to different market needs. Taste variations, sizing differences, brand-name and packaging changes are all necessary adaptations to suit customer tastes. Because basic candies are not usually mass advertised, "push" techniques emphasizing personal selling are used to get products through channels. Because of the intensive nature of candy distribution, much attention is placed on distributor selection, training programs, and relationships. In developing its U.S. market, ARCOR works with 160 distributors, wholesalers, and supermarkets, taking great care to supply different product lines to distributors where territories overlap. Throughout its many years of overseas selling, ARCOR has seen it all—political changes, economic volatility, trade barriers, but rarely have product supplies been affected by adverse market conditions. Outside of Argentina, the firm has six manufacturing plants, all in Latin America. Recent developments are an alliance with the U.S.'s Brach and a Canadian sales office. Future plans include licensing agreements with foreign producers, B2B web site ordering, and, once distribution is secured (as in China), foreign promotional campaigns.

Antipodean Law Services

As international businesses have expanded, so the need for global services, such as advertising, accounting, and legal advice, has expanded. In Asia, foreign corporations have invested over $1.2 trillion, creating demand for international service firms.

For Australian and New Zealand law firms, however, geographic proximity to the powerhouse nations of China (including Hong Kong), South Korea, Malaysia, Singapore, and Thailand has not created the sorts of demand for legal services that might be expected. Leading U.S. and UK law firms have dominated Asia, much to the chagrin of Australian and New Zealand companies. Antipodean lawyers are well-trained and can cope with the highly sophisticated demands of international companies. They are also much less expensive. One problem has been cherry picking. U.S. and UK firms have consistently "stolen" the best Australian and New Zealand lawyers to work for them. Another problem has been the inability of Antipodean companies to create a critical mass of foreign-based offices in Asia. Some firms, such as Australia's Freehills, have advised the Korean government on privatization, an area in which Australian firms have had considerable domestic experience. But the top six Australian law firms—Mallesons, Stephen Jaques, Freehills, Aliens Arthur Robinson, Clayton Utz, Minter Ellison, and Blake Dawson Waldron—have not been as influential internationally as they perhaps should have been. The international profiles of Australia and New Zealand were rising, having $113 billion and $31 billion of foreign direct investment within their respective borders, as well as $83 billion and $7 billion of their own investments in foreign markets.

The question was: How could Australian and New Zealand firms impact the Asian and global legal services market? What strategies could they follow to become more successful in international markets? One thing was certain: the longer they waited, the more difficult globalization would be.

The Utility Industry: Vivendi Water

France's Vivendi Water is the largest water treatment company in the world. A subsidiary of Vivendi SA, the utility and media conglomerate, Vivendi Environment is a global provider of municipal industrial, commercial, consumer water and wastewater treatment systems. It has over 180,000 employees in more than 100 countries, but globalization opportunities abound for Vivendi. Global privatization and deregulation trends have made countries and cities aware of private sector interests in utilities generally, and in water in particular. Trends toward higher environmental standards and expectations (clean air, water, etc.) have also helped the company. As international firms such as Merck, Pfizer, Unilever, Coca-Cola, and Nestle have expanded into developing markets, they have become acutely aware of the need to ensure quality water supplies. Then, too, firms in mining, metal processing, and manufacturing have increasing obligations to maintain environmentally friendly operations in the markets they service. When companies are not water experts, outsourcing water and wastewater treatments to firms like Vivendi is an easy option. The company prefers to work in politically stable countries, as partnerships with municipalities, governments, and companies are easier to maintain in those countries.

Korean Auto Globalization

For Korean carmakers Daewoo and Hyundai, the 1990s was a traumatic decade. Daewoo's joint venture with General Motors broke up in 1992. Hyundai's partnership with Ford lasted five years (1967–72). The Asian financial crisis and South Korea's IMF loan forced an opening up of the country's borders. For both firms, the domestic market was limited, with Hyundai and Daewoo having about 50 and 20 percent market shares respectively. Both needed to exploit the international marketplace. Both had resources, as they belonged to large business groupings (*chaebol*) that dominated Korean business (the four largest—55 percent of national GDP). Yet their globalization strategies were distinctly different.

Hyundai's strategy was based on building scale economies through exporting from the home market. Focusing on top quality R and D and manufacturing, its aim was to become a global top 10 auto maker and considerably boost its 1.15 million units per year output. It major focus was the North American market. To this end, Hyundai established R and D and manufacturing/assembly units in the U.S. and Canada respectively. Secondary targets were adjoining Asia-Pacific markets and Africa.

Daewoo's situation was different. It did not have Hyundai's large domestic manufacturing base. Neither did it want to go head-to-head with Hyundai and U.S. auto makers in the North American market. Its strategy was to acquire Polish auto firms FSL and FSO and Romanian company Rodae and focus its manufacturing efforts in Eastern Europe and its marketing efforts (thirty marketing subsidiaries) in Western Europe. As the 1990s drew to a close, Daewoo had grown its foreign production capacity from zero in 1986 to more than 1.2 million vehicles in nine countries. Hyundai, by contrast, had only 100,000 cars a year foreign capacity.

Both firms were ultimately interested in reaching two million units per year. Both needed foreign markets to achieve this objective. There, however, the similarities ended.

Questions

1. For each company, identify the major globalization drivers. Which do you think is the most important? Why? What do those drivers tell you about the industry?

2. For each company, identify the key success factors for their industries, that is, what they must do well to be successful in their globalization efforts.

Sources: Kimbrell, Wendy. "Global Goliar ll." *Candy Industry Supplement* (2001): 10–13. Ferguson, Nick. "Antipodean firms look for way out of isolation." *International Law Review* 20: 1 (January 2001): 41–44. Swichtenberg, Bill. "Global yet local: An interview with Andrew Seidel of Vivendi water." *Water Engineering & Management* (November 2000): 22–25. Kim, Bowon, and Yoonseok Lee. "Global Capacity Expansion Strategies: Lessons Learned from Two Korean Carmakers." *Long Range Planning* 34 (2001): 309–33. *World Investment Report 2001* (New York: United Nations, 2001).

Setting Up a Multilingual Web Site

Your manager has asked you to set up a multilingual web site for your office products business and has given you some basic country information to get started.

Country	Spoken language(s)	Commercial language(s)	Population (million)	GDP per capita ($)	Computer ownership/ 1000 people
Afghanistan	Pashto, Dari	Pashto, Dari, English	25	800	
Albania	Albanian, French, Italian	Albanian, French	3	810	
Algeria	Arabic	French	30	1550	6
Angola	Portuguese	Portuguese	12	380	
Argentina	Spanish	Spanish	36	8030	49
Australia	English	English	19	20640	469
Austria	German	German	8	26830	257
Bangladesh	Begali	English	126	350	
Barbados	English	English	0.25	12001	
Belgium	French, Dutch, German	French, Dutch, German, English	10	25380	315
Belize	English, Spanish	English	0.25	4566	
Bolivia	Spanish	Spanish	8	1010	
Brazil	Portuguese	Portuguese	166	4630	36
Bulgaria	Bulgarian	Russian, French, German	8	1220	27
Burma	Burmese	Burmese, English	44		
Cambodia	Khmer	French	11	260	
Canada	English, French	English	30	19170	361
Chile	Spanish	Spanish	15	4990	67
China (PRC)	Mandarin	Mandarin, English, Chinese	1239	750	12
Colombia	Spanish	Spanish	41	2470	34
Costa Rica	Spanish	Spanish	4	2770	
Czech Republic			10	5450	107
Denmark	Danish	Danish, German, English	5	33040	414
Dominican Republic	Spanish	Spanish	8	1770	
Ecuador	Spanish	Spanish	12	1520	20
Egypt	Arabic	French, English	61	1290	12
Ethiopia	Amharic	English, French, Italian	61	100	
Fiji	English	English	0.8	4321	
Finland	Finnish, Swedish	Finnish, Swedish, English, German	5	24280	360
France	French	French	59	24280	222
Germany	German	German	82	26570	297
Ghana	English	English	18	390	
Greece	Greek	Greek, French, English	11	11740	60
Guatemala	Spanish	Spanish	11	1640	
Guyana	English	English	0.7	3403	
Haiti	French	French	8	410	
Honduras	Spanish	Spanish	6	740	
Hong Kong	Mandarin Chinese, Cantonese, English	English	7	20763	298
Hungary	Hungarian	German, English, Russian, French	10	4510	75
Iceland	Icelandic	English	0.3	25110	
India	Hindi, English	Hindi, English	1000	440	3
Indonesia	Bahasa, Indonesian	Dutch, Chinese, English, Bahasa, Indonesian	204	640	9
Iran	Persian, Farsi	English, French, German	62	1650	52
Iraq	Arabic, Kurdish	English	22	?	
Ireland	Irish, English	English	4	18710	405
Israel	Hebrew, Arabic	English	6	16180	246
Italy	Italian	Italian, English	58	20090	192
Jamaica	English	English	3	1740	

Country	Spoken language(s)	Commercial language(s)	Population (million)	GDP per capita ($)	Computer ownership/ 1000 people
Japan	Japanese	Japanese, English	126	32350	287
Jordan	Arabic	English	5	1156	
Kenya	Swahili	English	29	350	
South Korea	Korean	English	46	8600	185
Kuwait	Arabic	English	2	?	
Laos	Lao	French	5	320	
Lebanon	Arabic	English, French	4	3560	
Luxembourg	French, German	English	0.5	33505	
Malaysia	Malay	English	22	3670	69
Mexico	Spanish	Spanish, English	96	3840	44
Morocco	Arabic	French, Spanish, English	28	1240	
Netherlands	Dutch	Dutch, French, German, English	16	24780	360
New Zealand	English	English	4	14600	328
Nicaragua	Spanish	Spanish	5	370	
Nigeria	English, Hausa, Yoruba, Ibo	English	121	300	6
Norway	Norwegian	English, German	4	34310	447
Pakistan	Urdu	English	132	470	4
Paraguay	Spanish, Guarani	Spanish	5	1760	
Peru	Spanish	Spanish	25	2440	36
Philippines	Filipino	English, Spanish	75	1050	17
Poland	Polish	English, French, German	39	3910	62
Portugal	Portuguese	Portuguese	10	10670	93
Puerto Rico	Spanish, English	Spanish, English	4	8000	
Romania	Romanian	English, French, German	23	1360	37
Rwanda	Kinyarwanda	French, English, Swahili	8	660	
Russian Federation	Russian	Russian, English, French, German	147	2260	
El Salvador	Spanish	Spanish	6	1850	
Saudi Arabia	Arabic	English	21	6910	57
Senegal	French	French	9	520	
Sierra Leone	Native dialects, English	5	140	458	
Singapore	Malay	English	3	30170	437
Rep. of South Africa	English, Afrikaans	English, Afrikaans	41	3310	55
Spain	Spanish	Spanish	39	14100	119
Sweden	Swedish	Swedish, English	9	25580	451
Switzerland	German, Italian, French	German, Italian, French, English	7	39980	462
Syria	Arabic, French, English	Arabic, French, English	15	1020	
Taiwan ROC	Mandarin Chinese	Mandarin Chinese, English, Japanese	22	12700	na
Tanzania	Swahili	English	32	220	
Thailand	Thai	English	61	2160	23
Tunisia	Arabic	French, English	9	2260	
Turkey	Turkish	French, English	63	3160	34
Uganda	Swahili, English	English	21	310	
United Kingdom	English	English	59	21470	303
United States	English	English	280	36200	511
Venezuela	Spanish	Spanish	23	3530	42
Vietnam	Vietnamese	English, French	77	350	9
Zambia	Icibema, Luapula	English	10	330	
Zimbabwe	Shona, Ndebele	English	12	620	

Questions

1. You have been given authorization to set up a four-language Web site for your initial business-to-business venture. Which languages would you select, and why? Justify your selections.

2. Your firm also does some specialty office equipment that is marketed directly to consumers. A two-language Web site has been proposed. Which two languages would you choose? Why?

3. Some thought is being given to regional strategies for warehousing and servicing. Which regions would you consider—first, second, third in order of priority?

Chapter Nine

Market Entry and Servicing Strategies

〜◦〜

EXPANDING INTO NEW MARKETS

Eli's cheesecake started to export from its U.S. base in 1994. Originally it used International Products, an export management company to help it gain access to the European market. Over time and after exhibiting at numerous European trade shows, the company built up exports of over $1 million. Along the way, Eli's had to adjust its product labeling to conform to metric requirements, and comply with EU certifications for milk-based products. Persistence paid off, and, in the late 1990s, the firm extended its penetration to other major European markets.[1]

In 1961, Japanese pharmaceutical manufacturer Sankyo established an office in New York, and used partnerships with U.S. drug maker Pfizer to establish its products in the world's largest pharmaceutical market. Over time, the company built up a sales force of over 1000 representatives to promote its wares. In 1996, Sankyo formed a 50–50 joint venture with the U.S.'s Warner-Lambert to develop and market drugs. In 2000, the firm split with Pfizer and proceeded to beef up its sales networks. Sankyo's objective is to build up to $1 billion in U.S. sales by 2007.[2]

Since the early 1990s, U.S. and European insurance companies have been expanding vigorously into developing markets. Where possible, companies such as AIG, Cigna, Chubb, and Allianz have set up their own affiliates in Latin America, Eastern Europe, and Asia. When these firms have encountered significant local rivals, they have used joint ventures, mergers, and acquisitions to penetrate markets and establish local connections.[3]

These examples illustrate the many strategies that international companies use to access and service foreign markets. Firms can service markets via exports from the home base (as with Eli's Cheesecake in Western Europe) or from foreign manufacturing sites (as sports shoes and equipment manufacturers do). A further option is to serve customer needs from within the foreign market via contractual arrangements such as licensing or franchising (McDonald's, KFC). Finally, they can make foreign investments through joint ventures (as Sankyo did) or through establishing subsidiaries or acquiring foreign competitors (as insurance companies have done).

Which market entry and servicing method is used depends on managerial assessments of industry, competitor, and market environments, as well as corporate needs and resources. These are among the most important decisions that international companies make. They represent significant resource commitments and often determine how well firms perform in individual markets.

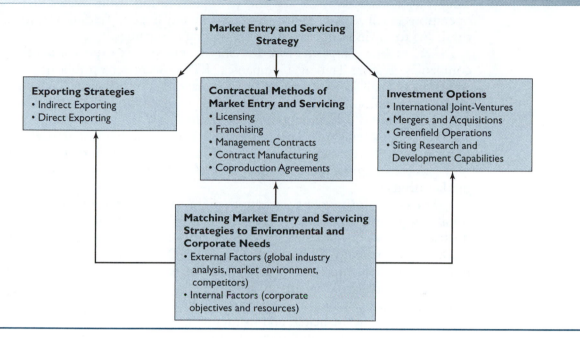

Hence, in this chapter, you will learn:

- How firms can service foreign markets through indirect exports (via third parties) or using direct exporting
- The ways that companies can contract with foreign firms to use home market technologies and/or marketing methods to produce goods and/or services in foreign countries
- What investment options are available to companies to manufacture in foreign markets, including joint ventures (usually with local partners), mergers and acquisitions, and custom-building their own subsidiaries
- What factors determine the choice of market entry and servicing strategy

INTRODUCTION: EXPORTING STRATEGIES

Indirect Exporting and Use of Trading Companies

Many firms lack the resources, expertise, and market contacts to cover world markets. When this occurs, many turn to trading companies to get their products into foreign markets and to handle the intricacies involved in gaining market access. Historically, trading companies originated in the sixteenth century where they were used to export the output of European colonial powers into the developing world and to import from those markets raw materials, spices, and materials back to the home market.

Today's trading companies provide market contacts, trade expertise, commercial financing, foreign distribution, and quality control for traded goods. They vary considerably in size and in sophistication from small independent operations (such as the Export Management and Export Trading Companies in the U.S.) to Japan's large sogo shosha trading companies.

U.S. trading companies and associations operate as export arms for small companies. Export Trading Companies (ETCs) were set up following a 1982 Act to help small U.S. firms find foreign markets, arrange sales, financing, and documentation, and perform as the firms' representatives abroad. Currently, these are about 178 ETCs operating from the U.S.[4] At the industry level, there are Webb-Pomerene Associations (WPAs). WPAs number about twelve in the U.S. and usually represent several manufacturers within a single industry where they direct foreign import enquiries to firms best suited to meet individual market needs.[5]

Taiwanese trading companies are the international arms of industry associations comprising independent producers, suppliers, and subcontractors in industries such as fashion shoes and furniture. Trading companies function as marketing agents and as information centers.[6] One trading company specializes in furniture trade with the U.S. and is known as the Export America Company. It plays an active role in furniture design for the U.S. market, helping Taiwanese producers custom-manufacture products for specific customers, arranging letter-of-credit financing, and maintaining quality standards.[7]

Mainland China trading companies are also mainly industry-centered. The Heilongjiang Textile Trading Company is organized into four departments (Yarn & Fabric, Garments, Linen products, and Knitwear). They perform sales promotions, locate suitable Chinese suppliers for specific customer needs, and arrange financing and shipping to foreign ports.[8]

Japanese trading companies were first established in the seventeenth century. Today there are about 70,000 trading companies, of which 300 are involved in international trade. The "big nine" sogo shosha maintain over 1000 overseas offices, and their combined annual turnover tops $350 billion. Mitsui alone has 153 offices worldwide in 88 countries. The accumulated international trade expertise of the network is such that they can buy and sell almost any products or services anywhere in the world. Their ability to find markets, perform complex barter transactions, and arrange credit and transportation has made them dominant in Japanese commerce and trade.[9]

Trading Companies and Global Supply Chains In Asia especially, trading companies link global demand and supply in many industries. They trade in market contacts and market knowledge. This gives them significant potential as supply-chain organizers. Li & Fung, a Hong Kong-based Trading company, functions as the supply-chain organizer for U.S. and European companies such as The Limited (clothing), Reebok (shoes and sporting accessories), Avon (cosmetics), and Tesco (supermarkets). This company arranges samples, sets up production schedules, and makes arrangements for delivery.[10]

Direct Exporting

Where firms have expertise in dealing with foreign customers and in financing and shipping goods abroad, direct exports to overseas markets are appropriate. Direct exporting is beneficial as companies deal face-to-face with foreign distributors and customers, learning as they go and building up international expertise. As markets develop and sales increase, marketing subsidiaries can be established to enhance market contacts and customer relations. Exports make three contributions to corporate strategies:

If you want to earn more—learn more.

—*William J. H. Boetcker*

1. For small- and medium-sized firms, exporting is a cheap and flexible way to develop foreign markets and to learn about customer needs. The Internet, in particular, has opened up world markets and gives companies competitive advantages by:
   * Being available 24-hours a day across time zones
   * Enabling web sites to feature promotional materials about companies, their products, and, in many cases, permitting on-site orders to be made
   * Facilitating international payments through electronic fund transfers and allowing cross-border consumer transactions via credit cards
   * Making written Internet communications the norm for messaging, thereby avoiding translation and other comprehension problems that can occur using, for example, the telephone[11]

2. For large international firms, export-import transactions are vital parts of their international operations. Global export strategies are used in industries where there are significant manufacturing scale economies. In these cases, global production is centralized to service world or regional markets. Autos, medical equipment, machine tools all use export-based strategies as they use a single production site to serve multiple markets. Additionally, industries with country-specific production advantages (French wines, Indian or Chinese teas, Italian fashions) place great reliance on export-based strategies.

3. Export and import strategies are key elements in global supply chains where materials and components are manufactured at specialized locations and shipped to other markets for final assembly. About one-third of world trade occurs between affiliates of the same international corporation, and two-thirds takes place between affiliates of different international companies.[12] Many industries, from autos to textiles, have regional or global supply chains and transship components between markets prior to final assembly.

For international companies, the mechanics of exporting and importing are basic. For those getting started in the export field, the paperwork and administrative detail involved in preparing export quotations, arranging financing, and shipping goods appear immense. Exhibit 9-1 shows the basic documents involved in getting goods into foreign markets and getting paid for them.

EXHIBIT 9-1
Basic Export Mechanics and Documentation

The export process begins with the *international proforma invoice,* or export quotation, to a prospective customer. This details the prices of goods to be shipped, cargo weights and dimensions, (which determine transportation costs), export packaging charges, inland freight costs (to the port or airport), freight-forwarder fees, dock and loading charges, ocean freight and insurance costs.

The prospective importer receives the quotation, and if all is in order, confirms the sale with the *international purchase order.* The importer uses the export quotation to arrange financing (see below), either to open a letter of credit at the importer's bank in favor of the exporter or to arrange for a bill of exchange (sight or time draft) in favor of the exporter. Where governments require *import licenses* (which are permissions to import), the importer uses the export quotation to obtain the required import license.

The exporter receives the international purchase order, packs the goods, and, often using a freight-forwarder, arranges shipment to the port and onto a carrier. Responsibility for the cargo is transferred to the trucking company via an *inland bill of lading.* At the port, the cargo is inspected and transferred to a cargo vessel that issues a *clean on board bill of lading* specifying that the goods have been safely placed onboard ship.

The exporter or freight forwarder collects the ocean bill of lading, the *international commercial invoice* (issued by the exporter), and other required documents. These may include *packing lists* (to facilitate customs clearances and prevent pilferage),

insurance certificates, certificates of origin (to verify place of manufacture for import duty assessment), and other, often industry-specific, documents. These are then sent to the importer's bank. The importer is notified when the goods arrive. They go to the bank, pay or sign for the goods, collect the title documents, and retrieve the goods at the port, paying the necessary duties. The importer's bank pays the exporter's bank, which then pays the exporter.

PAYMENT MECHANISMS

The two major means of payment are letters of credit and bills of exchange. Letters of credit are used when exporters and importers do not know each other very well or where there might be payment difficulties. On placing the order, the importer's bank opens an *unconfirmed irrevocable* (i.e., unchangeable) *letter of credit* in favor of the exporter. This specifies that the importer has the funds and credit to pay for the shipment. This document then goes to the exporter's bank who, for a small fee, will check the importer, the importer's bank, and hard currency availability in the market, and, if all is in order, issues a *confirmed irrevocable letter of credit.* This is the safest of payment mechanisms.

Bills of Exchange are "reverse checks" requiring payment and are issued through international banks. They may be payable immediately (a *sight draft*) or after a specified period (a *time draft*). These are used when exporters and importers know each other and mutual trust exists.

CONTRACTUAL FORMS OF MARKET ENTRY

Many firms find contractual modes of international business convenient means of servicing foreign markets. Under these arrangements, a company contracts with a foreign firm to render a service to that firm in a particular country or group of markets. The three most popular methods are licensing, franchising, and subcontracting production (outsourcing).

Licensing

Licensing allows a foreign-based firm to use a company's production processes, marketing logos, trademarks, or brand names for a defined time period in specific markets and for a pre-specified royalty fee. Companies use licensing to gain swift access to markets, but without significant upfront investments. Exhibit 9-2 shows three uses for licensing arrangements in varying situations. In the first, Danisco Cultor used licensing to extend the product life cycle for maltol in Asia, where the product had come under severe price competition from Chinese producers. In the second example, Ferrari Motorsports, allowed the licensee, TSS&P to use the prestigious Ferrari name and Italian associations to market a line of branded clothing. This afforded Ferrari royalties as well as free publicity as consumers bought its branded clothing, all without up-front investments. Third, Umbro used licensing as a global strategy weapon to combat the aggressive tactics of Adidas and Nike in the competitive sportswear field. The Manchester, England-based firm used licensees to compete with the sportswear giants without having to make major resource expenditures.

Franchising

Franchising is similar to licensing in that a protected trademark is contracted to a foreign company, giving it the right to use the trademark to produce or distribute a product or service.[13] The major difference is that while licensees have discretion in some aspects of the production or marketing of the product, franchisers exert considerable control over both the production process (with operating manuals, procedures, and quality standards) and marketing strategy (how the product or service is presented to customers). Consistency is the hallmark of franchised operations that include popular fast-food businesses (like McDonalds, KFC, and Pizza Hut), service outfits like Jani-King (a commercial cleaning service firm with 6500 franchise units worldwide) and industrial companies like Kott Koatings, which operates a 51-country franchise system in porcelain and fiberglass products.[14]

Franchising is a useful strategy where rapid international expansion is needed, but it requires significant amounts of investment capital (e.g., hotels). Hotel chains such as Hyatt and Holiday Inn require up to $100 million in real

> *The value of all things contracted is measurable by the appetite of the contractors, and the just value is that which they are contented to give.*
>
> —*Thomas Hobbes, 17th-century English philosopher*

> *The word* franchise *originally came from the French word meaning "to be free from servitude."*

EXHIBIT 9-2
Licensing and Global Strategy: Three Illustrations

1. **Danisco Cultor licenses maltol in India***

   Maltol is a widely used ingredient in the global flavor, fragrance, food, and beverage industries. As its patents expired in the U.S. and worldwide, Danisco Cultor, the global leader in maltol, sold its major brands, Velto and Velto-Plus, to its joint venture, Nicholas Piramal India, and licensed the production-process technology to them also. The process is ISO 9000 quality and ISO 14000 environmentally certified and complies with major global standards in food-ingredient production. Chinese overproduction of the food ingredient had caused prices to fall from $100 a kilo in 1997 to $20–30 a kilo in 1999. India had the potential to compete on a global low-cost basis, and the parent company continued to distribute the output via its existing global supply chain.

2. **Ferrari-branded clothing lines†**

   Ferrari knows high-performance sports cars, but capitalizing on its world famous name in the fashion business was beyond its expertise. So the company turned to TSS & P to design, manufacture, and market Ferrari clothing and accessories for a two-year period (1999–2001). Capitalizing on Ferrari's name and Italian fashion flair, the range

was to be marketed in upscale department stores, specialist motor-sport outlets, and the Internet.

3. **Umbro: Basing a global strategy on licensing‡**

   With the advent of international media and global TV exposure, soccer went from being the world's most popular sport to a global business. England's Umbro rode the wave, and 1992–95 were very successful years for the brand. The company identified sixteen global markets, and, in each, it signed the leading club. In England they had Manchester United. In Brazil they signed Santas. Then the predictable happened. In came Nike and Adidas. The latter were already into soccer. Nike went crazy and bought its way into the sport. In the ensuing struggle, Umbro lost its way. In April 1998, the company sold off or closed down all its manufacturing plants and distribution centers worldwide and established a global licensing business. In doing so, it capitalized on its soccer heritage that started in 1924. In the U.S., a growth market, retailers were calling for a third brand to counter Adidas and Nike. The Umbro name, suitably licensed worldwide, has become once again *the* lead brand in soccer and pushed the company back onto the profit side of the ledger.

*Peter Landau, "Danisco Cultor licenses Maltol in India to stay competitive," *Chemical Market Reporter* (September 20, 1999): 16–17.
†Anonymous, "Ferrari targets women in F1-branded clothes range," *Marketing* (April 1, 1999): 7.
‡Chris McEvoy, "The SGB interview: Steve Preston, Peter Draper," *Sporting goods Business* 32: 7 (April 1999): 27–29.

estate and capital expenditures per hotel. To speed up globalization, they moved from corporate ownership of hotels and resorts to ownership by franchisees. This placed the financial burden of foreign expansion on local business people.[15] Franchise management is mainly concerned with two issues: controlling foreign franchisees and coping with local problems.

Controlling Foreign Franchisees The issue of corporate control can be managed in two ways: by either concentrating or diluting ownership patterns in particular countries or regions.

Concentrating Ownership: The Master Franchiser This strategy concentrates ownership by having individuals supervise and develop a number of franchises within a country or region. Master franchisers are usually wealthy local business people who can afford to buy numerous franchises and exercise centralized control over market development, including the recruitment and training of individual franchise entrepreneurs. HFS is a leading franchiser of brand-name hotels (e.g., Howard Johnson, Day's Inn, Ramada), residential real estate (Century 21, Caldwell Banker, ERA) and rental cars (Avis). HFS licenses its brands to master franchisers who then locate interested entrepreneurs to build and manage local units.[16] This strategy works well when the "right" master franchisers can be selected. These tend to be individuals that are well-connected, know the local market, and are primary movers in their national business communities. Master franchisers work well in areas like Latin America, Middle East, and Asia where local connections are essential elements in all business deals. The master franchiser system is used by three-quarters of leading U.S. global franchise operations, but still has occasional problems including inadequate communications between master franchisers and franchisees, and master franchisers failing to maintain appropriate quality standards among franchisees.[17]

Diluting Ownership Patterns Some franchisers maintain control by owning a proportion of their foreign units or by fragmenting ownership patterns in overseas markets. McDonalds rarely concentrates ownership by using master franchisers in its 25,000 restaurant–117 country global empire.[18]

Managing Local Problems The second problem international franchisers face is dealing with local market environments, including archaic legal frameworks and bureaucracies, political unrest, and major cultural differences.

1. *Archaic legal frameworks and bureaucracies,* especially those relating to foreign investment regulations, are problematic, particularly in Asia and parts of Eastern Europe. But overall the trend is toward liberalizing foreign investment regulations, and countries such as Malaysia, Singapore, and Indonesia have all introduced legislation to encourage foreign franchise expansion. Other nations were opening up more cautiously. The Russian Federation's 1997 franchise law mandated that: (1) Franchises had the right to renew expiring contracts for the same terms as the original contract. (2) Franchisers must provide complete technical and consulting assistance throughout the contract period. (3) And franchisers can be held liable for franchisees' inadequate work or service performances.[19]

2. Political unrest is a problem for all international businesses, including franchises that depend on local business people and buoyant local economies. The 1997 Asian financial crisis caused hesitancy among franchisers looking to take advantage of Asia's growth potential. In Latin America, Colombia and Peru had their franchising (and foreign investment) prospects dimmed by guerilla activities and civil unrest in

the late 1990s. In the Middle East, Iraq, Iran, and Lebanon were similarly viewed as trouble spots.[20]

3. *Cultural obstacles* affect franchisers, particularly those in the culturally sensitive foods industries. McDonalds offers Kosher menus in Israel, Ruby Tuesday does not offer pork and alcohol products in Kuwait, and its Indian fajitas are vegetarian or chicken.[21]

Management Contracts

> One right and honest definition of business is mutual helpfulness.
>
> —*William Feather,*
> *U.S. author and publisher*

Management contracts are agreements whereby international companies, for a fee, train local employees and manage foreign-based facilities for a prescribed time period. Such contracts often include the setting up of foreign affiliates and include technical help in getting facilities up and running. Hilton Hotels used their hotel design skills and management experience to establish one of the world's premier hotel chains.[22] Similarly, Canadian firms Monenco AGRA and SNC-Lavalin used management contracts to break into major water resource projects in China.[23]

Contract Manufacturing

Contract manufacturing involves foreign firms using specific materials and/or processes to manufacture products or provide services at pre-certified quality and cost levels for third-party companies. Offshore manufacturing has flourished as developing countries in particular have embraced free-trade principles and encouraged export manufacturing. International firms, confident in their abilities to subcontract production while maintaining control over product development and marketing activities, have increased corporate dependencies on contract manufacturing in foreign markets. Contract manufacturing has become prominent in automotive and electronics industries, sports and leisure equipment (e.g., Nike, Reebok), retail apparel (Body Shop, Laura Ashley), and other sectors. Indeed, contract-manufacturing organizations (CMOs) have emerged as the production arms of many well-known international corporations.

The advantages of subcontracted production are:[24]

- *Flexibility:* In markets characterized by short product life cycles, rapid technological and customer-taste changes, contract manufacturers are in better positions to increase or decrease production at short notices, as most CMOs have several clients over which to maintain output levels.

- *Cost advantages:* CMO costs are lower than in-house manufacturing. Estimates place them at about half the costs of their least-efficient customers.

- *Manufacturing expertise:* CMOs bring considerable experience to bear on product design for manufacturing and product-testing procedures.

- *Resource outlays:* The costs of global expansion can be shared between CMOs and corporations. Telecommunications firms such as Lucent, Siemens, Nortel, and Alcatel encourage CMOs to bear the brunt of foreign production investments in return for major contracts.

- *Continuous improvements:* The manufacturing expertise accumulated by CMOs from their diverse client base allows them to suggest material and technological improvements for client products. Appliance and apparel manufacturers in particular have benefited from CMO suggestions.

- *Relationship advantages:* Manufacturing partnerships allow free exchanges of expertise. As trust builds, CMO cutting-edge manufacturing expertise can be translated into marketplace gains through higher margins, superior quality, and reduced time to market. This frees up corporate resources for use in R and D and downstream marketing strategies.

Subcontracting has disadvantages, though many can be avoided with careful management. These include:[25]

- *Responsibilities for subcontractor behaviors:* Nike's association with unfair labor practices in developing nations caused the company considerable embarrassment and adverse global publicity.

- *Creation of future competitors:* A major concern is equipping subcontractors with sufficient expertise to become marketplace rivals. Taiwanese bicycle producer Giant Manufacturing Co. stockpiled manufacturing expertise from U.S. producers Schwinn and Specialized Bicycle Components for nine years before launching its own line of branded bicycles. Knowing these dangers, international companies can take suitable precautions. Pentair power tools built a 75-subcontractor base in Taiwan but effectively isolated component subcontractors to prevent expertise buildups that could one day spawn rivals. Additionally, Pentair bans suppliers from accepting assignments from competing companies and safeguards key components that form the bases for products' competitive advantages.

> Mistrust carries one much further than trust.
>
> —*German proverb*

- *Quality control* can be a major concern in some, particularly developing, markets. Inspections of subcontractor facilities and appropriate vetting policies for upstream suppliers therefore become essential parts of the subcontracting process. In developed markets, ISO 9000 quality standards are used to benchmark subcontractor standards.

- *Changing parent company corporate cultures:* Taking manufacturing out of company supply chains and emphasizing R and D and marketing skills requires significant reorientations as firms change from capital-based businesses to outfits based on intellectual capital. Company prospects become dependent on brand-building, new product development, and R and D innovation. Relationships must be built and maintained with suppliers and channels. Friction with either group can cause major supply disruptions.

Coproduction Agreements

Coproduction agreements are manufacturing joint ventures, with partners retaining their independent marketing and distribution rights. U.S. company GE Silicones and Japan's Shin-Etsu Chemical entered a coproduction agreement to build and operate a plant in Thailand to supply key ingredients for both firms' silicone products businesses in Asia.[26]

INVESTMENT OPTIONS FOR SERVICING FOREIGN MARKETS

A little uncertainty is good for everything.

—*Henry Kissinger,*
U.S. Secretary of State

Companies make significant commitments to markets as financial investments are made in plant, equipment, and facilities in foreign countries. In-market investments bring their own sets of problems as firms interact directly with foreign governments, regulations, management styles, cultures, and supply-chain participants (suppliers, channels, customers). But they also have a number of benefits, the most significant of which are learning about markets and customers first-hand, and being able to monitor local rivals.

International Joint Ventures (IJVs)

Joint ventures occur when international corporations and local firms join forces to share ownership and management responsibilities in specially created enterprises. In some countries (e.g., China) IJVs are mandated for industry sectors in which governments have strategic interests (raw materials, key infrastructure developments, or "vital" technologies), or where they wish to build up local expertise. As importantly for some governments, IJVs also prevent total foreign control.

Typically for most IJVs, local partners provide market knowledge, familiarity with government regulations, local manufacturing facilities, and a trained workforce. Foreign partners bring process and product technologies, management expertise, capital, and access to international markets. Foreign equity participation varies from minority IJVs (10–49 percent ownership), through 50–50 relationships, to majority ownership (51 + percent).

Successful IJVs start with good negotiations of initial joint venture agreements, many of which typically take six months to two years to complete. Key topics include the following:[27]

Getting along with others is the essence of getting ahead, success being linked with cooperation.

—*William Feather,*
U.S. author and publisher

- *Equity structure* is important as majority interests imply control over IJV operations. Where local partners have controlling interests, international partners must be sensitive to their needs and avoid imposing their management and technological approaches on local executives. Similarly, international company control is not a mandate to dominate partnerships. In all cases, mutual trust and respect are hallmarks of successful IJVs.

Never have a partner unless it's absolutely necessary.

—*Victor Kiam, U.S. CEO*

- *Technology transfer arrangements:* International companies have many technologies available on a global basis. Appropriate technologies depend often on the international partner's assessment of market needs. Developing country governments and companies often demand "the best" technologies, but these work only when they match local market needs. In all cases, international companies are concerned about intellectual property protection issues, particularly in markets prone to piracy. Included in initial negotiations are controls over derivative technologies (i.e., technologies derived from original applications) and access to follow-on technologies.

- *Asset valuation problems:* How firms value land, buildings, equipment, and intangible assets (good will, brand names, etc.) can vary. International firms are cautious about local asset valuations, particularly when exchange rates are unstable. Valuation efforts are further complicated by accounting differences, especially in economies such as Eastern Europe, where market values have been distorted by years of communistic regimes.

- *Divisions of management responsibility* must be worked out to produce a cohesive team capable of resolving operational issues. Generally, personnel from both sides are included in all functional areas (R and D, manufacturing, marketing), but, almost inevitably, conflicts arise as to "who is really in control." Excessive parent company efforts to micromanage IJV affairs can also be problematic.

- *Financial policy and strategic objectives:* Both sides should agree on dividend and profit reinvestment policies. Typical conflicts occur, for example, over whether early IJV profits should be reinvested to foster further growth or repatriated to parent companies.

- *Blending of global corporate objectives with local goals:* International companies have obligations to other members of their corporate group, and local companies should be made aware up front of the IJV's role in the international company's global network. This includes issues such as manufacturing for other subsidiaries, allocating export rights for particular products or markets, and pricing issues for transfers within the international corporate network.

By the time that IJVs are up and running, conflict resolution processes should be in place. Open and continuous communications among parent companies and IJVs, and between IJV managers are the acknowledged key success factors for conflict resolution.[28]

Two problems that cannot be negotiated but which are responsible for many IJV breakdowns are cultural problems and changing relationships. In many (particularly developing) countries, for example, international executives often feel their managerial experience entitles them to take the initiative in decision making. Cultural stereotypes are formed that often lead to conflicts with local managers. For example, myths about Russian IJVs include claims that Russians are alcoholics, have inferior work ethics, and are incompetent managers who lack business savvy.[29] The second problem occurs when environmental or marketplace conditions change, making original agreements hard to fulfill. Casette 9-1 details IJVs that floundered under these circumstances.

Mergers and Acquisitions (M & A)

Foreign direct investment in plant, equipment, and management assets during 1999–2000 was over $1.2 trillion. Of this, over 75 percent (or over $866 billion) were mergers and acquisitions.[30] M & As provide quick access to markets and expertise. In highly competitive saturated markets, acquiring market-proven companies is often preferred to greenfield operations that must "go it alone" and build markets from the ground up. Yet M & As fail as often as they succeed, especially when inexperienced acquirers venture into foreign markets to takeover other companies.

Mergers, Acquisitions, and Corporate Strategy M & A strategies vary in accordance with their contributions to corporate strategies. Company M & A behaviors have been classified into seven types:[31]

1. *Carnivores* are companies for whom the M & A process is an everyday function. Nestle, Unilever, Electrolux, and GE fall into this category. These firms actively seek businesses that match or complement their major lines, take them over, and then integrate those activities that are useful to them and sell off nonmainstream activities to third parties.

2. *Dairy farmers* are conglomerates that buy and sell businesses to increase shareholder value. The UK company Hanson has been a primary exponent of this type of M & A behavior. These conglomerates impose planning and financial disciplines on acquisitions but otherwise allow the firms to continue as usual.

3. *Vegetarians* are infrequent opportunistic acquirers. They buy companies that they feel will be useful over the long-term. As a result, short-term acquisition motives are often hard to discern. Sony's and Matsushita's purchase of Hollywood-related businesses are examples. Short on M & A experience, vegetarians usually allow their acquisitions stand-alone freedom in day-to-day operations.

4. *White hunters* are old-style corporate raiders who frequently go for firms that are bigger than they are. Often unsuccessful in takeover bids, they provide "wake up calls" for under-performing managements. When successful, white hunters often dismember their acquisitions and sell off individual businesses to suitable partners in appropriate industries. Sometimes they are successful in building global businesses from small financial bases. An example was UK supermarket trolley maker WPP's takeover of U.S. advertising agency giant J. Walter Thompson.

5. *Gentleman shooters* make large acquisitions only after exhaustive research. They carefully evaluate their strategic needs, assess a number of candidates, and then go after their prey in a nonhostile manner. Infrequent acquirers, gentlemen shooters often have problems integrating their targets into their everyday operations. BMW's takeover of British auto firm Rover was one such acquisition.

> The dinosaur's eloquent lesson is that if some bigness is good, an over-abundance of bigness is not necessarily better.
>
> —*Eric A. Johnson,*
> *former president,*
> *U.S. Chamber of Commerce*

6. *Cross-breeders* are transnational mergers bringing together leading national companies to form regional (and sometimes global) power-houses in particular industries. In Europe, Asea of Sweden and Brown-Boveri of Switzerland pooled their assets to shoot for global leadership in heavy electrical equipment. Reed (UK) and Elsevier (Netherlands) did the same in publishing. They differ from mega-mergers in that the latter are already major global players; cross breeders seek the critical mass to attain that status.

7. *Global mega-mergers* became popular in the late 1990s as companies strived to build critical mass and presences in the international markets. Some examples:
   - Renault's $5.4 billion investment in Japan's number 2 car maker, Nissan

FIGURE 9.2
Mergers and Acquisitions Strategy and Implementation

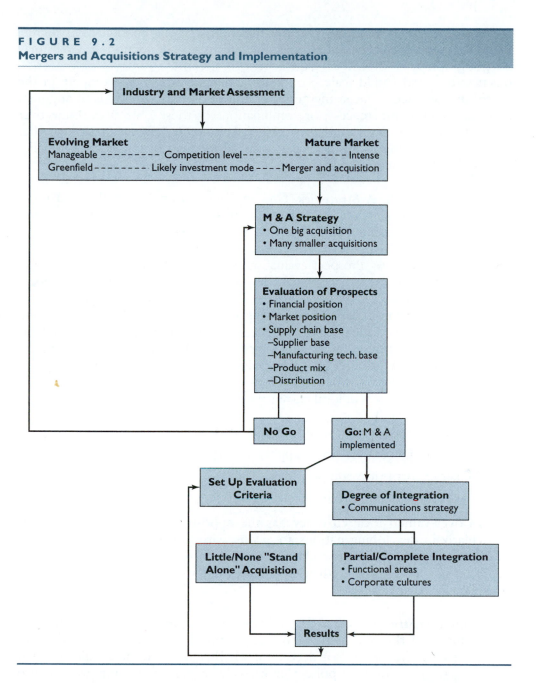

- German company Deutsche Bank's purchase of the U.S.'s Banker's Trust
- BP (formerly British Petroleum) and the U.S.'s Amoco
- In the telecoms industry, Vodafone and Airtouch completed a transatlantic merger, while AT&T and BT's joint venture (Concert Communications) started well but ran into conflicts over objectives.

In all cases, experienced acquirers know they must thoroughly evaluate the strategic prospects of potential acquisitions. Figure 9.2 shows the steps involved in this process.

M & A strategies begin with detailed industry and market assessments. From these evaluations, clear M & A objectives must be identified. Goals may be geographically oriented (gain access to specific countries or regions), business-oriented (build scale economies and critical mass to compete in the global marketplace—"mega-mergers," or add businesses or brands to augment corporate core competences), or combinations of these objectives. Objectives often dictate how firms implement M & A strategies, for example, whether they opt for one big acquisition (e.g., a mega-merger) or go for many smaller acquisitions (e.g., acquiring brands).

Implementing M & A Strategies This implementation is complex and time-consuming. There are three stages to the implementation process: evaluation of prospects, post-acquisition strategies, and M & A assessment.

Evaluation of Prospects Prospect evaluation is a four-step process. First comes a financial analysis to assess performance levels. Second is a strengths-weaknesses-opportunities-threats (SWOT) assessment. Then comes the third step, a cost-and-value chain analysis to evaluate pricing structures and margins. Fourth and finally, a competitive analysis summarizes the firm's prospects and what strategic issues need to be addressed if the acquisition proceeds. Exhibit 9-3 shows the issues to be addressed during prospect evaluations. Note the importance of exchange rates in evaluating foreign assets and performance. A weak local currency (i.e., increasing numbers of local currency units per international currency unit):

- Understates asset values and profits in hard-currency terms
- Makes labor costs and wages appear less expensive
- Makes export prices competitive
- Makes acquisition prices more attractive

An over-valued local currency has the opposite effects. Currency issues, particularly in developing nations are, along with governmental political policies, key concerns for firms making acquisitions. A post-acquisition currency depreciation, for example, adversely affects asset valuations on the acquirer's consolidated balance sheet.

Post-acquisition Strategies Once the evaluation is complete, a go/no-go decision can be made. If the price is right, the acquisition process can go ahead. After that, the next major decision is whether to leave the acquisition as it is (a stand-alone policy) or partially or completely integrate it into parent company operations.

1. Stand-alone policies tend to be used:[32]
   - Where the acquirer is inexperienced
   - When the acquisition has sound management, good results, and a sound strategic base
   - Where there is little or nothing to gain from integrating the acquired firm into the parent's structure

> Only the wisest and the stupidest of men never interfere.
>
> —*Confucius,*
> *6th-century* B.C.
> *Chinese philosopher*

EXHIBIT 9-3
Evaluating M & A Prospects

STEP 1: THE FINANCIAL ANALYSIS

- Sales, cost, and profit trends

- Ration analyses: profit on sales profit on assets, liquidity rations (current assets to current liabilities), receivables to sales, accounts payable to sales

- Stock price trends (where available), credit ratings

- Inventory levels, order books

- Asset valuations

- Financial position (cash in hand, etc.)

STEP 2: THE SWOT ANALYSIS

Evaluation of Strengths and Weaknesses

- Corporate expertise: low-cost manufacturing, quality levels, innovation, marketing skills

- Physical assets: global distribution; state of art production; land, mineral rights holdings; plant capacity

- Human assets: motivated, skilled employees, knowledgeable management, technical know–how.

- Corporate systems: corporate communication systems (Intranet, e-mail facilities), degree of supply-chain integration (with suppliers, distributors)

- Marketplace image/reputation: product reliability, order fulfillment, service records, brand reputation among distributors and customers "goodwill"

- Competitive capabilities/potential: distribution coverage, partnerships with key industry players (key suppliers, distributors), new product capabilities, manufacturing flexibility (custom orders, model changes)

PITFALLS

1. Where currencies are not stable, translations into hard-currency terms can be problematic.

2. Accounting differences: Use an experienced international accounting firm.

3. Legal framework robustness: Where legal/accounting frameworks are weak/not enforced, liberties may be taken.

4. Include national economic statistics (growth, inflation) to put financial performance into its proper economic context.

All these factors may be strengths or weaknesses.

Key Questions

If a strength, how can we capitalize on it?

If a weakness, is it significant? How much will it take to remedy it?

(*continued*)

EXHIBIT 9-3
Evaluating M & A Prospects   *(continued)*

Opportunity-Threat Evaluations

- Vulnerablity to economic conditions (industry-cycle trends)

- Pace of industry change: how well the firm is equipped to deal with it

- Rate of industry growth

- Power of suppliers, distributors, retailers

- Vulnerability to political change

- International exposure: trade/tariff protection, exchange rate effects on competition, domestic/foreign government trade policies

- Regulatory environment

- Attitudes toward environmentalism (ISO 14000, recycling, pollution)

- Rate of change of customer tastes

All factors can be threats or opportunities.

Those affecting individual industries should be classified according to potential impact (favorable/adverse).

STEP 3: SUPPLY CHAIN ANALYSIS

Cost structures should be broken down to identify the costs of supplier components, raw materials, manufacturing/converting, labor, administrative costs, R & D costs, distribution, marketing costs, service installation costs.

Should ideally be benchmarked against equivalent firms (same country, different countries) within the industry

STEP 4: COMPETITIVE POSITION AND EVALUATION

This comprises a summary of the positives in favor of an acquisition (internal strengths, competences, and favorable marketplace factors) and those reasons why M & A should not occur (internal weakness, unfavorable marketplace circumstances).

Usually this entails looking at what the company gains from the acquisition (expertise, markets, technologies, etc.) and evaluating this against the cost of acquisition PLUS the costs of integration PLUS the costs of correcting weaknesses and countering marketplace threats.

- When the two firms have significantly different corporate cultures, or where environmental differences are pronounced (e.g., developed-developing country firms)
- For ease of divestment, should the acquisition not work out

2. Integration strategies: For many acquirers, though, some degree of integration is necessary. For the integration to occur smoothly, differences in corporate cultures and modus operandi should be evaluated and differences bridged between the two companies. Exhibit 9-4 shows a framework to profile the operating environments for parents and acquisitions. Where there are major differences in operating environments, the stronger the case for stand-alone strategies or for only partial integration into the parent company. Where integration is forced on companies with major corporate culture and operating environment differences, significant problems result (as with the Daimler-Chrysler merger—see Casette 9-2).

Integrating functional areas can yield impressive payoffs as sales forces, distribution facilities, product assortments, manufacturing and service facilities can be amalgamated. The key factor affecting potential synergies is the extent of overlap in the firms' product assortments.[33] Where there are few overlaps, the potential for savings is decreased. Where product assortments are similar, hard decisions must be made about which product lines to keep and those to be discontinued.

Manufacturing integration benefits include rationalizing production facilities to take advantage of scale economies and running plants closer to full capacity. Outmoded facilities and technologies can be discontinued or spun off. Leverage with suppliers is increased, and new deals can be struck. A major problem with rationalization is labor. Worker layoffs become problematic in countries with strong trade unions and those with left wing (i.e., pro-labor) governments, such as parts of Europe, Japan, and the developing world.

The keys to successful integration are fourfold.[34] Experienced acquirers plan first, implement quickly, communicate frankly, and act correctly. These firms know what they are going to do with acquisitions prior to takeovers and waste no time executing their plans. Their first priority is to communicate their plans to acquired company personnel and outside stakeholders. These include owners or shareholders, financial institutions, suppliers, government officials, and distributors. Efforts are made to identify and keep key managers and employees. If cuts are made, generous severance packages are often necessary to maintain morale.

Hard decisions are forthcoming when acquired firms are underperforming. Parent company options depend on the reasons for the lack of results. If the parent feels that the acquired firm's strategy is flawed, but that implementation is adequate, steps are taken to replace top managers. If the overall strategy seems effective and execution appears lacking, then parent company scrutiny moves to middle management to remove roadblocks to implementation.

> To improve communications, work not on the utterer, but the recipient.
>
> —*Peter Drucker, U.S. author and management consultant*

> A casualty of a corporate merger describes the "mushroom treatment" that happened to his corporate personnel: "Right after the acquisition, we were left in the dark. Then they covered us with manure. Then they cultivated us. After that they let us stew for a while. Finally they chopped us off at the knees and canned us."
>
> —*Isadore Barmash, U.S. writer*

EXHIBIT 9-4

Plotting Operating Environment Differences Between Parent and Acquired Companies

Basic Driving Force	Parent Company	Acquisition
• Approval-driven (bureaucratic and mistake-avoidance driven)	_____	_____
• Momentum-driven (growth oriented)	_____	_____
• Personality-driven (dominant CEO/leader)	_____	_____
• Production-driven (eg., plant capacity utilization)	_____	_____
• Marketing-driven (total customer satisfaction above all)	_____	_____
• Finance-driven (numbers and profit/ROI orientation)	_____	_____
• Purpose-driven (shared values bond organization together)	_____	_____

Key Success Factors—what makes the company successful (examples)

	Parent Company	Acquisition
• Customer relationships	_____	_____
• Customer service/speed of response	_____	_____
• Coverage/efficiency of distribution system	_____	_____
• Product assortment	_____	_____
• Differentiated products	_____	_____
• Superior marketing (advertising, selling)	_____	_____
• Superior operations (manufacturing cost, quality control, forecasting, inventory turns)	_____	_____
• Superior innovation (R and D, new product development)	_____	_____

Competitive Advantage/ Internal Environment

Differentiation-based
High margins, many customer support staff, high marketing expenses, generous expense accounts and perks

Low cost-based
Low margins, fierce price competition, behaviors/strategies dictated by cost/ margin considerations

1   2   3   4   5   6

Corporate Culture

1. Operating environment

Short-time-frame projects	1	2	3	4	5	6	Long-time-frame projects
Consumer product oriented	1	2	3	4	5	6	Capital project orientation
Ideas from below	1	2	3	4	5	6	Direction from above
Confidence basis of approvals	1	2	3	4	5	6	Analysis basis for approach
Prima donnas tolerated	1	2	3	4	5	6	Dislike of mavericks
High margin/high tech	1	2	3	4	5	6	Low margin/low tech

2. Organizational Environment

Informal	1	2	3	4	5	6	Formal
Unpunctual	1	2	3	4	5	6	Punctual
Unstructured organization	1	2	3	4	5	6	Highly structured org.
Mistakes tolerated	1	2	3	4	5	6	Intolerant of mistakes
Risk takers	1	2	3	4	5	6	Risk adverse
Likes publicity	1	2	3	4	5	6	Shuns publicity
Highly individualistic	1	2	3	4	5	6	Conformist ("we") oriented
Subjective decision-making criteria	1	2	3	4	5	6	Objective decision-making criteria
Work pressures variable	1	2	3	4	5	6	Even pressures
External (marketplace) orientation	1	2	3	4	5	6	Internal orientation
Change oriented	1	2	3	4	5	6	Status quo-oriented

Source: Based on Mitchell and Holmes. *op cit.* 73–81.

M & A Assessment Many firms set short- and longer-term objectives for their M & A strategies. Immediate impacts are on revenue and profit projections (especially as they affect consolidated income and balance sheet statements), market share, and corporate image effects. Medium- and long-term (3–5 years) effects are less quantifiable but tend to include the following.[35]

- Did the acquisition reinforce corporate positions in core businesses? If yes, are there complementary acquisitions that can further bolster our overall market position?

- In retrospect, was the price of the acquisition excessive? What would the acquisition be worth if it were sold today?

- Was the strategic evaluation of the acquisition correct? Were there any unpleasant surprises that were not anticipated? Was the assessment of the acquisition's management correct?

- Has the parent company been able to leverage the acquisition's assets and products successfully in the marketplace?

- How well was the post-acquisition strategy managed? Did the integration process run smoothly? If not, why not?

> The trouble with experience is that by the time you have it you are too old to take advantage of it.
>
> —*Jimmy Connors, U.S. tennis player*

How well acquisitions perform depends very much on how the parent company manages it. Good parent companies set challenging but achievable objectives, impose reasonable financial and control disciplines to guide acquisition strategies, provide objective assessments of capabilities, and give acquired firms the resources and latitude to execute their strategies. Continuous communication is a key success factor in M & A strategy implementation.

Greenfield Operations

> To be independent is the business of a few only; it is the privilege of the strong.
>
> —*Friedrich W. Nietzsche, 19th-century German philosopher*

Greenfield operations occur when firms opt to custom-build foreign subsidiaries to suit their needs. The advantages of building versus buying (i.e., M & A) are, first, not having to deal with existing managements and facilities built for other purposes. Second, being able to start fresh in a market with the firm's own technologies, management styles, and corporate cultures. Third, greenfield operations give parent companies complete control of subsidiary development and market strategies. The disadvantages are having to build in-market relationships with suppliers and distributors from scratch, giving in-market competitors time to adjust their strategies and prepare for a new rival, and the risks of making major resource commitments and of financing losses until facilities reach their full market potential.

Companies are more likely to custom-build foreign facilities when:

- Financing needs are low, for example, in service industries (e.g., advertising agencies, accounting, consulting) where there are few or no major fixed investments to be made in factories, equipment, and distribution

- Markets are developing slowly and industry competition levels are low (in emerging markets, for example)

- Firms have leading edge products and process technologies and do not want to risk intellectual property theft that can occur with acquisitions or joint ventures (e.g., high tech firms)

- Companies have global brands and reputations they can leverage into local markets without outside help

- Strong corporate cultures are key factors in global success. In these cases, firms prefer to develop their human resources from the ground up to inculcate appropriate values and philosophies (Japanese firms, Body Shop, IBM, Procter & Gamble, Unilever).

Country Selection Criteria From the global industry analysis, country selection criteria for the siting of manufacturing facilities include:

- *Proven manufacturing capabilities in the global context:* The country is already the production base for a sizable proportion of global output. This ensures a workforce with proven competitive capabilities.

- *Significant market potential,* as evidenced by increasing national demand.

- *Major global competitors* are already present in the market.

- *A favorable business environment* is present (operating conditions, political risk factors, remittance, and repatriation of currencies, etc.). This also includes adequate infrastructures (ports, roads, utilities), international access (free-trade policies, reasonable exchange rates for imports, exports), and adequate factor supplies (raw materials, labor).

Site Location Within the Country Once the country selection process has been finalized, there are decisions about where to locate the facility within the market itself. Factors affecting this decision include:

- Government location incentives to place manufacturing investments in parts of the country in need of economic rejuvenation (economically depressed or underdeveloped regions).

- For consumer goods concerns, locating near economically significant centers (major towns, for example) facilitates distribution and market feedback.

- For industrial products, the availability of qualified personnel (engineers, skilled production workers) is paramount, with local universities and colleges being key labor sources. In many countries, local or regional centers of excellence (e.g., Silicon Valley in California for high tech) dictate where facilities should be sited.

- Where specialized resources are required, location options may be limited. Mining and extractive industries must locate around natural resource deposits; beer and mineral water investments are limited to areas with quality water supplies.

- In all cases, transportation and infrastructure facilities need assessing to ensure smooth running supply chains to national and international customers.

> Education is the chief defense of nations.
>
> —*Edward Burke, 18th-century British statesman*

Siting Research and Development Capabilities

Research and development (R and D) capabilities have become key success factors in sustaining competitive advantages in many global industries. As such, ensuring that such facilities are appropriately sited has become a top management concern in serving global, regional, and individual national markets.

Historical Patterns Up to the 1980s, most international commerce was concentrated in the Triad nations of North America, Western Europe, and Japan. In 1982 for example, while 30 percent of international firms' production was located outside the home market, just 12 percent of their research capabilities were in foreign countries. In those days, the role of foreign R and D amenities was straightforward: to adapt products and services to the needs of regional and individual markets. Basic R & D was performed in the home market to gain research scale economies, safeguard new product ideas, and facilitate communications with core functional areas such as marketing and manufacturing.[36]

Current R and D Strategies Today's globalized marketplace has caused international firms to be more focused in their worldwide R and D policies. Research and development facilities can be divided into three types: (1) research laboratories in traditional fields, (2) development laboratories, and (3) facilities in new emerging areas. Where these facilities are sited depends on their function. Where R and D facilities have important inputs to mainstream businesses, they are located in subsidiaries with significant market sizes and product ranges. In the research-intensive pharmaceutical industry, companies such as LaRoche and Novartis establish major research facilities in their largest markets (for example, the U.S. or Western Europe).

Where firms are exploring new technologies or products outside of mainstream areas, the key locational determinant is "competence regions." These are regions (often within major markets) that have developed expertise in specific research fields, and have top-quality researchers on hand at universities in areas with acknowledged scientific expertise and prowess.[37] Silicon Valley is centered around Stanford University and the University of California at Berkeley. Princeton University's industrial liaison programs in communications technology have attracted research lab facilities from Siemens (Germany), NEC, Matsushita, and Toshiba (all Japanese). Similarly, Texas Instruments and Hewlett-Packard have electronics R and D facilities around Kanto, Japan, to take advantage of the area's research expertise. In Europe, NEC and Canon have sites in London and Rennes (France) respectively.[38]

Development laboratories oversee product and service adaptations in overseas markets. The major locational driver is market size, though prospective sites are routinely screened for the availability of suitable workforces, finance costs, and appropriate technological environments. Development teams are often rotated through important research markets (e.g., Japan, U.S.) for updating and cross-fertilization of pure and applied research skills and ideas.[39]

As new markets in Latin America, Eastern Europe, and Asia opened up during the late 1980s and 1990s, international corporations began to rethink

R and D investments. Companies, often through acquisitions, obtained research assets that they needed to integrate into mainstream corporate R and D programs. The challenge was then to focus geographically dispersed activities into coherent global R and D policies. Coordination was achieved through shared information networks and through the rotation of key research personnel. Worldwide information systems were used to coordinate product development and R and D facilities at companies such as Boeing, ABB, and Motorola. In consumer-goods firms such as Procter & Gamble and Unilever, R and D activities are coordinated through routine rotation of key personnel as parts of global HRM practices and career development paths.[40]

Japanese electronics companies have loosened formerly rigid distinctions between research and development activities. Matsushita's overseas labs divide their work between "global projects" which cover R and D in major multimedia, mobile communication, and multi-language areas, and "local contribution projects" which include product modifications and the creation of new products for local markets. Sony went from a decentralized R and D culture to one where R and D synergies were encouraged through international division of labor for global projects.[41]

Managing the R and D Site   Two further managerial decisions about R and D facilities concern optimal sizes for individual sites and leadership issues.[42] Current research suggests that the optimal size for start-up R and D facilities for international companies is 35–40 employees. Over time, the optimal size increases to about 200–250 employees, including support personnel. This size appears appropriate for establishing research scale economies and for encouraging informal relationships to facilitate coordination and the cross-fertilization of ideas.

Leadership issues depend much on the site's function. Where pure research is the major objective, prominent local scientists or engineers are preferred to foster ties between the new site and the local scientific community. Where product development and adaptations are the main function, highly regarded managers are the best picks to cement relationships between head offices, local subsidiaries, and corporate manufacturing and marketing efforts. In all cases, R and D leaders tend to be respected scientists, engineers, or managers. They are skillful integrators of home office and local R and D efforts, have comprehensive knowledge of technological trends, and can move easily between their business and scientific communities.

> Respect a man, he will do the more.
>
> —*James Howell,*
> *17th-century English author*

MATCHING MARKET SERVICING STRATEGIES TO ENVIRONMENTAL AND CORPORATE NEEDS

How companies enter and service markets depends on external factors (industry market size, growth, market environments, and competitors) and internal factors such as corporate needs and resources. Figure 9.3 summarizes these influences on market entry and servicing strategies.

External Factors

External factors comprise analyses of global industry supply and demand trends, market environment assessments, and competitor evaluations.

FIGURE 9.3
External and Internal Influences on Market Entry and Servicing Strategies

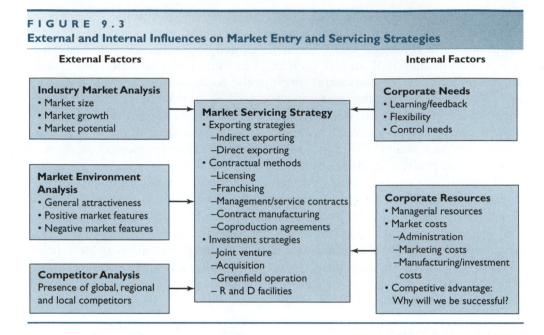

Global industry analyses presented in Chapter 6 show sector consumption patterns worldwide. Countries with significant market sizes and high market growth are candidates for major investments (joint ventures, greenfield operations, or acquisitions). Similarly, countries with significant market potentials (e.g., low per capita consumption rates), but with high growth rates, merit investment attention to gain early-mover advantages and to capitalize on market-growth opportunities. Where countries are close to their market-growth potentials (mature economies with little growth for example), joint ventures or acquisitions are favored to take advantage of local firms' market positions and contacts.

Medium and small markets are more likely to be serviced through joint ventures, contractual arrangements (such as licensing agreements), or exports. Where countries follow free-trade policies, exporting is a good option, especially if research shows high import-to-consumption ratios. Where there are trade barriers (and low levels of imports), contractual arrangements (licensing agreements, turnkey operations, coproduction arrangements) are more likely.

Market environment analyses are less important when firms are internationally experienced and have proven abilities to cope with foreign-market environments, and where foreign competitors have made inroads into particular markets (proving that market obstacles in their industries have been successfully overcome). However, when firms lack international experience, or, when they are pioneering industry pushes into new markets, environmental analyses become important inputs. For example:

- Where new products or technically innovative processes are involved, intellectual-property protection laws must be scrutinized, particularly in markets where counterfeit activities are prevalent.

- When trade policies may inhibit importation of key materials, components, or entire products

- Where undeveloped infrastructures make normal business activities difficult (e.g., financial transfers, product distribution, poorly educated workforces)
- When political or economic environments are unstable

Where markets are undeveloped or show sights of instability, most firms opt for export market entries initially to demonstrate market acceptance for its wares. Licensing or contractual agreements are used where importing is problematic (for example, when nations have trade deficits or inconvertible currencies). In other cases, where firms see market opportunities, joint ventures may be used to gain market access.

Competitive factors are playing increasingly important roles in market-entry decisions. Thorough market screenings alert firms to competitor presences and what facilities they have in particular markets. How industry rivals service markets help companies seeking competitive advantages. For example, if major competitors service a market through exports and independent distributors, a company can consider (1) buying into the independent distributors to take market exposure away from rivals, (2) establishing their own sales offices and sales forces to establish in-market access to customers, (3) investing in assembly or manufacturing operation to make customized output a competitive option.

Where market analyses show the presence of significant local or international competitors, joint ventures, global alliances, or acquisitions become viable entry methods. These strategies give incoming firms manufacturing resources, market and government contacts, and instant market presences.

Where competitors have established investments and market access, options are more limited. Firms can buy their ways in through joint ventures, global alliances, or acquisitions, or, if rivals are well-established, they can selectively attack product-line weaknesses via imports and build sales until significant investments are warranted. The rules of thumb for attacking competitor product lines are:

- If competitive advantage is built on established brands, superior service, or other differentiation criteria, attacks via good quality-low price imports can be disruptive and establish market beachheads.

- Where low prices are the competitive appeal, on-site investments and differentiation, perhaps via customization, can establish competitive advantages over market rivals.

Internal Factors

When firms commit resources to foreign markets, two sets of internal corporate factors contribute to their decisions. These are (1) what objectives they want to achieve and (2) what resources they have available.

Corporate Objectives Companies going into foreign markets use market-entry methods that are going to contribute to their long-term competitive advantages and corporate well-being.

Learning and market feedback are essential for companies wishing to build up global expertise, and, while some knowledge is gained via exporting and through contractual agreements, the best learning occurs in-market via joint ventures, greenfield operations, and acquisitions.

Flexibility is the ability of companies to switch resources quickly in response to corporate and marketplace needs. When investments are significant (as with equity investments or greenfield operations) flexibility is limited as commitments are made to in-market manufacturing and marketing resources. Contractual arrangements such as licensing, franchising, and turnkey operations are inflexible during the contracted period but become flexible as contracts are renewed. Because of their limited upfront capital needs, licensing, franchise, and other contractual arrangements facilitate fast rates of globalization. Exporting is perhaps the most flexible of market-servicing strategies. Companies can switch markets, change competitive stances, and adjust marketing mixes relatively easily as corporate and marketplace circumstances alter.

Control over products and manufacturing processes is important in many industries, especially in technical or marketing-intensive sectors. In these cases:

- Companies may prefer exporting to keep proprietary manufacturing processes in the home market to minimize rival opportunities to imitate products ("piracy") and production processes.

- Firms avoid minority joint ventures where they cannot maintain control over manufacturing-process technologies or branded products.

- Contractual agreements must be "watertight" with respect to technologies, technical improvements, product patents, brands, logos, and copyrights.

- Where companies have concerns over counterfeited brands, pirated technologies, or other intellectual property rights, market entry is likely to be through greenfield operations with total control or through exports and company-owned distributors.

Corporate Resources Corporate resources are always scarce, relative to what can be allocated to the international marketplace. As such, firms must tailor their market-entry strategies according to the human and technical resources available to them.

Managerial resources are scarce as companies take their first steps into global commerce. As a result, many firms use third-party expertise to sell their output. Export trading companies, export management firms, and general trading companies provide this knowledge. The major drawback is that firms learn little about foreign markets, as trading companies handle export documentation and financing and control access to market contacts.

International management expertise becomes a decisive factor in direct exporting and where contractual modes of market entry (licensing, franchising, turnkey operations, etc.) are used. The heaviest demands on managerial expertise occur when firms produce goods in-market using joint ventures, acquisitions, and greenfield operations. Setting up and managing foreign-based operations requires knowledge of local operating conditions, language and cultural skills, and financial expertise in integrating foreign ventures into corporate balance sheets and income statements.

Marketing and operating costs are involved in all entry strategies, with the possible exception of indirect exporting. For direct exporters, there are costs involved with employing international marketing managers and in promoting goods overseas (brochures, international trade shows, etc). Internet usage and web sites have facilitated the international promotions process and give economical worldwide exposure to companies. Contractual modes are relatively inexpensive, though there are legal costs in drawing up and executing contractual arrangements and in personal visits to service them. Costs are heaviest in joint venture, acquisitions, and greenfield operations. Physical-asset purchases are initial expenses (financing costs, plant building, equipment purchases, etc.); then there are ongoing expenses in managing assets once they are up and running. In joint ventures and acquisitions, these expenses are less, as local partners or acquired firms contribute physical and managerial assets. Greenfield operations are the most expensive, as marketing costs can be considerable as product lines are built up and promoted from scratch. Typically, firms carefully assess marketing and operating costs against market potential and market risks in their market-entry and servicing decision making.

Competitive advantage is a major factor in market-servicing decisions as firms seek to leverage home-market advantages into foreign-country environments. Effects vary according to the competitive advantage of the company.

- Where competitive advantage is based on global reputations and highly differentiated products (branded fashions, Coca-Cola, Pepsi, etc.) firms have the most options in market-servicing strategies. They can service markets initially via exports and build up sales and marketplace presence gradually. This approach works when competitor offerings are not major threats, and firms can add resources as market share increases. Where speed of globalization is a factor, or where corporate resources are limited, companies can license products or build franchise systems for low-cost capitalization of corporate or brand reputations.

- Where service contributes to competitive advantage (e.g., overnight delivery services such as FedEx, UPS), significant in-market presence is necessary and local offices become mandatory. Similarly, where post-sales service is important (as with autos, machine tools, industrial equipment), local service and sales subsidiaries are necessary investments.

- In some industries, national responsiveness and local appeals are key competitive advantages. This is the case for nondurable products such as food/drink, cosmetics, and general household goods (e.g., cleansers, soap powders). In these situations, on-site manufacturing and marketing facilities become essential as managements maintain close contacts with customers, distributors, and market trends.

- Where price competition and competitive cost structures are key success factors, firms have two options. First, where there are significant manufacturing scale economies, export-based strategies from central locations become feasible. This strategy works for industries ranging from bulk chemicals and commodities to specialized sectors such as industrial machinery and medical equipment. When manufacturing scale economies are minimal (as with restaurant franchises for example), investments in local supply chains become optimal strategies.

KEY POINTS

- How international firms choose to enter and service markets is a major factor determining their success within individual markets. There are three basic market-entry and servicing strategies: exporting, contractual methods, and investments.

- Exporting strategies involve manufacturing products in home or third-party countries and transporting them into target markets. Indirect exporters use intermediaries, such as export-management firms or general-trading companies, to handle the transportation, administration, and financing functions. Direct exporters perform these functions themselves.

- Contractual methods of market entry use contractual arrangements to permit foreign firms to service customer needs for predetermined fees. Licensing allows foreign companies use of home-market technologies to manufacture goods for use in specified markets. Franchising permits use of international companies' logos, brand names, manufacturing, and marketing methods to service local markets. Contract manufacturing occurs when foreign firms manage the production function but do not participate in any other supply-chain functions. The international company handles R and D, product design, and all marketing operations. Coproduction is an arrangement whereby two or more companies share manufacturing facilities but pursue independent marketing strategies.

- Investment options include joint ventures, where firms share ownership and management arrangements; mergers and acquisitions, whereby international firms take over local companies; and greenfield investments. In joint ventures and acquisitions, international companies gain swift access to local markets and expertise, but must work directly with local managements. Greenfield operations involve custom-building manufacturing and marketing facilities to suit corporate needs. This is expensive and takes time, but it allows firms to do things "their way."

- Manufacturing-site selection involves considerable research concerning suppliers, market demand, and infrastructure development, as well as local-factor supplies such as capital, labor, and raw materials. Where import-export operations are required, national trade policies, exchange rates, and international infrastructure facilities (ports, airports, etc.) need to be assessed.

- Research and development facilities have become major factors in maintaining competitive advantages worldwide. The R and D function has become complex. Major research facilities tend to be established in large markets in "competence regions" with acknowledged expertise in specific areas. Development laboratories oversee product and service adaptations to specific market needs, while a third type of R and D facility focuses on emerging market needs. Coordination and leadership concerns are important facets of worldwide R and D management.

- Matching market-entry and servicing strategies to external and internal corporate needs and resources is a complex task. Large and high potential markets tend to draw investments from international companies, though where markets are competitive or close to saturation, M & As are preferred. Where market environments are problematic, trade, contractual, or joint ventures are likely to be used to reduce risks and resource commitments. The presence of global or significant local competitors also affects market-entry strategy. Internal corporate needs and resources play important roles. Learning and market feedback are enhanced with in-market presences, though, while investments are often preferred, they can be costly and risk-laden, though they give good control. Companies need ample experienced executives to manage foreign-based operations. Finally, international firms' competitive advantages are important influences for differentiated goods and for companies using low-cost appeals.

ENDNOTES

1. Don Garbera, "Eli's Cheesecake marks 5 years on the continent," *Frozen Food Age* (June 1999): 14.

2. Lewis Krauskopf, Japanese Drug Maker Sankyo Seeks Inroads into American Pharmaceutical Industry," *Knight Ridder Tribune Business News* (June 21, 2002): 1–3.

3. Esther Baur, "World Target Practice," *Best's Review February* (2001): 44–47.

4. Vanessa Bachman, Office of Export Trading Companies (Washington D.C.: U.S. Department of Commerce, March 27, 2000).

5. James F. Mongoven (Washington, D.C.: Federal Trade Commission, April 6, 2000).

6. You-tein Hsing, "Trading companies in Taiwan's fashion shoe networks," *Journal of International Economies* 48: 1 (June 1999): 101–20.

7. Henry Wichmann Jr., "Private and public trading companies within the Pacific Rim nations," *Journal of Small Business Management* 35: 1 (Jan. 1997): 62–65.

8. Ibid.

9. Ibid.

10. Joanna Slater, "Masters of the Trade," *Far Eastern Economic Review* (July 22, 1999): 10–13.

11. "Sperka International," *Business America* (January 1998): 18.

12. *World Investment Report 1999* (New York: United Nations), xix.

13. Adapted from Farok J. Contractor and Sumit K. Kundu, "Franchising versus company-run operations: Model choice in the global hotel sector," *Journal of International Marketing* 6:2 (1998): 28–53.

14. John K. Ryans Jr., Sherry Lots, and Robert Krampf, "Do master franchisors drive global franchising?" *Marketing Management* 8:2 (Summer 1999): 32–37.

15. Contractor and Kundu, *op. cit.*

16. Jerry T. Williams, "Life in the Global Marketplace," *Franchising World* (Sept–Oct. 1997): 6–11.

17. Ryans, Lotz, and Krampf, *op cit.*

18. Ibid.

19. Leonard N. Swartz, "Exploring Global Franchising Trends," *Franchising World* (March–April 1997): 7–16.

20. Ibid.

21. Stand Delojer, "Ruby Tuesday going worldwide: Menus look similar around the globe, but there are adjustments," *News Sentinel* (Knoxville, Tenn., September 28, 1999): G5.

22. Curt R. Strand, "Lessons of a Lifetime: The development of Hilton International," *Cornell Hotel and Restaurant Administration Quarterly* 37: 3 (June 1996): 83–96.

23. Anonymous, "Canadians score in China," *ENR* (August 1, 1994): 14.

24. From Arthur P. Cimento, Michael Denham, Deepak Ramachandran, "What's behind the move to 'virtual manufacturing,'" *Machine Design* (Sept. 9, 1999): S2–S10.

25. Based on Weld Royal, "Contract manufacturing: perils and profits," *Industry Week* (November 1, 1999): 21–28.

26. Anonymous, "GE and Shin-Etsu join forces to make silicones in Thailand," *Chemical Market Reporter* (February 12, 2001): 3.

27. Based on Robert G. Miller, J. Jaspersen, and Fred Karmokolias, "International Joint Ventures in Developing Countries," *Finance & Development* 34: 1 (March 1997): 26–29.

28. Carl F. Key and Paul W. Beamish, "Strategies for Managing Russian International Joint Venture Conflict," *European Management Journal* 17: 1 (1999): 99–106.

29. Richard Reece, "Successful joint ventures in Russia," *World Trade* 11: 8 (Aug. 1998): 42–44.

30. *World Investment Report 2001* (New York: United Nations): 56.

31. Adapted from David Mitchell and Garrick Holmes, *Making Acquisitions Work* (London: Economist Intelligence Unit, 1996), chapter 3.

32. Based on Mitchell and Holmes, *op. cit.,* chapter 8.

33. Based on Mitchell and Holmes, *op. cit.,* chapter 7.

34. Mitchell and Holmes, *op. cit.,* chapter 6.

35. Based on Mitchell and Holmes, *op. cit.,* 88.

36. Rainer Voelker and Richard Stead, "New technologies and international locational choice for research and development units: Evidence from Europe," *Technology Analysis and Strategic Analysis* 11: 2 (June 1999): 199–209.

37. Ibid.

38. Walter Kuemmerle, "Building Effective R & D Capabilities Abroad," *Harvard Business Review* (March–April 1997): 61–70.

39. Voelker and Stead, *op. cit.*

40. Shaoming Zou and Aysegul Ozsmer, "Global product R & D and the firm's strategic position," *Journal of International Marketing* 7:1 (1999): 57.

41. Sadamori Arimura, "How Matsushita Electric and Sony manage global R & D," *Research Technology Management* (March–April 1999): 41.

42. Based on Kuemmerle, *op. cit.*

CASETTE 9-1
Managing the International Joint Venture (IJV)

Joint ventures formed between international and local companies are common, especially in developing markets where foreign firms need help getting established. Unfortunately, over half of IJVs fail. Here are four case studies: three failed, one is successful and ongoing.

1. HCL and Hewlett-Packard in India

In 1991, as the Indian market was opening up, Hewlett-Packard (HP) bought a 26 percent stake in HCL, India's largest computer conglomerate. Under the agreement, HCL became the distributor for HP servers and workstations built in India. At that time, tariffs on high-end computing equipment were 110 percent. But during the 1990s, the Indian market opened up. Duties went down to 32 percent, imports became financially viable, and new rivals entered the market. In the meantime, HCL's expertise base expanded, and the company developed the low-price mass-market segment for PCs, building a 50 percent market share of the rapidly expanding market and producing 15,000 PCs a month.

The HCL-HP partnership gradually fell apart. HCL executives complained that HP was treating the IJV "like any other HP division" and that its export efforts, at nearly $150 million a year, were being inhibited by the partnership. The IJV was discontinued in 1997. HP sold its stake for less than one-sixth of its original value and went about rebuilding the nationwide sales and marketing network it had lost in the HCL deal.

2. Ericsson's IJV in India

Ericsson's manufacturing IJV was established in 1971 with its Indian distributor of telecommunications equipment in a 74–26 percent ownership split favoring the Swedish company. Ericsson's reputation and technology were attractive to the local partner, and the latter's well-developed distribution system and local connections with India's defense department were key factors in Ericsson's development of the Indian market.

The IJV progressed well. No expatriates were employed in the joint venture, though frequent visits from Swedish personnel were encouraged and welcomed. Ericsson did not use its top-drawer technologies in India and local personnel were developed to take over production responsibilities. Over the years, IJV ownership arrangements were changed in favor of the local partner to comply with government regulations. While the major cultural differences between Swedish managers and local personnel were notable, informal communication and mutual trust prevented major conflicts. As the Indian market opened up after 1991, a new IJV was formed with the same partner, but with 51 percent of shares in Ericsson's favor. This IJV focused on the private sector, with local components increasingly used in the manufacturing of the major product, mobile phones. Ericsson, with local-partner approval, established a wholly owned subsidiary to expand its product assortment, which did not compete with IJV lines.

3. Kanthal IJV in India

Kanthal, a Swedish producer of alloys and heating materials, established its IJV in 1965 with an Indian engineer who had acted as the company's agent in India. It started as a 50–50 joint venture, but over time legal limitations reduced Kanthal's ownership to 40 percent. During this time, Kanthal exerted considerable influence over the IJV, supplying key material inputs and evaluating local-market prospects. Little learning took place between IJV participants, and Kanthal constantly pushed for the adoption of modern marketing techniques by its local partner.

Unhappy with the IJV's progress, Kanthal installed its own chief executive in 1986. Conflict ensued, and the partnership was dissolved in 1987. A new IJV was formed in the 1990s with Kanthal retaining 52 percent ownership. Remaining shares were distributed among 6000 local shareholders. Still, there were problems as Kanthal pushed for total control over production and marketing operations. Eventually this was obtained, and Kanthal's buildup of local contacts and market knowledge made local help unnecessary.

4. Procter & Gamble and Phuong Dong in Vietnam

P & G entered into an IJV with Phuong Dong Company in 1994 just after the Vietnamese market opened up, buying a 70 percent share in the Vietnamese soap company. After three years, it had over $30 million in debts. The Vietnamese government accused P & G of excessive expenditures on advertising and expatriate salaries. Market size had been overestimated. Start-up costs had been underestimated.

The government and Phuong Dong had expected the venture to be profitable very quickly. P & G responded by saying their initial plans, shared with the local partners, indicated that the market had not expected to be profitable for 5–7 years. Local commentators noted that Unilever, in a similar situation, had become profitable in less than two years. Unable to fund the losses, the Vietnamese parent company allowed P & G to buy out an extra 23 percent of the IJV to cover future debts, leaving the local firm with a face-saving 7 percent stake.

Questions

1. Why did the companies go in for IJVs instead of other market-entry methods?

2. What problems did these IJVs have? What caused them?

3. Prepare a list of do's and don'ts for IJVs based on these illustrations.

Sources: Anonymous. "Jaded with joint ventures." *Business Asia* (April 6, 1998): 5–6. Hyder, Akmal S., and Pervez N. Ghauri. "Managing International Joint Venture Relationships: A Longitudinal Perspective." *Industrial Marketing Management* 29 (2000): 205–18. Sidhva, Shiraz. "Goodbye, Partner." *Far Eastern Economic Review* (September 11, 1997): 62.

CASETTE 9-2
The Daimler-Chrysler Mega Merger

When Daimler Benz and Chrysler merged in 1998, optimism abounded on both sides. Chrysler was the world's most profitable and cost-efficient auto producer. Mercedes was the marquee quality name in the industry. The $36 billion merger was to produce the world's dominant global auto producer. Initial plans were ambitious. Twenty-eight integration teams were assigned to combine ninety-five areas of the joint business. Among the issues discussed and decisions made:

- Chrysler deferred its diesel engine development work to Mercedes.
- Fuel-cell research was folded into the Mercedes partnership with Canada's Ballard Power Systems.
- Resources were pooled to develop Mercedes' first American-style minivan.
- Production of the Mercedes M-class SUV began in the Steyr-Daimler-Puch factory in Austria, which also manufactures Chrysler minivans and Jeep Grand Cherokees.
- $500 million in purchasing savings came from pooling both companies' parts and materials procurement systems.
- Both companies' use of SAP AG (a German company) software made integration of their respective corporate information systems nonproblematic.

- Chrysler was strong in North America, Mercedes in Europe. Both companies were committed to global markets and were looking to stake out stronger positions in Asia.

- With the exception of the Jeep Grand Cherokee and the Mercedes SUV, company product lines had few overlaps.

But as the two companies got into the integration program, major problems surfaced. These included:

1. A mass exodus of key Chrysler executives occurred as Mercedes management began to dominate the mega-merger's decision-making apparatus. Chrysler costs escalated. Mercedes CEO Schrempp did not help matters when he publicly announced that he had always intended to make Chrysler a Daimler division and later called on Zetsche, a lifelong Mercedes stalwart, to turn Chrysler fortunes around. Disgruntled Chrysler executives began referring to their company as Daimler-Benz's twenty-third business unit.

2. Corporate culture differences became pronounced. At supervisory board meetings, Daimler executives arrived in chauffeur-driven Mercedes. Chrysler management arrived together in a single minivan. German management styles were formal and detail-oriented. Chrysler executives were less detail-oriented and did their decision making in informal, unstructured settings. The lean, cost-conscious Chrysler organization clashed with the quality-conscious engineering mindset of the German company. Chrysler perceived Mercedes as grossly overstaffed, with staff assistants to all senior managers. In the end, both companies admitted that their distinctive corporate cultures were too dissimilar to be meaningfully integrated.

The mega-merger took its toll in corporate finances. Losses at Chrysler were over $500 million in 2000 and were projected to rise to $2 billion in 2001. The group's cash chest shrank to $2 billion, compared to GM and Ford who each had about $13 billion in reserves.

In March 2000, DaimlerChrysler took a 34 percent stake in Mitsubishi Motors to complete its long awaited move into the Asian market. In addition to shoring up the company's geographic weakness in Asia, Mitsubishi was to bring much-needed small-car expertise to the group. Skeptics pointed out that Mercedes' inability to make money from its own smaller cars (the A-class and the Smart car) put this venture under a cloud: "the blind leading the blind." Competing against Toyota, Nissan, and Honda in Japan and Asia, Mitsubishi's small- and large-car prospects looked poor, and operating losses were over $600 million for 2000. Operating margins at less than 1 percent, and $14 billion in total debt seemed to confirm the Japanese company's dire situation. Mitsubishi Motors was placed under Rolf Eckrodt, chief of Daimler's Adtranz rail subsidiary. Finally, Japan's ailing economy and corporate traditions of lifetime employment, consensus decision making, and internal promotions looked significantly at odds with Daimler's modus operandi.

Questions

1. Using Exhibit 9.4, Plotting Operating Environment Differences Between Parent and Acquired Companies, plot the major differences in Daimler-Benz and Chrysler operating environments. What do you conclude?

2. Why is the Daimler-Chrysler merger not doing well?

3. What prospects do you see for the Daimler-Chrysler-Mitsubishi combo?

Sources: Naughton, Keith. "A mess of a merger." *Newsweek* (December 11, 2000): 54–56. Gardner, Greg, and David C. Smith. "The Global Hybrid." *Ward's Auto World* (December 1998): 48–49. Ostle, Dorothee. "Culture Clash." *Automotive News* (December 6, 1999): 1, 32. Tierney, Christine, and Ken Belsen. "Mitsubishi: Conquest or Quicksand for Daimler?" *Business Week* (September 25, 2000): 62–64.

Chapter Ten

Global and Multi-Market Strategies

BOOZE AND MONEY GO GLOBAL

Brands and money travel, and travel well these days.

The business of brand management has never been more worldwide in scope. This is apparent in many industries, none more so than in alcoholic beverages, traditionally national in scope but now moving global as tastes homogenize. Allied Domecq, a worldwide wine and spirit marketer, recognized the global brand movement and reorganized its corporate team into three brand divisions: a global whisky brands team that oversees worldwide branding strategies for Ballentines, Canadian Club, and Teachers, and a Euro Brands team that supervises Beefeater gin, Courvoisier brandy, Tia Maria liqueurs, as well as Cockburn's, Harvey's Bristol Cream, and Domecq sherries, ports, and fortified wines. Both are managed out of Bristol, England. The third division, Latin Brands, is based in the U.S. and is in charge of Allied Domecq's second biggest brand, Kalhua, which is marketed worldwide as a trendy cocktail ingredient.[1]

Trillions of dollars change hands every day in international money markets. When DuPont established its regional treasury in Singapore in 1992, the company knew there should be some advantages associated with centralizing its Asian financial dealings in a country with few foreign-currency trading restrictions. DuPont quickly found that centralizing its regional foreign exchange trading reduced costs associated with investment funding, currency conversions, and cross-border financing and facilitated the global communication of financial information.[2]

Other than globalizing the supply chain (discussed in the next chapter), nowhere are the advantages of corporate globalization more apparent than in the marketing and finance functions. For marketers, the global and regional nature of demand (for alcoholic beverages in the example above) can yield impressive economies as firms globalize their branding strategies and extend distribution into new markets. Allied Domecq identified those brands with global potential (whiskies, Kalhua) and headquartered them where they had "Made in" advantages ("British whiskies" and "Latin American" Kalhua). Other brands (gins, other spirits, and wines) were perceived as having regional appeal, with many receiving Euro Brand designations.

In the financial sector, Dupont was one of increasing numbers of firms recognizing that the globalization process had resulted not only in the freeing up of trade restrictions, but also the liberalization of world financial markets. This facilitated money movements within international corporations and allowed them to centralize and streamline their financial operations.

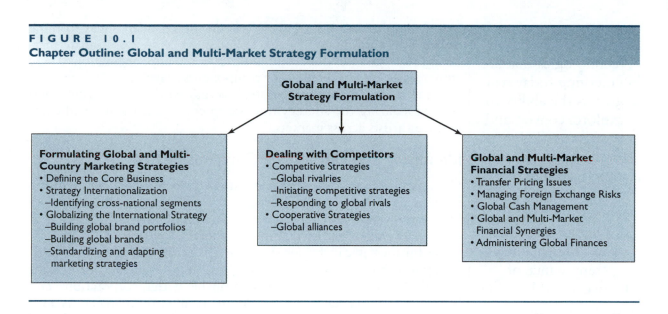

FIGURE 10.1
Chapter Outline: Global and Multi-Market Strategy Formulation

In this chapter you will learn:

- How the globalization movement has made firms acutely aware of the need to extend brands and strategies across multiple markets to take advantage of cross-cultural similarities in demand.
- The ways that international firms compete across national markets; and the strategies local companies use to counter threats from global competitors.
- How cooperative strategies with global rivals contribute to worldwide competitive effectiveness.
- The strategies international companies follow to reduce financial risks and manage the complexities of global money management.

FORMULATING GLOBAL AND MULTI-COUNTRY MARKETING STRATEGIES

Introduction

Globalization, as noted in Chapter 3, has affected world markets at many levels—its institutions, values, and behaviors. It also has had major effects on industries, business behaviors, and attitudes. In the marketing field, a major impact of globalization has been on customer tastes and preferences.[3] As Levitt noted:

"A powerful force drives the world toward a converging commonality, and that force is technology. It has proletarianized communication, transport and travel. It has made isolated places and impoverished peoples eager for modernity's allurements. Almost everyone everywhere wants all of the things they have heard about, seen, or experienced via the new technologies. The result is a new commercial reality—the emergence of global markets for standardized consumer products on a previously unimaginable scale of magnitude. Corporations geared to this new reality benefit from enormous economies of scale in production, distribution, marketing and management."[4]

Technologies that are emerging today will give us the ability to explore, convey, and create knowledge as never before. We have an opportunity that is given to few generations in history. If we respond . . . we can unleash a new renaissance of discovery and learning.

—*John Scully, chairman, Apple Computer*

Do what you know best; if you're a runner, run; if you're a bell, ring.

—*Ignas Bernstein*

The globalization movement has prompted many firms to think in terms of customer and market similarities as they formulate marketing strategies for global and multi-country implementation. These strategies consist of three major components: developing a core strategy, internationalizing that strategy across worldwide markets, and then globalizing the strategy to develop consistent themes and competitive thrusts across markets.

Identifying and Developing Core Businesses

Competition in today's worldwide marketplace is severe and requires companies to focus their efforts on what they do well—their core businesses where they have sustainable competitive advantages that can be leveraged across country markets. As noted in Chapter 7, these businesses can be identified as those that contribute significantly to corporate sales and profits, take full advantage of the technological and managerial resources available within corporations, and have significant potential for development in world markets. As a result, businesses outside of these core areas are carefully scrutinized and evaluated for possible divestiture. For example:

- PepsiCo spun off its Kentucky Fried Chicken, Pizza Hut, and Taco Bell fast-food chains to focus on its soft-drink core business.[5]

- French telecommunications equipment maker Alcatel sold off $2 billion of noncore businesses, including major media interests, to streamline its mainstream commercial business.[6]

- Canon's consistent focus on its copier, camera, and printer businesses enabled the company to expand its global interests and move from #866 to #62 in Fortune's global listings.[7]

- Even within industry niches, specialization often becomes necessary. U.S. motor-vehicle component manufacturers Dana and Eaton bought part of each other's component operations (Dana purchased Eaton's global axle and brake division; Eaton bought Dana's worldwide clutch business) to sharpen their focuses on core specialist activities.[8]

Once firms have their efforts fully focused on their core businesses, the task of formulating and implementing their marketing strategies begins.

Internationalizing the Core Strategy

Firms internationalizing their core strategies must first identify the cross-national segments that are the foundations for international expansions. These are based on similarities among customers, product uses, benefits, and markets. Then they must decide how quickly to internationalize—whether to enter markets one by one, regionally, or globally.

Identifying Cross-National Customer Similarities: Global Segmentation Criteria Global segmentation is the process of identifying cross-national customer groupings with similar needs and who respond in similar fashions to particular marketing mixes. Note that *similar* does not mean *identical*. There are always dif-

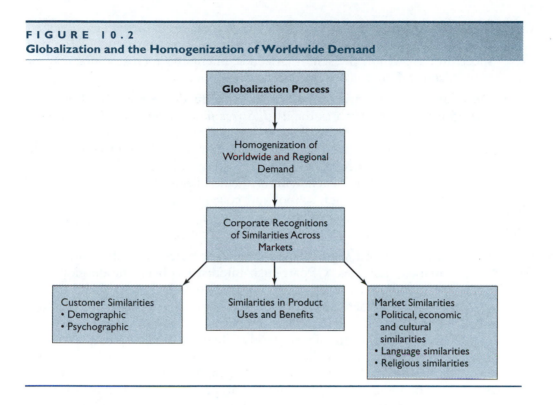

FIGURE 10.2
Globalization and the Homogenization of Worldwide Demand

ferences among customers at the national level. Management's task is to identify those global segments where customer similarities substantially outweigh the differences. Market segments should:

- Be identifiable (by geographic, demographic, or other criteria)

- Be reachable (through media)

- Have common responses to specific marketing approaches (i.e., have similar goals, dispositions)

- Give the company competitive advantages in serving particular segments.

> Anyone can see differences. It takes brains to gauge similarities.
>
> —*Anonymous*

Cross-national similarities become apparent as globalization results in demand homogenization across markets (see Figure 10.2). They can be classified according to three major criteria: customer similarities, product and service use and benefit similarities, and market similarities.

Customer Similarities: Demographic Criteria

- Age is a useful segmentation base for global markets, as consumption patterns are often dictated by life-cycle stages. Baby-related needs have enabled firms like Procter & Gamble and Johnson and Johnson to market infant products such as diapers (nappies) and baby food (Gerber, Heinz) on worldwide bases.

    Children have similarities worldwide. Taking advantage of these are toy manufacturers such as Mattel (dolls), Lego, and Nintendo. In the teenage market, music and fashions have been marketed worldwide since Elvis Presley, the Beatles, and the Rolling Stones hit the music scene in the 1950s and 1960s, and sports such as soccer and basketball have helped to globalize the athletic-outfitting market. At the other end of the age spectrum, growth in the senior-citizen segments have created markets for pharmaceutical products and assisted-living amenities.

- Occupational similarities have created worldwide markets for business-related print media, such as the *Wall Street Journal, Financial Times, Fortune, Business Week,* and the *Economist,* that keep executives abreast of national and worldwide business developments. In the professions, the link between occupations and education has resulted in global markets for learning materials in the medical fields (e.g., *Gray's Anatomy*), teaching areas (high school and college-level textbooks), as well as areas such as engineering (electrical, chemical, civil, industrial, agricultural, metallurgical, and aeronautical) architecture, and law.

- Income-based segments are important bases for global and multi-market strategies. Of particular interest has been the development of middle-income ("yuppy") segments worldwide. While definitions of middle class vary from market to market, the common denominator for all groups is discretionary income: that is, incomes over and above minimum levels. These income surpluses have created global markets for furniture (e.g., IKEA products), consumer durables such as washers, dryers, microwaves, TVs, CD players; labor-saving products such as prepared foods (frozen dinners, canned, packaged goods); "eating out" (franchises such as McDonalds, Pizza Hut, Kentucky Fried Chicken); and ethnic cuisines such as Chinese, Italian, Indian, and Greek foods.

- Gender-based products and services have evolved into global segments for women (fashions, cosmetics, literature, magazines, pharmaceuticals, female hygiene products, etc.) and for men (autos, magazines, books, etc.).

Customer Similarities: Psychographic/Lifestyle Criteria Similarities in global attitudes, interests, and opinions have resulted in discernible worldwide segments in lifestyles. In terms of consumer sophistication, three groups of consumers have cross-cultural similarities.

- *International sophisticates* are high- and middle-income consumers who have genuine interests in international products, fashions, and cross-cultural activities. Sophisticates often speak more than one language and have more in common with sophisticates of other nations than with their own compatriots.

- *Semisophisticates* are middle- and high-income consumers who know little about world affairs and foreign cultures. They are curious about international events but buy products from other countries only for status reasons.

- *Provincial consumers* may be poor or wealthy, more or less educated. They are nationalistic and have few interests in international products or world events. Provincial consumers often have active

Wealth is like seawater; the more we drink, the thirstier we become.

—*Arthur Schopenhauer, 19th-century German philosopher*

If women didn't exist, all the money in the world would have no meaning.

—*Aristotle Onassis, Greek shipping magnate*

Altogether, national hatred is something peculiar. You will always find it strongest and most violent where there is the lowest degree of culture.

—*Johann Wolfgang von Goethe, 18th–19th-century German poet* biases against foreign-made products and anything that is internationally related.

Other lifestyle groups have been identified. In the late-1990s, a 35-country–35,000-consumer survey identified six global groups, three with modern orientations: (1) Strivers (23 percent), who emphasized material and professional goals, (2) Fun seekers (12 percent), the young socialites, (3) Creatives (10 percent), whose major interests were in education, knowledge, and technology, and three traditionally-oriented groups: (4) Devouts (22 percent), for whom tradition and duty were important, (5) Altruists (18 percent), who were interested in societal welfare issues, and (6) Intimates (15 percent), who valued family and personal relationships above all else. These groups existed in all countries and regions, though proportions varied. Note the 55–45 percent split favoring those with traditional orientations.[9]

Global Segmentation Criteria: Product Features and Benefits While demographic and lifestyle descriptors provide useful bases for identifying common needs, ultimately product feature and benefit similarities drive multi-market strategies.

- *Product features:* In the auto industry, product features such as styling and performance drive global demands for high-performance sports cars like Maserati, Porsche, Jaguar, and Ferrari. Luxury features are the hallmarks of high-end BMWs, Rolls Royce, Mercedes, and limousines. Reliability has long been Toyota's major appeal, and economy features have been the mainstays of smaller cars, most notably Fiat in Europe and Daewoo and Hyundai in Asian markets. Japanese firms such as Matsushita, JVC, and Mitsubishi have carved out segments for televisions, radios, CD players, and other electronic products based on their technical features, reliability, and low-cost attributes.

- *Customer benefits* are closely allied to product features. For example, demand for labor-saving products increases with industrialization as more women join the labor force. Companies such as Whirlpool, GE, and Electrolux have based global expansion strategies for consumer durables based on this trend. Health and exercise benefits have made sports equipment producers more globally oriented. Common illnesses and health problems have globalized the pharmaceutical and healthcare industries for products ranging from headache remedies to AIDS vaccines to medical equipment. Industrial equipment manufacturers, from earth-moving equipment to industrial-process controls, have globalized as countries perceive the benefits of physical infrastructure improvements in roads, transportation equipment, telecommunications, gas, electric, and water treatment systems.

> In our factory, we make lipstick. In our advertising, we sell hope.
>
> —*Charles Revson, chairman, Revlon*

Market Similarities: Political, Economic, and Cultural Catalysts to Global and Multi-Market Segmentation Country similarities promote trade and exchanges of technologies.

- The formation of trade blocs such as the EU, NAFTA, and Mercosur has facilitated regional product and service flows. This has encouraged firms to adopt common strategies across multi-market areas and to build and market products on pan-regional bases. The fact that many trade-bloc members are at similar stages of economic development also results in increased potential for commercial and cultural exchanges.

- Language similarities, often remnants from colonial eras, facilitate commerce among nations and make multi-country strategies feasible. Multi-market language groups include English, commonly used outside of the UK in North American and former British colonies, Spanish in Latin America (except Brazil where Portuguese is spoken), Arabic over much of the Middle East, French in France and its former colonies in North and West Africa, and German across Germany, Austria, and parts of Switzerland.

- Religious similarities, while not overtly encouraging multi-market strategies, do homogenize outlooks on life across countries. Buddhism, Confucianism, and Taoism have collectively shaped the Asian character, and Islam and Hinduism have major effects on Middle Eastern and Indian lifestyles respectively. The migration of these religions across national borders (to the U.S. and Western Europe) also creates cross-cultural demand for some ethnic foods, clothes, and other products.

> England and America are two countries divided by a common language.
>
> —*George Bernard Shaw, 20th-century British playwright*

Commonalities among markets and regions are enhanced where there are multiple cultural overlaps. In Latin America, there are similarities of language (Spanish, Portuguese), religion (Catholicism), and economic development levels (all are emerging markets). Some Middle Eastern countries share the Islamic religion, the Arabic language, and oil-based economies. Western European countries have similar political structures (democracies with mixed economies), shared histories (former colonial powers and the world wars of the twentieth century), and, mainly, the same stage of economic development.

Speed of Internationalization: Single, Multi-Country, or Global Expansion Strategies Whether companies tackle international markets one at a time, by region, or on a global basis depends on:

- Availability of corporate resources
- Competitor strategies or likely reactions
- Corporate objectives
- Importance of individual markets

Where country markets are large or strategically important (e.g., big emerging markets such as India, China, Brazil), firms take their time to establish market beachheads that can be built upon in the future. For example, Philip Morris, attracted by Turkey's 43 percent smoking rate and a 5 percent market growth rate, put its corporate muscle behind a concentrated marketing effort in that country. Intensive lobbying was followed by a multimillion-dollar manufacturing investment and a massive marketing push to recruit the country's 130,000 mom-and-pop stores. The strategy paid off in the late 1990s as market share rose from 15 percent to 23 percent, mainly at the expense of local brands.[10]

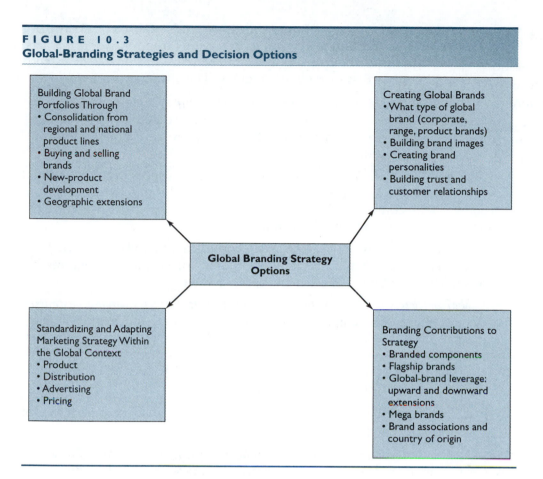

FIGURE 10.3
Global-Branding Strategies and Decision Options

Building Global Brand
Portfolios Through
• Consolidation from
  regional and national
  product lines
• Buying and selling
  brands
• New-product
  development
• Geographic extensions

Creating Global Brands
• What type of global
  brand (corporate,
  range, product brands)
• Building brand images
• Creating brand
  personalities
• Building trust and
  customer relationships

**Global Branding Strategy
Options**

Standardizing and Adapting
Marketing Strategy Within
the Global Context
• Product
• Distribution
• Advertising
• Pricing

Branding Contributions to
Strategy
• Branded components
• Flagship brands
• Global-brand leverage:
  upward and downward
  extensions
• Mega brands
• Brand associations and
  country of origin

Where competition is intense among international companies, first-mover advantages can be gained through multi-market launches. Procter & Gamble launched its Charmin toilet paper simultaneously in six countries—Germany, France, the U.K., South Korea, Hong Kong, and Mexico—using a single advertising strategy.[11] Similarly, in industries with rapidly changing technologies, global product launches are necessary. Fujitsu launched a global brand of UNIX servers simultaneously in Japan, Asia-Pacific, North America, and Europe.[12] In the same industry, Compaq's takeover of Digital to create the world's largest PC manufacturer prompted the acquirer to launch its first worldwide branding campaign to promote its service and engineering expertise in print and broadcast media.[13]

Globalizing the International Strategy

Having established beachheads in major markets, companies have two options. They can continue to operate on a market-by-market basis, or they can begin to integrate marketing strategies across countries to reap the synergies accruing to global branding and marketing. Major global branding options are laid out in Figure 10.3. Which choices firms make depend on the benefits accruing from the strategy.

Interdependence re-creates the world in the image of a global village.

—Marshall McLuhan, 20th-century Canadian author

Advantages and Disadvantages of Global Branding Strategies While globalization is an obvious trend in world markets, managers must be aware of both the benefits and pitfalls of extending brands across markets and regions. The advantages are:

- *Global approaches simplify the marketing task and reduce promotional costs.* McCann Erickson's standardized Coca-Cola campaigns have saved the soft-drink company an estimated $90 million in production costs.

- *Worldwide brand recognition* enhances success rates of global product launches and gives products multi-country momentum. This contrasts with staggered market rollouts that give competitors time to formulate counter strategies.

- *Good product ideas can be leveraged into multiple markets to gain first-mover advantages.* Finnish shampoo Timutei's success in its home market was quickly multiplied in other European markets.

- *Global products take advantage of worldwide similarities among customers.* Renewed corporate emphases on customer, product, and market similarities has given managers confidence to extend their wares into foreign markets. Nike appeals to youthful exuberance and encourages teens to express themselves. Europcar, Hertz, and Avis took advantage of the global stereotype of the hurried business person.

But global branding is not a panacea, and managers are aware of its disadvantages including:

- Standardized products and images are not sensitive to cultural differences. Where national differences are pronounced (as with food products), worldwide branding can be problematic.

- Misfortunes accruing to global brands (e.g., Nestle's infant food problems in developing countries) can reverberate across entire product ranges and tarnish corporate reputations on a worldwide scale.[14]

Building Global Product Portfolios Global brand portfolios are collections of brands that give international companies market influence in specific product areas. Portfolios enable firms to pursue multiple market segments, gain leverage over distribution channels, reap scale economies in advertising, sales, and merchandising, and facilitate new-product launches in related areas.[15]

International companies use four strategies to globalize brand portfolios. They can reorganize their brands from existing regional and national product lines, use mergers and acquisitions to augment existing lines, recalibrate their product lines through new-product development efforts, or build portfolios through geographic extensions.

Consolidation from Regional and National Product Lines Companies using regional and national product strategies can consolidate their brands under global umbrellas. In some cases, renaming and repackaging strategies can be used. Proctor & Gamble's relaunch of its Oil of Olay cosmetics line involved standardizing brand names and packaging of its European versions (Oil of Ulay and Oil of Olaz) and its Asian and South African products (Oil of Ulan).[16]

Heinz used a similar strategy to globalize its eight major product groups (seafood, food service, weight control, infant feeding, convenience meals, frozen foods, pet food, and sauces), many of which used different brand names across major markets. Each product line was recast as a global entity.[17]

Buying and Selling Brands through Acquisitions and Divestitures The buying and selling of global brands has become big business as companies adjust product portfolios to attain critical mass in their marketing efforts. The emphasis on global brands has caused some firms to drop or sell national or regional brands to focus on products with global brand potential. For example:

- Procter & Gamble sold France's #2 soap and shower product, Monsaron, to Sara Lee and its hair product, Petrole Hahn, to Eugene Perma. These sales allowed P & G to focus resources on its global brands.[18]

- Unilever sold its Harmony hair care brand to EMVI because of its limited appeal in the U.K. and Ireland. EMVI used this brand acquisition to bolster its personal-care products division in Europe.[19]

- Megamergers are another tool to build brand portfolios. The merger of drinks giants Guinness PLC and Grand Metropolitan PLC created a new company, GMG Brands, that, even after EU-mandated divestments of its Dewar's Whiskey brand and selected distributorships, still gave the group fifteen out of the top 100 global spirit brands.[20]

- Companies can use acquisitions to build brand portfolios in specific regions. Whirlpool bought Philips' European appliance division and gradually replaced the Philips name with its own. L'Oreal bought out the German brand Dralle and incorporated Laboratories Garnier brands into its lines to enhance its position in the Western European cosmetics business.[21]

> If you build up a business big enough, it's respectable.
>
> —*Will Rogers,*
> *U.S. humorist*

Building Global Brand Portfolios through New-Product Development Globalizing product lines requires significant belief in the universal appeal of company offerings on a worldwide scale. In many cases, internal factors such as duplication and cost cutting are as important as market appeal. The Ford 2000 reorganization unified North American and European divisions and created five vehicle centers with global responsibilities for developing and producing their type of car.[22]

Building global brands through new-product development runs the risk of customer dissatisfaction with standardized products. Honda faced this problem when its 1994 Accord was deemed too cramped for U.S. drivers, not stylish enough for the Japanese, and insufficiently sporty for Western Europe. The problem was solved using a variable frame that allowed the U.S. version to be upsized, high-tech sports features to be added to the Japanese model, and a short, narrow body to be designed to give European drivers a sportier drive. The versatile frame was also used to produce a minivan, a full-sized sports utility vehicle, and two Acura luxury versions.[23]

Building Global Product Portfolios through Geographic Extensions Where companies believe that brands have global potential, one option is to extend them across markets. Franchises such as McDonalds, KFC, and Pizza Hut have been successful users of these strategies since the 1960s. More recently, Taco Bell's

Mexican fast-food concept was extended into Asia by its parent, Tricon Global Restaurants. Targeting the 15–29 age group, the company took advantage of Asian preferences toward wrapped foods. Taco Bell went first into Singapore and Australia and then into the Philippines and China.[24]

Procter & Gamble took its Pringles potato chip brand into over forty countries throughout the 1990s and took the brand from near extinction to global status. A key success factor was its targeting of children ages 6–11 years to preempt global competitor Frito-Lay, which aimed at the 12–17 age group.[25]

Creating Global Brands For individual products and services, the task of creating global and multi-market reputations is not easy. The right product and services must be identified and considerable resources expended to create the right effects.

What's in a name? A 35 percent markup.

—*Vince Thurston*

Products and Brands: Key Differences[26] Few products become major brands. Still fewer become global brands. Everyday products are physical entities and are defined by physical attributes such as design, style, functionality, price, and performance that can be communicated (and forgotten) with ease. In contrast, a brand is a "covenant with the customer." They are built up over time. Longevity defines their innate quality and robustness. They command a marketplace following even during adverse circumstances. Their reputations are consistent and comprise the customer's total experience with a company and its products. The McDonald's hamburger franchise comprises its youthful orientation (with Ronald McDonald), the Big Mac, Ronald McDonald Houses for families of seriously ill children, and many local community support projects. Even high-profile lawsuits against the company have had little effect (hot coffee scalding a consumer in the U.S., environmental protests in the U.K.).

Types of Global Brands[27] There are three major types of global brands.

It is easier to add to a great reputation than to get one.

—*Publilius Syrus, 1st-century B.C. writer of Latin mimes*

- *Corporate (or Organizational) brands* use company reputations as centerpieces of global strategies. Such reputations are based on global expertise in their industries (e.g., Canon for R and D excellence), trustworthiness (Johnson & Johnson pharmaceuticals and consumer products), community orientations (e.g., Body Shop), innovation and technology (Gillette for razors, Intel for microprocessors), perceived quality (Nestle . . . "makes the very best"), and reliability ("you don't get fired for buying IBM").[28] Corporate brands work best when firms market vast arrays of products over multiple markets. For example, Mitsubishi markets tens of thousands of products worldwide, and Siemens sells over 100,000 products in 100 countries. For these companies, global reputations enhance marketplace performance by facilitating new-product launches and product-line extensions. Corporate brands also have internal advantages in molding and bonding corporate cultures. Japanese companies justify corporate advertising for its internal impact of encouraging employees "not to let the company down," while the Body Shop's hype-free, environmentally oriented reputation is a potent recruiting device for new franchisees.[29]

- *Range brands* are collections of product lines brought together under business-unit organizations and are often used with corporate branding initiatives. General Electric (GE) uses range branding to promote its eleven product divisions (GE Capital Services, Appliance Divisions, etc.), and Hewlett-Packard uses its Jet brand for printers.[30] Where a number of range brands fall under a corporate umbrella, they form the bases for megabrands. Calvin Klein fragrances and eyewear were leveraged out of the global clothing line, and Disney's global reputation for films helped launch its theme parks and consumer goods brand ranges.[31]

- *Product brands* contribute to and benefit from corporate and range branding strategies. Building global brands is a complex process, both at the corporate and individual brand levels.

Building Global Brand Images The most stable global brands in today's worldwide marketplace have long roots. They have been established for decades. At the corporate level, IBM, Shell, Siemens, and Mercedes built their global reputations throughout most of the twentieth century. In the post-1945 era, U.S. brands such as Coca Cola, Marlboro, Levi's, McDonalds, and KFC established their global brand presences in many parts of the world. In 2002, 65 of the top 100 global brands were U.S.-owned, and another 27 European.[32]

Since the 1990s, however, the globalization trend has made companies aware of the need to build global brands over shorter time spans. In individual countries, the route to strong national brands has been through mass-media advertising. But at the global level, this can be expensive and does not usually result in the depth of customer involvement necessary for brand status at the worldwide level.

> To disregard what the world thinks of us is not only arrogant but utterly shameless.
>
> —*Cicero, 2nd-century Roman general*

Creating Brand Personalities For companies starting the brand-building process, it all begins with measuring and evaluating brand personalities. Brand personalities have been measured along five major attributes.[33]

- Sincerity: incorporating down-to-earth, honest, wholesome, and cheerful sentiments (e.g., Campbells Soups)

- Excitement: using daring, spirited, imaginative, and up-to-date product images (Porsche, Absolut, Benetton, Calvin Klein)

- Competence: utilizing attributes such as reliability, intelligence, and success (IBM, Philips, Sony, *Wall Street Journal, Financial Times*).

- Sophistication: using upscale "snob" appeals (e.g., Lexus, Mercedes, Revlon, After Eight Mints)

- Ruggedness: incorporating strong, successful, masculine images (e.g., Levi's, Marlboro, SUVs)

These brand attributes have one thing in common: they all have high degrees of universal appeal and are potentially usable across a wide variety of markets.

> Conduct public relations as if the whole company depended upon it.
>
> —*Arthur W. Page, U.S. publicist*

Building Trust and Customer Relationships Once the brand personality has been identified, international companies have broad inventories of strategies to build and sustain customer relationships. These include:[34]

- *Clubs and usage programs:* for example, airline mileage programs, the Swatch Collectors Club, Nestle's Buitoni Club, Harley Davidson's Harley Owners' Group (HOG)

- *Public relations programs:* Nintendo, Sega, and Sony's video games generate massive amounts of publicity via TV programs, video-game magazines, press coverage, and Internet exposure.

- *Product shows and event stores:* Cadbury World in Birmingham, England, attracts a half-million visitors a year to view its history of chocolate making and numerous samples.

- *Publicity stunts:* Swatch hung 165-meter-long watches from skyscrapers in Germany, Spain, and Japan.

- *Event sponsorships:* Hugo Boss, a German producer of premium brand clothing, used sponsorships of Formula One motorcar racing, international tennis, golf, and ski competitions to reinforce the company's high-flying, cosmopolitan brand image.

In other cases, environmental circumstances and unique company situations have resulted in nonconventional brand-building strategies. In Europe's case, limited media options and the high advertising costs contributed to unconventional brand-building strategies. In all cases, though, companies built up customer involvement without resorting to conventional mass-media promotions.

How Global Branding Contributes to Strategy Once established, global brands can be leveraged to produce beneficial "halo" effects for other products, their corporate owners, or other companies and products.

- *Branded components* confer additional quality onto existing brands. "Intel Inside" signifies quality chips and superior internal reliability for PCs. Similarly, Nutrasweet artificial sweetener and Cadbury chocolate add their brand weights to products, using them as featured ingredients.

- *Flagship brands* "Silver Bullets" are star brands in the company's global portfolio. These are often market leaders in their sectors or give distinctive edges or auras to company products worldwide. The Walkman gave the Japanese company Sony high visibility in the consumer electronics market, the Mazda Miata is the jewel in Mazda's product line (e.g. "zoom, zoom, zoom" advertisements), and the Coca-Cola brand anchors that company's global lines. Such products give their companies marketplace visibility and are usually accorded star status in promotional and product development resources budgets.

- *Global brand leverage* allows companies through product extensions to add additional brands to their lines to reach new target markets and to respond to competitor moves. There are three types of extensions. (1) Line extensions increase product varieties to tap smaller or emerging segments. New-product ideas can be tested with extensions, or they can be used to block competitor efforts to upset mainstream markets. (2) Downward brand extensions bring in lower-priced products to attract value-conscious consumers and broaden corporate product mixes. Mercedes in the late 1990s brought out its SUV vehicle and its subcompact Swatchmobile and merged with Chrysler to gain access to mainstream automobile markets.

(3) Upward movement of brands into premium segments attracts customers wishing to trade up from companies' traditional lines. Nike, Reebok, and Adidas created top-of-the-line sports-shoe segments to cater to elite and non-price conscious athletes.

- *Megabrands* are an emerging trend as brand names are leveraged over entirely new business and product lines. Disney was an early user of this strategy, extending its brand name across theme parks and retail outlets. Richard Branson's Virgin brand has been leveraged out of its original vinyl record slot into airlines, financial services, and retail stores, and sports-shoe manufacturers have diversified into sports and casual wear.

> A nation's character is the sum of its splendid deeds; they constitute the one patrimony, the nation's inheritance.
>
> —*Henry Clay*

The danger of all brand diversifications is that they can dilute the market effectiveness of the original brand. Levi's western, rugged jeans-based appeal suffered with the introduction of more sophisticated clothing lines, and Gucci's prestigious leather goods appeal was tarnished by downward product-line moves into canvas goods and by licensing its name into watches, eyeglasses, and perfumes.[35]

Brand Associations and Country of Origin Some countries acquire reputations for specific products. In the alcoholic beverage industry, firms and brand names have become synonymous with their country of manufacturer (e.g., Scotch whisky, Tennessee bourbon, Italian Chianti, French champagne, German beer). Similarly, German engineering, British pop music, French/Italian fashions, Japanese product quality all give associated products competitive advantages in the global marketplace. In other cases, companies seeking global images denationalize their corporate identities. British Airways became BA, National Cash Register NCR, and the Hong Kong and Shanghai Banking Corporation HSBC.

Standardizing and Adapting Marketing Strategies: "Be Global, Act Local"

While in theory global strategies can be used unchanged across all markets (except for translation), in practice, firms fine-tune marketing-mix elements to optimize appeals in particular regions or markets. These adjustments can usually be made to strategies without undermining unifying global strategic themes.

Product Strategies Some marketing activities (e.g., brand names, product positioning, service standards, warranties, and advertising) are easier to standardize across markets than others. Mars, for example, was able to switch its U.K. candy bar name *Marathon* to bring it into line with its global counterpart, *Snickers*. Similarly, product positioning is easier to standardize when global segments are targeted. British Airways positioned itself as the business travelers' airline with a $150 million advertising campaign in 133 countries.[36]

Some aspects of product strategies require adaptation. In Russia, Thailand, and China for example, Pepsi's brand name was unreadable until translated into the local language. Some adaptations are necessary for goods to gain access to markets, but do not compromise global images. These include converting left-hand-drive cars to right-hand-drives in the U.K. or Japan; making required voltage changes for electrical products (110 or 220 volts); changing watch faces from

> A big corporation is more or less blamed for being big, but it is only big because it gives service.
>
> —*William S. Knudsen, former chairman, Ford Motor Company*

Roman numbers into Chinese, Japanese, or Arabic versions; and ensuring that legal requirements in labeling, packaging, and product specifications are met. All are necessary changes that do not alter basic strategies. Inter-Continental Hotels and Resorts tap the luxury segment for global travelers but are able to provide national cultural touches. For example, the Japanese traveler in Paris can order a Japanese breakfast or operate his or her computer on a Japanese telephone system.[37] Fast-food franchises add local items to standard menus. McDonalds serves wine in France, beer in Germany, and McSpaghetti in the Philippines.

Distribution Worldwide distribution has become streamlined with express-mail services, the Internet, and global retailers. Global marketers can use Internet resources to promote and distribute directly to customers. The advent of global and multi-market supply chains has enabled firms to customize output and develop high standards in customer service. PC makers in particular have taken advantage. Dell Computers pioneered the direct distribution mode of PC distribution. Compaq introduced kiosks at computer retails allowing consumers to custom-configure PCs for home or retail delivery within 7–10 business days. NEC ("Now" program) and Sony both ship direct to customers within twenty-four hours.[38] In the consumer-goods sector, Levi's has the ability to custom-produce and distribute clothing products directly.[39]

> Beat your gong and sell your candies.
>
> —*Chinese proverb*

Global retailers have facilitated international distribution by providing ready-made outlets for goods. Toys R Us has created distribution for toys and games in many new markets, and franchisers have provided global exposure for new varieties of food and other services.

Personal Selling and Sales Management These strategies are hard to standardize globally. Some standardization of sales training, presentations, and administration is possible in industries where product lines are more uniform globally, where channels are short, and where personal selling is the key element in the promotions mix (e.g., computers and electronic data processing). Where promotions are mass-media-oriented, distribution channels long, and product mixes more variable (as in general consumer goods), personal-selling and sale-management strategies are more prone to adaptation.

Head-office influence also varies by decision type. Strategic decisions involving resources (own sales force versus third-party independent sales force) and subsidiary sales targets carry more head-office influence. Sales-force structures, training content, and compensation packages are more moderately influenced, while sales presentations and administrative procedures are influenced by local market circumstances.[40]

> The advertising man is a liaison between the products of business and the mind of the nation. He must know both before he can service either.
>
> —*Glenn Frank, U.S. advertising executive*

Advertising Standardization of advertising strategy has been facilitated by the growth of global advertising agencies and global media. Global print media have developed for individual industries (e.g., *Computer World, PC World*) and for global segments such as business people (e.g., *Business Week, Financial Times, Wall Street Journal*). Regional and national versions have emerged for print media as well, such as *Esquire* (ten versions), *Good Housekeeping* (twelve versions), *Runner's World* (seven versions), and *Playboy* (nineteen versions), giving them regional and national appeals. Satellite technologies have broadened the reach for television audiences. BBC World reaches 60 million households, CNN International 221 million, ESPN Sports 242 million, and MTV 285 million households.[41]

Changes are often necessary as multi-country advertising campaigns are unfurled. Advertising messages are composed of two components: the advertising platform, which is the basic message theme, and the creative execution (how the message is presented). In many global campaigns, platforms are standardized as far as possible across markets, but subsidiaries are given latitude to alter creative presentations to suit local tastes. Unilever's Impulse fragrance for European teenagers had the same basic "boy meets girl with flowers" theme. But in France the creative execution had the boy and girl ending up in bed, in Italy a romantic relationship resulted; and in the U.K., humor was used.[42] In some cases, legal restrictions make changes necessary. Advertising to children is limited in Western Europe, and sex or female-related themes have to be toned down considerably in the Middle East where feminine modesty is required.

Pricing These strategies are difficult to standardize globally because of factor-price differences, transportation costs, and foreign exchange-rate discrepancies. Even within the EU with the advent of the euro, price differentials for common products persist within the European trading area, though these are expected to diminish over time.[43]

> *It may be the way the cookie crumbles on Madison Avenue, but in Hong Kong it's the way the egg rolls.*
>
> —Robert Orben,
> U.S. humorist

DEALING WITH COMPETITORS: GLOBAL AND MULTI-MARKET STRATEGIES

As internationalization and globalization strategies are put in motion, firms find themselves up against global, regional, and national rivals. Traditionally, this has meant competing against them, leveraging corporate advantages across markets, and responding to rivals' marketplace moves, both globally and locally. However, the advent of globalization has brought a new dimension to global and multi-market strategies—cooperation with rivals to exploit marketplace opportunities, and the 1990s saw the popularization of a new competitive weapon, global alliances.

Competitive Strategies

This review begins with looking at competitive strategies: global rivalries, the leveraging of competitive advantages across markets, the many strategies firms use to attack rivals, and how competitors respond to global attacks in the U.S., European, and emerging market theaters. Competitive options are illustrated in Figure 10.4.

Competitive Rivalries in Global Industries As markets have opened up, so global rivalries have spread over an increasing number of countries and industries. For example:

- Aircraft: Boeing (U.S.) vs. Airbus (Europe)
- Soft drinks: Coca-Cola (U.S.) vs. Pepsi (U.S.)
- Hamburger franchises: McDonalds (U.S.) vs. Burger King (U.K.)

> *You must not fight too often with one enemy, or you will teach him your art of war.*
>
> —Napoleon Bonaparte,
> 19th-century French emperor and general

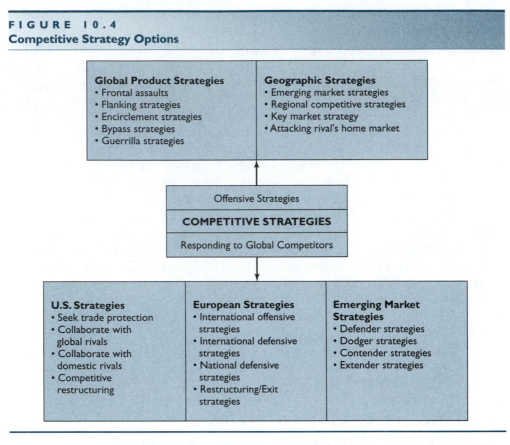

FIGURE 10.4
Competitive Strategy Options

- Luxury autos: BMW (Germany) vs. Mercedes (Germany) vs. Cadillac (U.S.) vs. Lexus (Japan) vs. Infinity (Japan)

- Consumer goods: Unilever (U.K./Netherlands) vs. Procter & Gamble (U.S.)

- Consumer electronics: Matsushita (Japan) vs. Toshiba (Japan) vs. Philips (Netherlands)

- Cellular phones: Motorola (U.S.) vs. Nokia (Finland) vs. Samsung (South Korea)

Rivalries among global firms are particularly acute because executives use competitor companies as reference points for marketing and geographic strategies.

Initiating Competition: Leveraging Competitive Advantages Across Markets The success of international companies to compete globally relies on their abilities to leverage their competitive advantages across world markets. Competitive advantage occurs when a company has an edge over rivals in attracting customers and defending their market positions against competitors.[44] Such competitive advantages are not easily imitated and are usually founded on technical excellence, customer loyalty, or superior organizational capabilities. Some sources of competitive advantage are:

- Developing a product that becomes an industry standard (Xerox)

- Superior customer service (Caterpillar parts, Federal Express)

- Achieving lower cost than competitors (Bic shavers)

- Mastering customized mass-production techniques (apparel and clothing manufacturers)

- Superior supply-chain management in translating customer needs into finished goods (Hewlett-Packard custom-built PCs)

- Brand names and corporate reputations (Nestle, Sony, Shell, Coca-Cola)

- Superior styling and features (Ralph Lauren, Maserati cars)

- Acknowledged technical expertise (Philips, Mercedes)

- Proprietary technologies (biotech companies, pharmaceutical firms)

- Renowned new-product development capabilities (Toshiba, Gillette)

- Convenient locations (on-site auto suppliers)

- Manufacturing the most reliable products (Toyota)

> I don't meet competition. I crush it.
>
> —*Charles Revson, former chairman, Revlon, Inc.*

Global competitors have a number of choices in attacking rivals. They can launch assaults on rival product lines across all markets, or they can focus their competitive efforts on particular regions or markets—a geographically oriented competitive strategy.

> When elephants fight, only the grass gets hurt.
>
> —*Swahili proverb*

Offensive Competitive Strategies When attacking global rivals in world markets, companies can select strategies that can be pursued globally or geographically across selected markets.[45] Global strategies include:

- *Frontal assaults:* When global rivals confront each other, they can opt for all-out offensives. Coca-Cola and Pepsi compete voraciously in global markets with taste tests, price wars, special promotions, and advertising. Reebok, Adidas, and Nike compete to gain sponsorships from leading athletes and teams, and airlines push to offer lower fares than rivals.

- *Flanking strategies* involve attacking market segments ignored or underserved by competitors. The wristwatch industry in the 1950s and 1960s consisted of high-priced mechanical watches and was dominated by Swiss producers. The advent of quartz and electronic watch technologies in the 1960s and 1970s saw prices fall and the Swiss position undermined by Japanese and Asian producers. A counterattack by the Swiss in the 1980s and 1990s used differentiation and low-cost techniques to attack Asian producers. The Swatch ("Swiss watch") was a notable global success as it repositioned watches as reliable low-cost jewelry.

> The enemy advances, we retreat; the enemy camps, we harass; the enemy tires, we attack; the enemy retreats, we pursue.
>
> —*Mao Tse-Tung, Chinese communist leader*

- *Encirclement strategies* are used when market leaders have limited product assortments, and rivals can use superior resources to produce greater product varieties to surround and crowd out the existing competitors. Japanese motorcycle manufacturers used product variety to extinguish major parts of the European and U.S. motorcycle industries in the push to global-market supremacy.

- *Bypass strategies* ignore existing market needs and products and focus on what firms perceive to be future customer needs. Environmental problems with the greenhouse effect and global warming prompted Honda and Toyota to introduce "green" cars with environmentally friendly gasoline-electric engines that have ranges of 70–80 miles per tank of gas.[46]

- *Guerilla strategies* are aimed at disrupting rivals' marketing strategies or stunting sales in major product or service lines. Pricing specials in the airline industry or special promotions opposite the launching of rival products are examples of guerrilla tactics.

Geographically based competitive strategies are more selective and involve focusing on specific regions or markets. They include:

1. *Emerging market strategies:* Marketplace rivals significantly influence where companies choose to allocate global resources—where they compete and with what intensity. This rivalry became more intense as Latin America, Asia, and Eastern Europe opened up during the 1990s: "Our major competitor is in that market—why aren't we?" The rush into emerging markets became justified as competitors rushed to gain footholds in major emerging markets. "First mover advantages" in these countries include:
   - First-time customer exposures to new products give companies advantages in product familiarity and a chance to build a loyal customer base ahead of competitors.

   - Being first gives firms the best choices of primary acquisition targets, the best suppliers, and the most appropriate distribution channels. It also allows key relationships to be built with local businesses and politicians.

2. *Regional competitive strategies* can be formulated to attack (or defend against) key regional rivals. Spanish banks targeted the Latin America banking industry for acquisitions in the mid-1990s. This strong regional investment attracted the attention of the Hong Kong and Shanghai Banking Corporation that promptly spent $2 billion to establish financial beachheads in Brazil, Peru, Mexico, and Argentina.[47]

   European unification has resulted in region-wide competitor assessments as rival products are distributed over the entire continent. Auto producers Audi, BMW, Jaguar, Mercedes-Benz, Saab, and Volvo must take regionwide account of each other's strategies as they position themselves at the premium end of the European car market.[48]

3. *Key market competitive strategies* are important as firms seek to undermine rivals in strategically important markets. Airbus, despite running even with Boeing in most international markets, found itself severely underpositioned in Japan, where its orders were one-sixth of Boeing's. Its response was to mount a major push to build close ties with major suppliers—Mitsubishi, Kawasaki, and Fuji Heavy Industries. These relationships were deemed essential in gaining Japanese sales and support for Airbus' new 550-seat super jumbo jet.[49]

4. *Attacking rivals in their home market:* Historically international corporations have had advantages in their domestic markets where they have established relationships with home-market customers and insider advan-

tages in meeting customer needs. There are also patriotic advantages where customers prefer home-market producers.

Attacking rivals' home-market bases is a key strategy to undermine global competitors that dominate their domestic markets. Fuji attacked Kodak in its home market by sponsoring the 1984 Los Angeles Olympic Games and gaining 50,000 new distribution outlets for its film, being the first company to introduce the disposable camera, attacking Kodak's sentimental approach to picture taking with a technological theme ("Pictures should be nostalgic; your film shouldn't"), and purchasing mass retailer Wal-Mart's six wholesale photo labs, a $400 million move that gave the Japanese company 15 percent of the American photo-processing market.[50]

Kodak reciprocated by mounting an assault on Fuji in Japan. However, the home-market advantage proved difficult to overcome, and Kodak made little headway against Fuji's 70 percent domestic market share. Frustrated, the company went to the World Trade Organization (WTO) with twenty-one charges of unfair trading practices and collusion between Fuji and the Japanese government. The WTO panel failed to uphold any of the charges.[51]

Responding to Global Competitors The superior resources and global know-how of international firms make them tough to compete against. Yet, to every strategy there is a competitive antidote. U.S. and European firms learned this lesson as they have faced the competitive onslaught of the Japanese and other global competitors during the 1980s and 90s.

U.S. Counterstrategies U.S. responses to global competitors take many forms, including:

- *Government-sponsored trade protection:* Initial responses, especially to import invasions, are to seek governmental relief in the form of trade protection. In 1998, low-priced steel imports into the U.S. from East Asia and the former Soviet Union, lead to the imposition of countervailing tariffs.[52] These tactics provided temporary relief until international pressures forced their removal in December 2003.

- *Collaborate with global rivals:* A second strategy is to cooperate with rivals and learn the secrets of their competitive advantages. American companies such as General Motors, Caterpillar, and John Deere all formed collaborative partnerships with Japanese competitors to gain access to superior manufacturing technologies and supply-chain management skills.[53]

- *Domestic collaboration:* A third strategy has been to form industry-wide cooperation groups, either on a domestic or a global basis. In the semiconductor industry, the U.S.-based Sematech consortium expanded to become a 15-firm semiconductor group from Europe, Asia, and the U.S.[54]

- *Competitive restructuring:* A fourth and more comprehensive approach has been to undertake top-to-bottom evaluations of

Carry the battle to them. Don't let them bring it to you. Put them on the defensive. And don't ever apologize for anything.

—*Harry S. Truman,*
20th-century U.S. president

The idea of imposing restrictions on a free economy to assure freedom of competition is like breaking a man's leg to make him run faster.

—*Morris R. Sayre,*
U.S. industrialist

Too often the American dream has been interrupted by the Japanese alarm clock.

—*Anonymous*

company and competitor marketing strategies. This involves complete assessments of supply-chain strategies from suppliers through to final demand at the customer level. This, as Motorola (U.S.) and Philips (Netherlands) found out, involved painful restructuring processes to shed non-core businesses and streamline global operations. Black and Decker revamped its power tool and other lines in response to a challenge from Japan's Makita Electric Works, and Xerox used Japanese management and production techniques to bring its costs in line with global competitors.[55]

European Responses[56] Global competition in the 1990s made many Western European companies aware of their strategic limitations. At that time, many were still country-based or only just developing European or globally-based strategies. As such, their strategic responses varied according to their state of preparedness for global competition.

- *International offensive strategies* were the response of choice for more globally oriented firms. Some, such as engineering conglomerate Asea-Brown-Boveri, opted for cost-leadership approaches to global markets. Others, such as French cosmetics giant L'Oreal or Italy's fashion merchandiser, Benetton, went for global-differentiation strategies. For these companies, offense was the best form of defense.

- *International defensive strategies* were oriented toward consolidating market positions within Europe. Firms such as Solvay (Belgium—chemicals) and Heineken (Netherlands) carved out specialist segments within Europe and fortified them against competitive attacks. Other firms such as Philips (Netherlands) and Germany's Siemens consolidated their regional positions with strategic alliances or takeovers.

- *National defensive strategies* were chosen by companies to maintain home-market dominance while contemplating international expansion moves. Some (such as German airline Lufthansa) focused their efforts on protecting their domestic-market position through economic consolidation and political influence. Others, such as British telecommunications company BT, went for customer-responsiveness strategies to preserve their market positions.

- *Restructuring or exit strategies* were undertaken by firms unable to sustain their market positions in increasingly competitive European theater of operations. Philips exited from its European appliance business (sold to U.S.'s Whirlpool) and from Defense Systems (sold to Thomson-CSF) and restructured to focus on its other core businesses.

Emerging Market Responses[57] For emerging market companies, the challenge of competing against the superior resource bases of international corporations is daunting. One strategy is to form partnerships with international rivals. But this involves losing their independence. To retain their identities, local firms must use their local knowledge of customers, marketplace conditions, and established relationships with channels and regulatory bodies to buy time as they transitioned to more competitive market practices. How local companies positioned themselves depended on two key factors: the extent of global-ization pressures in their industry, and whether their competitive assets were transferable into the international marketplace. These factors resulted in four competitive responses.

- *Defender strategies* work for companies where industry global-ization influences are low and where competitive assets are home-market-customized. Firms in these situations made the most of local knowledge to tap traditional segments and lever-age their distribution capabilities. For example, Bajaj, a local motor scooter producer, effectively countered Honda's entry into the Indian market as consumers retained their preferences for low-cost, durable machines that were easily maintained through Bajaj's vast distribution network. In China, Shanghai-Jahwa, a manufacturer of tradi-tional cosmetics, defended its market with low-cost products using local ingredients. Its Liushen ("six spirits") toilet water used locally produced pearl powder to counter summer ailments such as prickly heat.

- *Dodger strategies* are used by firms whose assets are home-market oriented, but which compete in industry sectors with high globalization pressures. These companies come under significant competitive pressures and either must use local expertise or political connections to avoid direct competi-tion. If these are unsuccessful, then joint ventures could be contemplated. Procter & Gamble's joint venture with Phuong Dong Soap in Vietnam re-sulted in 93 percent ownership after the local company lacked resources to create primary demand for consumer products in local markets.[58]

- *Contender strategies* are for larger local firms that can upgrade existing tech-nologies and eventually transfer competitive assets into foreign markets. Such companies initially adopt niche strategies to defend their home mar-kets until they can establish beachheads in overseas markets. Mexican giant Cemex used this strategy to become a major player in global cement mar-kets, and Indian PC producer HCL shed its joint venture with Hewlett-Packard to become a major producer of low-end PCs in the Asian region.[59]

- *Extender strategies* take advantage of local-market expertise and products to move into markets with characteristics similar to their own. Jollibee, a Philippine family-owned fast-food chain, took its seasoned hamburgers, noodles, rice, and fish menus abroad to cater to Philippine expatriates in Hong Kong, the Middle East, and California. Televisa, a Mexican pro-ducer of Spanish language soap operas, took its wares to Latin America, Spain, and Florida.

Cooperating with Competitors: Global Alliances

Another way of dealing with market rivals is to collaborate rather than compete with them. Global alliances (GAs) are cross-border collaborations among international companies that use other's re-sources and expertise. They became popular as international firms re-alized that they lacked resources to speedily expand into foreign mar-kets. Key aspects of GA management are laid out in Figure 10.5. Global alliances have the following characteristics; they:

> *A man cannot be too careful in the choice of his enemies.*
>
> —*Oscar Wilde, 19th-century Irish author*

> *The only safe way to destroy an enemy is to make him your friend.*
>
> —*Mark Twain, 19th-century U.S. author*

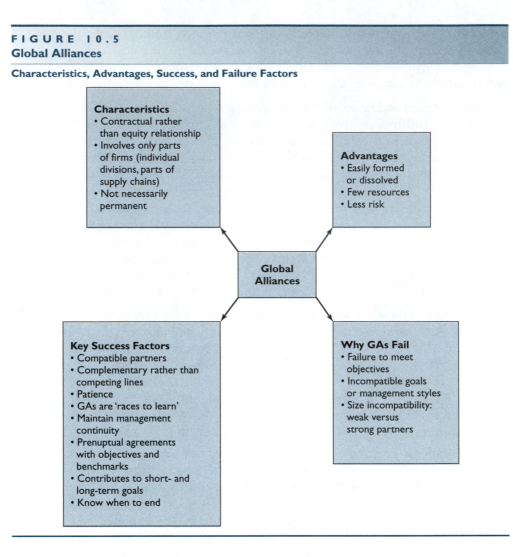

FIGURE 10.5
Global Alliances

Characteristics, Advantages, Success, and Failure Factors

Characteristics
- Contractual rather than equity relationship
- Involves only parts of firms (individual divisions, parts of supply chains)
- Not necessarily permanent

Advantages
- Easily formed or dissolved
- Few resources
- Less risk

Global Alliances

Key Success Factors
- Compatible partners
- Complementary rather than competing lines
- Patience
- GAs are 'races to learn'
- Maintain management continuity
- Prenuptual agreements with objectives and benchmarks
- Contributes to short- and long-term goals
- Know when to end

Why GAs Fail
- Failure to meet objectives
- Incompatible goals or management styles
- Size incompatibility: weak versus strong partners

1. Tend to be contractual agreements rather than equity-based relationships such as joint ventures

2. Often involve parts of corporate supply chains (e.g., technology development, market-access agreements, or shared production arrangements), rather than entire supply chains

3. Are not necessarily permanent (i.e., there are often time limits on relationships)

4. Often involve divisions of companies rather than entire firms[60]

Advantages of Global Alliances GAs are appealing as they tend to be flexible, nonpermanent relationships. They are easily formed (and dissolved), less risky, and require fewer resources than formal equity-sharing relationships. Companies such as software giant Oracle have many thousands of alliances, and the surge of agreements among international firms has resulted in what management guru Peter Drucker has termed a "worldwide restructuring" of international partnerships.[61] They work only when all partners get something out of the relationship. Reasons why GAs are formed include:

- *Technology and product development:* when speed-to-market is essential and major resource commitments are necessary (e.g., chip development, aero engines, aircraft manufacture)

- *Getting into related businesses:* Nestle used alliances with Coca Cola to produce beverages and with General Mills to market breakfast cereals in Europe.

- *Distribution-sharing agreements:* Star Alliances was an eight-airline group that gave individual airline customers access to global destinations.

- *Technology and market-access agreements:* Motorola exchanged technology with Toshiba to gain access to the Japanese market.

- *Shared production:* U.S. company Corning allied with German firm Siemens to produce fiber optic cable. Both firms maintained independent distribution.

- *Creating size and critical mass:* Fujitsu's agreements with Amdahl, Siemens, ICL, Nokio Oy, Advanced Micro Devices, Intellistar, and Sun Microsystems were aimed at creating sufficient size to compete with IBM.

Keys to Managing GAs Because of their flexibility and impermanent nature, cross-border alliances can be unstable. Companies and executives must work hard to maintain relationships over long time periods. The keys to alliance management are:

1. Pick a compatible partner and take time to get to know and trust them.

2. Choose a partner with complementary products and markets rather than one that competes head-on.

3. Be patient: Do not expect instant results or total compatibility—some conflict is healthy and normal.

4. Remember that GAs are "races to learn." Companies should absorb as much as possible about their partner's business while giving away as little information as possible. Firms do this by instituting designated technology sharing facilities, briefing employees about what technologies are off limits, or modularizing projects to preserve key core technologies.[62]

5. Maintain management-team continuity where possible.

6. Know at the outset what all parties want out of the alliance—objectives should be set out in a "prenuptial agreement" and benchmarks set to chart progress.

7. Be sure that alliances contribute to the building up of sustainable advantages (technologies, market access), rather than short-term goals (e.g., outsourcing key products because it's cheaper).

8. Know when a relationship is ailing or has accomplished its goals—then it must be terminated \or reformulated with new objectives.

Why Some GAs Fail About half of cross-border alliances are discontinued or fail to meet their objectives. The primary reasons for failure are incompatibilities between goals and management styles—especially when short-term profit

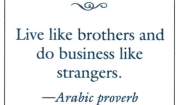

> Keep your friends close, but keep your enemies closer.
>
> *—Sicilian proverb*

> Live like brothers and do business like strangers.
>
> *—Arabic proverb*

orientations clash with long-term strategic objectives and where partners are unequal (one is much more powerful than the other). Weaker firms in this situation must give up more to maintain the strong partner's interest. Finally, managers must recognize that some alliances are overtures to acquisition. Japanese firms in particular use alliances to "get to know" foreign companies in order to see if they are worth acquiring.

GLOBAL AND MULTI-MARKET FINANCIAL STRATEGIES

As international firms extend their reaches in world markets, they become involved with increased numbers of national financial markets in their cross-border financial dealings. This affords them considerable flexibilities in leveraging their financial expertise and resource-switching capabilities to further corporate goals. Figure 10.6 summarizes the major options in global and multi-market financial strategies.

Transfer Pricing Issues

Of the $6+ trillion of trade occurring in world commerce, about one-third is between subsidiaries of the same corporation. While there are international and national rules governing the costing and pricing of products and services entering the international marketplace, firms enjoy some discretion as to the prices and margins they apply to intracompany transfers. Raising or lowering prices of goods shipped among subsidiaries affects the competitiveness and tax liabilities in national markets. Controversies arise between firms and nation states when

FIGURE 10.6
Global and Multi-Market Financial Strategies

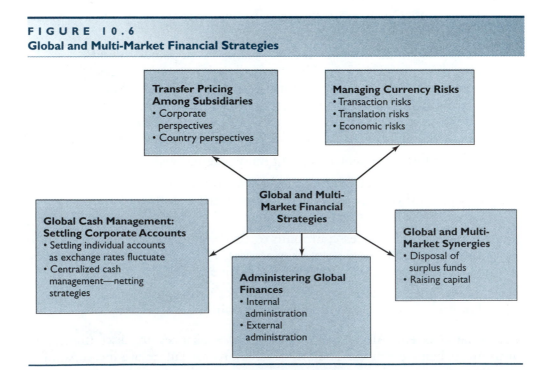

countries perceive that companies are manipulating intragroup transfer prices to their advantage.

Corporate Perspectives on Transfer Pricing Companies feel "justified" in manipulating transfer prices among subsidiaries for three reasons. First is when they encounter stiff price competition from local or international rivals in particular national markets. Where they lower prices to *meet* competition, few repercussions are likely. When they deliberately shave full-cost margins and prices to *undercut* competitors, they become vulnerable to dumping allegations. This occurs when foreign companies use predatory pricing practices to undermine national rivals and destroy market competition. For example, in 2003 U.S. furniture manufacturers filed a petition against Chinese furniture producers for severely undercutting domestic U.S. prices. The petition cited unfair subsidies, low labor costs, and unfair labor and environmental regulations.[63]

Second, where countries (such as Russia and India) either restrict or excessively (in corporate eyes) tax money remittances, such as profit repatriations, fees, or royalties, some firms have few qualms in manipulating margins in trade with that nation to squeeze out additional profits.

Third, many companies aim to minimize their global tax liabilities by manipulating tax earnings in various nations. Figure 10.7 lays out three options that international firms have in pricing products or services to optimize their worldwide tax situations. In Option A, goods are exported at cost (or at a diminished margin) from the high-tax jurisdiction to a nation where additional

FIGURE 10.7
Transfer Pricing Options for International Firms

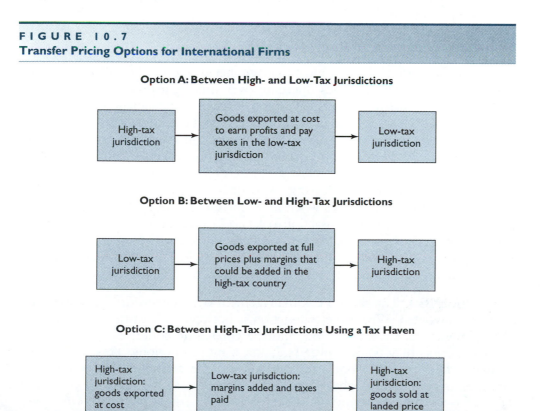

margins are added and taxed at a lower rate. Option B details goods exported at full price plus additional margins that normally would be earned in the importing country. Taxes are paid at the lower rate in the exporting nation rather than in the high-tax importing country.

Finally, Option C shows goods traded between two high-tax countries via a low-tax nation (tax haven) where margins are added and taxes paid in that jurisdiction. Note that the tax havens can be used to shield profits, assets, and other money streams and proliferate the global landscape. Argentina's transfer pricing laws list 88 nations with low or nonexistent income taxes. Many are island states like Bermuda, Nuie, Malta, Cyprus, Mauritius, and the Cayman Islands (advertised as the world's fifth largest financial center and housing forty-five of the world's largest banks). Tax havens account for 1–2 percent of the world's population but 26 percent of assets and 31 percent of net profits of U.S. international corporations.[64]

Country Perspectives on Transfer Pricing Nations generally dislike the idea of international firms "cheating them" out of revenues earned in their tax jurisdictions. Global standards (as set by the UN and the major industrialized nations) and country laws use the "arm's-length standard" for transfer prices. That is, goods and services should be priced as if the subsidiaries were unrelated. However, only about 40 percent of nations have penalties for transfer-pricing violators.[65]

Transfer pricing is projected to be the major tax issue between companies and nations in years to come. The dispute pitches corporate freedoms to earn profits and pay taxes where they choose against countries' desires to maximize national tax revenues.[66]

Managing Foreign Currency Risks

As firms expand globally, they must manage increasing numbers of foreign currencies, some of whose values fluctuate over time. Currency risks are rarely problematic for North American, Western European, and Japanese firms whose currencies, backed by strong economies, tend to be relatively stable over the long-term. In contrast, less-stable developing economies have more volatile currencies where there are often significant depreciations against the dollar, euro, and yen. Because of the increasing interests in developing markets, then, international firms have increasing exposures to weakening currencies that (1) can result in trading losses when local currencies can lose value during the course of a transaction ("transaction risk"), (2) foreign asset values go down when translated into strong parent-company currencies ("translation risks"), and (3) where new and continuing involvements in weak-currency countries expose firms to increasing currency exposures ("economic risks").

Transaction Risk Transaction risk management depends on the currencies and countries involved. Where the transaction is between two of these countries— U.S., Canada, Japan, Switzerland, and the euro-zone countries—forward currency contracts may be used over 1, 3, and 6-month periods. This locks in the exchange rate over the contracted period, and the exchange risk is borne by foreign-currency traders whose forecasting expertise allows them to come out "ahead" over the long-term.

When the transaction is with a weakening-currency country without forward exchange-rate arrangements, the exporter has three options. First, the exporter can insist on immediate payment or prepayment to ensure that there is no loss. Second (and the more usual option), exporters eliminate the time constraint, but have the importer pay the full hard-currency amount (in dollars, euros) over a specified time period, regardless of the exchange rate. This shifts the currency risk onto the importer who may have to use more local currency to buy the requisite number of euros, dollars, or yen. Third, exporters can build a premium into the price to compensate for the forecasted currency depreciation. For example, if a 5 percent local currency depreciation is anticipated, this is added to the dollar-euro-yen export price to compensate.

These methods work for individual transactions between independent businesses. Where businesses are interdependent (as with subsidiaries of international firms), pooling and netting schemes may be used (see next page under "Case Management—Netting Strategies").

Translation Risks Translation risks are asset depreciations that affect corporate balance sheets. These occur when asset values of investments diminish as local currencies depreciate. For example, a $1 million investment made in Costa Rica at 300 colons in time period 1 is a 300 million colon asset. That same investment in time period 2 when the exchange rate is 450 colons per dollar translates at an asset value of $666,667. When consolidated onto the group balance sheet, this represents a $330,000+ drop in assets. While translation downturns are really "paper losses," in that the foreign assets would have to be liquidated for the loss to materialize, they can impact financial performance measures such as return on assets goals.

Economic Risks Economic risks are transaction and translation risks projected over the long-term. Transaction risks affect corporate trading activities when, for example, home-market currencies show long-term appreciation tendencies, making home-market production-costs uncompetitive. Japanese, North American, and Western European firms have noted the steady depreciations of other nations' currencies and moved manufacturing out of home markets to developing countries. Long-term translation risks increase as increasing proportions of corporate assets get moved into weakening currency countries. One response has been for firms to opt for less asset-intensive forms of market involvement (e.g., licensing or subcontracting production instead of factory building).

Global Cash Management: Settling Corporate Subsidiary Accounts

With so many money and product movements among corporate subsidiaries, global cash management and settlements of corporate accounts are big issues. Fluctuating exchange rates can be a problem, as can the sheer complexity of managing so many cash exchanges. How firms cope with these is now discussed.

Settling Individual Accounts as Exchange Rates Fluctuate Chapter 2 discussed the general effects of exchange-rate realignments on money movements. The general conclusion was that companies preferred to work in currencies that were strong or strengthening, as these were natural hedges to maintain currency values. This principle is now extended to the cash-flow principles guiding corporate payables and receivables systems with fluctuating exchange rates. Note that one unit's accounts payable is another's receivable and that one affiliate's strengthening currency is the other's weakening currency. We examine this from two perspectives: the home market appreciating currency (examples 1a and 1b) and the home market depreciating currency (examples 2a and 2b). Remember, they are flip sides of the same issue.

- *Example 1a: Strengthening home-market currency—Accounts payable.* U.S. parent owes its Russian subsidiary $122,000, with the exchange rate moving from 27 rubles to an expected 35 rubles per dollar. This is a strengthening of the dollar and a weakening of the ruble (as might occur after a downturn in the Russian economy). If the Russian subsidiary receivable is paid immediately, the subsidiary gets 3,294,000 rubles ($122,000 × 27). If payment is delayed, it gets 4,270,000 rubles ($122,000 × 35). *Principle:* When a company is making payments from strong-currency countries to weakening-currency markets, it should DELAY payments.

- *Example 1b: Strengthening home-market currency—Accounts receivable.* The Russian affiliate owes its U.S. parent $18,370. For the affiliate, this is an account payable, for the home office, an account receivable. If it pays at 27 rubles per dollar, it must use 495,000 rubles to purchase the dollars ($18,370 × 27). If it opts to pay later, it must use 642,950 rubles ($18,370 × 35) to purchase the currency. *Principle:* When a payment must be made from a weakening-currency country into a strengthening currency, it should make payment immediately.

Examples 2a and 2b involve money movements between a Western European head office and its Japanese subsidiary, with an expected exchange rate moving from 115 yen per euro to 95. This is a weakening of the euro against the yen.

- *Example 2a: Weakening home-market currency—Accounts payable.* Its Japanese subsidiary has shipped a container of electronic components to the European head office that now owes the subsidiary 12,350,000 yen. Should the parent pay immediately or delay? If the parent pays immediately, it must expend 107,391 euros to purchase the requisite yen total. If it delays, the parent has to use 130,000 euros to secure that amount. *Principle:* When the home-market currency is weakening, accounts payable should be settled immediately.

- *Example 2b: Weakening home-market currency—Accounts receivable.* The European parent has receivables (is owed) 930,714 euros by its Japanese subsidiary. If the Japanese affiliate pays immediately, they must use 1,070,321,100 yen (115 × 930,714). If they delay, they must expend 88,417,830 yen to acquire the same number of euros. *Principle:* If the home-market currency is weakening, receivable payments should be delayed as long as possible.

Centralized Cash Management—Netting Strategies Payments among subsidiaries can be complex, so among countries with few or no capital-movement restrictions, many companies have moved toward netting strategies, using global or regional treasury centers to facilitate payments among subsidiaries. Under this system (illustrated in Figure 10.8), all subsidiary transactions are sent to global or regional treasury centers. The center then aggregates accounts payable and receivable and acts as a clearinghouse for money settlements. Each

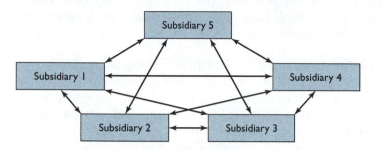

> **FIGURE 10.8**
> **Role of Regional or Global Treasury Units in Simplifying Intracompany Payments and Reducing Currency Transaction Costs**

Intracompany Payments Prior to Adoptioin of Global/Regional Treasury Unit
Ten sets of two-way payments to settle corporate accounts

Intracompany Payments After Adoption of Global/Regional Treasury Unit
Five one-way payments to settle accounts (either payment to or payment from the Treasury)

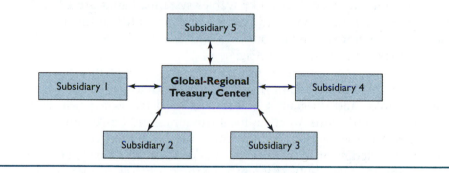

subsidiary receives a consolidated record of its transactions and a statement detailing whether it owes money to or should receive money from the treasury. The advantages of this system are that it greatly reduces the complexity of administering intracompany transactions. It also saves money spent on foreign exchange transactions and administrative expenses.[67]

Global and Multi-Market Financial Synergies

Having financial involvements and doing business in multiple markets gives international firms financial advantages in disposing of surplus funds and in raising capital.

Disposal of Surplus Funds International firms can pool surplus cash either regionally or globally. They can direct it either internally to markets in need of additional investments or they can invest it in any of the world's money or stock markets to maximize their returns. Siemens during the 1990s directed their surplus funds to the U.S. that had the dual advantages of being a strong-currency country and a growth market for the company's products.[68]

Raising Capital Similarly, when they need money for new investments, they can tap the world's financial markets where their reputation gives them funding terms advantages. Daewoo raised capital for its European expansion primarily from Western European money market. Similarly, GE Capital, by virtue of its size and reach, can raise money anywhere in the world.

Administering Global Finances

Companies have choices as to whether they administer their global finances internally through national, regional, or global treasuries, or externally using international or local banks.

Internal Administration Firms with heavily integrated global operations (and whose trading activities are mainly among group members) tend to work through corporate treasuries. Siemens Financial Services acts as its own internal bank, for example, coordinating 70 billion commercial payments throughout its 190 country network. Other companies use regional treasury centers. Cargill, an international agricultural, food, and industrial firm, processes transactions through treasuries in the U.S., England, and Singapore.[69]

External Administration Where corporations lack the expertise or resources to administer global receivables and payables systems, banks are used. This occurs particularly when firms are in the earlier stages of internationalization. U.K. retailer Tesco operates in nine countries and uses Citibank's regional facilities in central Europe and HSBC's in Asia.[70]

Some companies prefer to use national rather than international banks to manage their financial affairs. Fiat's corporate treasury liaises with prominent national banks, and oil giant Conoco uses local banks for cash collections. In China, India, and Latin America, local treasuries and banks tend to be used because of restrictions getting money into and out of their countries and because of their knowledge of local financial markets. Brazil's financial market restrictions during the late 1990s (foreign-exchange controls and prohibitions against intracompany netting and offshore accounts) caused many firms to totally localize their Latin American financial strategies.[71]

KEY POINTS

- The globalization process has enabled many international firms to extend products, services, and marketing mixes into foreign markets with relatively few adaptations.

- Formulating global and multi-market strategies involves defining core business strategies, internationalizing those strategies, and then globalizing them through the development of consistent themes and competitive strategies across markets.

- Core businesses are those that contribute to corporate profits, make full use of corporate expertise and resources, and have significant global potential.

- Internationalizing core strategies involves recognizing global similarities in customers and markets.

- Companies have choices as to whether they expand slowly, one market at a time, or more quickly by entering multiple markets or all world markets at the same time.

- Globalizing international strategies entails creating global brands and global-brand portfolios that are collections of brands in specific market areas.

- Total product standardization is rarely achievable, though most firms strive to standardize brand names and packaging as far as possible. Distribution, pricing, and promotional strategies are frequently adapted in "Be Global, Act Local" strategies.

- Global brands are "covenants with consumers" and can be classified into corporate brands, range brands, and individual brands. Many global brands have been established for decades. Others are created through mass-promotional (but not advertising) programs.

- International companies can deal with rivals by either competing against them or by cooperating with them through global alliances.

- Many global industries have major rivalries among a few large companies. Most international strategies are based on extending competitive advantages into foreign markets.

- Offensive competitive strategies can be product-based, using frontal, flanking, encirclement, bypass, or guerilla strategies, or geographically-based, targeting emerging markets, specific regions, key markets, or rivals' home markets.

- U.S. companies respond to global rivals by asking for trade protection, working with competitors, forming domestic collaborations, or restructuring themselves. European companies go for offensive or defensive international strategies, national defensive strategies, or exiting the industry. Emerging market firms can go for defender, dodger, contender, or extender strategies.

- Companies can opt to collaborate with market rivals through global alliances. Many alliances fail because of incompatibilities among partners.

- Global and multi-market financial strategies take advantage of corporate globalization in being able to manipulate intracompany trading margins for competitive or tax reasons via transfer pricing. Firms must also manage transaction, translation, and economic currency risks as they trade in volatile currencies, manipulate their global cash resources to take advantage of currency realignments, and, where possible, simplify cash management through netting strategies.

- Companies reap financial synergies globally through their access to world financial markets and administer corporate funds internally via regional or global treasury units or externally through use of international banks.

ENDNOTES

1. Alexandra Jardine, "A-D global teams axed in reshuffle," *Marketing* (July 8, 1999): 2.

2. Anonymous, "From cash management to cash generation," *Asiamoney* (May 1997): 10–13.

3. Based on George S. Yip, *Total Global Strategy* (Englewood Cliffs, N.J.: Prentice Hall, 1995): 4–7.

4. Theodore Levitt, "The Globalization of Markets," *Harvard Business Review* 83: 3 (May–June 1983): 92.

5. Scott Reeves, "Pepsi's Fizz," *Barron's* (January 12, 1998): 15.

6. Axel Krause, "Alcatel: Global Telecom Player," *Europe* (March 1996): 12–13.

7. Edward W. Desmond, "Can Canon keep clicking," *Fortune* (February 2, 1998): 98–106.

8. David Cullen, "Dana and Eaton swap component units," *Fleet Owner,* (August 1997): 10.

9. Tom Miller, "Global segments from 'Strivers' to 'Creatives,'" *Marketing News* (July 20, 1998): 11–12.

10. Suein L. Hwang, "Philip Morris muscles into Turkish market: Local brands lose as Marlboro Man makes most of advertising alliances," *Courier-Journal* (Louisville, Ky., September 20 1998): 1E.

11. Anonymous, "DMB&B's Global Brand Trios," *Adweek Southwest* (November 30, 1998): 8.

12. http://www.fujitsu.co.jp/hypertext/news/1998/nov/4-e.html

13. Lisa Campbell, "Global Branding ads for Compaq," *Marketing,* (June 18, 1998): 7.

14. Based on Jean Noel Kapferer, "Making brands work around the world," *Australian Financial Review* (September 1998): 12–21.

15. Patrick Barwise and Thomas Robertson, "Brand Portfolios," *European Management Journal* 10: 3 (Sept. 1992): 277–86.

16. Anonymous, "P&G to rename Oil of Ulay range," *Marketing* (November 5, 1998): 4.

17. Clare Conley, "Heinz turns focus onto Global Vision," *Marketing Week* (September 17, 1998): 23.

18. Anonymous, "Procter & Gamble sells Monsaron to Sara Lee and Petrole Hahn to Eugene Perma," *Les Echos* (November 2, 1998): 16.

19. Richard Rivlin, "City: Unilever severs link with Harmony."

20. Ernest Beck and Julie Wolf, "EU approves the merger of Guiness, Grand Met," *The Wall Street Journal Europe* (October 16, 1997): 3.

21. Jean Noel Kapfere, "Making brands work around the world," *Australian Financial Review* (September 1998): 12.

22. James B. Treece, "Ford: Alex Trotman's daring global strategy," *Business Week* (April 3, 1995): 96–102.

23. Keith Naughton, Emily Thornton, Kathleen Kerwin, and Heidi Dawley, "Can Honda build a world car," *Business Week* (September 8, 1997): 100–8.

24. Normandy Madden and Andrew Harnery, "US Multinationals: As Taco Bell enters Singapore, Gidget avoids the limelight," *Advertising Age International* (January 11, 1999): 13–14.

25. Judann Pollack, "Pringles wins worldwide with one message," *Advertising Age International* (January 11, 1999): 14–15.

26. Based on Jacques Chevron, "The Delphi Process: A Strategic Branding Methodology," *Journal of Consumer Marketing* 15: 3 (Summer 1998): 254–61.

27. Based on David A. Aaker, *Building Strong Brands* (New York: The Free Press, 1996).

28. Ibid., 119–35.

29. Ibid., 108, 111–14.

30. Ibid., 211, 242.

31. Ibid., 292–98.

32. Gerry Khermouch, "The Best Global Brands," *Business Week* (August 5, 2002): 92–99.

33. Aaker, 90, 120.

34. Based on Aaker, 187, and Erich Joachinsthaler and David A. Aaker, "Building Brands Without Mass Media," *Harvard Business Review* 75: 1 (Jan.–Feb. 1997) 39–50.

35. Orit Gradiesh and James L. Gilbert, "Project Pools: A fresh look at Strategy," *Harvard Business Review* 76: 3 (May–June 1998): 140–41.

36. Laurel Wentz, "BA's $150m campaign makes worldwide debut," *Advertising Age* (January 8, 1996): 33.

37. Alan Saloman, "Inter-Continental beckons homesick foreign travelers," *Advertising Age* (October 14, 1996): 24.

38. Tobi Elkin, "PC Makers ponder retail vs. direct and issues role in branding angles," *Brandweek* (June 22, 1998): 8.

39. Erick Schonfeld, "The customized, digitized, have it your way economy," *Fortune* (September 28, 1998): 114–24.

40. John S. Hill, Richard R. Still, and Unal O. Boya, "Managing the Multinational Sales Force," *International Marketing Review* 8:1 (1991): 19–31

41. Juliana Koranteng, "Global Media" *Ad Age International* (Feb. 8, 1999): 23–32.

42. Anonymous, "How Unilever's Impulse crosses borders," *Business Europe* (July 4, 1994): 7.

43. Anonymous, "Pricing for the Euro," *Business Europe* (April 21, 1999): 1, 3.

44. Adapted from Arthur A. Thompson and A. J. Strickland, *Strategic Management: Text and Cases,* 11th edition (Boston, Mass: Irwin-McGraw-Hill, 1997), 134.

45. Based loosely on Philip Kotler, Liam Fahey, and S. Jatusripitak, *The New Competition* (Englewood Cliffs: N.J.: Prentice Hall, 1985).

46. Emily Thornton, "Enviro-cars: The race is on," *Business Week* (Feb. 8, 1999): 74–76.

47. Michael Marray, "Good prices but is there a strategy?" *Euromoney* (July 1997): 20.

48. Bill Visnic, Andrea Wielgat, and Drew Winter, "The European Juggernaut," *Ward's Auto World* (Oct. 1998): 34–40.

49. Jeff Cole and Norihiko Shirouzu, "Airbus takes aim at Boeing's grip in Japan," *Wall Street Journal* (April 19, 1999): A3, A10.

50. Edward W. Desmond, "What's ailing Kodak? Fuji," *Fortune* (Oct. 27, 1997): 185–92.

51. Anonymous, "Kodak will still lose," *Industry Week* (Jan. 19, 1998): 13; and Daniel B. Moskowitz, "An even harder nut to crack," *International Business* 11, 1, (Jan.–Feb. 1998): 18–21.

52. "Business: In America's fiery furnaces," *Economist* (September 19, 1999): 73–75.

53. Philip Kotler, Liam Fahey, and S. Jatusripitak, *The New Competition* (Englewood Cliffs, N.J.: Prentice-Hall, 1985).

54. Jeff Dorsch, "It's a small semiconductor world," *Electronic Business* (April 1998): 36.

55. Kotler, Fahey, and Jatusripitak, 240–41.

56. Rene Samson, "Competing with the Japanese—Strategies for European Business," *Long Range Planning* 26: 4 (1993): 59–65.

57. Based on Niraj Dewar and Tony Frost, "Competing with Giants: Survival Strategies for Local Companies in Emerging Markets," *Harvard Business Review* 76: 2 (March–April 1999): 119–29.

58. Anonymous, "P&G Vietnam: Jaded with Joint Ventures," *Business Asia* (April 6, 1998): 5–6.

59. Shiraz Sidhva, "Goodbye, Partner," *Far Eastern Economic Review* (Sept. 11, 1997): 62.

60. Philippe Gugler, "Building transnational Alliances to create Competitive Advantages," *Long Range Planning* 26: 4 (1993): 36–41.

61. Debra Sparks, "Partners," *Business Week* (Oct. 25, 1999): 106–12.

62. Gary Hamel, Yves L. Doz, C. K. Prahalad, "Collaborate with your competitors—and win," *Harvard Business Review* 67: 1 (Jan.–Feb. 1989): 133–39.

63. Duncan Adams, "Group of US Furniture Manufacturers File Petition with Trade Commission," *Knight Ridder Tribune Business News* (July 16, 2003): 1.

64. Matthew Bishop, "The Economist Shelter. Globalization and tax: Gimme Shelter," *Economist* (Jan. 29, 2000): S15–S19.

65. Victor H. Miesel, Harlow H. Higinbotham, and Chun W. Yi, "International transfer pricing: Practical solutions for inter-company pricing," *The International Tax Journal* 28: 4 (Fall 2002): 1–22.

66. Anonymous, "Ernst & Young 2001 Survey: Transfer pricing again tops list of issues for multinationals," *Journal of International Taxation* 13: 4 (April 2002): 18–27+.

67. Christopher P. Holland, Geoff Lockett, Jean-Michel Richard, "The evolution of a global cash management system," *Sloan Management Review* 36: 1 (Fall 1994): 37–46.

68. Chris Wright, "Six perspective on financial management," *Corporate Finance* (May 2000): 4–10.

69. Jonathon Turton, "Seven different solutions to burning issues," *Corporate Finance* (May 2000): 11–19.

70. Wright, *op. cit.*

71. Susan Griffiths, "Managing treasury in Latin America," *TMA Journal* 19: 2 (March–April 1999): 28–32.

C A S E T T E   1 0 - 1
Global Branding, Rivalries, and Organizational Practices

Global, Euro, and National Brands: The Fight Continues

Global brands proliferate in many of the world's major markets. Their lure seems irresistible: scale economies in manufacturing and marketing reinforced with the latest technologies and marketing techniques. The homogenizing forces of world commerce have made the search for global segments as natural a management process as nation-based segmentation used to be for country-level strategies. Global media are in place to promote them, as are the multi-market channels to distribute them.

But local country brands continue to do well, even in Western Europe where globalization effects and a multitude of internationally-focused firms have combined with Europe-wide economic and political unification efforts to optimize conditions for successful global and euro-branding. Some examples:

- ICI is committed to establishing its Dulux paint brand worldwide, but the company has not replaced its best-selling French paint Valentine with the Dulux brand, as it has in other markets.

- The leading gin in Spain is not a global brand like Beefeater or Gordon's. It is the local brand, Larios, with a 60 percent market share.

- In France, the best-selling Scotch whiskies are not the world famous Johnny Walker or Ballentine brands; they are the British-sounding but locally produced brands, Label 5, Clan Campbell, and William Peel. Similarly in detergents, local French brands LaCroix (Henkel) and St. Marc (Benckiser) are primary competitors to global brands.

- Danone's leading biscuit (cookie) brand in Russia is Bolchevik, and in the Czech Republic it is Opavia.

Global Brand Rivalries: Nokia and Samsung

As global brands go, Nokia is up there with the Coca-Colas and Microsofts. The company, founded as a wood pulp company in Finland in 1865, did not get into electronics until 1966. Today, Nokia supplies over a third of the world's 900+ million cell-phone users, up from 19 percent in 1997. It produces in ten countries and markets its products in over 130. In contrast to other global brands, Nokia's rise to brand stardom has been meteoric in a market that grew at over 50 percent annually over 1996–2000, but which has shown signs of maturity over 2000–2002 as global demand has leveled off.

Nokia's reputation has been built on cellular phone style and technology. Its brand personality reflects the human-technology link, embracing individuality, quality, and freedom. Its corporate culture is based on hard-driving marketing and technological advances. Its newest product, the N-Gage, is typical. Aimed at the technology-conscious 18–35 segment, the N-Gage performs as a mobile phone, plays games, is an MP3 music player, and has an FM radio. Its U.S. launch is priced at $299. But it faces a formidable competitor in Korea's up-and-coming Samsung. Currently, Nokia's $600+ million global marketing budget is double Samsung's $300 million. But Samsung's has advantages: It has access to Asia's cheap labor pool; its Korean and Asian markets are prolific mobile-phone users and are sensitive to the latest technologies, and Samsung's diverse portfolio of electronic businesses give it immediate access to the a wide range of technologies. Its focus has been on high-tech and high-priced products.

Organizing the Multi-Country Marketing Effort

Cosmetics producer Elizabeth Arden's priorities were directed toward an organizational makeover to convert its twelve national subsidiary system into a pan-European operation. What the firm did was to create a European Supply Company (ESC) to manage Europe-wide media buying, retail and promotional strategies, brand management, and supply-chain purchasing and distribution. Supply-chain consolidation, for example, reduced working capital requirements (inventories, work-in-progress) by 50 percent. Prices and terms of trade began to move toward Europe-wide convergence, though payment terms differences were still apparent between Northern and Southern Europe. Company manufacturing and marketing functions were split away, with the ESC acting as group coordinator, bonding the business together via a shared service center to orchestrate uniform customer services, marketing, order processing, finance, treasury, supply-chain and information services. The ESC was based in Geneva, Switzerland, for tax reasons. General managers were maintained at the country level, though administrative headcounts were reduced by 60 percent at the national subsidiary level, and administrative costs were cut by 30 percent overall. Their function was to maintain and increase market share, collect intelligence, evaluate new product and service opportunities, and monitor customer sales and services. While many anticipated a desensitized regional structure, responsiveness to national needs actually improved.

Questions

1. Why are national brands continuing to do well in Europe? How should international firms treat their local brands?

2. Regarding Nokia and Samsung—do you think that Nokia is a true global brand? Why or why not? Relate Nokia's brand personality (human-technology link, individuality, quality, and freedom) to the mobile cell phone product. Regarding the Nokia-Samsung rivalry—which of the two do you think is better positioned for global dominance? Why?

3. What are the advantages and disadvantages to Elizabeth Arden's new organizational approach to its European operations?

Sources: Krempel, Marcie. "The Pan-European Company-Restructuring for a New Europe." *European Business Journal* 11: 3 (1999): 119–29. Kapferer, Jean-Noel. "Is there really no hope for local brands?" *Journal of Brand Management* 9: 3 (2002): 163–71. Lezzi, Teressa. "Fight to the Finnish." *Adageglobal* (June 2002): 14–15. Rogers, Daniel. "Handset Combat." *Marketing* (Sept. 2003): 22–25.

CASETTE 10-2
Making All the Right Moves: India's Tata Group

India's Tata group is a sprawling empire of over eighty companies ranging from steel, power generation, and cars to tea, hotels, and software. But the company faced its sternest challenge in the 1990s as India began to open its borders to foreign competitors, forcing this traditional family-based business empire to rethink strategies to become globally competitive.

Tata was not alone in making these adjustments. Mahindra and Mahindra, a family tractor business, faced major labor upheavals as it modernized its plants, but pushed through its agenda to become the world's fifth-largest tractor maker in the world by the turn of the millennium. Birla, another family-run conglomerate, focused its efforts on telecommunications and established a joint venture with the U.S.'s AT&T. Reliance Industries, with help from accounting firm Deloitte & Touche, became the first Indian business to raise $100 million in 100-year bonds in the U.S. market. Such modernization movements enabled India's family empires, as well as many others in Asia, to continue their dominance of their respective national markets for the foreseeable future.

But of all Indian family conglomerates, Tata has faced the greatest challenges in making appropriate changes. As one executive noted: "Tata is a microcosm of India. It's huge, sprawling, complex, full of heritage, and it needs to change. But it is difficult to change." But the company's approach to its steel business epitomizes Tata's determination to blend the old with the new to establish world-class business standards and compete in the international marketplace.

The company started to produce steel in the city of Jamshedpur about ninety years ago. Even today, the 80,000 workers still enjoy lifelong employment, free housing, education, and healthcare. Not surprisingly, the company hasn't had a strike in over six decades. But life at the plant has changed. Foreign companies helped with a vast modernization plan executed in three phases—1980–83, 1984–88, and 1989–94. The result was a transformation into one of the world's premier steel production facilities.

But major changes have occurred at the group level, and with 11 out of the 80 companies accounting for 85 percent of group revenues and 90 percent of profits, some focusing of group resources is oc-

curring. Tata realized it could not compete in some areas, such as toiletries, textiles, and cement, and is slowly adjusting its business portfolio. Its cement group, for example, was sold to France's Lafarge group in 1999. Seven businesses have been targeted for development: metals and minerals, automobile and engineering, chemicals, agro-business (tea), hotels, information technologies, and power generation. The automotive business, though, has become very cut-throat. Despite adopting Japanese manufacturing techniques and experiencing booming sales in the mid 1990s, cutbacks have been made and 4000 jobs lost. The passenger-car industry in India has undergone major upheavals as the world's premier automakers—all present in India—have overcapacity.

Tata has taken advantage of its many relationships with the outside world. Dating from India's closed economy years, Tata developed major relationships with premier Western companies anxious to gain footholds in the Indian market, including AT&T, Mercedes Benz, IBM, Cummins Engines, and many others.

Tata's strategies have not been limited to its domestic businesses. The Tata Group's international presence has been enhanced in a number of areas. The Taj Group of Hotels has 5300 rooms in forty-three hotels at major tourist locations throughout India. Its international spread extends to fourteen hotels and 3000 rooms in eight countries, including Washington, D.C., New York, and London.

The group has also taken advantage of India's expertise and natural advantages in tea production. Tata Tea Limited is the largest tea-growing company in the world, with over fifty tea estates producing 55 million kilograms of black tea annually. The company made a major international move when, seeking an upstream-brand presence in the West, Tata Tea bought Britain's Tetley group for $390 million in 2000.

Additionally, taking advantage of India's vast army of math, engineering, and science graduates, Tata Consultant Services and its Information Technology group established overseas presences in the U.S., Europe, Middle East, Australia, and Japan, as well as dominant positions in the blossoming IT sector within India.

∼⊸⊙⊸

The group is also aware that it will take more than just the family name to control its family concerns, especially as foreign companies are no big respecters of family pedigree. In the early days under the leadership of J. R. D. Tata, the group was held together by the Tata name and reputation. The Tata stake in some of its companies was in single digits (2 percent in Tata steel's case). After leadership passed to Ratan Tata in 1993, the group's labyrinth of cross-holdings has undergone change. Royalty levies for use of the prestigious Tata name were put into place (revocable in the event of an unfriendly takeover), and stakes in operating companies were increased to 26 percent with an eventual goal of majority (50+ percent) stakes by the time India's economy becomes fully open by 2005.

Questions

1. Have the Tatas made "all the right moves"? What were they, and what do you think is the underlying rationale for them?

2. Are there any weaknesses in Tata's strategy that may cause problems in the future?

3. What factors in India's market and operating environment may cause problems over the short- and medium-term (review Chapter 4 materials on India)?

Sources: "Mixing business with Pleasure." *Asiamoney* (Sept. 1996): 9–12. Chatterjee, Amit, and Tridibesh. "Staying Ahead of Global Competition: The Tata Steel Strategy." *Journal of General Management* 21: 1 (Autumn 1995): 71–88. "Reinventing Tata Series: Business." *Economist* (Feb. 17, 2001): 61–62. Engardio, Pete, and Shekhar Hattangadi. "India's Mr. Business." *Business Week* (April 18, 1994): 100–1. Press Reports. Slater, Joanna. "A Partnership brewing." *Far Eastern Economic Review* (May 17, 2001): 40–42.

Chapter
Eleven

Global and Multi-Market Supply Chain Management

~ॐ~

WHAT DO THESE COMPANIES HAVE IN COMMON?

In the mid-1990s, Bristol-Myers decided to coordinate the manufacturing and distribution processes of its 65 sites in 150 countries. This entailed consolidating materials procurement, finance and invoicing processes for over 200,000 products worldwide. A new information system was installed. Initially, $150 million was saved, and enhanced coordination resulted.[1]

Victor Fung is a Hong Kong businessman whose company, Li & Fung, works with 7500 suppliers in 26 countries to coordinate offshore manufacturing and distribution for 350 worldwide customers, including The Limited, Warner Brothers, Marks & Spencer, and Philip Morris. Clients come to the firm with product specifications, delivery dates, and target prices and leave the rest to Li & Fung.

The answer is that both companies used supply chains to integrate material, component providers, manufacturing, distribution, and customers on a worldwide scale. They had different approaches. Bristol-Myers reconfigured its internal organization to streamline its supply chain operations. Li & Fung acted as the external coordinator of offshore supply chains for large international companies that did not wish to become involved with the complexities of supply chain coordination. Both had the same objective: to become more efficient in worldwide operations and to take advantage of advances in information systems to be more responsive to changes in the worldwide marketplace. Both firms showed how important global and multi-market supply chains have become for international companies in their quests for competitive advantage.[2]

In this chapter you will learn:

- The nature of global and multi-market supply chains, the environmental and corporate catalysts promoting them, and the competitive advantages that accrue to firms from their development
- How firms integrate supply chains through linkages between suppliers and manufacturers, the configuring of their manufacturing systems, manufacturer-distributor links, and direct linkages with customers.
- The ways firms manage multi-country supply chains through information technologies, human resources, and new product development processes
- Deintegration decisions: why companies outsource supply chain components, and the advantages and disadvantages of these decisions

412

FIGURE 11.1
Global and Multi-Country Supply Chains: Topic Outline

Catalysts of Global and Multi-Market Supply Chain Development
- Environmental Catalysts
- Corporate Catalysts

Global and Multi-Company Supply Chains		
Integration Mechanisms	**Integration Options**	**Deintegration (Outsourcing) Strategies**

Information Technologies (IT)	Supplier-Manufacturer Linkages
	• Trends
	• Sourcing Strategies
	  –Home market sourcing
	  –Regional sourcing
	  –Worldwide sourcing
	• Supplier Integration
	  –Stages
	  –Relationships
		• Strategic Perspectives
		
		• Raw Materials
		
		• Components
		
		• Manufacturing

Multicultural Managers and Human Resources	International Manufacturing Systems • Factors Affecting Manufacturing Configuration • Evolution of International Manufacturing Systems • Managing Manufacturing Process Transfers Across Markets	• Logistics • Distribution • Information Technologies
New-Product Development Processes	Manufacturer-Distributor Linkages • Trends • Organizational Options	• Human Resources • New-Product Development
	Distributor-Customer Linkages • Electronic Data Interchange (EDI)	

INTRODUCTION: GLOBAL AND MULTI-MARKET SUPPLY CHAINS

Global supply chains are international networks linking suppliers, producers, distributors, and customers across national boundaries to facilitate product and service flows to ultimate users. In domestic markets, national cultures and common operating practices facilitate the integrating of supply chain participants and processes. As markets have globalized, so supply chain activities have been dispersed across countries to take advantage of low factors costs, national expertise in specific industry sectors, and material-resource differences to produce goods and services. The managerial challenge is to integrate these expertise and resource differences to produce goods and services with sustainable competitive advantages in world markets.

Environmental and Corporate Catalysts to Global and Multi-Market Supply Chain Development

Environmental Catalysts Environmental catalysts include the *free trade movement,* which allows companies to transship components, materials, and final

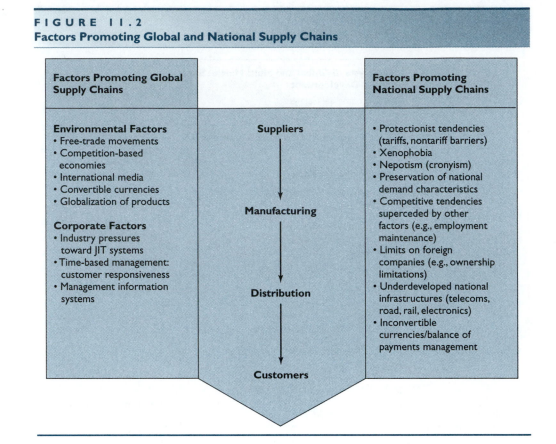

FIGURE 11.2
Factors Promoting Global and National Supply Chains

Factors Promoting Global Supply Chains		Factors Promoting National Supply Chains
Environmental Factors • Free-trade movements • Competition-based economies • International media • Convertible currencies • Globalization of products **Corporate Factors** • Industry pressures toward JIT systems • Time-based management: customer responsiveness • Management information systems	**Suppliers** ↓ **Manufacturing** ↓ **Distribution** ↓ **Customers**	• Protectionist tendencies (tariffs, nontariff barriers) • Xenophobia • Nepotism (cronyism) • Preservation of national demand characteristics • Competitive tendencies superceded by other factors (e.g., employment maintenance) • Limits on foreign companies (e.g., ownership limitations) • Underdeveloped national infrastructures (telecoms, road, rail, electronics) • Inconvertible currencies/balance of payments management

> Coming together is a beginning; keeping together is progress; working together is success.
>
> —*Henry Ford,*
> *U.S. motor magnate*

products between markets for sale or further processing. The *homogenization of global demand* has caused the erosion of country-level differences in consumption patterns. The formation of regional market blocs, such as the EU, have resulted in both the emergence of cross-national customer segments and some cross-border standardization of international marketing strategies. In addition, the *pressures of global competition* have forced companies to extend their best manufacturing and process technologies across increasing numbers of markets, thereby homogenizing supply chain strategies in world markets. Technological advances in *information systems, global media, transportation, and logistics systems* have also been major facilitators of supply chain integration.

Of course, not all countries can be included in multi-country supply chains. Markets with protectionist, xenophobic, or culturally chauvinistic tendencies must often be serviced on-site, with suppliers, manufacturing, distribution, and support systems localized through national supply chains. Still others combine elements of both global and national supply chains. Factors promoting each type of supply chain are summarized in Figure 11.2. The special conditions necessitating nationally-based supply chains are discussed fully in Chapter 13.

Corporate Catalysts: Global Supply Chains and Competitive Advantage Sustainable competitive advantages in the worldwide marketplace have become more difficult to sustain as cross-border transfers of products, technologies, and expertise have given more firms access to the latest technologies and management philosophies. Nevertheless, supply chain innovations and efficiency orientations contribute to competitive advantages for firms pursuing cost leadership and differentiation strategies.

Contributions to Cost Leadership Firms in cost-sensitive industries view efficient supply chains as cost-reduction vehicles. Costs can be minimized by:

- Giving producers access to more suppliers as free-trade movements reduce obstacles to offshore sourcing

- Reducing transportation delays as loading/unloading times exceed actual transport times. With antiquated supply chains, products are often stored and handled 2–5 times more than is necessary.

- Coordinating supply chain activities to reduce holding costs for materials, components, and finished goods[3]

- Consolidating manufacturing and distribution operations, enabling production and service costs to be reduced

- Giving firms access to purchasing scale economies as corporate bargaining power increases for components, materials, and services such as transportation

Contributions to Differentiation Advantages Supply chain contributions to differentiation-based competitive advantages occur with:

- Superior service levels as delivery times shorten, order-to-delivery cycles are reduced, responses to marketplace changes are quickened, and stock availability is improved. Unilever executives noted that delivery cycles, once measured in weeks or days, are now down to hours. Upgraded information systems have improved on time-in-full (OTIF) deliveries, and the use of just-in-time (JIT) systems in electronics and automotive industries have drastically cut down customer response times. Whirlpool's concentration of its finished products in distribution centers made stock-outs a comparative rarity.[4]

- New-product development advantages for supply chain participants (suppliers, distributors, customers) contribute ideas for product improvements and innovations. Independent operators have contributed enhancements in computer-chip design (for companies like Intel) and in software for firms such as Microsoft. Further, close coordination with suppliers and customers has reduced product-development times and increased new-product success rates.[5] Trust in suppliers has been identified as a key success factor in superior new-product development records.[6]

- Increasingly, as companies build global brands and reputations, product warranties and service become issues in boosting customer product confidence. Corporate abilities to quickly resolve post-sale problems have become major issues for quality-conscious customers, and tightly integrated supply chains help firms respond quickly to quality problems.

How much does it cost?

Combien est-ce? (French)

Wieviel kostet es? (German)

Quanto costa? (Italian)

Cuanto vale? (Spanish)

Skok'ko eto stoit? (Russian)

INTEGRATION OPTIONS

Supplier-Manufacturer Integration: "Upstream Relationships"

Today's international corporations outsource as much as 50–75 percent of final product costs, and internal acquisition costs can reach as high as 15 percent of total supply totals.[7] A key challenge, then, is cost containment. Most firms use supply chain hierarchies to keep outsourcing costs under control. Nissan, for example, has about 250 first-tier suppliers, who take components from 12,000 second-tier suppliers, who themselves are supplied by 30,000 smaller third-tier suppliers. First-tier suppliers are responsible for cost and quality controls over second- and third-tier suppliers and become the primary coordinators of upstream supply chain operations.

Trends Affecting Supplier–Manufacturer Relationships Integrating suppliers into manufacturer supply chains requires an understanding of corporate supply chain trends. Three major trends are apparent.[8]

1. *The decline of mass production:* Advances in manufacturing process technologies have made short production runs as cost efficient as mass manufacturing. Product-model changeover times have been reduced through computer-integrated manufacturing (CIM), with computer-aided design and manufacturing (CAD-CAM) contributing to this trend. Suppliers must match this flexibility and deliver customized components to manufacturing lines when needed.

2. *Reductions in processing time:* Just-in-time production methods have pushed companies to minimize manufacturing times, with suppliers providing components and materials just in time to be incorporated into final products. Demand-driven JIT systems give manufacturers advantages in customer service and in minimizing inventory and holding costs.

3. *Organizational changes:* Current trends are toward companies focusing on core competencies ("what firms do best") and outsourcing the rest. The advent of E-commerce and Internet-equipped supply chains has enabled firms like Nike to let consumers custom-order athletic shoes under its Nike iD program, with 2–3 week deliveries.[9]

> Remember that time
> is money.
>
> —*Benjamin Franklin,*
> *18th-century U.S. politician*

Global Sourcing Strategies International corporations can source raw materials and components either internally (within the corporate network) or externally (outsourcing).[10] Internationally, companies have three options in sourcing raw materials and components: within the market of manufacture; regionally, from neighboring countries; worldwide, with interregional shipments (e.g., between U.S.–Europe, U.S.–Asia); or combinations of these options. Table 11.1 contrasts conditions favoring each type of sourcing arrangement. Generally, where market needs are complex (e.g., multiple segments, customization needs, or short delivery times), shorter supply chains are optimal (national and/or regional). Similarly, where demand-pull JIT chains are necessary, shorter supply chains are preferred. Where more traditional "build for stock"

TABLE 11.1
Conditions Favoring National, Regional, and Global (Interregional) Sourcing

	National	———	Regional	———	Global
Market Needs					
Customer segments	Many	. . . .			Few
Delivery/Service	Yes	. . . .			No
Critical customization	Yes	. . . .			No
Production Needs					
Product variety	Yes	. . . .			No
Lead time (e.g., JIT or inventory-based)	Short	. . . .			Long
Production runs	Short	. . . .			Long
Logistics Needs					
Coordination	Less	. . . .			More
Transportation costs	Less	. . . .			More
Storage needs (e.g., warehousing)	Less	. . . .			More
Inventory needs	Less	. . . .			More

Based on Schary and Larsen, 26.

operations are the norm, longer supply chains can be used, as components and materials can be standardized and time is a less critical factor. Note though, that JIT systems can operate interregionally. GM-Toyota's pan-Pacific JIT system has functioned successfully since the mid-1980s.[11]

Sourcing Strategy 1 Maintaining home market suppliers is optimal for a number of reasons.[12] For example, where:

- Labor costs are small proportions of total costs. In many industries, direct labor costs are less than 10 percent of total costs. As a result, there are few advantages in going abroad, especially after transportation and other costs are factored in.

- Service and quick-response manufacturing are key competitive advantages. For example, Applied Digital Data Systems, an NCR subsidiary, found it more convenient and cost-effective to assemble its 4,000 different combinations of screen color, keyboard, and power-supply terminals in the U.S.

- Quality levels cannot be maintained in foreign plants. For example, Invalco, a U.S. producer of industrial flow meters and valves, moved its Mexican operation back to Kansas, despite a four-fold increase in wage levels.

- Patriotism and "Made in" advantages: Prominent U.S. retailer Wal-Mart claimed to have created or brought back 131,000 jobs through a renewed emphasis on "Made in USA" products. This patriotic appeal has enhanced Wal-Mart's image among nationalistic consumers in the U.S.

- Economic capital-intensive assembly processes: In the U.S., supercontractors have emerged as cost-effective alternatives, substituting capital and technology for labor-intensive assembly operations. Solectron of California assembles Hewlett Packard printers from components and ships them directly to customers. It also produced Egyptian entrepreneurs Zaki and Shlomo Raquib's super-modem when product development needs meant capital shortages for manufacturing facilities. In these situations, capital-intensive domestic assembly is cost-competitive when offshore labor costs are added to high intercontinental shipping costs.[13]

Sourcing Strategy 2 *Regional sourcing from neighboring countries:* This strategy works where free-trade agreements like NAFTA, EU, and Mercosur facilitate component- and raw-material movements among adjoining markets. Common technical standards are a plus, as are similar demand patterns for finished products. Where low labor-cost countries are parts of regional groupings (e.g., North/South America, Japan's use of Asian locations, Eastern/Western Europe), the combination of low labor rates and transportation costs can yield decisive cost advantages. Dana, a major supplier to the U.S.'s big three automakers, moves 150 containers of components per week from its Venezuelan plants to the U.S. Customs clearances are arranged electronically in fifteen minutes through Dana's forwarder, C. H. Robinson.[14]

Sourcing Strategy 3 *Global sourcing between regions:* Where raw material and component sourcing yields impressive cost economies, and transportation costs and trade barriers are minimal, worldwide sourcing between different regions becomes viable, especially for standardized components. The primary disadvantages are time-based, as low-cost ocean freight is used to minimize transportation costs. General Motors' 12,000-mile pipeline moves about 100,000 containers a year between five continents. One of its two logistics-support companies—Burlington—created three logistics centers in Tilburg (Netherlands), Romulus (Michigan), and Monterrey (Mexico). These centers coordinate the 2,500 global suppliers and 73 million kilos of freight in movements between North America, Europe, Middle East, and Africa. The other provider, AEI, coordinates shipments between North and South America and between North America and GM plants in China, Japan, Korea, Singapore, Indonesia, and other Asian locations. AEI's 500-office worldwide network is a key factor in the coordination of trans-Pacific shipments.[15]

Integrating Suppliers: A Six-Stage Process It takes time and patience to create global sourcing systems. Monczka and Trent discerned four stages of global sourcing.[16]

- *Stage 1:* Companies do all purchasing domestically. International goods, if bought at all, are purchased through foreign affiliates based in the home market.
- *Stage 2:* Foreign sources are tried when domestic sources prove inadequate.
- *Stage 3:* International sourcing becomes an integral part of corporate strategies, and worldwide sources of suppliers are aggressively pursued. Firms at this stage are confident of foreign suppliers' abilities to meet market needs.
- *Stage 4:* Global-sourcing networks are developed. Worldwide purchasing is coordinated across divisions and is represented at the highest organizational levels. Manufacturing materials and process technologies are coordinated across markets, and suppliers are selected on the basis of quality and global supply capabilities. At this stage, supplier expertise contributes to companies' competitive advantage, and cost advantages are sought from developing-country locations.

At the turn of the new millenium, two further stages can be discerned:

- *Stage 5:* Internet-integrated supplier-manufacturer relations: Companies with global sourcing needs use web-based programs to facilitate and consolidate foreign procurement policies. Tricon Global Restaurants (owners of KFC, Taco Bell, and Pizza Hut) centralized worldwide buying to allow its 30,000 units to order supplies through one clearinghouse in order to reduce procurement costs.[17]

- *Stage 6:* Complete supply chain integration: This involves integrating customers, distributors, manufacturers, and suppliers in a single global information-sharing system.

> One hundred organized men can always defeat one thousand disorganized ones.
>
> —*Lenin, 20th-century Russian leader*

Building Trust: The Evolution of Supplier-Customer Relationships Supplier-customer relationships evolve over time. One study suggests a five-phase model.[18]

- *Phase 1—Adversarial supplier-customer relations:* Initially, suppliers and manufacturers are antagonists. Price is the most important element in supplier selection. Arm's length relationships are customary, and suppliers are not involved in customers' manufacturing processes. Both sides get as much as they can out of the relationship.

- *Phase 2—The stress phase:* Competition becomes increasingly intense. Suppliers are subject to price and cost squeezes as buyers become more knowledgeable about component-cost structures. Short-notice deliveries, a forerunner of just-in-time, become more frequent.

- *Phase 3—The "resolved phase":* Supplier manufacturer collaboration begins as just-in-time principles are introduced. Price, quality, and reliability are key supplier-selection criteria, though little information is exchanged.

- *Phase 4—The partnership phase:* Suppliers and manufacturers exchange information and become involved in each other's supply chains. Components are delivered just-in-time, and suppliers are involved in manufacturers' new-product development processes.

- *Phase 5—Lean supply phase:* Supplier-manufacturer partnerships deepen, and suppliers are encouraged to become market leaders in their areas. They are expected to follow manufacturers abroad and establish production units close by. At this level of collaboration, six-sigma quality levels (where defects are measured in parts per million) are standard entry requirements.

> You don't get the breaks unless you play with the team instead of against it.
>
> —*Lou Gehrig, U.S. baseball player*

Integrating Subsidiary Suppliers into Global Manufacturing Networks Foreign subsidiaries represent major outlays in capital and executive manpower.[19] Therefore, international corporations go to great lengths to get the most out of their subsidiaries in order to enhance their contributions to worldwide manufacturing operations. Some of the ways that companies encourage this are:

- *Developing expertise in product improvements or new-product development:* Hewlett Packard's Guadalajara plant in Mexico not only assembles computers but also helps in the design of computer memory boards.

- *Acting as listening posts* in areas with known manufacturing expertise (e.g., watch-making around Jura on the French-Swiss border or textile machinery in northern Italy)

- *Upgrading of subsidiary marketing expertise* to encourage low-cost subsidiaries to service local demand as domestic markets develop

- *Using head office expertise to improve existing operations:* Hewlett Packard's Singapore plant redesigned the product it manufactured and reduced production costs by 50 percent.

- *Self-improvement programs* in JIT and TQM, together with close relationships with suppliers and customers, transformed NCR's Scottish factory from an average producer of ATM machines to a global innovator in that product category.

- *Developing superior sources of supply:* Sony's factory in Bridgend, Wales, was an assembler for Japanese suppliers. But over time it developed its own expertise, cut costs, and secured its own dependable base of European suppliers.

International Manufacturing Systems and Supply Chain Management

International companies use a variety of manufacturing systems to serve world markets, and, as supply chains become increasingly integrated across national boundaries, manufacturing operations have been customized to suit market conditions. As Table 11.2 shows, these systems vary from independent production plants to regional, multi-market, or global operations.

Evolution of International Manufacturing Systems Prior to global trade liberalization, international manufacturing systems tended to be *country-based* (i.e., production was in-market and built to serve national preferences) or *home-market-based* (with exports as the major market servicing mechanism).[20] As trade barriers diminished and/or market blocs rose to prominence, multidomestic and regionally uncoordinated manufacturing systems have given way to *regional specialization,* allowing individual factories to produce single-product lines for entire regions. Nestle uses this type of structure in servicing European markets from dedicated factories, and auto firms often concentrate single or related models at the same manufacturing site. *Regionally-integrated* production facilities specialize by component type, and system-wide shipments are coordinated for assembly and distribution from central processing centers. Hewlett-Packard's European PC operation consolidates subassemblies, such as keyboards and literatures, at its Luxembourg facility before transporting them to Germany, the Netherlands, or France for final assem-

TABLE 11.2
International Manufacturing System Configurations

Manufacturing System	Market Influences on Manufacturing Configuration	Product Line	Market Coverage	Supply Chain Emphasis
Multidomestic	Considerable variability in customer needs, fragmented industry, protected markets, variations in market standards	Broad and customized to individual market needs	Single market	Local supply chain
Regional Uncoordinated	Regional similarities in demand, still tariff/non-tariff barriers	Broad	Single or few markets	Local or regional
Regional Specialization	Few/no tariff/non-tariff barriers, factory specialization by product line and shipments to all regional markets	Narrow product line	Regional	Regional
Regional Integrated	Few/no tariff/non-tariff barriers, factory specialization by components, shipments regionally for assembly or distribution	Component specialization	Regional	Regional
Globally Coordinated Manufacturing Configuration	Standardized product mixes and manufacturing technologies, many small, local units (e.g., franchising)	Mainly standardized inputs	Local	Local
Global Specialization	Product specialization by subsidiaries ("dedicated factories"), shipments worldwide	Narrow, product-line specialization	Global	Global/regional
Global Integrated	Component specialization by subsidiaries, considerable intermarket shipments and final assembly close to customers	Narrow component specialization	Global	Global/regional
Global Exporter	Centralized manufacturing and export, steep experience curve and/or major scale economies involved (steel, shipbuilding, aircraft)	Broad	Global	Global/regional and local

Source: Adapted heavily from Shi, Y., and M. Gregory. "International Manufacturing Networks to develop global competitive capabilities." *Journal of Operations Management* 16 (1998): 195–214.

bly. Similarly, Euro-Bell assembles over one-million bicycle helmets per year from global and European sources for distribution within the EU.[21]

Similar organizational formats are used for *global manufacturing networks*. At one end of the spectrum, *globally coordinated* manufacturing configurations use the same small-scale production methods in all markets (franchises, fast food, hotels). This is a decentralized approach to manufacturing, with standardized processes and local supply chains. At the other end of the spectrum, the *global exporter* centralizes manufacturing as far as possible in one location to take advantage of concentrated technical expertise and gain scale economies. Shipbuilding and aircraft manufacturers are industries favoring this system.

Between these extremes are *globally integrated* production networks that take advantages of national and regional differences in production costs to manufacture at the most cost-effective sites. Japanese companies have configured many of their global manufacturing operations so that labor-intensive components are produced in developing markets, technology-intensive parts are manufactured in developed countries with skilled workforces, and high-tech component production occurs in Japan. All components are transshipped to end markets for assembly and sale.[22]

Global specialization occurs in multi-division firms where manufacturing for specific product lines is centralized and distribution is globalized from individual production sites. This is similar to the global-exporter organization, except that product lines are specialized rather than producing companies' entire product ranges. Scale economies are critical where competition is price-based. Chemical companies use this manufacturing format for specialty products. Manufacturing may also be concentrated where products or production processes are patented in order to safeguard intellectual property rights (specialty electronics, pharmaceuticals).

Transferring Manufacturing Capabilities Across Markets Once manufacturing networks are in place, international executives can focus on transferring production expertise abroad to ensure that worldwide quality standards are maintained. This involves transferring manufacturing processes to overseas plants and, as importantly, inculcating the proper mindsets into employees. *The Toyota Production System (TPS)* is acknowledged as one of the best worldwide. It comprises a set of values and processes that are virtually identical in all its markets worldwide.[23] The process has three fundamental principles:

1. Waste elimination is a top priority to ensure nonduplication of supply chain activities, starting with customer orders and ending with customer delivery and after-sales service.

2. The second principle—workflow maximization—levels off production peaks and valleys and ensures quick changeovers among models in order to minimize downtime.

3. The third principle is respect for people, with all employees becoming involved in the production process in order to maximize the quality of the end product.[24] This principle emphasizes the recruitment of appropriate workers: Toyota spends about $3000 on prospective employees as they move from employment applications through to actually landing jobs The company also invests in employee skills and in promoting teamwork.[25]

Cummins is a worldwide producer of diesel engines, automation products, and industrial power equipment with over forty plants in world markets. Despite this diversity of products, its global manufacturing practices in all businesses are based on ten basic practices.[26] The first two practices emphasize the *pull system* through which customer demand drives the manufacturing process:

1. Put the customer first.
2. Synchronize work flows.

Eight additional practices use group dynamics and customer orientations to maintain and improve quality levels.

3. Build quality in.
4. Involve people through teams.
5. Ensure that equipment is maintained and available when needed.

6. Create functional excellence in managing work stations.

7. Provide the right environment, such as efficient factory layouts to optimize workflows.

8. Treat suppliers as partners, and maintain positive relationships with stakeholders, such as colleges, to attract potential employees.

9. Follow sequential steps for all problem-solving activities, involving all interested parties for integrated solutions.

10. Emphasize continuous improvements in production processes. Cummins factory managers worldwide critique and grade each other's processes. The results have been major decreases in defects, scrap, lead times, and delivery times. Overall, productivity rose by over one-third.

Global Diffusion of Management Philosophies and Processes

Global and multi-market supply chains are only as good as the management philosophies, methods, and processes underlying them. While North American and Western European firms can initiate appropriate management philosophies and processes within home markets, their supply chains often stretch over many markets. Hence, the diffusion of philosophies and practices, such as just-in-time (JIT) and total quality management (TQM), worldwide is of paramount interest if supply chains are to be run efficiently on a global scale. For example, both JIT and TQM require considerable discipline throughout the supply chain. Supplier and manufacturing activities must synchronize with market demand, and weak links in quality orientations undermine global reputations for quality output. Therefore, international corporations place considerable emphases on diffusing JIT and TQM philosophies throughout their manufacturing and supply chains. For these types of processes, employee involvement and empowerment are important, and companies must equip employees with the skills and confidence to involve them in the customer-satisfaction process. When firms are successful in their employee-involvement activities, market orientations and business performance are improved.[27] There are three critical processes where managerial adjustments are often necessary: JIT, TQM, and, where major changes are necessary, reengineering processes.

> The magic formula that successful businesses have discovered is to treat customers like guests and employees like people.
>
> —*Thomas J. Peters,*
> *U.S. consultant and author*

Just-in-Time Just-in-time is defined as the successful completion of a product or service at each stage of the production process, from suppliers to customers, just in time for its use at minimum cost. JIT, which originated in Japan in the 1950s at Toyota, eliminates waste and maximizes the capabilities of suppliers, manufacturers, and distributors to eliminate imbalances between customer demand and production.[28] The ability to implement JIT processes varies across nations. One study showed that East Asian producers were strong in managing JIT methods, fully utilizing their strong supplier-manufacturer links. Constant supplier improvements and on-time deliveries were the norm. However, JIT implementation lagged among Nordic producers in Denmark, Sweden, and Finland. Firms in Taiwan, Korea, and Japan had more technology exchanges with supply chain partners, used more statistical controls in production, spent three times the money on worker education and training, and used more elaborate research techniques in evaluating customer demand.[29]

The power of the waterfall is nothing but a lot of drips working together.

—*Asian proverb*

Total Quality Management This is closely linked with JIT for smooth supply chain operations. For TQM to work effectively within firms, training, empowerment, and teamwork are essential. Japanese and Asian companies have consistently had the edge over Western firms in TQM, as lifetime-employment philosophies have allowed them to invest in worker training and build up teamwork. Asian job rotation methods of corporate training have also given employees broad appreciations of their production processes.

In some nations, however, employee empowerment can be a problem. Countries with histories of social-class distinctions (e.g., Latin America and parts of Asia) or those with authoritarian orientations have problems delegating initiatives to employees. Similarly, the TQM focus on customer satisfaction has been difficult to implement in undersupply economies where customer needs have less priority and in nations with histories of central planning.[30] Exhibit 11-1 shows major catalysts and obstacles associated with TQM implementation. Moves from autocratic to participative management styles are prerequisites for successful TQM implementation. Management-style change has been easier where educated work forces are available and where company training programs and frequent communications between managers and line workers are the norm.

Reengineering Reengineering of corporate structures and processes requires similar adjustments as those required to execute JIT and TQM programs. The experience of Eskom, the world's fourth-largest utility in South Africa was typical. The company had to reengineer its organizational chart to meet the needs of the expanding market for electricity. Eskom reorganized its businesses into three units (generation, transmission, and distribution) and then subdivided these into geographic units. Cross-functional management teams were then formed to formulate and implement strategies. This reorganization encountered significant problems, including the following:

- There was resistance to change at the lower levels of the organization where inadequate educational systems, ethnic diversity (among different tribal groups), and historic distrust between black and white groups created many problems, especially with trade unions.

- The transformation to team-driven organizations created uncertainties among employees and customers. Previously, the organization had been hierarchical and goal setting had been top-down. Under the new system, goal setting was decentralized to the group level, resulting in confusion about goal-setting procedures and workload distribution.

- The new work teams had problems working with central corporate managers to evaluate capital expenditures, demand forecasts, and environmental impacts on traditional communities.

- There were ongoing concerns about leadership roles in team-driven organizations. While senior managers talked about blending customer satisfaction goals (the business imperative) with employee self-actualization goals (the people imperative), the transition from hierarchical to participative organizations left a power vacuum as teams struggled to define objectives and roles.[31]

EXHIBIT 11-1
Implementing TQM: Key Success Factors

Key Success Factor	Cultural Catalysts and Obstacles
TQM starts at the top	Needs progressive senior managers who practice what they preach, and who reinforce quality principles throughout the organization. Autocratic or elitest management systems are usually too detached to do this effectively.
TQM focus on the customer	Needs constant communication flows from the marketplace, and no communication blocks within organizations.
TQM team organization	All employees need to be empowered to contribute. "No blame" corporate cultures are catalysts. Hierarchical corporate cultures are an obstacle.
TQM requires continuous training	Training programs for TQM are necessary at all organizational levels and for suppliers and distributors. Power-based relationships within the supply chain (management-workers, suppliers-manufacturers) are counterproductive.
TQM control	"What gets measured gets done." Realistic yardsticks and goals that relate to on-the-job activities are a "must"; scrap rates, defect rates, etc. must be communicated along with appropriate solutions.
TQM and continuous improvements	Constant pushes for improvement require employees to accept change as normal.

Sources: Guranu, Haresh. "Pitfalls in total quality implementation: the case of a Hong Kong company." *Total Quality Management* 10: 2 (March 1999): 209–28. Nasierowski, Wojciech, and Daniel F. Coleman. "Lessons from unsuccessful transfers of managerial techniques: Cultural impediments to the transfer of TQM practices." *International Journal of Management* 14: 1 (March 1997): 29–39.

Reengineering corporate processes is a significant challenge, particularly in developing-country circumstances. Ethnic fragmentation, traditional authority structures, and educational disparities are major challenges as corporations revamp organizational processes to meet marketplace needs.

Manufacturer-Distribution Linkages

Global and regional supply chains require global distribution as national distribution and retail chains are consolidated into multi-market networks. Within the last decade, there have been major changes in distributive networks, most notably affecting physical facilities (wholesalers, distributors, retailers, etc.) and transportation networks.

Changing Distributive Frameworks Six major changes have been apparent in the downstream distribution of goods and services.

1. *Increasing concentrations of retail ownership:* Within major regional markets, increasing competition and industry consolidations have led to increasing retailer power. In the U.S., big discounters, such as Wal-Mart, Big K-mart, Home Depot, and Toys R Us, have put increasing pressures on suppliers to conform to domestic and international needs. Within Europe, the supermarket and hypermarket concepts have become globally mobile. European retail chains, such as Rewe Zentrale, Makro, Aldi, Carrefour, Tesco, Sainsbury's, and Tenglemann, all wield considerable market power over suppliers. Manufacturers have countered this surge in retail power by making significant expenditures to create regional and global brands, by expanding into new markets, and by direct marketing to consumers. Generally, though, retailers and manufacturers have realized that cooperation between them (rather than competition) pays dividends.[32]

2. *Disappearing middlemen:* As trade barriers have declined and transportation systems have become efficient, wholesaling and middleman have diminished in importance. Within trade blocs like the EU, national distributors have become less necessary, and within individual markets, regional and local middlemen have disappeared. Advances in information technologies and data sharing have enabled large manufacturers to deal with stores directly, and, especially in Western Europe, independent retailers have banded together into buying groups to obtain superior discounts through volume purchases.[33]

3. *Changing consumer purchasing patterns:* As countries modernize and ownership of autos and refrigerators has risen, one-stop shopping has become prominent. While this has impacted supermarket shopping the most, consumers now have wider varieties of retail alternatives. Specialty discount stores in auto accessories, office equipment, computer services, furniture, etc. have emerged. Discount stores carry similar product mixes as specialty retailers but at lower prices.

4. *Information technologies:* Suppliers and distributors have become more aware of market trends through point-of-sale systems, product bar-coding, and electronic data interchanges (EDIs). This has contributed to shorter product life cycles and reduced holding costs within company supply chains.

5. *International retailing:* While there were early pioneers in the international retailing field (e.g., F. W. Woolworth), retailer global expansion strategies first took off in the late 1960s and early 1970s with the franchise rush into foreign markets. McDonalds and Kentucky Fried Chicken were among the first franchises to capitalize on the globalization of fast-food tastes. The 1980s and 1990s saw retailer globalization efforts expand as different retail formats (discount, department, hypermarket, mail order, Internet,

> Life is an instinct for growth, for survival, for the accumulation of forces, for power.
>
> —*Friedrich Nietzsche, 19th-century German philosopher*

> The world is a book, and he who stays at home reads only one page.
>
> *M. K. Frelinghuysen*

etc.) have become successful internationally. IKEA, Benetton, Boots, Laura Ashley, Carrefour, Printemps, Migros, Makro, and Marks and Spencer are among the many European retailers that have benefited from international expansion. Japanese retailers, such as Jusco/AEON (discount, drugs, mail order, supermarket), Takashimaya (department and specialty stores), Seiyu (supermarket), and Mitsukoshi (department stores), have also branched out, particularly in Asia, in order to take advantage of operating efficiencies and global commonalities in demand.[34] Current projections suggest that by 2009 the top 25 global retailers will control 40 percent of the worldwide retail market and the top 200 units 50 percent of the global market.[35]

6. *Emergence of global and pan regional carriers:* Privatization and deregulation trends have heightened competition and hastened consolidation in the trucking, airline, rail, and other transportation-based sectors. In Europe, this has resulted in the emergence of three types of transport organizations. First, national transport companies have formed alliances to offer pan-European services. The Swedish transport and forwarding company ASG joined with the Swiss firm Danzas to form a $6 billion logistics service giant with 800 offices in 40 countries.[36]

   Second, megacarrier groups have been formed to reap not only the scale economies associated with transportation, but to provide complete logistics services with terminals, warehouse operations, and integrated information and communications systems.[37] Third, some transportation operators have become niche carriers specializing in particular regions (e.g., Eastern Europe), specific industries (e.g., frozen foods, computers), or specialized services (express deliveries).

Manufacturer-Distributor Organizational Options Downstream product movements depend on industry and customer servicing needs. There are four major storage and retrieval systems: (1) classical, (2) transit, (3) direct, and (4) multi-country warehouse (see Figure 11.3).

1. *The classical system* entails bulk shipments going directly to subsidiary warehouses, where they are stored until sold. This results in low transportation costs because of the use of ocean freight and the consolidation of cargoes. Bulk shipments also lessen documentation requirements. Buffer stocks are kept to minimize stock-out probabilities. The classical system is costly to maintain, but it works for companies with broad product assortments where customer demand is stable and where customers want merchandise "from stock" immediately.

2. *The transit system* is used for small high-value shipments (computer, medical, and scientific equipment) between manufacturing locations and warehouses, which serve only as distribution centers. Storage costs are low because only safety stocks are kept, but transportation costs are often high because speedy forms of transport are used (such as air freight). Administration and documentation costs are also high because of small shipment sizes.

3. *The direct system* moves merchandise either directly from the production site to the customer or directly into a subsidiary's

> Businesses planned for service are apt to succeed; businesses planned for profit are apt to fail.
>
> —*Nicholas M. Butler,*
> *U.S. educator*
> *and Nobel Laureate*

FIGURE 11.3
Multinational Warehousing Systems

Classical Model's Physical Flow of Merchandise

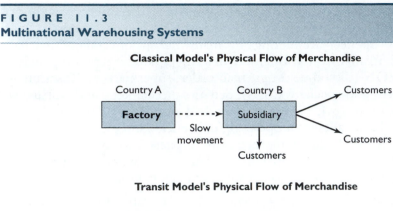

Transit Model's Physical Flow of Merchandise

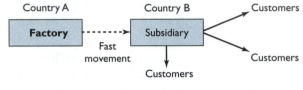

Direct System

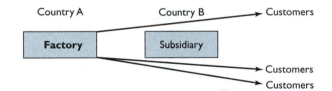

Multi-Country Warehouse

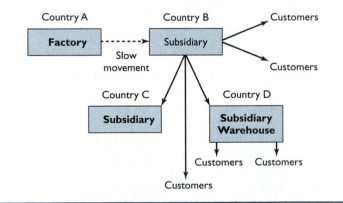

Source: Picard, Jacques, "Typology of Physical Distribution Systems in Multinational Corporations." *International Journal of Physical distribution and Materials Management* 12: 6 (1982): 30–33. Reproduced with permission.

distribution channel. Storage is centralized in the home market and minimizes subsidiary handling, storage, and shipping expenses. Direct systems work best with high-value goods (such as computers and electronic equipment) where customer demand is erratic or fragmented and where the products are custom made. Its disadvantages include high transportation costs (small, frequent shipments and no freight-consolidation economies). Quality control, labeling, and packaging must be performed at the central manufacturing site, often making multilingual labeling necessary. Finally, customers (or their authorized representatives) must personally clear the goods through customs and pay duties.

4. *The multi-country warehouse system* is used by companies with dedicated manufacturing sites where products or components need consolidating before final shipments to customers. Fixed costs are lower than they are for national warehousing systems, but there are higher variable costs due to transportation to and from warehouses. Multi-country warehouse systems are appropriate when products have low turnover rates, where there are numerous small-country markets in close proximity (for example, in continental Europe and Central America), and where there is much intracompany shipping of products and components.

Distributor-Customer Linkages

Electronic Data Interchange and Internet Systems Global and multi-country supply systems function best when they are closely aligned to customer demand (as in JIT and build-to-order systems). This entails reading demand signals, customizing output to meet current market needs, and streamlining distribution systems to lessen transit times and reduce (or eliminate) inventories. In the 1990s, electronic data interchange (EDI) emerged to fill this need.

EDI is the exchange of business information electronically between business partners, intermediaries, public authorities, and others in a structured format.[38] Corporate-based EDI systems relay point-of-sales data back to head offices (often via sales offices). Head offices scrutinize the information, analyze sales trends, and arrange for manufacture and shipping. Companies using cross-border EDI systems must often reconcile national differences in bar-coding systems. Within Europe, the U.K. food system used the tradacoms system, while continental Europe used the UN-based EANcom system. To reconcile these types of differences, there are movements toward global EDI bar-coding systems with the United Nations-based EDIFACT format.[39]

Internet systems are slowly replacing EDI as manufacturers seek to integrate downstream operations between production sites and distribution points. Ericsson, the Swedish telecommunications producer, uses Internet-based software to track deliveries from its 100+ factories worldwide to customers in over 130 markets.[40] Corporate Intranet systems keep head offices abreast of current sales and demand trends.

> In every instance, we found that the best-run companies stay as close to their customers as humanly possible.
>
> —*Thomas J. Peters,*
> *U.S. consultant and writer*

INTEGRATION MECHANISMS FOR GLOBAL SUPPLY CHAINS

For global and multi-market supply chains to function effectively, firms must have appropriate information technologies, executives capable of working in cross-cultural situations, and human-resource policies that can operate across markets. Additionally, corporate new-product development processes must be geared to the realities of the global marketplace.

Supply Chain Integration and Information Technologies

Internet capabilities have made data on supply chain activities and product movements available to all supply chain members, resulting in tighter integration among customers, distributors, manufacturers, and suppliers. Tightly integrated supply chains are particularly potent weapons when speed of manufacture and customization are viable competitive advantages. Dell Computer runs its European PC operations along these lines. Customer orders from company web sites or European call centers are accessed through the corporate Extranet (which allows selected outsiders to view corporate information). Suppliers then organize their component deliveries to coincide with Dell's JIT manufacturing schedule. Customers can also access and track their orders through to delivery.[41] Each of Dell's five geographic regions (U.S., Europe/Middle East/Africa, Latin America, Asia-Pacific, and Japan) has its own web site, customized for language and currencies. Between 35–50 percent of orders are placed online.[42] Speedy, customized output and well-orchestrated supply chains are gradually impacting increasing numbers of industries, such as jeans, autos, bicycles, and other sectors.

Obstacles to Internet-based Supply Chain Extensions In extending Internet-based systems to worldwide markets, firms face a number of impediments at the national-market and at the individual-consumer levels. *National-market obstacles* include:

- Infrastructure impediments, such as telephone line availability (in developing markets especially) and telecommunications costs. In Europe, telephone-line costs are five times those in North America, and web-surfing costs are twice those in the U.S.[43] National infrastructures are also obstacles when road, rail, and airline inefficiencies affect corporate efforts to upgrade product-delivery and service capabilities.

- Regulatory obstacles include commercial laws that affect advertising (for example, in Europe where Denmark bans advertising to children, France prohibits advertising in English, and Germany bans comparative advertising), privacy issues that involve the transfer of consumer data across borders, increased concerns about illegal transactions (offshore gambling sites, pornography rings, and cross-border movements of nonapproved drugs), and governmental distrust of outsider influences (e.g., Malaysia and China).[44]

- Economic issues as governments wrestle with taxation policies concerning Internet sales

- Currency convertibility as consumers attempt cross-border transactions from countries with soft (i.e., inconvertible or unacceptable) currencies

- Communications obstacles as multilingual nations strive to extend Internet services into culturally diverse areas

Consumer-based obstacles include:

- Ownership of personal computers and other Internet-access media (e.g., telephones)

- Credit-card ownership and consumer preferences for making cash payments

- Consumer buying patterns: Many consumers are reluctant to make purchases "sight unseen." Innovative strategies can overcome some consumer obstacles. GMAI-Asia installed 220 cell-phone retail outlets in China to enable consumers to place orders, and to return in a few days to inspect the purchase, pay for it, and take it home.[45]

Creating Multicultural Managers

As companies expand internationally, the need for management coordination of corporate activities increases. Creating multicultural executives becomes a corporate priority, and managing expatriate experiences properly becomes essential. As Black and Gregersen noted: "In today's global economy, having a work force that is fluent in the ways of the world isn't a luxury. It's a competitive necessity." They further note that 80 percent of mid-sized and large firms send managers abroad, and that 45 percent see expatriates as lynchpins for strategy implementation. As the annual cost of sending expatriates abroad runs into hundreds of thousands of dollars, it has become increasingly important for companies to manage foreign assignments as human resource investments.[46] The problem is particularly acute for U.S. firms whose 25–40 percent failure rate for expatriate assignments is much higher than the rates for European and Japanese companies. Failures are costly, not only with the direct costs of maintaining expatriate managers abroad, but indirectly as ill-equipped managers miss business opportunities and adversely affect customer, supplier, and government relations.[47]

International companies send managers overseas for three reasons. First, foreign assignments are essential preparation for leadership positions. Second, moving managers across markets allows the buildup of corporate networks that are so essential for integrating activities across markets. Third, expatriates are bridge builders in supply chain expansions, opening up new markets, transferring skills, facilitating mergers and acquisitions, and setting up new processes, technologies, or systems.[48]

> The whole object of travel is not to set foot on foreign land; it is at last to set foot on one's own country as a foreign land.
>
> —G. K. Chesterton,
> 19th–20th-century English
> journalist and author

Managing the Expatriate Assignment Successful companies manage overseas assignments in comprehensive fashions, focusing on selection, pre-preparation, enhancement of the expatriate experience, and the repatriation process. This process, well-managed, reduces the chances of executive turnover during and after assignments.

Executive selection: Identifying suitable candidates can be done formally through interviews, aptitude tests, etc., or through informal executive and peer assessments. Evaluations of spouses and families should also be made. Desirable qualities of expatriate managers include:

- Cultural empathy: A knowledge and appreciation of cultural differences, and broad tolerance levels to cope with and adapt to foreign behaviors are necessary. Foreign-language capabilities are part of this skill package.

- Interpersonal skills that enable individuals to recognize verbal and nonverbal communication cues ("personal sensitivity"), and a capacity to build trust with foreign nationals (trustworthiness, honesty, sincerity, integrity)

> Travel makes a wise man better and a fool worse.
>
> —Thomas Fuller,
> 17th-century English
> clergyman

- Ability to operate independently away from the home office
- Sensitivity to global events and the ability to assess those things that will impact corporate business
- Excellent competencies within their area of managerial expertise (marketing, R and D, production, etc.)[49]

> A danger half foreseen is half avoided.
>
> —*Thomas Fuller,*
> *17th-century English*
> *clergyman*

Pre-preparation for overseas assignments should include pre-assignment visits, language training, realistic job previews (with managers who have been on similar assignments), and cultural training for managers and families.[50] Shell International, which manages 5500 expatriates, noted that the greatest problems were associated with spouse careers, children's education, healthcare concerns, and creating realistic expectations about relocation moves.[51]

Enhancing the foreign experience: Foreign experiences are enhanced when companies "go the extra mile" to ensure that the foreign stay is enjoyable. Activities include:

- Finding mentors who have had experiences in the country and matching them with assignees
- Using technology such as e-mail and company newsletters to keep expatriates in touch with parent organizations
- Encouraging and helping spouses find work in foreign countries in order to keep them active and contribute to their sense of achievement while abroad
- Developing in-country relationships with other expatriate families in the foreign market
- Ensuring that "settling in" allowances are adequate with built-in safeguards against adverse currency fluctuations
- Providing career counseling so that expatriates fully understand how the foreign experience contributes to their career progressions

Coming home—the repatriation process: Companies with successful expatriate policies always ensure that the transition back to the home country is smooth. Monsanto's policies are typical. The company initiates the repatriation process some 3–6 months prior to coming home by assessing the experience and reviewing future openings within the company. This includes the expatriates' reports on how well the foreign experience went and how they feel their careers should progress from there. Finally, at a full debriefing session, all parties decide the best fit between the organization's needs and the individual's needs for future job prospects.[52] In general, the repatriation process is perceived to be a weak link in U.S. expatriate management policies.

Integrating Supply Chain and Human Resource Policies

As companies integrate their supply chains across markets, many firms review the human resource policies that overlay the process. Cross-border consistencies are sought in a number of areas, including:

1. *Recruitment and selection criteria:* Many firms prefer some consistencies among new hires. Sheer talent is a common criteria for many companies—

the "best and brightest minds regardless of academic background"; for technical firms, backgrounds in engineering or science are required. Where non-business graduates are employed, additional training in business and in human-resource and supply chain policies may be necessary.

2. *Reward systems:* Oracle Corp., the world's #2 software company, standardized its reward systems, first on a Europe-wide basis and then on a global basis, using revenues, margins, and employee- and customer-satisfaction scores. For European companies, EU integration and increasing labor mobility across Europe are prompting standardization moves, though national differences in payroll and social costs make total standardization difficult to achieve regionwide.[53]

3. *Global perspectives on HR policies:* Supply chain globalization works best when it is supported by consistent human-resource policies, yet relatively few HR managers get overseas assignments because their skills are often assumed to be market specific. Increasingly, though, firms are developing human-resource executives capable of functioning in overseas capacities. The methods firms use include:

   - Assigning HR practitioners to worldwide operating divisions and to global management teams to work with line managers

   - Placing HR managers and specialists to regional and country operating divisions abroad

   - Taking young line managers and giving them HR responsibilities in foreign markets

   - Rotating experienced line managers through foreign-based HR positions to broaden their experience bases before reaching senior line positions.[54]

4. *Labor-management relations:* Labor-force involvement in supply chains has become increasingly common. In the EU, labor-management consultation mechanisms (works councils) have been mandated for firms with over 1,000 employees and at least 150 in two or more member states.[55] Volkswagen's Latin American operation instituted a program to consolidate labor contracts among its 32,000 employees within the Mercosur trading area.[56] Clearly, as companies shift from national to multi-country supply chains, the stronger are the incentives to harmonize human-resource policies across markets.

> Most managements complain about the lack of able people and go outside to fill positions. Nonsense . . . I use the rule of 50 percent. Try to find someone inside the company with a record of success (in any area) and with an appetite for the job. If he looks like 50 percent of what you need, give him the job. In six months he'll have grown the other 50 percent and everyone will be satisfied.
>
> —*Robert Townsend, former president, Avis Rent-a-Car*

Global and Multi-Market New-Product Development Strategies

Increasing global competition and shortening product life cycles have placed increasing emphases on corporate new-product development processes to get new offerings into the marketplace as soon as possible. Where supply chains are integrated across countries, the process becomes complex. To launch products and services over multiple markets requires tapping creative energies worldwide. Thus, the development of new-product ideas requires significant amounts of cross-border coordination.

Generating New-Product Ideas on a Global Basis Encouraging worldwide participation in generating new product ideas can be done in several ways.

- The 3M Corporation actively encourages employees to generate new product ideas and develop them. About 30 percent of its global sales are from products less than four years old, and the company introduces about 500 new products per year. The company invests about 7 percent of its $15 billion of sales in R and D, with individual staff being allowed to allocate 15 percent of their work time on new-product ideas.[57]

- ASDA, the European supermarket chain, has its "Tell Archie" (Archie Norman, the ASDA CEO), system whereby employees are invited to submit new product ideas to top management. The system generates about 1000 suggestions per month.[58]

- Increasing numbers of firms (e.g., S. C. Johnson, Polaroid) use observational techniques to observe users in national markets. Through this method, companies gain critical insights regarding how customers actually use products. These insights are then used to modify existing products and or create totally new offerings. Whirlpool redesigned its appliance controls after observing users in multiple markets, and S. C. Johnson used an eleven-country study to revamp its floor-scrubbing and professional cleaning-product range to make them more user-friendly.[59]

- Many firms rely on their R and D departments to generate new ideas. Taking advantage of global trends toward health foods, Kellogg's, Zeneca, and Dupont have been working on "functional foods" that offer health benefits to consumers. Examples include tomatoes enhanced with the anticancer nutrient lycopene, eggs enriched with heart-healthy omega-3 fatty acids, and margarines with cholesterol-reducing ingredients.[60]

- Traditional market-research methods and intensive testing help firms diagnose market needs. Gillette's Sensor razor was almost two decades in development and underwent over 15,000 shave tests before its release.[61]

- Canvassing suppliers, distributors, and customers for ideas and improvements is particularly useful in technical fields such as consumer electronics and in durables such as washers, microwaves, and industrial products.

Implementing New-Product Development Programs While generating new-product ideas is important, commercializing them in a timely fashion is critical in today's competitive marketplace. Most often the obstacles to speedy, efficient new-product development processes are internal. Key success factors include:

- *Cross-functional new-product development teams:* Soliciting inputs from all supply chain participants—both internal and external—is important for coordination, as account must be taken of marketing, production, internal financial perspectives, and external suppliers, distributors and customers. Working together, supply chain stakeholders, including suppliers, distributors, and managers in key world markets, provide important input at all

> Nothing in the world is as powerful as an idea whose time has come.
>
> —*Victor Hugo, 19th-century French poet and novelist*

new-product development stages so that tradeoffs between customer expectations, manufacturing needs, and corporate resources are managed.

- *Maintaining the same product-design team* throughout the product life cycle provides continuity as products move through the various design phases and as they are modified for movement through world markets. Fujitsu's contract work with telecoms giant Nippon Telephone and Telegraph involved continuous new-product designs and modifications as equipment improvements were released into the Japanese, North American, and Western European telecoms markets.[62]

- *Early involvement of manufacturing* is essential, as about 70 percent of product costs are built in at early stages of the development process. "Design for manufacturing" helps engineering and production personnel anticipate problems. Product prototypes and initial manufacturing configurations can be worked out. Companies such as Hewlett Packard, Ingersoll Rand, and Seiko Epson use computer-aided design (CAD) and computer-aided manufacturing (CAM) to simultaneously develop products and their associated manufacturing systems.[63]

- *Use of common components:* New-product development time can be significantly reduced if designers do not insist on custom building components from scratch. Common product platforms and components facilitate development at Whirlpool appliances, and, in the auto industry, Honda, General Motors, and other firms use the same platforms and parts for multiple products.

- *Product design and recycling:* As more governments become conservation-oriented, (e.g., Germany, Netherlands), new-product developers are building reusable and recyclable components into product design, particularly in the computer and auto industries. Software packages are available to simulate disassembly of products at end-of-life and to identify costs and environmental impacts of products with specific design features. These "Design for Environment" softwares calculate financial returns from disassembly, disposal, reuse, and recycling alternatives.[64]

- *Appropriate organizational structures* facilitate commercialization and diffusion of new products through world markets. Product structures and strategic business units focus on rolling out the same or similar products throughout world markets, and with homogenizing customer tastes and borderless trade, more companies are moving to this type of structure. P & G's Organization 2005 transformed the old geographic structure into seven global business units (e.g., baby care, beauty care, and fabric and home care) capable of rapidly diffusing new products throughout world markets. The firm's new Pantene shampoo extension was introduced into fourteen countries in six months, about a quarter of the time necessary under the old structure. The internationalization of retailers such as Carrefour and Wal-Mart has also aided manufacturers' globalization efforts.[65]

> The achievements of an organization are the result of the combined efforts of each individual.
>
> —*Vince Lombardi, U.S. football coach*

> You can't evade the responsibility of tomorrow by evading it today.
>
> —*Abraham Lincoln, 19th-century U.S. president*

DEINTEGRATING THE GLOBAL SUPPLY CHAIN: OUTSOURCING STRATEGIES

Few companies are totally self-sufficient in their supply chain operations from raw materials through to customer sales. Indeed, current trends have been toward deintegration of supply chain activities, with firms focusing on core competencies that yield competitive advantages and outsourcing the rest, either domestically or internationally.

Strategic Advantages of Outsourcing

Firms can outsource any part of the supply chain: raw materials, components, manufacturing, logistics, distribution, information technologies, new-product development, or management functions. Most often, companies outsource to improve internal efficiencies, eliminate weaknesses, or capitalize on strengths. Outsourcing allows firms to:

- Focus on core competencies. Outsourcing nonessential or underperforming functions allows firms to zero in on what they do best—those processes, products, and components that add value to products or services and contribute to sustainable competitive advantages.

- Access world-class capabilities of other companies. In rapidly changing industries, most firms do not have the expertise or resources to be preeminent in all supply chain activities. Outsourcing allows them to tap outside expertise and use it to build superior products and services.

- Free up capital and resources and use them either to bolster other supply chain functions (e.g., new-product development in the pharmaceutical industry) or to strengthen the company's marketplace position (e.g., taking over a rival firm or diversifying into new products or markets).

- Reduce operating costs as dedicated suppliers become more efficient in supplying quality materials, components, products, or services at superior prices.

- Share or reduce marketplace risks. Outsourcing gives firms flexibility in moving between suppliers and reduces the risks of being caught with outdated manufacturing technologies in rapidly changing markets.

- Secure resources not available internally. Outside experts in related fields can be accessed via service contracts to evaluate or develop new technologies or processes (e.g., contract research with universities).[66]

> One that desires to be excellent should endeavor it in those things that are in themselves most excellent.
>
> —*Epictetus, 1st-century Greek philosopher*

Strategic Disadvantages of Outsourcing

Outsourcing involves reducing corporate-controlled assets and expertise and farming them out to third parties. Injudicious management or excessive use of outsourcing can result in serious long-term problems, including:

Loss of Core Competencies Key expertise or processes can be lost in the outsourcing process. For example, contracting with third parties to manufacture low-cost products or components can lead to the "hollowing out" of corporations as they lose management expertise or technological capabilities.[67] This expertise is difficult to regain if conditions change. Internationally, outsourcing allows foreign-based producers to build up production expertise and gain insights into customer needs and market trends, equipping them to become future competitors.

Control Problems Outsourcing supply chain functions and processes works effectively only when proper control mechanisms are in place. Control begins with selecting and evaluating vendor capabilities. This includes assessments of management expertise and commitment, past performance (with references), technologies, labor-force quality and commitment (including labor practices, wage rates, personnel and hiring policies, particularly in developing countries). For foreign vendors, national infrastructures need evaluating to assess transportation and delivery options, including ports, roads, and airfreight capabilities. Government trade policies (including export incentives and import controls) must also be reviewed, along with currency forecasts to assess trading prospects. Thorough screenings of companies and countries allow firms to anticipate and prepare for potential quality, price, and service problems.

Corporate and Home-Market Repercussions of Foreign Outsourcing Outsourcing, particularly to foreign firms, has internal and external repercussions. Internally, corporate morale suffers as domestic employees are deemed "not good enough," or "too expensive" (i.e., "overpaid for what they do"). Externally, company reputations can suffer as employees are displaced. In market forces-based economies, workforces are often regarded as expense items to be trimmed to maintain marketplace competitiveness. The U.S. auto industry has faced major labor problems as they have outsourced more and more of their supply chains. In other parts of the world, labor concerns make outsourcing a more deliberate process. In Western Europe, worker councils meet with management to assess major outsourcing decisions. In Japan, where workers are viewed as corporate assets, displaced workers are reassigned to avoid morale problems. Where foreign sourcing is mandated, Japanese firms are more likely to establish company-owned facilities to maintain supply chain control.[68]

Inadequate Supervision of the Supply Chain Process While outsourcing allows companies to reduce fixed assets and staff, it creates needs for experienced supply chain executives. Inadequate management of supply chain functions jeopardizes potential outsourcing benefits and can adversely affect product quality.

Outsourcing Individual Supply Chain Components: Pros and Cons

In addition to the strategic advantages and disadvantages of outsourcing, there are arguments for and against the outsourcing of specific supply chain components. These are summarized in Table 11.3 and discussed here.

> *People are always neglecting something they can do in trying to do something they can't do.*
>
> —*Ed Howe, 19th–20th-century U.S. journalist*

> *Don't expect. Inspect.*
>
> —*U.S. business saying*

> *Who steals my purse steals trash: 'tis something, 'tis nothing. But he that filches from me my good name robs me of that which not enriches him, and makes me poor indeed.*
>
> —*William Shakespeare, 16th–17th-century English dramatist and writer*

TABLE 11.3
Supply Chain Integration, Deintegration (Outsourcing), and Global Dimensions

Supply Chain Function	Insourcing (ownership, in-house)	Outsourcing (non-ownership)	Global Dimensions Insourcing/Outsourcing.
Raw Materials	Where raw material costs are high % of total costs (oil, plastics, food materials) or (quality) supplies are limited	Where raw materials are plentiful, many suppliers, competitive markets	Other countries have raw material deposits and/or comparative advantages in production
Components	Components are key inputs into final product, or scale economies are obtainable	Standard components or world class suppliers (e.g., Intel for chips, micro-processors)	Specialized labor required or low costs realizable
Manufacturing Fabrication/ Assembly	Specialized assemblies (e.g., autos), some customization needed (by country, customer)	Standardized assembly	Manufacturing requires specialized labor (D.C.s), or is cost sensitive (e.g., garment assembly in LDCs)
Logistics	Service levels are essential or a competitive advantage (e.g., Caterpillar)	Non-core activity/high cost	Logistics service providers have global networks, specialized transportation facilities, global expertise in product movements.
Distribution	Distribution outlets for customer service (e.g., financial services, some franchises)	Powerful channels, (e.g., retailers) or fragmented channel networks	Major investments necessary to secure global distribution, national/regional networks feasible for major markets
Supply Chain Support Functions			
New-Product Development	Key factor in marketplace success (Nike, fashions, aircarft, biotech)	Major investments required (electronics, chip design), rapid marketplace change	Many developers worldwide— pick and choose (software, textiles)
Human Resources	High caliber personnel essential, corporate culture a key success factor, training and development of in-house talent	Some functions may be outsourced (e.g., recruitment training) to focus on other HR activities (e.g., mergers and acquisitions or executive development)	Consistency and importance of corporate culture as global coordinating mechanisms

> Work out your own salvation. Do not depend on others.
>
> —*Buddha, 6th-century* B.C. *founder of Buddhism*

Raw-material outsourcing is common for most firms, due to the increasing competitiveness of global commodities markets for oil, iron ore, copper, zinc, aluminum, rubber, and so on. Ownership of raw-material sources makes sense when raw materials account for high percentages of producer cost structures or are key ingredients affecting product quality. Oil companies prefer ownership stakes in oil fields to control supply chain margins as the commodity moves from extraction through to end users. Similarly, in food manufacturing, ownership stakes are taken in agribusiness firms to ensure control over quality producers and to prevent rivals from gaining access to them.

Component outsourcing works where output is standardized and where many producers compete to supply original equipment manufacturers (OEMs). The more important the component, for example, when components contribute to OEM competitive advantages, the more likely they are to be produced "in house" under OEM supervision. Problems occur when companies outsource components critical to their competitive well-being. Hewlett Packard had problems when they became dependent on Japan's Canon for printer engines, and British computer maker ICL placed excessive reliance on Fujitsu components and technologies, ultimately leading to their takeover by the Japanese company.

Manufacturing outsourcing works best in markets characterized by constant changes in customer tastes (e.g., fashion garments) or in technologies (e.g., personal computers). Production outsourcing gives firms flexibility in responding to changing marketplace conditions and power over contractors with the granting (or taking away) of production contracts. Over time, where subcontractors prove trustworthy and reliable, ownership stakes may be taken or alliances forged to formalize their roles in corporate supply chains.

In these cases, firms maintain competitive advantages in diagnosing changing market trends. Control can also be maintained through ownership or control of retail channels (e.g., grocery chains), ownership of powerful brand names (e.g., sports shoes and accessories), or new-product development.

Logistics outsourcing became a major trend in the 1990s. Upstream, the efficient transportation of materials and components became essential as manufacturers switched to JIT production. Downstream, on-time delivery of spare parts and finished goods to customers contributes to competitive advantages in service. The globalization of demand and the availability of full-service logistics providers have made outsourcing logical, as companies must otherwise tie up significant resources in distribution assets. Such outsourcing agreements allow logistics service companies (LSCs) to effectively take over corporate transportation and logistics functions. Examples include FedEx Business Logistics Services' alliance with Laura Ashley, and Danish company DFDS's computers and auto parts network to service firms such as IBM, ICL, Apple, Ford, General Motors, and Toyota. In some cases, the logistics arms of manufacturing firms have been contracted out to third-party customers. Caterpillar Logistics Services—a subsidiary of the Caterpillar Group—operates global parts supply services for companies such as Land Rover, Massey-Ferguson, and Chrysler.[69]

The advantages of third-party logistics outsourcing include:

- Services on an "as needed" basis. This frees up capital that would otherwise be used for warehousing, transport vehicles, and material-handling equipment.

- Third-party logistics providers, in serving multiple clients, can leverage their knowledge, experience, and assets over a number of companies to gain superior economies of scope and scale.[70] This results in leaner supplier organizations while fully utilizing logistics providers' assets and facilities.

The disadvantages of third-party logistics outsourcing include:

- Lost of control over products/parts after leaving the supplier. This can be mitigated through use of product-tracking systems.

- The risk that service providers may become overstretched and be unable to maintain requisite service levels. This would be problematic where customer service was a key competitive advantage.

- Risks if the LSC was taken over or went out of business

- Problems meshing manufacturer-LSC organizations, their corporate cultures, information systems, and employee skills[71]

- Logistics companies' shipping schedules and standards may not be consistent with end-customer requirements.

- Downstream demand for products fluctuates so much that cost-effective logistics becomes difficult to achieve (e.g., excessive small shipments using high-cost transportation modes).

- Where warehousing or after-sales service facilities are necessary, logistics company facilities may not match manufacturer needs.

- It has been difficult to assess cost savings resulting from outsourcing decisions.[72]

Distribution outsourcing depends on the global reach of the outside operator and on how effectively the information systems of the manufacturer and operator can be integrated. Many companies maintain regional and/or national warehousing systems to maintain control and to ensure consistent flows of products and information. For some industries, control at the retail level is an essential part of their competitive advantage (e.g., for financial services). Similarly, for franchises and retailers, control at point-of-purchase is important and is maintained through ownership or contractual agreements.

For many companies, though, control at the retail level is not possible and must be left to independent operators. Here, the concentration of retailer power through chains simplifies product flows to retailers (e.g., order consolidations) but gives considerable purchasing power to retail purchasing departments. At the other end of the retail spectrum, fragmented retail structures elevate servicing costs but give manufacturers leverage in controlling brand exposure. In both cases, however, Internet servicing capabilities provide both manufacturers and retailers with increased sourcing and distribution options.

Information technologies (IT) have been outsourced increasingly as quantum leaps in IT technologies have made it difficult for firms to stay current with IT developments. Companies in Western Europe and North America spent $54 billion in IT subcontracts in 1998. This figure was expected to hit $77 billion by the year 2000.[73] Fears of becoming IT laggards are real as firms increasingly coordinate supply chains, maintain their vigilance of worldwide marketplace developments, and keep employees and stakeholders up to date with internal and external events.

Other advantages of IT outsourcing are:

- Allowing IT specialists to focus on shaping information architectures to suit management needs rather than spending time on day-to-day maintenance chores

- Having global IT specialists address IT international expansion needs. Staples, the U.S. office-supplies retailer, found Britain's ICL to be more efficient in keeping pace with the store's domestic and international growth rate of one new outlet every two days.[74]

The major disadvantage of IT outsourcing is that, once done, it becomes very difficult to move the IT function back in-house if problems arise. General

Motors' outsourcing of its IT function made the company totally dependent on external expertise and made the task of switching IT contractors extraordinarily difficult.[75]

New-product development functions are important enough for most international companies to maintain in-house control. In some technically-based industries, the subcontracting of new product needs occurs as additional expertise needs to be tapped. The advantages of this approach are:

- Maintaining a stable employee base rather than hiring/firing specialists at the termination of specific projects

- Subcontractors bring broader technical bases to the table; for example, computer firms bring in multi-industry expertise in technical-equipment design and the automation of manufacturing processes.

- Flexibility and speed in new-product development as new ideas do not have to wait for in-house resources to become available

- Production facilities can be prepared in-house as products take shape and market potentials are assessed.

Disadvantages to new-product development subcontracting are:

- Locating and selecting firms with appropriate technical credentials and available resources

- New-product parameters must be clearly specified with respect to technical specifications, investment cost limits, and timetables.

- Confidentiality must be maintained, especially in highly competitive industries where significant interactions occur among industry participants.

- Quality and performance parameters are difficult to guarantee.

- Future support must be optioned to ensure post-design problems are addressed and in the event that follow-on products are needed.[76]

Human resource management outsourcing became popular during the 1990s as international corporations streamlined their management ranks through downsizing. As mergers and acquisitions increased, HR professionals became increasingly involved with integrating acquired firms and establishing common corporate cultures across product divisions and geographic markets. Some nonessential HR activities (temporary staffing arrangements, checking of backgrounds and references, retirement plans, benefits, relocation services, etc.) were outsourced.[77]

> Put your personnel work first because it is the most important.
>
> —*Robert E. Wood, former president, Sears & Roebuck*

In international corporations, local HR professionals are essential to deal with country-level labor and employment laws. At head offices, HR departments have new mandates, such as corporate Intranets to maintain worldwide communications with workers and managers. They have also been charged with monitoring labor and employment policies of subcontractors, particularly in developing markets. Some outside help for international HR departments occurs for top-management recruiting ("headhunting") and for international compensation and benefit programs.[78]

KEY POINTS

- Global and multi-market supply chains are international networks linking suppliers, producers, distributors, and customers across national boundaries. Environmental catalysts, such as free-trade movements and demand homogenization, have promoted their development, as have catalysts such as corporate needs for cost leadership and differentiation.

- Manufacturer-supplier sourcing strategies can be nationally, regionally, or globally based and evolve slowly. Supplier-customer relationships also tend to evolve from arms-length antagonistic relations through to partnership arrangements.

- International manufacturing systems develop from single-market production systems to regional and global networks as trade barriers fall and firms transfer goods, components, technologies, and manufacturing methods between markets.

- Manufacturer-distributor linkages have been affected by changing distribution trends and needs, and electronic data interchange and Internet capabilities have enhanced distributor-customer relations.

- Global and multi-market supply chains are integrated through information technologies, the development of multicultural managers and human resource processes, and through multi-market new product development processes.

- Few firms own all assets within their supply chains, and outsourcing decisions are examined from general strategic perspectives and from the viewpoints of individual supply chain components.

ENDNOTES

1. Randy Weston, "Bristol-Myers CEO demands massive supply chain fix," *Computerworld* (November 17, 1997): 47, 52.

2. Joan Magretta, "Fast, Global and Entrepreneurial: Supply Chain Management, Hong Kong Style. An Interview with Victor Fung, *Harvard Business Review* 76: 5 (Sept.–Oct., 1998): 103–14.

3. Garrick Holmes, *Supply Chain Management,* London: Economist Intelligence Unit 1995 22.

4. Holmes, *Supply Chain Management,* 25–26.

5. For example, Vincent A. Mabert, John F. Muth, and Roger W. Schmenner, "Collapsing new product development times: Six case studies," *Journal of Product Innovation Management* 9: 3 (September 1992): 200–13.

6. Gary L. Ragatz, Robert B. Handfield, and Thomas Scannell, "Success Factors in Integrating Suppliers into new product development," *Journal of Product Innovation Management* 14 (1997): 190–202.

7. Holmes, 78.

8. Based on Philip B. Schary and Taqge Skjott-Larsen, *Managing the Global Supply Chain* (Copenhagen: Munksgaard International Publishers, 1995), 30–32.

9. Tim Wilson, "Custom Manufacturing—Nike Model Shows Web Limitations," *Internet Week* (Dec. 6, 1999): 1, 12.

10. Masaaki Kotabe, "Efficiency vs. effectiveness orientation of global sourcing strategy: A comparison of U.S. and Japanese multinational companies," *The Academy of Management Executive* 12: 4 (November 1998): 107–19.

11. Thomas F. Black, "NUMMI chalks up 15 years," *Automotive News* (May 24, 1999): 8ndd–8nee.

12. Edmund Faltermayer, "US Companies come back home," *Fortune* (Dec. 30, 1991): 106–8.

13. Peter Engardio, "Souping up the Supply Chain," *Business Week* (August 31, 1998): 110.

14. Kelly Hayes Madden, "Window on the World," *Distribution* (April 1997): 54–59.

15. Robert Bowman, "The 12,000 mile pipeline," *Distribution* (June 1996): 46–48.

16. Robert Monczka and Robert J. Trent, "Global Sourcing: A Development Approach," *International Journal of Purchasing and Materials Management* 27: 2 (Spring 1991): 2–9.

17. David O. Stephens, "The globalization of information technology in multinational corporations," *Information Management Journal* 33: 3 (July 1999): 66–71.

18. Based on R. Lamming, *Beyond Partnerships* (Englewood Cliffs, N.J., Prentice Hall).

19. Kasra Ferdows, "Making the Most of Foreign Factories," *Harvard Business Review* 75: 2 (March–April 1997): 73–88.

20. Based on Y. Shi and M. Gregory, "International Manufacturing Networks to Develop Global Capabilities," *Journal of Operations Management* 16 (1998): 195–204.

21. Jodie E. Melbin, "Vive La Logistique," *Distribution* (April 1996): 46–49.

22. Philip Kotler, Liam Fahey, and S. Jatusripitak, *The New Competition* (Englewood Cliffs: Prentice-Hall, 1985), 188.

23. Micheline Maynard, *The Global Manufacturing Vanguard* (New York: John Wiley & Sons, 1998), 23.

24. Alex Taylor III, "How Toyota defies gravity," *Business Week* (Dec. 8, 1997): 100–8.

25. Maynard, *op. cit.*, 116.

26. Ibid., 53–55.

27. James H. Martin, Beth Ann Martin, and Bruno Grbai, "Employee involvement and market orientation in a transition economy: Importance, problems and a solution," *Journal of Managerial Issues* 10: 4 (Winter 1998): 485–502.

28. K. Kristensen, J. J. Dahlgaard, G. K. Kanj, and H. J. Julh, "Some consequences of just in time: Results of a comparison between the Nordic countries and East Asia," *Total Quality Management* 10: 1 (Jan. 1999): 61–71.

29. Ibid.

30. Cristina Cosma and Charles Duval, "Total Quality Management in Eastern European Construction: the paradigm shift," *Total Quality Management* 9: 4/5 (July 1998): S38–40; and Haresh Gurnani "Pitfalls in total quality management implementation: The case of a Hong Kong Company," *Total Quality Management* 10: 2 (March 1999): 209–28.

31. Nicoline Boshoff and Pierre M. Van Zyl, "Empowered team based project management in developing countries," *Transactions of AACE International* (Morgantown, W. Va.: 1997): 171–76.

32. Schary and Larsen, *Managing the Global Supply Chain,* 196–97.

33. Schary and Larsen, 197.

34. Schary and Larsen, 198–200; and "Global 200 highlights," 55–57.

35. Anonymous, "On line buying's brave new world emerges," *DSN Retailing Today* 39: 10 (May 22, 2000): 15–16.

36. Schary and Larsen, 244.

37. Ibid., 245.

38. Schary and Larsen, 250.

39. Schary and Larsen, 251.

40. James A Cooke, "Making the Global Connection," *Logistics Management and Logistics Report* 38: 6 (June 1999): 47–50.

41. "Business and the Internet: You'll never walk alone," *The Economist* (June 26, 1999): B11–B21.

42. Margaret McKegney, "Dell adapts well to online sales," *Ad Age International* (May 2000): 26.

43. Anonymous, "Survey: E-Commerce: First America, then the world," *The Economist* (February 26, 2000): S49–S53.

44. Ibid.

45. Jill Jusko, " 'Net changes stripes for China," *Industry Week* (May 15, 2000): 14.

46. J. Stewart Black and Hal B. Gregersen, "The right way to manage expats," *Harvard Business Review* 77: 2 (March–April 1999): 52.

47. Maali H. Ashamalla, "International human resource management practices: the challenge of expatriation," *Competitiveness Review* 8: 2 (1999): 54–65.

48. Allan Halcrow, "Expats: the squandered resource," *Workforce* 78: 4 (April 1999):42–48.

49. Valerie Frazee, "Selecting global managers," *Workforce* 3: 4 (July 1998): 28–30.

50. Valerie Frazee, "No common thread in expat. selection," *Workforce* 3: 4 (July 1998): 9.

51. Anonymous, "Case Study: Shell International," *HR Focus* 75: 3 (March 1998): S–10.

52. Black and Gregersen, *op. cit.*

53. Anonymous, "Upward mobility," *Business Europe* (February 10, 1999): p. 1, 3.

54. Calvin Reynolds, "Global compensation and benefits in transition," *Compensation and Benefits Review* 32: 1 (Jan.–Feb. 2000): 28–38.

55. Anonymous, "Labor Relations: Five Years On," *Business Europe* (May 19, 1999): 7.

56. Thierry Ogier, "Mercosur: Regional Roadshow," *Business Latin America* (May 3, 1999): 6.

57. Holly Acland, "Harnessing internal innovation," *Marketing* (July 22, 1999): 27–8.

58. *Ibid.*

59. Tim Stevens, "Lights, camera, innovation," *Industry Week* (July 19, 1999): 32–38.

60. Amy Barrett, *et al.*, "Just like mom used to engineer," *Business Week* (Dec. 21, 1998): 82.

61. William C. Symonds and Carol Matlack, "Gillette's Edge," *Business Week* (January 19, 1998): 70–77.

62. "Global Manufacturing Strategies," *Business International Corporation* (New York, 1991): chapter 7.

63. Ibid., 98–99.

64. David S. Hotter, "A software approach to cutting new product costs," *Machine Design* 70: 7 (April 1998): 76–80.

65. Peter Galuszka, Ellen Neuborne, and Wendy Zellner, " P & G's hottest new product: P & G," *Business Week* (October 5, 1998): 92–94.

66. Anonymous "10 reasons to outsource," *Management* 45: 3 (April 1998): 45.

67. Robert Heller, "The dangers of Deconstruction," *Management Today* (Feb. 1993): 14–16.

68. Masaaki Kotabe, *op. cit.*

69. Masaaki Kotabe, 263–67.

70. Masaaki Kotabe, 250.

71. Masaaki Kotabe, 251.

72. Julian Keeling, "Pros and cons of outsourcing," *Traffic World* (January 18, 1999): 47–48.

73. Dean Emuti, Yunus Kathawala, and Matthew Monippallil, "Outsourcing to gain a competitive advantage," *Industrial Management* 40: 3 (May–June 1998): 20–24.

74. Judith N. Mottl, "IT outsourcing gives Staples the tools to grow," *Informationweek* (May 15, 2000): 112–16.

75. Bruce Caldwell, "Fortune One's outsourcing challenge," *Informationweek* (November 16, 1998): 57.

76. Greg Morin, "Going outside the company for product development," *Machine Design* (Dec. 9, 1999): 60–64.

77. Linda Davidson, "Cut away non core HR," *Workforce* (Jan. 1998): 40–45.

78. Calvin Reynolds, "Global compensation and benefits in transition," *Compensation and Benefits Review* 32: 1 (Jan.–Feb. 2000): 28–38.

C A S E T T E   11-1
Constructing and Evaluating Global and Multi-Market Supply Chains

Global and multi-market supply chains have resulted from free-trade movements and corporate needs to be cost competitive and to differentiate their goods and services from those of rivals. What follows are four descriptions of corporate supply chains. For each:

1. Draw the supply chains

2. Elaborate on each supply chain's features and how they contribute to each company's competitive efforts.

Capespan

Capespan was a South African supplier selling close to $1 billion of fresh fruits to thirty European markets. The company coordinated 3500 products and 1400 types of perishable agricultural products. But the European market had become ever more competitive as region-wide competition had produced more discriminating consumers and more powerful supermarket chains. As a result, Capespan revamped its supply chain process thus:

The process started with product delivery from farms to the packing house where produce was inspected, labeled, packed into cartons, and barcoded according to quality, treatment, and origin. The fruit was then moved to cold storage and then transported by ocean shipment to Europe. The cartons were scanned to facilitate movement on and off the ship. Cargo data was then sent to Capespan's European planners who decided which cartons were to be unloaded at each port for selected country markets. The ports accessed the network to confirm what cargoes were actually unloaded and contacted distributors to collect their merchandise. Country sales agents sent back daily reports about sales, inventories, and quality levels. Daily reports were then consolidated to provide growers with feedback concerning present and likely future sales levels.

Through this system, product defects and produce deterioration could be rapidly identified, special provisions made for retailer promotions, and adherence facilitated to country regulations concerning pesticides and chemical treatments. Future plans included electronic order placements to improve production planning.

Benetton

Benetton's supply chain to place $2 billion of fashion garments to 7000 retailers in over 100 countries was complex. Facing ten fashion changes per year, the company had to be flexible and quick on its feet to coordinate activities. Benetton had 180 suppliers feeding raw materials into its central manufacturing facility, where computer-aided design and material-cutting technology prepared the garment pieces. About 450 subcontractors assembled the pieces into garments, which were then factory-dyed to ensure consistency with the latest fashion colors and trends. Finished garments went to a company-owned distribution center. When needed, they were shipped directly to retailers. An outsourced freight forwarding system prepared the shipping documents and transportation was by third-party ocean and airfreight firms. Benetton used electronic data interchange between retailers, country, agents and corporate officers to monitor sales daily. Changes in consumer purchasing were quickly detected and adjustments made to garment types and colors throughout the supply chain.

Gillette's European Supply Chain

Gillette, the global producer of shavers and consumer products, rethought its supply chain as Europe unified. Key components were global sourcing of its strip steel from Japan's Hitachi and Britain's Avesta; plastics and packaging sources were European. The company employed a dedicated regional manufacturing system with blade cartridges being produced in Germany and disposable razors and toiletries being made at separate U.K. facilities. The company owned its distribution centers (which also performed postponement processes, such as custom packaging or national adaptations) with the Frankfurt, Germany, and Scandinavian distribution centers serving multiple markets.

National warehouses served geographically large countries, such as France, Italy, and Spain. Deliveries were made to national warehouses for independent retailers. EDI and computer linkages were in place to ensure timely deliveries and smooth linkages with independent retail outlets.

Ikea's Global Supply Chain

Ikea's furniture supply chain comprised 2,400 suppliers in sixty-five countries making 12,000 products. Nearly three-quarters were European-based, less than 5 percent were North American, and the remainder were sourced in Asia. Ikea had long-term relationships with most suppliers, but also selectively invested in a few key suppliers. The company owned fourteen distribution centers but maintained two independent warehouse centers in Belgium and Sweden. Its 158 stores were franchised and based in twenty-nine countries. The company also maintained its own direct distribution, with thirty-eight editions of its catalogs in seventeen languages being sent to consumers in twenty-eight countries. Its Internet system maintained a 140,000-customer database. A key feature for Ikea was customer involvement in the supply chain. Most products were customer-assembled. At headquarters, primary management functions were in demand analysis, new-product development, and supplier and franchise development. Information flows from retail franchises were fed back to distribution centers and headquarters. The Swedish head office provided feedback and technical assistance to suppliers.

Sources: Anonymous. **"Overcoming Communication Barriers."** *Transportation & Distribution* (October 1998): 91–94. **Dapiran, Peter. "Benetton: Global Logistics in action."** *International Journal of Physical Distribution and Logistics Management* 22: 6 (1991): 7–12. **Friedman Michael, Len Lewis, Richard Turcsik, Barry Janott, and Jenny Summerous. "Peoples in Excellence."** *Progressive Grocer* (April 2000): 22–48. **Holmes, Garrick. "Supply Chain Management: Europe's New Battleground London."** *EIU* (1995). **Schary, Philip B., and Tage Skjott Larsen.** *Managing the Global Supply Chain.* **(Copenhagen: Munkgaard International Publishers, 1995).**

CASETTE 11-2
Evaluating Outsourcing Decisions

Outsourcing activities is the route to global efficiency in worldwide operations. For each of the following three situations, evaluate the pros and cons of the outsourcing decision and decide whether each makes sense, and why.

1. McDermott International: In 1999, the New Orleans-based energy services and engineering company announced a ten-year, $600 million information technology outsourcing agreement with AT&T corporation. Under the agreement, AT&T would be responsible for IT design, implementation, and management services relating to its global information technology function. It would control McDermott's 10,000 PCs, 350 servers, its local-area networks (LANS), and some business applications. About 250 McDermott IT workers were transferred to AT&T as part of the deal.

2. Israeli medical equipment manufacturers ESC Medical Systems had experienced significant growth since its 1992 inception, moving rapidly from sales of $1.1 million in 1994 to $225 million in 1998. International operations in particular had flourished. Eighty percent of company output was from its two plants in Israel, the remainder occurring in Rugby, England, and Seattle, U.S. The company also maintained distribution centers in the U.S. and Europe and nine offices in six countries to sell its products in over fifty countries worldwide.

The company was experiencing some growing pains. Rapid expansion of sales had placed strains on its supply chain. Its distance from customers and from key component and material sources was becoming more of a problem for internal coordination. The company produced about twenty different medical equipment products, each about the size of a small refrigerator and priced at about $100,000 per unit.

The company was contemplating outsourcing its supply chain management to the Fritz Companies in the belief that it would shorten supply times and operating costs and allow it to focus on quality improvements and product developments. This involved an outside party that would:

- Manage inflows of components and materials to its plants, including tracking progress and arranging customs clearances

- Schedule ESC vendor deliveries to improve flows of raw materials, shorter cycle times, and reduce inventory

- Provide warehousing for finished goods and improved packaging and labeling processes, arrange shipment to end-use customers and ESC overseas distributors, and track foreign shipments to international customers and distributors

3. New-product development in the U.K. pharmaceutical industry: The U.K. pharmaceutical industry invests a world-leading 15 percent of sales in R and D to maintain the flow of new products vital to the industry's well-being. Historically, it has taken ten to twelve years to develop new medicines to standards of quality, efficiency, and safety required under international and variable national standards. Outsourcing this key function, though, is considered essential for pharmaceutical firms to enable them to focus on their core competencies, aiding innovation, reducing risk, and managing work peaks without adding to fixed costs. Financial imperatives included 7 percent market growth to 2005. This translated into almost $30 billion in new-product sales for each industry leader up to that time—or between 25–35 new drugs, each generating $1–1.5 billion in sales.

Sources: Celeshno, Martha L. "Keeping up with growth." *World Trade* 12: 6 (June 1999): 68–69. Osborne, John. "Pharmaceutical R&D spending expands at record pace." *Research & Development* 41: 10 (Sept. 1999): UK 14–16. Rosencrance, Linda. "10 year AT&T outsourcing deal dumped." *Computers World* (July 30, 2001): 1, 61.

Chapter *Twelve*

Managing Cultural Differences

∽

NEGOTIATING FACE-TO-FACE: WHEN CULTURE REALLY MATTERS

Few situations are as culturally loaded as face-to-face negotiations between executives of different nationalities. North American cultures developed from European immigrants, but their negotiating styles are often at odds:

- *North Americans use praise to soften up managers before they criticize them. Italians, French, and German managers don't, and view this approach as manipulative.*
- *The North American habits of informality, egalitarianism, spontaneity, and go-getter mentalities make British managers uncomfortable, as does the U.S. penchant toward nametags.*

  In Asia, North Americans also have adjustments to make. Sight-seeing, coffee and tea drinking, endless introductions and formalities, long periods of silence punctuated by frenetic group discussions on the other side of the table all serve to unnerve the most patient of North Americans.[1]

> ∽
>
> You never get a second chance to make a first impression.
>
> —*North American proverb*
>
> ∽

Face-to-face meetings among international executives are where much business gets done. Introductions are made. Impressions are formed. Relationships start to take shape, some to last a lifetime. As the world becomes ever smaller, so interactions among national cultures increase, and companies must rely more on relationships with other international firms to compete effectively in world markets. It is a truism to say that international managers cannot know enough about foreign cultures. How well managers understand their foreign counterparts is often the difference between getting international contracts and business and returning home from foreign trips empty-handed.

In this chapter, therefore:

- A framework for understanding intercultural behaviors—high-medium-low context cultures—is presented, along with discussions about their cultural underpinnings (the religious, political, economic, and social factors guiding these behaviors—the "whys").
- Then we flesh out this framework by examining negotiating characteristics found in North America, Latin America, Asia, and other regions, and how to organize international negotiations.

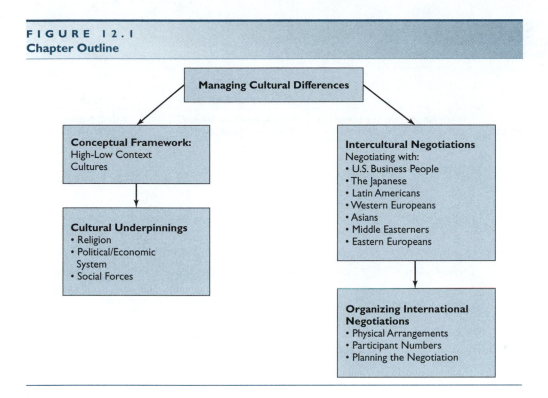

FIGURE 12.1
Chapter Outline

A FRAMEWORK FOR UNDERSTANDING BUSINESS AND INTERPERSONAL BEHAVIORS: HIGH-MEDIUM-LOW-CONTEXT CULTURES

Introduction

The high-low context classification, originally developed by E. T. Hall, offers a framework for understanding business and interpersonal relationships on a worldwide basis (see Table 12.1). The terms *high* and *low context* were originally used to describe the extent to which spoken statements conveyed the sum total of a message's content. In low-context cultures (such as the U.S., Germany), what is said is the sum total of this message ("the message speaks for itself"). Additional interpretations are not necessary. In high context societies (Asia, Latin America, the Middle East), what is said must be interpreted along with the sender's social status and background and the circumstances under which the message was conveyed (the "context").

This framework has been expanded (see Table 12.1) to include varieties of behaviors, values, and attitudes associated with particular societies. Note the parallels between the modern institutions and values (laid out in Chapter 3) and low-context behaviors. These reflect efficiency and competitive considerations in interpersonal relationships. Fully industrialized nations tend to exhibit competitive low-context behaviors. Developing nations, on the other hand, are more oriented to cooperative high-context behaviors.

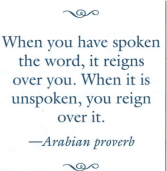

When you have spoken
the word, it reigns
over you. When it is
unspoken, you reign
over it.

—Arabian proverb

TABLE 12.1
Business and Interpersonal Relationships in High-, Medium-, and Low-Context Societies

	Context		
	Low	**Medium**	**High**
Country/Regional Examples	**North American, Scandinavian, Swiss, German**	**Greek, Spanish, Italian, French, Dutch, British**	**Asian, Arabic, Latin American**
Interpersonal Values, Attitudes, Behaviors			
Meeting people	Informal	Formal	Formal
Getting acquainted	Fast	Moderate	Slow
Depth of relationship	Shallow	Moderate	Deep
Trust in relationships	Little trust	Trust	Much trust
Limits on individual behavior	Legal	Legal/Social	Social
Reliance on lawyers	High	Moderate	Low/Zero
Meetings	Efficiency oriented	Mixture of business and social	Lengthy; much socializing
Business relationships	"At arms length," preferably objective and nonsociable	Some mixing of social/business through networking	Blusiness an extension of social relationship
Tolerance for mistakes	High	Medium	Low
Accountability for mistakes	At lowest level	At highest level	At highest level
Competition between individuals	Encouraged	Discouraged	Considered antisocial
Insider-Outsider distinctions	Low	Moderate	High
Patriarchal orientation	Low	Moderate	High
Individual orientation	High	Moderate	Lower
Social class distinctions	Low/moderate	Moderate	High
Tolerance for uncertainty	High	High	Low
Flexible Stereotype Orientation	LC-FS	MC-FS	HC-FS

LC-FS: Low-context flexible stereotype: Most people are low context (the national stereotype), but significant pockets of medium context inhabitants and smaller numbers of high context groups.
MC-FS: Medium-context flexible stereotype: Most people in Western Europe are medium context (British, French, Belgians, Italians); some are more low context (Germans, Scandanavia); some are more high context (Greeks, Spanish).
HC-FS: High-context flexible stereotype: National behaviors are rurally-oriented and high context; smaller pockets of medium context behaviors (migrants transitioning to urban behaviors); minority low-context behaviors of urbanites.

Source: Adapted from Hall, E. T. "How Cultures Collide." *Psychology Today* (July 1976): 67–74. Hofstede, G. *Culture's Consequences.* Beverly Hills, CA: Sage Publications, 1984.

One exception is Japan, whose fully industrialized status is accompanied by traditional high-context behaviors. Note also the intermediate positions of many Western European countries that are neither high nor low context cultures.

Low-Context Behaviors

Low-context behaviors, values, and attitudes are associated with capitalist, efficiency-oriented societies. These countries tend to be fast-paced, market forces-based societies where competitiveness is apparent in political systems (through democratic processes), in the marketplace (through corporate competitiveness), and socially (through mobile, materialistically based social-class systems). To counter competitive excesses, legal systems are well-developed to define acceptable behaviors at corporate and personal levels, and "watertight" contracts are customary. Mistakes are tolerated. Behaviors tend to be individually rather than group-oriented, and insider-outsider distinctions are less evident. Social-class barriers are low or nonexistent. High levels of economic activity draw women into national workforces, where recognition of their economic contributions drives emancipation between the genders. However, North American and some Western European societies exhibit low-context characteristics (as the flexible stereotype orientation in Table 12.1 shows). While low-context characteristics are mainstream (stereotypical) behaviors in some countries, there are significant deviations within those regions. For example, the U.S. is cast as a low context culture, but medium-context behaviors are more the norm in the agrarian-based Southern and Midwestern regions, and native American Indian cultures tend to be high context. These differences reflect local resistances to the diffusion of impersonal, competitive behaviors through the U.S. economy.

> A verbal contract isn't worth the paper it's written on.
>
> —*Samuel Goldwyn, U.S. movie producer*

High-Context Behaviors

High-context behaviors, values, and attitudes are traditionally-based and are to be found in Asia, the Middle East, and Latin America. These tend to be rurally based, less-competitive societies where cooperation, harmony, and stability are highly valued. Social relationships between individuals are emphasized, and trustworthiness is a key trait in business dealings. Even as comprehensive legal frameworks are developed to guide the transition to economic development, social rules still dominate interpersonal relationships. Stability and conformist behaviors are promoted through strict social-class divisions and societal responsibilities. "Surprises" are not welcomed, and outsiders are viewed with suspicion and mistrust until they "prove" their usefulness and loyalty. Excessive competitiveness, especially among individuals, constitutes grounds for social ostracization ("outcasts").

> You may be deceived if you trust too much, but you will live in torment if you do not trust enough.
>
> —*Frank Crane, U.S. businessman*

But as the winds of change sweep through traditional societies and as they become more exposed to external influences, behaviors and values become increasingly low context. Urban centers, with their more advanced infrastructures (media, transportation), educational amenities, products, and services, promote changes in lifestyles. Slowly, as modernizing influences diffuse from towns into rural areas, high-context behaviors come under pressure.

Medium-Context Behaviors

Medium context societies are to be found in the mainly industrialized nations of Western Europe. They are competitive in that Western European countries have fully functioning democratic processes, competition in the marketplace, and some movement between social classes. Business relations tend to be formal at first but barriers are broken down as relationships are formed and trust is established. Lawyers are used during negotiations, but usually at the end to draw up documents. They are rarely part of day-to-day discussions. Mistakes are tolerated, but scapegoats are rarely sought, and responsibility is often taken at the highest levels. Excessive individuality and competitiveness are frowned upon. Some snobbishness and elitism is apparent, though this tends to be educationally based (elite universities), rather than by birthright.

CULTURAL UNDERPINNINGS OF HIGH-MEDIUM-LOW-CONTEXT BEHAVIORS—THE "WHYS"

We noted in Chapter 1 that effective international executives not only know *how* to behave in foreign markets (the "do's and don'ts"), they also have some understanding of *why* people behave the way they do—the underlying cultural forces shaping everyday behaviors. While we have hinted at factors influencing high-medium-low-context behaviors, it is important to lay out these influences formally. Figure 12.2 shows major shapers of behaviors, values, and attitudes in low, medium, and high context societies.

Religion

Definitions and Overview Religion is defined as "A socially shared set of beliefs, ideas, and actions that relate to a reality that cannot be verified empirically yet affects the course of natural and human events—a way of life woven around people's ultimate concerns."[2] In North America and Western Europe, religions such as Protestantism and Roman Catholicism exert relatively little influence

FIGURE 12.2
Facors Affecting High-Medium-Low-Context Behaviors

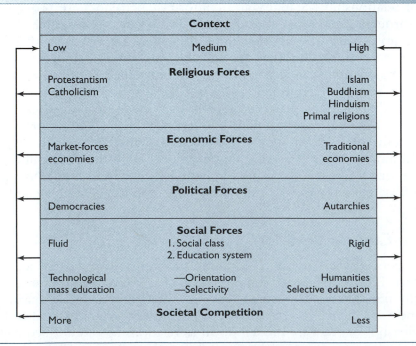

on daily behaviors. However, such is not the case in the rest of the world. For over four billion people, religion is important, either directly through daily prayer and rituals (e.g., Islam, Hinduism) or indirectly as religious and philosophical beliefs shape their daily behaviors, values, and attitudes (Buddhism, Confucianism, Taoism). Most importantly, knowledge of religious beliefs gives international managers key insights into societal priorities, behaviors, and values.

A brief historic overview of world religions (diagrammed in Figure 12.3) sets the scene for detailed discussions of individual faiths. Millions of years ago, when mankind hunted and farmed, the fates of individual communities were uncertain, and much depended on good hunting, good crops, animal and human reproduction. To aid good fortunes in these and other areas, many gods were created (gods of hunting, the sky, fire, reproduction, etc.). *Polytheistic religions* (those with multiple gods) have lasted millions of years and are still part of today's religious landscapes. In

> Religion is a central defining characteristic of civilizations.
>
> —*Samuel P. Huntington,*
> *political scientist,*
> *Harvard University*

FIGURE 12.3
World Religions: Polytheistic, Monotheistic, and Non-Theistic

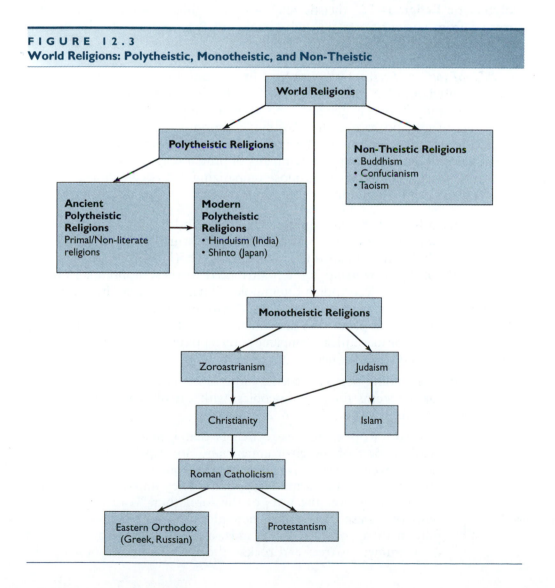

other societies, the notion of a single, omnipotent god took hold, and *monotheistic religions* began, most probably with Judaism and Zoroastrianism. Christianity and Islam descended from these beliefs. East Asia, however, moved in different direction, and in the sixth century B.C., there developed three religions—Buddhism, Confucianism, and Taoism—that were *non-theistic*. These religious philosophies were people- and nature-oriented, and supernatural deities were not centerpieces of their belief systems. All three were to have significant influences on Asian behaviors and values.

Polytheistic Religions Polytheistic religions are highly traditional faiths. They survived from ancient times through Greek and Roman times to the present day where they continue with tribal religions (e.g., native North and South American tribes) and in India (Hinduism) and Japan (Shinto).

Primal (or non-literate) religions have been around for over 3 million years and easily predate other major religions. They tend to be tribally-based and are passed on orally between generations.[3] Primal religions today are found in Africa (via magic and witchcraft), Australia (Aboriginal rites), Southeast Asia, the Pacific Islands, and among the Indian communities in North and South America. In modern societies, the remnants of primal religions survive with superstitions, astrology, and small groups emphasizing the occult. Some of their characteristics can be found in the following:

- Totemism is a belief system under which man and nature are perceived as one; plants and trees have "spirits," and rock formations are "alive." Distinctions between animate and inanimate objects ("nature") are perceived as artificial. Spirit worship is often attributed to these nonhuman objects (e.g., Native American Indian totem poles). Shamans are spiritual conduits between mankind and nature. These "witchdoctors" have specialized knowledge of local plants and herbs that can contribute to modern medicine. Many pharmaceutical companies are tapping these local knowledge sources to find cures for herpes and cancer.[4]

- Maintaining personal, social, and cosmic harmony are major spiritual concerns for primal peoples, with earthly concerns centering on rain, harvests, children, and health.[5]

- Ancestor worship relates to beliefs that human souls exist after death as part of the environment and are capable of influencing earthly events. Typically, they are benevolent when treated with respect but can be harmful if ignored. They impact social change, as "throwing over the ways of the forefathers" can be viewed as signs of disrespect. As such, new ideas must be introduced carefully in these societies. In Uganda, a $500 million dam was held up as numerous trees and rocks—the spiritual homes of ancestors

To forget one's ancestors is to be a brook without a source, a tree without a root.

—*Chinese proverb*

and local gods—had to be relocated through special ceremonies and sacrifices.[6]

Modern studies of primal religions and peoples have resulted in drastic changes from nineteenth-century attitudes when Western missionaries were dispatched to save the heathen "from themselves." Disenchantment with the complexities and disadvantages of industrial progress has resulted in respect for peoples who live in harmony with nature, who do not upset the ecological balance, and who represent mankind's past.[7]

Hinduism had its beginnings in 1500 B.C. when Aryan invaders swept into and occupied South Asia (today's India and Pakistan). With them, they brought their beliefs in gods and goddesses who ruled nature, and these beliefs over time were blended with local practices to produce Hinduism. Today, Hinduism has over 800 million adherents in India, or about 85 percent of the country's population. Worldwide, Hinduism claims in excess of one billion followers.

Hinduism's primary characteristics include:[8]

- Sanatana dharma: "The eternal way of conduct" that covers every aspect of life

- Sacred texts of the Vedas and the Upanishads that reveal the basic truths of life and the individual's place in the universe

- Samsara is a unifying Hindu philosophy in which birth, life, and death are all passing events in an eternal cycle of births and rebirths. The Hindu's ultimate goal is to attain moksha, or liberation from the samsara cycle. This is achieved by following a sacred code of conduct (dharma), including certain prayers and worship rituals, and behaving in a moral way to oneself, the family, and society.

- Hindus attach great importance to purity and freedom of pollution. These principles affect food preparations, social relationships, and spiritual well-being.

- The caste system divides the Hindu population into four major divisions: Brahmins (priests, professionals), Kshatriyas (rulers, administrators, soldiers), Vaishyas (peasant farmers, merchants), and Shudras (artisans). Caste affects many aspects of daily behavior, including marriage partners, food consumption, and social duties and obligations. Beneath these castes are the "untouchables," who historically have performed "unclean tasks" and who live in separate communities away from those who had "clean jobs." Hindus believe they can be polluted by lower castes if they are close to them, eat food prepared by them, or drink from the same well. The great reformer Mahatma Ghandhi renamed them *Harijans* (children of God). Today this group prefers to be called the *dalits* (depressed). The caste system has slowly broken down in the urban centers of modern

If I were asked under what sky the human mind has most deeply pondered over the greatest problems of life, and found solutions to some of them . . . I should point to India.

—Max Muller, 19th-century Orientalist

High thinking is inconsistent with a complicated material life based on high speed.

—Mohandas K. (Mahatma) Gandhi, 20th-century Hindu spiritual leader

India never confused democracy with egalitarianism.

—Huston Smith, religious scholar

India, and discrimination against the untouchables was officially outlawed in 1950. Some affirmative-action policies to reserve jobs and to provide educational opportunities for the *dalits* have been enacted. Still, caste discrimination is extensive in rural India where 70 percent of the population resides and where there are 3000 unofficial caste divisions.

- Hinduism places considerable emphasis on the family unit, looking after members in adverse circumstances, and sharing resources in good times.

Hinduism is a key factor in understanding India, its socially stratified environment, its orderliness, its eating habits, its duties, and the fatalistic lifestyles of much of its population. As noted earlier, its impact on daily life, particularly in rural sectors, is pervasive.

Shinto: Japan's state religion.[9] Shinto means: "the way of the kami" (gods) and came into being in the sixth century as Japanese national identity asserted itself over the "foreign" religions of Buddhism and Confucianism. Originally, legend dictates that the Japanese islands were formed from the gods Izanagi and Izanami. Their offspring was the sun god Amaterasu whose great grandson became the first emperor. Unlike other Asian-based religions, Shinto has no founder, sacred scriptures, religious philosophy, or explicit moral codes, but it has many deities, rites, shrines, and priests. Shinto is in every way a national religion that permeates everyday behaviors. Between the 1868 Meiji Restoration (which heralded the opening up of Japan to outside influences) and 1945, the religion was reformulated into State Shinto that emphasized the emperor as a kami. Today, Shinto's influence on behaviors are through affirmations of:

THE GLOBAL WEB

Visit the world famous Itsukushima Shrine at
www.hiroshima.cdas.or.jp.miyajima/
english/jinja/annai/annai.htm

- Tradition and the family as supremely important entities

- The love of nature and people's closeness and dependence on it

- Physical cleanliness: One must be clean in the presence of spirits.

- Matsuri: festivals honoring the spirits

Above all, Shinto requires its followers, as children of kami, to be sincere in relationships and to respect the rights of others. Historically, its philosophies have blended with those of Zen Buddhism (meditation, ritual correctness, tea ceremonies, landscapes, martial arts, acupuncture, and poetry), Confucianism (unselfishness, formalities, relationship orientations), and Taoism to produce a nation that is both uniquely Japanese and Asian in cultural outlook.

Monotheistic Religions The roots of single-god religions can be traced back generally to Judaism, from which Islam and Christianity developed; and Zoroastrianism, a set of sixth century B.C. Middle Eastern beliefs that many believe formed the basis of Christianity, including recognition of a single god; distinctions between God and Satan, heaven and hell, and angels and demons; judgment at death; resurrection of the body and life everlasting; and individual freedom to choose between good and evil. A later version (about first century B.C.) recognized a supreme deity (Mithra) who was born on December 25, an event witnessed by shepherds. This religion had congregational worship, and Sunday and December 25 were recognized as holy days.[10]

Judaism began with Abraham and the flight of the Israelites from Egypt. Sarah, Abraham's first wife, bore a son, Isaac, who remained in the Palestine and founded Judaism. Interestingly, Abraham's first son was by Hagar, a black servant, and was named Ishmael. Both were banished to Mecca, where Islam was founded.[11] Though Judaism has just 13 million followers today, its Ten Commandments still constitute the moral foundation for the Western world. Judaism is also unique in that it embodies a political entity (Israel), a language (Hebrew), and a culture, as well as a set of religious beliefs. Jews worldwide have been active participants in commerce and are bound together by a common destiny, purpose, and responsibility toward one another, much of it brought about by numerous persecutions by the Romans (up to A.D. 300), by the Europeans (fourteenth to seventeenth centuries), and the Nazis (twentieth-century Holocaust).

Christianity is the major religion in the low- and medium- context regions of North America and Western Europe, and worldwide numbers about 2 billion people. It comprises three main branches: Roman Catholicism (about 970 million followers), Protestantism (nearly 400 million), and Eastern Orthodoxy (over 200 million members). Of the major religions, Christianity has been perhaps the most adaptable to industrial societies, allowing commercial pursuits to coexist with (and sometimes supercede) spiritual concerns.

Historically, Christianity grew out of Judaism, and its sacred teachings spring both from the Jewish Old Testament and from the New Testament of the Bible, which records the life and teachings of Jesus. Most Christians believe that Jesus is God incarnate, sent to the world to enable people to gain salvation by repentance of their sins. As in Judaism, the Ten Commandments form the basis of moral law for Christianity. While in-depth discussions of the various Christian faiths goes beyond the confines of international business texts,[12] the link between Protestantism and capitalism is interesting. Martin Luther's sixteenth-century break with dominant Roman Catholic doctrines initiated a relationship between religion and commerce that became known as the *Protestant work ethic*. Developed also through the works of John Calvin, this Protestant philosophy emphasized that:[13]

- Protestants could approach God directly, that is, without the mediating influences of the Virgin Mary, ministers, or priests. This indirectly undermined the role of the church as the primary religious connection to God.

- Protestantism blurred distinctions between the secular and the religious life. Luther's thesis was that "*All* of life is a calling." Proper performance of secular actions was a religious obligation: "God accomplishes all things through you. Through you He milks the cow." This philosophy emphasized the individual rather than the church as the center of religious devotion.

- Calvinism emphasized that certain people were predestined to salvation and that productivity and income were signs of God's approval that individuals were predestined to be saved.

> Going to church doesn't make you a Christian any more than going to a garage makes you a mechanic.
>
> *—Laurence J. Peter, 20th-century U.S. author*

- Industry and frugality were part of the Protestant doctrine of asceticism. Therefore, accumulation of assets was encouraged. But Wesley noted: "after you have gained all you can and saved all you can, spend not one pound, one shilling or one penny to gratify either the desire of the flesh, the desire of the eyes, or the pride of life, or for any other end than to please and glorify God."

Whether Protestantism promoted capitalism or capitalism encouraged Protestantism, or whether both developed independently of each other, is a matter for philosophical debate. A distinguishing point between Christianity and other religions, however, has been its flexibility (particularly in Protestantism) in modifying religious practices in accordance with societal changes.[14] Other religions, as will be noted, have been more resistant to change.

Islam is the religion of Muslims. It dates back to the early seventh century A.D. and was established during the lifetime of the prophet Muhammad. It is practiced in about thirty countries, mainly in North Africa, the Middle East, and Asia, and has about 1.2 billion adherents. Indonesia has the largest Muslim population of any nation in the world, with almost 200 million worshipers. Islam is split into two major groups, the Sunnis (about 85 percent) and the Shi'ahs or Shi'ites (about 15 percent). In the Sunni branch, the lineage from the prophet Muhammad is passed down through hereditary rulers (kings, shahs, emirs). In Shi'ite countries, religious leaders are identified through their knowledge and practice of Islamic teachings (e.g., ayatollahs: "Reflections of God").

The major precept of Islam is submission to the will of Allah (Islam means "to submit"). Its primary text is the Qur'ān, which contains the divine revelations of the prophet Muhammad. The Qur'ān is the source of the various legal and social codes that constitute Islamic law. These codes are strict, and Muslims typically do not eat pork, drink alcohol, or smoke. In the strictest Islamic societies—such as Libya—there are no nightclubs, bars, or casinos.

Muslims have five main duties:

1. To profess the faith, that there is no God but Allah, and Muhammad is the prophet of Allah

2. To pray five times each day at specific times, no matter where one is

3. To abstain from food, drink, and worldly pleasures from dawn until dusk during the month of Ramadan

4. To give to the poor: Because Muhammad was himself an orphan, the Muslim faith dictates that all followers should give 2.5 percent of their annual incomes to the poor, a practice known as "Zakaat."

5. To make a pilgrimage (the Hajj) to the prophet Muhammad's birthplace, Mecca: Every able-bodied Muslim is encouraged to make at least one trip in his or her lifetime to Mecca in Saudi Arabia.

Islam dictates not only religious behavior but also social etiquette. Islamic societies are male-dominated. In Shi'ite countries (for example, Iran), women must cover themselves from head to foot and wear veils outside of their houses. In Saudi Arabia, women are not allowed to drive cars. Westerners doing business in Muslim countries must be aware that adherence to Islamic customs is mandatory, not to be compromised in any way (a cultural imperative). As such, marketing and operating strategies must accommodate the needs of Islamic traditions.

Islamic societies and cultural change: In the latter half of the twentieth century, Islamic countries have come into increasing contact with Western ideas and lifestyles. There have been three reactions to this cultural encroachment. First, some fundamentalist countries (such as Iran, Libya, Pakistan, Afghanistan, and Algeria) have at various times reacted strongly against Western intrusions and have imposed a total Islamic way of life on their citizens. This has been possible because Muslim philosophies embrace not only political and religious institutions (theocracies), but also dictate legal and social conventions through Islamic law and customs. Second, other nations (such as Turkey and Tunisia), have separated politics and religion and have embraced Western culture. Third, between these positions, some predominantly Sunni countries in the Middle East (Saudi Arabia, Egypt, Kuwait, etc.) have preserved their Islamic institutions but have accommodated selective aspects of Western lifestyles.[15]

Non-Theistic Religions Not all religions have gods as the focal points of their existences. In particular, East Asia is the home of three major religious philosophies: Buddhism, Confucianism, and Taoism. The influence of these religions cannot be measured, for example, through attendance at religious shrines or places of worship. Rather, their influences are measured through their impacts on their followers: their worldly philosophies, behaviors, values, and attitudes.

Buddhism was founded in the early sixth century B.C. by Siddhartha Gautama, a member of a wealthy warrior caste family in India. His search for spiritual enlightenment took him from his early self-indulgent lifestyle to one of self-mortification, where he denied himself all worldly pleasures and nearly starved himself to death. After much meditation, he became the "Buddha" (the enlightened one) and achieved an understanding of life based on the "Four Noble Truths":

1. Everything in life is suffering and sorrow.

2. The cause of suffering and sorrow is desire and attachment to worldly goods and goals, which bring disappointment, more sorrow, and more desire.

3. The way to end pain is to avoid desire.

4. The way to reach this end is to follow a Middle Way that falls between self-indulgence and self-mortification. It is called the Eightfold Path and is like a staircase with eight steps: right knowledge, right purpose, right speech, right action, right living, right effort, right thinking, and right meditation. This path leads to nirvana—total release from selfish cravings and

> Great men are they that see that the spiritual is stronger than any material force.
>
> —*Ralph Waldo Emerson, 19th-century American essayist*

desires and the achievement of release from the cycle of rebirths, a major precept of Hinduism, whence Buddhism came originally.

Today, Buddhism has over 400 million official adherents, though those influenced by Buddhist teaching (including China and Japan) are estimated at between 1–2 billion. Buddhism is split into two major groups, the Theravada and the Mahayana sects. Among some of the faster-growing Asian economies in the world (Japan, Hong Kong, Korea, Singapore, and Taiwan), Mahayana Buddhism is a major, and often dominant, religion. It emphasizes compassion, accessibility to the masses, and compatibility with outside influences. Theravada Buddhism is the stricter of the two sects, and it is strong in Sri Lanka and in the Southeast Asian nations of Vietnam, Laos, Cambodia, Burma, and Thailand. Theravada Buddhism—like Hinduism—stresses orderly societies and traditional class structures; heredity has a major role in determining social status and promoting strong family ties.

The central Buddhist philosophy emphasizes calmness, wisdom, and compassion. Buddhist movements worldwide have been associated with ecology, reforestation, animal rights, civil rights, hospice, and self-help movements.[16] Buddhism's emphasis on the spiritual rather than material aspects of life have perhaps contributed to the slow pace of economic development in countries such as Burma (Myanmar), Laos, Sri Lanka, and Thailand, though Japan's full-employment policy has been linked to Buddhist preaching that crime and immorality result from economic poverty.[17] Zen Buddhism, which is common in Japan, emphasizes meditation and ritual correctness and finds expression in the tea ceremony, ink landscapes, martial arts, and poetic imagery (e.g., the Haikus of Japanese poet Matsuo Basho: "a frog leaps in, the sound of water").

Confucianism: Confucius was born in China in 551 B.C. and died in 479 B.C. Respected but unappreciated while he lived, Confucius left a legacy that has led experts to call him "probably the greatest and most influential thinker in Chinese history";[18] and "the greatest single intellectual force among one quarter of the world's population."[19] His doctrine emphasized relationships between people and the creation of a harmonious and moral society. Confucianism is based on five ideals.

> As a solid rock is not affected by a strong gale, so strong persons are unaffected by praise or criticism.
>
> —*Siddhartha Gautama, the Buddha*

THE GLOBAL WEB

Experience a little Zen meditation at
www.do-not-zzz.com

- Jen: The ideal relationship between individuals is based on benevolence, humaneness, and love. People should be courteous, unselfish, and sympathetic in their dealings with others.

- Chun Tzu: The goal of individuals is to become the "ideal host" who devotes efforts to putting others at ease and becoming the "superior person."

- Li: The way things should be done: (1) appropriate titles and proper behaviors, (2) the doctrine of the mean—achieving harmony and balance between extremes, especially behaviors, (3) five constant relationships, between parent and child, husband and wife, elder and younger siblings, elder and junior friend, and ruler and subject, (4) the importance of respect for the family, and (5) for age (seniority). Li defined a pattern of respect and obedience that is still apparent in today's China and throughout much of Asia. The concepts of jen, chun tzu, and li form the basis of the Chinese (and Asian) "guanxi" system that commits family, friends, and associates to do what they can for each other and to reciprocate favors. Failure to do so results in loss of reputation ("face") and honor.

- Te: Rulers and those in authority should be obeyed, but leaders should merit the cooperation of their followers by demonstrating respect for them and a sincere devotion to the common good.

- Wen: The Arts of Peace; Confucius taught that ultimate victory went to the nation that demonstrated the highest culture (art, poetry, philosophy, architecture, etc.).

The effects of Confucianism have been profound. For 2,500 years, the Confucian classics were essential reading for Chinese politicians and civil servants. The respect that Chinese and Asians show each other daily is testament to this influence, as is Confucius' Golden Rule: "What you do not wish done to yourself, do not do unto others." Through such principles and beliefs, Confucianism has exerted tremendous influence on Asian values and behaviors.

Taoism (pronounced Daoism) is the philosophy of Lao-Tzu.[20] Similar to Confucianism (and founded at about the same time), Taoism has left an indelible imprint on Chinese and Asian mindsets. Embodied in Lao-Tzu's great work *Tao Te Ching* (*The Way and Its Power,* a book of only about 5,000 words), Taoist philosophies decreed that:

- Individuals should act in harmony with nature and not interfere with the forces of nature. This sets it apart from Western views that regard nature as an antagonist—to be controlled, dominated, and conquered. Taoism is said to have inspired the architectural achievements of Frank Lloyd Wright, and today it guides architects in Asia through Feng Shui, a philosophy that seeks to harmonize building construction with the natural environment.

- Taoists reject all forms of self-assertiveness and competition ("wu wei"—actionless action) and minimize energies "wasted" on desire, revulsion, grief, joy, delight, and annoyance. This is reflected in the Eastern stoicism (emotional calmness) found in today's Asia. Taoists preserve life's vital energies through diet, breathing exercises, meditation (to "empty the mind"), the martial arts, and acupuncture.

- Lao-Tzu was interested in the opposites of nature, reflected in his Chiao (relativity) principle and popularized under the yin-yang philosophy. Good-evil, masculine-feminine, right-wrong are viewed not as opposites (the Western view), but as complementary forces—one is meaningless without the other.

> The superior man does what is right, the small man what is profitable.
>
> The superior man thinks of others, the small man thinks of himself.
>
> The superior man accepts his lot calmly, the small man complains about everything.
>
> —*Confucian analects (sayings)*

> If there is righteousness in the heart, there will be beauty in the character. If there is beauty in the character, there will be harmony in the home. If there is harmony in the home, there will be order in the nation. When there is order in the nation, there is peace in the world.
>
> —*Chinese proverb*

Impact of Religion on Societal Behaviors The impact of religion on societal behaviors can be usefully divided into two parts: effects on low-context Western societies and the impacts of religion on high-context emerging and Eastern societies. In Western societies, secularization (or the loss of religious influence) dates back to the Age of Enlightenment in the eighteenth century when technology and industrialization first impacted Western Europe. Protestantism and capitalism are linked, in that hard work, the accumulation of assets, and thriftiness thrive under market-force conditions. Latin America (and Brazil in particular) has seen a steady stream of conversions from Catholicism to Protestantism since the 1960s. Some have attributed the 1980s and 1990s rapid economic development of the region to the Protestant upsurge.[21]

High-context behaviors emphasizing trustworthiness, interpersonal sociability, and societal stability have their origins in religions emphasizing a sense of community, family unity, and nonmaterial orientations. Eastern religions such as Hinduism, Buddhism, Confucianism, and Taoism, in particular, emphasize human virtues: humility, character, veracity (truthfulness), the ability to see things as they are (free from subjective distortions). These are all human traits that become warped under the pressures of competitive societies, where greed, envy, and delusions become acceptable human characteristics.[22] Hindu, Islamic, and Buddhist religions emphasize the spiritual aspects of life over all others, including commercial pursuits. In these societies, it is difficult for materialist needs to take hold (as they have in the West). Similarly, religious emphases on the family unit hinders labor mobility in pursuit of commercial opportunities, and resources are expended to support extended families rather than create demand for conspicuous consumption products.

From a societal perspective, religion serves as a "sacred canopy" shielding traditional societies from the discontinuities associated with a rapidly changing world. In rural parts of Asia, Africa, the Middle East, and Latin America, religion provides a reassuring link with the past that is idealized as "glorious, meaningful, without evil and enjoying supernatural approval." For communities, it provides a sense of identity and community that contributes to the strength, purpose and meaning of societies.[23]

> Science has not found a substitute for God.
>
> —*Henry Drummond*

Religion and change: In Islamic societies, Muslims lead God-centered lives, with religion as the centerpiece of political and legal systems. In Sunni traditions, the king, or shah is the spiritual as well as the political leader. Industrialization, secularization, and social change can threaten existing political, religious, and legal institutions. International companies tread warily in Muslim societies, with their strict conformance to religious traditions as the cornerstones of localized strategies.

Economic change and development have had some effects on specific religions. Mahayanan Buddhism is prevalent in societies influenced by Western cultures. Its fundamentalist counterpart, the Theravada philosophy, dominates in nations with less exposure to Western lifestyles. Similarly, Sunni Muslims have had more interactions with the West (through oil and commerce) than their fundamentalist Shi'ite counterparts.

Economic- and Political-System Effects

Industrialization and economic development embodies shifts from traditional communistic-based village societies to modern market forces-based economies and moves from autarchies (kings, chiefs, shahs, dictators, presidents-for-life, etc.) to democracies. In practice, the diffusion of competitive political processes and capitalist systems takes time and encounters significant resistance. As a result, mainstream high-context behaviors clash with competition-based low-context behaviors encountered in many international corporations.

The roots of high-context behaviors can be found in religious values (as discussed previously) and in traditional economic systems. Tradition-based economies are to be found in less-developed countries and in rural sectors of industrialized nations, where the full forces of competitive institutions and lifestyles have not yet materialized. In tradition-based economies and sectors, isolated villages and regional economies exhibit high-context behaviors as producers, merchants, distributors, and retailers trade in relatively stable economies. Business people live in close proximity to each other, and social dealings are naturally intertwined with commerce. The structure of traditional communities affords little duplication of business activities (one general store, single, specialized producers of everyday products), but social pressures prohibit excessive profit-taking, and exploitation is viewed as a highly antisocial behavior. In these circumstances, legal recourse in a business dispute is serious and occurs only as a last resort. Community orientation tends to be high, as individual prospects are closely related to the community as a whole. When adversity occurs, the community shelters the individual. When there are good times, surpluses are shared.

In most cases, as countries industrialize, competitive low-context behaviors diffuse from developed urban centers into rural parts (often taking decades or generations). Where governments limit or control outside influences, traditional high-context behaviors can remain the norm throughout industrialization. Such is the case of Japan where:

- Full employment rather than profit remains a primary concern of Japanese businesses.

- Lawyers are rarely used: there are 14,000 lawyers in Japan for 120 million people against about 1,000,000 in the U.S. for 280 million people.

- Price competition is rare, even though price levels are considerably higher in Japan than in other major industrialized economies.

- The benefits of high prices are distributed back to employees through bonuses and, in channels, large rebates from manufacturers to channel members. Only in Japan are prices likely to rise during recessions to maintain bonuses on decreased output.

- The interconnected nature of keiretzus (or industrial combines) insulates individual companies from excessively competitive behaviors and shelters them under corporate umbrellas.[24]

Western European nations have historically been mixtures of capitalist and socialist influences (though this is changing as the region becomes more market forces-oriented). The mixed-economy philosophy reflects the region's historic evolution. Western Europe from the 1850s to the onset of World War I in 1914 was highly capitalist. However, the 1920s and 1930s global depression demonstrated the disadvantages of capitalism, and, after 1945, European governments created extensive social-welfare systems to shield citizens from marketplace-dictated downturns. Industries vital to the national interest were nationalized. Competition in the social hierarchy remained muted as aristocracies and monarchies retained privileges and mobility among social classes remained limited. Swings between right- and left-wing governments since 1945 reflect the love-hate relationship Europeans have toward unbridled capitalism.

Social Forces

Social forces comprise two mainstream cultural components—*social class* and *education*. Social class has major effects on everyday behaviors. Where social-class systems are based on income and wealth, there are incentives to build up economic resources and move up the social hierarchy. The fluid nature of economically based systems makes social competitiveness a key feature of such societies ("who has the most toys"). In contrast, rigid hereditary systems stunt individual efforts to progress socially. Family name and pedigree count. Disrespect to those of higher social class standing is problematic, and social competitiveness is not encouraged (e.g., "old money" versus "nouveau riche" rivalries).

Education affects attitudes toward economic development and impacts individual movements among social classes (social mobility) in many societies. In industrialized countries, education contributes to income-earning potential. In developing countries, education is a major means of social improvement, and educational credentials are respected. The contribution of the educational system to economic development is important on two accounts. First, a nation's technological orientation determines the value placed on scientific and engineering achievement. Some countries, notably Germany, France, and Japan, emphasize science, mathematics, and technology. Nations that emphasize the arts, history, and the humanities tend to be less forward-looking (e.g., Middle Eastern countries with religion-based education systems). Second, national orientations toward education is a factor. Years of compulsory education, high school and university education availability, and, in developing countries, rural education facilities are all key factors in the buildup of national workforces and human capital resources.

Overall, high-low-context societies differ in their acceptance of competition. The low-context nations are often those that have competitive political systems (democracies), economic systems (capitalism), social-class systems, and educational systems. High-context societies tend to be less competitive on these dimensions, with elitism (family pedigree) heavily influencing political, economic, social, and educational opportunities.

INTERCULTURAL NEGOTIATIONS

Intercultural differences are most apparent during face-to-face negotiations. We refine the high, medium, and low context positions as we look at negotiating habits in various parts of the world. Most business transactions require some negotiations, and in international contexts, the face-to-face exchange of ideas and viewpoints is best achieved when both parties understand each other, because, although both parties share common goals in negotiation—to reach mutually acceptable agreements—how they achieve those goals often differs. Empathy, the ability to put oneself in another's shoes, is a distinguishing trait of effective intercultural negotiators.

Successful negotiating requires that participants know not only their own strengths and weaknesses, but also those of the other side. Knowledge about how others negotiate, therefore, becomes a key issue in reaching mutually acceptable agreements and, as importantly, establishing the rapport necessary to sustain long-term relationships.

Negotiating with U.S. Business People

U.S. business people belong to low-context cultures in which they are used to business dealings being conducted objectively, efficiently, and competitively. To maintain this sort of negotiating posture, Americans prefer informality (to minimize time-wasting formalities) and rationality (to keep personal opinions from playing critical roles in decisions). Americans also come from an economy driven by market forces, so they are competitive and generally use persuasive tactics and power overtly. Detailed contracts define commercial relationships, and lawyers are often key members of negotiating teams. Their decision making is individualized, though subordinates often provide key inputs (such as figures on sales, costs, and competitive analyses).

> Big print giveth and the small print taketh away.
>
> —*Bishop Fulton J. Sheen, U.S. clergyman*

Negotiating with the Japanese

The Japanese are archetypal high-context negotiators. Thus, their negotiation strategies are significantly different from the lower-context European and U.S. styles. Japanese society emphasizes harmony, cooperation, conformism, and long-term business perspectives. As such, the Japanese prefer personal trust rather than legal contracts as the basis for business relationships. In order to build trust with prospective partners, the Japanese want to know all about them—not just the product line, prices, and terms of sale and delivery, but all about the foreign company, its history, and its personnel. Their ultimate aim is to find out if foreign companies and their personnel have "integrity" or "inner worth." In short, are they worth doing business with? Is it worth spending the time to establish relationships with this firm? Successful negotiations require foreigners to understand Japanese views on sociability, use of lawyers and contracts, patience, business orientations, and negotiating habits.

Sociability When and how to get on good social relations with the Japanese requires patience and skill. It is true that sociability helps to move negotiations along, but when to become sociable is an issue. Some cultures, notably North American, attempt to get on a first-name basis early in order to create a relaxed atmosphere for the negotiations. This can cause problems in Japan where preliminary meetings are formal. Business cards are exchanged (a ritual in Japan), titles and pecking orders are made known, and negotiation procedures are established.

The situation changes once the day's negotiations are ended. Most foreigners go back to their hotels, dine, and prepare for the next day's negotiations. But at this point their Japanese counterparts are ready to socialize. After-hours drinking (largely subsidized by lavish entertainment budgets) is part of Japanese business etiquette. This is where the Japanese establish social rapport and put business relationships on a firm footing. The practice often makes Americans in particular uncomfortable because they are not used to mixing business with pleasure. In the United States, preferred business relationships are at arm's length, so that, if competitive pressures arise, there are no personal discomforts in terminating relationships. The Japanese objective is just the opposite. The Japanese build up personal elements in order to buffer the commercial relationship against unforeseen circumstances.

Use of Lawyers In competitive markets, laws are the major constraints on personal and company behaviors. In Japan (and other parts of the world), social codes take precedence over laws as the major determinants of societal behavior. These codes govern and spell out "acceptable" behaviors. The Japanese accept and conform to these codes, and lawyers and litigation are looked upon as "last resorts" (not as the first resort, as in some countries). So strong is the Japanese dislike of litigation that just having a lawyer present during the negotiation may cause the Japanese to view the foreign team with suspicion.

Patience Patience is a sign of strength in the East (and in many other parts of the world). But, in efficiency-oriented societies, it is often viewed as a weakness (time-wasting). Negotiators new to Japan may want to fly in, negotiate, sign a contract or agreement, and then move on. Experienced international executives know that this is generally not possible in Japan. The preliminary "getting to know you and your company" sessions take time. Presentations of business proposals are best paced to Japanese needs—slow, with many handouts and deviations from the plan. Fast-paced, brass-tacks presentations are often viewed as insincere.

Patience is also required in the post-presentation phase as the Japanese debate the proposed package and build a consensus among their decision makers. In many foreign companies, important decisions are made by top management and are made quickly. Implementation, however, takes a long time. In Japan, important decisions take time, but once made, they are quickly implemented.

Business Orientation Business orientation differences become apparent as negotiations move forward. Many foreign business people have but one motive—profits or profit maximization. Low profits cause stock prices to fall and precipitate takeovers or top management shake-ups. Japanese managers have no such concerns; their corporate financial structures are largely based on debt rather than equity, and their major obligations are to banks, not to shareholders. Once Japanese managers have satisfied the banks' interest, they pursue whatever objectives suit them. Primary Japanese concerns are to maintain employment and market share. This nonprofit maximizing perspective can cause problems in planning, goal setting, and strategy formulation. The Japanese, because they have few short-term-profit pressures, focus more easily on medium-term and long-term planning than do most foreign companies. Thus, during negotiations, while the foreign company is focusing on short-term objectives with profits as the primary benchmarks, while the Japanese are planning strategies over 3-, 5-, or 10-year periods.

Sequencing Negotiating Points Efficiency-oriented negotiating styles cause some business people (especially in the U.S.) to take up one point at a time, negotiate it, finish it, and go on to the next item. The Japanese, however, prefer to initiate discussions on a number of points, talking around and through topics, and then summarize the major points agreed upon at the end of the day, often in "letters of understanding."

Reaching an Impasse There comes a time in most negotiations when both parties disagree. In Japan, talking through disagreements is rare. The Japanese avoid open conflicts *at all costs*. Alert negotiators know that when negotiating problems occur, the Japanese become evasive and less communicative. At this point, a respected third party, or go-between, arbitrates between the two groups. Such people, often bankers or financiers, use shuttle diplomacy, moving between the two parties, comparing and modifying each group's position until a compromise is reached.

> The go-between wears a thousand sandals.
>
> —*Japanese proverb*

Use of Power In most negotiations, one company is clearly bigger and more powerful than the other. In highly competitive economies, "might is right" and power is recognized overtly and often is used to force concessions. In Japan, power is subtle—it is there but needs no display. In international situations generally, it is wise to avoid power plays. If companies perceive they are being bullied, or pressured, problems arise and relationships are undermined.

> Wise men talk when they have something to say; fools, because they have to say something.
>
> —*Plato, 4th-century* B.C. *Greek philosopher*

Silence Moments of silence frequently occur in negotiations with the Japanese, who are, by nature, patient people. Efficiency-oriented negotiators often have low tolerances for silence, and often fill the void by over-elaborating on details, volunteering additional information, or making concessions. In the Japanese case, what makes their silence unnerving is that it often alternates with frenzied conversations, as points of negotiating interest warrant instant conferrals.

Renegotiating The Japanese often like to renegotiate points. This preference tends to annoy time-conscious negotiators. This usually occurs when current negotiating points affect previously agreed-upon items, but occasionally to demonstrate good faith. Tolerance is necessary. Often renegotiations result in little or no change.

> If you understand everything, you must be misinformed.
>
> —*Japanese proverb*

Negotiating with Latin Americans

Latin Americans are generally more outgoing and more emotional than most other peoples. As Table 12.2 shows, Americans try to keep emotions out of business, while the Japanese suppress them in formal situations. But in Central and South America, emotions permeate everyday life and are part of the business and

TABLE 12.2
Japanese, North American, and Latin American Negotiation Styles

Japanese	North American	Latin American
Emotional sensitivity highly valued	Emotional sensitivity not highly valued	Emotional sensitivity valued
Hiding of emotions	Dealing straightforwardly or impersonally	Emotionally passionate
Subtle power plays; conciliation	Use of power legitimate and often overt	Great power plays; use of weakness
Loyalty to employer; employer takes care of its employees	Lack of commitment to employer; breaking of ties by either if necessary	Loyalty to employer (who is often family)
Decision making through group consensus	Teamwork provides input to a decision maker	Decisions come down from one individual
Face-saving is crucial; decisions often made on basis of saving someone from embarrassment	Decisions made on a cost benefit basis; face-saving does not always matter	Face-saving is crucial in decision making to preserve honor, dignity
Decision makers openly influenced by special interests	Decision makers influenced by special interests but often not considered ethical	Execution of special interests of decision maker expected, condoned
Not argumentative; quiet when right	Argumentative when right or wrong, but impersonal	Argumentative when right or wrong; passionate
What is down in writing must be accurate and valid	Great importance given to documentation as evidential proof	Impatient with documentation as obstacle to understanding general principles
Step-by-step approach to decision making	Methodically organized decision making	Impulsive, spontaneous decision making
Good of group is the ultimate aim	Profit motive or good of individual ultimate aim	What is good for the group is good for the individual
Cultivate a good emotional social setting for decision making; get to know decision makers	Decision making impersonal; avoid involvements, conflict of interest	Personal touch is necessary for good decision making

Source: Reprinted from Casse, Pierre. *Training for the Multicultural Manger: A Practical and Cross-Cultural Approach to the Management of People.* Washington, D.C.: Society for Intercultural Education, Training and Research, 1982. Used with permission.

negotiation processes. Overt disagreements are not avoided (as with the Japanese), and "sociable" disagreements often occur as inconsequential items are "over-negotiated." Insight and experience are needed to distinguish "sociable" debates from serious disagreements. On the surface, both appear to be similar.

Other negotiating tips to remember when in Latin America include the following.

Little or No Mixing of Business with Pleasure North Americans in particular are always "on the job." They like "business breakfasts" and "working lunches," and often, when abroad, they are "never off duty." Latin Americans make sharp distinctions between work and play. Hence, it is often difficult to talk business over lunch. Eating occasions in Latin settings are usually social times, and conversations about family, history, and current affairs occur as parts of the "getting to know you" routine.

Tomorrow is often the busiest day of the week.

—Spanish proverb

The Relative Unimportance of Work In Japan, work is the focal point of an individual's life, and in the United States, work is a major part. But, in Latin America, "one works to live, one does not live to work." Work tasks may be put off or made subordinate to family and other social pleasures, and nepotism (hiring relatives or friends) is often an accepted part of business. Social bonds play important roles in getting and keeping business. In common with the Japanese, Latin

Americans like to know with whom they are dealing, and personal friendships and mutual trust are often the difference between doing and not doing business.

Recognizing Social and Ethnic Distinctions, the "Patron" Latin Americans in general recognize social distinctions (though this is slowly changing). Lighter-skinned groups are, for better or for worse, thought of as "socially superior" to their darker-skinned compatriots. "Respect" is accorded to those in positions of power. The patron is "in charge" and makes major decisions, often unilaterally, without subordinate input.

Negotiating with Western Europeans

Culturally, Western Europeans tend to fall into medium- or low-context categories. The British, French, Spanish, Italians, Portuguese, Dutch, and Belgians are medium-context, and the Germans, Swiss, and Scandinavians tend to be more low-context. Low-context Europeans emphasize objectivity in business dealings, focusing on contracts, "plain talking," and efficiency. Medium-context Europeans (especially the French, Spanish, Italians, and Portuguese, and, to a lesser extent, the British and Dutch) place more emphasis on personal relationships and trust, shying away from confrontations. Because low-context behaviors have been discussed under U.S. negotiating, the following discussion focuses on the medium-context countries.

Procedures Europeans are fond of procedures and guidelines, but, unlike Americans, they observe them not for efficiency's sake, but to give structure to business dealings. Agendas and protocols are established early on to ensure smooth negotiations and to confirm the meeting's purposes.

Titles The formal exchanges of titles, positions, and functions are protocols most Europeans observe (though it is less obtrusive in Scandinavia). Introductions, with titles, establish initial pecking orders within negotiating teams. Generally, formal barriers are broken down quickly (although more slowly among the Germans and Swiss), and sociability is substituted.

Negotiating Sequence Like the Japanese, Europeans generally recognize the interrelatedness of problems and the difficulty of focusing on isolated negotiating points. Thus, several points are often negotiated simultaneously. Negotiations in Europe tend to be shorter than in Japan but longer than in the United States

Legal Contracts Europeans use legal contracts to summarize major areas of agreement. Because trust is important, "water-tight" contracts may be viewed with suspicion.

Negotiating Postures In meetings medium-context Europeans can be viewed as elusive. E. R. Eggers notes the following French-American contrasts, many of which apply to other Europeans as well.[25]

> *The first thing we do, let's kill all the lawyers.*
>
> —*William Shakespeare, 16th-century English playwright*

  1. Americans think in a straight line; the French think in a circle. Americans mistrust complicated things and try to oversimplify;

the French mistrust simple things and overcomplicate. French negotiators spend time defining the problem, whereas Americans devote their energies to solving them.

2. The French mistrust items in which Americans have the most confidence—income statements (because in France the purpose is not to show how much money has been made, but to demonstrate to the government how little has been made), the telephone (the French believe important business should be conducted face-to-face, so that proposal makers can be evaluated along with their proposals), the law, and the press (what is laid out in formal print is not necessarily true and certainly not sacrosanct).

3. American executives tend to forget what they wrote in a letter; French executives remember what they left out. In correspondence, Americans include lots of details, and the French purposely leave them out.

4. Small is beautiful. The French and Europeans generally believe that small companies can be as efficient as large ones, mass-production goods are inferior to custom-made products, and planning processes consist of many smaller plans.

5. Life's pleasures to the French are nondurable pleasures such as eating and vacations. To Americans, they are tangible items, such as houses and automobiles.

Overall, medium-context Europeans are probably closer to the Japanese in negotiating style and technique than they are to the Americans. They have confidence in people rather than in "cold" facts and figures; they are less profit conscious (though this is changing). They negotiate with more flair and are hard to pin down on crucial points. There are also a number of country-specific characteristics.

- *Italians* are capable of the same dramatic flair as Latin Americans. They tend to be conscious of their external image and the impressions they create *(bella figura)*. They use emotional arguments well, and, similar to the French, enjoy negotiating as an intellectual exercise. They can be hard to pin down on specific points, and Italian negotiating styles can vary from being very obliging *(simpatico)* to abrasive. Presentations made to Italians should be elegant, organized, clear, and exact. Style and appearances are important, and patron-like autocratic decision making is often the norm.

Other European negotiating stances more directly reflect their low- and medium-context cultural designations.[26]

- *Dutch and German* business people are competitive negotiators. German executives in particular are technically oriented, disciplined, and orderly. Presentations can be direct and factual without giving offense. Similarly, Dutch and Germans do not emphasize the personal side of business relationships, unlike southern Europeans; commerce and social aspects are usually separated. But like many Europeans, they are suspicious of overbearing profit orientations.

- The *British* conduct business in an orderly and proper manner. They are polite but usually reserved, especially at first. They are uncomfortable when faced with openly ambitious or aggressive counterparts. Similarly, the British rarely emphasize superior finances or market positions. They consistently understate things and have a subtle and indirect mode of speech that demands attention and sensitivity from listeners.

- *Spanish* business negotiations require patience. Friendship is an important part of business relationships, which are assiduously cultivated over long lunch sessions, with little or no business being discussed.

- *Greek* negotiators are in many ways similar to negotiating with the French. Personal relationships are very important, whether at the family, business, or political level. Candor is appreciated, though it is best wrapped in silvery-tongued oratory. Finally, Greeks regard contracts as evolutionary, not limited to written contractual specifications. Additional obligations, under the spirit of the relationship (but outside of the written agreement), may be required. Similarly, it should be understood that unanticipated circumstances may force deviations from contractual obligations.

Negotiating with Asians

While it is difficult to generalize over all the eastern and southern Asian countries (often because of differences emanating from their religious outlooks), there are some similarities among these countries. Most are high-context societies, which are largely tradition-based and emphasize personal relationships over written contracts. There are, however, some common elements in their general business practices and attitudes.

- *Respect for the past:* Tradition-based practices are not instantly discarded just because new practices are superior. This respect for time-honored traditions makes change difficult. People considerations in particular are major factors in organizational change. Employees tend to be viewed as human capital assets rather than expense sheet items. This makes downsizing efforts difficult to implement, making them last, rather than first, resorts in business restructuring decisions.

- *Importance of the family:* Family-run businesses dominate in developing countries, and their commercial motives often differ from those of large Western organizations. Hiring preference is routinely given to family, relatives, and friends, and the profit motive, while present, often is tempered by other considerations, such as social obligations.

- *Patience and humility:* Asian societies generally stress different personal qualities from those admired in the West. Eastern peoples (perhaps due to Taoist philosophies) value stoicism—not showing outward signs of emotion, especially anger—and the virtues of patience and humility. Aggression and impatience are viewed as immature emotions. Sincerity and integrity are highly valued. Asians, however, are commercial pragmatists, though their attitudes and demeanors, even under adverse conditions, reflect mutual respect and desires for trust and cooperation.

Negotiating with Middle Easterners

Middle Eastern countries, such as Saudi Arabia, Kuwait, Qatar, United Arab Emirates, Iran, and Iraq, share many characteristics. Their peoples are predominantly Arabic speaking; many of these countries are kingdoms and largely Muslim. These last two elements affect business transactions. Exhibit 12-1, "Portrait of an Arab Negotiator," shows similarities to other high-context Asian nations. The Arab mediator resembles the Japanese go-between; both perform similar functions in their negotiating environments. Characteristics of Middle Eastern negotiating patterns are religiously, socially, and personally based.

Conflict situations are avoided at all costs (as in Japan), and much store is set on eloquent and (to outsiders) overly elaborate modes of speech. Respect for both individuals (however menial) and institutions (especially the family) are extremely important. In contrast to Western business people who view the future as controllable and moldable, Muslims believe that human beings only incidentally determine the future and that no one is to blame when things do not work out. Accountability, therefore, is difficult to pin down. For Muslims, events occur "Inshallah": if God wills it.

Social formalities and courtesies based on a hereditary aristocracy are important in most Arabic countries. Many of them are monarchies, and most have cliques of powerful families that control many commercial interests. These families (as in Saudi Arabia) are often royally appointed and command much respect. They are not "just businessmen." The extended family is important in business, with relatives having preference over friends. Profit, while desirable, is but one of many business goals that include maintaining jobs, commercial and social relationships, and corporate prestige.

Time consciousness: Like Latin Americans, Arab businessmen are not as time-conscious as their Western counterparts, because efficiency does not equate with money or status. As in Japan, negotiations take lots of time, with many formalities (tea and coffee drinking especially) occurring before business is discussed.

Negotiating with Eastern Europeans: The Russian Case

While perestroika and glasnost have recast the economic order in the former Soviet Union, Russian negotiating habits, culminating from their core values and beliefs, have been shaped by the region's inhospitable climate and centuries of oppressive, cynical governance.[27] Traditional traits of pessimism and stoicism have made Russians cautious and reticent negotiators, but with a tenacious streak when covering key points. Key characteristics:

- Russian teams tend to be comprised of experienced veterans. They are disciplined and speak with one voice ("the party line").

- They customarily present starting-position draft outlines. Included in these are "throwaway" points that can be used as bargaining chips. Concessions are made point for point ("we'll give you this if you concede that"). Russian negotiators try to yield minor concessions in return for major ones.

- Willingness to compromise without a *quid pro quo* is viewed as a sign of weakness. Russian teams have the discipline to maintain silence (like the Japanese) on key points.

EXHIBIT 12-1
Portrait of an Arab Negotiator

Those Arabs who are Muslim and are involved in negotiation believe in using the traditional way to settle disputes—namely, to use mediators. A successful mediator is someone who:

1. Protects all the parties' honor, self-respect, and dignity

2. Avoids direct confrontations between opponents

3. Is respected and trusted by all

4. Does not put the parties involved in a situation where they have to show weakness or admit defeat

5. Has the necessary prestige to be listened to

6. Is creative enough to come up with honorable solutions for all parties

7. Is impartial and can understand the positions of the various parties without leaning toward one or the other

8. Is able to resist any kind of pressure that the opponents could try to exercise on him ("In sum, the ideal mediator is a man who is in a position, be-

cause of his personality, status, respect, wealth, influence, and so on to create in the litigants the desire to conform with his wishes")

9. Uses references to people who are highly respected by the opponents to persuade them to change their minds on some issues ("Do it for the sake of your father")

10. Can keep secrets and in doing so gains the confidence of the negotiating parties

11. Controls his temper and emotions (or loses it when and where necessary)

12. Can use conferences as mediating devices

13. Knows that the opponents will have problems in carrying out the decisions made during the negotiation

14. Is able to cope with the Arab disregard for time

15. Understands the impact of Islam on the opponents who believe that they possess the truth, follow the Right Path and are going to "win" because their cause is just

Source: Excerpt from Patai, Raphael. *The Arab Mind*. New York: Scribner, 1983. Copyright 1973, 1976, and 1983 by Raphael Patai. Reprinted with permission of Charles Scribner's Sons.

- Russians prefer general agreements with details to be worked out later (unlike Americans and Germans who work out agreements in detail, point by point).

- They view negotiations as they do their national pastime, chess. They argue current points but plan several moves ahead.

- Like the Japanese, relationships can be built up via after-meeting drinking sessions. Building relationships is a major key to creating win-win situations.

- Russians continue to be suspicious about Western profit motives. Sales and accounting figures should be laid out in transparent fashions to reassure them that no advantage is being taken.

ORGANIZING INTERNATIONAL NEGOTIATIONS

All negotiations have increased chances of success when they are properly organized and the participants are both well-prepared and experienced. The following discussion provides some perspectives on the importance of planning, preparation, and conduct during the international negotiations process.

Planning and Preparation

Planning begins with the realization that negotiations are the beginnings of relationships, and where investments are involved, the stakes are high and have long-term consequences. Early planning and thorough preparations are essential, and involve a number of important decisions.

- *Where to negotiate* is the first major decision. Negotiations in foreign markets often require significant travel times, jet-lag, different cuisines, and acclimatization. Negotiating in the domestic market gives the cultural advantage to the home team as the other side has to worry about making appropriate adaptations.

- *Assembling the right team:* The best negotiators are those with significant international experiences who are comfortable dealing with foreign cultures. When traveling abroad, managers from the local country are invaluable because of their cultural knowledge, language capabilities, and contacts. Where investments are contemplated, those likely to be running the local operation should be included to build contacts and relationships. When high-level negotiations involve top foreign managers, the visiting team should have executives of equivalent status. Where negotiations are protracted, efforts should be made to maintain the same team throughout. Finally, though small teams are cost efficient, larger teams command respect and instill a sense of importance to the negotiations.

> Match eagles with eagles.
>
> —*Malaysian proverb*

- *Preparation:* It is impossible to be over-prepared. Traveling teams should take as much information with them as possible, and know as much about the other side as they can. This includes questions to be asked about the foreign company and its situation. Clear objectives should be laid out, including what the foreign firm expects from the negotiation (technology, job creation, societal concerns).

Conducting the Negotiation

- *Relationship building:* Relationships in North America and parts of Western Europe are easily formed (and dissolved). In the high context nations of Latin America, Middle East, and Asia, it takes weeks, months or longer to develop first personal, then business relationships appropriate for long-term dealings.

- *Recognize the power brokers:* In all negotiations, there are decision makers who must be influenced and persuaded. Most times, these executives participate in the negotiations. Other times, there are other influential parties, such as government officials (in China) or trade unions (in Western Europe) whose opinions are important.

- *Showing respect:* Regardless of the relative sizes of the negotiating firms, both should treat the other side with the utmost respect. Arrogance is avoided at all costs.

- *Reading body language:* High-context cultures tend to be very adept at recognizing nonverbal cues. Eyes and facial feature movements signify pleasure, displeasure, surprise, and discomfort. When shown, they indicate sensitivities and possible pressure points in the negotiation process. Eastern stoicism ("poker faced" calmness) gives Asian managers advantages in negotiations with Western managers.

- *Negotiating style:* Low-context cultures tend to have efficient, confrontational negotiating styles. There are often recognizable "winners" and "losers." High-context cultures tend to be slow and deliberate, they take up to two or three times as long to negotiate an agreement. In these parts of the world, "win-win" agreements work best, with no "losers." Conflict and embarrassment are avoided.

Reaching an Agreement

Reaching agreements in high-context cultures take time, as managerial consensus is a lengthy process, plus outside parties (e.g., governments) may need to be consulted. First meetings rarely result in lengthy contractual agreements, and short, general letters of agreement are customary outcomes. High-context cultures regard such agreements as the *beginnings* of a relationship. Often, they signal the *start* (not the end) of serious negotiations. Further, they do not view contract or agreement terms as "written in stone," and may not honor them if circumstances change. Competitive, legalistic low-context business people, however, view contracts as sacrosanct, and prefer long, detailed documents.

Some Conclusions: What Is a Good Negotiator?

What characteristics distinguish successful negotiators from average negotiators? One study of British negotiators offers some insights.[28]

- Both average and successful negotiators spend the same amount of time planning. The difference is in *what* is planned.

- Good negotiators develop twice as many alternatives as less-effective negotiators. This leaves them with more options when negotiations deviate into uncharted waters.

- While the main objective of negotiations is to reduce and reconcile different interests, experienced negotiators spend much more time on areas where there is common ground and agreements are possible, rather than devoting excessive time to topics where obvious differences exist. Experienced negotiators also "nibble away" at differences rather than tackling them head on.

- Skilled negotiators spend more time exploring long-term issues and their effects than do average negotiators. This practice puts companies emphasizing short-term objectives at a negotiating disadvantage.

> Negotiation in the classic diplomatic sense assumes parties are more anxious to agree than to disagree.
>
> —*Dean Acheson,*
> *U.S. diplomat*

- Good negotiators are flexible in setting goals. They define goals within ranges (for example, a return on investment of 10 to 20 percent) rather than as definite targets ("We must get a minimum 14 percent return").

- Unskilled negotiators have definite sequences of points to cover, ranked usually by their order of importance. Skilled negotiators go into meetings with a series of issues to tackle but do not have a predetermined sequence. The second method makes it more difficult for the other side to determine what the opposite negotiating team considers as the critical issues. This method also maintains a balance among the issues, thereby minimizing the chances that either side will hurt the negotiations by applying pressure on sensitive issues.

- Successful negotiations generally go through four phases: (1) building up rapport, (2) learning about the proposed agreement, including its technical, legal, and business aspects, (3) bridging differences through reason, persuasion and, occasionally, argument, and (4) making concessions and drawing up agreements.

KEY POINTS

- The concepts of high-, medium-, and low-context cultures are introduced, with efficient and competitive low-context behaviors of industrialized nations contrasting with trust-oriented and cooperative high-context cultures found in many developing nations.

- The major cultural underpinnings of low-context cultures are Christianity (and Protestantism in particular) and politically, economically, and socially competitive societies. High-context cultures have heavy religious orientations and less-competitive economies.

- Religions can be divided into those with those with many gods (polytheistic: e.g., primal religions, Hinduism, Shinto), a single omnipotent god (monotheistic: e.g., Judaism, Christianity, Islam), no major deities (nontheistic: Buddhism, Confucianism, Taoism).

- Face-to-face negotiating is where cultural differences become critical and national characteristics are important.

  U.S. business people are efficient, competitive negotiators who prefer arm's-length dealings.

  Japanese negotiators build relationships through after-hours socializing. Legal matters are deemphasized, patience is rewarded, long-term perspectives are taken, and conflict is avoided.

  Latin Americans tend to be more emotional and autocratic in their decision making and build relationships over lengthy lunches and dinners.

  Western Europeans like procedures, titles, and orderly agendas. German and Dutch negotiators are efficiency-oriented like North Americans. Medium-context Europeans are more relaxed, and are relationship-builders, particularly in the south (Greece, Spain, Portugal).

Asians use negotiations to build relationships and are concerned with long-term and employment issues. They are patient negotiators who avoid conflict situations.

Middle Eastern negotiators are also relationship builders who avoid open conflicts. Much emphasis is placed on courtesy and social formalities.

Russians are cautious, strategic negotiators who push hard to identify and capitalize on factors that can be leveraged to their advantage.

- International negotiations should be carefully planned concerning pre-trip preparation, negotiating team composition, negotiating style, and agreement expectations.

ENDNOTES

1. Partly based on Lalita Khosla, "You say tomato," *Forbes* (May 21, 2001): 36–37.

2. Vern Terpstra and Thomas David, *The Cultural Environment of International Business* (Cincinnati: Oh.: Southwestern Publishing, 1991), 79; and Huston Smith, *The World's Religions* (Harper San Francisco, 1998), 183.

3. Huston Smith, 232.

4. Thomas M. Burton, "Magic Bullets: Drug Company Looks to Witch Doctors to Conjure Products," *Wall Street Journal* (July 7, 1994): A1.

5. Smith, 238.

6. Marc Lacy, "Traditional Spirits block $500 million dam plan in Uganda," *New York Times* (September 13, 2001).

7. Smith, 242–43.

8. Based on V. P. Kanitar and W. Owen Cole, "Hinduism," in Peter B. Clarke, ed. *The World's Religions* (Pleasantville, N.Y.: Reader's Digest Association, 1993); www.easc. indiana.edu/pages/. . .asia/1995/general/Japan/Shinto/htm.

9. John Breen, "Shinto," in Clarke, ed., *The World's Religions*, 124–43.

10. S. A. Nigosian, *World Faiths* (New York: St. Martin's Press, 1990): 62–77.

11. Smith, *op. cit.*

12. For excellent readings and contrasts among major Christian faiths, see: Clarke, ed., *The World's Religions*; or Huston Smith, *The Illustrated World's Religions*, (San Francisco: Harper Collins, 1994),

13. Vern Terpstra and Kenneth David, *The Cultural Environment of International Business*, 2nd edition (Cincinnati Oh.: Southwestern Publishing, 1991), 104–5.

14. Terpstra and David, 106.

15. Peter B. Clarke, "Islam," in Clarke, ed., *The World's Religions,* 118.

16. Peggy Morgan, "Buddhism," chapter 8 in Clarke, *op. cit.*

17. John S. Hill, "The Japanese Business Puzzle," *Journal of General Management* 15, 3 (Spring 1990): 20–38.

18. Michael Jordan, *Eastern Wisdom* (New York: Marlowe and Company, 1998), 172.

19. Huston Smith, *The World's Religions* (HarperSanFrancisco, 1998), 158.

20. Based on S. A. Nigosian, *World Faiths* (New York: St. Martin's Press, 1990); John T. Loftin, *The Big Picture: A Short World History of Religions* (Jefferson, N.C.: McFarland & Company, 2000); and Smith, *op. cit.*

21. John Marcom, Jr., "The Fire Down South," *Forbes* (October 15, 1990): 56–71.

22. Smith, 246.

23. Clarke, 13.

24. John S. Hill, "The Japanese Business Puzzle," *op cit.*

25. E. Russell Eggers, "How to Do Business with a Frenchman," in *Culture and Management,* Theodore D. Weinshall, ed. (New York: Penguin Books, 1977), 136–39.

26. Adapted from David Altany, "Culture Clash: Negotiating a European Joint Venture Agreement Takes More Than Money . . . It Takes Savvy," *Industry Week* (October 2, 1989): 13–14, 16, 18, 20.

27. Richard D. Lewis, "How to Handle the Russian Bear," *Management Today* (September 1995): 90–91.

28. Neil Rackham, *The Behavior of Successful Negotiators* (Reston Va.: Huthwaite Research Group, 1976).

CASETTE 12-1
West Meets East over the Negotiation Table: Contrasts and Causes

Even after many decades of commercial interactions, Asian negotiating styles are an anathema to most workers. In the 1980s, the U.S. Department of Commerce estimated there were twenty-five failures for every successful Japanese-American negotiation. While, hopefully, this percentage rate has improved over the past two decades, both Western and Asian negotiators continue to surprise each other. Often, they are aware of what negotiation behavior to expect, but still lack an understanding of their cultural underpinnings. Based on Chapter 12 materials, we present a framework for comprehending East-West negotiating behavior. Note that the focus here is on U.S./Western European behavior on the one hand, and Eastern Asia (Japan, China and Korea) on the other. What do you think are the rationales for these negotiation positions? Do you see any elements that might be unusual? Summarize what the key success factors are for successful East-West negotiations.

∽◍∾

East-West Negotiation Contrasts

RATIONALE	EASTERN POSITION	WESTERN POSITION	RATIONALE
	Team Composition / Size		
	Large team (4+)	Small (3 or less)	
	Objectives		
	To initiate a relationship	To sign a business deal	
	Preparations		
	Company analysis history and background, also individual background / detail	Business analysis Financial aid Strategic analysis	
	Women		
	Usually only as secretaries, translators	More likely to be included	
	Introductions		
	Respected third party introductions "go between"	Cold calling acceptable	
	Formal titles and protocols are used	Often opt for informality, first names as quickly as possible	
	Negotiation Behavior		
	Eye contact avoided	Eye contact preferred	
	Emotions / Body Language		
	Poker faced, much reading of body language	Not as important to keep emotions hidden	
	Negotiation Skills / Attributes		
	Modesty, good listening skills, pragmatism; self-restraint, broad perspective	Able to move discussions forward, good advocate	
	Negotiations Sequencing		
	Circular logic: discuss many issues at same time issues often renegotiated	Linear logic: one issue at a time	
	Persuasion / Conflict Resolution		
	Meeting of the minds; persuasion should be subtle, best done outside of formal meetings; negotiation breaks or after hours	Important part of any negotiation; talk through conflicts—can be resolved through debate	

∽◦∾

RATIONALE	EASTERN POSITION	WESTERN POSITION	RATIONALE
After-hours Socializing			
Part of Asian business etiquette	"Do we have to?"		
Japanese entertainment expenses 1–2% GDP versus 1–0% for national defense			
Use of Time / Silence			
Much time taken to get *complete* understanding of issues, all angles looked at. Silence often follows other's presentations	Pros and cons, make a decision, move on		

Concluding the Negotiation

RATIONALE	EASTERN POSITION	WESTERN POSITION	RATIONALE
Contracts / Agreements			
Should be 2–3 pages "Gentlemen's agreement"; details are avoided and are less important	Should be long, legalized, and detailed		
What Is Left Out			
Will be followed through in the spirit of the agreement	Is dangerous, can be manipulated		
Concessions			
Early concessions viewed as weaknesses; concessions occur later once the stability of the situation is understood and concessions viewed as necessary	Early concessions to speed up negotiation process and establish good faith; late concessions less likely		

Sources: Park, Tongsun, and Rosalie Tung. "Negotiating with East Asia: How to attain 'win-win' outcome." *Management International Review* 39: 2 (1999): 103–22. Martin, Drew, Paul Herbig, Carol Howard, and Pat Borstorff. "At the Table: Observations on Japanese Negotiating Style." *American Business Review* 17: 1 (Jan. 1999): 65–71. Harris, Philip R. and Robert T. Moran. *Managing Cultural Differences* 5th Edition. Houston Tex: Gulf Publishing Company, 2000.

CASETTE 12-2
Negotiating Cross-Border Acquisitions in a Changing Europe

As Western Europe unified economically and politically, companies within the region prepared for the expanded European market in many ways. Some firms were already global. Others expanded their domestic operations into other European markets. But for many firms facing competitively saturated national markets, the major growth option was mergers and acquisitions (M & A)—a strategy that gave acquirers instant international presences and market clout.

But the M & A process is complex, even in a region that in one day (13 October 1997) saw $120 billion in cross-border mergers and acquisitions. Much research and negotiation is required to consummate a successful M & A deal. Despite a gradually emerging European identity, national pride and rivalries are still apparent, and regional M & As are tough to negotiate unless managers are well-prepared. In Germany, only three hostile takeovers had occurred since 1945. In France, combinations of trade unions and governments had stymied many foreign acquisitions. A major key to European M & As was to take the "hostile" out of hostile takeovers. Here's how one Italian company, Societa Metallurgica Italiana (SMI), worked to achieve this objective.

SMI in the 1960s was a medium-sized converter of refined copper and scrap, with 3800 employees producing 63,000 tons of copper products each year. By the late 1990s, SMI had become a leader in the European industry, producing eleven times its 1960s tonnage with 2.3 times the employees; it had fourteen plants regionwide and a turnover of $3 billion. SMI achieved this position by negotiating three key acquisitions, one in its native Italy, the others in France and Germany.

Within the Italian market, SMI's key rival in the 1960s was Finmeccanica. Owned by the Italian government, the company had heavy losses (a fact duly publicized by SMI). At this time, privatization was not popular, and Finmeccanica was adamantly opposed to being taken over by its primary domestic rival. Yet SMI completed the takeover in three years. SMI did this by negotiating a win-win deal whereby the company promised to make investments in Finmeccanica to bring the company out of the red, and, if it was successful, to acquire the firm at a predeter-mined price. It was a risky strategy, but SMI had confidence in its turnaround abilities. The trade unions were won over by promises of new investments, and the government by the prospects of not having to subsidize Finmeccanica anymore.

The second major acquisition was also an Italian competitor, Trafilerie e Laminatoli di Metalli SpA (TLM), which was owned by Trefimetaux, a French company, which itself was owned by Pechiney of France. First, SMI talked with members of the TLM management team. Then approaches were made to Pechiney (not Trefimetaux, who would have adamantly opposed the deal). Pechiney was mainly an aluminum producer. Its copper interests constituted just 10 percent of group turnover. Pechiney was interested, but an Italian takeover would have been considered an affront to French corporate pride. To counter this, SMI created a new parent company, Europa Metalli (EM). SMI had the major controlling interest, but Pechiney was given a 16 percent ownership stake and representation on EM's board. This was the 1980s, a time of change. Trefimetaux started to make major losses in its copper converting operations. Jacques Chirac and a pro-business government were elected in France. After Trefimetaux received assurances about jobs, Pechiney was able to negotiate a deal with the French government, and TLM and Trefimetaux became part of the Europa Metalli group. From the time SMI had shown an initial interest in Trefimetaux and TLM to the time that they joined the group, a decade had passed.

The most difficult negotiation was the acquisition of Kabelmetal AG, SMI's major German competitor. This was the copper-products division of the MAN conglomerate that manufactured trucks and precision machinery. Through mutual acquaintances at the German firm Allianz, preliminary meetings with the MAN group established the viability of the acquisition. Then the major negotiation, with Kabelmetal's Vorstand, was undertaken. The Vorstand was the executive management board appointed by a supervisory board (itself comprised of shareholder and employee-elected officials). It was heavily oriented to employee and trade-union interests and had power of veto for major strategic moves. Its cooperation was critical if the acquisition was to occur, and similar groups had stopped many takeovers of German firms. Many presentations to this group were undertaken with a focus on the new unified Europe and the need for strong European firms to counter outsiders. While there were obvious linguistic and management-style differences between the groups, the vision of a strong European copper conversion group proved critical, and the deal was approved. The holding company, Europa Metalli, was renamed KM Europa Metal, and a seven-person Vorstand was selected to help oversee group operations. This process took two years.

Question

Identify the critical factors in the negotiation processes in which SMI participated. Which do you think is the most important, and why?

Source: Sebenius, James K. "Negotiating cross-border acquisitions." *Sloan Management Review* 39: 2 (Winter 1998): 27–41.

Chapter Thirteen

Localization Strategies: Managing Stakeholders and Supply Chains

GETTING TO GRIPS WITH THE REAL CHINESE MARKET

Everyone knows that China is a potential-laden market. But to reap the benefits of the nation's 1.3 billion population, firms must get into rural markets that account for about 70 percent of its population. Coca-Cola knows this. Rural Chinese consumers drink just three Coke products per year compared to sixty in urban markets such as Beijing and Shanghai.

But this is easier said than done. Finland's Nokia and Switzerland's Swatch have made strenuous efforts to move westward. But, as with many companies, they find that rural China presents many new headaches. The country's huge geographic area makes for a fragmented media landscape: 3,000+ TV stations (2,000 in the U.S.), 1,800 radio stations, 1,000+ newspapers and 7,000+ magazines. Then there are regional dialects and variations in behaviors, etiquette, and advertising rules. Distribution problems plagued Whirlpool as a lack of national retail chains forced the company to negotiate with local retailers who wanted all sorts of "sweeteners" to carry the firm's brands. Even then they had to compete with Korea's LG and Germany's Siemens as well as local brands such as Wuxi Little Swan and Little Duck. Product lines had to be reassessed. TV manufacturers found that smaller rural houses and incomes made little color TVs a better buy than bigger versions.[1]

This vignette demonstrates the many obstacles international firms face, especially in developing markets and especially outside of developed urban markets. As noted back in Chapter 1, the diffusion of new ideas, products, technologies, and lifestyles is particularly slow in developing-market rural areas. As a result, international companies, faced with other global rivals and local competitors, "go local"—they adapt to whatever market conditions they find to enhance the effectiveness of localized operations and marketing strategies. In China's case, the stakes are high. The market is huge (over 1.3 billion people) but it is not an affluent market. While international corporations can target China's middle classes, the mass market is rural and poor. Even in developed countries, some degrees of localized strategies must be used. How they do this is the subject of this chapter.

In this chapter, you will learn:

• How international firms build insider relations with key stakeholders in local markets—governments, business communities, environmental, consumer groups, and the press.

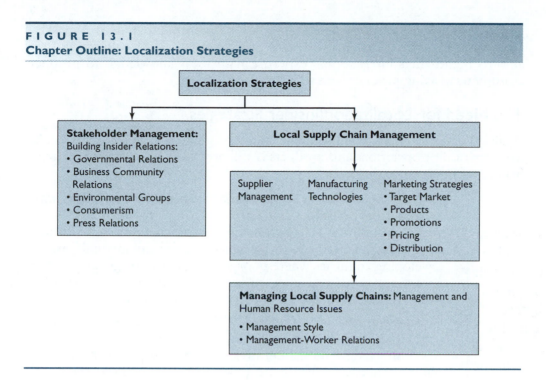

FIGURE 13.1
Chapter Outline: Localization Strategies

- The ways companies factor local considerations into supplier relations and into manufacturing and marketing strategies, and how management styles vary around the world.

INTRODUCTION: THE IMPORTANCE OF LOCALIZATION STRATEGIES

All companies, even those pursuing global or regionally based strategies, must deal with local market circumstances to varying extents. Exporters and arms-length contractual arrangements (e.g., licensing) have their distributors, customers, or contractors in foreign markets and must compete against local rivals. For these firms, local knowledge and international expertise adds up to competitive advantages. For companies with investment commitments, the importance of "acting local" is also important. Foreign companies are guests in overseas markets, and even though they contribute jobs and technologies and add to the varieties of goods and services available to customers, ultimately they must behave appropriately and respect local traditions and cultures. This is particularly important in emerging markets where international companies are catalysts to social change—a process that must be handled delicately and with tact. Modern technologies and lifestyles take time to diffuse through national markets, and international firms must be patient as this occurs.

International firms are also ambassadors for their countries of origin. Disrespect for local cultures reflects poorly on parent-company

I traveled a good deal all over the world, and I got along pretty well in all of those foreign countries, for I have a theory that it's their country and they have a right to run it like they want to.

*—Will Rogers,
19th–20th-century
U.S. humorist*

global reputations. Local stakeholders must be accommodated, and marketplace success occurs as companies make adaptations to local cultures and are able to blend their international expertise with local knowledge to produce customer-satisfying products and services.

The Need for Localization/Insider Strategies

While globalization forces impact all nations to greater or lesser degrees, the need to localize operations and products is still present. Their desirability stems from:

> A Canadian is someone who drinks Brazilian coffee from an English teacup and munches on a French pastry while sitting on his Danish furniture having just come home from an Italian movie in his German car. He picks up his Japanese pen and writes to his member of Parliament to complain about the American takeover of the Canadian publishing business.
>
> —*Campbell Hughes,*
> *Canadian publisher*

- *Slow diffusions of technologies and products within individual markets:* National cultures remain intact when modernization and westernization tendencies take time to reach significant portions of country populations. In particular this occurs in rural parts of developing countries where poor infrastructures or geographic circumstances limit or isolate customer groups from outside influences: products, media, and other commercial activities.

- *Xenophobia:* Dislike or mistrust of foreigners causes customers to prefer localized products and output. Countries with long histories and strong national cultures, for example, often have xenophobic tendencies. These are reflected at the highest levels with government contracts being given to local contractors and at the consumer level when "made in" preferences are toward locally made products.

- *"Insider" contacts are necessary for marketplace effectiveness:* This occurs where local business connections are essential to gain access to key materials, suppliers, distributors, etc., or political permissions are needed to establish businesses or run day-to-day operations (e.g., investment permissions, trade permits). In China, insider contacts (*guanxi*) are generally acknowledged as essential to operate in the PRC, and royal connections are major facilitators in the Middle East.

- *Major cultural dissimilarities* are apparent between an international company's national culture and that of the local country culture. For example, adaptations are usually necessary to bridge East-West differences in customer tastes.

- *Governmental protection of national cultures* can occur to shelter citizens from outside influences such as westernization or modernization. Countries with heavy religious orientations (e.g., Buddhism, Hinduism, Islam) have reservations about Western lifestyles that are perceived to undermine centuries-old religious philosophies.

Market-Servicing Strategy and Localization Potential

How firms service markets determines or influences how far they can localize their operations and output. Exporting into a country affords some opportunities to use insider contacts, as national distributors help companies adapt offerings to local preferences. Similarly, while contractual arrangements such as licensing or franchising rely on borrowed technologies, processes, logos, or trademarks, global operators such as McDonalds or Pizza Hut allow local franchisers to deviate from standardized programs.

The potential for localized programs and products is greatest when firms have in-market manufacturing (as in joint-ventures, local acquisitions, greenfield operations). In-market investments allow full immersion and participation in local cultures and afford the best learning opportunities. This involves managing local stakeholder groups and partial or complete localizations of company supply chains.

MANAGING LOCAL STAKEHOLDER RELATIONS

Stakeholders are organized groups that influence, directly or indirectly, a firm's local operations. As firms acquire global reach and set up operations in foreign markets, they must cater to a host of local stakeholder needs. Unlike home markets where stakeholder influences are known, companies must assess stakeholder needs on a market-by-market basis and devise strategies to address their concerns. Overall, firms have two basic strategies. First, they can maintain low profiles and rely on anonymity to stay out of trouble. Second, they can adopt proactive plans to establish dialogues with key stakeholder groups, including governments and national and local regulatory agencies, local business and financial communities (for supply-chain and funding purposes), local communities, the press, environmental groups, and consumer activists.

Building Government Relations

Relationships with governments begin as companies develop country short lists for investment consideration. Preliminary negotiations between governments and companies are conducted to evaluate investment incentive packages and possible production sites. In the pre-investment period, international firms have the advantage in choosing between alternative sites. As negotiations proceed, governments are interested in how the international firm will contribute to local and regional economies. Once investments are made, firms establish programs to build solid company-government relations. These include:

> A government that is big enough to give you what you want is big enough to take it all away.
>
> —*Barry Goldwater, U.S. senator*

- *Job creation and technology transfer programs:* While acquisitions are common forms of market entry in highly competitive markets, governments, particularly in developing countries, prefer market commitments that upgrade local firms' competitive abilities (e.g., joint ventures) or those that add to their country's asset base (e.g., greenfield investments).

- *Producing for the local market* and encouraging national supplier development is a strategy that curries favor with local governments. German firm Siemens boasts that 80 percent of merchandise sold in host countries are produced there. Its U.S. operation has about sixty production plants employing about 35,000 Americans.[2]

- *Establishing relationships with local educational institutions:* Mercedes' move into Vance, Alabama, was accompanied by the establishing of liaisons with local academic institutions. Siemens sponsors research at 150 educational institutions worldwide not only to tap local research talent but also to attract top students to the company.[3]

- *Appointing local boards of directors to oversee national operations:* Swedish-Swiss company ABB uses local boards to supervise local operations and act as liaisons among country and global business-unit managers.[4]

- *Corporate philanthropy programs* build solid community relations. Hitachi USA dedicates 1.5 percent of its pretax profits to a charitable foundation for arts, education, and economic development and encourages employee volunteer programs for food, clothing, toy drives, literacy programs, recycling, and prenatal nutrition. Pharmaceutical company Pfizer donates products and materials to the Red Cross. Microsoft makes software contributions to schools worldwide, and, in China, Hewlett-Packard provides employee housing as part of its employment package.

- *Establishing strong corporate identities* gives firms advantages in all stakeholder dealings. Monsanto's "without chemicals, life itself would be impossible" is a strong statement legitimizing the company's commercial activities and contributions to mankind. "Hitachi is committed to working for a better tomorrow" attests to the company's commitment to progress.

- *Consistency, longevity, and commitment to local markets* generally reflect positively on companies. Companies such as the pharmaceutical firm Pfizer, Fluor-Daniel (the engineering and construction outfit), and the U.K.'s Unilever have maintained presences in major markets over long time periods, through good times and bad. They have also been scrupulous in maintaining global reputations for good citizenship.

> The most serviceable of all assets is reputations . . . it works for you automatically . . . 24 hours a day. Unlike money, reputation cannot be bequeathed. It must be acquired.
>
> —*Otto Kahn*

Building Business-Community Relations

International companies, through their presence and their technological contributions, have major effects on national and local business communities. Where they source locally, they provide quality benchmarks for national suppliers and sensitize them to world standards of competition. In China, estimates suggest that every dollar spent by international corporations adds $2.50 to China's economy via supplier expansions. General Motors, Volkswagen, and Ford, in particular, have helped create major supplier networks.[5] Motorola's manufacturing and supplier strategy has helped local businesses and workers overcome outdated management philosophies from the communist era. For example:

- All the company's 12,000 Chinese employees receive an average of two weeks of training a year on topics such as total quality control and total customer satisfaction. The company spends $2 million per year to bring management practices up to international levels.

- A supply network of 100 local firms gets $750 million in orders but also provides training to boost quality levels. Defective product levels in 1999 were one-seventh of those in 1996.[6]

Executives from international companies build relationships with local managers via trade associations and Chambers of Commerce. Presentations to local business groups and dialogs help establish international managers as contributors to local economies. Such groups are also valuable sources of commercial intelligence.

Environmental Groups

There is little doubt that worldwide industrialization has adverse effects on the global environment. In particular, global warming and environmental protection issues continue to impact corporate strategies at global, regional, and local levels. The global warming thesis posits that greenhouse gases, most notably carbon dioxide from the combustion of fossil fuels, accumulate in the atmosphere, trap heat, and warm the planet. As global industrialization continues, some scientists have prognosticated that unless greenhouse emissions decrease, dire consequences are possible for future generations.[7] The European Union, prompted by the "Green" environmentalist movement, has pushed member countries first to stabilize their carbon dioxide emissions (by the year 2000) and then to cut them by 15 percent from their 1990 levels.[8]

At the nation-state level, countries vary in their abilities to enact environmental laws and then to police them effectively. The problem is particularly acute in Southeast Asia. Malaysia and Indonesia, in particular, suffer from poor enforcement of environmental laws that are circumvented by bribery and political influence.[9] In Western Europe, the Friends of the Earth group launched Europe's first chemical-release web site. In the U.S., the Environmental Defense Fund Scorecard logs chemical industry emissions on an Internet site.[10]

The global warming issue has become more urgent as deforestation limits nature's ability to convert carbon dioxide back into oxygen. Government actions in Brazil have retarded the logging industry's progress into the Amazon forests. In Asia, however, environmental groups estimate that Cambodia's forests will be gone by 2003, that the forests in the Philippines and Malaysia will disappear by 2010, and that Indonesia's forests will be decimated within three decades.[11] In response, an international environmental organization, the Forest Stewardship Council, has attempted to restrict indiscriminate logging by issuing FSC stamps that certify that lumber has been cut only from sustainably-managed forests.[12]

Many international companies have responded positively to environmental concerns. Some examples:

> The nation behaves well if it treats natural resources as assets that it must turn over to the next generation, increased and not impaired in value.
>
> —*Theodore Roosevelt, 20th-century U.S. president*

- In the auto industry, Ford's pickup and sports utility vehicles had their emissions reduced to appease environmental groups,[13] and Toyota produced an environmentally friendly auto using an electric and a gasoline motor. The company is also attempting to develop trees and plants that absorb toxic gases more efficiently.[14]

- In the 1990s, IBM, through efficient waste management, reduced its carbon dioxide emissions by 6 million tons, with a $525 million savings, and Johnson & Johnson committed to a 25 percent reduction in energy consumption by the year 2000.[15]

- British Petroleum decided that working with environmental groups was the best way to demonstrate the company's commitment to environmental protection.[16]

Consumerism

The excesses of capitalistic competition have caused the emergence of consumer groups in most nations to contest corporate claims concerning products and responsible strategies. In developed markets, such as North America and Western Europe, consumer organizations publish magazines like *Which?* (U.K.), *Consumer Reports* (U.S.), and *Consumentengids* (Holland). These magazines aim to improve shopper knowledge of marketplace products and to influence government legislation and corporate decision making. They maintain independent testing laboratories to evaluate product performances, product contents (ingredients, etc.), and price-value relationships ("best buys").[17] Nevertheless, controversies persist, including:

> How to improve goods or services? Learn to complain, politely and firmly, when you receive what you believe are inferior goods or services.
>
> —*Stanley Marcus, U.S. merchant*

> Nature knows no indecencies; Man invents them.
>
> —*Mark Twain, U.S. author*

- The mass-market advertising of prescription drugs in the U.S.,[18] while in Western Europe there have been increased calls for transparency and accountability in pharmaceutical testing and regulation. This includes falsification and suppression of data, circulation and use of substandard drugs, and misrepresentations of negative findings.[19]

- The use of genetic engineering to modify agricultural crops has attracted consumer-activist attentions in Europe. While genetically modified soya, oilseed rope, and maize crops are widely cultivated, resistance to their use in Europe has been widespread.[20] Protagonists claim that the use of genetically modified crops in the developing world has increased production in unattractive climates in India and Pakistan. New strains of wheat, corn, and rice have been developed to increase crop yields and resistance to disease. The hope is that modified crops and plants can ultimately reduce pesticide and fertilizer use.[21]

In developing markets, the aim of consumer groups and some governments is to protect inexperienced consumers where protective legislation is not in place. Government and commercial media in China PRC attacked foreign corporations such as KFC, McDonald's, Sony, Samsung, Sharp, Daewoo, Wal-Mart, and Microsoft, accusing them of substandard products, services, and false advertising. Such adverse publicity prompts most international firms to investigate complaints and take corrective actions.[22]

Public Relations and the Press

Public perceptions of business activities and corporations are influenced through the popular press. At national levels, anti-business news, especially when it concerns foreign companies, invites backlashes at governmental and consumer levels. In the Czech Republic, the national press vilified foreign direct investment and portrayed them as job-cutting expatriate fat cats threatening the "Czech Way." A response by CzechInvest, the country's foreign investment agency, presented counterarguments by noting that foreign manufacturers were creating one new net job every ten minutes. Further, international firms supported 10,000 Czech-based suppliers (representing 10 percent of the national labor force), accounted for 60 percent of manufactured exports. Two-thirds of them had Czech managing directors.[23]

As national economies have become market forces-oriented, freedom of the press and independent news coverage make corporate PR and media relations essential management functions. Corporate and brand images can be molded by proactive public relations policies. In Latin America, foreign companies have been encouraged to build relationships with journalists, publicize firm-related human interest stories, support surveys and research efforts, and become involved in fund-raising, social causes, and sponsorships.[24]

Mishandled public relations cause corporate embarrassment and, at worst, damage to global reputations. Coca Cola's 1999 product-recall scare in Western Europe did both. Peculiar odors from Coke products prompted a 14-million Coke case recall over five countries. European press ran rumors that Coke cans were contaminated with rat poison. Poor handling by the company resulted in adverse publicity. For a company as quality and image conscious as Coca Cola, the experience was humiliating.[25]

> *Four hostile newspapers are more to be feared than a thousand bayonets.*
>
> —*Napoleon Bonaparte, 19th-century French emperor and general*

SUPPLY CHAIN MANAGEMENT

The Benefits of Supply Chain Localization

From a supply chain perspective, localization brings many benefits to international firms, including:

- *Development of local raw-material sources and component suppliers:* This strategy is effective because local materials can be cheaper and better and can contribute to customer appeal.

- *Corporate learning* occurs as international firms accumulate experience from different manufacturing and marketing locations. Learning also occurs as firms custom-build products for national markets and tap local expertise.

- *Marketing strategy localization* works where national cultures are strong and heavily influence local behaviors. In such markets, Western or modern appeals are less effective, and localized marketing mixes are necessary. Asia, the Middle East, and Russia have been markets where localized strategies pay dividends.

Supplier Management

Supplier management can be viewed from two perspectives: (1) from the home market perspective when companies source complete products or services from foreign locations, and (2) from the foreign market perspective when firms have in-market manufacturing and must put together completely localized supply chains.

Control Issues and Subcontracted Foreign Production International firms face major challenges also as they subcontract production to countries where labor laws are non-existent or are not enforced. Nike came under fire in the late 1990s when its offshore contractors were found to be employing underage workers in Asia. Pressure from consumer organizations forced 200 American and European firms to adopt good-behavior codes for foreign factories that included the elimination of child labor and improvement of health, safety, and environmental standards. Asia's problems are particularly acute, with over 150 million child workers engaged in manufacturing jobs.[26] Casette 13-2 explores some ethical dilemmas associated with child-labor usage. Many companies opt for UN-sponsored ISO 14001 certifications to ensure compliance with environmentally friendly manufacturing practices and with SA 8000, which establishes social-accountability standards for worker health and safety on a worldwide basis.[27]

> We hold these truths to be self-evident, that all men are created equal, that they are endowed by their Creator with certain unalienable rights, that among these are life, liberty and the pursuit of happiness.
>
> —*Thomas Jefferson, 3rd president of the United States (Declaration of Independence)*

In-Country Supply Chain Management Securing materials and components is the first step in local supply chain management. Country-based suppliers have several advantages, including: (1) simplifying supply chain management by shortening communication lines, (2) allowing manufacturers to work with vendors to customize materials and components to meet local customer needs, (3) currying favor with governments as local-company supply capabilities are upgraded and hard currencies preserved which otherwise would be used to import materials, (4) alleviating company concerns about managing international supply lines that are subject to disruptions such as dock strikes, currency problems, and import restrictions. Coca Cola, for example, was forced out of Sudan when a U.S. embargo prevented it from importing vital concentrates and chemical mixtures.[28]

But there are costs and problems involved in developing local suppliers.

- *Financing concerns:* Local firms supplying international firms often lack the finances needed to bring their output up to required standards. McDonalds requires its Eastern European vendors to invest heavily to ensure steady supplies of milk, hamburger buns, meat, and potatoes. The firm estimates the cost of establishing potato suppliers at $20 million.[29]

- *Quality:* Efforts to maintain global product-quality standards meet local resistance when cheaper but poorer-quality alternatives are available. Pizza Hut had these problems in establishing Cypriot and Czech operations.[30]

> It is a funny thing about life; if you refuse to accept anything but the best, you very often get it.
>
> —*Somerset Maughan, 20th-century English novelist*

- *Establishing supply chain disciplines:* Getting raw materials and component suppliers to meet the time and service requirements of JIT processes is problematic in economies not used to catering to manufacturer and customer needs. McDonalds India used joint-venture connections and Western-based logistics providers to oversee linkages between contract farmers (unusual in India) and regional distribution centers to provide JIT services to local restaurants.

- *Establishing global standards of manufacture* for local suppliers: Auto parts manufacturers setting up in Mexico initially found only eight local firms producing to ISO 9000 quality standards.[31] Similarly, the ISO 14000 standard on environmentally friendly manufacturing systems (demanded by manufacturers such as IBM and Volvo), caused adjustment problems for their iron and steel suppliers.[32]

- *Geographic and physical infrastructure obstacles* impose severe restrictions on the adoption of efficient supply chains. In Asia, especially outside of urban centers, poor inland infrastructures and unreliable transport systems cause producers to maintain high parts inventories and lead to longer manufacturing cycles. Further, the use of traditional intermediaries can also be problematic.[33]

- The key to building local suppliers in any country is *patience*. Consequently, international corporations do not expect instant change, nor do they expect instant returns from their supplier investments. Rather, they build relationships and help suppliers build up their capabilities. Pelit, a Turkish patisserie and chocolate manufacturer, worked with Anglo-Dutch multinational Unilever to become a supplier of ice cream coatings in Turkey, then later in Europe and the Middle East.[34]

Managing Local Manufacturing Operations

Managing in-country production facilities bring its own sets of challenges to international firms, especially where they under-research market investments.

Elevated Cost Structures Many companies are unprepared for unexpected operational costs. In Western Europe, cost structures are elevated by government payroll taxes for social security, retirement, and health and education systems that can increase hourly wage rates by 50–100 percent. In developing countries, cheap wage rates can be offset by increased costs due to low productivity rates, quality problems, and poor infrastructures (energy costs/availability, transportation problems).

> Taxes are what we pay for a civilized society.
>
> —*Oliver Wendell Holmes,*
> *19th–20th-century*
> *U.S. jurist*

Education/Labor Availability National education infrastructures (schools, technical colleges, universities) must deliver adequately trained labor for businesses. In particular, technical, engineering, and scientific personnel must be developed. Lower wage rates in China, Vietnam, and Indonesia forced the Thai government to focus its efforts to train technically competent workers in order to attract technology-intensive industries.[35]

Labor Laws These laws must be obeyed, especially with respect to worker hours, safety, pay, and benefits. In developing nations, in particular, child labor, 7-day work weeks, and 10–15 hour work days are often endemic problems. Most international companies set the standards in developing markets for worker treatment, adhering to national laws (even when local rivals do not), and using home-market standards where possible. In developed countries, well-defined laws lay out company-worker relations, hiring/firing policies, and workplace conditions. In Western Europe, for example, employees are well-protected and layoffs can be problematic.

Employee Recruitment and Selection In developed nations, recruitment criteria tend to be education and experience-based, though education-system differences (e.g., technical, professional qualifications) can cause problems. In developing nations, attracting educated elites can be problematic, as government posts (in Japan) and prestigious local firms (e.g., Tata group of companies in India) are attractive employment alternatives. At the factory level, educational proficiencies can be deficient (e.g., basic literacy skills), and variable ethnic and linguistic backgrounds (e.g., in multi-lingual/dialect nations in Africa or parts of Asia) can cause shop-floor conflicts. Countering this, many firms use local referrals to find new employees, though they must be careful not to open themselves up to charges of nepotistic hirings.

Appropriate Manufacturing Technologies The transfer of advanced technologies into emerging markets can be problematic. In Zimbabwe, Australian mining company BHP was forced to sell its stake in its platinum mine when the firm realized that its capital-intensive technologies would not work in Zimbabwe's labor-intensive mining environment. The firm decided that the task of upgrading unskilled workers would be too costly.[36] Some corporations modify their operating requirements and procedures for use in less-advanced markets. Dutch electronics giant Philips varies its developing-country manufacturing technologies so that equipment can be adapted to small scale production, needed tools and auxiliaries are available, and capital needs are kept as low as possible. These adaptations were used in twenty Philips' plants in the developing world.[37]

> Man must be disciplined, for he is by nature raw and wild.
>
> —*Immanuel Kant,*
> *19th-century*
> *German philosopher*

Factory Discipline Many factors conspire to frustrate international firms intent on instilling Western-style efficiency and shop-floor discipline. In developing countries, the shift from inefficient rural lifestyles to regimented factory and work environments causes adjustment, turnover, and absentee problems (e.g., Africa). Where income is not a primary determinant of social status (e.g., Latin America), worker motivation can be reduced. In some nations, however, work ethics and discipline are superior. One attraction of Asia has been the Confucian work ethic that makes Asian workers highly productive.

Maintaining Production Efficiency Levels For companies maintaining JIT or even regular manufacturing schedules, there are a number of problems that can be overcome with careful planning.

- *Encouraging home market or international suppliers to set up close by* (or even in) foreign manufacturing facilities. This occurs frequently in the auto industry, with Mercedes and Toyota expecting trusted suppliers to follow them into foreign markets.

- *Infrastructure problems:* Production sites located in or around major cities (e.g., Hong Kong, Mexico City, Los Angeles) can expect traffic congestion problems and supply delays. Where factories are located in rural development regions, particularly in developing nations, infrastructure and climatic problems (e.g., monsoons) should be factored into production schedules.

- *Time orientation problems:* In countries where efficiency and work ethic orientations are questionable (*mañana* in Latin America, *Inshallah*—"If God wills it" in the Middle East), time delays must be factored into production timelines.

Localizing Marketing Operations: Multinational Strategies

Multinational marketing strategies involve making adaptations to target markets, products, promotions, pricing, and distribution to suit local customers and environmental conditions. Few products (even global brands) can be marketed identically across all countries. The question then becomes how far to take adaptation strategies.

Target Markets Target markets must first be identified. When companies localize strategies, they acknowledge that differences among national markets are important and that customized marketing strategies are necessary to gain competitive advantages. This is often the case when international firms from advanced countries enter emerging markets and must bridge major developmental differences. In these (and some developed) countries, segmentation criteria must be adjusted to fit local circumstances. For example:

- *Income differences* must take account of lower purchasing-power capabilities. Here mass-market products and services must appeal to low-income segments, and product cost structures must be adjusted to ensure that profitability targets can be met. For example, computer manufacturers in India and China simplify personal computer designs to enhance mass-market appeals.

- *Educational levels* are important for complex products and services requiring in-depth customer knowledge for effective use. Companies marketing high-tech consumer goods (e.g., computers, software) and complex services (e.g., financial goods such as insurance) must carefully target educated customers to assure proper comprehension and use.

- *Geographic differences* within countries often require marketing adjustments. Even within developed countries like the U.S. and U.K., regional variations are apparent (for example, north-south differences in both markets). In France, geographic regions have distinctive tastes and often have their own dialects (e.g., Provence, Brittany, Alsace, Catalonia, and Basque areas).

In developing markets, ethnic and racial segments must be geographically documented to make appropriate adaptations to labeling, brand names, product usage instructions, and other product components.

From Montreal to Munich to Melbourne, the world is too large and filled with too many diverse people and firms for any single marketing strategy to satisfy everyone.

—David L. Kurtz,
U.S. educator and writer

We will have differences. Men of different ancestries, men of different tongues, men of different colors, men of different environments, men of different geographies, do not see everything alike. Even in our own country, we do not see everything alike.

—Lyndon B. Johnson,
36th president
of the United States

EXHIBIT 13-1
Religious Influences on Architectural Design in Asia

Western companies building corporate offices in Asia are aware of the influence of feng shui ("wind water"). Buildings must be designed to harmonize with the spirits of nature, and while Westerners are skeptical of its effects, Western developers in China, Taiwan, and Hong Kong have known buildings to remain unoccupied for years because they were built along bad feng shui principles, and post-hoc spiritual surveys of offices, factories, and bank buildings can result in outlay of millions of dollars. Some examples of feng shui influences:

- Hong Kong's Regency Hotel put in a large glass window to allow dragons from Kowloon to pass through to drink and bathe in Hong Kong's harbor.

- Advertising agency FCB's Hong Kong office had to put in a shocking pink carpet that clashed aesthetically with FCB's corporate blue color scheme.

- Triangular, T-shaped, or cul-de-sac lots should be avoided for building, with preference being given to rectangular lots.

- Entrances should not face northeast or southwest, and the three most important entrances—main gate, main door, and the back door—should be balanced.

- Staircases should not face entrances, nor be located in the center or northwesterly part of buildings.

Feng shui's influence on interior design has caught on in the U.S., especially for restaurant design, where it helps direct the flow of energy through a restaurant to enhance its profitability, bolster its physical identity, and improve patron comfort and enjoyment.

Sources: Lip, Evelyn. "Feng Shui for Business." Singapore: Time Life Books. 1989. Mack, David. "Feng Shui: Ancient Chinese Art Is Cutting Edge Design." *Nations Restaurant News* (Dec. 22, 1997): 22–24. Grey, Robert. "The Feng Shui Audit." *Campaign London* (Oct. 9, 1998): 3–4.

- *Religious differences* are important as they affect marketing offerings to customers. Effects on food consumption (e.g., no pork in Islamic nations; no beef in Hindu countries) are important, and lifestyle products (e.g., apparel and female modesty) are examples. Exhibit 13-1 shows how Asia's feng shui philosophy (a Taoist concept) influences architectural designs and office layouts in that region.

- *Customer purchasing differences* are apparent in many countries. Automobile and refrigerator ownership affect purchasing behaviors. Daily purchasing of food items contrasts with one-stop shopping habits that are the norm in many developed markets. These factors affect product-size decisions, for example. Decision processes are important as male-female influences on big-ticket purchases vary, as do children's influences on food purchases.

- *Urban-rural differences* are important, especially in developing markets. Urban consumers tend to be more sophisticated, are better educated, and have greater exposure to modern amenities and infrastructures. Outside urban centers, additional adaptations are often necessary to accommodate rural needs.[38]

Product Strategy Product strategy decisions concern product-mix assortments (what products should be marketed in individual countries) and, for individual products, how far they should be adapted.

Product-Mix Decisions Upon entering a new market, international firms must decide what products to sell. They have two options. Where companies see similarities in country demand (similar needs, target markets), they can transfer in products from the home market or third-party markets, test them, adapt them where necessary, and market them. The advent of globalization has made product transfers the most popular strategy, and they average over 80 percent of product lines in foreign subsidiaries.[39] Unilever has a stable of starter brands it can use in most international markets. Procter and Gamble's product staples include Camay soap, detergents Tide and Ariel, hair-care products (Pantene), feminine protection (Always), diapers (nappies—Pampers), and Fairy dish liquid.

A second option is to custom build products for individual markets. This usually occurs as subsidiaries build sales and become familiar with customer and market preferences. Unilever's Latin American strategy includes not just their global product lines, but also downscale versions ("economy products") of their soap powders and ice-cream businesses to appeal to less-affluent segments.[40] Kelloggs created a strongly flavored local cereal brand, "Mazza," in India to supplement its international brands.[41]

When companies use acquisitions to gain market access, they must decide how to handle local brands. In Argentina, Proctor & Gamble gradually replaces local products with established global brands. The company replaced local diaper (nappy) and feminine-protection products with Pampers and Always from its global brand portfolio.[42]

Product Adaptation Strategies These involve making changes to goods transferred from other markets. Managers have two options. They can make minimal changes to preserve brand identities; this works when firms are building global brand portfolios. Brand names and packaging appearance are preserved as far as possible, but other product components may be changed to suit customer and market circumstances. The second option is to rethink the entire product to maximize its local appeal. This involves scrutinizing:

> When the product is right, you don't have to be a great marketer.
>
> —*Lee Iacocca,*
> *former CEO, Chrysler*

- *Measurement units:* Metric measures are common throughout world markets (except the U.S., Liberia, and Myanmar/Burma). Grams and kilograms replace pounds and ounces, and liters are used instead of pints and fluid ounces.

- *Package size:* For consumer goods, smaller sizes are necessary in developing markets to compensate for lower consumer purchasing power. For example, Unilever's standard washing-powder pack in Europe is 2 kilograms; the largest size in Vietnam is 500 grams.[43] Food-product sizes are often adjusted upward to cope with the feeding of extended families (from 2–3 to 6–8 servings).

- *Package appearance* may be revamped. Unilever switched its Viso washing powders into a red package to stand out in dimly lit Vietnamese shops. The product became a nation-leading brand within six months.[44]

- *Ingredient changes:* Again in Vietnam, Unilever included bo ket, a local seed, in its Sunsilk shampoo, which became a national market leader in its segment. The company also locally sources 60 percent of raw materials and 90 percent of packaging materials.[45]

- *Usage instructions* not only must be translated into local languages, but adapted where necessary to conform to legal guidelines to prevent product misuse ("idiot-proofing").

- *Labeling* changes are usually necessary to conform to national or regional (e.g., EU) requirements. Ingredients, dates of manufacture, name of manufacturer, expiry dates are typical requirements in most countries and are particularly important in the chemical, food, and pharmaceutical industries.

- *Packaging protection* has to be reviewed with respect to its durability (shelf-life expectations) and recyclability. Campbell Soup launched its Deliciously Good range of ready-to-eat soups in Europe with a sixteen-month duration paper-and-foil package.[46] In many parts of the world, packaging must be recyclable. Hungary, as part of its EU entry preparations, set packaging companies targets of 45 percent recycled-material use in manufacturing to avoid paying environmental product fees. This has affected companies like Sweden's Tetrapak and soft-drink producers like Coca-Cola and Pepsi, who must use returnable bottles.[47]

- *Product features* may need reassessing. Low-suds features of detergents used for machine washes are changed in developing markets where hand washes make high-suds features desirable.

- *Product warranties* must be reviewed for technical and durable household products and provisions made for servicing and warranty maintenance. In the computer industry, Compaq allied with Digital/Unisys to provide regional support systems using the latter's networks in Japan and Latin America.[48]

- *Brand name changes:* Some brand names do not travel well. Unilever changed its Fish Fingers name to "Fish Oh Fingers" to accommodate Japanese difficulties in pronouncing the original brand name.[49]

Advertising Adaptations While many international companies try to standardize advertising for global brands, local circumstances often make message changes necessary. Adaptations occur for many reasons:

> You can tell the ideals of a nation by its advertisements.
>
> —*Norman Douglas, 20th-century English author*

- *Legal problems* affect advertising as governments worldwide seek to protect consumers against unscrupulous commercial interests. Tobacco and alcohol products are severely restricted throughout most of the world, and pharmaceutical advertising is heavily regulated. China's rules are typical, with no advertising to children, no doctor or expert testimonials, no comparisons, no representations about effectiveness, and only over-the-counter (rather than prescription) drugs can be promoted.[50]

- *Consumer-education differences* make changes necessary. In countries with low literary rates, ads are often simplified and lengthened (infomercials about product use).[51] At the other end of the education spectrum, European and Japanese consumers appreciate subtle, soft sells rather than hard-hitting "lowest common denominator" approaches found in markets like the U.S.

- *Target market changes* necessitate new messages. In the Chinese beer market, Heineken repositioned its product to broaden its appeal from expatriates to the general population with a "pure freedom" slogan.[52]

- *Non-meaningful message contexts:* A Chesebrough-Pond's skin-care commercial was withdrawn from the South African market after native Africans did not make the connection between a dried-out leaf and skin care.

- *Greater consumer impacts:* Some advertising platforms are maintained while creative executions are adapted to enhance their consumer impacts. Master Card's "There are some things money can't buy, for everything else there's Master Card" has been used worldwide, but with actor and situation changes customized for individual markets.

- *Cultural differences* are extremely important for personal products and in culturally sensitive regions. In Iran, extreme sensitivity is required for promotions. A poster advertising lingerie had no woman and no mention of the product: only a plain green package with the words *soft and delicate.* Shoe promotions could show only below-ankle shots. A silver spoon serving ice cream was pulled because silver spoons were perceived as symbols of decadent aristocracies.[53]

- *Media availability and popularity* affect advertising strategies. Many countries restrict advertising, either by not allowing it at all (e.g., Libya, Myanmar), restricting it to certain times of the day (parts of Western Europe), or banning it from vulnerable audiences (e.g., children). Media popularity can cause reorientations. India has low television-ownership levels, making cinema advertising particularly effective in that market.

Good marketing practices require stringent screening of advertisements in all markets. Personal products (cosmetics, female hygiene products, contraceptives, underwear) need special attention, and advertisements in deeply religious markets always need rigorous pretesting. National advertising associations are useful for promotional screening purposes.

Sales Promotion Adaptations Sales promotions (SP) consist of methods and techniques to promote products, build patronage, and reward customers for brand-loyal behaviors.[54] Sales promotion techniques include premiums (usually small gifts), coupons, games, contests, sweeps, rebates, samples, and the like. They are commonly used in advanced markets and are popular marketing tools worldwide. However, sales promotions must conform to governmental laws restricting their use. Some examples:

- Western Europe and Germany in particular have perhaps the most restrictions on SP in the world. In Germany, "Buy one, get one free" is not allowed; neither are price-off coupons. Games, sweeps, and contests are severely restricted, as are on-pack and near-pack premiums. Major EU reforms to remove restrictions and harmonize sales-promotion regulations were underway in the new millennium.[55]

- Major Latin American markets have relatively permissive sales promotional environments, and most SP methods are legal in Brazil, Chile, and Colombia. However, sales promotion effectiveness varies by market. In Brazil, for example, premiums, games, contests, gifts with purchases, and samples are popular, while coupons and refunds are less effective.

- Worldwide, most countries have legislation governing the use of games, contests, and sweeps. Restrictions include obtaining special government permissions, publicizing exact details of offers, and special taxes (e.g., Italy).

Adapting Sales Management Practices The global forces impacting marketing management also affect sales management aspects of the promotions mix.[56] Where product mixes are similar across markets, potential exists to standardize the sales management practices promoting them. But, for many industries, environmental factors affect local management practices. Localizing influences include:

- *Effects of geography and market potential on sales force structure:* Many international firms are from high-potential developed markets where sales forces are specialized by territory, product, and customer-types. Foreign sales forces in smaller markets (e.g., Scandinavia) must often be organized more economically, with larger sales territories and less specialization by product or customer-type.

- *Ethnic divisions* within countries such as India require companies to recruit sellers with appropriate language/dialect skills. Locally recruited salespersons are also preferable because of their community contacts.

- *National education systems* affect recruitment and selection practices. In developed markets, university graduates can be recruited into sales positions. However, in many, especially developing countries, university education is limited to wealthy, privileged elites, making their recruitment into sales positions difficult.

- *National legislation on compensation packages* makes benefit packages hard to standardize. Western European governments dictate generous packages to cover medical expenses, social-security allowances, and bountiful maternity and vacation policies. In developing-market contexts, inadequate benefit packages cause firms to supplement basic salary packages. Swedish Match's Southeast Asian sales forces receive clothing and additional allowances to bolster morale and pride in being part of the company family. Collectivist orientations can affect compensation schemes. In Japan, though individually based sales incentives are becoming acceptable, most sales bonuses are based on the sales force performance as a whole.

- *Social status influences* can affect sales management activities. Sales presentations to senior managers in high-context societies tend to be muted and respectful in deference to corporate seniority. Similarly, sales meetings and seminars are subdued to avoid conflicts between sellers and senior managers. Finally, in nonconfrontational cultures, sales training is conducted with ritualistic decorum to avoid "loss of face" to either trainees or mentors.

- *Cultural contexts* affect buyer-seller relationships and presentation styles. The high-context cultures of Latin America, the Middle East, and Asia require sellers to develop relationships with buyers. This requires time and personal and corporate commitments to the servicing of such relationships. In Western Europe, buyer-seller relationships run deeper than in the low-context U.S. Client entertaining outside of office hours is often customary and obligatory, especially for big-ticket sales.

High-low context cultures affect party-selling activities of companies like Avon, Mary Kay, and Electrolux. In Western Europe, for example, such selling is "low key" to avoid taking advantage of personal relationships. In Asia, social relationships are the basis for successful selling (though much decorum is required in the sales process).

Distribution, Logistics, and Transportation These decisions are often the most vital component of local marketing strategies. Generally (as noted in the Chapter 5), distribution strategies are dictated by population concentrations within markets and national infrastructures (which parts of the country can be served economically, and which transportation methods should be used—roads, rails, or air). Distribution issues in Latin America, Eastern Europe, Asia, and Africa illustrate the challenges of getting goods to customers in these regions.

Latin American distribution[57] is dominated by the sheer geographic size of the region, which goes from the subtropical north to the frozen south near Antarctica. Major road systems tend to run north-south down the eastern and western seaboards. Road conditions are generally poor, though privately-run toll roads are better. Railroads and ports are passing from public ownership into private hands, making inter-modal transportation arrangements easier to implement.

The liberalization of Latin American markets brought a surge of foreign direct investment in transportation and physical distribution, and foreign logistic providers have upgraded the region's transportation and warehousing facilities. Local firms have worked with foreign companies such as GATX Logistics, American Consolidation Services, and UPS World Logistics to build warehousing facilities and improve administrative procedures, quality standards, and information systems.[58] The region has also attracted major international retailers. French hypermarket specialist Carrefour is Brazil's largest retailer with fifty stores nationwide. The company uses local suppliers (97 percent are Brazilian), decentralized decision making, and low prices to enhance its competitive appeal.[59] Both Chile and Peru have also attracted multinational retail chains, principally from the U.S. and Western Europe, where they compete against local chains in urban areas and mom-and-pop stores in rural parts.

Many companies, realizing the importance of distribution, have established their own facilities. In Colombia, Colgate Palmolive established a number of warehouses throughout the country to quicken retail deliveries, and France's Yoplait centrally distributes its products to around 35,000 stores in Colombia.[60]

Eastern European distribution reflects the slow transition from command to market-forces economies. In Central European countries such as Hungary, Poland, and the Czech Republic, urban-based distribution systems approach Western standards of efficiency. Outside of towns, and as firms move eastward to Russia, the Ukraine, Romania, Bulgaria, and the former USSR republics, old-style management and distribution practices make product movements arthritic and unresponsive to market needs.

Companies have two major approaches to physical distribution in Eastern Europe. The first is to set up local subsidiaries and custom-build transportation and distribution networks from the ground up. German company Schenker & Co. and the Swiss firm Panalpina follow this route, which gives firms good control of their distribution in the more advanced, reform-minded markets of Central Europe. As firms move eastward, a second approach, using independent local distribution partners, is required, as bureaucracy, corruption, and personal contacts become important factors in physical distribution. Local distributors and transporters are preferred as they deal more easily with documentation and other problems (custom clearances, insurance, local language translations, etc.).[61]

International firms must work hard to establish and maintain their Eastern European channels of distribution. In the pharmaceutical industry, foreign firms supply 70 percent of medicines and pharmaceutical raw materials in Russia, yet 4000 local distributors dominate market access. Margins are high, as are stock levels. Distributors are financially weak, and much financing of stocks is necessary.[62]

In Romania's highly traditional distribution structure, wholesaling is dominated by 150 large concerns, few of whom have national coverage. These wholesalers tend to be financially weak and carry broad yet shallow product assortments (i.e., many product types, little variety). Its retail sector resembles the U.S. or Western Europe in the 1940s or 1950s. There are few Western-style supermarkets—and none outside the capital, Bucharest. Store chains, some with over sixty outlets, all have low turnovers, limited product mixes, and high margins. Many Romanian retailers are informal, low-overhead operations; these include kiosks (over 100,000 of them), open-air markets, and street tables. The keys to distributing products successfully in Eastern Europe are careful distributor selection; slow, deliberate expansion; strong sales forces; credit extensions; and the use of promotions rather than price as a competitive weapon.[63]

Asian distribution presents challenges for international companies as they distribute products over large geographic areas. Importers typically use up to forty carriers to service the entire region. High distribution costs put major pressures on margins, especially given the region's relatively small groups of affluent customers and increasing marketplace competitiveness. In particular, the variability in dealing with modern urban distribution systems contrasts with antiquated systems in rural areas. India is typical. Travel documents for goods vary for each of India's twenty-two states, causing administrative hassles and, often 5–6 hour waits at state borders. Retailers are small and have limited space for stock.[64] Distribution is dominated by the neighborhood grocery store—the kirana shop that comprises a high percentage of the 5 million or so retail outlets. Western-style supermarkets, by contrast, number about 400 and account for about 1 percent of national retails sales. The success of the kirana shop is due to the following factors:

- Proximity: Indian housewives lack transport, and kirana shops are convenient for daily shopping.

- Kirana shops provide informal credit, personal service, and home delivery.

- Prices are economical because property values and overheads are low and some price competition is apparent.[65]

Gaining access to distribution remains a significant key success factor for international firms in the Indian market. Local TV manufacturers consistently outsell the Japanese, Korean, and European giants (Matsushita, Sony, LG, Grundig, Thomson) because of their market coverage and reputations. As a result, many manufacturers establish joint ventures (such as GE and Godrej in appliances and Parle and Coca-Cola in soft drinks) to secure access to local distribution.

Western firms trying to do it "their way" have had mixed success. Both Levi Strauss and Reebok tried to sell their wares through exclusive shops, but they went back to multibrand outlets because Indian consumers preferred to shop and compare. On the other hand, Swedish company Oriflame and the U.S.'s Avon and Tupperware have successfully used party selling techniques with Indian housewives.[66]

China has many of the same distribution problems as India. Infrastructure problems mean that many transportation companies must be used to secure national distribution. Wholesalers and distributors are plentiful, and in many industries, products pass through three wholesalers (organized geographically—national, provincial, local levels), each taking significant markups.[67] There are numerous regulatory restraints, especially against foreign participation in distribution and retailing activities. Partly because of these restraints, international firms view Chinese distribution as especially uncontrollable.[68]

Geographic size and infrastructure deficiencies make international companies wary of establishing their own transportation and logistics networks. Many outsource these activities to European and U.S. logistics firms operating in China. Though expensive, these companies offer quick, reliable deliveries, low damage rates, and electronic data links.[69]

In other Asian markets, geographic size and infrastructure problems are not so pronounced, and companies can establish their own distribution networks by building supply-chain relationships with Asian distributors and retailers. Anglo-Dutch consumer goods firm Unilever is an experienced implementer of such strategies. In Vietnam, the company built its network from 50 agents and 30,000 shops to 300 agents and 80,000 outlets. Retailers were provided with product display cabinets and received regular weekly visits from distributors.[70] In Pakistan, the company's Wall's Ice Creams were sold by vendors on bicycles fitted with iceboxes; retail outlets were supplied with special freezer cabinets to keep ice creams frozen even through frequent power outages.[71]

International retailers such as Wal-Mart and Carrefour have been successful in Asia, though local adjustments have been necessary. Typical problems have included the following:

- Most Asians lack the income, transport capacity, and domestic storage for bulk buying. Wal-Mart's Indonesian mega-store, an hour's drive from Jakarta, has suffered, as has International Mega Mart's facility in Shanghai, China.[72]

- Local adjustments to fit consumer purchasing habits have been key success factors. Toys R Us and the U.K.'s Marks and Spencer localized their product

> *Businesses planned for service are apt to succeed; businesses planned for profit are apt to fail.*
>
> —*Nicholas M. Butler, U.S. educator*

assortments. The nineteen Asian venues of Toys R Us have been particularly popular in Taiwan, Singapore, and Hong Kong.[73]

- Political backlashes have occurred as the operating habits of international firms have disrupted traditional lifestyles. The Chinese government banned door-to-door selling in 1998, hurting Amway, Avon, and Mary Kay in particular. Foreign investments in Chinese distribution and retailing have been severely restricted.[74]

- Distribution in Japan employs about 20 percent of the working population, and protecting the labyrinth of multiple wholesalers has been a priority of the Japanese government since 1945. Price competition has been kept to a minimum to preserve employee bonus systems, and competition within distribution channels has been limited to new-product introductions. The 1990s saw some movement away from distribution employment maximization toward price competition, though much remains to be done.[75]

African distribution is extremely variable. At the upper end of the retailing spectrum, South Africa has many varieties of stores, and increased industrialization has affected lifestyles and shopping habits. With more women entering the work force, the trend is toward convenience shopping, with retailers responding with wider product assortments to facilitate one-stop shopping.[76] Small-store formats have been successful, and specialized retailers have emerged in the toys, books, baby goods, and bedding sectors.[77]

More typical in rural areas are the bazaars and street vendors found in Uganda and throughout much of the developing world. Animals are slaughtered and butchered to order. Fresh vegetables are stacked up, and store-minders call out their prices. Plastic bowls, T-shirts, magazines, and other Western artifacts are available in limited supplies.[78]

Pricing Pricing in international markets varies according to whether country markets are serviced from outside (via exporting) or if they have in-market presences (local manufacturing).

Export pricing works where there is little competition in foreign markets and exporters are not disadvantaged by the additional charges brought about by extra packaging, transportation costs, and import duties. Such costs routinely add 10–50 percent onto product prices, with importers and distributors determining final prices charged to customers and exporters having little control. Where export volumes justify the expense, exporters can set up marketing subsidiaries and sales networks to exert better control over final prices.

> A thing is worth whatever the buyer will pay for it.
>
> —*Publilius Syrus, 1st-century* B.C. *author*

In-market pricing strategies are variable according to market conditions. In competitive market-driven economies such as North America and Western Europe, price is a primary competitive weapon. Price information is readily available through company lists (for industrial goods) or through media advertisements (for consumer products), and governments have agencies to monitor unscrupulous business dealings such as price gouging (excessive prices due to unusual conditions such as monopolies).

In Western Europe, the introduction of the euro has resulted in companies like Sun Microsystems adopting pan-European pricing policies. Pricing inconsistencies in basic products such as foods and office equipment, with cross-border variations up to 100 percent of final prices, are diminishing. Internet-based business-to-business transactions have been most affected as European firms have been able to shop and compare among rival producers. Companies have been rethinking their segmentation strategies and using packaging variations and other forms of differentiation to blur cross-border product and price comparisons.[79]

In many parts of the world, however, price is less of a competitive weapon. In countries like India, Taiwan, and Colombia, some resale price maintenance is practiced in order to maintain margins and reduce sales fluctuations due to heavy price competition. In countries such as China and Japan, price competition is constrained in order to maintain stable markets and avoid job layoffs. In these nations (and in many others), distribution channels are less efficient, and price competition upsets established distribution patterns and relationships. China in the late 1990s set price minimums on twenty-one industries to restrain competition and prevent layoffs for non-price competitive companies.[80] Japan's retail prices are set high to preserve the bonus system in their distributive industries.

In emerging markets and especially outside of urban areas, haggling is the primary price-setting mechanism, with prices settled by verbal interactions between buyers and sellers. Such practices are common in Latin America, Africa, and Asia.

> There are two fools in every market; one asks too little, one asks too much.
>
> —*Russian proverb*

MANAGING LOCAL SUPPLY CHAINS: MANAGEMENT AND HUMAN RESOURCE ISSUES

National supply chains must be staffed and managed, and local management practices usually complement localized supplier-manufacturer-distributor-customer processes. As international corporations have moved into foreign markets, they encounter local human-resource practices that challenge their corporate models. From Table 3.5, traditional-modern contrasts in management and worker relations help put international differences into context.

Management Styles

A *traditional management style* emphasizes output and employment maximization. Leadership styles are autocratic, with top-down orientations in communications and decision making. Workforce turnover tends to be low, and lifetime employment is often the norm. With this orientation, seniority and corporate loyalty are the keys to individual progression within the corporate hierarchy. Lack of marketplace competition deemphasizes customer satisfaction and marketplace responsiveness as corporate objectives. This management style developed in stable markets shielded from the uncertainties associated with modern competitive industries.

> If you've got them by the balls, their hearts and minds will soon follow.
>
> —*Charles Colson, assistant to President Nixon*

A *modern management style* tends to be profit-oriented, with increased communications within corporations and greater employee inputs into decision making. Nevertheless, employees compete for corporate resources, and rewards tend to be results-based. The North American managerial style most closely resembles this profile. Western European companies are moving toward the competitive model, though some traditional elements still remain. Latin American, Asian, Eastern European, and African models are more closely aligned to the traditional model.

North American Management Styles Management styles in North America were culled from the pioneering values of nineteenth-century domestic expansion. As colonization took root and populations moved from east to west coasts, self-reliance, independence, and a willingness to shape environments according to their needs were essential qualities for survival. The breaking away in 1776 from British rule established a social order in the U.S. that was free from "accidents of birth." Citizens determined their own places in society through hard work and achievement ("to do is to be"), rather than through family pedigree (aristocracies: "to be is to do"). Today, these values are hallmarks of North American management styles.

The U.S. orientation toward shaping their own destinies ("making things happen") makes American business people adept at planning, and the self-reliance trait causes them to prefer accountability on an individual rather than a group basis.

North American management styles are based on merit and internal competition rather than seniority and corporate harmony needs. This can be traced back to the societal competitiveness at the political level (through fiercely competitive elections), at the economic level (through interfirm rivalries), and at the personal level (with the economically-based social-class system). The high living standards of North America are testament to the effectiveness of the capitalist philosophy. However, the spread of market forces-based business practices and competitive management philosophies to other nations remains a contentious issue.

>
>
> You don't die in the U.S., you underachieve.
>
> —*Jerzy Kozinski*

> America: The only country in the world where failing to promote yourself is regarded as being arrogant.
>
> —*Gary Trudeau, political cartoonist*

Western European Management Styles Western European management styles have been historically shaped by social distinctions, notably blue- versus white-collar employees, and recognitions of different skill levels among workers (unskilled, skilled occupations). Many of these hierarchical distinctions are still apparent in today's Europe.

The *French management style* can be termed elitist, with graduates from the *grandes ecoles* being admitted automatically to cadre ranks of professional managers, and the President Directeur Generale (PDG) wielding significant power in determining the strategic direction of the corporation. Managerial training is somewhat traditional and involves rotations through departments to give executives company-wide perspectives that pay off over the individual's career-long commitment to the company. Management is viewed as an intellectual and professional pursuit, and mathematics, engineering, and scientific backgrounds are viewed as essential.[81]

German management styles share many French characteristics, with high levels of numeracy required, functional rotations, and (especially among elite German firms), lifelong employment opportunities. Collegiality and teamwork are valued, though formal hierarchies exercise subtle restraints on individual initiatives.[82] Historically, many leading German companies have been family owned or controlled through bank-held interests. This has sheltered German managers from strict shareholder-profit orientations and given companies latitude in strategic choices and HRM activities.

French and German firms generally follow *stakeholder capitalist models,* whereby shareholders are one of many stakeholder groups to be satisfied. Other stakeholders include suppliers, labor, distributors, customers, as well as government, environmental, and press groups. This Continental management style emphasizes employment longevity and movement down the human-resource experience curve.[83]

However, this system has come under pressure as European competition stiffens under the impetus of economic and political unification. Shareholder interests, downsizing, and restructuring have become part of the management lexicon in Continental Europe for companies like Veba and Hoechst (Germany), Elf Acquitaine and Danone (France), ENI in Italy, and Nokia in Finland.[84] Firms have become less hierarchical and more oriented toward networking, teamwork, joint problem solving, and the free communication of ideas.[85]

U.K., Dutch, and Scandinavian management styles are more likely to follow shareholder rather than stakeholder interests, and decisions are based on shareholder considerations rather than broader concerns. As such, management styles and human-resource policies are based on the "economic-contractual" model of market-determined wages and executive movements among competing companies.

Overall, relative to North American styles, European managers still tend to have closer relationships with stakeholders (especially governments and labor), reflecting their socialist histories. Management structures are still somewhat hierarchical, though participative decision styles are spreading. European managers tend to have greater tolerances for cultural diversity, a "people orientation," and a propensity toward negotiated compromises and "managing between the extremes."[86]

Latin American Management Styles Management styles in Latin America exhibit many traditional characteristics, though these are breaking down as modernization and international management influences diffuse through the region. The boss (patron) is in charge and makes all major decisions. Workforces, especially outside of modernizing urban centers, are stable—but not efficiency-oriented. Loyalty is highly valued, and maverick behaviors are viewed with suspicion. Considerable respect is accorded to senior employees. Criticism of peers and "betters" is muted, and titles and protocols are observed in ritualistic fashions.

> Tomorrow is often the busiest day of the week.
> —*Spanish proverb*

In Latin America's case, autocratic management styles mirror society at large. Latin American society is still highly stratified. The availability of education, especially at university levels, is limited to elites. However, change is on the way. Educational opportunities are being made available to broader spectrums of the population, and, as industrialization creates demand for executives, merit rather than privilege is becoming the criterion for advancement. Top-management elitism is expected to erode as lower-level managers earn the opportunity to participate in corporate decision making.

Asian Management Styles—Japan Within Asia, Japan's approach to management has attracted the most attention over the years and has been the model for many Asian companies. Its major characteristics—market share/employment goals, participative decision making, seniority orientation, subjective evaluative criteria, lifelong employment, and generalist (rather than specialist) management training—are largely traditional. But they have been effective. Japanese management styles propelled the country to leadership positions in many global industries and have been emulated by top U.S. and European corporations. But how did the Japanese management system evolve? The religious and philosophical underpinnings of Asian society provide valuable clues.

> *If he works for you, you work for him.*
>
> —*Japanese proverb*

- *Shinto,* the indigenous Japanese religion, requires its followers to be sincere in relationships and to respect the rights of others.

- *Buddhism* preaches the virtues of full employment through the doctrine that crime and immorality result from economic poverty.

- *Confucian philosophies* emphasize that man's inner stature is enhanced through contributions to national and societal causes. The seniority orientation, common in many Asian societies, is spelled out in Confucius' five unequal relationships (ruler and subject, husband and wife, older and younger brother, senior and junior brother, and father and son).[87]

Other historic and geographic influences on Asian and Japanese management styles include:

- *A history of wet rice farming* which for efficiency reasons had to be undertaken in large groups (twenty or more). This cultivated group skills in production that live on in Japanese corporations in quality circle and management groups.

- *Land scarcities and small dwellings* that have made the Japanese acutely aware of the need for social harmony.

- In Japan's case, *geographic isolation* made the Japanese racially one of the purest of world countries and contributed to a high level of national patriotism.[88] This nationalism promoted protectionist policies that shielded the Japanese market from destructive price competition and enabled firms to focus on corporate harmony and long-term strategic goals.[89]

Management Styles in India Indian styles have a number of traditional and Hindu characteristics. As Exhibit 13-2 shows, the stratified nature of Indian society gives companies autocratic tendencies; families rather than jobs are viewed as important, and fatalistic perspectives are common.

Eastern European Management Styles Until the 1980s Gorbachev era of perestroika and glasnost (and for a period thereafter), communist governments set employment, wages, prices, and production levels in accordance with five-year plans. At this time, managers were trained in science and engineering and were appointed on the strength of their communist party affiliations. As a result, old-style Russian managers had the following characteristics:

> ## EXHIBIT 13-2
> ### Managing for Success in India
>
> ❦
>
> Indian management is hierarchical and has its origins in the Hindu caste system discussed in Chapter 12. Managers and workers are usually acutely aware of social differences that in society at large determine whom they should marry and associate with. Other differences include:
>
> - Working to support their families rather than to meet corporate objectives or achieve personal recognition
>
> - Fatalistic perspectives (perhaps related to Hindu and Muslim beliefs) that make commitments to deadlines precarious ("If it can be done by then—fine; but I don't totally control the situation")
>
> - Criticism of any kind is indirect to protect relationships between givers and receivers; it is subtle, lengthy, and may involve use of a third party (like mediators and go-betweens in intercultural negotiating).
>
> - Top-down communications may be very direct ("do this by 4 P.M."), reflecting the authority structure. Western approaches ("I'd be very much obliged if you could . . .") are viewed as indecisive.
>
> - Colleagues from different caste backgrounds may not cooperate well, as, despite managerial equality, social inequalities may result in suggestions being ignored (if from the lower caste) or assumed superior (if from the higher caste person).
>
> **Source: Adapted from Frazze, Valerie. "Working with Indians."** *Global Workforce* **(July 1998): 10–11.**

- Managerial objectives tend to be focused on technologies (especially in defense of military-based sectors), employment (ensuring that jobs were maintained), and production goals (regardless of whether demand existed for products).[90]

- The effects of macro factors such as inflation on wages, costs, and prices were ignored or under-appreciated.

- Despite collectivist philosophies that emphasized the good of the organization or the group, managers used their positions to further personal goals and to maintain their own power and leadership positions.

- There was a widespread avoidance of responsibility and lack of accountability among Russian managers. Unsolved problems were passed around organizational levels. Information was hoarded ("information is power") rather than circulated.

- Labor-management relations were characterized by mutual distrust.

- Job descriptions, specifications, and evaluations were noticeably absent, and pay awards tended to be uniform or arbitrary.[91]

But in the 1990s, change started to occur. Increasingly, managers obtained business educations, began to understand how market economies worked, and English became the foreign language to know. Increasing numbers of Western-educated Russian managers became available, modern management methods took hold, and the Russian work ethic improved.[92]

Slowly, the Russian management style has evolved under Western influences, and companies entering the Russian market have adopted one of two approaches to human resource and managerial strategies. The first is the "imported model" that involves the direct application of Western methods to Russian affiliates, including:

> The only solution for the problem of communism is pure, unadulterated capitalism.
>
> —*William J. H. Boetcker*

- Linking business strategy and performance indicators (market share, profitability) with HRM policies. Forecasts and plans are primary drivers of recruiting strategies, and selection processes include psychological and aptitude testing.

- Adopting parent-company schemes of professional development, including competency assessments, career planning, development assignments, and periodic reviews.

- Using Russian nationals as trainers to speed up the introduction of new methods and schemes, with increased investments in training and development.

The second approach is the localization model. This includes using some old-style Russian management philosophies. Management and personnel needs are filled on an ad hoc basis. Managerial development is informal and implemented through coaching and job rotation, and managerial compensation schemes include non-cash items such as cars, subsidized or free meals, club memberships, and medical insurance.[93]

African Management Styles—"Ubuntu" While it is yet to emerge as an economic power, companies have slowly started to invest in Africa in anticipation of its development potential. As a result, recent attention has been focused on African management styles. "Ubuntu," as it is known, takes African culture into account, and has the following characteristics:

- Western managements are exclusive, in that they focus on individuals and their self-fulfillment. African managers see themselves as parts of groups (tribal, clan, companies), and their aim is to establish themselves as part of the group.

- Western managers work for themselves, with profit as the major motivation for work. African managers see profit as the residue accumulating from products and services that are useful to society.

- Decisions are best made by consensus, with account taken of both majority opinions and dissenting voices. Post-agreement opposition to decisions is viewed as confrontational and to be avoided.[94]

The parallels between Ubuntu and Asian management styles are notable. Both have collective orientations that place societal and group needs above those of individuals, and both de-emphasize profit maximization.

Management-Worker Relations

A special component of management style is management-worker relations. These are important for international companies, as subsidiary managers are

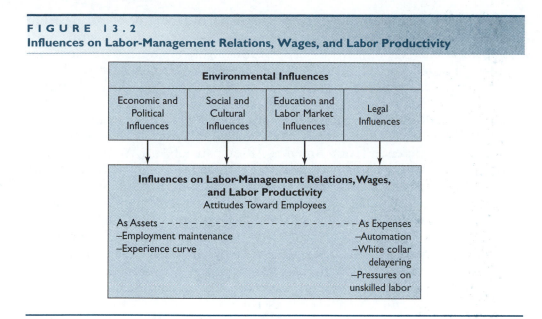

FIGURE 13.2
Influences on Labor-Management Relations, Wages, and Labor Productivity

key intermediaries between head office and local operations and must convert head-office goals and orientations into local output. Worldwide, labor (both blue and white collar) can be treated as assets to be nurtured and encouraged or as expenses to be minimized. As Figure 13.2 shows, political, economic, social, cultural, educational, labor market, and legal influences affect this relationship.

Economic and Political System Differences Many international companies operate in competitive marketplaces where there are continual pressures to contain costs and upgrade manufacturing efficiencies. In these contexts, labor is often viewed as an expense, and management-labor relations can be antagonistic. In the U.S. and Western Europe, restructurings and downsizings are regular occurrences, and trade union resistance is customary. In Western Europe, extensive unemployment and social-welfare programs cushion labor as these adjustments are made, but management-labor conflicts are still common.

Management-labor problems arise as countries open up their economies to international competition. In the U.S., trade unions and environmentalists have opposed free trade because of its employment effects and child-labor issues in developing markets. In Western Europe, economic restructuring has strained national welfare systems. In industrializing countries, governments have been pressured to upgrade national welfare, pension, health care, and education systems to cope with the new economic realities. China's late 1990s push toward a market economy included provisions for national health, pension systems, and retraining centers to absorb the labor-market shock as state-owned enterprises streamlined and became unable to perform stewardship functions for workers (houses, company pensions, education systems).[95] In almost all cases, labor unrest has resulted, despite government efforts to buffer the effects of increased global competition.

> Management and union may be likened to that serpent of the fables who on one body had two heads that fighting each other with poisoned fangs killed themselves.
>
> —*Peter Drucker,*
> *U.S. business consultant*
> *and author*

National economic and political priorities set the tone for corporate labor policies. In pro-labor countries, such as much of Western Europe, firms must balance efficiency concerns with "fair" treatment of employees. In France, for example, it is very difficult to fire workers. In the market-forces-oriented U.S., the major moves have been to push the unemployed back into the workforce.

Social and Cultural Differences These differences make some adaptations inevitable, particularly in emerging markets. Where countries have long histories of social class differences (Latin America, Africa, parts of Asia, Western Europe), white- and blue-collar distinctions tend to be maintained, and "us versus them" mindsets strain management-worker relations. Separate dining facilities, and perquisites (perks), are visible reminders of management-worker differences. Use of titles, elaborate protocols, and strict hierarchical reporting structures highlight status differences in organizations. But management-labor differences tend to erode as marketplace competitiveness increases, and pressures mount to sidestep protocols, streamline decision making, and quicken corporate response times to marketplace changes.

> I understand why some American companies fail to gain the loyalty and dedication of their employees. Employees cannot care for an employer who is prepared to take away their livelihood at the first sign of trouble.
>
> —*Sadami Wada,*
> *vice-president*
> *Sony Corporation*

Countries with collectivist/group orientations (such as Asia, Africa) regard employment preservation as corporate and national economic objectives. As noted earlier, since 1945, Japanese companies have striven to maintain full employment and regard employees as assets. This is not unusual, especially in developing economies where firms have paternalistic attitudes toward labor and jobs are preserved wherever possible. Problems occur when international firms try to lay off workers in economies used to lifetime employment and paternalistic attitudes toward labor. Anglo-Dutch firm Unilever and U.S. semiconductor maker ChipPAC had major labor problems when they tried to lay off workers in China.[96]

Education and Labor Market Differences National education systems equip citizens with skills to make them productive employees in industrial settings. Labor market problems occur when national education systems are insufficiently developed to provide skills in appropriate areas. Countries at low levels of development have surpluses of unskilled labor (as rural to urban migrations create worker surpluses) and shortages of well-educated employees. National shortfalls can create problems. In Mexico's case, industrialization has been stunted by a national average of five years of formal education.[97] In other cases, efforts to upgrade educational infrastructures have paid dividends. National emphases on science, math, and engineering have made India and other Asian nations attractive sites for high-tech companies.

In developed economies, rising educational levels and standards of living have put unskilled labor in a disadvantageous position. Cost considerations have pushed labor-intensive industries to developing nations, leaving domestic service industries as the only major users of unskilled labor. In high-cost labor nations, governments strive to enhance worker skills to make them employable in high value-added industries. Those lacking skills must often rely on trade unions and political protection (through tariff and non-tariff barriers) to preserve jobs, though worldwide free-trade movements make such moves at best only short-term job-protection measures.

Legal Factors The more governments legislate workplace issues, the fewer the conflicts between management and labor. The International Labor Organization (ILO) provides countries with draft frameworks for labor laws and keeps statistics and reports about labor activities around the world. At the regional level, the EU provides consultation guidelines for management and labor relations for international firms within its jurisdiction.

> *Industrial relations are like sexual relations. It's better between two consenting parties.*
>
> —*Lord (Vic) Feather, British trade union leader*

Most countries have labor laws, though the extent to which they protect labor and trade-union rights varies. Most national labor laws cover:

- Minimum wage levels and fringe benefits
- Employment discrimination issues (age, gender, disabilities)
- Work week (hours worked, overtime issues)
- Sickness, maternity benefits
- Conditions of employment and job termination
- Legal status of trade unions and industrial dispute issues
- Management-labor issues
- Worker health and safety policies (including child labor laws)

However, having legal frameworks in place is one thing, enforcing them effectively is another. Developing-nation governments in particular have problems monitoring businesses, especially outside of urban areas. Their challenge is to frame labor law requirements to balance worker needs for employment stability with economic policies opening up markets to international competition. Clashes between organized labor and pro-business groups are common. In Latin America, the 1970s saw major extensions of legislation for labor entitlements and worker protection. This trend continued in the 1990s with protections of worker collectives, preventions of mass dismissals, work-week legislation, and payroll-financed social security and employment systems. However, there was major opposition and significant labor unrest as labor markets became increasingly competitive.[98]

KEY POINTS

- All international companies must deal with local market conditions to greater or lesser extents, regardless of whether they export to the market, have contractual agreements within the market, or have manufacturing and/or marketing investments there. In all cases, they must manage local stakeholders (governments, business communities, local communities, the press, and environmental/consumer groups).

- Supply-chain localization benefits firms by simplifying raw material and component sourcing; anticipating manufacturing problems and managing local production processes; enhancing market appeals through localized product, promotion, distribution, and pricing strategies; and maintaining locally-attuned management styles and harmonious management-labor relations.

- Supplier management is important when (1) companies subcontract manufacturing to foreign producers and are unable to control local hiring or work conditions; (2) there are problems financing local suppliers, maintaining quality, establishing global manufacturing standards, instilling appropriate supply chain disciplines (e.g., JIT), and overcoming physical infrastructure problems (e.g., unreliable transportation systems).

- Local manufacturing systems must overcome problems associated with (1) unanticipated costs, (2) inadequate worker education, (3) local labor laws and their enforcement, (4) employee recruitment and selection, (5) factory and shop floor discipline, (6) maintaining efficiency in production schedules in the face of infrastructure deficiencies and poor worker attitudes.

- Multinational marketing strategies entail identifying local target markets and adapting product mixes (transfers, custom-built goods, and services), individual products (measurement units, sizing, packaging, labeling, instructions, warranties, etc.), advertising messages, sales promotions, sales management strategies, pricing and distribution strategies to local market conditions.

- Management styles are adjusted to local needs, with modern, profit, and efficiency-oriented management styles being prominent in North America and parts of Western Europe, and traditional styles, emphasizing employment maintenance, seniority, loyalty, and lifetime employment characterizing Latin American, Asian, Eastern European, and African managements, though, in all cases, modernizing influences are taking hold in these regions.

- Management-worker relations vary from treating employees as expense-sheet items to being regarded as corporate assets. Political, economic, social, cultural, education, labor market, and legal factors are major influences on labor-management relations.

ENDNOTES

1. Craig Simons, "Marketing to the Masses," *Far Eastern Economic Review* (Sept. 4, 2003): 32–34; Ben Dolven, "Into China's New Frontier—Foreign Brands, successful in cities, head for tough rural markets," *Wall Street Journal* (Feb. 23, 2003): A10; Dallas *Asiainfo Daily News* (Sept. 7, 1999): 1.

2. Alan S. Parker, *Going Local: How Global Companies Become Market Insiders,* (London: Business International: Economist Intelligence Unit, 1991), 69.

3. Parker, 71.

4. Parker, 45.

5. Erik Guyot, "Foreign Companies bring China more than jobs," *Wall Street Journal* (Sept. 15, 1999): A26.

6. Ibid.

7. Anonymous, "Global warming education," *Oil & Gas Journal* (June 7, 1999): 19.

8. Anonymous, "A Warming World," *Economist* (June 28, 1997): 41–42.

9. Anonymous, "An Asian pea-souper," *Economist* (Sept. 27, 1997): 40.

10. Alex Scott, "Friends of the Earth launches toxic release website," *Chemical Week* (Feb. 17, 1999): 20.

11. Bruce Gilley, "Sticker Shock," *Far Eastern Economic Review* (Jan. 14, 1999): 20–23.

12. Ibid.

13. Anonymous, "Green Fords," *Time* (May 31, 1999): 78.

14. Emily Thornton, "Only God and Toyota can make a tree," *Business Week* (March 30, 1998): 58.

15. Anonymous, "Global Greenings," *Buildings* (Oct. 1998): 100.

16. Jenn Bendell and David Murphy, "Strange bed fellows: business and environmental groups," *Business and Society Review* 98 (1997): 40–46.

17. Colin Brown, "Consumer Activism in Europe," *Consumer Policy Review* 8: 6 (Nov–Dec., 1998): 209–12.

18. Diane West, "Nader raids DTC ads," *Pharmaceutical Executive* 19: 4 (April 1999): 5–9.

19. Kevin Gopal, "Truth, lies and confidences," *Pharmaceutical Executive* 17: 1 (Jan. 1997): 26–28.

20. Anonymous, "Sowing the seeds of discontent," *Director* (July 1998): 42.

21. Thomas G. Dolan, "Long Live the Revolution," *Barron's* (Sept. 15, 1997): 62–63.

22. Dexter Roberts, "Blazing away at foreign brands," *Business Week* (May 12, 1997): 58–60.

23. Anonymous, "To FDI For," *Business Eastern Europe* (Jan. 11, 1999): 1.

24. Anonymous, "Latin America: New Media, new message," *Business Latin America* (March 15, 1999): 7.

25. Nikhil Deogun, et al., "Anatomy of a Recall: How Coke's Controls Fizzled out in Europe," *Wall Street Journal* (June 29, 1999): A1, A6.

26. Shada Islam, "Minor concerns," *Far Eastern Economic Review* (June 18, 1998): 25–26.

27. "Viewpoint: Beyond compliance; social accountability can protect companies and profits," *Asiaweek* (April 13, 2001): 1–3.

28. Anonymous, "Africa: Coca-Cola bubbles along," *Crossborder Monitor* (June 24, 1998) 8.

29. Anonymous, "Settling in for the long haul," *Crossborder Monitor* (May 13, 1998): 8.

30. Anonymous, "Quick bites, slow profits," *Business Eastern Europe* (March 4, 1996): 7.

31. Anonymous, "Desperately seeking suppliers," *Business Latin America* (May 20, 1996): 1.

32. Amy Zuckerman, "Using ISO 14000 as a trade barrier," New Steel *Iron Age* (March 1999): 77.

33. Bill McKnight, Richard Miskewicz, Yan Liu, "Asia supply chains: The Hong Kong/China Connection," *Transportation and Distribution* (June 1997): 79–82.

34. Susan Tiffany, "Turkey's Pelit branches out," *Candy Industry* (March 1998): 22–27.

35. Anonymous, "Southeast Asia's learning difficulties," *Economist* (Aug. 16, 1997): 30–31.

36. Anonymous, "Zimbabwe: BHP exits," *Country Monitor* (July 14, 1999): 12.

37. S. Benjamin Prasad, "Technology Transfer: The Approach of a Dutch Multinational," *Technovation* 4: 1 (1986): 3–15.

38. This has been empirically verified; see Richard R. Still and John S. Hill, "Effects of Urbanization on Multinational Product Policies," *Columbia Journal of World Business* 19 (Summer 1984): 62–67.

39. John S. Hill and William L. James, "Product and Promotion Transfers in Consumer Goods Multinationals," *International Marketing Review* 8:2 (1991): 6–17.

40. Anonymous, "Latin America: Unilever responds to down turn," *Country Monitor* (July 23, 1999): 12.

41. M. Kahn, "Breakfast in Bombay isn't just Corn Flakes," *Advertising Age International* (Oct. 19, 1998): 15.

42. Pablo Maas, "Foreign Command," *Business Latin America* (June 21, 1999): 7.

43. Anonymous, "Against the Odds," *Business Asia* (Jan. 11, 1999): 4–5.

44. Ibid.

45. Ibid.

46. Suzanne Bidlake, "Campbell expands in Europe's soup market," *Advertising Age International* (Nov. 9, 1998): 13.

47. Sarah Roe, "Green Light," *Business Eastern Europe* (March 22, 1999): 1.

48. Anonymous, "Compaq, Digital defend service alliance," *Computer Reseller News* (April 15, 1996): 3, 208.

49. John S. Hill and William L. James, "Effects of selected environmental and structural variables on international advertising strategy," *Current Issues and Research in Advertising* 12: 1–2 (1989): 135–53.

50. Normandy Madden, "Drug ad rules are Chinese Puzzle," *International Advertising Age* (Oct. 19, 1998): 30.

51. Miriam Jordan, "In Rural India, Video Vans sell toothpaste and shampoo," *Wall Street Journal* (Jan. 1996): B1, B5.

52. Normandy Madden, "Brew rivals shift their images and agencies," *Advertising Age International* (Oct. 19, 1998): 22.

53. Peter Waldman, "Please don't show you lingerie in Iran, even if it's for sale," *Wall Street Journal* (June 21, 1995): A1.

54. This section based on *PROMO Magazine: Special Report* (Aug. 1998): 512–17.

55. "Removing restrictions in sales promotions: Proposal for new regulation," *European Business Journal* 14: 1 (2002): 54–55.

56. John S. Hill, Richard R. Still, and Unal Boya, "Managing the Multinational Sales Force," *International Marketing Review* 8: 1 (1991): 19–31.

57. Based on Toby B. Gooley, "Things are Looking up," *Logistics* (Aug. 1998): 79–84.

58. Toby B. Gooley, "US 3rd parties hit the road to Rio," *Logistics* (Aug. 1998): 87–91.

59. Anonymous, "Carrefour: growing amid competition," *Business Latin America* (April 27, 1998): 7.

60. Anonymous, "Colombia's chain of distribution rattles MNCs," *Crossborder Monitor* (Dec. 4, 1996): 1–2.

61. Anonymous, "Shopping for Shippers," *Business Eastern Europe* (March 1, 1999): 6–7.

62. James Arnold, "Bitter Pills," *Business Eastern Europe* (Feb. 22, 1999): 3.

63. Anonymous, "Benckiser tackles antiquated distribution," *Crossborder Monitor* (Jan. 20, 1999): 12.

64. Amy Zuckerman, "Managing the unmanageable," *Distribution* (Feb. 1999): 40–41.

65. Anonymous, "Corner Shop," *Business Asia* (March 9, 1998): 4–5.

66. Ibid.

67. S. T. Kluk, W. Z. Xu, W. C. Ye, "Distribution: The Chinese Puzzle," *Long Range Planning* 31: 2 (1998): 295–307.

68. Anonymous, "Stuck in the Middle," *Business Asia* (Jan. 11, 1999): 6–7.

69. Ibid.

70. Anonymous, "Nothing if not thorough," *Business Asia* (Jan. 11, 1999): 5.

71. Anonymous "Licking the opposition," *Business Asia* (Feb. 22, 1999): 5.

72. Anonymous, "Retail retrenchment," *Business Asia* (Aug. 26, 1996): 1–3.

73. Ibid.

74. Anonymous, "Requiem," *Business China* (Jan. 4, 1999): 2.

75. Emily Thornton, "Revolution in Japanese retailing," *Fortune* (Feb. 7, 1994): 143–46.

76. Joan Muller, "Specialist shopping is latest trend," *Finance Week* (Oct. 2, 1998): 30.

77. Karola McArthur, "South Africa: Retail Industry Profile," *Stores* (Feb. 1999): 543–44.

78. Richard C. Morais, "The world's first department store," *Forbes* (Dec. 29, 1997): 110–11.

79. "Pricing for the Euro," *Business Europe* (April 21, 1999): 1–3, (May 5 1999): 4.

80. Dexter Roberts, "So much for price competition," *Business Week* (No. 30, 1998): 28–29.

81. Jean Louis Barsoux and Peter Lawrence, "The Making of a French Manager," *Harvard Business Review* (July–Aug. 1991): 58–67.

82. Based on Anthony Ferner, "Country of origin effects and HRM in multinational companies," *Human Resource Management Journal* 7: 1 (1997): 19–37.

83. Ibid.

84. Janet Guyon, "Europe's new capitalists," *Fortune* (Feb. 5, 1999): 104–8.

85. Francesco Caio, "The Catalyst for a New Organization," *Harvard Business Review* (Jan.–Feb. 1999): 49.

86. R. Calori and B. Dufour, "Management European Style," *Academy of Management Executive* 9: 3 (1995): 61–71.

87. From John S. Hill, "The Japanese Business Puzzle," *Journal of General Management* 15: 3 (Spring 1990): 20–38; and Richard D. Lewis, "Wizened and Wiser," *Management Today* (May 1996): 100–1.

88. Hill, 20–23.

89. Hill, 34–38.

90. Linda M. Randall and Lori A. Coakley, "Building successful partnerships in Russia and Belarus: The impact of culture on strategy," *Business Horizons* (March–April 1998): 15–22.

91. Ruth May, Carol Bormann Young, Donna Ledgerwood "Lessons from the Russian Human Resource Experience," *European Management Journal* 16: 4 (1998): 447–59.

92. Stanislar Shekshnia, "Western Multinationals' Human Resource Practices in Russia," *European Management Journal* 16: 4 (1998): 460–65.

93. Ibid.

94. Anver Versi, "The Ubuntu system of management," *African Business* (Dec. 1998): 7–8.

95. Dexter Roberts, Mark L. Clifford, and Matt Miller, "Overhauling China Inc.," *Business Week* (Aug. 25, 1997): 54–55.

96. Craig S. Smith, "China's workers challenge status quo," *Wall Street Journal* (June 9, 1999): A20.

97. Geri Smith and Elizabeth Malkin, "Mexican Makeover," *Business Week* (Dec. 11, 1998): 50–52.

98. Arturo S. Bronstein, "Labour law reform in Latin America: Between state protection and flexibility," *International Labour Review* 136: 1 (Spring 1997): 5–26.

CASETTE 13-1
Localization Strategies in Rural India

Rural markets in developing nations are one of the final frontiers for international companies as they expand their global marketing presences. These markets are important because they are today's battlegrounds for tomorrow's consumers. India's 700+ million and China's 900+ million are among the many sets of rural consumers being targeted worldwide. Yet the task of reaching and appealing to these consumers requires that firms customize their approaches, as market conditions and environments are so different from the home markets of most companies. India's market is typical. About 70 percent of its 1 billion population are rural-based. Of these, about 7 percent of households have flush toilets, 20 percent have running water, a third have electricity and a television, and half are illiterate. There are hundreds and (including dialects) thousands of languages. Infrastructure linkages with regional and major urban metropolises are often weak. Traditions are strong. The Hindu religion dominates daily lifestyles. Local hierarchies based on landholdings and caste are very influential. Decision making tends to be patriarchal and seniority-oriented.

But the winds of globalization are blowing, and, with education being increasingly widespread, TV and satellite channels becoming available, and migrants returning to their rural roots after sampling urban and industrial life, companies are not waiting for modern lifestyles to diffuse. Using combinations of modern and unorthodox methods and media, most are stepping into rural markets to gain decisive first-mover advantages and make impacts on new (and fairly inexperienced) consumers who will eventually become full-time members of the consumption society.

The strategies used to reach rural customers are many and varied. "Folk media" are big. Traveling live shows entertain and promote products. Village magic shows introduce the virtues of Tiger biscuits to children. A puppet show aimed at sugar-cane farmers contains ads for Round Up, a weedicide. At weekly cattle and trade markets, Unilever-produced shows entertain and educate inhabitants about Lifebuoy toilet soap and associated products and use ultraviolet lamps to show dirt and germs on hands. In a country where bathing and cleanliness are key elements of the Hindu religion, the message strikes home. Similarly, cosmetics are not common in rural India, but a major indulgence, especially for women, is hair care. Indians account for about 14 percent of the world's population but about 28 percent of the world's hair. Hair-care products, therefore, receive special attention.

Effective use of folk media is complemented with careful research. Hindustan Lever, in particular, goes to great lengths to profile its rural clienteles, their religion, demographics, affluence, literacy and education levels, and dialects. Their outreach group, Lever & Ogilvy, have their fifty teams of performers customize performances according to rural community needs. To ensure empathy, management trainees spend up to two months living in a rural village. And R and D teams spend time applying science to cost-effective soaps, ice creams, and other products.

One of the greatest challenges in rural marketing is to tempt consumers into abandoning traditional consumption patterns and converting product nonusers into users. For this task, the sachet has become the marketer's weapon of choice. Hindustan Lever's

⤛⤜

shampoo sachets are distributed in 400,000 of India's 600,000 villages and 90 percent of the people buy their shampoos in this form, where they cost as little as 2 rupees (about 5 cents in U.S. money). Similarly, perfumes, powered drinks, detergents, tomato paste, jam, shaving lotion, medicines, and mosquito repellents are also sold in sachet form. In this way, consumers can sample "modernity's allurements" within their $100 per year family incomes.

Other strategies work in rural markets too. The close-knit nature of village communities makes personal selling viable. Hindustan Lever trains women from villages of less than 2000 residents to party-sell their products to neighbors and friends. Colgate-Palmolive uses samples and half-hour infomercials to lure rural consumers away from traditional dentifrice habits, such as tooth cleaning with charcoal powder or using twigs from the neem tree. One half-hour promotion has a bride pulling away from her husband on their wedding night because of bad breath.

Questions

1. Contrast the rural Indian market environment with what might be expected in a developed market. Are there any commonalities?

2. Why are "folk media" effective?

3. Why are rural markets "today's battlegrounds for tomorrow's consumers"?

4. You are preparing to go to India for the first time on a business trip. What would you study first, and why?

5. Are international companies taking advantage of unsophisticated or inexperienced consumers? Are they force-feeding modern consumption behaviors onto consumers? Explain.

Sources: Balu, Rekha. "Strategic Innovation: Hindustan Lever." *Fast Company* **(June 2001): 120–36. Jordan, Miriam. "In Rural India, Video Vans Sell Toothpaste and Shampoo."** *Wall Street Journal* **(Jan. 10, 1996): B1, B5. Bailay, Rasul. "Small Packets, Big Business."** *Far Eastern Economic Review* **(Jan. 23, 2003): 40–41. "India: Marketing to Rural India."** *Businessline Islamabad* **(Oct. 11, 2001): 1. "A Rural Pitch for the Big Brands"** *Business Islamabad* **(July 3, 2002): 1.**

CASETTE 13-2
Child Labor—Is It a Matter of Perspective?

⤛⤜

During the 1700s, just as the British industrial revolution was getting under way, children started to be employed by manufacturers. They worked for lower wages. They rarely caused trouble. Their small, nimble fingers were ideal for tending machines. Their meager wages helped support unemployed parents. Children were also commonly used when the United States started to industrialize in the late 1700s. They were deprived of the chance to attend school. It was not until 1802 that the British Parliament passed a law regulating child labor. Children under fourteen years were not allowed to work at night, and workdays were limited to twelve hours. In 1819, the law was extended to include all (not just pauper) children. Germany was the second nation to pass national child-labor laws in 1839. In the U.S., about 40 percent of all factory workers in New England were between the ages of seven and sixteen years. In 1836, Massachusetts passed the first state child-labor laws. Many states followed the Massachusetts' example, but enforcement was lax because of the large number of poor families and government reluctance to offend employers. The first federal law limiting child labor was passed in 1916, but it was declared unconstitutional by the U.S. Supreme Court in 1918. It was not until 1938 that the Fair Labor Standards Act was passed to limit child-labor work hours.

Fast forward to India entering the new millennium. The newly emerging Asian economy has the highest number of child workers in the world, with between 14–30 million children between the ages of seven and sixteen being employed.

Fourteen-year-old Nancy is typical. She has been an embroiderer since she was six years old. Two of her sisters are carpet weavers. She would like to go to school, but she has to work to pay school fees for her other brother and sister so that they can become educated. They live in the Kashmir in Northern India. Ongoing territorial and religious disputes between Hindu India and Muslim (Islamic) Pakistan has driven off tourists who used to provide livelihoods for local families, including Nancy's father.

Also in India, about 50,000 girl children, mainly 7–14 years old, are employed in the hybrid cotton-seed industry that supplies U.S. and European multinationals, such as Novartis, Hindustan Lever, Advanta (formerly ITC Zeneca) Proagro, and Mahco-Monsanto. They employ 8,000, 20,000, 3,000, 2,000, and 15,000 children respectively. Their region accounts for 70 percent of the country's cotton seed production. Dr. Venkateswarlu, a consultant, noted that the special physical dexterity of children is well-suited to the cottonseed emasculation and pollination processes. Girls are preferred because their wages are lower than those of boys and adults, long hours can be worked (9–12 hours a day), and girls are easier to control—they do not rebel against employers or complain about work conditions. The children are offered chocolates and biscuits as incentives, and they are taken to town twice a month to see a movie. But they are also exposed to poisonous pesticides used on cotton crops, with health problems such as headaches, convulsions, and respiratory ailments among the problems experienced.

The International Labour Organization (ILO), a special UN agency, estimates that there are over 250 million child laborers worldwide. The ILO mandates that fourteen years is the minimum age for industrial work. The organization further notes that the worst forms of child labor are not in the manufacturing sector, but in child prostitution, drug trafficking, military groups, and hazardous work. Children, for example, are commonly used in Tanzanian mines to plant explosives hundreds of feet underground.

In Cambodia, Deth Chrib sits in front of a sewing machine sixteen hours a day, seven days a week. She is thirty years old, with five children. Her husband left her two years ago. For Deth, it is the best job she ever had. She survived the Khmer Rouge regime from 1975–79, when 2 million Cambodians died from overwork, starvation, torture, and executions. At five years of age, she was forced to do manual labor. Deth went to the city to seek a better life, but was forced to become a prostitute. Now she earns $60 a month, in-

cluding overtime, four times what Cambodian judges and doctors make. Her employer, June Textiles (a Singapore corporation), employs 3800 workers. Three-quarters of its output goes to Nike and the Gap. Unfortunately, a BBC TV crew documented a fourteen-year-old worker at the June factory (one year below the minimum 15 years old age). Nike and Gap, stunned by the adverse publicity in the developed world, were threatening to terminate the June contract. The 200 garment factories in Cambodia employ 150,000 workers. For them, recruitment is not a problem. Despite the low wages, firms can easily recruit and employ adults. All require identity papers, but fake papers can be obtained for $30 locally.

That Nike and Gap are responsive to what happens in the home market is not surprising. Both had been involved in developing world sweatshop controversies, along with firms such as Liz Claibourne, Timberland, Reebock, and Wal-Mart. Wal-Mart, the symbol of Main Street USA, had been criticized by Domini 400 Social Index (DSI) for not adhering to its stated policy of favoring vendors who have social and political commitments to basic principles of human rights. Their problem had been a Chinese supplier of handbags that had subjected its workers to 90-hour work weeks, beatings by factory guards, exceptionally low wages, and prison-like conditions. Shareholder responses to these criticisms had been less than sympathetic. On the day of the DSI accusation, Wal-Mart shares had risen. One analyst termed the announcement a "non-event," while a shareholder noted that if the factories did not exist, the only alternatives might be prostitution or selling drugs. Wal-Mart noted that the company's agent and third-party monitors had conducted over 7000 factory audits in the year 2000.

The ongoing controversy about child and sweatshop labor highlights differences between developed and developing country perspectives on labor conditions, and the tightrope that international companies must walk in seeking low-cost sites for price advantages and their responsibilities to third-world citizens.

Questions

1. Summarize the perspectives of the three major parties: the international corporation, third-world workers, and developing-country governments. Is anyone right? Why or why not?

2. What are the consequences for international companies and local governments in monitoring and strictly adhering to local labor laws?

3. Should developed country governments and media acknowledge that developing nations have the right to use child labor as the developed world had done in its early stages of economic development?

Sources: Bowden, Bill. "Wal-Mart: Profits vs. Conscience." *Northwest Arkansas Business Journal* 5:5 (2001): 1–4. Chon, Gina. "Dropped Stitches." *Asiaweek* (Dec. 22, 2000): 1–5. Lovgren, Stefan, Rena Singer, David Enrich. "All that glitters." *US News and World Report* 131: 6 (2001): 24–28. Parekh, Roopesh. "Working for Children." *The World Today* 57: 8–9 (Aug.–Sept. 2001): 12–13. Anonymous. "Nancy's Life: A job for life." *The World Today* 57: 8–9 (Aug.–Sept 2001): 9. Anonymous. "India: Even Multinationals employ girl children for a profit." *Businessline* (June 21, 2001): 1. Brody, David. "Child Labor." *The World Book Encyclopedia* Chicago: World Book Co. C-Ch; 1.

CASETTE 13-3
The Case of the Efficiency-Oriented Gringo

Tim Grant was in his third month at the company's subsidiary just outside of Buenos Aires, Argentina. His firm, an international manufacturer of auto parts, had sent him to its major Latin American affiliate to gain experience in international operations and to informally assess why the subsidiary, acquired just eighteen months ago, was having problems integrating its activities with those of the parent company. Jim, an MBA specializing in finance, had two years of Spanish under his belt, and, while the language had not proven to be a major problem, adjusting to Latin American management styles had left him frustrated.

"They're just not efficiency-oriented," he complained to his boss in Toledo, Ohio, in a long telephone conversation. "Meetings start late, finish late, and totally mess up my daily schedule. Operations aren't a whole lot better. A major parts shipment was due to be sent to the U.S. plant Monday of this week. By Wednesday, it was still sitting on the warehouse dock. I went down there to see what the problem was. It turns out the warehouse supervisor was on vacation for the week, and his assistant wouldn't let the shipment out without his boss's authorization. I called the warehouse supervisor's boss, but he seemed annoyed to be brought in: 'It'll get there, si Dios quiere (if God wills it), Señor Grant,' was his response.

"And our meetings, especially with government officials, and even with upstream suppliers—well, it takes forever to get down to business! Even though they've known each other a long time, half of every meeting is formal introductions, handshakes, and how everyone's family is doing. Half the meeting's over before we get down to business, and even then, no one talks details. Everything is on a general level.

"Then there's our planning sessions. Boy, it's tough to get these guys to think about the future. Head office was hoping our three-year plan would have been completed by now, but it's hard to focus them on the bottom line. They're content to know that revenues should cover costs and that we'll make a profit. 'Señor Grant,' they say, 'we provide jobs for 1,500 people and give their families a good living. Our benefits are good, and the factory soccer team is having a good season.' I explained to them that the head office was planning to expand distribution of their components into European distribution channels. We can employ more people, but it will involve building a new facility, most likely over the soccer field area. There was a long silence. Everyone looked at Señor Garcia, the big boss. He said it was an interesting idea and that he would look into it. That was six weeks ago. I've heard nothing since. You'd think their big ambition in life was to stay small."

Question

Sketch out the major contrasts between the U.S. and Latin American management styles. Why do you think the Argentine management team behaves the way they do?

CASE 6

Hewlett Packard Company in Vietnam[1]

❧

*I*n September 1995, John Peter, a marketing manager of Hewlett-Packard Asia Pacific (HPAP) was evaluating HPAP's long-term strategic investment options for doing business in Vietnam. HPAP was a subsidiary of the Hewlett-Packard (HP) Company, and its headquarters was located in Singapore. Vietnam had recently adopted an open-door policy after the U.S. lifted its embargo on the country in February 1994. The country had a population of over 70 million, and foreign investment in the country had climbed steadily to reach almost US$12 billion by the end of 1994.

An environmental and market analysis revealed that the information technology (IT) market in Vietnam had potential. However, the market was currently small, and market growth was uncertain. Several business units within HP had begun to distribute some HP products in Vietnam. John needed to make a recommendation on whether the HPAP should enter the Vietnam market in a more strategic fashion, that is, to give serious consideration of Vietnam as a major market for HP. If so, what form should the market entry take, and how should it be done?

The Country of Vietnam and Its Business Environment

Vietnam was situated in the east of the Indochina Peninsula with a total land area of 330,363 square kilometers (see map in Figure 1). It shared borders with China in the north, Laos in the west, and Cambodia in the southwest. The coastline in the east stretches 3400 km. The country had fifty-six provinces. Its major cities included the capital city of Hanoi, Ho Chi Minh City (formerly Saigon), and the port cities of Haiphong and Danang. The official language was Vietnamese.

HISTORY For over a thousand years, from 111 b.c. to a.d. 939, Vietnam was governed as a Chinese province, Giao Chia. After it liberated itself, Vietnam frequently had to resist Chinese invasions. The country remained free from foreign control until 1885, when the French brought all of Vietnam under its rule. After the Japanese surrender in August 1945, Ho Chi Minh, founder of the Vietminh, proclaimed the independence of the Provisional Democratic Republic of Vietnam.

France's refusal to give up its colony led to a protracted war. China and the Soviet Union backed the Vietminh, while the U.S.-backed the French. In subsequent years, the U.S.-backed Ngo Dinh Diem, took power in the South. A united front organization, called the National Front for the Liberation of South, was formed to oppose Diem. The conflict escalated and turned into an American war, with the U.S. deploying 500,000 troops in Vietnam by 1968. The Southern forces collapsed after the U.S. withdrawal, and on April 30, 1975, the communists entered Saigon, and Vietnam's 30-year war of independence was over.

After the fall of Saigon, the North proceeded to reunify the country. Vietnam subsequently found itself treated with suspicion and, after its invasion of Cambodia in late 1978, was isolated by the international community. After the final withdrawal of Vietnamese troops from Cambodia in late 1989, the process of normalization of economic ties with ASEAN, Western Europe, North-East Asia, Australia, and New Zealand began to gather pace. In late 1991, after the Paris agreement on Cambodia, diplomatic and economic relations with many countries, including China, were fully normalized.

POLITICAL ENVIRONMENT The supreme organ of state power in Vietnam was the National Assembly, which performed functions such as promulgation of laws, ratification of the annual and long-term plans for economic and social development, budget planning, election of top officials, and selection of the cabinet members. The government was the executive body responsible for the enforcement of the laws of the country issued by the National Assembly.

Until the mid-to-late 1980s, the leadership of the Vietnamese Communist Party (VCP) held orthodox Marxist-Leninist beliefs, which viewed the world as a mortal struggle between imperialist and revolutionary camps. In the late 1980s to early 1990s, due partly to the fall of the Berlin Wall, the Vietnamese Political Bureau acknowledged the need for Vietnam to participate

FIGURE I
Map of Vietnam

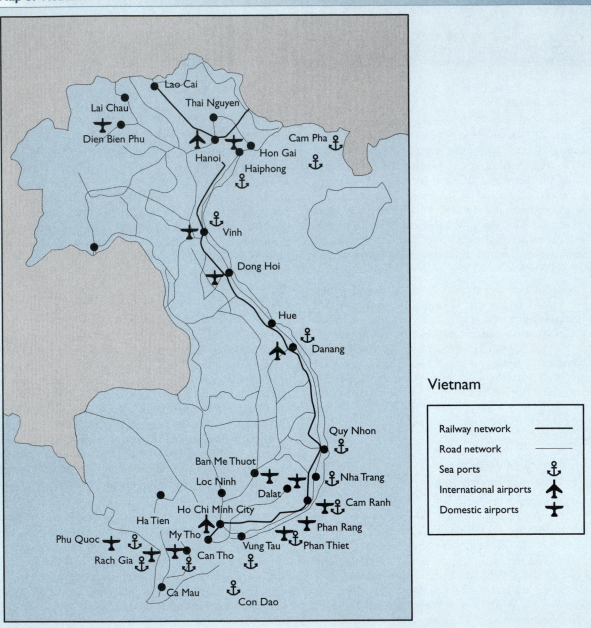

Vietnam

Railway network	———
Road network	——
Sea ports	⚓
International airports	✈
Domestic airports	✈

actively in the global capitalist economy, since the social-ist organization for economic cooperation (COME-CON) was becoming less relevant. The leadership sought to achieve a breakthrough in trade with the capitalist countries and an expansion of external cooperation, in-cluding the taking out of loans for capital investment and the promotion of joint venture projects.

Elements of the old worldview, however, continued to coexist with the new one. The aging leadership con-tinued to adopt an autocratic political system, and there was conflict between a closed political system and the economy opening up. This resulted in continuing de-bates and shifts in emphasis from struggle against imperi-alism to economic interdependence.

THE PEOPLE AND WORKFORCE The population of Vietnam was approximately 71 million people, 70 percent of them under thirty-five years old. The population growth was

2.2 percent. The population was basically rural and was concentrated in the two main rice-growing deltas: the Red River in the north and the Mekong in the south. The river delta population was almost entirely ethnic Vietnamese (Kinh), who made up 87 percent of the total population. The minority groups (including Khmer, Cham, Muong, and Thai peoples), whose cultures and languages were quite distinct from those of the Kinh Vietnamese, were found in the upland areas. The overseas Chinese community, which was largely concentrated in the South, was depleted by the decision of many to leave the country, often as "boat people." This community had partly recouped its position in the economy since the late 1980s, largely on the strength of its links with Hong Kong and Taiwan.

Vietnam was under-urbanized by comparison with many other developing countries in Southeast Asia. The largest city was Ho Chi Minh with a population of well over 4 million. The capital, Hanoi, had a registered population of 3.1 million. The level of primary education was comparatively high. The population, especially in the north, was basically literate, with a literacy rate of over 90 percent. The average wages in Vietnam and some neighboring countries are shown in Table 1 below.

ECONOMIC ENVIRONMENT Vietnam was the largest among the three Indo-Chinese nations, accounting for about 44 percent of total land area and 75 percent of the combined population of the region. The country was endowed with oil reserves and extensive mineral resources. It was an agro-based economy with the agricultural sector absorbing 70 percent of the work force (numbering about 32 million people) and contributing some 40 percent to the GNP and nearly 40 percent to total exports. Since 1989, Vietnam had become an important rice exporter and was the world's third largest rice exporter, after Thailand and the United States.

Light industries, including textiles, garments, footwear, paper, food processing, electrical, and electronics, though scattered throughout the country, were more concentrated in the south. Heavy industries, including iron and steel, power generation, cement, mining, chemicals, fertilizers, and machine tools were mainly concentrated in the north.

In the past, Vietnam relied mainly on the former Soviet Union and Eastern European countries for trade and economic cooperation and assistance. All of its foreign aid and one-half of its export markets vanished with the collapse of the Eastern bloc in 1991. However, the country survived this crisis, and economic growth rebounded to an official 8.3 percent in 1992 after a mild slowdown to around 5 percent in 1990. Inflation eased from about 700 percent in 1986 to 17.5 percent in 1992. Foreign investment approvals rose by 73 percent in 1992 and accounted for 26.2 percent of total investments. Export rose by 19 percent to US$2.5 billion, while imports climbed by 9 percent during the same year. For the first time in several decades, Vietnam was estimated to have registered a trade and current account surplus in 1992. Table 2 shows some key economic indicators for Vietnam from 1991 to 1994.

The government encouraged greater exports and imports. Exports were encouraged, and only a few items were subject to export duty, which had been kept low. The import of capital goods and materials for domestic production was encouraged, while the import of consumer goods, which could be produced at home or were considered luxurious, were discouraged. The list of items subjected to export and import prohibition or quota had been substantially cut down. Greater autonomy had been given to companies and enterprises in their export and import business. State subsidies and price control on export and import had ended except for some major items. The country established its first Export Processing Zone, named Tan Thuan, in Ho Chi Minh City in 1991.

Vietnam had diversified its export and import markets to other parts of the world. As a result, about 80 percent of total trade was now with Asia Pacific countries, with Singapore, Japan, Hong Kong, South Korea, Taiwan, Australia, and Thailand as the main trade partners. Meanwhile, widespread tax reforms and improved collection had raised government revenue by 82 percent. Reflecting these strengths, the Vietnamese currency, the Dong,

TABLE 1
Monthly Minimum Wage Rates of Selected Countries in Asia

Countries	Monthly Wage Rates (US$)
China	50
Hong Kong	525
Indonesia	80
Malaysia	290
Philippines	95
Singapore	600
Taiwan	650
Thailand	165
Vietnam	35

TABLE 2
Key Economic Indicators for Vietnam (1991–94)

Year	GDP Growth	Industrial Growth	Services Growth	Agricultural Growth
1991	6.0%	10.0%	2.2%	8.2%
1992	8.6%	15.0%	7.2%	8.3%
1993	8.1%	12.0%	4.4%	13.0%
1994	8.5%	13.5%	4.5%	12.5%

TABLE 3
Exchange Rates of the Dong

Year	Exchange Rates (Dong per US$)
1989	4,000
1990	5,200
1991	9,390
1992	11,181
1993	10,641
1994	11,080

appreciated almost 5 percent against the U.S. dollar in 1993, in contrast to 1991, where its value was almost halved (see exchange rates of the Dong in Table 3). Vietnam had normalized relations with the World Bank, the International Monetary Fund (IMF) and the Asian Development Bank (ADB) and had attracted many sources of bilateral and multilateral financial support. Vietnam joined ASEAN in July 1995.

Vietnam had received about $12 billion in foreign direct investment. Of this, $4.3 billion was in manufacturing, $2.2 billion in tourism and hotels, $1.2 billion in services, and $951 million in transportation and communications. The top seven investing nations were Asian, with Taiwan, Hong Kong, and Singapore each having over $1 billion in FDI. Joint ventures accounted for about 74 percent of the foreign investments, totally foreign-owned companies accounted for 11.0 percent, and business cooperation contracts accounted for 15 percent.

The lifting of the U.S. trade embargo on Vietnam in February 1994 brought benefits, such as direct access to U.S. technology and investment, and smoother access to soft loans and aids from multilateral institutions. A survey of 100 American companies by the US-ASEAN council (reported in the *Business Times of Singapore* on February 5, 1994) indicated that trade and investment opportunities in Vietnam were worth US$2.6 billion in the first two years following the lifting of the embargo. Foreign investment had climbed steadily and reached US$11.99 billion (from 1,201 projects) as of the beginning of January 1995.

The government had set the target growth rates of 3.5 to 4 percent for the agriculture, aqua-culture, and livestock husbandry sectors and 7 to 8 percent for the industrial sector. The food processing industry would give priority to the development of the Mekong and Red River Delta regions in order to upgrade the quality of processed agro-products and aquatic products to export standards. In the production of consumer goods, attention would be paid to the rehabilitation of current equipment and installation of new ones to improve the quality of manufactured products. Electronics assembling and manufacturing facilities would be established. Oil and gas exploitation on the continental shelf would be carried out, and an oil refinery would be constructed. The min-

ing, cement production, steel, and mechanical industries were also targeted for development.

Despite the positive economic outlook, some economic observers had pointed out several problems. The low savings rate and lack of hard currency constrained investment growth. Vietnam had an estimated US$15 billion of foreign debt, and the foreign exchange reserve constituted only about one month of imports. Three-quarters of export revenues were generated from only two sources—unprocessed farm products and crude oil. The inflation rate in Vietnam had ranged from a high of 400 percent in 1988 to a low of 15 percent in 1992. The forecast for 1994 to 1998 was 40 percent. The Vietnam currency, Dong, was not a fully convertible currency. The official exchange rate had depreciated from 5,200 Dong per U.S. dollar to 9,390 Dong per U.S. dollar in 1991 (see Table 3). The 6,000 state-owned enterprises appeared inefficient. They used 85 percent of the total fixed capital, 80 percent of total credit volume, 100 percent of savings, 60 percent of forestry output, and 90 percent of trained and high-school educated people, but they contributed less than 15 percent of total GDP in 1992.

FOREIGN EXCHANGE AND INVESTMENT REGULATIONS Previously, in Vietnam, all transactions had to pass through the state export and import corporations. Beginning in 1980, however, provinces, cities, and individual enterprises were given some freedom to sign contracts with foreign traders. Exchange control was administered by the State Bank, which had branches in Hanoi and Ho Chi Minh City.

On January 1, 1988, a new foreign investment law was promulgated to supersede the one dating from 1977. The new code allowed foreigners to own up to 100 percent of a venture, against a previous maximum of 49 percent. The old requirement that foreign investors should take a minimum 30 percent stake in joint ventures was retained. Priority areas for investment specified in the code were production for export and import substitution. Investors were expected to meet their own foreign exchange needs. The duration of a venture with foreign capital generally might not exceed twenty years, but it could be extended in special cases.

Corporate income tax had been reduced from between 30 percent and 50 percent in the old code to between 15 percent and 25 percent in the new one. There was provision for tax holidays of up to two years after the company made a profit. A statute governing labor relations and remuneration in foreign-invested companies was issued in 1990. Some main provisions in the statute specified the minimum wages, working hours, day of rest and holidays, minimum working age, rights to join a union, and labor arbitration process. The State Committee for Cooperation and Investment was created to manage and administer all foreign direct investment in 1988.

Land in Vietnam could not be purchased, only leased for a period, which depended on the duration of investment. The cost of land lease ranged from US$0.50 to US$18.00 per square meter per year in 1995.

INFRASTRUCTURE AND BANKING SYSTEM The existing telecommunications system in Vietnam was found by many to be expensive and inefficient. The country relied mainly on waterways for transportation. The port facilities were felt to be backward and might hinder the distribution system, especially when volume increased with the expected surge in economic activities. Many observers from the financial sector felt that the banking system, though reformed, was still far from those in capitalist countries and might cause delays and confusion, especially in the handling of foreign exchange remittances.

The Vietnamese government had directed the state to invest in the construction of infrastructures, such as water supply and drainage systems in big cities, in-town traffic projects, improvement of seaports, and upgrading of airports in major cities. There were plans to construct new hydro-power plants and thermo-power plants with a target production of 16–17 billion KWH for 1995.

Information Technology Market in Vietnam

MARKET CHARACTERISTICS The computer industry in Vietnam was in its infancy. The 18-year-old trade embargo imposed by the United States had effectively prevented computer technology from being transferred into the country by any of the major computer manufacturers and restricted heavily on any capital inflow. Since the number of computer installations currently was small and located mostly in Ho Chi Minh City, many businessmen viewed the computer industry as an emerging industry with good market potential. There were not many competitors in the market, and there were no clear leaders in the market yet. Distribution channels for the industry were also not fully developed.

An analysis of Vietnam's IT end-user market showed that the government, together with its related agencies and institutions, made up 35 percent of the market, followed by multinationals (35 percent), small and medium enterprises (25 percent), and small home or office users making up the remaining market. The buyers in the foreseeable future would be the public sector and major foreign companies. The deal sizes were forecast to be large as the government departments and foreign companies made initial investments in information technology infrastructure.

Different types of computers, such as personal computers, minicomputers, RISC-based workstations, and mainframes, could be used by businesses in their operation in Vietnam. The price differences among them would be an important consideration for these different business customers in their buying decision. Skilled local expertise in IT in Vietnam was somewhat limited. The Vietnamese workforce, however, was hardworking and well-educated and could possibly be trained quickly.

Computer products had limited intrinsic proprietary attributes, and most innovations were easily imitated. Computer products, thus, were increasingly becoming less differentiated. The market, especially the low-end segment, tended to have fierce price competition, and switching costs from one manufacturer to another was low. The Vietnamese users tended to favor U.S. brands of computers, even though brand loyalty for the product area was currently not strong.

There were problems associated with the lack of normalized ties between the U.S. and Vietnam, although the trade embargo had been lifted. As a result, American banks were not able to provide credit, although financing for their operation was a necessity in doing business in Vietnam. This was because hard currency was still hard to come by. American IT companies such as UNISYS had invested heavily in at least two large IT bids, only to find that their European and Japanese competitors had the edge against them when it came to extending credit. This problem might be resolved in the near future, as U.S. Secretary of State, Warren Christopher, had recommended that ties with Vietnam be normalized.

As in other Asian countries, *guanxi* was an important factor in doing business in Vietnam. *Guanxi* is a Chinese term denoting the use of personal connections, relationships, or networks to win business deals, forge business ventures, or get business approvals for government authorities. Local and regional competitors could have a better understanding of such culture and practices, and they could have built up their own networks, since they entered the market before the trade embargo was lifted.

VIETNAM'S IT-2000 PROGRAM Vietnam planned to propel itself into the twenty-first century through a billion-dollar program called IT-2000. It was based on a similar development model created in Singapore. The IT-2000 called for expenditures of up to two billion dollars over the next five years to set up the hardware necessary to create a national data communications network, establish a domestic industry in component manufacturing, and educate over 5000 Vietnamese in the use of computer technology. The government adopted the IT-2000 on August 4, 1993, designating it a national initiative. The Ministry of Science Technology and Environment had been given the formidable task to oversee the plan.

Part of this plan was to create on-line computer networks for almost all government agencies and the financial sector, build the Vietnam Education Research and Development Network (VERDNet), and provide each secondary school and university student in Vietnam with access to an integrated computer complete with Vietnamese educational software. The IT-2000 also addressed government policies for financial management and support. The State Bank of Vietnam and the Ministry of Finance were desperately in need of an integrated nationwide data processing network to manage the chaos of transactions in banking, financial markets, and tax collection.

The Minister of Science, Technology, and the Environment, and chairman of IT-2000, Dr. Dang Hua, was quoted as saying, "The purpose of IT-2000 is to build a foundation for basic information demands in the management of government and socioeconomic activities, and to develop the IT industry to a level where it can help in national development. We have stated very clearly in the master plan for IT-2000 that an integrated system of different computing networks must be built, with strong enough software and database systems which are able to service the government and other key activities. Some domestic services will be integrated with international systems."

CUSTOMER GROUPS IN THE IT MARKET Two segmentation approaches, by industry and by benefits, were adopted to examine customer groups in the IT market. The industry segmentation identified the high growth business segments of the Vietnamese economy which, from HP's experience in other countries, might be heavy and early adopters of IT. The benefit segmentation further defined the characteristics and needs of these segments.

INDUSTRY SEGMENTATION
Financial Services The Vietnam government had increasingly liberalized foreign bank participation. As of beginning 1995, investments totaling US$1.77 billion had been made in financial and commercial services. Apart from the lucrative trade finance business, which was forecast to expand rapidly, other financial services, especially venture capital, leasing, and project financing had potential too. In the short-to-medium term, this was generally the segment most Vietnam watchers and experts deemed likely to experience explosive growth. Funds from lenders were desperately needed to fuel the growth of the economy. In addition, the government was trying to encourage savings to create a pool of investment money. The financial industry had long viewed IT as a competitive advantage, and, thus, IT investment in this segment was expected to pick up strongly. Due to the mission-critical nature of financial applications, financial customers demanded a high level of support services.

Telecommunications Vietnam's telecommunications infrastructure was still in its infancy. Explosive growth was expected here as well, especially in mobile communications and high-speed data communications links for businesses. The postal and telecommunications sectors were still very much a monopoly in Vietnam today, so any investor wanting to offer a public telecommunications service would have to work with VNPT, the Vietnam Post and Telecommunications Department. Some recent announcements of foreign joint ventures in the telecommunications sector are shown in Exhibit 1.

Hotel and Tourism Vietnam had increasingly become a new tourist destination, and business travels continued to surge. This would create demand for hotel facilities, as well as spark the growth of a retail sector. Some international hotel groups, such as the Accor Group and Pullman International Hotels, and some Singapore companies, had begun a number of hotel projects in Vietnam. As of beginning 1995, foreign investment projects totaling US$2.235 billion had been made in this sector.

Manufacturing Vietnam was an attractive location for labor-intensive industries, due to low wages and a relatively skilled and productive workforce. The government encouraged export-oriented and resource- or agricultural-based manufacturing such as assembly operations for electronic goods, garment, and food-processing industries.

Utilities There would be explosive growth in this area as Vietnam sought to build her power infrastructure to cope with the demands of a modern economy. The Phu My thermal-power plant project, worth US$900 million, was expected to provide 600 megawatts of power.

Oil and Gas There were extensive offshore crude extraction activities going on. The Vietnamese government wished to promote local refining of crude oil. Many joint ventures with the various international and regional oil extraction and refining companies like BHP, Mobil, Shell, and Petronas were already in place. Total foreign investments as of beginning 1995 in this sector totaled US$1.3 billion.

Government The government was expected to play a major role in influencing the use and penetration of IT in the Vietnamese economy. With its IT-2000 plan, the Vietnamese government hoped to follow in Singapore's footsteps and accelerate the country's entry into high technology.

MARKET COMPETITION IN THE IT MARKET Table 4 shows selected information on some major players in the IT market.

Digital Equipment Corporation or DEC was a leading supplier of networked computer systems, software, and services. Its areas of differentiation were open systems, client-server knowledge and experiences, and multivendor experiences. Its strategy was to invest in technical research, build up technical capabilities, and focus on training.

During the past few years, DEC's financial results had been poor and DEC made a net loss of US$2 billion in 1994. DEC's poor performance caused the ouster of DEC's founder and CEO, Ken Olsen. His replacement

EXHIBIT 1
Foreign Joint Ventures in the Telecommunications Sector

FRANCE

Alcatel Alsthom said it had been selected by the Ministry of the Interior to supply the first private national communications network in Vietnam. The contract covered the supply, installation, implementation, and maintenance of a service integration network, which would eventually cover the entire country and represent 50,000 lines. The first part of the network was to be operational in March 1995.

SWEDEN

Three Swedish companies and Vietnam's Posts and Telecommunications Department had applied for a license to set up a US$340 million mobile phone network covering the whole of Vietnam. They hoped to install and operate a cellular telephone and paging system connected by hubs in Hanoi in the north, Danang in the center, and Saigon in the south by the end of 1995. The Swedish companies were reported to be Industriforvaltings, Kirnevik, and Comvik International, and they said their combined investment would be US$159 million.

CANADA

Montreal-based Teleglobe Inc. said its cable systems arm and Telesystem International Wireless Services Inc. had signed a deal to study the feasibility of a multiregional wireless and communication service and coastal submarine fiber-optic cable system in Vietnam. The study would cost US$720,000, and the project itself would cost US$100 million.

TABLE 4
Some Players in the IT Market

Company	1994 Annual Revenue (US$m)	1994 Net Income (US$m)	1993 Net Income (US$m)	Number of Employees	Revenue per Employee (US$)
IBM	62,716.0	−8,101.0	−4,965	267,196	234,719
Hewlett Packard	24,991.0	1,599.0	1,177.0	98,400	253,974
DEC	13,450.8	−2,156.1	−251.0	78,000	172,466
Unisys	7,742.5	565.4	361.2	49,000	158,010
Compaq	7,191.0	462.0	13.0	10,043	716,021

from within was Robert Palmer, who had since sold off a number of DEC's non-core divisions, like the disk-drive operation, database software, and the consulting unit. He sought to focus on DEC's core hardware business and increase margin by adding value in networking. Palmer had positioned DEC to take advantage of key trends, such as mobile computing and video on demand. Palmer had also shifted most sales to indirect distribution channels and sought to slash costs by signing on computer resellers as key partners. Salomon Brothers Inc. expected DEC's new Alpha system sales to soar in 1995 by 84 percent to US$1.7 billion and by another 55 percent in 1996.

In 1992, DEC had 45 percent of its turnover in the U.S., 40 percent in Europe, 10 percent in Asia-Pacific (including Japan), and 5 percent in Canada. Alpha still faced a long-term problem: the chip had not won a single influential convert among computer makers. That could ultimately prove fatal when it came time to fund the mind boggling cost of succeeding generations of chips. Most industry analysts believed that Palmer's accomplishments of the past year had merely brought DEC to the point where it was ready to compete again. If Palmer could not make DEC stand out with his networking strategy, the company risked following the path of another former industry number two, Unisys Corp., which now served mostly its old customers, and its revenue was shrinking slowly. Digital had a strong client base in government, banking and finance, insurance, and telecommunications. DEC had also done projects in health care, transportation, utilities, and retail. DEC currently had a representative office in Hanoi. So far, their main area of activity seemed to be on large internationally funded tenders. They had appointed three distributors in Vietnam as sales outlets and as service providers.

International Business Machine (IBM) Despite losses amounting to over US$8 billion in 1994, IBM was still the world's largest information systems and services company. In 1995, IBM CEO Lou Gertsner had engineered a turnaround. Recently, IBM purchased Lotus Corporation for US$3.5 billion. IBM's worldwide revenues had declined since 1990, slipping to US$62.7 billion in 1994. In 1992, IBM had 1,500 consultants worldwide. While these consultants provided support to all industries, their key focus was on finance, retail and manufacturing.

IBM's key area of differentiation was its ability not only to provide insights, experience, and specialized skills to its customers, but also to deliver results and increase the value of IBM products and services to customers. Its strategy was to focus on customer relationships and develop an account presence. Its global organization allowed IBM to bring its best intellectual capabilities to bear on any project. IBM, however, was still encumbered by a mainframe image it might never completely shake. Still in recovery mode and uncertain about its strategic directions, IBM supported more than a half-dozen operating systems, as well as dual desktop hardware platforms with PowerPC and X86.

IBM had set up "IBM Vietnam" in Hanoi in 1995. The operation provided sales and marketing support to distributors and dealers, as well as to customers. They had also appointed their dealers as service providers for hardware repair and support.

Unisys Unisys was the ninth-largest systems and PC vendor in the world in 1994. Unisys manufactured and marketed computer-based networked information systems and software. The company also offered related services, such as systems integration and IT outsourcing. As such, its strategy was to provide a full spectrum of services and solutions. It sought to develop leading-edge hardware and technology in open systems.

Unisys specialized in providing business-critical solutions based on open information networks for organizations that operated in transaction-intensive environments. In 1992, Unisys generated 49 percent of its revenue from the U.S., 30 percent from Europe, 9 percent from Canada, 5 percent from Asia-Pacific, and 7 percent from Japan. For international projects, local resources were normally relied upon. Vertically, Unisys focused on airlines, public sectors, financial services, and telecommunications. Horizontally, they focused on networking and online transaction processing. Unisys had also established a representative office in Vietnam. With a fifteen-person marketing staff based in the country, it ap-

peared that they had adopted an aggressive strategy in Vietnam. In 1995, they installed their equipment for the banking sector in the country for SWIFT (Society for Worldwide Interbank Financial Telecommunications) transactions. Unisys was targeting to set up an operation (subsidiary) in Vietnam in 1996.

Compaq In 1994 Compaq completed yet another record year with sales of US$10.9 billion, up 51 percent from the previous year. Net income grew by a healthy 88 percent to reach US$867 million. As the leading manufacturer of PC systems (desktops, portables, and servers), Compaq was currently positioned to tackle both the consumer and corporate computing markets and was now a major player in the commercial server market.

The reasons for Compaq's success to date included aggressive expansion of distribution channels, efficient manufacturing, ability to bring new products and technologies into the market early, ability to deliver top-quality products and ability to include added-value features in its products.

Hewlett Packard in Southeast Asia

THE HEWLETT PACKARD COMPANY In January 1939, in a garage in Palo Alto, California, two graduates from nearby Stanford University, William Hewlett and David Packard, set up a company called the Hewlett-Packard (HP) Company with an initial capital of US$538. They marketed their first product (invented by Bill), a resistance-capacity audio oscillator. HP's initial emphasis was on instrumentation. It was not until 1972 that the company finally acknowledged that it was in the computer field, with the introduction of its first business computer, the HP3000.

In 1995, HP was a sprawling corporate giant with annual sales in excess of US$25 billion and about 90,000 employees worldwide. It was involved principally in the manufacture, supply, marketing, and distribution of computer-based products, test and measurement products, medical and analytical products, electronic components, and Information Technology-related service and support. In 1985, HP was ranked by a *Fortune* magazine survey as one of the two most admired companies in America. In 1995, the bulk of the company's business, a good 76.6 percent of the net revenue, came from computational products and services.

Years ago, Bill Hewlett and Dave Packard developed a set of management objectives for the company. With only slight modification, these became the corporate objectives of HP and were first published in 1957. These objectives gave a clear idea as to how the company viewed itself and its position in society.

These corporate objectives formed the basis of what was known as "The HP Way," which sought to create a work environment geared to produce capable, innovative, well-trained, and enthusiastic people who could give their best to the company. HP's guiding strategic principle had been to provide customers with devices superior to any competitive offering in performance, quality, and overall value. To this day, HP corporate strategy was pursued with three measures in mind:

- Getting the highest return out of the company's most important asset, its people

- Getting the best output from a given technology

- Giving the customer the best performance for price paid

HP's MARKET POSITION AND CAPABILITIES HP had established its presence in countries like Hong Kong, Singapore, Japan, Taiwan, and Korea for more than twenty-five years. It had extensive experience in entering into emerging Asian markets such as China, Indonesia, and the Philippines. Though a subsidiary of an American company, HP Southeast Asia had a largely Asian management team. They shared similar norms, practices, beliefs, customs, and languages with many local markets. Nevertheless, HP was still an American company with its own stringent code of business and the requirement to comply with American laws.

Over the years, HP had built up many major customer accounts, many of which were multinational corporations with offices worldwide. It had developed a strong reputation and brand identity. The HP name was synonymous with quality products and high technology, albeit at a premium price. HP could not be as aggressive in product pricing due to its higher cost structure and overheads. For many years, HP had been rated tops in many independent customer-satisfaction surveys conducted by organizations like Datapro and IDC.

HP had a large network of subsidiaries and associated companies in different countries in the Asia Pacific. It

was, thus, able to source for raw materials and parts in these countries at the cheapest prices, manufacture at locations with the lowest costs, and establish an efficient distribution and warehousing network to transport products from manufacturing sites to markets.

Table 5 shows some information related to the turnover and earnings of HP from 1989 to 1994. In the brutal, fast-paced world of IT, customers looked for financial stability to ensure that vendors would still be around when their projects were completed, especially for large multiyear, infrastructural projects.

HP was a diversified company and had products and services in computation, measurement, and communications. This gave it a breadth that few computer vendors could match. The autonomous units dealing with measurement, communications, and computers in the HP set-up, however, often acted as separate companies and, thus, created functional silos that might not effectively leverage HP's knowledge and diversity.

HP was the industry leader in open-systems technology and solutions, and it had a specialized knowledge and extensive experience in this area. HP moved into RISC4 long before DEC, IBM, and other rivals and was now collecting the dividends. HP was strong in client/server computing involving PCs, workstations, and large systems and servers. HP opened up its proprietary HP 3000 systems, and it had become a whirlwind of success.

While HP served a cross-section of the IT industry, it had in particular established a significant presence in three industry groups: manufacturing, telecommunications, and financial services. In addition, HP also had large installed bases in industries such as retail, hospitality, government, and health services. In manufacturing, HP was the dominant worldwide supplier of UNIX systems accounting for 45 percent of this market. HP had a wide range of customers in the manufacturing sector, which remained HP's largest vertical market.

TABLE 5
Income and Earnings of HP from 1989 to 1994 (US$ million)

	1989	1990	1991	1992	1993	1994
Revenue	11,889	13,233	14,494	16,410	20,317	24,991
Cost of revenue	6,091	6,993	7,858	9,152	12,123	15,490
Gross profit	5,808	6,240	6,636	7,258	8,194	9,501
Research and devt.	1,269	1,367	1,463	1,619	1,761	2,027
Mkgt, gen. and admin.	3,327	3,711	3,963	4,224	4,554	4,925
Operating income	1,212	1,162	1,210	1,416	1,880	2,549
Other income/exp.	(61)	(106)	(83)	(79)	(96)	(126)
Pretax income	1,151	1,056	1,127	1,338	1,784	2,423
Income tax	322	317	372	449	606	824
Net income	829	739	755	556	1,177	1,599

HP sought to use the distribution channel as a means to support its customers. In 1988, HP sold its products primarily through a direct sales force. HP foresaw the rapid fall in gross margins as standardization, volumes, and competitiveness increased and developed two distinct sales strategies, one for volume sales where sales were indirect and took place through sales channels, and the other direct, providing value sales to large HP target accounts around the world. While many high-tech companies viewed distribution channels as their customers, HP had identified end-users as its customers. HP recognized that the computer industry had become a demand-driven (pull) environment, and HP had sought to create demand for its products among end-users. HP tracked consumer buying preferences very closely and responded quickly to changes in the market

HP's Businesses in Southeast Asia

Hewlett Packard Southeast Asia had its headquarters in Singapore with fully-owned subsidiaries in Singapore, Malaysia, and Thailand. In Indonesia, Philippines, and Brunei, HP appointed distributors. In addition, HP had a joint venture in Indonesia with its distributor, Berca. Called HPSI, it was primarily an IT services company.

In Southeast Asia, WCSO was represented by the Southeast Asia (SEA) Customer Support Organization, whose role was to provide services and support in satisfying customer's needs in financing, implementing, and operating their IT operations. The SEA Customer Support Organization managed the following product lines:

PL72—Hardware Support for Computer Systems and Networks

PL3D—Software Support for Computer Systems

PL71—Support for Personal Computers and Peripherals

PL6N—Outsourcing Services

PL6L—Network Integration Services

Product Lines 72, 3D, and 71 were the traditional maintenance services that HP had provided for buyers and users of its computer systems and was primarily focused on post-sales maintenance. In recent years, these businesses had experienced declining growth rate. Prices of computer products continued to drop, even as their performance improved. This trend was especially prevalent in the hardware maintenance business. Support expenditure, typically capped at a percentage of total IT expenditure, was thus greatly affected by this trend.

Product Lines 6N and 6L were the newer businesses WCSO had set up to counter the slower growth of the traditional maintenance businesses. They required higher investment and typically had lower profitability. The selling model for these product lines were also different, requiring more direct selling, as it was not always possible to leverage support revenues off computational product sales as was more often the case in the traditional maintenance businesses.

CURRENT STATUS OF HP'S BUSINESS IN VIETNAM Since the lifting of the U.S. embargo on February 3, 1994, different business units in HP had taken initial and ad-hoc steps to develop their businesses in Vietnam in response to the current changes taking place in the country. The CSO, CPO and TMO had signed up distributors in Vietnam to distribute their products. The CSO currently had one main distributor, the High Performance Technology Corporation (HiPT). HiPT was 100 percent privately owned. One of the owners, Dr. Binh, had good contacts with the Vietnamese government. CSO was ready to appoint a second distributor (the Peregrine Group) for the south of Vietnam. TMO had also appointed a distributor, Systems Interlace, while CPO had appointed several wholesalers and resellers in Vietnam. Projected orders from these product organizations were expected to hit US$10 million at the end of October 1995. HP's computer support business, WCSO, was not represented in Vietnam in 1994.

Hewlett-Packard and its CSO distributor in Vietnam, the HiPT, officially opened a Center for Open Systems Computing Expertise in Hanoi on July 1, 1995. Its establishment was part of a formal memorandum of understanding which HP and the Ministry of Science, Technology, and the Environment (MOSTE) had signed in March 1995. MOSTE was the body responsible for the promotion and development of information technology in Vietnam. The center would assist MOSTE's goal of developing a pool of qualified IT professionals to implement the Vietnam IT-2000 plan, based on the open-systems concept.

Perspectives on the Vietnamese IT Market

In January 1995, John made a business visit to Vietnam to assess first-hand the business climate and investment opportunities and to provide ideas on how WCSO in Southeast Asia should plan its overall investment strategy in Vietnam, rather than the current ad-hoc involvement of its CSO, CPO, and TMO in the Vietnamese market. The first stop was Ho Chi Minh City, a bustling city of 5 million people, 1 hour and 25 minutes from Singapore by air.

MEETING WITH DR. VO VAN MAI (MANAGING DIRECTOR OF HiPT) Dr. Vo Van Mai was the Managing Director of High Performance Technology (HiPT), HP's distributor in Vietnam. He was educated in Hungary. Dr. Mai expected the IT market in Vietnam to hit US$300 million by the year 2000. The market size had doubled each year for the past few years and Dr. Mai expected the IT market to grow even more rapidly in the next two years.

Currently, IT took the form of mainly personal computers (PCs) with some limited local area networks. Vietnam, being an IT greenfield, looked likely to adopt client-server technology in a big way, bypassing legacy and proprietary systems common in most developing and developed countries. The PC brands available in Vietnam included Compaq, HP, ACER, Wearnes, AST, Digital, Unisys, and IBM.

Dr. Mai felt that the most attractive segments of the IT market would be finance, utilities, telecommunications, petrochemicals, and airlines. Today, within Vietnam, the primary means of data transmission was using phone lines and modems. Between Hanoi and Ho Chi Minh City, more sophisticated and higher bandwidth transmission methods were available through Fiber Optic Links and X.25.

IBM had a representative office in Hanoi and Ho Chi Minh City, with staff strength of ten. They had six to seven distributors in Vietnam and it was known that they had applied for a license to operate a service operation in Vietnam.

Dr. Mai's conclusions were that it would be three to four years before the Vietnamese market became really significant in IT revenues. He felt that the next two years would be critical in establishing a presence and building relationships and awareness of products and services. Obtaining budgets for IT expenditure was still a problem. The government's IT-2000 plan, however, was a clear indication of the government's commitment to IT.

MEETING WITH ROSS NICHOLSON (GENERAL MANAGER OF DHL WORLDWIDE EXPRESS) Ross Nicholson felt that it had access to good market information as DHL had been operating in Vietnam since 1988. DHL worked through the Vietnam Post Office as the Vietnamese government still controlled the provision of mail and postal services tightly. Nicholson was assigned to Vietnam as a technical advisor in April 1994. Ross told us that things had not boomed as expected since the American embargo was lifted. Some obstacles, like chaotic taxation laws and investment risks, still plagued potential investors. In the short-term, the Mexican peso incident was likely to affect investor outlook, especially in emerging economies like Vietnam. In his opinion, the Asians, especially Japanese, were moving in very quickly. Hotels in Hanoi were usually full of Japanese.

In Nicholson's opinion, the finance industry had the highest prospects for growth in the immediate future. Presently, agriculture was DHL's biggest customer for the provision of shipping facilities. In time, more technologically advanced production activity would take place. DHL would then have the opportunity to sell logistics services to these new entrants, leveraging on their long experience in the Vietnamese market. DHL would like to get itself integrated into these companies, which would

be very happy to listen because they were in start-up mode.

Nicholson believed that there would not be anything spectacular for two to three more years. He cited the lack of skilled IT personnel as one of the obstacles to IT growth. Still, he felt that it was well worth the investment of establishing a presence in Vietnam now, so that when the boom came, companies like DHL would be well-positioned to capitalize on the ensuing growth. DHL currently used a stand-alone PC for its IT needs. This was certainly not suitable for the anticipated growth. Ross intended to upgrade to a nationwide system comprised of two HP 9000 E45s.

MEETING WITH DR. TRUENE GIA BINH (MANAGING DIRECTOR OF FPT) The Corporation for Financing and Promoting Technology (FPT) was a wholly-owned government company incorporated under the auspices of the Ministry of Science, Technology, and the Environment (MOSTE). Dr Binh, the managing director of FPT and son-in-law of a prominent general in Vietnam, elaborated on the difference in status between a representative office and an operating office. Basically, a representative office could only acquire goods required for the operation of the office. It was not allowed to receive payment for any products or services rendered but could provide marketing and support services as part of its distributor support service. Commenting on the attractiveness of the IT market, Dr. Binh felt that the financial sector would be very attractive, due to the high growth prospects and the prominence placed on it by the Vietnamese economy in the next three to four years.

MEETING WITH HAI CHAO DUY (DIRECTOR OF TECHNICAL SERVICES AND OPERATIONS, VIETNAM MOBILE TELECOMMUNICATION SERVICES) Hai Chao Duy expressed that he looked forward to a long-term relationship with HP. He mentioned the tremendous opportunities in Vietnam Mobile Telecom Services (VMS) to build networks. Today VMS supplied cellular services to 9000 subscribers in Ho Chi Minh City and Hanoi. The IT projects needed to facilitate the provision of cellular services were in operation, transmission, business support, finance, end-user computing, and e-mailing. He also mentioned that the next project would involve some management-system software for the telecommunication network.

MEETING WITH NGUYEN TRANG (CHAIRMAN OF HCMC COMPUTER ASSOCIATION) Nguyen Trang was a very influential personality in IT and chairman of the Ho Chi Minh City Computer Association. The Vietnam IT-2000 plan would be driven centrally from Hanoi. The city also had a board, which would oversee the implementation of the IT-2000 plan. That plan had been approved, and Mr. Nguyen revealed details regarding two other projects.

One was IT applications for municipal and government administration in the areas of transportation and traffic control, financial control, industrial administration, land property, city planning, trade services, and manpower development.

The other was governmental IT infrastructural development. This included the setup of units such as the Center for System Analysis and Design and the Center for Manpower Development, and projects such as the feasibility study for Ho Chi Minh EDI, a museum for IT development, and an Internet gateway for Vietnam. In his estimate, the market size of the Vietnamese IT industry would be US$500 million by the year 2000.

Market Entry Decision Options

Vietnam represented a promising market with untapped potential. There were, however, risks. Despite all the recent rapid progress toward a free economy, the basic political structure in Vietnam had not changed. Although Vietnam had recently adopted an open-door policy, economic development in the country was only beginning to take off, and the pace and direction of reform was still uncertain. Although economic growth was robust, the economy recently suffered from high inflation, and the dong was expected to depreciate against the U.S. dollar. There were gaps in Vietnam's legal framework with two instances where business firms were subjected to different interpretations of the law by authorities at different levels in the government, which resulted in different applications of the same law. This had caused uncertainties and delay in the business setup.

Although the information technology (IT) market in Vietnam had potential, the market was currently small, and market growth was uncertain. HPAP Management needed to weigh the positive and negative factors before deciding if the company should enter the Vietnam market in a more strategic manner.

MAJORITY JOINT VENTURE WITH LOCAL PARTNER HP could use the joint-venture strategy to enter the Vietnam market. In Southeast Asia, a HP joint venture existed in Indonesia where an agreement was entered into with Berca, her distributor, to set up a service company, HPSI. Berca retained the primary responsibility for the sale of HP products, while HPSI was charged with providing HP services to the marketplace. This option required less initial investment, compared to the direct-presence strategy, thus, reducing the risk involved. A local joint-venture partner could be a valuable resource where *quanxi* was vital for doing business.

DISTRIBUTION (INDEPENDENT PARTNER) HP could appoint one or more independent organizations as distributors, as well as service and support providers. In the initial years, it was likely that products from each business unit would be sold through only one distributor, although the same distributor might be chosen for the products of more than one business unit.

This strategy offered a quick start-up for HP and was especially suited for the off-the-shelf, mass-market, plug-and-play type of products offered by CPO. To be successful, HP needed to commit resources to train and develop the distributor to build up their service capability. The disadvantage of this strategy was that it would result in the cultivation of future competitors for support services. Where services in many other markets were concerned, HP had not found a way to provide support to its mission-sensitive and mission-critical end-users through channel members and still maintained the high quality and responsiveness which customers required. In addition, the margins on services were high, and services contributed significantly to HP's profit. The profit was likely to drop if HP allowed its channels to sign support contracts directly with the end-users.

DISTRIBUTION (EX-HP EMPLOYEE START-UP) A modified form of the entry strategy was to appoint a start-up company founded by ex-HP employees as its distributor. These ex-HP employees could be trusted to deliver quality service. In the future, this company would probably be more obliged to pay off the goodwill shown by HP in giving it the opportunity to be HP's service provider in Vietnam. When HP decided to establish a direct presence in Vietnam, the former employees could also be rehired as key managers in the new subsidiary.

COOPERATIVE VENTURE FRANCHISING Investment in the form of a cooperative venture was also viable. HP could initially franchise the support services and provide advisory services to a partner on how to establish and manage a support business. HP could act as a supplier of spares to its Vietnamese partner. HP would not have to take the risks incurred in direct investment, and trade ties could still be forged because of the special relationship with a local firm. At present, Singapore firms like Rothmans of Pall Mall (cigarettes) and Cold Storage (retail supermarkets) had established such ventures with Vietnam firms Agrex Saigon and Saigon-Intershop, respectively.

DIRECT PRESENCE HP could have a direct presence in Vietnam by setting up a subsidiary or representative office to provide marketing, sales support, and management services. This strategy required the largest investment and commitment of resources. It also offered maximum control and flexibility and the best payoff. HP's direct presence in the market would allow it to keep in touch with customers. HP would gain invaluable access to markets and customers. To reduce the risk, uncertainty, and investment requirement, it was possible to start off with limited staff on a smaller scale and increase staffing as required.

DECISION TIME John knew he had to make a decision soon. Many of HPAP's competitors had already made strategic moves in Vietnam. If HPAP did not act quickly, they might be left behind.

Questions

1. What aspects of Vietnam's history and geography would contribute to HP's evaluation of the market?

2. Evaluate Vietnam's general business environment—its political, economic, and international positions. Based just on these factors, what market entry method would you recommend, and why?

3. Examine current industry and competitive conditions in Vietnam. What would you conclude?

4. What corporate factors would be instrumental in the market entry decision (what the company would like to achieve versus the constraints facing it)?

5. Recommend a market entry strategy and justify it.

Note

1. Reprinted by permission from the *Case Research Journal*. Copyright 2000 by Geok Theng Lau and the North American Case Research Association. All rights reserved.

CASE 7

Responding to Competition: Alcoholes De Centroamerica, S.A. de C.V.[1]

On a summer afternoon in 1995, Sr. Emin Barjum watched the faded-yellow Toyota pickup truck pull away from his loading dock in Tegucigalpa, Honduras. Sr. Barjum, founder and president of the Honduran liquor manufacturer *Alcoholes de Centroamerica* (ALDECA), wondered if his plan would work. The truck was laboring under a load of *Yuscaran,* a competitor's brand of *aguardiente*. Sr. Barjum had purchased the *Yuscaran* for delivery to his most important customers, the large liquor distributors in San Pedro Sula, a major industrial city in northern Honduras.

Sr. Barjum was doing this because *Grupo Cobán,* a large conglomerate that had been able to establish a virtual monopoly in the Guatemalan *aguardiente* market, was planning to expand its business into Honduras. As an initial step in this process, *Grupo Cobán* had begun offering incentives to the largest San Pedro Sula liquor distributors in exchange for carrying its brands. Sr. Barjum was attempting to send a subtle message to these distributors. He wanted them to believe that ALDECA, which accounted for up to 80 percent of their business, could distribute its brands, as well as those of the competition, directly to retailers. Sr. Barjum felt that this warning would provide leverage in his dealings with the distributors and might discourage them from doing business with *Grupo Cobán*. To make his message even stronger, Sr. Barjum was providing the *Yuscaran* to his distributors at a very low price. The distributors did not realize that ALDECA was actually losing money on each bottle of *Yuscaran* it delivered to San Pedro Sula.

Sr. Barjum also faced other problems in August 1995. In addition to the *Grupo Cobán* threat, the market for *aguardiente* was shrinking slowly, because Honduran preferences were shifting to lighter alcohols like wine and beer. Also, *Licorera de Boaco,* a Nicaraguan distillery with production facilities in Honduras, had proposed a merger. After a year of study, a decision had to be made soon. The merger would give ALDECA additional capacity and could help fight the *Grupo Cobán* threat, but it would result in less direct control over marketing and operations. Was the additional capacity worth the loss of control? What other strategies might work? Sr. Barjum

went back inside his office to speak with his son, Salomon "Tony" Barjum, about their company's future.

History of *Alcoholes de Centroamerica*

Emin Barjum returned home in 1965 to Tegucigalpa, the capital city of Honduras, after receiving a BBA from the University of Pennsylvania and an MBA from the University of California at Berkeley. He began looking for business opportunities while working for the Honduran government's Economics Ministry. Sr. Barjum noticed that there was a lack of good-quality industrial alcohol in Honduras. To fill this gap, he founded ALDECA in 1967, with initial financing coming from the Barjum family and a group of friends. The plant was designed with the help of a Mexican consulting firm. Because the minimum efficient scale was greater than the local demand for industrial alcohol, Sr. Barjum had to go into the liquor business to make the project feasible. He obtained technical advice on fermentation, distillation, and other aspects of alcohol manufacturing from a retired Cuban distiller who lived in Miami, Florida. ALDECA then began producing small quantities of rum, vodka, gin, Scotch, and an inexpensive liquor called *aguardiente*.

With production established, Sr. Barjum began marketing his liquor by loading as many cases as possible into his car and driving northward from Tegucigalpa. Those early sales trips were very difficult, because Honduras had only 1,000 kilometers of roads (barely 100 kilometers were paved). At first, Sr. Barjum sold only a few cases per trip. However, his marketing efforts soon began showing results. He persuaded the owners of many northern cantinas to begin carrying ALDECA's rum and *aguardiente*. Sr. Barjum was successful in part because he was the only distillery owner who called directly on customers; other distilleries used sales people. ALDECA's sales grew each year.

When Sr. Barjum began producing alcohol, there were about sixteen distilleries in Honduras, most of which were relatively small in terms of output and market share. Sr. Barjum believed that "it was easier for us to compete then, since we had many small competitors instead of a few very large ones." ALDECA's entry into the market changed liquor manufacturing in Honduras.

Most of the competitors had been using raw sugar in the fermentation process, which was quite expensive. ALDECA, however, produced lower-priced products made with black strap molasses. In 1995, only eight distilleries remained in Honduras; the rest had gone out of business. About half of the survivors were forced to change to molasses to remain cost competitive.

ALDECA prospered until 1972, when a large Nicaraguan distillery, *Licorera de Boaco,* entered the Honduran rum market. Hondurans preferred internationally produced rums, and sales of ALDECA's rum declined rapidly. As a result, ALDECA changed its focus to *aguardiente* production. By the early 1990s, the company had developed a presence in the *aguardiente* market throughout the country and had captured approximately 50 percent of the market share. However, northern Honduras was ALDECA's most important market, comprising nearly 85 percent of its sales.

The Honduran *Aguardiente* Industry

THE PRODUCT, ITS CONSUMERS, AND PLACE OF CONSUMPTION *Aguardiente* is a clear, inexpensive, very strong liquor that is generally purchased by the glass in small cantinas by poor, uneducated males between the ages of twenty-six and forty-five. The small, family-owned cantinas usually have a maximum of six tables and a small bar. "The cantinas are traditionally the place where men meet after work to have a few drinks," states Sr. Barjum. "They are basically a haven for men." Women traditionally avoided consumption of *aguardiente,* because those women who drank it were considered immoral. The serving size is typically 125 milliliters (approximately one-half cup), and the average consumer drinks three servings per cantina visit. About 60 percent of *aguardiente* consumers drink it straight, while roughly 40 percent follow it with lemon, salt, or a sip of a soft drink.

The product is traditionally sold to the cantinas in 750-milliliter and one-liter bottles, from which the bartenders pour drinks for their customers. A trend is developing, however, toward smaller, 125-milliliter bottles. Some customers prefer the small bottles because, when they purchase one, they are guaranteed that the bartender did not "water-down" the product. However, production of *aguardiente* in the smaller bottles is quite expensive, and price is an important factor in the purchase decision. The "best" combination of taste (smoothness) and strength (alcohol content) typically determines a consumer's brand preference.

THE COMPETITORS There were three major players in the Honduran *aguardiente* market in the mid-1990s: ALDECA, which sold approximately 2.5 million liters of its brands per year; *Destilleria Buen Gusto,* which sold approximately 2.5 million liters of *Yuscaran* per year; and *Licorera de Boaco,* which sold 700,000 liters of its brands per year. There were several smaller competitors in Honduras, as well as many black-market operations.

While ALDECA commanded nearly half of the legal Honduran *aguardiente* market, the company did not fare well "brand-to-brand" with *Destilleria Buen Gusto*'s *Yuscaran* brand. A recent ALDECA marketing survey revealed that, in the city of San Pedro Sula (within ALDECA's core northern market), 57 percent of the respondents preferred *Yuscaran* over ALDECA's *Caña Brava.* Sr. Barjum notes that, "If we combine all of our brands, then we win. But, brand against brand, they have a better share."

THE GENERAL ENVIRONMENT IN HONDURAS Honduras is located in Central America between Guatemala, El Salvador, and Nicaragua. Although the Honduran political environment had been stable in recent years, more than 150 internal rebellions, civil wars, and governmental changes had occurred in Honduras since 1900. Its six million people live in a country that is approximately the size of Louisiana (see Figure 1) and depend primarily on agriculture for employment. In the mid-1990s, Honduras was among the poorest countries in the Western hemisphere, with per capita income of approximately $630 (U.S.). The country suffered from high population growth, high unemployment (15 percent) and underemployment (36 percent), high interest rates (approximately 36 percent), and high inflation (averaging 22 percent between 1990 and 1994). A weak infrastructure was also a problem. For example, there were only 1,700 kilometers of paved roads in 1995, and water and electric service were very unreliable. Agriculture employed 34 percent of the population but accounted for 18 percent of GDP. Industry and services were 32 and 50 percent respectively of GDP and occupied 21 and 45 percent of the workforce. Between 55 and 70 percent of the population were officially below the poverty line, with the lowest 10 percent of people having 0.4 percent of the wealth and the highest 10 percent having 44.3 percent. Honduras had 2.45 million radios and 570,000 TVs. Literacy rates were over 70 percent but much lower outside of urban areas.

A lack of hard currency for foreign exchange was also a problem. In 1994, the Honduran Central Bank mandated that commercial banks, exchange houses, and businesses could not retain foreign currency. Rather, they were required to sell foreign currency to the Central Bank within twenty-four hours of its acquisition in exchange for lempiras, the Honduran currency. The Central Bank then auctioned the foreign currency on the open market, but quotas limited the amount anyone could purchase per day. It took businesses quite some time, therefore, to obtain the currency necessary for foreign transactions.

FIGURE I
Regional Map of Central America

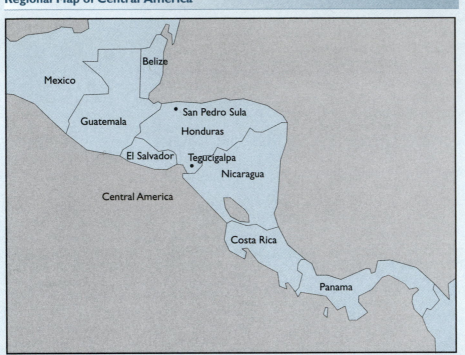

TABLE I
ALDECA's Top Management Team

Name and Position	Age	Years at Company	Education	Experience
Emin Barjum—Owner and General Manager	53	28	MBA, University of California at Berkeley, and BBA, University of Pennsylvania	Company President
Salomon Barjum ("Tony")— Assistant General Manager	23	1	MBA and BBA, University of Texas at Arlington	Started here
Armando Leonel Aguilar— Production Manager	26	2	Chemical engineer and MBA, Honduras University	Assistant Production Manager at a sugar mill
Ileana Zelaya—Head of Laboratory	24	1	Chemical engineer, currently getting MBA, Honduras University	Head of lab at another company
Lesbia Argentina Nunez de Flores— Head of Accounting	41	21	CPA, Honduras University	Started here
Julio Valladares—Sales Manager	40	4	High school graduate	10 years in sales (liquor)

Alcoholes de Centroamerica in 1995

PERSONNEL In 1995, Sr. Barjum was joined by his son, Tony, who was "learning the business" after completing a BBA and MBA at the University of Texas at Arlington. Sr. Barjum's daughter, Patricia, provided some marketing advice to ALDECA as needed. Other top managers at ALDECA included Armando Leonel Aguilar, Production Manager; Ileana Zelaya, Head of Laboratory; Lesbia Argentina Nunez de Flores, Head of Accounting; and Julio Valladares, Sales Manager. Table 1

highlights the education and experience of ALDECA's top managers. The remainder of the eighty-four employees filled clerical and production positions. ALDECA had little trouble filling these lower-level positions because of the high Honduran unemployment and underemployment rates, as well as ALDECA's higher-than-average pay scale.

The importance of having a qualified, in-house chemical engineer was highlighted in the early 1990s, when Sra. Zelaya discovered a virus living in the fermentation tanks. The elimination of this virus enhanced the efficiency of the fermentation process and increased ALDECA's production capacity by nearly one-third.

PRODUCT LINES ALDECA produced seven brands of *aguardiente: Caña Brava* (its highest quality and best-selling brand), *Tic-Tac, Catrachito, Costeño, Torero, Favorito,* and *Bambu*. The multibrand strategy was developed in part, Sr. Barjum notes, because "each cantina will carry only two or three brands. That's one of the reasons we're trying to get a lot of brands into the market, to confuse the markets. That way, our brands could stock a whole cantina."

ALDECA also manufactured small amounts of vodka and wine on a manual production line. A separate Barjum-controlled company produced a line of cosmetics (perfumes, deodorants, and lotions) made from excess alcohol. *Aguardiente* production, however, remained ALDECA's specialty, though sales were showing signs of decline (see Table 2).

PRODUCTION PROCESS ALDECA produced all of its alcohol from black strap molasses, which was obtained from a few large sugarcane plantations in northern Honduras. Sr. Barjum signed contracts with these producers each year at the beginning of the harvest to ensure that ALDECA had enough molasses to last the entire year. However, since the molasses producers often promised more than they could manufacture, shortages were common toward the end of the year. ALDECA's attempts to resolve this problem were ineffective. Transportation costs prohibited the company from acquiring molasses from other countries, and large-capacity tanks, pipelines, and pumps would be very costly. Furthermore, it was impossible for ALDECA to build additional storage tanks in its current location because the land adjacent to the distillery had become developed in recent years.

Upon receiving the molasses from the manufacturers, ALDECA mixed the molasses with yeast and stored it in tanks, where it was allowed to ferment. After ALDECA's chemical engineer, Ileana Zelaya, determined that the

mixture had achieved the proper level of fermentation, the molasses was pumped into distilling units, where it was converted into alcohol. The alcohol was then pumped into large vats, where it awaited the bottling process.

Following a standard practice in Honduras, ALDECA recycled all of its bottles. The bottling process began at an enormous bottle-washing machine. Once the used bottles were washed, they were moved one-by-one through the filling machine, then to the capping machine, and on to the labeling machine. They were then placed in boxes of twelve and stored for shipment.

Although it may appear that ALDECA's production process was highly automated, it was still relatively labor-intensive. The bottles returned by the distributors were loaded manually into the bottle washer. After each bottle was filled, it was visually inspected for purity. Then each bottle cap was started by hand before being tightened by the capping machine. Next, safety seals were secured by hand. Finally, the full bottles were boxed and stored manually.

In 1995, ALDECA was still using most of the same equipment with which it began production. Despite its age, the equipment remained simple, safe, efficient, flexible, and trouble-free. The bottling line was seldom interrupted by mechanical failures, and the interruptions that took place were usually solved within a few minutes.

MARKETING Marketing ALDECA's *aguardiente* was difficult. Nearly all *aguardiente* consumers were illiterate, so common vehicles for advertising, such as newspapers and magazines, were ineffective. Advertising on television was also ineffective, because the customers generally had no access to televisions. ALDECA used some radio advertising since many cantinas (and some customers) had radios.

Most of ALDECA's marketing efforts, however, involved point-of-sale advertising. Each year, ALDECA developed a poster featuring a female model in a bathing suit. A twelve-month calendar appeared at the bottom of the poster so that, according to Sr. Barjum, "the cantina owners will leave the poster on the wall all year." One year, ALDECA's advertising company failed to put the year itself on the calendar. As a result, that particular calendar remained on the walls of many cantinas for several years, even though the day/date designations were wrong! ALDECA also distributed to the cantinas, free of charge, disposable plastic cups with ALDECA's various product logos on the front and the serving sizes marked on the sides. Less successful marketing campaigns, such as neon signs for distributors and metal signs for cantinas, were attempted at various times.

ALDECA tried to improve the effectiveness of its advertising campaigns by hiring a well-respected local marketing firm to evaluate and revise its advertising. ALDECA gave this firm detailed information that included consumer demographics, as well as frequency,

TABLE 2 Liters of *Aguardiente* Sold by ALDECA, 1987–94	
1987	1,944,000
1988	2,177,000
1989	2,342,000
1990	2,449,000
1991	2,801,000
1992	2,711,000
1993	2,554,000
1994	2,445,000

amount, and location of consumption. The marketing firm then developed a multimedia campaign (television, radio, and print) that focused on a man consuming *aguardiente* at home. Sr. Barjum was disappointed with the result of the marketing firm's work, because "we had given them all of the marketing information we had, but they came out with a campaign which was completely out of the environment where people drink *aguardiente*."

New product testing and introduction were handled through ALDECA's sales department. A sales representative typically visited the cantinas with the new *aguardiente* and offered the cantina owners several free bottles in exchange for permission to conduct a brief taste test. The free bottles were provided to the cantina owner as a show of goodwill, as well as to offset revenues lost by the cantina during the test. The sales person then offered cantina patrons free samples of the new product and asked for their opinions on how the new product compared to their favorite brands. A follow-up sales call was made later to secure the cantina's order.

FINANCIAL PERFORMANCE A cursory look at ALDECA's sales figures might lead one to believe that its bottom line had been suffering. Total factory sales dropped from 22 million lempiras in 1991 to 12 million lempiras in 1994. However, this drop reflected an intentional response by ALDECA to changes in the taxation of *aguardiente* by the Honduran government. Until April 1992, the price at the factory of ALDECA's *aguardiente* included a flat tax of 4.5 lempiras per liter. In April 1992, the Honduran government implemented a new tax system requiring that tax be paid on a percentage of the selling price at the factory.

To remain competitively priced, ALDECA altered its transfer pricing. The company began selling its *aguardiente* to an in-house distributor at a lower price, thereby reducing the effect of taxes on the final price to wholesalers. The in-house distributor then provided ALDECA with the dividends shown at the bottom of ALDECA's income statement. Table 3 shows the price movements of ALDECA's *Aguardiente* brands. Table 4 provides more detailed information about ALDECA's financial performance.

TABLE 3
ALDECA *Aguardiente* Prices, 1990–95 (in *lempiras* per 12–bottle case)

	1990	1991	1992	1993	1994	1995
Cana Brava	104	Not Available	116	122	152	156
Tic-Tac	86	Not Available	98	110	132	138
Catrachito	91	Not Available	103	110	128	124
Costeno	95	Not Available	107	114	129	115
Torero	99	Not Available	111	117	135	124
Favorito	85	Not Available	97	104	121	115
Bambu	85	Not Available	97	104	116	93

TABLE 4
Alcoholes de Centroamerica Income Statements, 1990–95 (in lempiras)

Ventas (Sales)	1990	1991	1992	1993	1994	1995 through 4/30
Aguardientes y rones (Aguardiente and rum)	16,166,341	20,412,604	13,309,216	8,638,207	9,448,812	3,759,387
Otras bebidas (Other drinks)	87,702	157,122	182,237	131,180	123,080	74,440
Vinos (Wines)	49,720	38,880	97,268	118,564	95,642	56,230
Otros productos (Other products)	860,260	115,764	1,062,047	1,262,978	1,959,433	844,051
Otros ingresos (Other income)	438,591	512,147	364,106	454,011	484,937	225,735
Total ventas (Total income)	17,602,614	22,276,507	15,014,874	10,604,940	12,111,904	4,959,844
Devoluciones y rebajas s/ventas (Returned sales)	29,154	15,979	11,369	12,321	7,913	1,957
Total ventas e ing netos (Net sales)	17,573,460	22,260,528	15,003,505	10,592,619	12,103,991	4,957,887
Costo de ventas (Cost of goods sold)	13,826,979	16,957,738	8,591,248	4,898,314	6,397,587	2,798,326
Utilidad bruta (Gross income)	3,746,481	5,302,790	6,412,257	5,694,305	5,706,404	2,159,561
Gastos de fabrication (Manufacturing costs)						
Salarios (Salaries)	212,244	330,425	403,930	407,991	437,602	134,938
Sueldos (Wages)	93,656	132,244	126,339	110,098	166,959	85,331

TABLE 4
Alcoholes de Centroamerica Income Statements, 1990–95 (in *lempiras*)—Continued

Gastos de fabrication (Manufacturing costs)	1990	1991	1992	1993	1994	1995 through 4/30
Vacaciones (Vacation)	12,390	15,751	20,265	21,782	27,876	10,820
Prestaciones sociales (Severance pay)	39,000	16,057	57,873	55,215	50,972	38,184
Depr. maquinaria (Dept. of Equip.)	76,369	95,731	126,147	164,541	193,052	64,357
Depr. otras instalaciones (Dept. of Installations)	10,304	15,553	16,562	22,587	32,030	10,677
Mantenimiento (Maintenance)	155,334	225,031	232,628	177,324	223,830	39,741
Combustibles (Fuels)	4,110	70	8,128	2,776	64,275	13,328
Miscelanea (Misc.)	6,027	13,768	14,286	13,413	17,488	5,360
Materiales (Materials)	30,671	48,230	10,909	14,725	5,586	1,171
Herramientas (Tools)	2,668	8,066	3,877	1,573	4,316	181
Energia electrica (Electricity)	75,737	145,582	183,817	215,922	213,482	72,745
Agua (Water)	71	3,382	10,206	11,279	4,145	2,114
Vigilancia (Security)	64,408	155,468	199,906	218,460	220,762	96,396
Regalias (Licensing fees)	38,282	28,569	48,144	36,882	6,019	0
Marcas de registros (Brand registration fee)	2,499	1,419	2,501	22,187	3,338	1,171
Total (Total)	823,770	1,235,346	1,465,518	1,496,755	1,671,732	576,507
Gastos de ventas (Selling expenses)						
Sueldos (Wages)	8,423	20,256	43,616	46,600	49,050	12,700
Comisiones (Commissions)	76,713	0	0	0	0	0
Vacaciones (Vacations)	466	566	1,566	1,833	2,300	800
Prestacioines sociales (Severance pay)	0	0	0	0	0	0
Depr. vehiculos (Depreciation of Vehicles)	34,609	32,296	62,475	77,954	70,791	23,597
Combustibles (Fuels)	62,499	103,425	89,378	112,819	126,278	38,182
Mantenimiento (Maintenance)	39,855	125,614	129,591	77,034	108,265	58,199
Seguros (Insurance)	25,981	37,705	37,716	33,701	38,014	39,733
Otros gastos vehiculos (Other vehicle expense)	23,966	24,634	32,441	31,864	38,950	11,484
Fletes (Transportation fees)	187,674	265,800	103,092	155,563	225,189	93,456
Cuentas incobrales (Bad dept, exp.)	0	0	93,197	35,377	77,688	0
Gastos de viaje (Travel expense)	11,438	16,479	23,473	28,001	20,175	2,405
Promocion (Advertising)	254,662	351,225	520,997	506,214	622,613	43,151
Otros gastos de venta (Other selling expenses)	48,258	77,305	61,251	54,486	43,542	7,878
Miscelaneos (Misc. expenses)	475	599	2,682	586	484	136
Impuestos distr. s/ventas (Taxes)	23,436	46,990	55,088	54,982	60,353	21,218
Total (Total)	797,915	1,102,894	1,256,563	1,216,814	1,483,692	352,939
Gastos admin. y grales (Administrative expenses)						
Sueldos (Wages)	189,707	219,926	238,788	246,322	284,979	115,513
Vacaciones (Vacations)	6,663	5,341	5,305	5,169	8,172	1,689
Prestaciones sociales (Severance pay)	27,066	0	0	0	566	0
Benef. empleados (Empl. benefits)	96,926	133,039	133,962	168,490	195,830	52,610
Depr. edificios (Building exp.)	12,075	12,075	12,075	21,634	26,965	8,988
Depr. Mobiliario (Dept. Furniture)	12,880	9,360	10,108	16,331	20,127	6,709
Mantenamiento (Maintenance)	11,426	22,565	23,931	15,676	28,142	10,106
Seguro (Insurance)	22,232	28,731	34,626	29,532	29,532	24,359
Arrendamiento equipos (Lease–buyback expense)	0	20,060	60,979	53,123	39,193	0
Gastos de viaje (Travel exp.)	0	34,905	34,928	25,892	38,254	10,072
Honorarios profesionales (Legal fees)	15,061	52,524	33,625	20,870	19,210	56,308

(continued)

TABLE 4
Alcoholes de Centroamerica **Income Statements, 1990–95 (in** *lempiras***)—Continued**

Gastos admin. y grales (Administrative expenses)	1990	1991	1992	1993	1994	1995 through 4/30
Dietas y gastos de repres. (Representation fees)	32,100	47,600	56,000	63,600	78,600	30,900
Papeleria y utiles (Office supplies)	22,133	21,037	20,717	17,634	29,493	16,779
Correro, telgrafo, telefono (Telephone and mail)	11,909	18,157	25,771	19,907	38,008	11,827
Donaciones (Donations)	22,300	35,989	46,650	17,850	21,235	11,028
Miscelaneos (Miscellaneous)	19,551	43,496	39,444	44,719	41,104	13,192
Otros impuestos distritales (Taxes)	5,776	11,043	11,089	10,639	11,813	0
Otros gastos (Other expenses)	0	0	0	0	0	0
Total (Total)	507,805	715,848	787,998	777,388	911,223	370,082
Gastos financieros (Financial exp.)						
Interese pagados (Interest paid)	75,589	56,668	51,884	53,852	6,722	83,887
Gastos bancarias (Bank comms.)	103,185	10,462	50,286	1,169	0	9,728
Total (Total)	178,774	67,130	102,270	55,021	6,722	74,159
Gastos no deducibles (Non-deductible expenses)						
Aportaciones INFOP (Training Institute tuition)	5,819	7,791	9,157	9,168	11,369	1,911
Multas, reparos, y otros (Penalties)	378	989	423	352	128	0
Total (Total)	6,197	8,780	9,580	9,520	11,497	1,911
Total gastos (Total expenses)	2,314,461	3,129,998	3,621,929	3,555,498	4,084,866	1,375,598
Utilidad antes del I/S/renta (Net income Before taxes)	1,432,020	2,171,792	2,790,328	2,138,807	1,621,538	783,963
Impuestos S renta estimado (Taxes)	523,876	823,073	1,071,835	809,715	597,306	0
Utilidad despues del I/S/renta (Net income after taxes)	908,144	1,349,719	1,718,493	1,329,092	1,024,232	783,963
Dividendos recibidos (Dividends received)	159,904	161,973	173,098	213,414	693,365	423,000
UTILIDAD NETA (Net income)	1,068,048	1,511,692	1,891,591	1,542,506	1,717,597	1,206,963

The Honduran *Aguardiente* Market in 1995

In the early 1990s, demand for *aguardiente* began to shrink after fifteen years of relative stability. As a result, ALDECA produced only 2.4 million liters in 1994, compared with 2.8 million liters in 1991. Sr. Barjum explains the possible reason for this decline:

> We feel that there is a market for softer, or less alcoholic, beverages, like wine or beer. We found out that the demand for beer in Honduras is 260 million 12-ounce bottles per year. Wine imports have increased considerably. We don't have the exact figures because they aren't published, but we feel certain that these products have been taking some overall market share.

There were indications that demand for *aguardiente* was declining throughout Central America. As a result, competition within the industry was becoming more in-

tense by the mid-1990s, as distilleries looked for ways to maintain profitability. Because of this, ALDECA was faced with a potential new competitor from Guatemala, as well as a merger offer from another Honduran distillery.

A NEW THREAT A Guatemalan conglomerate, *Grupo Cobán,* had recently made attempts to enter the Honduran *aguardiente* market. Sr. Barjum believed that *Grupo Cobán* was a major threat to ALDECA, because it "has a monopoly on the Guatemalan *aguardiente* market, producing 15 million liters per year. They have total control in Guatemala. They own a bank and a sugar mill. They also have an interest in the Pepsi Cola™ manufacturing facilities in Guatemala, as well as beer. In addition, they have a cost advantage with respect to raw materials; both molasses and fuel oils are cheaper in Guatemala."

Grupo Cobán purchased a small distillery in Honduras, as well as the rights to use several brands of *aguardiente* that have been popular there. Sr. Barjum explains,

> They [*Grupo Cobán*] have purchased relatively new facilities. That is a disadvantage because they had to put up a lot of money for them. Right now, they are testing the market and testing what competitive reactions will be. If they give credit to distributors, for example, what are we going to do? If they give away bottles, how will we react? They are at that stage. They have not really come in full-strength. I think they are just at the initial testing stage.

Grupo Cobán's initial attempts to enter the Honduran market came in the form of enticements to ALDECA's distributors. *Grupo Cobán* executives offered one particularly attractive incentive; for initial orders, and for orders expanding a distributor's volume, *Grupo Cobán* would provide the reusable bottles free of charge. Normally, distributors wishing to carry a new manufacturer's *aguardiente* were required to either pay for the bottles up-front or to provide acceptable used bottles for exchange. This represented a large initial cost for the distributors. *Grupo Cobán*'s incentive shifted this cost from the distributor to the manufacturer. After the initial order is sold, the distributor would simply exchange the empty bottles to cover the bottle cost for the next order. However, while the bottles of most *aguardiente* manufacturers were interchangeable, thus minimizing the distributors' switching costs, *Grupo Cobán*'s bottles were unique. Therefore, the distributors could recover the value of these bottles only by reordering *Grupo Cobán* brands.

Recently, *Grupo Cobán* invited ALDECA's four largest distributors in the San Pedro Sula area to visit *Grupo Cobán*'s facilities in Guatemala. Two of the four declined that offer. The two distributors that accepted the offer reported some of the details of the meetings to Sr. Barjum. They were informed that *Grupo Cobán* was in the initial marketing stages in Honduras, confirming Sr. Barjum's suspicions. Later, *Grupo Cobán* was planning to introduce two new *aguardiente* brands into the Honduran market, each having a traditional Honduran name.

Unknown to ALDECA's distributors, *Grupo Cobán* had a history of entering markets in this way, then bypassing local distributors after its brands became established. Several of ALDECA's distributors indicated that they were considering *Grupo Cobán*'s proposal, and Sr. Barjum was very concerned. He had been gathering and analyzing information on *Grupo Cobán*'s entry into the Honduran market and identified several alternative courses of action for ALDECA. He explains,

> We can respond in-kind. To a certain extent, we can give credit to the wholesalers. We can

also lower our prices. But, I'm trying to figure out some unique way to respond. One way might be to go to our distributors and tell them that they cannot take on different brands. If they choose to go with *Grupo Cobán*, then they can forget about us; we will begin selling directly to the cantinas. But, that would require a lot of changes in our marketing department. We don't have too much experience with retailing.

AN OPPORTUNITY ALDECA also had the opportunity to merge with another Honduran distillery, *Licorera de Boaco*, which had recently approached Sr. Barjum with a merger proposal. *Licorera de Boaco* was also concerned about *Grupo Cobán*'s entry into the Honduran *aguardiente* market and felt that a merger was the best way to handle the situation. According to Sr. Barjum,

> We have been off and on for about two years with the possibility of closing down our plant and manufacturing all of our products in their facility, under our supervision, but using their technical procedures. We would give them all of our equipment, but we would keep the land and buildings. But, we are used to making decisions without talking too much with our board of directors. This merger would mean that any decision would have to be mutually agreed upon. They have been in the market for about fifteen years and haven't really been successful. They have good marketing and distribution, but they have not done a good job with the product.

In 1995, ALDECA was running at 80 percent of capacity. ALDECA's plot of land was surrounded by other development and was too small for additional construction. Any large increase in output would require a shift in production to a different location. *Licorera de Boaco*, however, had the ability to produce three times more alcohol than ALDECA, and they had the potential to produce it at 15 to 20 percent lower cost. Sr. Barjum notes,

> If we united with *Licorera de Boaco*, that would mean that we would have larger storage facilities, or we could build larger storage facilities because they have more land than we have. That would give us an advantage of being able to get better prices for molasses because, at certain times of the year, the sugar mills are really pressed for storage. At that time, you will find two or three of them competing with each other. The thing is, though, I'll be frank with you. If I'm going to merge, I don't want more problems than I had to begin with. I'm going to have to look closely at their operation from the start and see what problems

they are having. It is going to be more difficult for us, because I'm going to have their
production problems. Tony cannot take care
of that, because he is just starting to learn.
I'll have to worry about that myself. I'll also
have to be concerned with their marketing
problems.

A major marketing problem was that *Licorera de
Boaco* had not been able to establish a strong brand name
for its *aguardiente*. If ALDECA chose not to merge,
however, *Licorera de Boaco* may have continued to try to
build strong brands themselves. Says Sr. Barjum,

They have their own sugar mill, they have 85%
control of the Nicaraguan market, they have
the technical know-how, and they have banks
in the United States. So, they are a very powerful company. They also own the franchise for
MasterCard™ in Central America. Financially,
I think they may be more powerful than
Grupo Cobán, and we are in the middle. We
are like the cheese between the two slices of
bread . . . everyone is trying to get us. So
that's one of the reasons we thought about the
possible merger with these people. But, that
would mean we would have to close down
shop here. Some of our personnel would be
taken over there, and some of them would
not. So, we would have to pay approximately
1.2 million lempiras in workers' compensation.

Some of the conditions of the merger proposal were
as follows:

1. ALDECA would shift all of its production equipment to the *Licorera de Boaco* distillery.

2. The consolidated firm would have exclusive rights
   to the brand names of both ALDECA and *Licorera
   de Boaco* for ninety-nine years.

3. The board of directors of the new firm would have
   seven members, three from ALDECA and four
   from *Licorera de Boaco*.

SR. BARJUM'S VIEW OF THE FUTURE   Sr. Barjum sat in his office with his son, Tony, late into the night trying to
come to some conclusions about their situation. "I am
reacting on a day-to-day basis," Sr. Barjum explained. "I
have not determined where I want the company to go in,
say, five years. How are we going to meet the new competition that is coming into the country? Maybe the way
we've operated in the past is not correct for today."

They decided to call a meeting of their most important distributors to discuss the issue. Tony wanted to tell
the distributors directly of *Grupo Cobán*'s usual form of
market entry and then give them an ultimatum: "Our
brands or theirs, but not both." But what if the distributors did not believe that ALDECA could enforce the ultimatum? Sr. Barjum favored discussing the problem with
the distributors and explaining to them some of the options that ALDECA was considering, like distributing
aguardiente directly to the cantinas themselves. The im-
plied threat should be enough to persuade the distributors to avoid *Grupo Cobán*'s brands. Sr. Barjum hoped
that the distributors did not know that ALDECA could
ship only competitors' products, like the pickup-load of
Yuscaran, at a loss.

Questions

1. What are the key characteristics of the Honduras economy? How do they affect (a) business generally, and
(b) ALDECA specifically?

2. Review ALDECA's financial statements in Table 4. What
trends do you see? How is ALDECA doing?

3. What are ALDECA's strengths and weaknesses? What
opportunities and threats face them?

4. How should ALDECA respond to the competition?
What strategies would you recommend and why?

Note

1. Reprinted by permission from the *Case Research Journal*. Copyright 1999 by Richard L. Priem and
K. Matthew Gilley and the North American Case Research Association. All rights reserved.

CASE 8

Negotiating Across the Pacific[1]

❦

Bill Wright, vice president of US Fortune, had just finished a telephone conversation with Edward Tang, general manager of Asia-Pacific Consulting Group, during which Tang had informed him that their stalled negotiations with BBT could lead to an international lawsuit. Eight months earlier, Beijing Bio-Tech (BBT), an animal-feed manufacturer from China, asked Tang to help locate a supplier of feed grade lecithin in the U.S. Tang, working with Wright as an intermediary, initiated negotiations between NutriNex, a U.S. lecithin producer, and BBT. The negotiation had been long and very difficult, and the transaction was not completed as planned.

The evening of July 16, 1997, found Bill reflecting on what had happened during the past eight months. He felt trapped and did not know what to do, but knew that he had to deal with the situation quickly. Edward had suggested to him that he should get the negotiation back on track, but Bill did not know if that was possible. However, Bill realized that if negotiations were not successful, the Chinese might launch a lawsuit against him.

Background: Participants and Transaction

Asia-Pacific Consulting Group (APCG) was a Philadelphia-based company specializing in export management, cross-cultural training, and foreign language-related services such as translation. The company's clients were from all over the United States and a dozen foreign countries, especially in Asia. This was because APCG's two founding partners, Edward Tang and his wife Joyce, were originally from China and had maintained extensive relationships in Asia.

Beijing Bio-Tech Co. Ltd. (BBT) was a joint venture set up by a Taiwan-based multinational company and a Beijing-based company affiliated with China's Ministry of Agriculture. BBT specialized in research, development, and production of nutrition, feeding, and breeding products for aquaculture. Since its establishment in 1990, BBT had made substantial progress in product innovation and marketing and became a leading aqua-biotech company in China. To recognize its accomplishment, the city government of Beijing named BBT a "Most Admirable Foreign-Funded Enterprise" for each of the last four years. Mrs. Ming Kuo, general manager of BBT, was featured in a publication as one of the "Outstanding Females in Contemporary China."

In November 1996, Ming Kuo contacted APCG and requested assistance in locating a supplier of feed-grade lecithin in the United States. The product was a core feed additive ingredient for fresh-water fish and shrimp, which was BBT's main product line. In the past, BBT purchased lecithin from two sources, a Chinese manufacturer that operated in China and a Hong Kong distributor that supplied U.S.-made lecithin. BBT preferred the U.S. products because they had more consistent quality. However, involving the Hong Kong distributor made the price very expensive. The average price of lecithin in the market was $3,700 per ton, ranging from $3,500 to 4,300. As far as the Asian markets were concerned, margins for middlemen could be as high as 40 percent. BBT currently purchased about 50 metric tons of lecithin annually. It intended to increase the purchase by 100 percent in the next year and then by 10 percent in the subsequent years. Eliminating the middleman and establishing a direct relationship with a U.S. supplier were important goals for BBT.

On November 12, 1996, Ming Kuo wrote a letter to APCG explaining the company's criteria for selecting the supplier: "We are looking for a long-term relationship with a reliable supplier. This means that we would consider the first purchase as a trial, hopefully both sides will be satisfied and decide to continue the relationship." While quality and price were important, on-time delivery was especially crucial. "Our season starts in late August and we must have the lecithin in our plants by that time," Mrs. Kuo stated.

As Edward Tang and his wife Joyce read the letter, they became excited. APCG had been involved in about a dozen international trade deals, but only a few of them had come through. This time the Tangs not only knew the Chinese company's reputation, they also interacted on several occasions with Mrs. Kuo and enjoyed a good personal relationship with her. In fact, it was the relationship that brought the business to APCG. As Mrs. Kuo stated: "As a Chinese, I like to do business with people I know." Access to hard currency usually posed a major challenge to foreign firms selling to China. The Chinese currency was not convertible, and Chinese importers had to purchase the foreign currency necessary for authorized imports, which was always troublesome. However, hard currency would not be a problem in this case because, like all joint ventures with investment from Taiwan, BBT was given a Sino-foreign joint-venture status and, therefore, was allowed to retain foreign currency contributed by the "foreign" (Taiwanese, in this case) partner or earned by the joint venture. As the Tangs knew, BBT enjoyed a high credit standing and never had payment problems in international trade. The Tangs also realized this might be a big deal, and, if this transaction did succeed, it could evolve into a continuous business.

In 1996, the United States was the world's leading supplier of lecithin due to its superior technology as well as its abundant domestic soybean supplies. Although China had made an effort to develop its own lecithin production, its technology was far behind. More importantly, lecithin was produced from soybeans, but there was little room for China to expand its soybean production in order to manufacture lecithin on a large scale. With limited arable lands, China had to concentrate on grains more suitable for human consumption, such as wheat and rice.

To locate sources of lecithin, the Tangs started with the U.S. Department of Agriculture, trade associations, and published industry directories. Then, with a short list of potential suppliers, they began calling companies. It was not too long, however, until they realized that these companies did not like to deal with middlemen. They said that they were definitely interested but would like to communicate directly with the buyer. With this concern, Edward called Bill Wright.

Bill Wright and His Working Plan

Bill Wright was executive vice-president and a director of US Fortune, an investment bank that had operations across the East Coast. US Fortune was a well-established company. Edward Tang had met Bill through a client who was Bill's close friend. Bill Wright had been with US Fortune for over twenty years, and, because of this, he was very well connected in the business community. As a senior executive, he currently had little involvement in the company's daily operation and was able to develop other business interests outside US Fortune. Particularly, Bill held substantial stakes in several food and drug-related firms. To take care of these businesses, Bill frequently traveled to Europe. However, he had never dealt with Asian countries.

Bill Wright was thrilled with the opportunity. BBT was a reputable Chinese company, and lecithin trade was a very profitable business. Most importantly, Bill had a long-time client, NutriNex, which happened to be a major manufacturer of lecithin.

NutriNex was located in the Midwest. It was a major player in the industry and had started exporting several years ago. Dr. Robert Fisher, NutriNex's CEO, knew the huge potential of the Chinese market. The company had been looking for an opportunity to enter the market at that time. However, NutriNex had been unsuccessful thus far because of the difficulties of establishing contacts in China. Therefore, when Bill called, Dr. Fisher could hardly believe it. "I am delighted to help," he said calmly. "Bill, just let me know what you want me to do." As they were talking, Bill already had a plan wherein he and the Tangs acted as middlemen between NutriNex and BBT (see Figure 1).

FIGURE 1
Bill Wright's Working Plan: The Players and Roles

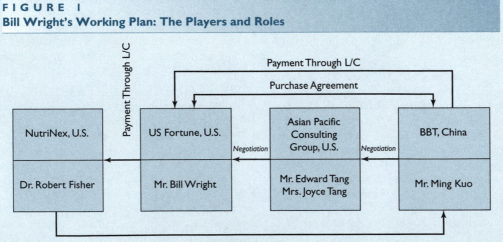

In practice, a middleman had two options in an export or import transaction. First, the middleman could work on a commission basis without taking title to the goods; his job was to provide a bridge between the buyer and seller. Second, the middleman could act as a real buyer and reseller and actually take title to the goods. In doing so, the middleman could be able to avoid the financial burden by means of back-to-back letters of credit (L/C). With this procedure, the buyer issued a L/C to the middleman who then issued another L/C to the supplier. The first L/C involved an amount larger than the second L/C; the middleman retained the difference as profits. Under the first option, the middleman's role was terminated after the buyer and seller were connected and a predetermined amount of commission was paid to the middleman. Quite often, a middleman did not want the buyer and seller to interact directly so that they would depend on his mediation in any further transactions. This was the main reason why some middlemen, often the experienced ones, took the second option.

Bill sensed that the purchase of BBT was likely to become a repeat business. He did not want to just take a commission and go away. Over the phone, he told CEO Fisher that he would like to handle the transaction through the following process:

1. Bill Wright should negotiate with the Chinese buyer for a purchase agreement and appear in the agreement as the SELLER.

2. The Chinese buyer should issue a letter of credit to Bill Wright.

3. Upon receipt of the L/C from the Chinese buyer, Bill Wright should then issue another L/C to NutriNex.

4. NutriNex should make the shipment after receiving the L/C from Bill Wright.

In the next hour, Bill sent a fax to Dr. Fisher to confirm their conversation. "OK, if this is how you want to do it," replied Dr. Fisher over the phone.

Letters of credit (L/C) was a basic method of receiving payment for products sold abroad. A letter of credit added a bank's promise of paying the exporter to that of the foreign buyer when the exporter has complied with all the terms and conditions of the letter of credit. In a typical export process, only one letter of credit was necessary; the foreign buyer applied for issuance of the letter of credit to the exporter. The process specified in Bill Wright's working plan involved two letters of credit (see Figures 2 and 3).

As agreed upon by Bill Wright and Robert Fisher, NutriNex would arrange shipping of the goods from its manufacturing facility directly to Xin Gang, the Chinese port where BBT would pick up the goods. At NutriNex factories, the lecithin would be loaded in a container,

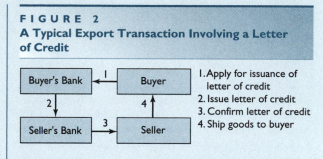

FIGURE 2

A Typical Export Transaction Involving a Letter of Credit

1. Apply for issuance of letter of credit
2. Issue letter of credit
3. Confirm letter of credit
4. Ship goods to buyer

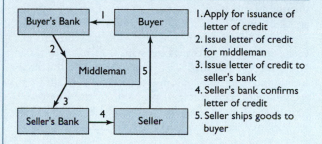

FIGURE 3

Export Process Involving Back-to-back Letters of Credit

1. Apply for issuance of letter of credit
2. Issue letter of credit for middleman
3. Issue letter of credit to seller's bank
4. Seller's bank confirms letter of credit
5. Seller ships goods to buyer

which then was carried by a truck to a port in California. At the port, the container was put on an ocean carrier. In normal situations, it took three to four weeks for a container to get from a U.S. port to China. At the Chinese port, BBT unloaded the goods to trucks. It took about an hour from the port to BBT's facilities in Beijing by trucks.

The Tangs had no problem with the arrangement. The only question was: Should they tell Ming Kuo everything? They knew that Mrs. Kuo intended to deal with a manufacturer, but they also knew that Bill did not want the buyer to establish direct contact with the supplier. In the end, the Tangs decided not to complicate the situation. "While the goods are not from Bill, Bill knows NutriNex's president. We should be OK," they said to each other. They did not tell BBT that the ultimate supplier was not Bill Wright but NutriNex.

Economic and Cultural Environment in China

Bill Wright's past overseas experience was largely limited to Europe. He felt that he needed to gain a broad perspective about what was going on in China. He called the Tangs with many questions. He realized that China had been one of the fastest growing economies in the world in recent years. This dynamic growth could be attributed largely to China's policy of reforming its economy and opening up to the outside world, which began in 1979. One of the most striking features in the changing economic system was the steady growth in the number of foreign-funded enterprises. He was aware that BBT, which was his Chinese counterpart in the transaction, was one of many enterprises jointly owned by Taiwanese and Mainland Chinese companies.

Bill Wright had heard that China's rapid economic growth and bold reform measures pointed to enormous market potential in China, and particularly that the Chinese had a high regard for American products. However, he just now realized how large the Chinese market for American manufactured lecithin could be. According to the Tangs, the Chinese consumers, with increasing purchasing power, had been demanding more and better products from the aquacultural sectors. Because of this, a number of aqua-biotech companies had recently emerged in the areas of research and development, production of nutrition, feeding, and breeding products for aquaculture. These Chinese companies, however, had to face a major challenge posed by China's limited per capita natural resources. For instance, with scarce arable lands the Chinese had used soybean mainly for direct human consumption. Coupled with lack of advanced technologies, currently and probably in the foreseeable future, the Chinese aqua-biotech companies had to rely on imported lecithin to meet the growing needs for quality feed additives.

Having talked to the Tangs, Bill realized that the Chinese people had a cultural system that was quite different from that in the U.S. and other Western countries. In conducting business, the Chinese paid much attention to building *guanxi,* that is, the intricate and pervasive network of personal relations. The Chinese culture also emphasized "face," or a person's credit, honor, and reputation. Embarrassment, failure, or contradictions lead to loss of face. Importantly, the Chinese concepts of *guanxi* and face were not universal, but highly situational and reciprocal. When a Chinese acted, he normally anticipated a return. And a Chinese would deal with a party as that party dealt him. The Chinese would say: "If you are good to me, I will be ten times better to you; but if you are bad to me, I will be ten times worse to you!" Hence, Chinese were morally justified to either repay or retaliate upon another person depending how that person treated him.

Similarly, face could be traded. A person doing a favor for someone was said to be giving face and the person who had received a favor was expected to give face in return. The notions of *guanxi* and face were evident in a Chinese business negotiation context. As observed by many Western negotiators, the Chinese took longer to make decisions. They apparently were more concerned with long-term associations and invested time in building a good working relationship. Because of this, they attached great importance to sincerity and reputation on the part of the foreign party. The Chinese seldom used the word *no,* because they tried to save face for both par-

ties. They proceeded cautiously and slowly at the negotiation table, because they tried to avoid mistakes that would embarrass them.

Bill was especially amazed by the Chinese' attitude toward legalistic approaches in business. Consistent with their attention to human relations and face, Chinese traditionally shunned legal considerations. Instead, they stressed the moral principles of everyday living and carefully managed relationships in business settings and among social groups. Even in today's international business environment, the Chinese preferred not to have lawyers involved in the negotiation process. To a large extent, they relied on personal trust instead of legal documents as the foundation of business relationships. For the Chinese, negotiation was an ongoing process and did not end with a signed contract. When disagreements occurred, they often sought compromise and consultation through a third party who was trusted by both sides. Legalistic measures were used only as a last resort.

While describing Chinese negotiation styles, the Tangs tried to illustrate some of the salient differences between the Chinese and Americans. Compared to Chinese emphasis on personal relationships, Americans took a factual approach toward negotiation and considered it as a place simply for problem solving. Unlike their Chinese counterparts, American negotiators separated people from issues and felt comfortable with confrontation. During the negotiation process, they were expected to give and take and even engage in hard bargaining. However, when a legal contract was signed, the negotiation reached the endpoint that both sides had to follow. The approaches toward conflict resolution were also different between the two people. While a typical Chinese approach was emotion-confounded, situational, and sometimes circuitous, a typical American approach was factual-based, legalistic, and generally straightforward.

The Ball Was Rolling

It did not take long for Bill to draft a purchase agreement. The only difficult part of the job was to determine the amount of commissions. In this transaction, there were two intermediaries: APCG and Bill Wright. Bill wanted to build in $20,000, which would be split equally between APCG and himself.

The total cost for a 40-foot container of lecithin, including insurance and freight, was $56,000. Edward figured that a commission over one-third of the sale price, exactly 38 percent, was too high to be acceptable and expressed his concern immediately. After listening to Edward, Bill replied: "Well, this is the normal way we do business in this country. The best price is the maximum you can charge yet the buyer is willing to pay. Who knows, maybe the Chinese will think it's okay!" "What if the Chinese think it's too expensive?" asked Edward. He was afraid that this price would scare BBT away. He then suggested to reduce the commission and give a more generous offer that he believed would signal goodwill to the Chinese buyer. "I understand that," Bill insisted, "but why don't we just start with this price. We can always back off some if BBT thinks our price is too high."

On February 16, 1997, APCG sent a fax to inform BBT of the price quoted by Bill Wright. Four weeks passed, but there had been no answer from BBT. Edward decided to call Mrs. Kuo. Mrs. Kuo first apologized for not responding and then said: "You should know how I feel—when a price quote seems way too high, we don't believe the seller is serious."

Edward felt embarrassed and said: "I am sorry, but I thought you might know how Americans start a negotiation. Believe me, they are really serious about this transaction." "Why should I know how Americans negotiate, Edward? Ming Kuo replied. "You went to American school, but I didn't. So you have better understanding on how they deal with these matters than I do. Well, since you've said that, I don't mind giving them a try. But please—tell them this time is for real. By the way, I am now thinking of a 20-foot container, not the 40-foot. Do you think they will do that?" Edward replied: "Ok, let me talk to Bill."

"How can they change from a 40-foot to 20-foot container, and why did it take them a month to respond!" Bill was upset while talking to Edward over the phone. Edward replied: "Bill, I told you that we should lower the price to be real. Now, if you listen to me this time, this is what we should do—get back to them as quickly as possible, agree to take an order for a 20-foot container, and lower the price. What I'm suggesting is that we show them that we are flexible and try very hard to work with them. Remember, I told you that BBT is not just looking at this single deal, they are trying to find a partner to work with for a long time."

On April 2, Bill sent a fax to Edward, informing him that Dr. Fisher from NutriNex agreed to take an order for a 20-foot container. Bill also agreed to quote a lower price to BBT, with the total commissions being reduced to $6,000. Edward was pleased with the news and sent a message to BBT on the same day. Twenty-four hours later, Ming Kuo called Edward. She was grateful for the effort made by APCG and agreed with the price. She promised that she would ask her Import Manager, Rong Zhang, to proceed immediately.

However, another week passed before Edward received the response from Rong Zhang of BBT. Mr. Zhang apologized for the delay and explained why. Since the tariff on lecithin was very high to manufacturing firms like BBT, the company had been negotiating with a licensed foreign trade company, Beijing International Trading Co. Ltd., to handle the import process. Under the Chinese government's import/export regulations, this trading company would pay lower tariffs for importing a product like lecithin than would BBT.

It was not until late May when Bill Wright and BBT could start serious discussions on the contractual terms. After several rounds of negotiation on items such as product name and packaging, the contract was finalized. Bill Wright signed the contract as "Executive Vice-President, US Fortune, Inc." The contract followed rather standardized format in international trade. It stipulated "Shipment within 30 days upon receipt of Buyer's Irrevocable, Transferable L/C issued from a reputable international bank or equivalent."

But Finally Dropped

On June 9, 1997, Bill faxed the signed contract to BBT. BBT signed the contract and faxed it back to Bill two weeks later. On July 3, BBT opened a L/C from Bank of China. On July 7, Bill received the copy of the L/C.

As he called on NutriNex to arrange delivery, Bill could hardly believe what he heard from Dr. Fisher. He was told that the delivery time requested couldn't be met because something had happened, which was outside the control of NutriNex. According to Dr. Fisher, there had been heavy rains, which caused a serious flood in the midwestern states. The flood created delays in transportation and ultimately slowed down the manufacturing of lecithin. At that time the company was experiencing a backlog of orders. "When you first talked to me about the deal, I said we would ship the goods to the buyer within three weeks. Now, it is going to take at least two months," said Dr. Fisher. Bill said he understood the situation but insisted NutriNex should figure out a way to make the delivery. "I am sorry, Bill," replied Dr. Fisher. "But there is no way my company can deliver this time." He pointed out that if there was a signed contract between Bill and NutriNex, they would have had to ship the goods on time, but there was no contract.

Listening to Dr. Fisher, Bill was shocked by the plain fact that he, not NutriNex, was obligated to make the delivery according to his contract with BBT. In the contract, he himself was the seller. "Why did I dare to sign the contract?" he asked himself. Yes, he had the verbal promise from Dr. Fisher and he believed his friendship with Dr. Fisher provided the assurance, but he didn't have a signed contract with Dr. Fisher, and NutriNex did not have to deliver.

Bill took the corporate jet to visit Dr. Fisher at NutriNex's headquarters. He believed that Dr. Fisher was able to help if he wanted to; NutriNex was so big that it should have no problem to fill a 20-foot container. However, Dr. Fisher offered no help. NutriNex's new delivery schedule was two months and even this delivery time could not be guaranteed until "We've received the order," said Dr. Fisher.

No Way Out?

When Bill came back to his office from the trip, he had several messages from Edward on his answering machine explaining that BBT had been waiting for the delivery. Bill sent a fax to BBT, informing the Chinese of the inevitable delay. He explained how the production was delayed by the weather and proposed to amend the contract with a new delivery time schedule.

It took only one day for Bill Wright to receive a fax from BBT. "We understand the difficulty due to the natural disaster," the fax stated. "However, our manufacturing season is approaching and we cannot afford a delay."

Bill Wright was now desperate, and decided to visit Dr. Fisher again. However, nothing had changed and NutriNex could not deliver to China at the moment. Bill sent another fax to BBT, indicating that he simply could not deliver on time.

BBT returned a fax to Bill the next day. It stated that Bill had violated the contract and caused the Chinese company a loss amounting to $13,450, as a result of an emergency purchase and the fund lockfee for the L/C in the bank. BBT therefore asked Bill to (1) apologize for the mistake, (2) compensate them for the loss, and (3) provide details of the amendment.

On July 21, Bill replied with a fax. He first stressed that the delay was unavoidable because of high demand and the rains and then gave another reason for the delay: "As you know, we have been dealing with you through our associates at APCG . . . . They have been out of town . . . . I did not feel that it was proper for me to contact you directly until I had spoken to them," and finally apologized for the delay. He suggested making an amendment to the original shipment time, 40–60 days instead of 30 days after receipt of an updated L/C from BBT. He did not mention the loss compensation issue.

Edward received a phone call from Mr. Zhang. He said Mrs. Kuo was very upset by Bill's response. He then asked Edward to pass the following message to Bill: BBT would initiate a lawsuit if it could not get a fair solution from Bill Wright.

Cross-Cultural Agent at Work

Edward translated the message very carefully when he talked to Bill on the phone, but he did not mention the word "lawsuit." He still hoped Bill could realize the seriousness of the situation: "No matter what happened, the contract had a delivery date and you didn't deliver," said Edward. "Ed, you know what? When you first talked to me like this, I kind of blamed myself too, then I said, wait a minute, if they moved reasonably fast when we started the negotiation, there wouldn't have been a delay," Bill argued. "Please understand that when we began this process, it was over four months ago. At that time shipment was two to three weeks after placing an order. As you know all commodities are subject to supply and demand forces." Finally, Bill replied: "Ed, I am sorry for their loss and I have apologized for the delay. But I have no control over the weather and I didn't ask them to lock funds at the bank."

While disappointed with what Bill had said, the Tangs decided to save the deal at any cost. That night, Joyce Tang called Mrs. Kuo at home. She told Mrs. Kuo that the responsibility was definitely Bill Wright's. However, she suggested that Mrs. Kuo try to get some good out of the bad since things had already happened: "See, you've already borne a loss. If you quit here, you've got nothing. Although this season's gone, if you don't give up, I am sure they will work very hard to deliver on time for your next season. Think about the time and money you've already spent. As long as their lecithin is good, that means that you did not waste all your money, and I promise to help you work with the manufacturer directly next time."

After a long silence, Mrs. Kuo replied: "Well, you're probably right; but we just think this American is too arrogant, he's made a mistake but blamed the flood. You're asking me to look forward, but I haven't received a true apology from Bill Wright! He needs to change his attitude if we are to continue doing business together. By the way, Joyce, you should have told me if I was dealing with a real seller or not!"

Having talked with Mrs. Kuo, Edward was more frustrated than ever. He knew that for the problem to be settled, Bill had to do something. However, Bill was not listening to him. Edward decided to make a dramatic move as he started dialing Bill's phone number in the middle of the night.

"Bill, we need to talk. I know you're upset. You know this is not just your problem, don't you? I'm on the phone all the time, and I realize I've already lost face with Mrs. Kuo. But I try to say to myself, 'things already happened, you've got to face it.' Now, no matter what really caused the problem, the fact is that we didn't deliver, so that means we broke the contract. Bill, I don't want to tell you this, but I was told BBT is preparing a lawsuit."

"Fine. Tell them I will see them in court!" Bill reacted immediately.

"Wait a minute, Bill. You know I'm here to help. Remember, I told you before that the Chinese don't like to go to court? I really don't believe Mrs. Kuo wants to take this step. What they want is a real apology, don't you ever understand this, Bill? Please! You've probably never dealt with the Chinese before. If you can show them that you are sorry about their loss and want to do something, you can calm them down and many times you'll make friends out of such situations. Bill, are you listening?"

After another uncomfortable pause, Bill said, "Well, what exactly do you want me to do, Ed?"

"You know, Bill, we are a team, and I made mistakes too. I'm thinking that we can offer to sign a new contract for next season. In the next contract, we could reduce the price, basically the commissions, yours and mine. Then we can say, 'Look, we're really sorry for what happened. We can't compensate you at this time, but we will help you by dropping all commissions in the new contract. We know this won't be enough to cover all your losses, but that's what we can do to help. We will work very hard to make sure things like this won't happen again in the future. And we would like to have a very productive working relationship. I think that by doing this it would stop them from going through with the lawsuit."

Lawsuit . . . Impossible?

Bill Wright was shocked to hear that BBT was going to sue. According to his notes, the Chinese culture deviated from a legalistic mentality. In resolving disagreements, Chinese used courts only as a last resort. "Are they really going to sue me just for this amount of money?" Bill asked himself. As this question came to his mind, Bill rushed to find the copy of the purchasing agreement. In the agreement, there was no mention of possible court procedures. Yet, the agreement stated that the seller should not be held responsible for any losses sustained by the buyer due to natural causes. Remembering all of this, Bill did not believe that BBT could win the case if they went to court in the United States. So, if BBT wanted to enter a lawsuit and win, they had to appeal to a court in China. If Bill did not agree to appear in a Chinese court, then the lawsuit would not take place.

Questions

1. Who is responsible for the failure of the transaction?

2. Advise a U.S. company about doing business with the Chinese and then how the Chinese should deal with U.S. business people.

3. Is there anything that can be done to save the transaction?

Note

1. This case by Xiouhua Lin of Penn State Great Valley and Jian Guan of Penn State Delaware County. It originally appeared in the *Case Research Journal* (Fall 2001): 41–51. Reproduced with permission.

CASE 9

Stakeholder Management: Shell Oil in Nigeria[1]

On November 10, 1995, Nigerian novelist and environmental activist Ken Saro-Wiwa was executed by hanging in a Port Harcourt prison. Just eight days earlier, he had been convicted by a military tribunal on what many observers considered trumped-up charges that he had ordered the murder of political opponents. Protests by many world leaders and human rights organizations had failed to prevent the Nigerian military regime from carrying out the death sentence.

Saro-Wiwa's execution provoked a profound crisis for the Royal Dutch/Shell Group of Companies. In its wake, some environmentalists and political leaders called for an international boycott of Shell's gasoline and other products. The World Bank announced it would not provide funding for Shell's liquefied natural gas project in Nigeria. Several groups, including the London Royal Geographic Society, voted to reject the company's charitable contributions. In Canada, the Toronto provincial government refused a $900,000 gasoline contract to Shell Canada, despite its low bid. Some even called for the oil company to pull out of Nigeria altogether. Alan Detheridge, Shell's coordinator for West Africa, told a reporter in February 1996, "Saro-Wiwa's execution was a disaster for us."

Just what was the connection between Saro-Wiwa's execution and Shell Oil? Why did the company find itself suddenly, in the words of the *New York Times,* "on trial in the court of public opinion"? Had the company done anything wrong? And what, if anything, could or should it do in the face of an escalating chorus of international criticism?

"The Group"

The Royal Dutch/Shell Group was the world's largest fully integrated petroleum company. "Upstream," the conglomerate controlled oil and gas exploration and production; "midstream," the pipelines and tankers that carried oil and gas; and "downstream," the refining, marketing, and distribution of the final product. The company also had interests in coal mining, metal mining, forestry, solar energy, and biotechnology. In all, the Anglo-Dutch conglomerate comprised over 2,000 separate entities, with exploration and production operations in dozens of countries, refineries in thirty-four, and marketing in over one hundred. Royal Dutch/Shell was, in both its ownership and scope, perhaps the world's most truly transnational corporation.

In 1994, Royal Dutch/Shell made more money than any other company in the world, reporting astonishing annual profits of $6.2 billion. The same year, the Anglo-Dutch conglomerate reported revenues of $94.9 billion, placing it tenth on Fortune's Global 500 list. Assets were reported at $108.3 billion and stockholders' equity at $56.4 billion. With 106,000 employees worldwide, it had the largest work force of any oil company in the world.

This highly successful global corporation traced its history back over more than a century and a half. In the 1830s, British entrepreneur Marcus Samuel founded a trading company to export manufactured goods from England and to import products, including polished sea shells (hence, the name "Shell"), from the Orient. In the early 1890s, Samuel's sons steered the company into the kerosene business, assembling a fleet of tankers—each named for a different shell—to ply the fuel through the Suez Canal to Far Eastern ports. At about the same time, a group of Dutch businessmen launched the Royal Dutch Company to drill for oil in the Dutch East Indies, sold under the "Crown" brand name. In 1907, Royal Dutch and Shell merged their properties in order to survive competitive pressures from Rockefeller's Standard Oil. Royal Dutch retained a 60 percent interest; Shell, 40 percent. The resulting organization came to be known as the Royal Dutch/Shell Group of Companies, or, sometimes, simply "the Group."

In the 1950s and 1960s, the company had diversified, increasing its holdings in chemical manufacturing, coal mining, and metal mining. By the 1990s, however, like many large conglomerates, the Group had begun to refocus on its core competencies in oil and gas. A 1995 internal strategy memo expressed the view that the contribution of fossil fuels to the world energy supply would continue to grow until around 2030, after which fossil fuels would give way gradually to solar, wind, hydro power, and biomass, as these alternative energy sources became relatively cheaper. "It is not up to us . . . to choose the 'winning' technologies," the company concluded. "But . . . our first attention will now be devoted to the robust maintenance of our core business . . . the market for fossil fuels."

Over the years, Royal Dutch/Shell had developed a highly decentralized management style, with its far-flung subsidiaries exercising considerable autonomy. The company believed that vesting authority in nationally based, integrated operating companies—each with its own distinctive identity—gave it the strategic flexibility to respond swiftly to local opportunities and conditions.

The corporation was governed by a six-person board of managing directors. Reflecting its dual parentage, the Group maintained headquarters in both London and The Hague. The chairmanship rotated periodically between the president of Shell and the president of Royal Dutch. In 1995, the chairmanship was held by the Dutch president, Cornelius A. J. Herkstroter, an accountant and economist who had held positions in the company in Asia and Europe. Decision making was by consensus, with no dominant personality. Few, if any, Royal Dutch/Shell executives were well-known outside the company. The company cultivated a style that was both conservative and low-profile. One senior executive commented, "If you want to get ahead at BP [British Petroleum, a long-time rival], you've got to get your name in the paper, but that's the best way to get fired at Shell."

Shell Nigeria

The Shell Petroleum and Development Company of Nigeria—usually called Shell Nigeria—stated its corporate objective simply. It was "to find, produce, and deliver hydrocarbons safely, responsibly, and economically for the benefit of our stakeholders."

The Royal Dutch/Shell Group had begun exploring for oil in West Africa in the 1930s, but it was not until 1956 that oil was discovered in the Niger delta in southeastern Nigeria. In 1958, two years before Nigeria's independence from Britain, Shell was the first of the major oil companies to commence operations there. Nigerian oil was of very high quality by world standards; in the industry, it was referred to as "sweet crude," meaning that only minimal refining was required to turn it into gasoline and other products.

In 1995, Shell Nigeria was the largest oil company in the country. The company itself was actually a joint venture with the Nigerian federal government, which, in the form of the state-owned Nigerian National Petroleum Corporation (NNPC), owned a 55 percent stake. Royal Dutch/Shell owned a 30 percent stake in the joint venture; the remaining 15 percent was owned by two European oil companies strategically aligned with Shell: Elf (French—10 percent) and Agip (Italian—5 percent).

Although the Nigerian government was the majority owner in the joint venture, its role was confined mainly to providing mineral rights; Shell built and managed the lion's share of the oil operations on the ground. Other players in the Nigerian oil industry, including Mobil and Chevron, mainly operated offshore. Of all the multinational oil companies in Nigeria, Shell had by far the most visibility.

Shell Nigeria's operations were huge, not only by Nigerian standards, but even by those of the parent firm. In 1995, Shell Nigeria produced an average of almost one million barrels of crude oil a day (about half of Nigeria's total output) in ninety-four separate fields spread over 31,000 square kilometers. It owned 6,200 kilometers of pipelines and flow lines, much of it running through swamps and flood zones in the Niger delta. In addition, the company operated two coastal export terminals, at Bonny and Forcados. By its own assessment, Shell's operation in Nigeria was "arguably [the company's] largest and most complex exploration and production venture" anywhere in the world outside of North America. The Nigerian operation provided about 14 percent of Royal Dutch/Shell's total world oil production—and probably a larger share of its profits, although financial data for Shell's subsidiaries were not separately reported. Its significance to the parent firm was indicated by the fact that several chief executives of Shell Nigeria had risen to become managing directors of Royal Dutch/Shell itself.

Shell Nigeria employed about 2,000 people. Ninety-four percent of all employees, and about half of senior managers, were Nigerian. Few employees, however, were drawn from the impoverished delta communities where most oil facilities were located; for example, by one estimate, less than 2 percent of Shell Nigeria's employees were Ogoni—the ethnic group from the Niger delta of which Saro-Wiwa was a member. The percentage of local people was higher—20 to 50 percent—on Shell's seismic crews, which did the dirty and dangerous work of drilling and blasting during oil exploration.

Shell's financial arrangements with the Nigerian government dated from the 1970s, when world oil markets had been restructured by the emergence of newly assertive oil-producing regions—first Libya and later OPEC, of which Nigeria was a member. The arrangements were highly beneficial to the Nigerian government. For every barrel of oil sold by Shell Nigeria, 90 percent of net revenues (after expenses) went to the federal government, in the form of taxes and royalties. Shell, Elf, and Agip split the remaining 10 percent.

Although Shell and the Nigerian government worked hand in glove in the oil industry, relations between the two were often strained. Although usually unwilling to comment publicly, Shell seemed to resent the Nigerian government's large take and was frustrated by its frequent failure to pay revenues due its corporate partners. Endemic corruption in Nigerian society was also a frequent irritant. Brian Anderson, Shell Nigeria's managing director (chief executive), once in a moment of apparent candor complained bitterly to journalists of the "black hole of corruption acting like a gravity . . . pulling us down all the time."

"The Giant of West Africa"

Nigeria, the Group's, at times, troublesome partner, has been called the "giant of West Africa." Located on the North Atlantic coast between Benin and Cameroon, Nigeria was slightly more than twice the size of California, and, with 98 million people, the most populous country on the continent. Nigeria's gross domestic product of around $95 billion placed its economy second, smaller only than South Africa's. The economy was heavily dependent on petroleum: [oil and natural gas sales produced 80 percent of federal government's revenue, and over 90 percent of the country's foreign exchange. Thirty-seven percent of all exports and 50 percent of oil exports went to the United States, more than to any other single country.

Nigeria was a land of stark socioeconomic contrasts. The nation's military and business elites had grown wealthy from oil revenues. Yet most Nigerians lived in poverty. The annual per capita income was $250, less than that of Haiti or China, and in the mid-1990s, economic distress in many parts of Nigeria was deepening.

A legacy of colonialism, in Nigeria as elsewhere in Africa, was the formation of states that had little historical basis other than common colonial governance. In the Nigerian case, the modern nation was formed from what had been no less than 250 disparate ethnic groups in traditional society, many with little by way of cultural or linguistic ties. The nation was comprised of three main ethnic groups: in the north, the Hausa-Fulani; in the southwest, the Yoruba; and in the southeast, the Ibo. Together, these three groups made up 65 percent of the population; the remaining 35 percent was made up of scores of smaller ethnic groups, including the Ogoni. The military in Nigeria—and, not coincidentally, the federal government—had always been dominated by the Hausa-Fulani.

In 1967, the Ibo and their allies in oil-rich southeastern Nigeria attempted to secede as the independent state of Biafra. The resulting civil war, that lasted three years, was eventually won by federal forces. A major outcome of the Biafran conflict was the emergence of a powerful federal government with weak states' rights and a deep mistrust of any move toward regional autonomy.

Since its independence from Britain in 1960, Nigeria had been ruled by military governments for all but nine years. Several efforts—all eventually unsuccessful—had been made to effect a transition to permanent civilian rule. In June 1993, then-military dictator Ibrahim Babangida annulled the presidential election, suspended the newly created national assembly, and outlawed two fledgling political parties. In his memoirs, Saro-Wiwa likened Nigeria's halting attempts to democratize to "a truck [that is] completely rusty, without a roadworthiness certificate or an insurance policy; its license has expired. Yet its driver insists on taking it out on an endless journey."

In November 1993, yet another military man, General Sani Abacha, took power in a coup. The Abacha regime has been called "indisputably the cruelest and most corrupt" government in Nigeria since independence. A specialist in African politics summarized the situation in Nigeria in testimony before the Senate Foreign Relations Committee in 1995:

> [The] current government appears indifferent to international standards of conduct, while dragging the country into a downward spiral of disarray, economic stagnation, and ethnic animosity . . . . [It] has curtailed political and civil rights to an unprecedented degree in Nigerian history, magnified corruption and malfeasance in an endemically corrupt system, and substantially abandoned responsible economic management . . . . [F]ormal lapses in macroeconomic management have been accompanied by an upsurge in illicit activities, including oil smuggling, narcotics trafficking, and a prodigious cottage industry engaged in international commercial fraud.

In 1993, inflation was running close to 60 percent annually, foreign debt was growing, and the country's balance of payments was worsening.

Nigeria in 1995 was by many accounts the most corrupt nation in Africa, arguably, in the world. Fabulous oil wealth and a lack of democratic accountability combined to create a society where almost everyone was on the take. General Abacha himself was reputedly a billionaire. The state-owned oil company, the NNPC, incredibly, did not publish annual accounts; by one estimate, as much as $2.7 billion was illegally siphoned from NNPC coffers annually. White elephant projects—like a multibillion dollar project to develop a steel industry in a country that had neither high-grade coal nor iron ore, and a new Brazilia-like capital built from the ground up in Abuja in central Nigeria—drained public monies while enriching those lucky enough to receive government contracts. Local officials tried to get their cut. By one observer's account:

[Traveling in Nigeria, one] is assailed with re-
quests for payments for everything from getting through the airport to being given directions in a government ministry to having
somebody talk to you. . . . And it has been
aggravated at the level of petty corruption by
the situation of economic decline . . . and
the plummeting real wages of many Nigerians,
so that people simply have no alternative but
to take these sorts of inducements in order to
get by.

Corruption was so rampant in Nigeria, the *Economist*
concluded in an editorial, that "the parasite . . . has almost eaten the host."

The Ogoni People

Saro-Wiwa's people, the Ogoni, were in many ways victims both of oil development and of the Hausa-Fulani
dominated federal government. Ogoniland was a small
area—a mere 12 by 32 miles—that had the misfortune to
be located in the Niger delta, right on top of one of the
world's greatest oil reserves. A distinctive ethnic group,
numbering about half a million in the mid-1990s, the
Ogoni spoke four related languages and shared a common animistic religion. Prior to the arrival of the British
in 1901, a stable Ogoni society based on fishing and
farming had existed in the delta for centuries.

Ogoniland was the site of tremendous mineral wealth,
and yet, over the years, the Ogoni had received virtually
no revenue from its development. Somewhere on the
order of $30 billion worth of oil was extracted from
Ogoniland's five major oil fields between 1958 and
1994. Yet, under revenue sharing arrangements between
the Nigerian federal government and the states, only
1.5 percent of oil taxes and royalties was returned to the
delta communities for economic development—and most
of this went to line the pockets of local officials.[2]

The Rivers State, that included Ogoniland, was
among the poorest in Nigeria. No modern sanitation systems were in place, even in the provincial capital of Port
Harcourt. Raw sewage was simply buried or discharged
into rivers or lakes. Drinking water was often contaminated, and water-related diseases, such as cholera,
malaria, and gastroenteritis, were common.

Ogoniland's population density of 1,500 per square
mile was among the highest of any rural area in the
world—and much higher than the Nigerian national average of 300 per square mile. Housing there was typically
constructed with corrugated tin roofs and cement or,
more commonly, dirt floors. Only one fifth of rural housing was considered by authorities to be "physically
sound." Approximately 30–40 percent of delta children
attended primary school, compared with about three-
quarters in Nigeria as a whole; three-quarters of adults

were illiterate. Unemployment was estimated at 30 percent. A British engineer who later returned to the delta
village where oil was first discovered in Nigeria commented, "I have explored for oil in Venezuela, I have explored for oil in Kuwait, [but] I have never seen an oil-
rich town as completely impoverished as Olobiri."

In 1992, in response to pressure from the Ogoni and
other delta peoples, the Nigerian government established
an Oil Mineral Producing Areas Development Commission (OMPADC), funded with 3 percent of oil revenues.
These funds (double the prior allocation) were earmarked for infrastructure development in the oil producing regions, mainly the delta. In 1993, the group spent
$94 million, with about 40 percent going to the Rivers
State. Although some projects were initiated, the World
Bank later criticized OMPADC for "poor dialogue with
other institutions and communities" and "no environmentally sustainable development emphasis."

Shell Nigeria gave some direct assistance to the oil-
producing regions. In 1995, the company's community-
development program in Nigeria spent about $20 mil-
lion. Projects included building classrooms and
community hospitals, paying teacher salaries, funding
scholarships for Nigerian youth, and operating an agricultural station. According to one study, however, almost
two-thirds of the community development budget was
allocated to building and maintaining roads to and from
oil installations. Although open to the public, these roads
were of little use to most delta residents, who did not
own cars. Moreover, Shell made little effort to involve
local residents in determining how its community development funds would be spent. The World Bank concluded that "[in] spite of . . . large investments, the impact of . . . oil company investments on improving the
quality of life in the delta has been minimal."

Ken Saro-Wiwa: Writer and Activist

Ken Saro-Wiwa, leader of the Ogoni insurgency, was in
many respects an unlikely activist. A businessman who
later became a highly successful writer and television producer, he had a taste for gourmet food, fine literature,
sophisticated humor, and international travel. Yet, in the
final years of his life, he emerged as a world-renowned
advocate for sustainable development and for the rights
of indigenous peoples who was honored by a Nobel
Peace Prize nomination and receipt of the Goldman Environmental Prize.

The British novelist William Boyd, a close friend, described Saro-Wiwa this way:

Ken was a small man, probably no more than
five feet two or three. He was stocky and
energetic—in fact, brim full of energy—and
had a big, wide smile. He smoked a pipe with
a curved stem. I learnt later that the pipe was

virtually a logo: in Nigeria people recognized him by it.

Saro-Wiwa was born in 1941 in Bori, an Ogoni village in the delta area east of Port Harcourt, into a large, supportive family. A brilliant student, he was educated first at Methodist mission schools in Bori and later, with the aid of government scholarships, at Government College, Umuahia, and the University of Ibadan, where he studied literature with the intention of becoming an academic.

When the Biafran civil war broke out in 1967, Saro-Wiwa, then a graduate student and lecturer at the University of Nigeria, declared his support for the federal government. As one of the few educated Ogoni to side with federal forces, he became part of what he later called "a sort of Cabinet of a government-in-exile" for the delta region, then under Biafran control. After federal forces had recaptured the delta, Saro-Wiwa was appointed civil administrator for the oil port of Bonny. His position during the Biafran conflict—that ethnic minorities in Nigeria, like the Ogoni, would do better by seeking full democratic rights in a federal state than through succession—prefigured his later views.

In 1973, then 32, Saro-Wiwa left government service to launch his own business. After four years as a successful grocer and trader, he took the proceeds and began investing in real estate—buying office buildings, shops, and homes. In 1983, having acquired sufficient property to live comfortably, Saro-Wiwa turned to what he called his "first love," writing and publishing. He proved to be a gifted and prolific writer, producing in short order a critically acclaimed novel, *Sozaboy: A Novel in Rotten English,* a volume of poetry, and a collection of short stories.

In 1985, Saro-Wiwa was approached by a university friend who had become program director for the state-run Nigerian television authority to develop a comedy series. The result, a show titled *Basi & Co.,* ran for five years and became the most widely watched television show in Africa. Reflecting Saro-Wiwa's political views, the program satirized Nigerians' desire to get rich with little effort. The show's comic protagonist was Basi, "a witty rogue [who] hustled on the streets of Lagos and was willing to do anything to make money, short of working for it."

By the late 1980s, Saro-Wiwa had become a wealthy and internationally known novelist and television scriptwriter. His wife, Hauwa, and four children moved to London, where his children enrolled in top British private schools. Saro-Wiwa joined his family often, making many friends in the London literary community who would later work doggedly, although unsuccessfully, for his release.

In 1988, Saro-Wiwa undertook a nonfiction study of the Nigerian civil war, later published under the title, *On*

a Darkling Plain. The work reawakened his interest in politics and in the plight of his own Ogoni people. In a speech at the Nigerian Institute of International Affairs in Lagos in March 1990, marking the book's publication, Saro-Wiwa used the subject of his historical study to lay out a theme that was to become central to the rest of his life's work:

> Oil was very much at the centre of the [Biafran] war. . . . Twenty years [later] . . . the system of revenue allocation, the development policies of successive Federal administrations, and the insensitivity of the Nigerian elite have turned the delta and its environs into an ecological disaster and dehumanized its inhabitants. The notion that the oil-bearing areas can provide the revenue of the country and yet be denied a proper share of that revenue because it is perceived that the inhabitants of the area are few in number is unjust, immoral, unnatural, and ungodly. . . . The peoples of Rivers and Bendel States, in particular, sit very heavy on the conscience of Nigeria.

On a Darkling Plain, not surprisingly, ignited a storm of controversy in Nigeria, and *Basi & Co.* was canceled shortly after its publication, as was a column Saro-Wiwa had been writing for the government-owned weekly *Sunday Times.*

Movement for the Survival of the Ogoni People

While working on his book on the civil war, Saro-Wiwa experienced a vision in which he was visited by the Spirit of the Ogoni, a fetish god in traditional society. He later described this experience:

> I received a call to put myself, my abilities, my resources, so carefully nurtured over the years, at the feet of the Ogoni people and similar dispossessed, dispirited, and disappearing peoples in Nigeria and elsewhere. The Voice spoke to me, directing me what to do and assuring me of success in my lifetime and thereafter. I was adequately warned of the difficulties which this call to service would entail and the grave risks I would be running.

The cancellation of his TV series and newspaper column seemed to propel Saro-Wiwa further into political activism. In August 1990, he met with a group of Ogoni tribal chiefs and intellectuals in Bori, where they drafted and signed an Ogoni Bill of Rights. This document, while reaffirming the Ogoni people's desire to remain part of Nigeria, called for political autonomy; cultural, religious, and linguistic freedom; the right to control a "fair proportion" of the region's economic resources; and higher standards of environmental protection for the Ogoni people. The document was addressed to the president of the Federal Republic and to the members of the Armed Forces Ruling Council.

Shortly thereafter, drafters of the bill of rights met to form an organization to press their demands. The group chose the name Movement for the Survival of the Ogoni People (MOSOP). Although Saro-Wiwa was the main organizer, he felt that he would be most effective as a writer and press coordinator, so he was named "spokesman." Garrick Leton, a tribal chief and former cabinet minister, was named president.

From its inception, MOSOP adopted a philosophy of nonviolent mass mobilization. In a speech in December 1990, Saro-Wiwa spelled out the organization's strategy:

> Some, looking at the enormity of the task, must ask, "Can we do it?" The answer, unequivocally, is YES. . . . The next task is to mobilize every Ogoni man, woman, and child on the nature and necessity of our cause so that everyone knows and believes in that cause and holds it as a religion, refusing to be bullied or bribed therefrom. . . . This is not, I repeat NOT, a call to violent action. We have a moral claim over Nigeria . . . Our strength derives from this moral advantage, and that is what we have to press home.

MOSOP's earliest organizational efforts focused on educational work and appeals to the military government and to the oil companies. The organization published the Ogoni Bill of Rights and organized a speaking tour of the region to present it to the Ogoni. Saro-Wiwa traveled abroad to the United States, Switzerland, England, the Netherlands, and Russia, where he met with human rights and environmentalist groups and government officials to build support for the Ogoni cause. MOSOP also issued a propagandistic "demand notice" calling on Shell and the NNPC to pay "damages" of $4 billion for "destroying the environment" and $6 billion in "unpaid rents and royalties" to the Ogoni people.

Environmental Issues

A central plank in the MOSOP platform was that the oil companies—particularly Shell—were responsible for serious environmental degradation. In a speech given in 1992 to the Unrepresented Nations and Peoples Organization (UNPO), Saro-Wiwa stated MOSOP's case:

> Oil exploration has turned Ogoni into a wasteland: lands, streams, and creeks are totally and continually polluted; the atmosphere has been poisoned, charged as it is with hydrocarbon vapors, methane, carbon monoxide, carbon dioxide, and soot emitted by gas which has been flared twenty-four hours a day

for thirty-three years in very close proximity to human habitation. Acid rain, oil spillages, and oil blowouts have devastated Ogoni territory. High pressure oil pipelines crisscross the surface of Ogoni farmlands and villages dangerously.

> The results of such unchecked environmental pollution and degradation include the complete destruction of the ecosystem. Mangrove forests have fallen to the toxicity of oil and are being replaced by noxious nypa palms; the rain forest has fallen to the axe of the multinational oil companies, all wildlife is dead, marine life is gone, the farmlands have been rendered infertile by acid rain, and the once beautiful Ogoni countryside is no longer a source of fresh air and green vegetation. All one sees and feels around is death.

Shell disputed these charges. In a comment on "environmental issues" posted on the Internet, the company stated:

> We have never denied that there are some environmental problems connected with our operation and we are committed to dealing with them. However, we totally reject accusations of devastating Ogoniland or the Niger delta. This has been dramatized out of all proportion.

Shell argued that the land it had acquired for operations comprised only 0.3 percent of the Niger delta; and that the region's environmental problems had been caused mainly by rising population, overfarming, and poor sanitation practices by local residents. Moreover, Shell charged, many of the oil spills in the area had been caused by sabotage, for which they could not be held responsible.

The Niger delta was one of the world's largest wetlands, a vast floodplain built up by sedimentary deposits at the mouths of the Niger and Benue Rivers. It was an ecologically complex area composed of four zones: coastal barrier islands, mangroves, fresh water swamp forests, and lowland rainforest. In a comprehensive study of environmental conditions in the Niger delta completed in 1995, the World Bank found evidence of significant environmental problems, including land degradation, over fishing, deforestation, loss of biodiversity, and water contamination. Most of these problems, however, were the result not of oil pollution but rather of overpopulation coupled with poverty and weak environmental regulation.

The World Bank did find significant evidence of air pollution from refineries and petrochemical facilities and also of oil spills and poor waste-management practices at and around pipelines, terminals, and offshore platforms. It concluded, however, that "oil pollution . . . is only of moderate priority when compared with the full spectrum of environmental problems in the Niger Delta."

Of the environmental problems associated with the oil industry, the World Bank reported, the worst was gas flaring.

Natural gas is often produced as a byproduct of oil drilling. In most oil-producing regions of the world, this ancillary gas is captured and sold. In Nigeria, however, gas was routinely simply burned off, or "flared," in the production fields. In 1991, over three-quarters of natural gas production in Nigeria was flared—compared with, say, less than 1 percent in the U.S. or a world average of less than 5 percent. In 1993, Nigeria flared more natural gas than any nation on earth.

Gas flaring had several adverse environmental consequences. The flares produced large amounts of carbon dioxide and methane, both greenhouse gases and contributors to global warming. Residents in the immediate vicinity of the flares experienced constant noise, heat, and soot contamination. The flares, which burned continuously, lit up the night sky in much of the delta with an eerie orange glow. One British environmentalist commented poignantly after a fact-finding visit to the delta that "some children have never known a dark night, even though they have no electricity."

During the early 1990s, Shell Nigeria was involved in a joint venture known as the Nigeria Liquefied Natural Gas project. The aim of this scheme, in which Shell was a 24 percent shareholder, was to pipe natural gas to ocean terminals, liquefy it, and ship it abroad in special ships at super-cooled temperatures. In late 1995, the fate of this venture was still unclear.

Contrary to charges made by some of Shell's critics, Nigeria did have some environmental regulations in place. In 1988, the federal government had promulgated the Federal Environmental Protection Agency Decree and, in 1991, had followed with a set of National Environmental Protection Regulations. These laws, which were enforced by the federal Department of Petroleum Resources, required industry to install pollution abatement devices, restricted toxic discharges, required permits for handling toxic wastes, and mandated environmental impact studies for major industrial developments.

Civil Disturbances in Ogoniland

During the early 1990s, civil disturbances in Ogoniland and nearby delta communities, many directed at Shell, escalated. Shell later posted on the Internet descriptions of some of these incidents. Three examples of Shell's posted accounts follow:

Umuechem, 1 November 1990

[This] incident happened when armed youths invaded and occupied a rig location and nearby flowstation, chasing off staff who were not given the opportunity to make the location safe. The youths demanded N100 million [*naira*, the Nigerian currency, at that time worth about $12.5 million], a new road, and a water scheme. Attempts to talk with the youths, who were armed with guns and machetes, failed.

In response, Shell staff called the Nigerian police, which sent in mobile police units. In the ensuing riot, at least one policeman and seven civilians in the village of Umuechem were killed. Shell concluded its posting, "The Shell response to the threatening situation was made with the best intentions and what happened was a shock to staff, many of whom had friends at Umuechem."

Ahia, 7 March 1992

A gang of youths . . . stormed . . . a drilling rig in the Ahia oil field . . . looting and vandalizing the facility and rig camp. Rig workers were held hostage for most of the first day while property worth $6 million was destroyed or stolen. The rig was shut down for 10 days and the Ahia flow station was also shut down. . . . [A protest leader] raised the issue of the 1.5 percent derivation of oil revenues to the oil producing communities by the government, the need for a new road, and rumors of bribery by Shell of a paramount chief . . . .

In this incident as well, Shell called the police; this time, no injuries resulted.

Nembe Creek, 4 December 1993

A gang of armed youths attacked Nembe production camp as staff slept at 4 A.M., ransacking and looting offices, a workshop, stores, switchboard, mess, kitchen, and recreation block—and attacking and beating up staff. Eight staff were assaulted and wounded. The gang also shut down five swamp flowstations and invaded a nearby drilling rig and oil service barge. Among the demands the youths made were that Shell should take over the construction of a stalled road project being built by the government, provide electricity, employ [local] people as managers and directors of Shell, and sandfill an area of cleared swamp.

Again, Shell called the police. The incident was resolved without injuries. The cost to Shell was estimated at $3 million, and production was shut down for five days.

Most of the civil disturbances followed a similar pattern, as these examples suggest. A group of young men, armed with whatever weapons were readily available, would attack one of the many far-flung oil installations in

TABLE 1
Community Disruptions in Shell's Niger Delta Operations

	Number	Days Lost
1989	34	28
1990	95	28
1991	102	243
1992	85	407
1993	169	1,432
1994	84	1,316

the delta. Employees would be attacked, equipment would be sabotaged, and the group would make demands. The demands would be denied, and the company would call in police. Violence against civilians sometimes followed.

Shell's summary data on patterns of community disturbances in the Niger delta, shown in Table 1, reveal a pattern of escalating violence throughout the early 1990s, peaking in 1993. Shell estimated that the company sustained $42 million in damage to its installations in Ogoniland between 1993 and the end of 1995, as a direct result of sabotage.

The relationship between these incidents and MOSOP was complex. Saro-Wiwa's group explicitly rejected violence and repeatedly disavowed vigilante attacks on Shell or other companies; Saro-Wiwa himself frequently toured Ogoniland to restore calm. Yet publication of the Bill of Rights and MOSOP campaigns focusing attention on injustices suffered by the Ogoni clearly had the effect of escalating expectations within Ogoni society. In this context, many young unemployed Ogoni men simply took matters into their own hands. In a democratic society, demands for electricity, roads, jobs, and piped water would find political expression. In Nigeria, where the state was run by the military and no parliamentary process existed, these demands became directed against business.

On January 3, 1993, MOSOP held a massive regional rally to mark the start of the Year of the Indigenous Peoples. The rally, held at successive locations across Ogoniland, was attended by as many as 300,000 people—three-fifths of the Ogoni population. Protesters carried twigs, a symbol of environmental regeneration.

Two weeks later, Shell abruptly announced that it would withdraw from Ogoniland. It evacuated all employees and shut down its operations. Company officials gave a terse explanation: "There is no question of our staff working in areas where their safety may be at risk."

The "Militarization of Commerce"

As civil unrest escalated in Ogoniland, Shell by some accounts began to work more and more closely with the Nigerian police, especially with mobile police units known as the supernumerary police. Shell defended this practice:

> It is normal practice in Nigeria among leading commercial businesses for supernumerary police, trained by the Nigeria Police Force, to be assigned to protect staff and facilities. Violent crime is a daily occurrence in Nigeria. Over the last two years there have been more than 600 criminal incidents against SPDC's [the Shell Petroleum Development Corporation of Nigeria] staff and operations. One in 10 of these included the use of weapons. The problem of ensuring maximum protection for its staff and facilities remains a matter of grave concern to SPDC.

Shell also provided material and logistical support to police protecting its facilities. The company publicly acknowledged that it provided firearms to mobile police units. The company explained:

> [Shell Nigeria] does not own any firearms. However, it does purchase side arms on behalf of the Nigerian police force for police personnel who guard the company's facilities against general crime. This is a requirement of the police force and it applies to all oil companies and other business sectors that require police protection against the high rate of violent crime in the country . . . .

Several human rights organizations claimed that Shell provided more than handguns to the police. A representative of the Nigerian Civil Liberties Organization reported that Shell-owned cars, buses, speedboats, and helicopters were regularly used to transport police and military personnel to the site of civil disturbances. Human Rights Watch reported that Shell was meeting regularly with representatives of the Rivers State police to plan security operations.

After General Abacha took power in November 1993, he apparently decided to take a hard line with the Ogoni insurgency in an effort to induce Shell to resume operations.

One of his first acts as chief of state was to assemble a special Internal Security Task Force, comprised of selected personnel from the army, navy, air force, and police and headed by Maj. Paul Okuntimo, to restore order in Ogoniland. According to internal memos, later revealed, between Okuntimo and the military governor of Rivers State, the purpose of the task force was to ensure that those "carrying out business ventures in Ogoni land are not molested." A memo dated May 12, 1994, read in part: "Shell operations [are] still impossible unless ruthless military operations are undertaken for smooth economic activities to commence." Under the subheading "Financial Implications," Okuntimo advised the governor to put "pressure on oil companies for prompt regular inputs as discussed." Shell later denied giving any support to Okuntimo's operation.

In May and June 1994, intense violence erupted in Ogoniland. Amnesty International, which collected eyewitness accounts, reported that Okuntimo's paramilitary force entered Ogoniland, where it "instigated and assisted" interethnic clashes between previously peaceful neighboring groups. The units then "followed the attackers into Ogoni villages, destroying houses and detaining people." In May and June, the Ukuntimo's force attacked thirty towns and villages, where its members "fired at random, destroyed and set fires to homes, killing, assaulting, and raping, and looting and extorting money, livestock, and food," according to the Amnesty International report. As many as 2,000 civilians may have been killed. In August, Okuntimo held a press conference where he "boasted openly of his proficiency in killing people and of payments made to himself and his men by Shell to protect oil installations" and "justified the use of terror . . . to force the Ogoni into submission."

In 1995, Okuntimo's efforts notwithstanding, Shell had still not returned to Ogoniland. All its other oil production operations in the Niger delta were being conducted under round-the-clock military protection. Claude Ake, a well-known Nigerian political economist, described the situation in a chilling phrase: "This is a process," he wrote, "of the militarization of commerce."

Divisions Within MOSOP

In 1992 and early 1993, failure of MOSOP's efforts to win voluntary concessions from the military government or from Shell and deepening civil unrest in Ogoniland precipitated a split in the organization's leadership. MOSOP president Garrick Leton and his supporters favored a conciliatory approach, working with military authorities to suppress violence in exchange for various favors from the regime. Saro-Wiwa and his followers, while not condoning violence, were opposed to any cooperation with the military. In the early months of 1993, Saro-Wiwa sought to build an "alternative power base" for his position. He organized the National Youth Council of the Ogoni People (NYCOP), "to give discipline and direction to militant young Ogonis," as well as other groups for women, teachers, religious leaders, students, and professionals. Leton bitterly resented this move, say-

ing, "This is where the trouble started, with these parallel organizations. He [Saro-Wiwa] was doing things all on his own. He didn't want us elders any longer."

The split came to a head over the presidential elections of June 1993, which were later annulled by Babandiga. Leton's faction favored participation, Saro-Wiwa's, a boycott. The matter was put to a vote, and Saro-Wiwa's followers won. Leton and his supporters, who included Edward Kobani, of whose murder Saro-Wiwa was later accused, resigned from MOSOP. Saro-Wiwa was elected president.

In late 1993, an anonymous leaflet appeared in Ogoniland. It accused Shell of offering a multimillion dollar reward to any "vultures" who could destroy MOSOP and Ken Saro-Wiwa. The term *vulture* was often used by militant youth to describe conservative leaders suspected of collusion with the military government. No one ever claimed responsibility for the leaflet.

The Arrest, Trial, and Execution of a Martyr

On May 21, 1994, just a little over a week after Okitumo's "smooth operations" memo, Saro-Wiwa was en route to a MOSOP rally, where he was scheduled to speak. On the way, his car was stopped at a military roadblock, and he was ordered to return to his home in Port Harcourt. He never attended the rally.

Later that same day, a group of Ogoni chiefs, who were allied with Leton's faction, met at one of their homes, a concrete block bungalow in the Gokana district. Their meeting was interrupted by a young man outside revving his motorcycle. One of the chiefs, Edward Kobani, went outside to see what he wanted. According to testimony at Saro-Wiwa's trial, the young man on the motorcycle said, "So it's true the vultures are meeting. . . . Ken . . . said that the vultures are sharing out money from Shell and the government."

Within an hour, the young man had returned with several hundred youths. The youths denounced the "vultures" and demanded that they come out. Albert Badey, Samuel Orage, Theophilus Orage, and Edward Kobani emerged. They were promptly assaulted and bludgeoned to death. Edward's brother, Mohammed, ran out the back door, across the garden, and into a shrine for the Spirit of the Ogoni. Mohammed, who later testified at the trial, reported:

> I am an Ogoni man, and I know churches are just window dressing. If I had gone into a church or mosque they would have killed me there. But, because of their fetish belief, they were afraid if they [went] into the shrine . . . the repercussions would be on their families for generations.

In the nick of time, the police arrived and drove off the mob; Mohammed Kobani survived the attack.

The following day, May 22, Saro-Wiwa and several other leaders of MOSOP were arrested. In a televised press conference, the military governor of Rivers State blamed the MOSOP leaders for the murders. Saro-Wiwa and his colleagues were detained in a secret military camp outside Port Harcourt, where they were chained in leg irons and denied access to medical care. It would be eight months before they were formally charged.

During Saro-Wiwa's imprisonment, his brother, Owens Wiwa, met on three occasions with Shell Nigeria's managing director Brian Anderson to seek his help in securing Ken's release. Wiwa later gave an account of these meetings that was posted on the Internet. Anderson told him, Wiwa reported, that it would be "difficult but not impossible" to get his brother out of prison. Anderson allegedly said, "if [MOSOP] can stop the campaign [against Shell] we might be able to do something." Wiwa refused. Wiwa also reported that he had asked Anderson if the company had made payments to Okintumo. "The answer he gave is that '*I* [emphasis added] have never approved payment to Okuntimo.' He did not deny that Shell was paying Okuntimo. I think he knew about it, and the people in London knew about it."

While later acknowledging that meetings between Anderson and Wiwa had taken place as part of an effort at "quiet diplomacy," Shell denied Wiwa's specific allegations as "false and reprehensible."

In November, General Abacha appointed a Civil Disturbances Special Tribunal to try the case of the MOSOP leaders. Established by special decree, this tribunal was empowered to impose the death penalty for previously non-capital offenses in cases involving civil disturbances. The decision of the court could be confirmed or disallowed by the military government, but defendants had no right of judicial appeal. Amnesty International and many other human rights organizations denounced the tribunal for violating standards of due process guaranteed by Nigeria's own constitution and by international treaties.

Saro-Wiwa's trial for murder began in February 1995. Government witnesses testified that Saro-Wiwa had relayed a message to his youthful supporters, after the roadblock incident, that "the vultures who connived with the security forces to stop me from addressing you are now meeting . . . [to share] money sent them by the federal government. . . . Go to the meeting place and deal with the vultures."

Saro-Wiwa's defense attorneys countered that Saro-Wiwa had been at home at the time and had had nothing to do with the killings. The defense team also presented evidence that two key prosecution witnesses had been bribed by the government with Shell contracts and cash in exchange for their statements implicating Saro-Wiwa. Shell later adamantly denied bribing witnesses, saying, "We have not paid cash, awarded contracts or used any other means to try to influence events surrounding the cases before the Tribunal."

In June, Saro-Wiwa's defense team withdrew from the case in protest after repeated rulings by the presiding judge favorable to the prosecution and after being denied access to the defendants in custody. Saro-Wiwa refused to cooperate with the attorneys appointed by the court to replace them. Trial observers reported that from this point on, Saro-Wiwa appeared to view the proceedings as a "farce" and took little interest in them, "skim[ming] a newspaper or star[ing] blankly ahead as though he were a mere bystander at the performance around him."

On November 2, the tribunal found Saro-Wiwa and eight other MOSOP leaders guilty of murder and sentenced them to death. Six defendants were acquitted. On November 8, Shell issued this statement, in response to international appeals that it seek a commutation of the sentence:

> We believe that to interfere in the processes, either political or legal, here in Nigeria would be wrong. A large multinational company such as Shell cannot and must not interfere with the affairs of any sovereign state.

Two days later, Saro-Wiwa and eight MOSOP associates were hanged at Port Harcourt prison. His last words on the gallows were: "Lord, take my soul, but the struggle continues."

"With Deep Regret"

> Shell issued a statement on the executions that read, in part: It is with deep regret that we hear this news. From the violence that led to the murder of the four Ogoni leaders in May last year through to the death penalty having been carried out, the human cost has been too high.

Shell told reporters that it had approached the government privately after Saro-Wiwa's conviction to appeal for clemency on "humanitarian grounds." It would have been inappropriate, however, the company said, to have intervened in the criminal trial. The company also declined to comment further regarding human rights in Nigeria. A spokesperson stated:

> We can't issue a bold statement about human rights because . . . it could be considered treasonous by the regime, and the employees could come under attack. It would only inflame the issues.

The company also defended its actions in the months leading up to Saro-Wiwa's execution. Shell representatives stated that it would have been wrong to have sought to influence government policy on environmental protection, Ogoni autonomy, or other issues of concern to MOSOP. With respect to the actions of the Nigerian police, the company argued that it would have been improper to provide its own armed security. An executive told the news media, "Our responsibility is very clear. We pay taxes and [abide by] regulation. We don't run the government."

Shell also vigorously resisted calls by some human rights activists and environmentalists that the company withdraw from Nigeria. If it left, the company argued, whatever organization took over its operations would probably operate with lower environmental and safety standards, and the jobs of its Nigerian employees would be imperiled.

Whether or not Shell's position was justified, its public disclaimers did little to slow down the public controversy swirling around the company. By mid-1996, the company was facing a growing international boycott, the possibility that it would have to abandon plans to proceed with its liquefied natural gas project, and persistent demands that it withdraw from Nigeria altogether. The crisis threatened the company's shareholders, employees, franchisees, and customers—not only in Nigeria, but throughout the world.

Questions

1. Who are Shell's stakeholders? How important is each to the company?

2. Who is responsible for the plight of the Ogoni people?

3. How have Nigeria's political, economic and cultural circumstances affected Shell's operations and policies?

4. Could or should Shell have influenced the Saro-Wiwa verdict or punishment?

Notes

1. This case by Anne T. Lawrence of San Jose University. It appeared in *Case Research Journal* (Fall/Winter 1997): 1–21. Reproduced with permission.

2. The revenue-sharing arrangements in place in Nigeria had their origins in the system of land rights in precolonial Africa. In traditional societies, such as the Ogoni prior to colonization, families and communities had held land rights collectively, with elaborate norms governing use. Elements of this system of land ownership remained in modern Nigeria, where all mineral rights were vested in the federal government, with residents continuing to enjoy the right to use land for farming, fishing, and the like. Accordingly, under Nigerian law, oil companies that expropriated land for exploration or drilling were required to compensate residents for loss of their use of the land (for example, for the value of lost crops), but not for the value of oil or natural gas extracted. Thus, unlike—say—the United States, where discovery of a "gusher" on a farmer's land might make him an overnight millionaire, the discovery of oil in Nigeria had the consequence of enriching the government, not individual residents of the Niger delta where oil was found.

CASE 10

Lion Nathan China[1]

In China, anything is possible, everything is difficult.

—Anonymous

This is not a destination in China, this is a journey. This is going to be a forever thing.

—Jim O'Mahony, Managing Director,
Lion Nathan China

In April 1999, Paul Lockey, Chief Financial Officer of the international brewing company Lion Nathan Limited (LN) was really quite perplexed as he prepared his mid-year report for the Board. Lockey realized that higher losses from their China operations were going to wipe out LN's profits from elsewhere. Competition was intensifying in the Chinese beer market, particularly at the higher-margin premium end, markets were extremely volatile as consumers tried new brands, and the economy was cycling downward. With overcapacity in the beer industry, consolidation was underway. Was the new deal to brew and market Beck's premium beer under license going to provide the leverage needed to survive the shakeout? How could Jim O'Mahony's China team deliver in the world's most exciting market?

Company History

In 1999 Lion Nathan Limited (LN) was an international brewer with three geographic divisions in New Zealand, Australia, and China. With a portfolio of over fifty brands, the company owned and operated ten breweries in these three countries. To achieve greater international scale, LN also exported beer to fifty countries and licensed three brewers in Europe to produce and distribute Steinlager and Castlemaine XXXX. Through its 45 percent Japanese equity partner, Kirin Brewing Company, LN was part of the fourth-largest brewing group in the world.

Lion Nathan Limited was formed in 1988 when Lion Corporation merged with New Zealand's largest retailer, L. D. Nathan & Co. At this time the Chief Executives of the two companies, Douglas Myers at Lion and Peter Cooper at Nathan, decided the best thing to do was to get an outsider who came from neither culture to run it. As a result of an international search, Kevin Roberts was appointed in 1989 to manage the day-to-day operations as Chief Operating Officer (COO). Roberts had significant international experience with consumer product brands from his days with companies such as Proctor & Gamble, Gillette, and PepsiCo. Roberts noted almost immediately:

> It was very evident to me, after being here ten seconds, that for a consumer products company to be exclusively dependent on New Zealand made no sense, because there were no consumers here. And that was not going to change. We were in a lot of businesses where we had no core competency. Our core competency, I decided, was going to be brand building. So we sold off all non-core businesses and focused on beer, our core business in New Zealand. We bought established regional breweries and ran them. We acquired Alan Bond's breweries, and transformed ourselves in a twelve-month period from being a top ten New Zealand conglomerate to the biggest beverage producer in Australasia. We simultaneously brought in a lot of international people to drive the culture, drive performance, build brands. We hired stellar people from offshore and New Zealand who became the core of the management group.

In 1993, with limited growth in the New Zealand and Australian markets, LN began looking further afield for growth opportunities in America, Europe, and Asia. Like many other multinational consumer product companies at this time, they found the world's largest consumer market—China. According to Roberts "China represented the single best opportunity for a number of reasons, including size of market, growth potential, low barriers to entry, and no established big guy in there." Two years and forty brewery evaluations later, LN entered this market in April 1995 with a 60 percent joint venture in Wuxi. This initial investment was made in one of the wealthiest cities in the heart of the Yangtze River Delta—China's fastest growing beer market (Figure 1). Buoyed by success, LN increased its shareholding in this brewery to 80 percent in 1996 and made a major commitment to

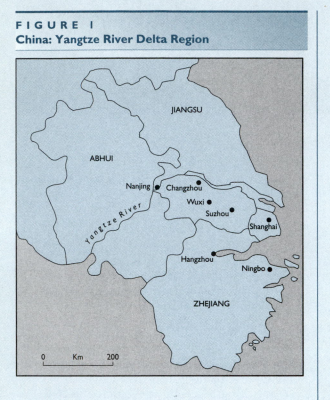

FIGURE I
China: Yangtze River Delta Region

build a brand new $178 million[2] brewery 30 kilometers away in the Suzhou Industrial Park. Construction of this 200 million liter world-class brewery was completed under budget and ahead of schedule. Commercial production began in February 1998, and the premium brand Steinlager was launched in September. In April 1999, LN announced a licensing agreement with German brewer Brauerei Beck and Co to brew and market Beck's international premium beer. The addition of a high-margin brand to its portfolio was important to utilize brewing capacity at Suzhou and to extend its market reach beyond the Yangtze River Delta.

LN's ownership structure changed in April 1998 when the Japanese brewing group, Kirin Brewery Company, acquired a 45 percent share in the company. Kirin had its own small brewing and soft-drink businesses in China, as well as selling the Kirin lager beer in over forty countries, particularly in North America, Europe, and Asia.

Gordon Cairns, who became CEO in April 1998 when Douglas Myers stepped up to Chairman of the Board, described LN's charter as "profitable growth." With growth of 5.5 percent in volume, 3.6 percent in revenue and 7.5 percent in earnings, he called 1998 a "watershed year" for LN. Speaking at the company's annual meeting, Cairns reported:

In China, we are investing to develop the business that will be generating profits in the medium term. As a shareholder, you obviously believe in the game plan. But let me draw your attention to five reasons that differentiate us as a stock. Firstly, we are virtually a pure beer company. Secondly, everywhere we compete we are investing to build brands. We believe beer is a regional business, with few truly global brands. Fourthly, a key success factor is for us to be the lowest cost producer, everywhere we compete. And finally, we are measured, managed and motivated by shareholder value, where what we do, should earn greater than the cost of capital.

The Brewing Industry in China

In 1998 there were over 600 brewers in the highly fragmented Chinese brewing industry producing 17.8 million tonnes of beer. The sheer size of this beer market, servicing a population of 1.2 billion people, coupled with the growth potential due to increasing per capita consumption, attracted many international brewers to China. However, growth rates had decreased dramatically from over 20 percent per year in the 1980s, to 12.5 percent on average between 1992 and 1997, and near 6 percent growth was projected from 1998 to 2001. Beer consumption had risen to average 14 liters per capita in 1998, but this was still low compared with average consumption of 30–40 liters in the Asian region, 87 liters in New Zealand, and 95 liters in Australia. The demand for beer was influenced by macroeconomic factors such as levels of unemployment and disposable income. Government rulings on items such as entertainment spending, were also key to understanding beer consumption on public premises such as restaurants, bars, and hotels. However, this aggregate level of analysis was of limited value in China as there were quite different patterns of consumption throughout this vast country, particularly between urban and rural communities. For example, per capita beer consumption was 21 liters in the affluent urbanized Yangtze River Delta (YRD) region, and closer to 29 liters within the leading city of Shanghai (the "golden chalice"). Therefore, each region in China was considered a different market. Beyond the economic factors, provincial government requirements and limited transportation infrastructure for efficient distribution acted as specific constraints for multiregion or national participation. In addition, some uncertainty was created for foreign brewers by the government's signal of possible restriction of the proportion of beer sold by foreign firms to 30 percent, as it was not clear if, when, or how this would be implemented.

The major segments in the China beer market were linked to the quality and price of the beer. Table 1 shows the key segments with their retail price points, market size in 1998, and market projections for 2001. Market share proportions for each segment in the Yangtze River Delta and Shanghai are shown in Figure 2. There were only eighty breweries in the country with capacity over 50 million liters; eighteen of these had over 100 million liters capacity. The ten largest domestic brewing groups accounted for less than 20 percent of the total market. Table 2 shows the major international brewers operating in China in 1998, with their origin, type of investment, production capacity, and beer brands. Profiles of the major competitors are provided in Exhibit 1.

The low end of the China beer market was the largest segment served by several hundred small, state-owned, domestic brewers. Many of these breweries suffered from problems of quality, were unable to achieve efficient operations, had insufficient capital for any improvements and were unable to return a profit. With low-priced products and high distribution costs because of limited transportation networks, these brewers typically served a geographically limited, local market. The situation in this market segment was summarized by media commentator, Denise McNabb, as follows:

Inefficient and undercapitalized, loss-making breweries are in their death throes as the gov-

TABLE 1
China Beer Market Segments

	Retail Price Points[1] (RMB)	China 1998 (Tonnes)	China 2001 (Tonnes)	Examples
Imported Premium[2]	10.0	40,000	50,000	Heineken[3]
Premium	5.0–6.0	722,000	920,000	Beck's/Budweiser/Carlsberg
Mainstream	2.0–3.50	2,100,000	2,800,000	Reeb/Rheineck
Low-end	Under 2.0[4]	14,900,000	14,500,000	GuangMing[5]
		17,762,000	18,270,000	

[1]Off-premise retail price points in Chinese reminbi (RMB), NZ1.00 = 4.67 RMB at 30 April 1999
[2]With 0.2% market share, this category was usually included in with other premium beer
[3]Retails for 12.50 RMB (NZ$2.67)
[4]Most are priced close to 1.0 RMB (NZ$0.214)
[5]Retails for 1.90 RMB (NZ$0.406)

FIGURE 2
Yangtze River Delta and Shanghai Market Share

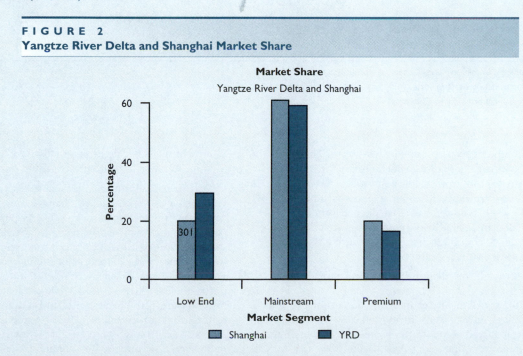

TABLE 2
Major Brewers and Brands in China, 1998

Brewers	Origin	Investment Type[2]	Capacity[1]	BRANDS Premium	Mainstream	Low End
Anheuser-Busch	U.S.	JV in Wuhan / 5% in Tsingtao	250	Budweiser		
Asia Pacific	Singapore	JV in Shanghai	200	Tiger	Reeb	
	Holland	Imported / JV in Hainan / JV in Fuzhou	200 / 100	Heineken Heritage		
Asahi	Japan	JV in Hangzhou	600	Asahi		
Beck's	Germany	JV in Fujian	150	Beck's		
Carlsberg	Denmark	JV in Shanghai	180	Carlsberg	Karhu	
Changzhou	Local					Guangyulan
Fosters	Australian	JV in Shanghai	120	Fosters Haoshun		Guangming Pujing Shanghai
Interbrew	Belgium	JV in Nanjing / JV in Guangzhou	80		Jinling	
Linkman	Local					Linkman
Lion Nathan	NZ	WFO in Suzhou / JV in Wuxi	200 / 120	Steinlager Carbine	Rheineck Taihushui	
Kirin	Japan	JV in Shenyang	120	Kirin		
Miller	USA	JV in Beijing	200	Miller		
Pabst Blue Ribbon	USA	JV in Guangdong	350		Pabst	
San Miguel	Philippines	JV in Baoding	600	San Miguel		
South African	South Africa	5 breweries—North	950			Snowflake
Suntory	Japan	JV in Shanghai	200	Suntory	Suntory	
Tianmuhu	Jiangsu		50			Tianlun Tianmuhu Huaguang
Tsingtao[3]	Qingdao	5 breweries	800			Tsingtao
Zhanjiagang	Jiangsu		70	Dongwu		Zhangjiagang

[1] Capacity is in million liters. Capacity utilization is generally low.

[2] International ownership varies for these joint venture partnerships.

[3] Largest local brewery in China

ernment stops propping them up in line with cost cutting reforms, which include the removal of housing and medical subsidies. Ugly price wars are expected to emerge as the tiny state-owned brewers make last ditch efforts to stay alive by selling below cost on already thin margin prices of 1.9 renminbi [about NZ40 cents] for a 640-ml [quart] bottle

Brewers in the mainstream segment provided a higher quality beer, at a slightly higher price (average 2.5 RMB, NZ$0.53). With higher margins, but major executional challenges in sales and distribution, the mainstream segment attracted some of the more adventurous international brewers, including Asia Pacific Breweries with its Reeb (i.e. beer spelt backward), Carlsberg with Karhu, Lion Nathan with Taihushui and Rheineck, and Suntory from the Japanese brewer Suntory (Table 2 and Exhibit 1).

As Figure 2 illustrates, the mainstream and premium segments in the YRD and in Shanghai were significantly larger than the national average; these segments were expected to continue to grow, while the overall market was static. In the coastal cities region, the premium segment was estimated to be 7 percent of the market. Gross margins from 40–60 percent were needed in the brewing industry to cover marketing (30–100 percent), freight and warehousing (10–15 percent), and administration and other overhead expenses (10–40 percent). Assuming comparable production costs for mainstream and premium beer, the margins for premium beer were significantly higher (50 percent). However, profitability was

EXHIBIT 1
Key Players in the China Beer Industry

While almost all of the world's major breweries have sought to establish a presence in China, there are significant differences in the competitive position and strategies of the various key players.

ANHEUSER-BUSCH

This American company was the world's largest brewer selling its premium Budweiser brand in sixty countries around the world. The company was aiming for 20 percent of the world's market share. Anheuser-Busch entered the China market with a joint venture (80 percent) in Wuhan (on the Yangtze River for transportation access) in 1994; 1160 km by road, and 1400km by rail, to Shanghai. Establishing a small stake in Tsingtao, China's largest domestic producer and exporter of beer, provided local connections for Anheuser-Busch and a status partner for Tsingtao. Budweiser was the leading premium beer brand with 30 percent of the China market in 1998. In China, the company built on high levels of ambient awareness of its brand from television, movies, sports, and sponsorship. In addition, Anheuser-Busch invested heavily in marketing to build brand equity; it also used its dominant international brand and resources to establish deals for access to on-premise retailers. By raising the costs to compete, Anheuser-Busch reduced the ability of most competitors to obtain profits from the premium beer segment in China, which lead to industry rationalization.

ASAHI

Founded in 1889, 90 percent of the Japanese Asahi Breweries' sales were from its flagship brand, Asahi Super Dry, which was marketed in over thirty countries. Asahi produced specialty beer including a black draft, Asahi Kuronama and a low-calorie beer for women, Asahi First Lady. The company also operated about 130 restaurants and sold other beverages, including soft drinks, wines, fruit juices, and whiskey. Growth in international activities through alliances were being developed in Europe and North America. In 1998, Asahi was a major player in the premium segment (estimated at 7 percent share of the China market) with very large scale capacity (600 million litres). The company had joint ventures in Beijing, Quanzhou, and Hangzhou. Asahi was investing heavily in television and media to develop its premium brand. However, its foreign image positioning was not as distinct as the American or European premium brands. Further development of distribution and trade networks was required to further increase sales volume.

BECK'S

Founded in 1873 by a master builder with a passion for brewing beer, the German Brauerei Beck & Co produced and sold its premium Beck's beer around the world. The company had a strong international focus with divisions in Finland, Greenland, Great Britain, U.S., Canada, Venezuela, Taiwan, and Puerto Rico. The Beck's brand was differentiated with a distinctive shaped bottle and positioned as a top-quality, world-class premium beer. The company had strict quality guidelines for raw materials and the brewing process, to achieve its unique quality and flavor. In China, Beck's beer was brewed under license at Putian (100 km from Shanghai by road) and sold in over forty cities, primarily located along the coast from Shenyang to Guangzhou. From mid-1999, the production and marketing of Beck's brand was to be taken over by Lion Nathan China.

CARLSBERG

Carlsberg, a Danish company, had global brewing operations in 140 markets, brewing *(continued)* in forty countries; 80 percent of sales from overseas markets. The company's brewery construction division entered China in the mid-1980s, renovating forty breweries. In 1994, Carlsberg established a joint venture brewery (with a Hong Kong trading partner) in Huizhou, Guangdong province, for its premium brand beer (1600 km from Shanghai by road). The company built a new brewery in Shanghai in 1998 and successfully launched a new mainstream brand (Kaihu).

FOSTER'S

This Australian brewer entered China in 1993 with joint ventures in Shanghai and Guangdong, adding a third brewery in Tianjin in 1995. Foster's strategic intent was to become the largest brewer in China with a national network of breweries, selling Foster's premium lager and several mainstream brands. In Shanghai the company invested heavily in signage—the Foster's signs were in many key central city display areas, but the premium beer was not widely available. To curb continuing losses in Asia, Foster's admitted an "over aggressive" strategy in China and in 1998 announced plans to cut back. Sale of its breweries in Tianjin and Guangdong were announced in 1999, allowing the company to focus on the Shanghai market.

HEINEKEN

Heineken, the largest European brewer, operated in over 170 countries, with shares in over sixty brewing companies. Heineken was a global beer brand with a high level of ambient awareness from TV coverage, movies, sports, and sponsorship. In China, Heineken beer was imported and sold as superpremium, working with Asia Pacific Breweries joint ventures in Haikou (Hainan province) and Fuzhou. The company used local mainstream brands to achieve cost effi-cient volumes, while building its premium brand. Heineken was aiming for national coverage of key hotels in China and was prepared to wait while the premium segment grew, but it was not interested in lowering its prices to increase sales volume.

KIRIN

Kirin, the fourth-largest brewing group in the world, attempted initially to enter the Chinese market through a licensing arrangement, but then formed a joint venture with a local brewer at Zhuhai in Guangdong province. Kirin's premium beer was positioned as a high-quality beer because it was brewed with a single filtration process (and therefore had a higher extract loss than standard brewing processes), targeting Japanese expatriate consumers and their Japanese association. Kirin's beer was also produced under license at Shenyang, in northern China, by South African Breweries. Kirin, with a 45 percent equity stake in Lion Nathan, was planning to have some beer brewed under contract at Lion Nathan's brewery in Suzhou. Apart from its brewing operations, Kirin had joint ventures to produce and sell other beverages (e.g., soft drinks and fruit juices) in China. At home in Japan, Kirin had fifteen breweries and captured 40 percent market share; it also sold over 300 beverage products in categories such as soft drinks, tea, coffee, wine, and spirits. Kirin had partnerships in pharmaceutical plants and research laboratories. Other joint venture and subsidiary businesses were in food service and restaurants, transportation, sports and recreation, engineering, building management, and business systems.

SAN MIGUEL

The largest brewer in the Philippines, San Miguel, began a five-year overseas expansion into the Asian region in 1998 aiming to

EXHIBIT 1 (*continued*)

brew the most beer in Asia and to be in the top 10 brewers in the world (by volume). The company had four breweries spread across China (including joint ventures in Baoding, Guangzhou, and Shunde) producing its premium beer, plus operations in Indonesia and Vietnam. Following the Asian economic crisis and losses in its China operations, San Miguel's new CEO announced plans (late 1998) to cut back loss-making businesses and focus on regaining market share in its domestic beer market. Talks with four international brewing companies (Anheuser-Busch, Carlsberg, Heineken, and South African Breweries) were underway to find a partner for its China breweries. San Miguel had a portfolio of businesses in food and beverages.

SOUTH AFRICAN BREWERIES

South African Breweries had sixteen brands providing 98 percent of the domestic beer market in South Africa and international operations spread throughout Africa, Asia, and Europe. The company's entry strategy in China involved buying into a local brewery with a joint venture agreement, then upgrading the operations and brands, rationalizing costs and building distribution infrastructure. This approach was replicated five times in the northern region of China, establishing large-scale capacity for local mainstream and low-end brands. In 1999, the company had two joint ventures in Shenyang and one in each of the following—Dalian, Chengdu, and Jilin. Each area was treated as an independent regional market. Bottled water was also produced and sold by its joint venture on the Hong Kong-Guangzhou border.

SUNTORY

Suntory was Japan's leading producer and distributor of alcoholic and nonalcoholic beverages. The company was also involved in pharmaceuticals, restaurant operation, sports, music and film, resort development, publishing, and information services. Approximately two-thirds of its annual international sales were from the food and nonalcoholic beverages and 20 percent from alcoholic beverages. In 1984, Suntory established China's first joint venture specializing in beer; in 1994 the company extended its alcoholic beverages to include whiskies and brandies. This company had a large joint-venture brewery in Shanghai and a small brewery at Lianyungang (65 million liters). It sold a premium brand with very low volume, however, in the mainstream segment in Shanghai, Suntory was in second place (selling 50,000 tonnes in 1998) behind Asia Pacific's Reeb beer. The company used extensive market research to develop its positioning and promotion imagery.

TSINGTAO

China's largest domestic brewer, Tsingtao, was founded in 1903 by British and German businessmen and taken over by the Qingdao Municipal People's Government in 1949. From its head office and five major breweries in Qingdao in Shandong province, plus a few affiliates around the country, Tsingtao provided nearly 3 percent of the total Chinese beer production in 1998. In addition, Tsingtao exported beer to over thirty countries, which provided foreign exchange to import raw materials, packaging, technology, and equipment. The company responded to intensifying competition from foreign brewers by increasing its production capacity and revamping its sales and distribution network. Tsingtao [beer was the best-selling domestic brand, sold at a premium to other domestic beer because of its popularity and reputation for award-winning quality taste.

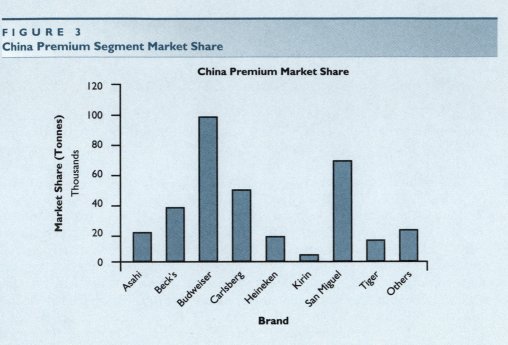

FIGURE 3
China Premium Segment Market Share

elusive in this industry, with marketing expenses running between 30–120 percent of sales.

The premium segment was most attractive for international brewers because of the higher margins and the long-term potential in the China market. Most of the brewers were involved with joint ventures or licensing contracts for domestic brewing with local partners (Table 2). Figure 3 shows the premium market share for the top 10 brewers in China. By 1999, with overcapacity intensifying competition and economic growth declining, several of these foreign brewers were cutting back their involvement, putting breweries up for sale (e.g., Foster's), and reconsidering their future options in China (e.g., San Miguel). The imported premium segment was a niche segment for the most expensive beer brands. Rather than taking advantage of lower cost production within China, Heineken's premium beer was imported and, therefore, incurred higher transportation and production costs, but also realized a substantially higher selling price.

Seasonality had a major impact on the beer market in China. [Consumption of premium beer, primarily on licensed premises such as restaurants, bars, and hotels, did not show as much seasonal variation as sales of mainstream beer. However, to understand these beer-consumption patterns, it was necessary to appreciate the perception of beer in China. Steve Mason, who had been LN's business development manager (China) and then marketing director in China for two years before becoming LN's corporate marketing director, explained:

Beer is seen to be a healthy drink, nutritive, low alcohol, no social downsides. Historically strong alcohol beverages have been drunk, like white spirits or rice wine-based drinks that might be, say 60%, or 15–20% alcohol. Central government encouraged breweries as a moderation thing. So beer is seen as a beverage. It's not seen as a liquor or alcohol. So it's seen as a beverage choice—what will I have? A beer or a Pepsi or a cup of tea? . . . With the communal society in China there is a lot of emphasis put around meal times. Beer in conjunction with food is the habit. So you don't just go out to have a drink. Beer is an auxiliary to food.

Further, beer was a "cooling" beverage typically consumed warm, on a hot summer day. In winter a "warming" drink such as rice wine was preferred, so sales of off-premise beer declined dramatically from October. Frank Gibson, who was the company's Strategy Director within China, elaborated on the nature of Chinese beer:

Chinese beer is clear and lager-like, drunk mainly in the humid summer months. This reflects its German heritage—the main brewery schools are still taught in the German mold. Even though more Chinese households now have refrigerators, it is not drunk cold, as this is considered unhealthy by Chinese.

Mainstream beer was generally purchased in small quantities (one or two bottles) from a nearby street stall and carried to a multistory apartment block home. There was a myriad of small off-premise retailers in China running kiosks, commonly known as "mom and pop" stores. Mason described the scale of these stores as follows:

FIGURE 4
Yangtze River Delta Beer Industry Structure

Regional Market Architecture Highly Fragmented

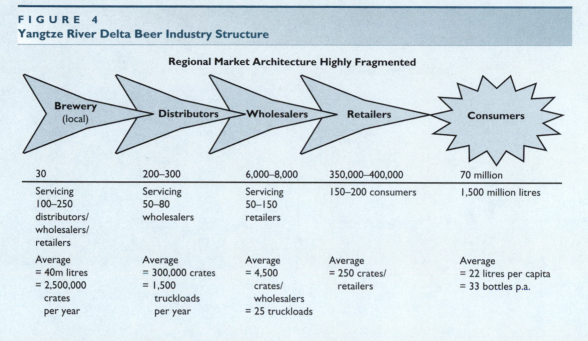

Brewery (local)	Distributors	Wholesalers	Retailers	Consumers
30	200–300	6,000–8,000	350,000–400,000	70 million
Servicing 100–250 distributors/ wholesalers/ retailers	Servicing 50–80 wholesalers	Servicing 50–150 retailers	150–200 consumers	1,500 million litres
Average = 40m litres = 2,500,000 crates per year	Average = 300,000 crates = 1,500 truckloads per year	Average = 4,500 crates/ wholesalers = 25 truckloads	Average = 250 crates/ retailers	Average = 22 litres per capita = 33 bottles p.a.

The "retail outlet" is often nothing more than a shelving unit stuck to the front of someone's house. There are fewer than a dozen bottles of beer of various brands, some cans of soft drink, chewing gum, washing powder, sweets, and a shelf within a shelf containing packets of cigarettes and cheap lighters. In the doorway, an old lady sits knitting in the winter haze.

LNC sources estimated that there were 350,000–400,000 retailers of beer in the Yangtze River Delta region. Thirty local breweries operated in this region, servicing the population of 70 million via 200–300 distributors and 6,000–8,000 wholesalers. The structure of the YRD beer industry from production to consumers is summarized in Figure 4.

Premium beer was primarily consumed in restaurants, bars, and hotels. Status was a major influence on consumption in this segment. Restaurants were prolific in this socialistic society. Steve Mason, who did LN's early research on the Chinese beer market and later became the Chief Marketing Officer, explained, "As face is extremely important in China, you will drink internationally famous high-quality beer when entertaining clients or staff at restaurants." Therefore, the levels of government and corporate entertainment budgets acted as a driver for this segment of the beer market.

Market-share statistics for the top brands in each beer segment for the five key cities in the YRD from 1996–98 are shown in Table 3. Even within this small regional sample, the volatility of the beer market was evident. New brands skyrocketed from obscurity to dominance within a few months with strong advertising, sales promotion, distribution, and support. However, with numerous competing brands and limited brand loyalty, leading brands could also disappear just as quickly. Therefore, developing brand equity was a key challenge for competitors in this industry.

The Macro Environment in China

After record growth for nearly two decades, China's economic growth rate fell below the government's 8 percent of GDP target in 1998, with slower export growth, falling retail prices, and weaker consumption; the level of per capita GDP was $2,800 at this time. By comparison, Australia's economic growth estimate was 4.7 percent in 1998, with $23,600 GDP per capita; and New Zealand had −0.4 percent growth estimate and $18,500 per capita GDP. However, the scale of expansion that China offered as a consumer market was exponential. By 2000, there would be 160 cities with a population over 1 million people, 250 cities with annual income levels high enough to support consumerism, and 260 million people able to afford packaged consumer products, hence, the world's largest market in many categories including beer and biscuits.

There were still many major challenges ahead for the Chinese government on the road to a free-market economy. The financial system was reported by *The Economist* to be a mess, but the currency was not considered to be overvalued against a basket of its trading partners:

There is no doubt that China is stuck with a cluster of financial time-bombs. Its state banks

TABLE 3
Yangtze River Delta Key Cities: Market Size for Key Brands, 1996–98 (All figures in tonnes)

Shanghai   420,000

Premium			70,000	Mainstream			230,000	Low End			120,000
	1996	1997	1998		1996	1997	1998		1996	1997	1998
Budweiser	11,000	16,000	15,000	Reeb	133,152	88,154	70,182	Guangming	37,000	40,000	49,000
Becks	18,600	18,800	10,836	Suntory	5,800	43,030	50,000	Zhonghua	8,000	6,000	7,000
Carlsberg	2,800	2,900	2,800	Rheineck	0	10,407	22,000	Qianjiang	6,600	4,000	4,500
San Miguel	1,800	1,500	1,400	Karhu	0	0	10,000	Shanghai	31,840	31,331	30,000
Tiger	2,335	2,961	3,903	Qingdao[1]	26,000	24,200	25,000	Donghai	12,320	9,900	10,000
Heineken	650	700	750	Pabst	3,000	2,300	2,400	Swan	17,017	14,115	14,000
Kirin	600	620	600								

Suzhou   105,000

Premium			15,000	Mainstream			50,000	Low End			40,000
	1996	1997	1998		1996	1997	1998		1996	1997	1998
Budweiser	3,360	6,200	1,000	Taihushui	10,000	16,050	14,664	Zhangjiagang	30,000	27,696	8,000
Becks	4,200	4,100	800	Linkman	2,000	1,500	500	Dongwu	7,000	6,200	4,000
Carlsberg	840	550	200	Rheineck	0	1,700	10,345	White Swan	15,000	12,602	6,000
San Miguel	240	650	200	Reeb	1,500	2,200	5,000	Shajiabang	14,000	12,200	4,000
Tiger	60	160	100	Sankong	5,000	4,720	1,000	Bawang	6,000	4,020	5,000
Heineken	60	220	200	Wumin	3,000	2,200	800	Weili	4,000	3,700	1,000
Qingdao[1]	200	300	600	Pabst	100	100	100				

Wuxi   92,000

Premium			11,000	Mainstream			54,000	Low End			27,000
	1996	1997	1998		1996	1997	1998		1996	1997	1998
Budweiser	1,500	2,200	2,900	Taihushui	27,000	29,384	30,000	Zhangjiagang	15,000	13,800	12,000
Becks	3,300	3,000	2,000	Shanjuan	10,000	10,916	10,000	Fuli	6,000	5,850	4,000
Carlsberg	500	450	234	Rheineck	0	3,550	2,934				
San Miguel	650	600	550	Linkman	2,000	1,800	1,000				
Heineken	100	130	156	Guanyulan	1,300	1,200	200				
Qingdao[1]	400	500	700	Pabst	350	400	350				

Nanjing   114,000

Premium			26,000	Mainstream			70,000	Low End			18,000
	1996	1997	1998		1996	1997	1998		1996	1997	1998
Budweiser	4,300	6,000	11,500	Jinling	33,070	33,613	27,000	Zhangjiagang	800	500	300
Becks	3,500	2,500	1,000	Yali	11,860	38,175	25,000	Tianmuhu	1,000	700	300
Carlsberg	1,200	800	400	Rheineck	0	1,700	17,000	Shenquan	10,000	9,500	9,000
San Miguel	1,200	800	400	Qingdao[1]	2,900	2,950	3,000	Tiandao	4,000	4,500	5,000
Heineken	30	40	50	Pabst	6,400	3,000	1,500	Tianjin	3,000	3,500	4,000
Hansha	450	300	200								

Changzhou   70,000

Premium			4,000	Mainstream			36,000	Low End			30,000
	1996	1997	1998		1996	1997	1998		1996	1997	1998
Budweiser	800	1,200	1,000	Guangyulan	32,622	26,214	20,000	Tianmuhu	11,100	26,214	27,000
Becks	1,500	1,400	1,400	Linkman	2,896	2,959	10,000	Zhangjiagang	2,400	2,300	2,400
Carlsberg	230	250	200	Taihushui	3,200	3,800	3,939				
San Miguel	150	280	250	Rheineck	0	40	1,659				
Heineken	15	25	20	Qingdao[1]	500	350	400				
				Pabst	400	350	400				

[1]Qingdao is priced at RMB3.5 and is categorized as sub-premium (overseas Chinese spelling is *Tsingtao*).

are insolvent, and they have few reliable borrowers. The competence and power of financial supervisors are stretched too thin, while mismanagement and fraud are stripping state assets. The central government has mounting financial liabilities, not least to pay for welfare and for infrastructure meant to sustain growth, but its grip on tax revenue is even shakier.

Reforms were underway, subsidies were being removed, but there were major performance problems in the state sector, as described in *Fortune* magazine:

> The major roadblock: a largely unreformed state manufacturing sector, numbering 300,000 enterprises, that employs 70% of the urban work force (109 million workers), but generates only 30% of industrial output. Officially, around 40% of these enterprises are losing money; the true figure is certainly much higher.

Reform packages typically included restructuring the state owned enterprise's (SOEs) operating systems, establishing social security systems and reemployment projects. However, allowing loss-making SOEs to continue operating avoided some of the social problems engendered by high unemployment levels. Nevertheless, the gap between rich and poor was increasing. There was an urban drift; according to a World Bank study, 80 million people had moved to the cities in search of work.

> China's landlocked hinterland, remains for the most part, an overcrowded world of poor peasants, rapacious officials and indolent factory managers, with walk on parts for disaffected ethnic minorities. It's here where foreign investment is thinnest, that Premier Zhu Rongji must overcome the toughest resistance to reform.

Improvements were being made to the transportation infrastructure, particularly between key cities in the coastal regions. Yet, difficulties with interregional and urban distribution were unlikely to be resolved quickly, as demand for transportation was increasing at a faster rate than the new capacity. With limited private ownership of motor vehicles and poor public transportation systems, the number of small-scale stores was increasing. The number of supermarkets was also increasing in the larger cities, but less than 10 percent of grocery sales were made in these "large format" stores.

Patterns of consumer demand in China were found to vary by age and social activity. Price sensitivity increased with age. Consumers under thirty years were least sensitive to price and most responsive to marketing: "they are most likely to be familiar with advertising, especially on television, and to base their purchase decisions on its messages." Within this segment, the majority were socially inactive, sticking close to home and family. The socially active minority group, who spent a lot of time on entertainment and travel, "perceive advertising as truthful, prefer branded products, and put a high value on attractive and comfortable retail environments." The influx of new products to Chinese stores provided these consumers with endless opportunities to experiment with different products and brands. Consumers over forty-five years, influenced by their experiences in China's Cultural Revolution, were "highly sensitive to price and respond negatively to new products and most forms of marketing."

Lifestyles and culture in China were strongly based on relationships. Stemming from the Confucian view, family relationships were very important. This meant respect for elders, deference to authority, rank consciousness, modesty, ancestor worship, and harmony (avoidance of direct confrontation) were stressed. There was a cultural focus on team effort and enhancing group harmony. The group process was not just based on authority; it also strongly focused on consensus. For the collectivist Chinese, their family, including extended family and friends, was the prime group toward which allegiance was owed and paid. In the business context, having a good relationship (*guanxi*) network in China was the single most important factor for business success. *Guanxi* was the intricate, pervasive network of personal relationships which Chinese people cultivated with energy and imagination. The *guanxi* was not just a relationship network but one with obligations. In contrast to Western society where social order and business practices were regulated by law, the Chinese were willing to bend rules in order to get things done. It was regarded as reasonable and acceptable to find ways to avoid the consequences of rules, so that Chinese with *guanxi* connections could circumvent government regulations for their own benefits and for those to whom they owed an obligation.

China was a major player within the broader Asian region. Diplomats and other officials were lobbying actively for China's admission to the World Trade Organization. Media commentators were optimistic that this would occur by 2002. While rules for market access and tariff levels in many industries would be reviewed, increased uncertainty was expected during the transition period as new regulations and procedures were established. Throughout the Asian region, fluctuations in economic and political stability within specific countries created ripples for neighboring nations, including China. For example, the economic crisis in Korea in 1997 had major impacts on trading partners throughout the region. Similarly, political instability in Indonesia had social and economic consequences extending beyond this country.

Lion Nathan China LNC

LN's research identified the Yangtze River Delta (YRD) as the best region for its entry to China. Ex-McKinsey consultant, Paul Lockey, whose responsibilities included LN's corporate strategy and corporate finance, explained:

> With a population of 70 million, the Delta is an area of relative wealth, high growth and above-average beer consumption. It has a rapidly developing infrastructure including new highways along key corridors, express rail services and a supply and service industry base suitable for foreign ventures.

LN's entry strategy was to take a small, measured step into an existing brewery with an upgrade path, learn, and then build on the experience. The Taihushui Brewery at Wuxi was a profitable joint venture with good plant and astute management. LN's $50 million investment was used to double capacity to 120 million liters, improve the quality and the shelf life of the beer, introduce new packaging, expand distribution, and develop sales capabilities. David Sullivan, who was on LN's managing team for this joint venture and responsible for establishing processes, systems, and controls, explained LN's approach at Wuxi:

> We brought in a Sales Director, who was an expatriate Hong Kong Chinese, out of Coca-Cola, to try and build some sales skills into the workforce. We leveraged the expatriates like Steve Mason [LN's corporate marketing officer] to come in and improve the Taihushui brand, change the packaging a little bit, bring in new advertisements, look at how we communicated with the consumer, and do some research, basically bringing Western sales and marketing practices into the business.

> We had a very good relationship. It started well. We valued the business at a fair price. We immediately doubled the size of it. We retained the workforce. We didn't do anything that created an unfair, unreasonable work environment for the local staff. We very much approached it from—"we're here to learn and we're here to teach." So you teach us about the local market, and we'll teach you about marketing. So, in the finance area, for example, we said, "This is what we want you to report, and this is how we want you to do it. Now, let us show you how to do it and teach you why it is important for us," rather than saying "Do this" or "Our guy will do this." So we put a lot of trust in them, and they put a lot of trust in us.

Confidence was developed from this first experience in China, the expansion programme was successful, sales and profits grew, and LN increased its ownership in this joint venture to 80 percent.

LN's second step into China was a bold commitment to build a large world-class brewery in nearby Suzhou. Located within a 70-square kilometer special-development zone, Suzhou Industrial Park (SIP), established by the Chinese and Singaporean governments in 1994, enabled LN to create a privileged asset. Wholly foreign ownership, which was highly restricted for breweries elsewhere in China, was a unique advantage that SIP offered for early investors. As Steve Mason, LN's Chief Marketing Officer, explained:

> To be able to talk about wholly foreign-owned sounds significant, but not particularly awesome. But in China it really, really is awesome. The autonomy to be able to make your own decisions and to be able to act on those decisions—the significance of that autonomy of action is absolutely awesome.

Efficient transportation links were available from Suzhou by air, road, rail, and canal to Shanghai and other key YRD cities. SIP provided utilities, such as water, power, and telecommunications, for industrial and residential usage. Other key support services for investors included a one-stop service for company incorporation and construction permits, local customs clearance, and warehousing and distribution. This infrastructure and SIP's services were important for LN's "green field" project. The company also saved $50 million on import duties for plant and equipment; this duty-free policy ceased in 1997. A turn-key approach, driven by performance-based contracts and international sourcing of materials, enabled LN to complete the "single best facility in China" in just sixteen months. Speaking at the official Suzhou opening ceremony in September 1998, Jim O'Mahony, Managing Director of Lion Nathan China, LNC, said, "We have built the capability to achieve our objective of being the leading brewer in the Yangtze Delta." Production capacity of the state-of-the-art brewery was 470 million bottles of beer per year or more than 1 million bottles per day.

Lion Nathan China: Strategy

The vision of Lion Nathan China was "to become the leading brewer in the Yangtze River Delta by 2000 and the market leader in the Shanghai-Nanjing corridor." Three core values were emphasized in the company's formal and informal activities—passion, integrity, and realism. LNC's strategy for competing in China was updated in 1997 with input from the international strategy specialist consultancy firm, McKinsey & Co. LNC's five-point strategy involved (1) displaying market leadership in the mainstream beer segment within the Shanghai-Nanjing corridor of the Yangtze River Delta, (2) developing a differentiated brand portfolio including premium and mainstream brands, (3) selling premium beer outside the YRD, (4) out-executing the competition, and (5) leading industry consolidation.

Reflecting on LNC's strategic position in February 1999, after eighteen months as Managing Director for China, O'Mahony said:

> We are focusing on five key cities in the Shanghai to Nanjing corridor, south of the Yangtze river. We are number 1 or number 2 in three of those cities already [in mainstream beer] . . . but Shanghai is going to be a real battle.
>
> We have four brands now in our portfolio: Taihushui, meaning "water of lake Tai," is a high-quality mainstream beer for blue-collar workers; Rheineck, launched in 1997, with a foreign name and packaging linked to Germany, is positioned as a more outgoing mainstream beer for blue- and white-collar markets; Carbine is a dark, niche beer positioned at restaurants—so it's a beer with food. Then we have Steinlager, launched in September 1998, positioned as a trendy premium beer in a curvy bottle for sale in night venues and upmarket restaurants. The gap in our portfolio is a premium beer in the status segment occupied at the moment by Budweiser, Beck's, Tiger, San Miguel, and Carlsberg. Our objective is to forge an alliance with another international player to get access to a major premium brand. We are just about ready to make an announcement. Then we'll have done the portfolio work.
>
> We've been constrained in terms of moving outside the Delta because of lack of a premium brand that can actually do it for us. . . . Apart from 3 million kiwis, nobody's ever heard of Steinlager. But when we announce the deal with the international alliance partner, as it is already a brand that's got presence throughout China, we'll have an immediate volume that we can "piggy back" Steinlager onto.
>
> We started with a zero base, and we are building capabilities and developing infrastructure to compete in this region. This is proving to be as difficult as all the others. We've had a massive recruitment exercise followed by intensive training. We had no systems in place, so we had to build all the basic systems for the business, including accounting systems, credit collection, invoicing, and sales reporting. But I think we are in line with plan. I think we are doing as well as anybody else in China.

> We believe the long-term success of the beer industry in China is based on consolidation. Our alliance will not only achieve our goal, but also lead the way for major consolidation. We are hoping there will be a domino effect to drive industry consolidation.

Adopting a regional strategy in the Yangtze Delta was not only consistent with the company's expertise in its home markets, it also aligned closely with understanding of the economic drivers in brewing. CFO Lockey explained that LNC was "a small player in global terms, but we are the biggest where we are." He believed the company was "well-positioned with the lowest-cost position and among the largest capacity." However, continued growth was not without its problems, as Lockey elaborated:

> Sustaining growth at 70% [as in 1998] is quite extraordinary. A lot of that growth has come from entering new cities. You have to recognize that there are only so many cities you can enter. At that point you have to compete more aggressively in the cities you are already in. There are some dynamics about just how far you can go. In the mainstream market, for instance, you can only ship the beer about 300 kilometers before the freight costs just kill profits. Whereas in the premium market it is a little bit different. The product is heavy, relative to its value, unlike shampoo or microchips. So worldwide this tends to be a business where local production is a dominant factor.

Lion Nathan China: Structure and Systems

In addition to the two breweries at Wuxi and Suzhou, LNC had a head office and sales team based in Shanghai. Eight of O'Mahony's senior management team were located at the Shanghai office. Many of these key staff were relatively new to these executive positions. However, the company's staff-rotation policy meant that expatriates from Australia or New Zealand had at least five years' experience in two or three breweries before joining the China team. In addition, all of the local Chinese managers had previous experience in the beverage or consumer-products industries.

Taking an uncompromising stand on fundamental business practices was a feature of the corporate culture. Motivated by the desire for high performance, the corporate team initiated a project in 1996 to capture best practice and apply it universally across the business. The "Lion Nathan Way" was described by O'Mahony, who joined LN in 1991 and leads this development, as follows:

> The Lion Nathan Way is the "way we do things around here." It says three things—

what we do, how we do it, and why we do it. And it covers marketing, sales, HR, operations, finance, IT. They're not intended to be big binders that sit of the shelf, they're intended to be live documents. Each of them has a self-paced training module that goes with it. This is something that spans the whole of Lion Nathan.

This resource was particularly useful for LNC with induction and training of new staff and also provided guidelines for the full range of core business processes and activities from financial reporting through to developing advertising copy and conducting consumer research.

Lion Nathan China: Human Resources

People were critical for success of this business in China. Finding staff was not considered a problem by LNC in Shanghai; jobs were highly sought after in this progressive city, as employment provided the work permits needed to relocate into this area. To select new staff, LNC looked for applicants with previous retail experience, ambition, and ability. The company preferred recruits who were generally under thirty years old, with more than two years experience in another multinational corporation. Performance targets were established for each person and a remuneration package including bonuses/rewards negotiated. Status and loyalty were key elements of the Chinese culture that influenced employment positions, promotions, and relationships, as Graham Stuart, LN's corporate Strategy Director (from February 1999), who had five years experience working for LN in China, explained:

> Ambitious young staff are prepared to work extremely hard towards long-term personal goals, especially those involving promotion and status. Western distinctions between personal and professional issues are not commonly understood in China. The hierarchical relationship between an employee and his/her boss is also intrinsically personal. Loyalty can be expected from employees as long as promises are kept. However, if they are dissatisfied, then they will feel this "contract" had been broken and may leave the company. Typically they do not complain or ask for any explanation.

According to Stuart, the main reasons for employees leaving jobs in China were (1) being offered more money elsewhere, (2) pressures at work becoming too great, and (3) replacing expatriates with locals. The company had training systems in place to ensure new staff not only understood their specific tasks but also appreciated key corporate plans. Commenting on staff retention, Stuart said;

"Retention of staff is not considered an issue for us in China, as we are still in a rapid-growth phase."

Mindful of costs during the early stages of LNC's investment in China, the company leveraged knowledge and skills of key staff from Australia and New Zealand by flying them in for specific projects and then home again. This project-based team approach was successful for introducing new systems and processes, as well as transferring and developing new skills within the local companies. This approach was also cost-effective, as resident expatriates were significantly more expensive than local staff with their higher salaries, accommodation needs, transport costs, plus needs for additional English-speaking support staff. Although the number of expatriates increased during the Suzhou construction phase, LNCs commitment to localize and build capabilities continued; by February 1999, LNC had only eight expatriate staff.

Rotating key staff throughout the company had many benefits for the company and the individuals concerned. Sullivan explained:

> It transfers skills into the Chinese team, it continually raises or benchmarks your standard against what we're doing back home. It's also development that the person then takes back home. Every person that we've sent to China from our business in Australia or New Zealand has come back saying they learned so much. The environment is so different. They are so challenged. They're given a lot of responsibility to actually make things happen, and they've found it invaluable. So this is why we've tended to try to use that project-based teamwork approach, rather than having a big bench of expatriates.

Lion Nathan China: Production

LNC's focus on brewing high-quality beer in Wuxi provided an initial source of differentiation in the mainstream market, as the local breweries did not have the equipment, technology or the systems to produce a consistent beverage. The addition of a large-scale, technologically advanced, world-class facility at Suzhou enabled LNC to produce at low cost. As LN's Board Chairman, Douglas Myers effused at the official opening of the Suzhou brewery in September 1998:

> This brewery is a vital component in our China strategy. Without it, we would not have the capacity we need to continue our rapid growth. Nor would we have the capability to brew and package the high-quality premium brands necessary for profitability. The Suzhou Brewery is also an important asset as the beer

market here undergoes very rapid change. It sets us apart as a brewery of the highest quality and lowest costs. Together with our first-class sales force, it gives us a strong position in the Yangtze River Delta.

Capacity at Suzhou was also expandable as the plant design allowed for a mirror operation to be built on the same site. In 1998, LNC utilized one-third of the new plant's capacity (60,000 tonnes), which allowed for 100 percent volume growth in 1999. Brewing Beck's premium beer under license was expected to contribute a significant proportion of this new volume. LNC was also preparing to use some of this spare capacity brewing Kirin's premium beer.

The process of brewing beer was well-known and documented. With sophisticated technological support, much of the craft of brewing had been routinized into precise scientific processes that were able to be computer controlled. Fernando Coo, Suzhou's Technical Department Manager, discussed LNC's brewing systems:

> Our production systems are internally accredited with Class A ratings and externally validated by our ISO accreditation. The quality of raw materials is critical for beer attributes such as taste and color. Availability and cost of raw materials have a major impact too. Beer is made from malted barley, hops, water, yeast, and water. We get barley from Australia, Taiwan, Hong Kong, and Northern China, rice from Jiangsu province, and three different varieties of hops from New Zealand. Water, which is 90% of the beverage, is sourced locally (with assistance from SIP), filtered and stored in tanks on site. Every beer has its own strain of yeast, which is grown from a 10 ml sample for 8–10 generations, and then a fresh batch is started. We are able to use the same suppliers for our breweries at Wuxi and Suzhou. At the other end of the process, we sell the grain residues that have been extracted as cattle feed.

Quality was monitored at every stage of the brewing process. Further, to ensure the consumer enjoyed consistent quality, the company worked to improve the shelf life of its beer and enforced strict rules for the product's life: LNC's beer was aged for thirty days before it was released, and it was destroyed if not sold within eighty-four days.

Lion Nathan China: Sales and Distribution

Producing large volumes of top-quality beer to match local taste palettes was comparatively straightforward for LNC and other international brewers entering the China market. However, developing sales and distribution networks within this environment was significantly more challenging and complex than experiences elsewhere. LNC developed different systems for its two major market segments: (1) selling mainstream brands for off-premise consumption through "mom and pop" stores and supermarkets, and (2) selling premium brands for consumption on-premise in restaurants, cafes, hotels, and bars.

LNC's off-premise system involved selling mainstream brands from five warehouses to 400 wholesalers, who then sold the beer to 70,000 retailers. Sales teams were established for the five YRD target cities with account managers assigned to each wholesaler and merchandising managers providing the supporting merchandise (e.g., posters, price boards, shelf displays) for the retailers (to create consumer demand).

> The primary wholesaler is a man with a truck and a storage shed amid an enclave of houses down a track. He distributes the beer to the next-tier wholesaler who stacks up a bike or rickshaws with heavy loads for distribution to small open-fronted shops [kiosks].

Although beer sales in supermarkets were increasing (2 percent of total beer sales in 1998), the vast majority of off-premise beer was sold through "mom and pop" stores. These were typically small kiosks with a few shelves of basic household consumables such as soft drinks, beer, sweets, soap powder, and cigarettes. Located every few meters down many of the narrow streets, these cash-only stores provided a subsistence living. O'Mahony described the context for beer distribution:

> Most people in China go to the store next door, and they buy whatever they need to buy for that day or that half-day. They go to the wet markets and buy what they need to buy in the wet market, the fruit market, or whatever. Now until that changes we're not going to see much of a change in the distribution infrastructure in China. The people live in very concentrated areas. Public transport is OK, but people don't have cars. They can't afford taxis. So they are not going to carry bag loads of shopping long distances. They are going to buy very small quantities, frequently, and from the closest place to where they live as possible. We'll get in our car and drive 5 or 10 kilometers to buy whatever we want. These guys won't. They will walk 100 meters. The normal quantity of beer purchased is one or two bottles at a time. Because carrying one and a half kilos (which is two bottles) more than a short distance, if you are a frail old Chinese woman (the primary off-premise shopper) . . . is not something you are going to do.

The physical difficulties of frequent deliveries of crates of beer by tricycle through narrow congested streets from the wholesaler to the retailer were handled by contractors. LNC negotiated contracts with wholesalers annually, but did not do direct store delivery of the returnable bottles and crates of mainstream beer.

Shanghai, a city of 13 million people in 6,340 square kilometers, was projected to be the leading consumer market in the twenty-first century. Although it offered a real challenge, LNC had 41,000 retail outlets systematically mapped and allocated to sales teams. Albert Chu, General Manager for Mainstream Beer Sales, had 160 permanent sales staff for this dynamic city. Chu outlined his ideas on this challenge as follows:

> I was National Sales Director for Johnson & Johnson before joining LNC. I learned that increasing the proportion of stores stocking a product to 85% is needed to provide significant benefits from scale and market share. . . . I am very keen to push the Rheineck brand to that level of coverage. I'd also like to increase our carton sales through supermarkets.

The process of making sales was highly social and time-consuming, requiring continuous communication, camaraderie, and cajoling. Major responsibilities were vested in regional sales managers to achieve aggressive sales targets. For example, Tommy Wang, one of LNC's top-performing regional sales managers, lead 71 staff servicing 84 wholesalers and 14,000 retailers in urban Shanghai; and in Suzhou, Steven Zhu had a team of 68 staff for sales to 40 wholesalers, 250 secondary wholesalers and 10,000 retailers. The on-premise system for selling premium brands involved the use of distributors to sell beer to wholesalers, as well as making some direct sales to large retail accounts. LNC's sales managers had oversight of account managers who worked with the distributors. Sales representatives were employed to interact with wholesalers and retailers. Distributors typically carried a number of premium brands, with the exception of Anheuser-Busch specialists who were "voluntarily" exclusive. Selection of distributors and wholesalers was critical for success as O'Mahony explained:

> There is always a big fight annually to get the best distributors and the best wholesalers. We have a system of annual contracts that run January through December. There is an annual rebate for hitting volume targets. We are in the middle of negotiating the 1999 contracts right now [2 February]. It is a competitive process. Distributors and wholesalers have catchment areas; they have loyal retailers and then there are floating retailers. So capturing the best distributors and wholesalers is critical. After that its brand strength and how much support you are prepared to put into it. Off-premise retailers will stock a much wider range of brands

than on-premise. Bars, particularly Western-style bars, may have 50 beers, but the regular restaurant will have only two or three beers.

Higher margins for premium beer attracted many international breweries to China; this gave retailers the power to choose from numerous foreign brands. In addition, consumers typically drank the beer recommended by the restauranteur or bar patron, as Frank Gibson, LNC's Strategy Director, reported:

> People go out to a good restaurant, and they want to impress their friends, so they want to buy a foreign beer. Unfortunately, at this point in time, they really don't care what sort of beer it is, as long as it's foreign. They don't care if it's Beck's or Budweiser or San Miguel. So the restauranteur has an enormous amount of power over what gets drunk. Research shows that nine out of ten times the restaurateur can dictate what the consumer will drink. So this gives the trade a lot of power. There is an increasing number of competitors, a very fragmented channel, and no brand equity, so the trade can exercise a lot of leverage over the breweries. They don't have to take your beer. You don't have to have every beer in a restaurant. You only have to have two, basically. Most have only two or three. In premium, the vast majority of restaurants will only have two. So they don't have to take your beer. . . . This increases the cost of entry for any foreign players who want to get in. They've got to pay a lot of money below-the-line.

Higher margins for premium beer extended the distribution zones for these brands. Furthermore, improved intercity transportation infrastructure made it easier to supply beer to a broader region. Marketing Beck's, a top-tier premium brand, with LNC's other brands, was expected to significantly improve LNC's access to retail outlets within the YRD and to springboard distribution well beyond the delta; Beck's was already sold in over forty cities along the coast from Shenyang to Guangzhou. Distribution systems were generally a tablestake in most developed markets, but in China mastering logistical difficulties would be advantageous.

Lion Nathan China: Marketing

Like Procter and Gamble, LN had a portfolio of brands, rather than a single brand based on its corporate name. This provided flexibility to select and adapt beer brands for Chinese markets. As O'Mahony noted, "Unlike Budweiser or Carlsberg or Foster's, we don't have to push a particular brand." Launching a new brand, even in just one region of China, was extremely costly. CEO Gordon Cairns reported at the annual general meeting that

37 cents in every dollar earned in China was being invested in building brands. Steve Mason, Chief Marketing Officer, explained the company's approach to marketing:

> We do market research and use very sophisticated psychographic profiling to position and promote our brands in all three countries. We are always measuring the health of our brands and monitoring the effectiveness of our advertising. Our approach has always been to study and learn iteratively about positioning in each market. We really try to build on our experiences.

In the mainstream segment, Taihushui, which was acquired with the Wuxi brewery, was upgraded and relaunched in 1996 as a high-quality local beer for everyday drinking with comfort and affiliation messages. According to Mason, these messages were designed to convey a sense of closeness and belonging—"because it is from around here, you should feel comfortable drinking it." Taihushui was a market leader in Wuxi and Suzhou and had the second-highest market share in Changzhou (Table 3). Although a very strong performer, this brand was geographically locked.

Rheineck, which was from the New Zealand portfolio, was adapted and launched very successfully in 1997 as a pan-delta brand positioned as a beer "you drink with friends." LNC targeted a younger profile of more upwardly mobile consumers, with images of good times with good friends. Rheineck was an affordable foreign lager beer, brewed locally. In this mainstream segment, the economics of returning bottles and crates constrained geographic expansion. As the market share figures in Table 3 show, Rheineck rocketed into second or third place in these key YRD cities. Building on experience with Taihushui, LNC achieved significant volume growth within twelve months in Nanjing (17,000) and Shanghai (22,000). Sullivan described LNC's mainstream growth:

> We said there's growth . . . if we bring in a quality product and put in the right relationships with the wholesalers, do the right merchandising, get the brand out in front of the customer, get consumer awareness, then there's market share available without going beyond price. So we actually sell for a higher price than the local brands, and we've got significant growth in those markets.

Rapid turnover in popularity of beers was particularly obvious in the premium segment where many major international competitors battled for on-premise market share; positioning of these international brands was generally based on status. Mason outlined LNC's promotional strategies for each premium brand, as follows:

> We launched Steinlager as a progressive premium beer for the "new generation" in Shang-

hai in September 1998. This was a New Zealand lager with German connections which we adapted for the Chinese palate. To differentiate this beer and position it as trendy, we used a curved green bottle, labeled it as an "international awards winner" and offered it in up-market Western-style bars, hotels, and restaurants. We also had a dark-colored niche beer, Carbine, which was sold in restaurants positioned as "a beer with food." This was a mild stout beer, which was named using a brand from Queensland. This premium beer was reformulated and introduced to encourage winter consumption of beer using imagery of energy, warmth, and powerfulness.

The addition of Beck's beer to the portfolio of premium brands which LNC brewed and marketed, was expected to provide significant leverage in the future. Although Beck's volume and market share in the key YRD cities had declined significantly from 1997, the brand was still ranked number two behind Budweiser in four of these cities and was number one in Changzhou (Table 3).

Significant investments were involved to promote brands and obtain access to retail outlets. Image building activities—advertising, signage, event sponsorship, or merchandising, to build brand equity—were categorized as "above-the-line" expenditure. There were also "below-the-line" expenses for transactional deals with the trade, which were standard practice to gain access in China. With overcapacity in the on-premise segment, the costs to compete were increasing. As O'Mahony explained,

> A restaurant will typically stock two or three premium beers. They know that there are seven or eight producers of premium beer out there. It becomes an auction for which beers will be stocked. It comes down to who pays the most money. So, therefore, the costs to compete have risen. You know whether it's a listing fee or whether it's promotional support, whether it's paying for new signage, redecoration of the restaurant, whatever it happens to be. . . . The other thing that has happened is the costs of TV advertising have risen as a result of demand. Again, when you've got seven or eight players looking for the same spot on TV, then you have to pay more for it.

Gibson described the below-the-line dealing required for access to restaurants:

> You're selling to restaurateurs; you're not selling to consumers. You're trying to convince the restaurateur to stock your beer and push it on to consumers. It's all sales driven. It's all about push. You get in there and you do deals

with distributors who've got the best coverage, because you want the distributors who deal with the most restaurants directly. You go in there and do deals with the restaurateur. You give him push girls (who provide information and hand out promotion materials), and you give him so many ashtrays, and so many glasses, and so many beer mats, uniforms, etc. So that's been the focus until now. Increasingly the focus will be more on above-the-line marketing.

Increasing consumption and driving market share were critical activities for success in this market. LN's ex-COO, Kevin Roberts, speaking in his new role as CEO of Saatchi & Saatchi the worldwide advertising agency, described the status of brands in China:

The Chinese have not been exposed to brands at all. So every brand promise that makes sense to them, hey, they'll try it immediately. They think it's cool. They believe it. They are not cynical. A brand to them screams quality. So the way to build brand equity is to advertise the living hell out of a property and communicate it . . . have consistency of delivery . . . and you have to become part of them. You cannot advertise down to them with Western characters.

Furthermore, Roberts advocated the Coca-Cola strategy to drive consumption—"make it *Available* everywhere, make it *Affordable* and make it *Acceptable*."

Lion Nathan China: Financial Control

In 1998, sales revenue for LNC increased 91 percent to $56.2 million on volume growth of 73 percent; this result was impressive in a beer market growing at less than 5 percent. James Brindley moved into LNC's Finance Director role in November 1998, after six months in Shanghai working as a Planning Manager for David Sullivan. He recognized the need to balance shareholders' short-term needs and the company's long-term returns:

We're playing in the premier league now. We've got to realize that it's a big game. We've got to act like a big player, not like a small amateur player. And that takes courage. Our NZ$30 million loss is nothing to the likes of Anheuser-Busch and the other big players. And you know, beer in China is not a profitable business. Margins are very low, and it's very competitive. The economy is in a terrible state. Pricing is very hard to maintain. So all these things are stacked against us in the short-term. But that could turn in two years with a few exits, income growth, the economy turning around . . . then we could be doing very

well. Getting a partner is a great leap forward because it helps share the risk in these early years.

Commenting on the financial dilemma the company faced, CFO Lockey said:

The faster we grow, the more we lose. In the broadest sense, the faster we grow, the more chance we have of winning, but in the short-term the more we would lose. We can improve our financial performance by slowing down.

As margins for premium beer were 50 percent higher than mainstream beer, increasing the proportion of premium beer LNC sold was a top priority. Brewing Beck's beer under license in Suzhou would also help to utilize brewing capacity and accelerate break-even. Geographic expansion to new cities offered volume and sales growth, but there were major set-up costs involved in establishing a sales force in a new city. As O'Mahony indicated, "every time you open a sales office you could be looking at $1 million loss in year one." This would typically be followed by achieving break-even in year two and making a profit in year three. Another dynamic factor influencing profitability was the stage of brands in their lifecycle; new brands required significantly more investment than older brands. LNC also faced challenges on a daily basis arising from the cash-flow nature of the beer business. Brindley explained:

Most of the cash collection is by hand. Salesmen go to the wholesaler's office and collect a wad of cash, bring it back in to the office, and deposit it. So it's very high risk. It's very hard work. And it's a real challenge. Paying debts isn't a top priority here. We are really doing quite well on cash collection, but it's very hard work.

Seasonality was another major factor influencing this business. Brindley explained its impact on LNC as follows: "In August [summer] we sold 27 million liters of beer—nearly 1 million liters a day. In December we sold 1 million liters of beer. So a month's sales, equals a day's sales." There was a huge investment in bottles and crates to service peak sales; off-season (from October) the empties were returned and stacked high all around the plant. Bottles typically cost 0.8RMB and 3 percent were written off annually. Carton beer was more expensive, because the bottles were not returned. Brindley was concerned about the financial implications of the government's ruling for beer to be sold only in approved new bottles:

By 1st April every bottle has to be a B bottle made of safety glass. So with the number of bottles in the marketplace and the actual glass manufacturing capacity in China, it will take 11 years to make that number of bottles. But they expect it to be done by 1st April. So we may have to spend $10 million changing over our bottles. Mainstream beer is sold in returnable 640 ml bottles. But it's impossible to get your own bottles back. Actually, we won't care whose bottle we get back as long as it has a B on it. The old labels are washed off in the washer anyway.

Lion Nathan China: The Future?

With the partnership deal to brew and market Beck's beer signed on the table, LNC's Strategy Director, Gibson, reflected on the lengthy process that had been followed to put this international licensing agreement in place. He commented, "The strategy is all set now. We've nailed the final piece of the puzzle. My job is all done." Another key player, Graham Stuart, who had been actively involved in all the developments in China, moved in February 1999 from LNC's General Manager Sales and Marketing, to LN's corporate Strategy Director role. His brief was to look forward—"What's next for LN?" Stuart was excited to be beginning this task of searching for new opportunities and new horizons for LN.

However, the company's financial performance and future depended on success in China. The competitive landscape was changing, competition was intensifying in the Chinese beer market, and the economy was slowing down. In 1998, LNC had achieved record growth in volume and sales in this difficult market. Yet Lockey recognized that the challenges in China were far from over. Could O'Mahony and his senior management team continue to deliver on aggressive growth targets? How was LNC going to ensure success in this volatile market? Was it time for another bold move? Could LNC lead consolidation in the Chinese brewing industry? If so, how?

Reflecting on LNC's future options, Sullivan enthused:

> What can we do to drive the industry forward? We can communicate with other brewers. We can talk about how we compete in a profitable way. We can look for alliances with other brewers that don't have competing portfolios. We could license other premium brands and produce them in Suzhou. We can leverage

suppliers. We can raise the bar on quality: glass standards, labeling, packaging. We can acquire other breweries. We can acquire other brands. We can encourage other brewers to acquire other brands. We don't look at Wuxi to grow massively; we look for growth outside of Wuxi. And then expanding out from the traditional base . . . trying to grow seasonality, or extending the shelf life, getting people drinking more beer in winter . . . getting premium products into more restaurants, and mainstream into more shops.

Questions

1. What are the dominant economic and business characteristics of the Chinese beer industry?

2. Profile the following and, where appropriate, contrast to what would be found in Western markets:

- Chinese economy and its economic structure
- Chinese beer market and consumption habits

What implications do you see for Lion Nathan?

3. Examine Table 3, market sizes for the Yangtze River Delta region. What do you conclude? Who are Lion Nathan's major rivals in the region?

4. Prepare a profile of Lion Nathan's major competitors.

5. Examine Lion Nathan's human resource policies and corporate culture. Do they clash with China's mainstream culture?

6. Review Nathan Lion's marketing strategy and prepare some recommendations for implementation.

Notes

1. This case by Delwyn N. Clark of the University of Waikato in New Zealand. It originally appeared in *The Case Research Journal* (Spring 2001): 1–33. Reproduced with permission.

2. New Zealand dollars: exchange rate NZ$1.00 = U.S.$0.5628 at April 30, 1999.

Index